FOREWORD

by Derek Dooley MBE, Chairman of Sheffield United Football Club

I was delighted to be asked to write the foreword to this Encyclopedia of Sheffield United Football Club which is a welcome addition to the growing number of books exploring our Club's long history.

The book will add to our knowledge and refresh our memories of games and players of the past but a book such as this is not just about personal memories, for a great deal of the contents will cover a period before the reader made their first visit to 'the Lane' and became a Blades fan. Those early years will always provide a feast of reminiscences but our attachment and passion for the Blades will grow ever more deeply as we build up an understanding of our club's story through listening to those who remember earlier days and books such as this.

The United heroes of the past who brought distinction to our club remain part of the club today and will remain so forever. The players of today are our current heroes but they play in the shadows of those who have gone before. Bill Foulke, Tommy Morren and 'Nudger' Needham, George Utley, Bill Brelsford and Albert Sturgess, Billy Gillespie, George Green and Fred Tunstall are in the distant past but some of our oldest supporters can still recall Jack Smith, Jack Pickering, Ernest Jackson and 'Jock' Dodds.

I remember my days as a player and games against United stars such as Jimmy Hagan and Joe Shaw. Few players have their skill however; there are others that I remember such as Harry Latham and Cec Coldwell, who bring different qualities to the game and win the respect of colleagues and supporters and earn their place in United's heritage. Later, I would admire the development of players such as Len Badger, Mick Jones and Tony Currie and am proud to have played some part in United's history in what is now, nearly thirty years.

Great players and managers and many that were not so good; great games and strange games. All have their place in the growing panorama of our history which this book covers. Dip into it and enjoy the story of our Club as I have done.

INTRODUCTION

I am positively certain that all supporters of Sheffield United Football Club, young and old, male and female, have, at some time or another, been involved in an argument concerning a player, whether from the past or present!

I know from experience that in numerous pubs and clubs, inside street cafes, bars and restaurants, at schools and colleges, at home, in office blocks, on the work floor, at various grounds, in cars, on trains and buses, even when travelling in an aircraft or walking down the road, perhaps sitting on the beach, discussions have taken place about certain players (and a few managers) who have been associated with The Blades down the years.

Some of these for sure have turned into heated arguments, with questions being asked but no definite answer given. As a result wagers have been laid as to who is right and who is wrong!

Some questions revolve round the obvious, such as (a) When did he join the club and where from? (b) How many goals did he score? (c) Where did go after leaving The Blades? (d) Did he play for England (or Wales etc)? (e) Was he a defender or midfielder, a left or right-winger? or (f) Did he play in a Cup Final?

Hopefully this elaborated Encyclopaedia of the Blades can answer most, if not all of those questions, as well as offering you a lot more information besides. It will also satisfy that laudable curiosity without a shadow of doubt.

On the following pages you will find multitudinous authentic personal details of almost every single player who has appeared for the Blades in a competitive League and Cup match from 1889 up to and including the 2002-03 season and there are details, too, on several footballers who guested for the club during the two World War periods.

There is also information about the men who have managed the Blades down the years.

For easy reference, virtually all of the players who have served with the club are included and have been listed in A-Z order, with the date and place of birth and death given, if clarified, although occasionally it has only been possible to ascertain a certain year with regards to when he was actually born and when he died. In some instances the date of death has not been included at all, although the word deceased has been added as an alternative.

Also included in the pen-picture portraits are details of the junior and non-League clubs that player served, any transfer fees involved (if known), honours won at club and international level, plus the respective senior appearance and goalscoring records (for United) which appears at the head of each individual players' write-up. An asterisk (i.e *) alongside any figure (s), indicates that the player was still adding to his appearance and/or goals tallies at the time the book was published.

Virtually throughout this book, the name of the club - Sheffield United - is referred to as either the Blades or United. Very few abbreviations have been used, but among the more common ones are the obvious: FC (Football Club), FAC (FA Cup), FLC (Football League Cup), apps (appearances), sub (substitute).

Where a single year appears in the text (when referring to an individual player's career), this indicates, in most cases, the second half of a season: i.e. 1975 is 1974-75. However, when the figures (dates) such as 1975-80 appear, this means seasons 1975-76 to 1979-80 inclusive and not 1974-80.

If you spot any discrepancies, errors, even omissions, I would appreciate it very much if you could contact me (via the publishers) so that all can rectified in any future publications appertaining to Sheffield United Football Club. If you have anything to add, this, too, would be welcome as people tend to reveal unknown facts from all sources when football is the topic of conversation.

Tony Matthews
2003

Statistical Information
The statistics entered in each of the individual player's profile are for the following:
* Premiership matches (1992-2003)
* Football League matches (1892-2003: Divisions 1, 2, 3 & 4)
* FA Cup fixtures (competition proper & qualifying rounds: 1889-2003)
* Football League Cup games, under various sponsorship (1965-2003).
* Also other competitions including: Midland Counties League, Northern League, Associate Members Cup, Full Members Cup, Birmingham Cup, Sheffield & Hallamshire County Cup, Sheffield Challenge Cup, Steel City Cup, Simod Cup, Sheriff of London Charity Shield, Test Match, Zenith Data Systems Cup, Play-Offs, Watney Cup, Anglo-Italian & Anglo-Scottish Tournaments and matches played during WW1 & WW2

ACKNOWLEDGEMENTS

Firstly this book could not have been published without the generous agreement of Denis Clarebrough (Sheffield United Football Club historian) and Andrew Kirkham (Club statistician) who gave me permission to reproduce much of their original research which has been previously published in 'Sheffield United Football Club, The First 100 Years' and 'The Complete Record of Sheffield United Football Club 1889-1999' and in the United match programmes since 1983. Also many thanks to Denis for checking and re-checking the manuscript.

I must say a special big 'thank you' to my good friend John Russell from Waterlooville, Hampshire who has helped enormously with the statistical work contained in this book. I also acknowledge the assistance afforded to me by Kevin Cookson (Press Officer, Sheffield United FC), David Barber (of the Football Association). Zoe Ward (FA Premier League).

Thank you, too - and 'sorry' darling for the inconvenience caused - to my loving wife Margaret who once again has had to put up without me for hours upon end whilst I've been sat typing away on the computer keyboard, thumbing through old reference books, matchday programmes and soccer magazines, checking and re-checking the thousands of statistics and stories.

And there is also a huge thank you to Derek Dooley MBE for agreeing to write the foreword to this book.

Last but by no means least I must give a sincere thank you to everyone who has worked on the book at Britespot Publishing, especially to Roger Marshall, Paul Burns and Chris Russell more so to Roger and Paul who jointly agreed to publish the book.

* The majority of old (and some not so old) pictures used in this book have come from scrapbooks, photograph albums and certain programmes, owned by ex-players, Blades' supporters (young and not so young) and serious collectors of footballing memorabilia. Neither myself or the publishers, have been able to establish clear copyright on some of these pictures and therefore the publishers (Britespot) would be pleased to hear from anyone whose copyright has been unintentionally fringed.

Bibliography
I have referred to several books to clarify certain relevant statistics, facts and figures, player's details and, indeed, stories and match reports from past seasons regarding Sheffield United FC. There is some conflicting information in these sources and I have made judgment as to which is likely to be correct.

Here is a list:
Association Football & The Men Who Made It: 4 vols.
(A Gibson & Pickford)
AFS Who's Who: 1902, 1903, 1907 & 1909
The Encyclopaedia of Association Football (M Goldsworthy)
England v. Scotland (B James)
English Internationals Who's Who: 1872-1972 (D Lamming & M Farror)
FA Official Yearbooks
Football In Sheffield 1964 (Percy M Young)
Football League Directory: 1985-89
Footballers' (PFA) Factfile (B Hugman/AFS) 1995-2002
Rothmans Yearbook (Vols. 1-32)
Sheffield United Football Club: 1899-1999: A Complete Record
(D Clarebrough & A Kirkham)
The Official Centenary History of Sheffield United Football Club: the First 100 Years (D Clarebrough)
Where Are They Now? (Andy Pringler & Neil Fissler) 1996

Magazines Etc.
AFS Football Recollections & AFS Bulletins (various)
Sheffield United 'home' programmes (various: 1897-2003)
Charles Buchan Football Monthly: 1954-70
Sheffield United Football Club. 100 Greats (Denis Clarebrough)
Shoot Magazine: 1970s
Soccer Star: 1960s
* I have also referred to various club histories and Who's Who publications, certain autobiographies and biographies of individual players and managers and football reference books in general for confirmation of various factual points.

First published in Great Britain by
Britespot Publishing Solutions Limited,
Chester Road, Cradley Heath,
West Midlands, B64 4AB

December 2003

© Copyright: Tony Matthews/Britespot Publishing, 2003

ISBN 1 904103 19 7

Cover design: © Britespot Publishing Solutions Limited
Photos: Empics and Colorsport

Printed and bound in Great Britain by
Butler & Tanner ltd
Caxton Road
Frome
Somerset
BA11 1NF

FOOTBALL LEAGUE DIVISION 1
Champions: 1897-98
Runners-up: 1896-97, 1899-1900

NATIONWIDE LEAGUE DIVISION 1
Play-off beaten finalists: 2002-03

FOOTBALL LEAGUE DIVISION 2
Champions: 1952-53
Runners-up: 1892-93, 1938-39, 1960-61, 1970-71, 1989-90

FOOTBALL LEAGUE DIVISION 3
Runners-up: 1988-89
Promoted (in 3rd place): 1983-84

FOOTBALL LEAGUE DIVISION 4
Champions: 1981-82

FA CUP WINNERS
Winners: 1898-99, 1901-02, 1914-15, 1924-25
Runners-up: 1900-01, 1935-36
Semi-finalists: 13 times, the last in 2002-03

FOOTBALL LEAGUE CUP
Semi-finalists: 2002-03

FOOTBALL LEAGUE NORTH
Champions: 1945-46

MIDLAND SECTION - SUBSIDIARY COMPETITION
Champions: 1916-17, 1918-19
Runners-up: 1915-16

MIDLAND SECTION - PRINCIPAL TOURNAMENT
Runners-up: 1915-16, 1917-18

SHEFFIELD & HALLAMSHIRE COUNTY CUP
Winners: 1920-21, 1923-24, 1925-26, 1929-30, 1930-31, 1932-33, 1951-52, 1952-53, 1953-54, 1956-57, 1957-58, 1958-59, 1959-60, 1963-64, 1964-65, 1966-67, 1968-69, 1973-74, 1977-78, 1979-80, 1980-81. Also 1938-39 (shared with Sheffield Wednesday).

4

SHEFFIELD UNITED FC: 1889-2003
ROLL OF HONOUR

THE OFFICIAL ENCYCLOPAEDIA OF SHEFFIELD UTD

CONTENTS

A	6-21
B	22-49
C	50-70
D	71-81
E	82-85
F	86-103
G	104-114
H	115-131
I	132-135
J	136-142
K	143-148
L	149-157
M	158-177
N	178-188
O	189-191
P	192-204
Q	205
R	206-216
S	217-241
T	242-250
U	251-253
V	254
W	255-272
Y	273-276
Z	277

ABANDONED MATCHES

Here is a list of abandoned matches involving United:

Date	Comp	Opponents	Time	Reason	Score
28.12.1889	Friendly	Doncaster Rovers (a)	80 mins	Darkness	(0-2)
07.04.1890	Friendly	Crewe Alexandra (h)	75 mins	Rain	(1-1)
25.12.1891	Friendly	W Arsenal (h)	75 mins	Fog	(3-3)
27.02.1892	SCC S/F	Kilnhurst (a)	61 mins	Player dispute	(4-0)
27.12.1892	Div 2	Burton Swifts (h)	68 mins	Fog/poor light	(2 1)
28.12.1895	Div 1	Burnley (a)	65 mins	Rain	(0-1)
27.03.1899	FAC SF	Liverpool (n)	45 mins	Crowd on pitch	(0-1)
06.01.1900	Div 1	Blackburn Rovers (a)	36 mins	Weather	(0-0)
10.02.1900	FAC Rd 2	Wednesday (h)	53 mins	Snow	(0-0)
06.03.1909	Div 2	W Arsenal (a)	72 mins	Waterlogging	(0-3)
11.01.1913	FAC Rd 1	Huddersfield T (a)	75 mins	Snow	(2-1)
23.12.1916	WW1	Grimsby Town (a)	60 mins	Fading light	(0-2)
30.04.1927	Div 1	Bury	40 mins	Player death	(1-0)
04.01.1919	WW1	Hull City (a)	75 mins	Poor light	(1-6)
20.01.1945	WW2	Lincoln City (a)	14 mins	Snow	(0-0)
12.09.1970	Div 2	Millwall (a)	25 mins	Rain	(0-0)
04.03.1972	Div 1	Coventry City (a)	62 mins	Poor light	(2-0)
08.04.1975	Testimonial	Barnsley (a)	72 mins	Snow	(3-3)
23.05.1984	Friendly	Sabah FA XI/Malaysia	83 mins	Tropical storm	(3-2)
30.01.1987	Friendly	Aston Villa (h)	45 mins	Ice	(1-0)
06.03.1992	Friendly	Kilmarnock (a)	60 mins	Heavy rain	(0-1)
16.03.2002	Div 1	West B Albion (h)	82 mins	Too few players	(0-3)

Fact File

* United's Sheffield County Cup semi-final against Kilnhurst (away) in 1892, ended in controversy when the home side (4-0 down at the time) walked off the pitch after 61 minutes - annoyed with the referee's decisions. The score was allowed to stand and the Blades progressed into the Final.
* In March 2002, the Nationwide League Division One game between United and promotion-chasing West Bromwich Albion was abandoned after 82 minutes with the visitors leading 3-0. Preston referee Eddie Wolstenholme called a halt to proceedings because the Blades had insufficient players on the pitch - only six. Three had been sent-off and two went off injured. The score was allowed to stand.
* United (like many other clubs up and down the country) had several League games postponed during the harsh winter of 1947. They played their last Football League fixture that season on 14 June - having started the programme on 31 August 1946. (The match was the Championship decider)
* United's 3rd round FA Cup-tie with Bolton Wanderers, scheduled to take place in early January 1963, was finally played on 6 March - two months late!

ABLETT, Gary Ian

Defender: 12 apps.
Born: Liverpool, 19 November 1965
Career: Liverpool (apprentice 1981, professional November 1983), Derby County (on loan, January 1985), Hull City (on loan, September 1986), Everton (£750,000, January 1992), BLADES (on loan, March 1996), Birmingham City (£390,000, June 1996), Wycombe Wanderers (on loan, December 1999), Scunthorpe United (on trial) and Blackpool (on a free transfer, January 2000). He retired in May 2001 through injury.
Gary Ablett helped Liverpool win the First Division championship in 1988 and 1990; the FA Cup in 1989 and the FA Charity Shield in 1988. He was then both an FA Cup and Charity Shield winner with Everton in 1995.
Capped once by England at both 'B' and Under-21 levels, he was a composed left-sided defender, cool and calm under pressure and amassed over 300 appearances in total for the two Merseyside clubs. Injuries began to interrupt his performances during the latter stages of his career.

ACCRINGTON

United's playing record against Accrington:
Test Match

Venue	P	W	D	L	F	A
Neutral	1	1	0	0	1	0

Accrington, founded in 1876 by players from the local cricket club and not to be confused with Accrington Stanley, were one of the original 12 members of the Football League in 1888. The Lancashire club spent just five seasons in the competition before bowing out. Accrington had always had a fragile relationship with their cricketing colleagues who formed the committee. Despite drawing crowds of 8,000 to their Thorneyholme Road ground, the cricket committee refused to allow any permanent stands to be built, insisting the temporary ones could be dismantled after each game. Cricket was king at this stage, despite the football team's success, so when Accrington were relegated following their Test match defeat by the Blades (see below) the cricket club was unsure how the loss of revenue would effect the club overall. Resignation was inevitable; the professionals left and the team reverted to amateur status, playing in a local League. Ironically Accrington then found their 'own' ground, Moorhead Park, sharing it with a junior side 'Stanley Villa.' In 1896 Accrington FC folded, Stanley Villa now becoming Accrington Stanley, taking over Moorhead Park, adopting the disbanded club's colours (scarlet and black) and even their nickname, 'T 'Owd Reds.' It's a small wonder the clubs have been confused ever since! That Test Match was played at Nottingham on 22 April 1893, and the Blades won 1-0 thanks to Jack Drummond's goal) to gain promotion to the First Division.
Player Wilson Greenwood was associated with both clubs.

ACCRINGTON STANLEY
United never played Accrington Stanley, a Football League club from 1921 to 1962.
Players with both clubs include: Stan Fazackerley, John Pears and Percy Thorpe.

ADDISON, Colin
Inside-forward: 110+2 apps. 26 goals
Born: Taunton, Somerset 18 May 1940
Career: Cliftonville FC/York, York City (junior, July 1955, professional at Bootham Crescent, May 1957), Nottingham Forest (£12,000, January 1961), Arsenal (£45,000, September 1966), BLADES (£40,000, December 1967), Hereford United (player-manager, October 1971, retired as a player May 1973, remaining as manager until May 1974). Durban City/South Africa (manager, January 1975), Notts County (assistant-manager, December 1975 to October 1976), Newport County (manager, January 1977 to May 1978), West Bromwich Albion (assistant-manager/coach to Ron Atkinson, July 1978 to May 1979), Derby County (manager, May 1979 to January 1982), Newport County (manager, January 1982 to May 1985), Kuwait & Qatar (as a coach), Celta Vigo (manager, April 1986 to April 1987), West Bromwich Albion (assistant-manager/coach, September 1987 to October 1988), Atletico Madrid (assistant-manager/coach, October 1988, then manager, December 1988 to June 1989); FC Cadiz/Spain (manager/coach, March-July 1990), Hereford United (manager, July 1990 to May 1991), Al Arabi (coach 1991-92), Merthyr Tydfil (manager, October 1994), Yeovil Town (manager), Merthyr Town (manager, July 1996), Swansea City (manager, autumn 2001-March 2002), Forest Green Rovers (manager, October 2002).
A positive inside-forward, aggressive with good ball control, Colin Addison helped the Blades in promotion to the First Division in 1971. Two years later he was forced to retire in 1973 after breaking his leg. He had an excellent career, amassing well over 400 League and Cup appearances and netting more than 230 goals. He was Forest's top scorer three seasons out of four in 1960s; guided Hereford to that magnificent FA Cup victory over Newcastle in 1972 and was highly successful as a coach. He became Merthyr's fourth manager in 15 months when he joined the Welsh club in 1994, and Swansea's eighth in 10 years when he moved into the hot-seat at The Vetch Field in 2001. Addison now lives in Hereford.

Sheffield United team group: (back row, l-r) Ian McKenzie, Len Badger, Bill Dearden, Tony Currie, Geoff Salmons, John Tudor; (middle row, l-r) John Flynn, Dave Powell, Graeme Crawford, Alan Hodgkinson, Frank Barlow, Colin Addison; (front row, l-r) Paddy Buckley, Alan Woodward, Eddie Colquhoun, Gil Reece, John Barnwell

7

ADMISSION PRICES

When United commenced playing League Football in 1892, the minimum admission charges for
admission to a home game were 6d (3p) to the ground and one shilling (5p) for a seat.
The 6d charge remained as the standard entrance fee until after World War One (1919-20)
when it was increased to one shilling (5p) with the seats at 1s 6d (9p).
Throughout the twenties and thirties and, indeed, until 1942-43, that (bob) shilling admission price remained in force. Then the
admission fee was raised from one shilling to 1s 3d (around 7p).
In 1951-52 the minimum charge was upped again, this time to 1st 6d (9p) and subsequent charges rose
steadily: 1955-56 to 2s (10p); 1960-61 - 2s 6d (13p); 1965-66 - 4s (20p); 1968-69 - 5s (25p).
By 1972-73 the price was up to 50p; soon afterwards fans were asked to pay 60p, then it was 80p, and
finally up to £1.00...And then even higher to £1.70 (more than double for a seat) by 1982-83.
Thereafter it rose steadily through the eighties - £1.50, £2.00 and up £2.50.
In the late 1990s, the fans were paying £11 each (£17 a seat) and when the 21st century arrived it was £12 per match.

Season Tickets

* An 1890s ground season ticket to watch Sheffield United cost the supporter ten shillings (50p).
* At the turn of the century (1900) the price had risen to one guinea (£1.1s £1.05).
* After WW2 (1946-47), Centre stand season tickets were priced at £5 a time.
* They were over £6 each in the mid-1950s; £8 8s in the early 1960s and a decade later the first £20 tickets
* were issued in 1982-83, a centre stand season ticket at Bramall Lane could be purchased for £80 and a decade after that fans were
being asked to pay between £180 and £279 (with ground season tickets available at £170).
* The most season tickets sold by United for one season is believed to have been around 12,000 for their first Premiership campaign.
Prior to that the 'record' was 4,721 in 1968-69 one of few totals known. During the period 1994-2003 the average season ticket sale
has been 8,500.

Complimentary Tickets

For Football League matches, the visiting club can normally claim in the region of 40 complimentary tickets - 25 for use by the players,
manager and coach - and 12 for the Directors. However, there is no set limit on how many complimentary tickets the home club can
issue.

AGANA, Patrick Anthony

Striker: 154 apps. 52 goals
Born: Born in Bromley, Kent 2 October 1963
Career: Weymouth (August 1985), Watford (£35,000, August 1987), BLADES (£45,000, February 1988), Notts County (£750,000,
November 1991), Leeds United (on loan, February 1992), Hereford United (March 1997).
Striker Tony Agana was one of manager Dave Bassett's first signings for United. He formed a splendid partnership with Brian Deane
when helping the Blades rise from the Third Division into the First in double quick time. He scored over 50 goals in more than 150
first-class appearances for the Blades. He gained a semi-professional cap for England before joining Watford. He helped Notts County
win the Anglo-Italian Cup at Wembley in 1995 and reach the Play-offs a year later. He quit top-class football in the summer of 1997
with 80 goals to his credit in 358 senior games (at club level).

AGE

Oldest

The oldest player to appear for the Blades' in a major competitive Cup match is Albert Sturgess (born 21 October 1882) who was 40
years, 113 days old when he made his last League appearance for the club on 10 February 1923 v. Huddersfield Town (Division 1) on
10 February 1923.
Billy Gillespie (born 6 August 1891) was 40 years, 25 days old when he played in his final League game for the Blades v. Blackpool on
31 August 1931 (Division 1).
Jimmy Hagan was 39 years, 236 days when he lined up in his 391st and last League game versus Derby County (Division 2) on 14
September 1957.
Jack Pickering is the fourth oldest, aged 39 years, 14 days in 1948 and Jack Smith was 39 years, 9 days when he last played in 1949.
Reg Wright, United's 'A' team trainer at the time, was 39 years, 8 months of age when he played at right-back for the Blades in a WW2
game v. Doncaster Rovers (a) in September 1940.

Youngest

Dennis Thompson (born on 2 June 1925) made his first team debut for United at the age of 16 years, 103 days in a WW2 game v.
Mansfield Town on 13 September 1941.
Stephen Hawes (born on 17 July 1978) stepped up into the first XI at the age of 16 years, 10 months for a friendly against FC
Viterbese in Italy on 18 May 1995.
Hawes then went on to become United's youngest-ever League player when he made his bow in the First Division against West
Bromwich Albion at the age of 17 years, 47 days on 2 September 1995.
Other youngsters include: Joe Shaw, aged 16 years, 285 days (April 1945); Simon Stainrod, aged 17 years, 55 days (March 1976);
Julian Broddle, 17 years, 62 days (January 1982); Gary Hamson, 17 years, 67 days (October, 1976), Barry Wagstaffe (April 1961) and
Kevin Lewis, aged 17 years, 97 days (December 1957).
* When United beat Harrogate Railway Athletic 5-1 in a friendly in March 1991, one of their goals was scored by 14 year-old trialist
Terry Harris.
18 year old from Dublin - Docherty - came on as a substitute for United in the 0-0 friendly draw at Immingham in April 1992.
Teenage winger Geoffrey Taylor also played in this same game.

Age Concern

* Stanley Matthews had just celebrated his 48th birthday when he played for Stoke City against Sheffield United at Bramall Lane on 23
February 1963.
* 17 year-old Tony Hoyland made a scoring League debut for United v. Leicester City (h) in March 1950.
* Goalkeeper John Burridge was 41 years, 338 days old when he became Scarborough's oldest League player v. Doncaster Rovers in

November 1993. In December 1995 he played for Scarborough in an Auto-Windscreen Shield game v. Notts County a week after his 44th birthday. 'Budgie' is also Darlington's oldest League player, aged 44 years, six days in December 1995 (ironically v. Scarborough) and he's the oldest player appear in the Premiership, aged 43 years, five months, 11 days for Manchester City v. QPR on 14 May 1995. Burridge played in his last FA Cup-tie for Darlington on 12 December 1995, aged 44 years, nine days. He served the Blades from 1984-87.

* Kevin Gage, aged 17 years, 15 days, became Wimbledon's youngest first-team player when he made his League debut v. Bury on 2 May 1981. He signed for the Blades in 1991.
* Ian 'Chico' Hamilton made his League debut for Chelsea v. Tottenham Hotspur in March 1967, aged of 16 years, 138 days - the Blues' youngest-ever footballer. He moved to Bramall Lane in 1976.
* Blades' centre-forward Arthur Brown was 18 years, 10 months, 23 days old when he made his international debut for England v. Wales on 29 February 1904.
* Joe Cockroft was almost 37 years, five months old when he made his First Division debut - for United v. Preston North End in November 1948. He had played regularly in lower Divisions prior to that with Rotherham United (3 games), West Ham (251) and Sheffield Wednesday (87).
* Former Forest goalkeeper Dave Beasant was almost 44 years of age when he made his debut for Brighton & Hove Albion against Walsall in February 2003.
* In May 1964, future United manager Howard Kendall was, at the time, the youngest player ever to appear in an FA Cup Final - for Preston North End against West Ham United.

AGGREGATE SCORE

All ties in rounds 1, 2, 3, 4, 5 and 6 of the 1945-46 FA Cup competition were played over two-legs - the first and only time this has been agreed. The Blades beat Huddersfield Town 3-1 on aggregate in the 3rd round before losing 4-3 to Stoke City 4-3 over two legs at the next stage.

Two-legged ties were introduced to the League Cup for season 1979-80, the Blades losing 4-2 on aggregate to Doncaster Rovers in the opening round.

The Blades beat Grimsby 8-4 on aggregate in the 2nd round of the League Cup in 1982-83...they took out Rotherham 8-2 on aggregate in the opening round in 1985-86...beat Stockport County 6-1 over two legs in round 2 in 1994-95 and knocked Lincoln City out 6-2 on aggregate in 2000-01

Everton beat the Blades 6-2 over two legs in the 2nd round in 1984-85 while Stockport beat them 7-3 on aggregate in a 2nd round encounter in 1996-97.

Several two-legged matches were played by Blades during WW2. They beat Liverpool 7-6 on aggregate in February 1942 (winning 5-1 at home after losing 5-2 away) and Rotherham United 8-5 over two legs in April 1942 (5-2 away, 3-3 at home) both 'encounters' coming in the Football League Wartime Cup.

ALDERSHOT

United's playing record against the Shots:

Football League

Venue	P	W	D	L	F	A
Home	2	2	0	0	3	0
Away	2	0	1	1	1	2
Totals	4	2	1	1	4	2

FA Cup

	P	W	D	L	F	A
Home	1	0	1	0	0	0
Away	1	0	0	1	0	1
Totals	1	0	1	1	0	1

Watney Cup

	P	W	D	L	F	A
Away	1	1	0	0	6	0

In 1991, after being voted out of the Football League where they had played since 1932, moving no higher than the Third Division, Aldershot FC folded. But their supporters refused to accept their days were over and quickly formed Aldershot Town (1992) Ltd, entering a team at the very bottom of the footballing pyramid system while continuing to use their old Recreation Ground for home matches. Progress has been made and now the 'Shots stand just two promotions away from winning Football League status.

The 'old' club enjoyed its heyday during WW2 when, as the centre of the British Army, most of the country's top-line players were posted in the town and often the 'Shots would turn out star-studded teams that included the likes of Wally Boyes (Sheffield-born), Matt Busby, Dennis Compton, Stan Cullis, future Blades' manager Joe Mercer, United's own Jimmy Hagan, Jack Rowley and goalkeeper Frank Swift.

The Blades were blasted out of the FA Cup in the 3rd round by the Shots in 1978-79, losing 1-0 at The Recreation Ground after a 0-0 draw at Bramall Lane.

The first League game between the clubs took place at 'the Lane' in December in 1981 (Division 4). The Blades won 2-0 and later in the season drew 1-1 in the return fixture.

Tony Currie and Alan Woodward both scored twice when the Blades 'bombarded Aldershot 6-0 in a Watney Cup-tie in August 1970. Among the handful of players who have served with both clubs we have David Barnes, Francis Joseph, Dennis Longhorn, Bert Menlove, Mark Morris and George Raynor, while Blades' manager Neil Warnock also played for the 'Shots, likewise Jimmy Sirrel who was also a trainer at The Recreation Ground. Jimmy Hagan guested for the 'Shots during WW2.

ALDERSON, John Thomas

Goalkeeper: 137 apps.

Born: Crook, County Durham 27 November 1891. Died: Sunderland, 17 February 1972.

Career: Crook Town, Shildon Athletic, Middlesbrough (as an amateur), Newcastle United (£30, February 1913), Crystal Palace (£50, May 1919), Pontypridd (July 1924), BLADES (May 1925), Exeter City (May 1929). Later employed as Torquay United trainer (from November 1930), he also assisted non-League side Worcester City (September 1931-April 1932) before returning to serve as player-coach with Crook Town ((to May 1934).

Capped by England against France in Paris in 1923, 'Jack' Alderson was a competent 'keeper of splendid consistency who took over

9

from Charlie Sutcliffe between the posts at Bramall Lane and eventually handing over his duties to Norman Wharton in 1929. Whilst with Palace he accomplished the rare record of saving eleven penalties out of 12, including two in one game. He represented the Southern League (1920) and Welsh League (1924) and helped Palace win the Third Division title in 1921. Alderson became a farmer in the North-East after retiring from football.

ALLCHURCH, Leonard

Right-winger/inside-forward: 146 apps. 37 goals
Born: Swansea, 12 September 1933
Career: Swansea Boys, Swansea Town (amateur, November 1949, professional, October 1950), BLADES (£12,500, March 1961), Stockport County (September 1965), Swansea City (July 1969), Haverfordwest (season 1971-72). After appearing in 272 League games for Swansea (49 goals scored) Len Allchurch helped the Blades clinch promotion at the end of the 1960-61 season by grabbing vital goals. A Welsh schoolboy international, and for so long in the shadows of his more illustrious brother, Len nevertheless made almost 600 League games, his debut coming v. Grimsby Town in 1951.
A quick-thinking player with excellent ball control and a deceptive body-swerve, he usually lined up on the right-wing, but could also play as an inside-forward where he proved to be a smart finisher, using both feet. He gained the first of his 11 full international caps for Wales against Ireland in Belfast in 1955 when he lined up alongside his brother and with the Charles brothers, John and Mel - the first time two sets of brothers had ever appeared for the Principality. He actually ended his playing days with brother Ivor at Haverfordwest - and after hanging up his boots Allchurch took over a hotel in Swansea and later ran a successful leather goods business.
* There was also another Allchurch brother, Sid, who gained amateur caps for Wales.

ALLISON, Wayne Anthony

Striker: 23+23 apps* 7 goals*
Born: Huddersfield, 16 October 1968
Career: Halifax Town (apprentice, April 1985, professional July 1987), Watford (£250,000, July 1989), Bristol City (£300,000, August 1990), Swindon Town (£475,000, July 1995), Huddersfield Town (£800,000, November 1997), Tranmere Rovers (£300,000, September 1999), BLADES (July 2002).
Journeyman striker Wayne Allison (6ft 1in tall) was a Second Division championship winner with Swindon Town in 1996 and he reached the milestones of 175 goals and 650 senior appearances at club level during the 2002-03 when he had four different partners in the Blades' attack - Steve Kabba, Paul Peschisolido, Dean Windass and Carl Asaba. A totally committed performer, he is known as 'Big Chief.'

ALMOND, John

Inside-left/centre-forward: 125 apps. 21 goals
Born: Darlington, 6 November 1876. Died: 1912 (after a short illness).
Career: Darlington, Bishop Auckland, BLADES (September 1896), Gainford FC (May 1901), Millwall Athletic (November 1901), Doncaster Rovers (season 1903-06).
Fair-haired Jack Almond - who displayed plenty of all-round attacking skills - spent five seasons at Bramall Lane during which time he averaged a goal every six games and helped United win the First Division championship and the FA Cup in successive seasons (1898 & 1899).

ALTRINCHAM

United's playing record against Altrincham:
FA Cup

Venue	P	W	D	L	F	A
Home	1	0	1	0	2	2
Away	1	0	0	1	0	3
Totals	2	0	1	1	2	5

Formed a couple of years after United (in 1891) Altrincham became one of England's best-known non-League sides, twice winning the FA Trophy at Wembley in 1978 & 1986, and finishing runners-up in 1982, while also causing plenty of upsets in the FA Cup and claiming two Northern Premier League titles, in 1980 and 1981
United were humiliated by non-Leaguers Altrincham in the 1st round of the FA Cup in 1981-82. After struggling to hold on for a draw at Bramall Lane in front of 12,433 spectators, the Blades succumbed to a 3-0 defeat at Moss Lane where the attendance was almost 10,000.

AMATEUR CLUBS

Between 1889 and 1925 United played three of the country's leading amateur teams, the Casuals, the Corinthians and the Old Carthusians.
Here is a breakdown of those matches:

v. Casuals

Venue	P	W	D	L	F	A
Home	6	3	2	1	25	10
Away	4	2	0	2	5	5
Totals	10	5	2	3	30	15

v. Corinthians

Home	9	4	2	3	24	22
Away	9*	3	3	3	13	10
Totals	18	7	5	6	37	32

v. Old Carthusians

Away	1	1	0	0	2	0

* Including two Sheriff of London Charity Shield matches

Fact File
* United met the Casuals twice in the space of four days in December 1891, losing 1-0 away and drawing 3-3 at home in friendly matches.
* In December 1890 and December 1891 the Blades beat the Casuals 7-0 and 7-2 respectively in friendlies at Bramall Lane.
* United beat the Corinthians 5-3 at home and 4-0 away in December 1898 and April 1900.
* A crowd of 38,167 saw United beat the Corinthians 5-0 in a home 1st round FA Cup-tie in January 1925. Harry Johnson scored four times.
* The game against the Old Carthusians was played in January 1896 when United won 2-0 (away).
* In the annual Sheriff of London Charity Shield in 1898, United and the Corinthians shared the trophy after two draws: 0-0 and 1-1 (both at The Crystal Palace).
* Several amateur players have been associated with the club over the years

AMATEUR PLAYERS

Before professionalism was introduced to the game on a permanent basis (it was finally recognised by the FA in July 1885 after years of debate) many talented amateur footballers paraded their skills up and down the country and like a lot of other clubs, United were privileged to have some of these players represent the club. Among them were George Aizlewood, William Beardshaw, Edward C Benson, Thomas BA Clarke, Richard Creighton, Robert Fenwick, George J Groves and Bernard L Shaw.

Between 1902 and the late 1920s several more donned the famous red and white stripes, among them Fred Milnes (1902-05), Jimmy Raine (1904-05), Dr J Brown-Sim (1908-09), Ernest Ibbotson (1908-09), AR 'Dicky' Leafe (1911) and Jack Roxburgh (1925-27). And there were also quite a few amateurs who played the odd game for the Blades during WW2, some of whom later turned professional at Bramall Lane.

John Fulford, an amateur with the club, was killed on active service in WW2. Jack Chafer (as a guest) was another amateur WW2 player with the Blades.

Amateur forward Bill Hudson scored on his League debut for the Blades v. Chelsea in 1953.

Two Blades players have been capped by Scotland at amateur level - 1980s centre-half Ken McNaught and 1920s centre-forward Jack Roxburgh.

Tommy Morren, a future United centre-half, gained an FA Amateur Cup winners medal with Middlesbrough in 1895.

Mansfield Town fielded six amateurs v. Sheffield United in a WW2 game in December 1942. Jack Stone scored five goals as the Blades won 6-2.

Billy Russell was still an amateur with the Blades when he made his League debut against Charlton Athletic in August 1957, scoring in a 3-1 defeat. He won four caps for England at amateur level.

ANDERSON, Peter Thomas
Forward: 31+2 apps. 12 goals
Born: Hendon, 31 May 1949.
Career: Hendon, Luton Town (professional, February 1971), Tampa Bay Rowdies (May 1976), BLADES (£80,000, September 1978), Tampa Bay Rowdies (May 1979), Millwall (December 1980, retired in May 1983).
A smart footballer with good pace and telling shot, Peter Anderson scored 34 goals in 181 League outings for the Hatters before moving to Bramall Lane.

ANDERSON, William
Left-back: 27 apps.
Born: High Westwood, Newcastle-upon-Tyne, 12 January 1913. Died: Radcliffe-on-Trent, 19 February 1986.
Career: Medomsley Juniors, Chopwell Institute, Nottingham Forest (August 1931), BLADES (February 1932), Barnsley (May 1935, retired through injury six months later); Lincoln City (trainer July 1945, manager from January 1947 to January 1965, then general manager), Nottingham Forest (assistant-manager, October 1966 to January 1975), Arsenal (scout, February 1975), Ipswich Town (Scout 1976-77).
Bill Anderson didn't have much success as a player - making only 37 League appearances in total - with his debut for United coming against Wolves in October 1933. After retiring he did exceedingly well as a manager, guiding Lincoln City to two Third Division (North) championships (1948 & 1952) before handing over his duties to Roy Chapman.

ANGLO-ITALIAN CUP
United entered this competition in 1994-95, playing four games as follows:

24 August	v. Udinese	(h) 1-2	Att. 7,497
6 September	v. Piacenza	(a) 2-2	Att. 4,744
5 October	v. Ancona	(h) 3-3	Att. 1,827
15 November	v. Cesena	(a) 4-1	Att. 3,200

* United failed to qualify for the next stage.

Full record:

P	W	D	L	F	A
4	1	2	1	10	8

Andy Scott top-scored with three goals.

* Five players were sent-off during the United v. Udinese Anglo-Italian Cup game at Bramall Lane in August 1994. Besides a trio of Blades' men, Nathan Blake, Glenn Hodges and Charlie Hartfield, Udinese's Kozminski also saw red while United's manager Dave Bassett was 'sent-off' after protesting from the touchline. The game ended in a 2-1 win for the Italians.

11

ANGLO-SCOTTISH CUP

United played in this competition six seasons running: 1975-81 inclusive.
Their full record was:

P	W	D	L	F	A
23	11	4	15	30	41

Prior to 1975 this competition was known as the Texaco Cup (see under separate category).
Fact File
1975-76 - After a 3-1 home win over Blackburn Rovers and a 1-1 draw at Blackpool the Blades were defeated 3-1 by Manchester City at Maine Road.
1976-77 - Three successive 1-0 defeats - at home to Newcastle United and Middlesbrough and away at Hull City - ruined United's hopes of glory this season.
1977-78 - Following successive away wins at Oldham Athletic (3-2) and Hull City (2-0) the Blades caved in by losing 8-4 on aggregate to Notts County (going down 5-4 at home and losing 3-0 away).
1978-79 - Two quick defeats at the hands of Oldham Athletic 1-0 at Boundary Park and Bolton Wanderers by the same score at Burnden Park was followed by an academic 2-1 home victory over Sunderland as the Blades failed to qualify for the next stage.
1979-80 - Five straight wins: 1-0 v. Mansfield Town (h), 1-0 v. Cambridge United (a), 1-0 v. Notts County (a) and then double of 2-1 (h) and 1-0 (a) over Dundee took the Blades into the Final. There they met another Scottish side, St Mirren who proved far too strong and they duly blunted the Blades by drawing 0-0 at Bramall Lane and winning 4-0 at love Street to carry off the trophy.
1980-81 - No joy on this occasion as United failed to progress beyond the first phase, losing 1-0 at Chesterfield and then by the same score at Grimsby, despite beating Hull City 2-1 in between times at Bramall Lane.

ANNAN, Walter Archibald

Full-back: 28 apps.
Born: Bathgate, 1880.
Career: West Calder FC, St Bernard's, Sunderland (1903), BLADES (December 1903), Bristol City (April 1905), Burslem Port Vale (July 1911-May 1912).
Scotsman Archie Annan, tough and competitive, spent sixteen months at Bramall Lane during which time he made almost 30 senior appearances. He had over 150 outings for Bristol City.

ANTHONY, Graham John

Midfielder: 0+3 apps.
Born: South Shields, 9 August 1975
Career: BLADES (trainee, August 1991, professional July 1993), Scarborough (on loan, March 1996), Swindon Town (non-contract, March 1997), Plymouth Argyle (non-contract, August 1997), Carlisle United (November 1997), Barrow (August 2000).
Unable to get into the Blades' first XI, Graham Anthony moved to Swindon Town in 1997 after spending six years at Bramall Lane. He made 69 League appearances for Carlisle.

APPEARANCES

Here are lists of the top appearance-makers in major competitions for Sheffield United down the years (substitute appearances have been included in the totals):

Football League/Premiership
(qualification 300 apps)
632 Joe Shaw
576 Alan Hodgkinson
538 Alan Woodward
464 Ernie Needham
458 Len Badger
448 Billy Gillespie
439 Graham Shaw
437 Fred Tunstall
410 Cecil Coldwell
393 George Green
373 Bernard Wilkinson
363 Eddie Colquhoun
361 Jimmy Hagan
353 Albert Sturgess
347 Jack Smith
344 Jack Pickering
340 Tom Sampy
332 Simon Tracey
313 Tony Currie
313 Harry Johnson

Other Major
competitions
(qualification 100 apps)
218 Harry Latham
210 Walter Rickett
194 Jack Pickering
153 Albert Nightingale
150 Ernie Jackson
141 Bill Archer
137 Albert Sturgess
133 Fred White
130 Fred Furniss
124 Harold Pantling
121 Bill Brelsford
120 Jack Smith
118 George Utley
112 Tommy Sampy

Football League Cup
(qualification 20 apps)
32 Alan Woodward
30 Len Badger
24 Alan Hodgkinson
22 Tony Currie
22 Simon Tracey
21 Tony Kenworthy
21 Paul Stancliffe
21 Dane Whitehouse
20 Brian Deane
20 Eddie Colquhoun
20 Colin Morris

FA Cup
(qualification 35 apps)
53 Joe Shaw
52 Alan Hodgkinson
49 Ernie Needham
44 Billy Gillespie
41 Cecil Coldwell
41 Bill Foulke
40 Harry Thickett
37 Billy Bennett
37 Fred Priest
37 Graham Shaw

All Senior Matches
(qualification 300 apps)

714 Joe Shaw	479 Cecil Coldwell	342 Joe Kitchen
639 Alan Woodward	442 Jimmy Hagan	341 Paul Stancliffe
563 Billy Gillespie	438 George Green	336 Brian Richardson
561 Jack Pickering	433 Fred Furniss	335 Harold Gough
554 Ernie Needham	431 Eddie Colquhoun	333 Albert Cox
541 Len Badger	427 Harry Latham	324 Bill Cook
512 Albert Sturgess	417 Bill Brelsford	314 Ted Burgin
498 Graham Shaw	400 Ernie Jackson	310 Keith Edwards
498 Jack Smith	397 Bernard Wilkinson	310 Harry Thickett
491 Fred Tunstall	382 Simon Tracey	305 Gerry Summers
483 Tom Sampy	376 Tony Currie	302 Derek Pace
	368 Harold Pantling	301 Paul Garner
	357 Tony Kenworthy	301 Jimmy Simmons
	352 Bill Foulke	

Consecutive Appearances
The following players made 100 or more consecutive League appearances for the Blades during the seasons indicated:

203 Jack Smith*	1935-48
148 Alan Woodward	1967-72
136 Tony Currie	1968-72
126 Len Badger	1969-72
125 Joe Lievesley	1904-08
119 Derek Pace	1959-63
118 Brian Richardson	1960-64
106 Bob Cain	1894-98
106 Alan Hodgkinson	1965-68
102 Ted Burgin	1949-52

*Smith's tally includes three at the start of the ill-fated 1939-40 season.

Ever-Presents
Alan Woodward, with a total of five, holds the record for most ever-present campaigns for United: 1968-69/1969-70/1970-71/1973/74 & 1974-75. Jack Smith and Len Badger both had four seasons as ever-presents.

In season 1952-53, five players - Ted Burgin, Fred Furniss, Joe Shaw, Alf Ringstead & Derek Hawksworth appeared in all 42 League games for the Blades.

The longest spell with there being an ever-present in United's ranks is 12 years: 1990-91 to 2002-03 inclusive.

United's defence of goalkeeper Alan Hodgkinson, full-backs Cecil Coldwell, and Graham Shaw and half-backs Brian Richardson, Joe Shaw and Gerry Summers, along with centre-forward Derek Pace, played in the first 21 matches of the 1958-59 season.

Appearance Fact File
* The Shaw brothers, Graham and Joe, amassed a total of 1,212 competitive appearances for the Blades (1,071 in the Football League alone).
* Goalkeeper John Burridge appeared in 917 first-class matches during his 20-year career.
* Dennis Mortimer, too, appeared in more than 700 competitive games as a professional, including 590 in the Football League.
* Alan Woodward scored on his 500th League appearance for the Blades in a 3-2 win over Southampton in October 1977.
* Joe Shaw made his 600th League appearance for the Blades against West Ham at B.Lane on 6 February 1965. A year later he played in his last competitive game for the club on the same ground.
* Belarus striker Petr Katchouro holds the record for most substitute appearances by a United player, 57...(see under SUBSTITUTES).
* The most players called up for action by United during a full League season is 41 - in 1997-98 (46 matches).

One Match Wonders
Here is a list of some of the many players who made just one League or major League or FA Cup appearance for the Blades:
Ted Anderson (1905-06), Wattie Anderson (1899-1900), Max Ashmore (1957-58), Peter Bennie (1893-94), Chris Bettney* (1996-97), John Bisby (1905-06), John Blair (1897-98), Billy Booth (1907-08), Dr Jim Brown-Sim (1908-09), Pat Cassidy (1907-08), George Cole (1937-38), Mervyn Day (1991-92), John Ebbrell (1996-97), Archie French (1897-98), Harry Green (1925-26), Charlie Heeley (1902-03), Bill Hibberd (1898-99), Billy Hudson (1953-54), Ernie Ibbotson (1908-09), Gary Kelly (2002-03), Lewis Killen* (2001-02), Frank Lindley (1912-13), Dick Lowe (1937-38), Jim McCormick (1956-57), Hugh McNaught (1906-07), Ryan Mallon* (2001-02), Mark Mellors (1907-08), Carl Muggleton* (1995-96), Ernie G Needham (1912-13), Nathan Peel * (1991-92), Jim Raine (1904-05), Stan Rhodes (1951-52), JW Richardson (1895-96 - one goal), Charlie Saul (1900-01), Jim Senior (1894-95), Nigel Steanc* (1979-80), Bill Sykes (1919-20), Stan Taylor (1923-24 - one goal), Tyrone Thompson (2002-03), Jack Thorpe (1895-96), George Turnbull (1927-28), Charlie Weatherspoon (1950-51), Paul Wood* (1987-88) & Wilson (FAC, 1889-90).
* Appearance made as a substitute.

Career Appearance Records
The following players (all of whom were associated with the Blades) had excellent records in League football with over 550 appearances under their belts:

771 John Burridge	(1969-95)	632 Joe Shaw	(1948-66)	576 Alan Hodgkinson	(1953-71)
730 Stuart McCall	(1982-2003)	611 Stephen Charles	(1980-96)	565 Brian Deane*	(1985-2003)
714 Glenn Cockerill	(1976-98)	608 Dean Saunders	(1982-2001)	564 Peter Beagrie*	1983-2003)
685 Keith Curle	(1981-2002)	607 Bob Hatton	(1964-83)	553 Keith Edwards	(1975-91)
676 Paul Stancliffe	(1976-95)	605 Andy Goram	(1981-2003)	* Still adding to total in 2003
664 John MacPhail	(1973-95)	600 David Kelly*	(1983-2003)	
620 Paul Simpson	(1983-2003)	599 Ray McHale	(1970-87)	
562 Bruce Rioch	(1964-84)	599 Ian Rush	(1979-99)	
642 Mervyn Day	(1973-94)	594 Gordon Cowans	(1976-97)	
641 Chris Kamara	(1975-95)	590 Dennis Mortimer	(1969-87)	

13

Fact File

John Burridge appeared in 915 competitive matches all told (and well over 1,000 if you include friendlies, tour games etc). MacPhail appeared in 805 games.

NB: For United players' wartime appearances, see under WARTIME FOOTBALL.

ARCHER, William Henry

Centre-half: 141 'other' apps
Born: Scunthorpe, 5 February 1914. Died: 1992.
Career: Grantham, BLADES (first as a guest, January 1940 and then signed Feb 1941), Lincoln City (May 1945), Doncaster Rovers (season 1946-47).
A WW2 guest player from Sincil Bank, defender Bill Archer gave the Blades excellent service during the hostilities.
He never made the first XI with Lincoln but did appear in 14 League games for Rovers.

ARNOTT, Kevin William

Midfielder: 151+2 apps. 15 goals
Born: Gateshead, 28 September 1958
Career: Sunderland (junior, April 1974, professional September 1976), Blackburn Rovers (on loan, November 1981), BLADES (June 1982), Rotherham United (on loan, March 1983), Chesterfield (on loan, November 1987), Vasalund/Sweden (May 1987).
A very capable and effective midfield player with a splendid right foot, Kevin Arnott also possessed excellent vision and was at his best when his colleagues around him were also playing well.
He helped the Blades win promotion in 1984 and scored 16 goals in 133 League games for the Wearsiders.

ARSENAL

(originally Royal Arsenal & Woolwich Arsenal)
United's playing record against the Gunners:

Premiership

Venue	P	W	D	L	F	A
Home	2	0	2	0	2	2
Away	2	0	1	1	1	4
Totals	4	0	3	1	3	6

Football League

Home	44	24	12	8	97	60
Away	44	9	7	28	49	106
Totals	88	33	19	36	146	166

FA Cup

Home	4	2	0	2	6	8
Away	5	1	2	2*	8	8
Neutral	2	0	0	2	0	2
Totals	11	3	2	6	14	18

League Cup

Home	3	2	0	1	4	2
Away	2	0	1	1	0	2
Totals	5	2	1	2	4	4

*Includes the void 1999 FA Cup-tie (see below).

Formed by workers at the Royal Arsenal, Woolwich, in 1886, the Gunners began in Dial Square (name of one of the workshops) and included two former Nottingham Forest players, Fred Beardsley and Morris Bates. Beardsley wrote to his old club seeking help and they provided the new club with a full set of red jerseys and a ball. The club developed fast, turning professional in 1891 and joining the Football League two years later (elected to the Second Division). When WW1 broke out Arsenal were back in the Second Division (having suffered relegation after promotion) but when peacetime football started up again in 1919 they found themselves back in the top flight and they've stayed there ever since! (They went into the First Division when it was increased from 20 to 22 clubs).

The Blades and the Gunners first played against each other in a friendly at The Kennington Oval cricket ground in March 1891. Honours finished even at 1-1.
The first two League games between the clubs took place in 1904-05 (Division One). The Blades won 4-0 at home but lost 1-0 in London. The Blades claimed a remarkable 6-2 win at Highbury in 1920-21 (their only away success of the season). A 'young' Harry Johnson hit a hat-trick.
The first-ever radio commentary game featured the Blades against Arsenal at Highbury in January 1927. It finished in a 1-1 draw. The commentator was George Allison, later to become Arsenal's manager.
United led the Gunners 4-0 after 13 minutes of their home League game in January 1928. Going in 4-2 up at half-time, the Blades swept on to record a wonderful 6-2 victory, Harry Johnson scoring four times.
Arsenal won home League games by 8-1 and 9-2 in April 1930 and December 1932 respectively. Jack Lambert scored a hat-trick in the first victory and weighed in with a fivetimer in the second while Cliff Bastin netted three times. This latter defeat is United's heaviest reverse in top flight football to this day. But United were certainly unlucky; they were without their injured goalkeeper John Kendall for part of the match, Len Birks taking over between the posts.

Second Division United were beaten by Arsenal in the 1936 FA Cup Final, Ted Drake scoring the only goal in the 74th minute in front of 93,384 spectators (receipts of £24,857).

An aggregate total of more than 104,000 spectators saw the two 5th round FA Cup games between Arsenal and Second Division United in February 1959. The Blades won the replay at Bramall Lane 5-0.

Bernard Shaw (2) and Graham Shaw (3) were full-back partners for the Blades for the first time against Arsenal at Highbury in March 1965 (Division 1).

The Blades raced into a 4-0 lead inside the first 17 minutes of their home First Division game with Arsenal on 4 September 1973. The final score was 5-0.

Then, four-and-a-half years later, the Blades found themselves 4-0 adrift after just 17 minutes of their home 3rd round FA Cup-tie with Arsenal in January 1978. They lost 5-0.

The Arsenal-United 5th round FA Cup-tie at Highbury on 13 February 1999 was declared void after the Gunners had scored what was agreed to be an 'unsporting' goal in their 2-1 victory. The game ran its full course of 90 minutes but afterwards the FA decided to replay the contest (10 days later) and Arsenal again came out winners by the same score.

The biggest League Cup crowd the Blades have played in front of - 44,061 - saw the Gunners held to a 0-0 draw at Highbury in October 1971.

In 1996, having lost their Premiership status, United beat Arsenal 1-0 in a 3rd round FA Cup replay at Bramall Lane. Aussie striker Carl Veart scored the all-important goal.

Seven years later Neil Warnock's Blades side came so close to reaching the Final when they lost 1-0 in the semis to Arsenal in front of more than 59,000 spectators at Old Trafford, Freddie Ljungberg scoring the all-important goal after referee Graham Poll had failed to penalise Sol Campbell for a foul on Wayne Allison and then baulked Tongue as he tried to intercept a pass in midfield.

As manager, Herbert Chapman, a former United player, guided Arsenal through the club's greatest phase between 1930-36, bringing three successive League titles and FA Cup glory to Highbury. Joe Mercer played for Arsenal and manager United while Brice Rioch played for the Blades and was boss at Highbury. Stewart Houston was also a Blades player and later assistant-manager at Arsenal.. Among the players who served with both clubs we have Colin Addison, John Barnwell, Bob Benson, Fred Cheesemuir, Alf Common, Jimmy Dunne, Alex Forbes, Ralph Gaudie, Harold Hardinge, Charlie Hartfield, Colin Hill, Peter Kyle, Joe Lievesley, Scott Marshall, Brian Marwood, John Matthews, Trevor Ross, Wilf Rostron, John Ryan, Paddy Sloan and Jack Wilkinson.

ARTIFICIAL PITCHES

Other than playing the occasional friendly/tour game abroad, the first time United displayed their skills on an artificial pitch at competitive level was against Luton Town at Kenilworth Road in a 2nd round League Cup-tie on 8 October 1985. That evening a crowd of almost 9,000 saw the hatters win 3-1, Keith Edwards having the pleasure of scoring the first 'astro' goal for the Blades.

ASABA, Carl Edward

Striker: 63+17 apps* 12 goals*
Born: London, 28 January 1973.
Career: Dulwich Hamlet, Brentford (August 1994), Colchester United (on loan, February-match 1995), Reading (£800,000, August 1997), Gillingham (£600,000, August 1998), BLADES (£92,500, March 2001).

Carl Asaba drew up a fine goalscoring record with the Bees before his big-money move to Reading. At 6ft 2ins tall and 13st 5lbs in weight, he is ideally built for a striker but was plagued by injury during the 2002-03 season when his manager wanted him most! He came back towards the end of the campaign (in readiness for the Play-offs) having scored the 100th goal of his senior career while netting a hat-trick in Blades' 4-2 away League win at Brighton & Hove Albion on 19 October 2002. He certainly played his part in the 5-4 aggregate semi-final win over Nottingham Forest and also lined up against Wolves at Cardiff's Millennium Stadium in the Final.

ASHTON, Edward

Right or left-winger: 39 apps. 5 goals
Born: Kilnhurst, Yorkshire, 19 January 1906. Died: 1978
Career: Kilnhurst WMC, Mexborough Town, Barnsley, BLADES (£1,250, October 1936), Carlisle United (April 1938), Barnsley (season 1939-40).

Teddy Ashton, who was 30 years of age when he joined United in 1936, netted 70 goals in 289 League games for the Tykes. Small but strong and tireless with qualities of subtlety and ball control. He loved taking on defenders and gave the Blades useful service for some eighteen months before moving to Carlisle. He did not figure after WW2.

ASSOCIATE MEMBERS CUP

United's record in the AMC is:

Venue	P	W	D	L	F	A
Home	2	2	0	0	5	4
Away	2	1	0	1	1	1
Totals	4	3	0	1	6	5

United entered this competition - the forerunner to the Sherpa Van Trophy -in season 1983-84. They beat Rotherham 1-0 at Millmoor in their opening fixture, accounted for Bradford City 2-1 at Bramall Lane in their second and after defeating Scunthorpe United, also at home) 3-2 in the quarter-final, the Blades succumbed to Hull City in the semis, beaten 1-0 at Boothferry Park.

Only 12,971 spectators watched those four ties. Keith Edwards and Paul Garner topped the scoring lists with two goals apiece.

15

ASTON VILLA

United's playing record against the Blades:

Premiership

Venue	P	W	D	L	F	A
Home	2	0	0	2	1	4
Away	2	0	0	2	1	4
Totals	4	0	0	4	2	8

Football League

Home	58	27	16	15	110	81
Away	58	8	12	38	54	141
Totals	116	35	28	53	164	222

FA Cup

Home	2	0	0	2	0	3
Away	1	0	0	1	1	4
Neutral	2	1	1	0	5	2
Totals	5	1	1	3	6	9

WW2

Home	1	0	1	0	2	2
Away	1	0	0	1	2	3
Totals	2	0	1	1	4	5

Birmingham Cup

Away	1	0	0	1	0	3

Aston Villa, one of the founder members of the Football League in 1888, started life in 1874 when a group of cricket enthusiasts from the Villa Cross Wesleyan Chapel, Aston, Birmingham, decided to form a football section. Their first game was against Aston Brook St Mary's Rugby side, the match itself being split into two codes, rugby in the first half, soccer in the second. The round ball game was preferred and within a few years Aston Villa were one of the biggest names in the country, winning the FA Cup in 1887 and 1895 as well as claiming five League titles in the space of six seasons (1893-1900).

The first time the Blades met Villa in the Football League was in 1893-94 (Division 1). United won 3-0 at Bramall Lane but lost 4-0 at Perry Barr. Villa went on to win their first championship.

On 12 November 1894, Villa's Perry Barr ground was completely under water but the referee ordered the League game to be played. Several players left the field during the course of the match and at one stage United were down to seven men. A handful of Villa players went off to change their shirts and take hot drinks while a bottle of brandy was passed around among the players. Villa's Jack Devey donned an overcoat at one point and his colleagues Charlie Athersmith and goalkeeper Tom Wilkes both borrowed umbrellas from fans. A crowd of 7,000 saw Villa win 5-0.

In January 1898, a record crowd at Villa Park (43,000) saw United win 2-1 on their way to the League Title. After Villa had led with a Fred Wheldon penalty, Jack Cunningham equalised on 80 minutes and then the same player snatched the winner in the last minute.

There was a terrific battle involving the Blades and Villa for the League title in 1900. In the end Villa won the prize (50 pts to 48) after United only collected one point from their last two matches.

United started 1902 off in great style, beating Villa 6-0 at home on New Year's Day. (Did the opposition have a hangover I wonder?)

Only 4,850 fans saw the end-of-season League game in April 1913 when Villa (FA Cup winners) beat United 4-2 at Bramall Lane. This is the lowest attendance for a League game between the two clubs.

Fourteen goals were scored in the two League games in 1931-32; United won 5-4 at Bramall Lane, Villa 5-0 in Aston.

United led Villa 5-1 in a home League game in December 1935. The visitors fought back to 5-4 and even missed a penalty!

Between 1902 and 1946 United managed to record only one League win over Villa, losing 26 of 30 fixtures, including 16 in successive seasons.

Derek Pace scored a hat-trick (against his future club) when Villa beat the Blades 3-2 in April 1956. His first goal came after just 10 seconds.

When United won 3-1 at Villa Park in February 1960, former Villa player 'Doc' Pace scored a hat-trick. That was Villa's only home defeat of the season as they took the Second Division title.

When Villa beat the Blades 2-0 in August 1992, it was their first League success at Bramall Lane for 31 years (since September 1961).

The Blades completed their first League double over Villa for more than 60 years when they recorded 2-1 home and away wins in 1962-63, Pace again scoring against hiss old club in the win at 'the Lane.'

Villa were the first English club to field two German-born players in a League game when they introduced Stefan Beinlich and Matthias Breitkreutz against United (home) on 27 January 1993.

United's first home defeat in the Premiership was at the hands of Villa on 29 August 1992...the visitors won 2-0.

The Blades knocked Villa out of the FA Cup in a semi-final replay at Derby in 1901, winning 3-0 after a goalless draw at Nottingham. Allan Evans, playing at centre-forward, scored six goals for Villa's reserves against United's second XI in a Central League game at Villa Park in February 1978. The Blades lost 10-0!

Several internationals have been associated with both clubs over the years, including: Earl Barrett, Michael Boulding, Gordon Cowans, RE 'Bob' Evans, Willie Hamilton, Trevor Hockey, Paul McGrath, Dennis Mortimer, Bruce Rioch, Dean Saunders and Peter Withe ...also among the many other players who have worn the colours of the Blades and Villa we have Billy Brawn, John Burridge, Bobby Campbell, Franz Carr, Mervyn Day, Kevin Gage, Dean Glover, Ian 'Chico' Hamilton, Jimmy Harrop, Peter Kyle, Ken McNaught, Derek Pace, John Roxburgh (amateur international), Simon Stainrod and Carl Tiler, while Joe Mercer was manager of both clubs.

ATKINS, Robert Gary

Central-defender: 48+6 apps. 3 goals
Born: Leicester, 16 October 1962.
Career: Enderby Town, BLADES (July 1982), Preston North End (February 1985-May 1991).
After helping the Blades win promotion from Division Three in 1984, Robert Atkins - strong and competent - went on to appear in more than 200 first-class games for the Lillywhites over a period of six years.

ATTENDANCES
The all-time record crowd at Bramall Lane is 68,287 for the United v. Leeds United 5th round FA Cup-tie on 15 February 1936.
A record attendance for a League game at Bramall Lane - 59,555 - saw the Sheffield derby between United and Wednesday on 15 January 1927.
The largest crowd to watch the Blades play a home League Cup-tie has been 39,614 v. Leeds United in the 3rd round on 10 October 1978.

Record Crowds
This is how the Bramall Lane attendance record has been broken over the years, bearing in mind that the early figures were only approximate:

100	The XI v. The 22	Cricket	30.04.1855
1,000*	Yorkshire v. Sussex	Cricket	27.08.1855
2,000	Sheffield v. London	Representative	02.12.1871
8,000	Heeley v. Wednesday	Challenge	10.03.1877
9,000	Sheffield v. Glasgow	Inter-City	09.02.1878
12,000**	Blues v. Reds	Practice Match	14.10.1878
20,700	Yorkshire v. Australia	Cricket	28.06.1884
22,688	PNE v. West B Albion	FAC S/F	16.03.1889
23,000	Notts Co v. Sunderland	FAC S/F	25.02.1891
25,000	Aston Villa v. Sunderland	FAC S/F	27.02.1892
27,000	United v. Wednesday	Division 1	16.10.1893
28,600	United v. Wednesday	Division 1	26.12.1896
30,000	Liverpool v. Aston Villa	FAC S/F	20.03.1897
37,389	United v. Wednesday	Division 1	27.12.1897
38,408	United v. Wednesday	Division 1	26.12.1908
40,118	Manch Utd v. Newcastle U	FAC S/F	27.03.1909
42,912	United v. Wednesday	Division 1	25.10.1914
51,016	United v. Bradford PA	FAC Rd 2	31.01.1915
51,500	United v. Burnley	Division 1	27.12.1920
50,060	United v. Cardiff City	Division 1	25.12.1923
54,531	Aston Villa v. Burnley	FAC S/F	29.03.1924
57,197	United v. West B Albion	FAC Rd 4	07.03.1925
62,041	United v. Sunderland	FAC Rd 4	30.01.1926
68,287	United v. Leeds Utd	FAC Rd 5	15.02.1936

* Cricket matches around this time usually attracted audiences of 1,000 spectators on average per day.
** It is thought that up to 8,000 more spectators entered the ground illegally. This was the first floodlit football match anywhere in the world.

Lowest Attendances at Bramall Lane (games involving United):

500	United v. Darwen	Division 2	15.10.1892
676	United v. Doncaster Rovers	County Cup	08.12.1980
750	United v. Blackburn Rovers	Division 1	09.01.1897
826	United v. Doncaster Rovers	County Cup S/F	05.05.1980
1,151	United v. Rotherham Utd	County Cup	06.11.1934
1,400	United v. Rotherham Utd	County Cup S/F	06.05.1981
1,500	United v. Mansfield Town	WW2 EM	08.06.1940
1,600	United v. Rotherham Utd	County Cup S/F	05.10.1936
1,827	United v. Ancona	Anglo-Italian Cup	05.10.1994
2,000	United v. Sheffield FC	FAC Rd 3Q	11.11.1889
2,000	United v. Rotherham Town	FAC Rd 4Q	21.12.1889
2,000*	United v. Burnley	FAC Rd 1	18.01.1890
2,500	United v. Millwall Athletic	FAC Rd 1	02.02.1895
2,500	United v. Rotherham Utd	York/Humberside Cup	10.08.1989
2,981	United v. Chester City	Sherpa Van Trophy	13.12.1988
4,014	United v. Nottingham Forest	Division 2	27.04.1935
4,075**	United v. Bury	League Cup Rd 2/2	20.09.1995
4,931	United v. Derby County	Division 1	28.04.1934
5,000	United v. Darwen	Division 2	15.10.1892
6,647***	United v. Crystal Palace	Division 2	17.03.1987
7,004+	United v. Fulham	FAC Rd 3	13.01.1986

* Some references indicate that this attendance was 1,500.
** Lowest League Cup crowd at 'the Lane.'
*** United's lowest post WW2 League attendance.
+ The lowest post WW2 FA Cup attendance at 'the Lane.'

Other low attendances at 'the Lane' (games not involving United):

100	Sheffield v. Hallam	Representative	29.12.1862
200	Sheffield v. Hallam	Representative	12.02.1861
500	Hallam v. Norfolk	Representative	05.03.1867
500	Garrick v. Wednesday	Friendly	15.02.1868
500	Sheffield v. North Wales	Representative	15.01.1877
500	Sheffield v. Staffordshire	Representative	15.12.1877
500	English v. Scottish	Benefit Match	17.01.1898
500	Gainsborough Trinity v Ilkeston	FA Cup	28.11.1910
650	Sheffield v. Shropshire	Representative	30.10.1873
700	Sheffield v. Royal Engineers	Friendly	20.12.1873
800	Wednesday v. Staveley	FA Cup	21.12.1881

(See also under matches at Bramall Lane).

United's average home League attendances: 1890-91 to date:

1892-93	2,659		1966-67	20,599
1893-94	9,063		1967-68	22,497
1894-95	8,001		1968-69	15,480
1895-96	7,783		1969-70	17,840
1896-97	8,650		1970-71	25,254
1897-98	12,298		1971-72	33,189
1898-99	10,323		1972-73	23,509
1899-00	11,199		1973-74	22,917
1900-01	13,378		1974-75	22,555
1901-02	13,611		1975-76	23,549
1902-03	12,427		1976-77	16,779
1903-04	16,419		1977-78	15,489
1904-05	14,895		1978-79	16,339
1905-06	13,943		1979-80	16,584
1906-07	12,724		1980-81	12,772
1907-08	13,537		1981-82	14,892
1908-09	13,805		1982-83	11,764
1909-10	13,968		1983-84	12,881
1910-11	13,687		1984-85	12,055
1911-12	14,549		1985-86	10,798
1912-13	16,705		1986-87	9,992
1913-14	21,503		1987-88	10,207
1914-15	14,947		1988-89	12,222
1919-20	24,160		1989-90	19,988
1920-21	27,619		1990-91	21,451
1921-22	26,143		1991-92	22,096
1922-23	20,595		1992-93	18,801
1923-24	23,670		1993-94	19,577
1924-25	20,762		1994-95	14,463
1925-26	19,149		1995-96	12,901
1926-27	22,662		1996-97	16,638
1927-28	19,482		1997-98	17,946
1928-29	22,395		1998-99	16,243
1929-30	19,711		1999-00	13,718
1930-31	19,996		2000-01	17,211
1931-32	20,795		2001-02	18,020
1932-33	14,296		2002-03	18,069
1933-34	15,902			
1934-35	14,166			
1935-36	18,428			
1936-37	21,136			
1937-38	21,927			
1938-39	26,022			
1946-47	29,537			
1947-48	35,094			
1948-49	34,386			
1949-50	30,764			
1950-51	27,488			
1951-52	31,185			
1952-53	31,027			
1953-54	31,313			
1954-55	23,880			
1955-56	23,581			
1956-57	21,803			
1957-58	19,243			
1958-59	19,580			
1959-60	18,037			
1960-61	18,487			
1961-62	22,526			
1962-63	22,775			
1963-64	21,654			
1964-65	20,006			
1965-66	19,405			

NB:

Division 2: 1892-93;	Division 1: 1893-1934;
Division 2: 1934-39;	Division 1: 1946-49;
Division 2: 1949-53;	Division 1: 1953-56;
Division 2: 1956-61;	Division 1: 1961-68;
Division 2: 1968-71;	Division 1: 1971-76;
Division 2: 1976-79;	Division 3: 1979-81;
Division 4: 1981-82;	Division 3: 1982-84;
Division 2: 1984-88:	Division 3: 1988-89;
Division 2: 1989-90;	Division 1: 1990-92;
FA Premiership: 1992-94;	Division 1: 1994-2003.

Wartime Average Home Attendances:

1915-16	7,539
1916-17	7,361
1917-18	10,012
1918-19	13,872
1939-40	7,558
1940-41	3,323
1941-42	7,387
1942-43	12,278
1943-44	13,830
1944-45	11,023
1945-46	24,844

Attendances of over 50,000 at Bramall Lane:

68,287	United v. Leeds Utd	FAC Rd 5	15.02.1936
62,041	United v. Sunderland	FAC Rd 4	30.01.1926
62,022	United v. Grimsby Town	FAC Rd 5	11.02.1939
59,692	United v. Sheffield Wed	FAC Rd 6	12.03.1960
59,555	United v. Sheffield Wed	Division 1	15.01.1927
57,197	United v. West B Albion	FAC Rd 4	07.03.1925
57,000	United v. Burnley	FAC Rd 6	10.03.1962
56,495	United v. Norwich City	FAC Rd 6	28.02.1959
55,847	United v. West B Albion	FAC Rd 5	15.02.1958
54,531	Aston Villa v. Burnley	FAC S/F	29.03.1924
52,640	United v. Nottingham Forest	FAC Rd 6	03.03.1928
52,199	United v. Rotherham Utd	Division 2	13.10.1951
51,893	United v. Derby County	Division 1	08.11.1947
51,745	United v. Everton	FAC Rd 3	21.02.1925
51,644	United v. Sheffield Wed	Division 2	21.01.1950
51,516	United v. Sunderland	FAC Rd 5	18.02.1956
51,500	United v. Burnley	Division 1	27.12.1920
51,075	United v. Sheffield Wed	Division 2	08.09.1951
51,016	United v. Bradford PA	FAC Rd 2	31.01.1915
50,859	United v. Stoke City	FAC Rd 4/2	28.01.1946
50,827	United v. Sheffield Wed	Division 2	26.02.1938
50,723	United v. Arsenal	Division 1	24.08.1953
50,586	United v. Preston N End	Division 2	27.12.1949
50,500	United v. Burnley	Division 1	27.12.1920
50,264	United v. Liverpool	FAC Rd 4	22.01.1938
50,060	United v. Cardiff City	Division 1	25.12.1923

Attendances of over 63,000 for United games:

114,815	United v. Tottenham H	FAC Final	20.04.1901(CP)
93,384	United v. Arsenal	FAC Final	25.04.1936(W)
91,763	United v. Cardiff City	FAC Final	25.04.1925(W)
80,000	Chilean WC XI v. United	Friendly	05.06.1966(S)
76,912	United v. Southampton	FAC Final	19.04.1902(CP)
75,364	United v. Sheff Wed	FAC S/F	03.04.1993(W)
73,833	United v. Derby County	FAC Final	15.04.1899(CP)
71,779*	United v. Bolton Wds	FAC S/F	24.03.1923(OT)
69,473	United v. Wolves	Div 1 PO Final	26.05.2003(MS)
69,360	United v. Huddersfield	FAC S/F r	02.04.1928(MR)
69,250	United v. Huddersfield	FAC S/F	24.03.1928(OT)
68,287	United v. Leeds United	FAC Rd 5	15.02.1936(BL)
65,754	United v. Southampton	FAC S/F	28.03.1925(SB)
65,385	Sheff Wed v. United	Division 2	05.01.1952 (H)
64,383	United v. Crystal Palace	Div 1 PO Final	26.05.1997(W)
63,016	Sunderland v. United	FAC Rd 5	14.02.1931(RP)

Key: BL - Bramall Lane; CP - Crystal Palace; H - Hillsborough; MR - Maine Road; MS - Millennium Stadium (Cardiff); OT - Old Trafford; RP - Roker Park; S - Santiago, Chile; SB - Stamford Bridge; W - Wembley
* Probably much bigger as thousands of fans entered ground illegally.

Low Away Crowds (first team matches - all levels)

40	Fiorenzuola v. United	Fr, Italy	26.07.1998
50	Parma XI v. United	Fr, Italy	21.07.1998
75	E'Quip R XI v. United	Fr, Italy	23.07.1998
100	Grantham v. United	Friendly	02.08.1983
100	Grantham v. United	Friendly	01.08.1985
150	El Ahi v. United	Fr, Dubai	03.02.1994
200	Barrow v. United	Friendly	26.02.1986
200*	Al Ain v. United	Fr, Dubai	06.02.1994
200	Grimsby T v. United	WW1 MS	23.12.1916
200	Glossop v. United	Friendly	13.05.1987
200	Immingham v. United	Friendly	06.04.1992
218	Ski IL v. United	Fr, Norway	04.08.1993
300	Greta FC v. United	Friendly	15.10.1984
300	TSV Havelse v. United	Fr, Germany	24.07.1989
300	Moss IK v. United	Fr, Norway	03.08.1993
300	Denaby Utd v. United	Friendly	23.10.1990
350	Altrincham v. United	Friendly	11.08.1990
400	Raith Rovers v. United	Friendly	03.08.1982
400	Falkirk v. United	Friendly	07.08.1982
400	Krylbo v. United	Fr, Sweden	08.08.1988
400	TSV Friesen v. United	Fr, Germany	25.07.1989
404	Poole Town v. United	Friendly	29.12.1981

431	Barnsley v. United	CC S/F	17.05.1982
450	Bradford City v. United	WW1 MS	11.12.1915
500	Lincoln City v. United	WW1 MS	20.01.1917
500*	Lincoln City v. United	In Gibralter	24.05.1976
500	Clyde v. United	Friendly	31.07.1981
500*	Doncaster R v. United	Friendly	12.08.1983
500	Darlington v. United	Friendly	10.08.1984
500	Ljusdals v. United	Fr, Sweden	01.08.1988
500	Hagfors v. United	Fr, Sweden	03.08.1988
500	Vassunda v. United	Fr, Sweden	07.08.1988
539	Sutton Utd v. United	Benefit	15.11.1993
600	Harrogate RA v. United	Friendly	11.03.1991
600	Ullensalker v. United	Fr, Norway	02.08.1993
600	Marsala v. United	Fr, Italy	21.05.1995
620	Berwick Rgrs v. United	Friendly	11.08.1982
630	Queen of S'th v. United	Friendly	01.08.1981
700	TuS Celle v. United	Fr, Germany	23.07.1989
700	Langangen v. United	Fr, Norway	01.08.1991
700	Viterbese v. United	Fr, Italy	18.05.1994
711	Tulsa Renegades	Fr, USA	22.05.1991
741	Lincoln City v. United	Benefit	23.04.1991
800	Orkdal FC v. United	Fr, Norway	29.07.1995
850	Averoy FC v. United	Fr, Norway	26.07.1995
870	Huddersf'd T v. United	WW2 NR	02.11.1940
900	Nordstern v. United	Fr, Switz'd	29.07.1978
900	Skegness T v. United	Friendly	30.07.1985
900	Kongsvinger v. United	Fr, Norway	29.07.1993
959	Barnsley v. United	WW2 NS	18.10.1941
976	Barrow v. United	Friendly	07.12.1981
1,000	Bradford PA v. United	Benefit	04.05.1927
1,000*	Jersey XI v. United	Friendly	15.05.1986
1,000*	Skegness T v. United	Friendly	31.07.1989

* Estimated attendance

Lowest Away Crowds (in major competitions)

1,050	West B Albion v. United	Division 1	30.04.1901
1,325	Wimbledon v. United	Division 1	07.04.2003
1,379	Lincoln C v. United	LC Rd 1/2	23.08.2000
2,439	Colchester Utd v. United	Division 3	04.04.1981
2,555	Shrewsbury T v. United	Division 2	17.11.1987
2,842	Wrexham v. United	FAC Rd 1	19.11.1983
3,058	Hereford Utd v. United	Division 4	17.02.1982
3,979	Wimbledon v. United	Premiership	20.02.1993

Other low attendances, perhaps under 1,000, could well have been registered in other tour games in Holland 1955, 1957, 1960, 1961, Switzerland 1960, Cyprus 1974, Sweden 1982, 1984, 1991, 1992 and 1997, Norway 1991, 1995 and 1997, Switzerland 1994 and in Northern Ireland 1996 as well as for friendlies against non-League opposition in the U.K.
The Yorkshire & Humberside Cup game between United and Halifax Town was played behind closed doors at Huddersfield's Leeds Road ground on 22 August 1988.

Attendance Facts & Figures
* Attendance figures were not officially registered at Football League head-quarters until 1925 and therefore several crowd figures prior to that may not be precise as a lot were estimated by the home team and also by the newspapers.
* United's best away League Cup crowd has been 44,061 v. Arsenal at Highbury on 26 October 1971 (round 4). The smallest League Cup turnout has been 4,075 v. Bury on 20 September 1995 (round 2/1st leg).
* A record County Cup crowd at Bramall Lane of 39,698 saw the United-Sheffield Wednesday clash in 1925-26, while an overall best of 49,980 saw the County Cup clash at Hillsborough on 12 February 1949.
* A crowd of 30,464 saw the Wednesday v. United Zenith Data Systems Cup encounter at Hillsborough in November 1989 and a WW2 crowd of 52,836 witnessed the League North Cup-tie at Newcastle United's St James' Park ground in April 1944.
* There have been excellent attendances at testimonial matches for two United players: 29,166 for Jimmy Hagan's night out in 1956-57 and 29,500 for Joe Shaw's evening in 1964-65.
* United's best home League attendance in the 'old Third Division

was 42,526 v. Sheffield Wednesday on 5 April 1980, while in the 'old' Fourth it was 24,593 v. Bradford City on 30 March 1982.

* The meagre attendance of 20,470 for the 1901 FA Cup Final replay at Bolton was due to thousands of supporters staying away in fear of being crushed, thus leaving hundreds of meat pies unsold which had to be given away free of charge. The first game at Crystal Palace had attracted a crowd of 114,815 - the biggest ever to watch a United team in action. (Some references indicate there were 110,805 fans present for that game).

* Although the official attendance figure was given as 71,779, the 1923 FA Cup semi-final between Bolton Wanderers and United at Old Trafford may well attracted a crowd of 90,000 or more as thousands entered the ground illegally.

* A record post WW2 attendance at Bramall Lane of 59,692 saw the United v. Sheffield Wednesday 6th round FA Cup-tie in March 1960.

* The record attendance for a Sheffield derby - 65,327 - assembled at Hillsborough on 5 January 1952 when United beat the Owls 3-1 in a Second Division game after Ted Burgin had saved Redfern Froggatt's penalty.

* Only 5,587 fans saw the United-Bristol City League Cup clash on 7 October 1986 - the lowest crowd for a major game at Bramall Lane since February 1895.

* A record League crowd of 23,500 saw United beaten 3-1 by Sunderland at their Newcastle Road ground in March 1898.

* There was also a record crowd of 30,000 for the Newcastle United v. Blades First Division game at St James' Park in October 1899.

* The biggest crowd for a United home game during WW2 was that of 50,809 for the 4th round FA Cup clash with Stoke City at Bramall Lane on 28 January 1946, It is believed another 10,000 fans may well have forced their way into the ground illegally.

* A crowd of 48,483 saw the United v. Aston Villa LCN S/F at Bramall Lane on 22 April 1944 and 52,836 attended the LCN 3rd round tie v. Newcastle United at St James' Park on 8 April 1944

* A record attendance at Belle Vue - 28,560 - saw United draw 0-0 with Rovers in a Second Division game in April 1936.

* Only 2,429 loyal supporters attended the Huddersfield Town v. Blades Second Division match in February 1933 - the lowest for a League game at Leeds Road.

* A record Anfield crowd of 51,859 saw the Liverpool-United 3rd round FA Cup-tie in February 1923 (the Blades won 2-1).

* The attendance of 1,329 for the Wimbledon v. United First Division game at Selhurst Park in April 2003, was the lowest for a League game involving the Blades (at home or away) for 102 years....since the fixture with WBA at The Hawthorns in April 1901.

ATTERCLIFFE

The Blades beat Attercliffe 6-0 in a home Sheffield County Cup game in January 1890. Billy Calder led the scoring spree in front of just 650 hardy supporters.

United also beat near neighbours Attercliffe 2-0 in the Wharncliffe Charity Cup in March 1892.

Early United secretary John Nicholson was also the secretary of Attercliffe FC.

ATTREE, Albert

Bert Attree played against his 'own' club - Doncaster Rovers - in a friendly match on 28 December 1889. The Blades arrived at the ground with only 10 men and Attree agreed to full the gap. Rovers won 2-0.

AWAY FROM HOME

* United have played away Football League matches against 97 different clubs in 100 seasons on 124 different club grounds.

* United's best season away from home was in 1981-82, the club's only one in Division Four, with 12 wins out of 23 matches.

* Their best in the top flight was nine wins (in 1946-47) out of 21 matches, although the championship-winning campaign of 1897-98 was the best in relative terms with weight wins and four draws and only three defeats.

* The Blades' best goal tally is 41 (in 23 matches) in 1981-82, while their best in the top Division is 38, in season 1946-47 (21 matches played).

* United's worst season on the road was their first relegation campaign of 1933-34 when they registered just one win and suffered 18 defeats from 21 starts. They also conceded 76 goals and suffered their heaviest defeat to date - losing 10-3 at Middlesbrough.

* In their first ever League season of 1892-93, United technically claimed their best away record (from games played) with six wins and 27 goals (from just 11 matches).

* United's best away win in the Football League (goals scored) is 10-0 v. Burslem Port Vale in December 1892 (Division 2).

* The Blades' biggest away win a Cup game is 6-1 at Scarborough on 5 September 1889. they also won 5-0 at Newcastle United on 10 January 1914.

* Their heaviest Cup defeat on the road (in any major competition) has been that of 13-0 in an FA Cup-tie in February 1890.

* United have never failed to register at least one away win in the Football League per season (the nearest coming in 1920-21 & 1933-34 (with just one success).

* During one spell in the late 1930s United could win away but not at home, so they decided to treat home matches as away ones! On the Saturday morning all the players met and took a bus into Derbyshire, lunched and then returned to Bramall Lane in time for the kick-off. The little dodge met with immediate success,

21

Sheffield United v.s Lincoln City 28 January 1961

22

Programme December 26 1904.

BADGER, Leonard

Right-back: 539+2 apps. 8 goals
Born: Sheffield, 8 June 1945
Career: BLADES (juniors, June 1960, professional August 1962), Chesterfield (January 1976-May 1978).
Len Badger played four games for England Schoolboys and was also honoured by his country's Youth team (winning the European International Youth Tournament in 1963, starring in the vital 3-0 win over Scotland at Wembley) before going on to win 13 Under-23 caps (his first in a 3-3 draw with Scotland in February 1964) as well as representing the Football League. He is also United's youngest-ever captain. Not blessed with great strength or physique, he nevertheless developed into a splendid full-back with fine positional sense and good ball control. He helped the Blades gain promotion from Division Two in 1971 (as an ever-present) and had amassed well over 540 senior appearances by the time he left Bramall Lane for Saltergate in 1976. Badger admits that Bolton, Liverpool and England international Peter Thompson was the Winger he ever faced..."He used to give me loads of trouble; I could never contain him or get near him half the time."

BADGE

The badge currently embroidered on the United players' jerseys was first used in 1977. The design itself incorporates the name (Sheffield United Football Club) and the club's colours of red, black and white. Also the year the club was formed (1889) plus two crossed scimitar blades and the white rose of Yorkshire.
Many years earlier the club badge/logo depicted two cricket balls and bats, a set of stumps and a football with two hands joined, thus indicating the unity between the two sports (soccer and cricket) which was played at Bramall Lane.
Occasionally, for the odd big match, like the 1925 FA Cup Final, United players have had the Sheffield coat of arms on their jerseys. Indeed, this was prominent for more than a decade prior to 1977.

BAILEY, Thomas Graham

Full-back: 23 apps.
Born: Dawley, Shropshire, 22 March 1920.
Career: Donnington Wood FC, Huddersfield Town (professional, March 1937), BLADES (March 1948-May 1949).
Graham Bailey, tough and resolute, made 244 first team appearances for the Terriers (33 in the Football League) before, during and after WW2.

BAINES, Reginald

Inside or centre-forward: 11 apps. 6 goals
Born: York, 3 March 1907. Died: suddenly in 1974 when holidaying abroad.
Career: York City (Midland League days), Selby Town, Scarborough, York City (September 1931), BLADES (£500, May 1933), Doncaster Rovers (January 1934), York City (August 1937), Halifax Town (season 1938-39).
Reg Baines was a typical old-fashioned, hustling goalscoring centre-forward who netted 93 times in 140 first-class matches in three separate spells with the Minstermen., scoring on his FL debut at Carlisle in 1931. He set a new club scoring record of 29 goals in 1931-32 that stood until 1952 when Billy Fenton weighed in with 31. He struggled to come to terms with a higher level of football (despite scoring six times for the Blades) and in 1934 moved to Doncaster, helping the Belle Vue club gain promotion to the Second Division the following season. After notching 43 goals in 80 League games for Rovers he returned to Bootham Crescent where his presence was immense as the Minstermen reached the quarter-finals of the FA Cup, Baines grabbing five goals during that excellent run, including a hat-trick in a 3-2 win over West Bromwich Albion. He ended his playing days The Shay in 1939. A more than useful club cricketer, Baines played many seasons for Rowntrees CC, the chocolate company where he worked for 50 years.

BALL

The laws of Association Football state that the matchball will not be more than 28 inches and no less than 27 inches in circumference, while the weight at the start of the game must not be more than 16 ounces nor less than 14 ounces.

BALL, John

Inside or centre-forward: 14 apps. 4 goals
Born: Hazel Grove near Stockport, 29 September 1899. Died: 1989.
Career: Silverwood Colliery FC (Sheffield Association League), BLADES (July 1919), Bristol Rovers (May 1921), Wath Wanderers (August 1922), Bury (June 1923), West Ham United (July 1929), Coventry City (May 1930), Stourbridge (season 1931-32).
A former miner, John Ball, was doing well with the Blades until a bad leg injury forced him back into non-League football with Bristol Rovers in 1921. Then, after playing in the Midland League for a season, his career underwent a remarkable transformation when he signed for Bury in 1923 ...and his fairytale was complete when he was chosen to play for England against Ireland in Belfast in October 1927 and he gave an impressive display as a makeshift goalie after former Blades' 'keeper Ted Hufton had broken his arm. He appeared scored 93 goals in 203 League games for the Shakers.

BARCLAY, Robert
Inside-forward: 264 apps. 77 goals
Born: Scotswood, 27 October 1907. Died: 1969
Career: Bell's Close Amateurs, Scotswood FC, Derby County, BLADES (£3,500, June 1931), Huddersfield Town (£7,000, March 1937 with Eddie Boot), Hurst FC (retiring in 1946).
Bobby Barclay was a clever ball player with exceptional distribution qualities although at times he failed to display his best form with the Blades for whom he played in the 1936 FA Cup Final, and then two years later returned to Wembley for the 1938 Final with Huddersfield. Unfortunately he was a loser on both occasions. He was capped three times by England against Scotland and Ireland in 1932, when he scored against both nations, and versus Scotland (again) in 1936.

BARKE, John Lloyd
Right-half/centre-half: 7 apps.
Born: Nurncargate, Notts, 16 December 1912. Died: Kirkby-in-Ashfield, 7 March 1976.
Career: Nottinghamshire Boys, Annessley Colliery FC, Chesterfield (amateur, June 1930), East Kirby Welfare, Bleakhall United, Mansfield Town (as a trialist), Scunthorpe & Lindsey United (August 1933), BLADES (May 1933, professional December 1934), Mansfield Town (£80, June 1937, caretaker-manager, August 1944-May 1945), Denaby United (player-manager, August 1947), Sutton Town (player-manager, season 1950-51), Ilkeston Town (player-manager to May 1952), Belper Town (player-manager during 1952-53) and Heanor Town (player-manager from August 1953, finally retiring from football in May 1954).
Despite being a willing worker and a solid tackler, and making a sound enough League debut against Hull City in 1935, John Barke failed to establish himself in the first team at Bramall Lane and left the club for Mansfield for just £80, half of which was his accrued share of benefit. He amassed 244 appearances for the Stags, twice helping them win the Notts FA County Cup (1938 & 1939) while also guesting for several clubs in and around the Nottinghamshire area during WW2. He later did well as a player-manager on the non-League circuit.

BARLOW, Frank Charles
Defender/midfielder: 137+7 apps. 3 goals
Born: Sheffield, 15 October 1946.
Career: BLADES (junior, April 1962, professional September 1965), Chesterfield (August 1972-May 1976); later coach at Birmingham City.
Able to play in most defensive positions as well as midfield, preferring to be in the centre of the park, Frank Barlow was an England Schoolboy international before signing for the Blades in 1962. A player's player, he became the 'brains behind the team's performances and spent the seven years at Bramall Lane during which time he helped United gain promotion in 1971 before transferring to Chesterfield. He quit League football in 1976 with over 260 appearances under his belt.
* Barlow gained entrance to Sheffield University to study chemistry.

24

BARNES, David
Full-back: 107 apps. one goal
Born: Paddington, London, 16 November 1961.
Career: Coventry City (apprentice, April 1977, professional May 1979), Ipswich Town (£25,000, October 1982), Wolverhampton Wanderers (£30,000, October 1984), Aldershot (August 1987), BLADES (£50,000, July 1989), Watford (January 1994), Colchester United (August 1996-May 1997).
When strong-tackling full-back David Barnes, a former England Youth international, joined the Blades from Aldershot in 1989, he had already amassed more than 200 competitive appearances. He took over the number '3' shirt from Wilf Rostron and helped United win promotion from Division Two in 1990.

BARNES, William
Inside/outside-left: 26 apps. 8 goals
Born: West Ham, London, 20 May 1879. Died: 1962.
Career: Leyton FC, Thames Ironworks, BLADES (July 1899), West Ham United (May 1902), Luton Town (August 1904), Queen's Park Rangers (July 1907), Southend United (May 1913).
Billy Barnes was mainly a reserve team player at Bramall Lane and when Walter Bennett was ruled out of the 1902 FA Cup Final replay through injury, he stepped up and scored the winning goal. Soon afterwards he left the Blades for West Ham for whom he made over 50 appearances. He played Southern League football for each of his last three clubs, notching 37 goals in 234 outings for QPR. He netted twice on his League debut for United in a 5-0 home win over Everton in December 1899.

BARNSLEY
(formerly Barnsley St Peter's)

United's playing record against the Tykes:

Football League

Venue	P	W	D	L	F	A
Home	25	13	7	5	46	22
Away	25	7	10	8	38	34
Totals	50	20	17	13	84	56

FA Cup

	P	W	D	L	F	A
Home	1	0	1	0	2	2
Away	2	1	1	0	1	0
Totals	3	1	2	0	3	2

League Cup

	P	W	D	L	F	A
Home	1	0	0	1	1	3

WW1

	P	W	D	L	F	A
Home	7	5	0	2	19	7
Away	7	2	3	2	10	10
Totals	14	7	3	4	29	17

WW2

	P	W	D	L	F	A
Home	12	10	2	0	24	9
Away	13	4	1	8	26	32
Totals	25	14	3	8	50	41

Sheffield & Hallamshire County Cup

	P	W	D	L	F	A
Home	15	11	4	0	46	15
Away	20	6	4*	10	30	41
Totals	35	17	8	10	46	56

* United won 5-4 on penalties after a 0-0 draw in 1982 semi-final.

Many clubs owe their inception to the church and Barnsley is among them. Formed in 1887 by the Rev. Thomas Preedy, curate of Barnsley St Peter's, they went under that name until it the latter part was dropped in 1897, a year before the Tykes gained entry to the Football League (Division 2).

Locked together at 3-3 in a Second Division home game with Barnsley in January 1938, United quickly went into overdrive and raced on to register a splendid 6-3 victory.

United were 2-0 and then 3-1 down to the Tykes in a Second Division game at Oakwell in September 1951. But they came back strongly to win 4-3 in front of 25,577 fans.

The Blades whipped Barnsley 6-1 at Oakwell and 5-0 at Bramall Lane to complete a splendid League double in 1956-57. Colin Grainger scored a hat-trick in the first game.

United repeated that 5-0 scoreline at 'the Lane' the following season and claimed a successive double with a 3-1 win at Barnsley.

In a WW2 game at Oakwell in February 1943, Barnsley led United 2-1 with six minutes remaining. The final score was a 4-2 win for the Blades.

All three FA Cup games were played in 1989-90, United finally going through into the 6th round after two replays thanks to Tony Agana's extra-time penalty winner at Oakwell.

The Blades beat the Tykes 9-2 in the Final of the Sheffield & Hallamshire Co.Cup in 1931.

Dave Bassett and Nigel Spackman have managed both clubs; Glyn Hodges and Jim Iley both played for the Blades and later managed the Tykes; Neil Warnock played for Barnsley and is now Blades' manager

Ted Ashton, Bill Batty, Percy Beaumont, Carl Bradshaw, Ian Bryson, Bill Calder, John Curtis, Jack Drummond, Jan-Aage Fjortoft, George Jones, John Lang, Jim McGuire, Ray McHale, Joe Mitchell, Tom Morren, Albert Rawson, Ernie Robinson, Tommy Sampy, Oliver Tummon, Carl Tiler, David Tuttle, George Utley, Mitch Ward, are among the players who have served with both Yorkshire clubs.

BARNSLEY, Andrew
Defender: 89+6 apps.
Born: Sheffield, 9 June 1952
Career: Denaby United, Rotherham United (June 1985), BLADES (£25,000, July 1986), Rotherham United (December 1988), Carlisle United (August 1991-May 1993).
Versatile defender Andy Barnsley career in League football realised 243 appearances (5 goals).

BARNWELL, John
Wing-half/inside-forward: 13 apps. 2 goals
Born: High Heaton, Newcastle-upon-Tyne, 24 December 1938
Career: Newcastle Schools, Bishop Auckland (amateur, June 1953), Arsenal (amateur August 1955, professional November 1956), Nottingham Forest (£30,000, March 1964 BLADES (£20,000, April 1970, retired in June 1971 through injury); Hereford United (coach, summer 1972, remaining at Edgar Street for 13 weeks); Peterborough United (coach 1974, then manager from May 1977-November 1978), Wolverhampton Wanderers (manager, November 1979-January 1982), Saudi Arabia (in a coaching capacity, 1982-83), AEK Athens (manager-coach, August 1983 - banned from working in Greece, January 1984), Notts County (manager, June 1987-December 1988), Walsall (manager, January 1989-March 1990), Northampton Town (consultant to player-manager Phil Chard, 1992-93). In July 1996 he was appointed Chief Executive of the Football League Managers Association while also controlling team affairs at Grantham Town.

Has a player, John Barnwell was a powerful, workmanlike inside-left who scored 24 goals in more than 160 games for the Gunners before having by far his best spell in the game with Forest whom he served splendidly for six years, making over 200 first-class appearances. When he retired in 1971 he had netted almost 50 goals in 327 League games and had gained England Youth and Under-23 international honours (winning one cap in the latter category) while also representing the Army during his National Service with the RASC in the 1950s.After that Barnwell developed into a very efficient manager, leading Wolves to victory in the 1980 League Cup Final (over Nottingham Forest) and to the FA Cup semi-finals in 1979, the year he almost his lost his life in a horrific car crash in which he suffered a fractured skull. He was also involved to two huge transfers - selling Steve Daly from Wolves to Manchester City for £1.43 million and then signing Andy Gray from Aston Villa for £1.15 million in the space of a week at the start of the 1979-80 season. He was voted 'Midland Sports Personality of the Year' in 1979-80.

25

BARRASS, Malcolm Williamson
Centre-half: 21 apps.
Born: Blackpool, 15 December 1924
Career: Ford Motors FC (Manchester Works League), Wolverhampton Wanderers (on trial), Bolton Wanderers (August 1944, professional November 1944), BLADES (£4,100, September 1956-May 1957); Wigan Athletic (player-manager, 1957-59), Nuneaton Borough (1959-62); later settled in the Bury area where he worked as a sales representative while also helping out both Pwllheli and Hyde United as trainer.
Malcolm Barrass cost Blades' manager Joe Mercer over £4,000 in 1956. A traditional big weighty centre-half who had played for Bolton Wanderers v. Blackpool in the 1953 FA Cup Final, he was appointed captain but proved far too slow and was released after just one season. Capped by England against Wales in a Victory international at West Brom in 1945, he went on to gain three full caps (v. Wales and Ireland in 1951 and Scotland at Wembley in 1953) and represented the Football League. He appeared in 357 competitive games for the Trotters (27 goals scored).
* His father, Matt Barrass, played for Blackpool, Manchester City and Sheffield Wednesday.

BARRETT, Earl Delliser
Defender: 5 apps.
Born: Rochdale, 28 April 1967
Career: Manchester City (juniors 1983, professional April 1985), Chester City (on loan, March 1986), Oldham Athletic (November 1987), Aston Villa (£1.7 million, February 1992), Everton (£1.7 million, January 1995), Sheffield United (on loan, January 1998) and finally Sheffield Wednesday (February 1998-May 1999).
A stylish defender, able to play at right-back or as a centre-back, Earl Barrett appeared in exactly 150 first-class games for Aston Villa before transferring to Everton. Capped three times by England, he also represented his country at 'B' & Under-21 levels and played for the Football League side. He gained a Second Division championship in 1991 with Oldham and a League Cup winners' medal in 1994 with Villa, picking up a Charity Shield prize with Everton in 1995. Barrett made over 400 League appearances in all.

BARROW
Barrow, elected to the Football League in 1921 (Division 3 North) remained in the competition for 50 years before losing its status in 1972, replaced by Hereford United, despite finishing above Stockport County and Crewe Alexandra at the bottom of the Fourth Division.
Almost 20,500 fans saw the Blades beat the Cumbrian side 5-0 in a 3rd round FA Cup-tie at Bramall Lane in January 1956.
John Burridge, John Cunningham, Keith Eddy, Tony Field , George Handley, Andrew McLaren, Jim Shankly, Norman Wharton and Peter Withe all played for both clubs.
Andy Beattie was secretary-manager of Barrow and later assistant-manager of United.

BARTON, Harold
Right-winger: 290 apps. 74 goals
Born: Leigh, Lancashire, 30 September 1911
Career: Whitegate Juniors (Blackpool), Liverpool (November 1928), BLADES (£1,600, June 1934-May 1946); guested for Bradford Park Avenue, Chesterfield, Lincoln City, Rotherham United and Sheffield Wednesday during WW2.
Harry Barton was a skilful winger with speed, control and craft, although he lacked total commitment and at times was rather inconsistent in his overall play (as crowd hostility tended to destroy his confidence). A former butcher's boy, he netted 25 goals in 101 outings for the Merseysiders including four in an FA Cup-tie v. Chesterfield in 1932 and a hat-trick in a 7-4 League win over Everton the following year. After making his debut for United against Preston at the start of the 1934-35 season and was a member of the 1938-39 promotion-winning side and remained at Bramall Lane until FAC final 1936.

BATTERSBY, Anthony
Forward: 6+9 apps. 2 goals
Born: Doncaster, 30 August 1975.
Career: BLADES (YTS, April 1992, professional July 1993), Southend United (on loan March 1995), Notts County (£150,000, January 1996), Bury (March 1997), Northampton Town (on loan, September-October 1990), Lincoln City (August 1998), Stevenage Borough.
Tony Battersby was unable to get regular first team action at Bramall Lane but after leaving the Blades he fared better at a lower level and in season 2002-03 reached the personal milestone of 300 career appearances

BATTY, William
Inside-forward: 40 apps. 8 goals
Born: Kilamarsh, Sheffield, 13 July 1886. Died: 1974.
Career: Thornecliffe FC, Mortonley, High Green Swifts, BLADES (April 1907), Bristol City (March 1910), Lincoln City (briefly), Swindon Town (seasons 1920-22), Barnsley (May 1922-May 1923).
Bill Batty was a well-built forward who cracked home a stunning 25-yard goal on his League debut for the Blades against Blackburn Rovers (home) in September 1907 (won 4-2) and although at times he looked very useful, he failed to hold down his place in the side and was subsequently transferred to Bristol City.

BEAGRIE, Peter Sydney
Forward/wide-midfielder: 95+3 apps. 11 goals
Born: Middlesbrough, 28 November 1965
Career: Middlesbrough (April 1983, professional, September 1983), BLADES (£35,000, August 1986), Stoke City (£210,000, June 1988), Everton (£750,000, November 1989), Sunderland (on loan, September 1991), Manchester City (£1.1 million, July 1997), Bradford City (£50,000, July 1997), Everton (on loan, March-April 1998), Wigan Athletic (free transfer, February 2001), Scunthorpe United (July 2001).
Renowned for his back-flip somersault after scoring a goal, soccer journeyman Peter Beagrie has had a wonderful career. Capped twice by England 'B' and twice at under-21 level, he has now accumulated in excess of 725 senior appearances, scoring over 80 goals. He made his League debut as a substitute for Middlesbrough v. Oldham Athletic in October 1984, scoring his first goal on the last day of that season v. Shrewsbury Town.

26

BEARD, Mark
Full-back: 26+19 apps.
Born: Roehampton, 8 October 1974.
Career: Millwall (junior, April 1992, professional March 1993), BLADES (£117,500, August 1995), Southend United (on loan, July 1998 and again October-November 1997, signed permanently on a free transfer, July 1998), Kingstonian (May 2000), Southend United (October 2001, released May 2003).
Combative full-back Mark Beard never really established himself in the first XI at Bramall Lane. He joined Southend for a fourth time in the autumn of 2001, staying at Roots Hall for a further two years.

BEAUMONT, Percy
Centre-half: 62 apps. 4 goals
Born: Mexborough, 3 September 1897. Died: 1967
Career: Mexborough Rovers, BLADES (March 1918), Barnsley (March 1921), Southend United (August 1926-May 1927).
Percy Beaumont, able-bodied, good in the air, showed his worth in the latter stages of WW1 before making 20 League appearances in the first peacetime campaign of 1919-20 when he lined up with Bill Brelsford and Harry Pantling in the half-back line. Injured and then in and out of the side during the next campaign he was transferred to Barnsley for whom he appeared in well over 140 senior games.

BECTON, Francis
Inside-left: 13 apps. 3 goals
Born: Preston, 25 March 1895. Died: Merseyside, 6 November 1909.
Career: Fulwell FC, Fishwick Ramblers, Preston North End (July 1891), Liverpool (£100, March 1895), BLADES (October 1898), Bedminster (June 1899), Preston North End (October 1900), Swindon Town (May 1901), Ashton Town (June 1903), New Brighton Tower (albeit briefly), retiring through poor health in 1905.
A creative inside-forward who was able to bring the best out of his wingers, Frank Becton was the best known of a prominent soccer family - brothers Jack (Middlesbrough Ironopolis), Martin (Preston North End & Watford) and Tommy (also PNE as well as Newton Brighton, Sunderland and Bristol Rovers, among others) all played competitive football. He was a star performer with the Merseysiders, scoring 37 goals in 74 appearances and helping them win the Second Division title in 1896 before switching to Bramall Lane in 1898 An England international, capped twice against Ireland in March 1895 (scoring twice in a 9-0 win) and Wales in March 1897, he also represented the Football League. Becton died from tuberculosis as did many sporting folk from the Victoria and Edwardian eras.

BEER, William John
Inside/centre-forward: 91 apps. 21 goals
Born: Poolsbrook near Chesterfield, 4 January 1879. Died: March 1941.
Career: Staveley Town. BLADES (amateur 1896), Chesterfield Town, BLADES (professional, August 1898), Small Heath/Birmingham (£700, January 1902, retired through injury in May 1910). After leaving football he spent many years working as a sheep farmer in Australia before returning to England to become a licensee in 1920, later taking over as manager of Birmingham, a position he held for almost four years, from May 1923 to March 1927.
An FA Cup winner with the Blades in 1899, Billy Beer was a very skilful player of explosive reflexes and subtle imagination. He had balance and strength, a fluent body-swerve and booming shot. A penalty-expert (when allowed to take them) it is on record that he never missed from the spot. He was also a talented musician and it is said that he was lured south (to the Midlands) by the promise of a job as a church organist. He is possibly the only footballer to have composed a cantata.

BEESLEY, Paul
Defender: 186+9 apps. 9 goals
Born: Liverpool, 21 July 1965
Career: Marine FC (Liverpool), Wigan Athletic (September 1984), Leyton Orient (October 1989), BLADES (£375,000, July 1990), Leeds United (£250,000 August 1995), Manchester City (February 1997), Port Vale (December 1997-January 1998), West Bromwich Albion (on loan, March-May 1998), Chester City (seasons 1998-2000).
Signed by Blades' manager Dave Bassett for a club record fee in 1989, Paul Beesley was a rugged, quick-tackling defender who, for certain periods, was the enigma in a United side that enjoyed the long ball game as he liked to play himself out of trouble, despite not being good with his distribution. Nevertheless he was a great aide to his co-defender Brian Gayle and was hugely popular with thee fans. He missed out on an FA Cup semi-final appearance in 1993 before his subsequent transfer to Elland Road. He made 155 League appearances for Wigan.

27

BENEFIT, CHARITY & TESTIMONIAL MATCHES

Here is an unofficial list of benefit, charity, testimonial and fund-raising matches Sheffield United have taken part in over the years. Some of these games were also competitive fixtures (i.e. Football League or County Cup games etc).

Date	Fixture/score	Beneficiary
24.04.1893	Wednesday 0 United 0	JC Clegg
18.01.1894	Aston Villa 4 United 0	H Devey
18.02.1895	English 3 Scottish 1	W Hendry
24.04.1895	Blackwell 2 United 3	R Cockayne
02.03.1896	Wednesday 0 United 5	A Mumford
09.04.1896	United 0 Preston NE 0	S Dobson
23.04.1896	United 1 Burton Swifts 0 (n)	Lord Mayor's Fund
07.04.1897	Gainsborough T 0 United 2	J Scott
21.04.1897	Clowne 2 United 7	Colliery Acc. Benv. Fund
17.01.1898	English 1 Scottish 1	R Cain
12.04.1898	United 1 Newton Heath 4	M Whitham
27.12.1898	United 5 Corinthians 3	E Needham
15.01.1900	United 5 International XI 1	A Watson
27.12.1900	Aston Villa 5 United 1	H Spencer
14.01.1901	United 6 Aston Villa 2	H Thickett
21.01.1901	United 2 Celtic 2	W Foulke
03.05.1902	Wednesday 3 United 0	Ibrox Park Disaster Fund
01.01.1903	Reserves 0 Wednesday Res 3	T Morren
09.11.1903	United 4 Derby County 2	F Priest
25.12.1903	Reserves 2 Wednesday Res 2	H Johnson/F Priest
29.12.1904	United 1 Corinthians 2	W Bennett
17.02.1906	United 1 Derby County 0	B Lipsham/B Wilkinson
26.01.1907	United 2 Stoke 0	E Needham
26.12.1907	Reserves 0 Wednesday Res 2	W Parker
28.03.1908	United 1 Manchester City 2	A Brown
13.03.1909	United 3 Notts County 2	J Lang/Wilkinson
12.02.1910	United 1 Nottm Forest 4	C Johnson/Lievesley
28.01.1911	United 1 Blackburn Rovers 1	R Benson
02.03.1912	United 1 Blackburn Rovers 1	J McGuire/B Wilkinson
15.03.1913	United 4 Derby County 1	J Smith/W Hardinge
15.11.1913	Oldham Athletic 1 United 2	H Matthews
07.02.1914	United 1 Sunderland 0	J Kitchen/A Sturgess
04.04.1914	United 5 Burnley 0	RE Evans
03.05.1919	Manchester City 1 United 0	FA War Fund
10.05.1919	United 3 Manchester City 2	FA War Fund
17.05.1919	Hull City 0 United 2	Hull Hospital Cup
23.09.1922	Nottingham For 1 United 0	RJ Masters
11.10.1922	Hartlepools 0 United 2	F Priest
19.04.1923	United 0 Wednesday 2	G Waller
18.09.1924	United 2 Wednesday 2	J Nicholson
04.05.1927	Bradford PA 1 United 4	F McLean/HW Taylor
28.04.1931	United 6 Grimsby T 0 (n)	Spalding Nursing Home Cup
27.04.1932	Darlington 1 United 6	J Waugh
18.04.1933	United 2 Sheffield Wed 1	S Gibson
03.04.1935	Sheffield Wed 0 United 0	C Craig/D Steele
20.08.1938	Sheffield Wed 4 United 1	FL Jubilee Fund
19.08.1939	Sheffield Wed 2 United 4	FL Jubilee Fund
25.05.1942	Chesterfield 1 United 2	Red Cross
21.08.1943	United 3 Sheffield Wed 2	YMCA Fund
27.04.1954	Northampton T 1 United 1	B Collins
26.09.1956	Worksop Town 1 United 0	St John's Ambulance Fund
01.10.1956	Sheff U/Wed XI 7 Leeds XI 1	L Browning
17.04.1957	Wisbech Town 0 United 4	G Bailey/G Nicholas
02.05.1957	Boston United 2 United 3	F Tunstall
06.11.1957	Rhyl 1 United 4	J Rodgers/S Wilson
26.03.1958	Hereford United 2 United 3	C Thompson
10.03.1958	Sheffield XI 3 Internat'l XI 4	J Hagan
05.11.1962	Hearts 2 United 2	W Bauld
15.12.1964*	Select XI 3 United/Stoke XI 3	J Noble
29.03.1965	United 5 All Star XI 6	J Shaw
31.10.1966	United 5 All Star XI 5	C Coldwell
25.09.1967	Sheffield Wed 3 United 2	R Springett
13.05.1968	Chester 2 United 3	J Butler/E Morris
10.09.1968	United 2 Sheffield Wed 2	A Hodgkinson
25.04.1968	Sheffield wed 3 United 3	G Young
10.05.1971	Swansea Town 3 United 5	L Allchurch
20.03.1973	United 1 Sheffield Wed 1	L Badger
09.05.1974	United 3 Sheffield Wed 3	A Woodward
08.04.1975	Barnsley 3 United 3	B Murphy
06.05.1975	Watford 2 United 2	J Williams
10.05.1976	United 0 Sheffield Wed 0	H Latham
16.05.1977	Lincoln City 2 United 2	P Freeman
10.04.1978	Worksop Town 0 United 0	D Birkenshaw
17.10.1977	Sheffield XI Nott Forest XI 1	J Harris
12.09.1978	Norton Woodseats 0 United 2	WR Rogers
04.03.1980	United 9 Select XI 1	E Colquhoun
26.03.1980	United 4 Select XI 2	M Speight
17.11.1980	United 8 Select XI 4	J Flynn
23.03.1981	Truro City 1 United 9	K Solomon Memorial
18.04.1983	United 1 Ipswich Town 1	L Tibbott
14.11.1983	United 1 Sheffield Wed 1	C Coldwell
13.05.1984	Lincoln City 3 United 3	British Olympic Appeal
06.05.1986	United XI 3 Sheff Wed XI 4	A Kenworthy
08.05.1986	Chesterfield 2 United XI 1	E Moss
15.09.1986	Sheffield Wed 3 United 1	M Smith
05.10.1986	United XI 7 Waterman's XI 5	A Currie
05.08.1987	United 0 Sheffield Wed 3	World Student Games
12.09.1988	United 1 Sheffield Wed XI 3	C Morris
11.05.1990	Brentford 4 United XI 2	R Booker
17.08.1990	Sheffield Wed 3 United 0	L Madden
12.11.1990	Yeovil Town 0 United 2	A Stone
05.03.1991	Grimsby Town 0 United 2	J Fraser
23.04.1991	Lincoln City 2 United 0	A Roberts
18.03.1992	Sheffield XI 1 FF Malmo 6	P Stancliffe
04.05.1992	United 2 Ex-Blades XI 3	B Smith
06.05.1992	Barrow XI 0 United 3	R Wilkie
08.05.1992	Frickley Athletic 4 United 4	M Wright
08.08.1992	Rotherham Utd 0 United 1	P Henson
14.12.1992	Worksop Town 3 United 1	S Fowler
09.08.1993	United 0 Sheffield Wed 1	D Dooley
06.09.1993	Mansfield Town 1 United 2	W Dearden
15.11.1993	Sutton United 3 United 2	P McKinnon
12.12.1994	Staveley XI 3 United 4	J Booth (descendants of)
07.05.2001	United 9 Sheff Utd All Stars 5	D Whitehouse

*This game featured a Doncaster/Stockport XI v. Sheffield United/Stoke City XI

Facts & Figures

* The game at Hillsborough in August 1990 was also billed as the First Steel City Challenge Cup Final.
* The 'friendly' with Barnsley at Oakwell in 1975 was abandoned after 72 minutes.
* Blades' goalkeeper Simon Tracey was scheduled for a testimonial game v. Middlesbrough in August 2003.

BENJAMIN, Ian Treacy
Midfielder/striker: 8+2 apps. 3 goals
Born: Nottingham, 11 December 1961.
Career: BLADES (apprentice, April 1977, professional May 1979), West Bromwich Albion (£125,000, May 1979) Notts County (February 1982), Peterborough United (August 1982), Northampton Town (August 1984), Cambridge United (October 1987), Chester City (July 1988), Exeter City (February 1989), Southend United (March 1990), Luton Town (November 1992), Brentford (September 1993), Wigan Athletic (September 1994), Bury Town, Ilkeston Town, Kettering Town (July 1996), Chelmsford City, Corby Town, Raunds Town, Warboys Town, Soham Town Rovers, Wisbech Town (January 2002).
Tall midfield/striker Ian Benjamin did exceedingly well in the lower Divisions, amassing over 560 appearances (149 goals)...this after just 10 first team appearances for the Blades and being frozen out at The Hawthorns. An England Youth international, he helped Northampton win the Fourth Division championship in 1987 when he was also voted the Cobblers' 'Player of the Year.'

BENNETT, Jesse
Full-back: 10 apps.
Born: Dronfield, Sheffield, April 1901.
Career: Dronfield Woodhouse, BLADES (August 1928), Coventry City (May 1932), Northampton Town (July 1933, retiring through injury, May 1936).
Jesse Bennett was basically a reserve during his four years at Bramall Lane. He later played 25 League games for Coventry and 56 for Northampton.

BENNETT, Walter
Outside-right: 234 apps. 70 goals
Born: Mexborough, Yorkshire, 1874. Died: 6 April 1908.
Career: Mexborough Town, BLADES (January 1896), Bristol City (April 1905), Denaby United (season 1907-08).
A powerfully built England international right-winger (two caps gained v. Wales and Scotland in 1901) Walter 'Cocky' Bennett loved to take on defenders at pace and whip over dangerous crosses on the run. He was also regarded as one of the hardest shots in the game when he chose to fire in on goal. Although he was a rather moody character and lacked consistency to a certain degree, he was still a tremendous asset to United's brilliant side around the turn of the 20th century, helped the Blades win the League title in 1898 and the FA Cup twice, in 1899 and 1902, as well as playing in the 1901 losing Final and collecting a Second Division championship medal in 1906. Bennett was sadly killed in a colliery accident in 1908.

BENSON, Robert William
Right-back: 285 apps. 21 goals
Born: 9 February 1883. Died: London, 19 February 19116.
Career: Dunston Villa, Shankhouse FC, Swalwell, Newcastle United (£150, December 1902), Southampton (£150, September 1904), BLADES (£150, May 1905), Arsenal (November 1913, retiring from competitive football in April 1914).
Unfortunately with full-back competition so high at St James' Park Bob Benson made only one League appearance for the Magpies (v. Liverpool in March 1903). After 22 games for Saints he moved to Bramall Lane where he developed into a big, bold defender. Indeed, he was described in one biography as being 'a terror to opposing forwards'. Equally adept on either flank, he was famous for his penalty-taking whereby he used to ask a colleague to place the ball on the spot and then run up the field (perhaps 80 yards or so) from his full-back position to wallop his shot at goal. Capped by England against Ireland in Belfast in February 1913, Benson also played in three unofficial Test Matches in South Africa in 1910, was an international trialist (also in 1913) and represented the Football League. Sadly Benson died of a burst blood vessel in the arms of trainer George Hardy in the dressing room at Highbury after collapsing whilst playing in a war-time game in 1916 (he had been engaged on munitions work in Woolwich, London and had not played for some time and was, in fact, called into action as a late recruit when the Gunners found themselves a man short). He was buried wearing an Arsenal shirt.

BENSTEAD, Graham
Goalkeeper: 70 apps.
Born: Aldershot, 20 August 1963
Career: Queen's Park Rangers (junior, July 1979, professional in July 1981), Norwich City (£10,000, March 1985), Colchester United (on loan, August 1987), BLADES (March 1988), Brentford (£60,000, July 1990), Rushden & Diamonds (June 1994), Brentford again, (July 1997).
The career of England Youth international goalkeeper Graham Benstead took off when he joined Norwich in 1985. He spent 13 years at Carrow Road, appearing in more than 240 League and Cup games. A fine shot-stopper on his day, he lost his place in the Blades' side to Simon Tracey after helping the team gain promotion from Division Three in 1989.

BENT, Marcus Nathan
Forward: 56 apps. 24 goals
Born: Hammersmith, London, 19 May 1978.
Career: Brentford (trainee, June 1993, professional July 1995), Crystal Palace (£150,000, January 1998), Port Vale (£375,000, January 1999, BLADES (£300,000, October 1999), Blackburn Rovers (£1.3 million, November 2000), Ipswich Town (£3 million, November 2001).
Marcus Bent appeared in more than 90 first-class games for the Bees. After some excellent displays for United - scoring a goal almost every other game - he was sold to Blackburn where he struggled hard to hold down a regular first-team place. As a result he was transferred to Ipswich in 2001. Capped twice by England at Under-21 level, Bent has the ability to do the unexpected and get away from defenders through a quick turn in the box or a deft change of pace and he can shoot too, from any angle.

BIGGAR, Frederick William
Goalkeeper: 14 apps.
Born: Blaydon-on-Tyne, 1877. Died: 1935.
Career: Birtley FC, BLADES (March 1900), West Ham United (June 1902), Fulham (August 1903), Watford (July 1904), Rochdale (1910-15).
Billy Biggar was signed as cover for Bill Foulke. He was given little opportunity to show his worth and moved to West Ham. He later played in 217 Southern League games for Watford, being an ever-present from 1906-09.

29

BIRCHENALL, Alan John

Forward: 123+1 apps. 37 goals
Born: East Ham, London, 22 August 1945
Career: Thornyewood Athletic, BLADES (apprentice, June 1962, professional, June 1963), Chelsea (£100,000, November 1967), Crystal Palace (£100,000, June 1970), Leicester City (September 1971), Notts County (on loan, March 1976), San Jose Earthquakes (summer 1976), Notts County (September 1977), Memphis Rogues (summer 1978), Blackburn Rovers (July 1978), Luton Town (March 1979), Hereford United (October 1979, Trowbridge Town (player-manager, July 1980-May 1983); later returned to Filbert Street to work as an energetic P.R.O

Alan Birchenall scored over 60 goals for the Blades' intermediate team during 1963-64 before making his senior debut in a 1-0 win at Stoke on 2 September 1964 after just eight Central League outings. A tall, extrovert blond striker, he produced some fine displays over the next few years before being transferred to Chelsea. Capped four times at Under-21 level by England, he was successfully converted into an industrious midfielder player who scored 74 goals in 458 League games for his eight English clubs.

BIRD, Donald William Carlton

Left-winger: 18 apps. 4 goals
Born: Llandrindod Wells, 5 January 1908. Died: Essex, 1987
Career: Llandrindod Wells FC, Cardiff City (January 1930), Bury (June 1931), Torquay United (July 1932), Derby County (August 1934), BLADES (December 1935), Southend United (October 1937, retiring in 1938).

Dickie Bird was a useful, steady left-winger who failed to establish himself at Ninian Park or Gigg Lane but did well at Torquay, scoring 15 goals in 74 League games for the Devon club. He scored United's all-important goal in the 1936 FA Cup semi-final win over Fulham but was left out of the side for the Final against Arsenal in preference to Bert Williams. He quit League football a year after leaving Bramall Lane.

BIRKS, Leonard

Right-back: 220 apps.
Born: Fenton, Stoke-on-Trent, 6 October 1896. Died: Shirehampton, 22 March 1975.
Career: Butts Lane Star, Port Vale (May 1920), BLADES (£2,350, October 1924), Plymouth Argyle (February 1931), Bristol City (April 1933), Yeovil & Petters United.

Len Birks was an energetic, stylish full-back, exercising fine judgement and smart ball control. No slouch in the matter of speed, he was a regarded as a 'clever tackler' but was at times rather too casual, being prone to a defensive error! He played in more than 100 first-team games for Port Vale.

BIRMINGHAM CITY

(formerly Small Heath)
United's playing record against the Blues:

Football League

Venue	P	W	D	L	F	A
Home	48	29	8	11	107	63
Away	48	12	9	27	47	85
Totals	96	41	17	38	154	148

FA Cup

Venue	P	W	D	L	F	A
Home	2	0	2	0	2	2
Away	3	0	0	3	2	7
Totals	5	0	2	3	4	9

League Cup

Venue	P	W	D	L	F	A
Home	1	0	0	1	2	3

WW1

Venue	P	W	D	L	F	A
Home	3	1	1	1	4	4
Away	3	0	0	3	2	13
Totals	6	1	1	4	6	17

The Blues are amongst United's oldest League rivals, both clubs being elected to the newly-formed Second Division in 1892.
In 1875, some cricket enthusiasts who were largely members of the Trinity Church in Bordesley Green, determined to continue their sporting relationships throughout the year by forming a football team - Small Heath Alliance. The early games were played on waste ground in Arthur Street. In 1888 'Alliance' was dropped and four years later 'Blues' gained entry (with the Blades) to the Football League (Division 2), having done well in the Alliance. In 1905 they changed to Birmingham and during WW2 added City to their title. Blues have been playing at their current St Andrew's ground since 1906, having moved there from Muntz Street.
The first League meeting was at Bramall Lane in September 1892, United winning 2-0 (Jack Scott and Harry Hammond the scorers). The Blades drew the return fixture 1-1 at Muntz Street, the only point dropped by Blues at home all season.
United scored five times in the first 18 minutes of their home League game v. Blues in February 1923. They went on to win 7-1, registering the last five goals from crosses by David Mercer. 'Young' Harry Johnson netted four times to secure the Blades' best-ever win over Blues.
Blues beat United 3-0 at St Andrew's on the last day of the 1963-64 season to retain their First Division status. Graham Shaw kept goal for the Blades for 75 minutes (Hodgkinson off injured).
In season 1969-70 United beat Blues 6-0 at 'the Lane' in a second Division fixture; Colin Addison (2) was one of five goalscorers. The following season saw Blues visit Sheffield and lose 3-0, Gil Reece scoring two brilliant goals, as the Blades strove to clinch promotion. In their opening home match of the 1996-97 League season the Blades played out a thrilling 4-4 draw with Blues. The visitors led 2-0 before United bounced back to gain a 4-2 advantage with some vintage football, only to be concede two late goals scored by future Lane players, Paul Devlin and Jonathan Hunt, in a breathtaking encounter.
Other players who have served with the Blades and the Blues include Billy Beer and Steve Bruce (who have also managed both clubs), Gary Ablett, Edgar Bluff, Alonzo Drake, Charlie Field, George Gallimore, Don Givens, Roger Hansbury, Bob Hatton, Fred Hawley, Trevor Hockey, David Holdsworth, Henry Howard, Andy Kennedy, Martin Kuhl, Marcelo, Chris Marsden, Dennis Mortimer, Peter Ndlovu, Jack Peart, Paul Peschisolido, Albert Rawson, Bruce Rioch, Phil Starbuck, Paul Tomlinson, Roy Warhurst, Steve Wigley, Walter Wigmore and Peter Withe. Howard Kendall played for Blues and managed the Blades while Frank Barlow and Geoff Vowden have also been associated with both clubs, likewise Jim Smith (manager of Blues). Lou Macari was Blues' boss and later a scout for United.

BIRMINGHAM CUP

The Blades entered and reached the Final of this Midland competition in season 1895-96, playing four matches, the details as follows:

Rd 1	v. Wolves (home)	won 2-0	Att. 2,250
Rd 2	v. Walsall (away)	won 5-2	Att. 5,500
SF	v. Derby County (away)	won 2-0	Att. 4,000
Final	v. Aston Villa (away)	lost 3-0	Att. 5,250

* Tom Egan top-scored with five goals.

Full record:

Venue	P	W	D	L	F	A
Home	1	1	0	0	2	0
Away	3	2	0	1	7	5
Totals	4	3	0	1	9	5

BLACK, Russell Palmer

Forward: 10+4 apps.
Born: Dumfries, 29 July 1960
Career: Gretna, BLADES (June 1984), Halifax Town (August1986-May 1988).
Scotsman Russell Black remained at Bramall Lane for two seasons. He went on to score 14 goals in 72 League games for the Shaymen.

BLACKBURN ROVERS

United's playing record against the Rovers:

Premiership						
Venue	P	W	D	L	F	A
Home	2	0	0	2	2	5
Away	2	0	1	1	0	1
Totals	4	0	1	3	2	6
Football League						
Home	67	33	20	14	136	75
Away	67	20	13	34	84	124
Totals	134	53	33	48	220	199
FA Cup						
Home	2	1	1*	0	4	3
Away	2	0	1	1	1	2
Totals	4	1	2	1	5	5
WW2						
Home	1	1	0	0	2	1
Away	1	0	1	0	0	0
Totals	2	1	1	0	2	1
Others						
Home	1	1	0	0	3	1
Away	1	0	0	1	0	1
Totals	2	1	0	1	3	2

* United won 5-3 on penalties after a 2- draw.

One of England's most famous football clubs, Blackburn Rovers were formed by a group of Public School old boys who called a meeting in 1875 at which the colours blue and white were immediately adopted. The leading light was John Lewis, later founder of the Lancashire FA and a top class referee who officiated in two FA Cup Finals as well as becoming vice-President of both the FA and the Football League.

Rovers, founder members of the Football League in 1888, won the FA Cup five times before the end of the 19th century and have played at Ewood Park since 1890, having moved there from their Leamington Road ground

United met Rovers for the first time at League level in season 1893-94 (losing 4-1 away before gaining revenge with a 3-2 home win, courtesy of Ernest Needham's penalty). In fact, the Blades remained undefeated in their first 12 home matches against Rovers.

In January 1897, United blitzed Rovers 7-0 at Bramall Lane to record their best ever League win over their Lancashire rivals. Centre-forward George Walls netted a second-half hat-trick in front of just 750 hardy spectators, the lowest attendance of the season and, indeed, United's lowest in top flight football to this day, and the second lowest in all home League matches. A week earlier 30,000 had packed into 'the Lane' to witness the Sheffield derby!

In season 1926-27 the two League games between the clubs produced 15 goals, United doubling up with wins of 4-3 at Ewood Park and 5-3 at 'the Lane.'

In March 1930, with the Blades battling out of their skin to avoid relegation, were beaten 7-5 at home by Rovers - the only recorded instance of such a scoreline to top-flight football (with only one other in Division One).

A crowd of 42,216 saw United draw 0-0 with Blackburn at Bramall Lane in April 1939 to clinch promotion to the First Division.

United ran up their best League win on Rovers' soil in 1951-52 when both teams were in the Second Division, Alf Ringstead scoring twice in a 5-1 victory.

Nearly 30,000 fans saw Jimmy Hagan score his 100th League goal for United in a 2-1 win at Blackburn in February 1953.

On Boxing Day 1957, Blades' manager Joe Mercer introduced centre-forward Derek Pace, a £12,000 signing from Aston Villa, for the home game with Rovers. He scored after just eight minutes of a 4-2 win and went on to become one of the club's greatest-ever marksmen.

In 1970-71 (the promotion campaign from Division Two) the Blades doubled-up over Rovers with a 5-0 win at 'the Lane' and a 3-1 success at Ewood Park...and seven different players scored the eight United goals.

Keith Edwards scored his 200th League goal for United against Blackburn at Ewood Park on 19 April 1986 (Division 2). It was no use as the Blades were sliced open to the tune of 6-1.

Thanks to some heroics by goalkeeper Alan Kelly, United beat Rovers 5-3 on penalties in a 6th round FA Cup replay at Bramall Lane in March 1993 (it was 2-2 after extra-time). The first game at Ewood Park had finished goalless.

Kevin Arnott, Marcus Bent, Alan Birchenall, Nathan Blake, David Bradford, Walter Brayshaw, Viv Busby, Franz Carr, Gordon Cowans,

31

John Curtis, Matt Dickens (United reserve), Tony Field, Terry Garbett, Mike Heaton, Alan Kelly, Andy Kennedy, Neil Logan, Nicky Marker, Andy Morrison, Albert Nightingale, Mark Patterson, Mike Speight, Phil Starbuck, Frank Talia and Jamie Thomas are among the players who have served with both clubs, while Ken Furphy and Howard Kendall have been managers at 'the Lane' and Ewood Park. Jim Iley was a Blades' player and Rovers manager.

BLACKPOOL

(South Shore)

United's playing record against the Seasiders:

Football League

Venue	P	W	D	L	F	A
Home	26	15	5	6	51	38
Away	26	8	6	12	35	39
Totals	52	23	11	18	86	77

FA Cup

Home	2	1	0	1	3	3
Away	5	4	0	1	10	4
Totals	7	5	0	2	13	7

League Cup

Home	2	1	0	1	2	2
Away	2	0	1	1	0	3
Totals	4	1	1	2	2	5

WW2

Home	1	1	0	0	4	2
Away	1	1	0	0	2	1
Totals	2	2	0	0	6	3

Others

Home	1	0	0	1	1	2
Away	1	0	1	0	1	1
Neutral	11	6	1	4	22	17
Totals	13	6	2	5	24	20

There is reference that a football club (Victoria FC) existed in Blackpool in 1880 but the current club, it seems, was formed by ex-pupils of St John's School seven years later. This group of men, including the Rev. N S Jeffrey, Sam Bancroft, W J Brown, Dick Swarbrick and Dick Worthington - held a meeting at the Stanley Arms Hotel in July 1887 and introduced Blackpool St John's. In their first season, playing at Raikes Hall Gardens, St John's won both the Lancashire Junior Cup and the Fylde Cup. Things developed fast and in 1896 the 'Seasiders' gained entry to the Football League. A year later the club moved to The Athletic Ground and in 1899 combined forces with South Shore FC (retaining the full name of Blackpool) while also having a brief spell back at Raikes Hall Gardens before switching to their present home, Bloomfield Road.

The Blades first met Blackpool in a 1st round FA Cup-tie in 1892, winning 1-0 away.

The first League meeting between the clubs did not take place until Christmas Day 1930 when the 'Pool won 3-1 only for the Blades to gain sweet revenge 24 hours later by winning 5-1 at 'the Lane' with Jimmy Dunne scoring twice. This is United's best win of the 29 so far registered over the 'Pool at senior level. Their heaviest defeat, also 5-1, was suffered in a League game at Bramall Lane in April 1977. By beating United 3-1 at Bramall Lane on the last day of the 1931-32 season, Blackpool avoided being relegated to the Second Division.

The Blades completed seven League doubles over Blackpool...in 1932-33 (1-0 at home & 3-0 away), 1948-49 (3-2 & 3-0), 1954-55 (each by 2-1), 1961-62 (2-1 & 4-2), 1979-80 (3-1 & 3-2), 1981-82 (3-1 & 1-0) and 1988-89 (4-1 & 2-1).

In February 1906, United paid Blackpool £250 to switch their 2nd round FA Cup-tie to Bramall Lane. The move back-fired as the Seasiders won 2-1 in front of just 10,219 spectators (receipts: £310).

Stanley Matthews paid his first visit to Bramall Lane for a Division One game in April 1948. A crowd of 48,150 saw the Blades win 2-1.

Over an amazing four-week period from mid-May to mid-June 1965, United played Blackpool 11 times in New Zealand (see under BOAC Trophy).

Of those matches, the Blades won six to Blackpool's four with one game drawn. Prior to going to NZ, United and Blackpool had drawn 3-3 in a friendly in Vancouver.

In that 1964-65 the two teams also met each other twice in the First Division. United were beaten 3-1 at Bramall Lane and drew 2-2 at Bloomfield Road.

Players who have been associated with both clubs down the years include: Gary Ablett, John Burridge, 'Jock' Dodds, Peter Duffield, George Farrow, Bob Hatton, Garry Jones, Gary Kelly, Tom McAlister, Colin Morris, Andy Morrison, Mark Patterson, John Reid, Paul Richardson, Walter Rickett, Eddie Shimwell, Paul Simpson, Jamie Thomas, Percy Thorpe and Harry Warren.

BLACKWELL, Ernest

Goalkeeper: 92 apps.
Born: Sheffield, 19 July 1894. Died: 1964
Career: Scunthorpe & Lindsey United, BLADES (May 1914, retired in September 1924)
Ernie Blackwell played well for Scunthorpe before moving to Bramall Lane. He was forced to give up the game at the age of 30 on medical grounds...due to a combination of illness and injury.

BLAIR, John Guthrie

Inside-forward; 34 apps. 7 goals
Born: Neilston, Scotland, 23 August 1905. Died: Kilmarnock, 1 January 1972.
Career: Third Lanark (1922), Tottenham Hotspur (April 1926), BLADES (£3,000, November 1927), Fordsons FC (November 1929-31).
John Blair scored in the second minute of his Blades' debut against Cardiff City. A clever Scottish forward, he perhaps lacked urgency at times, but was always likely to create an opening and even find the back of the net himself. He scored 16 goals in 32 games for Spurs and after leaving Bramall Lane played non-League football for a couple of years before returning to Scotland.

BLAKE, Nathan Alexander

Striker: 60+15 apps. 35 goals
Born: Cardiff, 27 January 1972.
Career: Chelsea (trainee), Cardiff City (professional, August 1990), BLADES (£300,000 February 1994), Bolton Wanderers (£1.5 million, December 1995 with Mark Patterson, valued at £500,000, moving to Bramall Lane as part of the deal), Blackburn Rovers (£4.25 million, October 1998), Wolverhampton Wanderers (£1.4 million, September 2001).
Striker Nathan Blake scored 40 goals in 164 games for Cardiff, gaining two Welsh Cup winners medals in successive seasons and helping them lift the Third Division title in 1993. He continued to show his ability in front of goal at Bramall Lane, finding the net every other game before his big-money transfer to Bolton in 1995. After helping the Wanderers reach the Premiership as First Division champions in 1997, he switched to nearby Blackburn before re-entering the Nationwide League with Wolves in 2001, helping the Black Country team reach the Play-off Final two years later (meeting the Blades at Cardiff's Millennium Stadium). A Welsh international (capped 22 times at senior level, once by the 'B' team, five times by the Under-21's and also as a Youth player) Blake, tall, aggressive and a fine header of the ball, ended the 2002-03 season with more than 150 goals under his belt in well over 500 senior appearances (at club and international level).
* Blake was the first player sold by United manager Howard Kendall who, by all accounts, was not happy with the striker's overall work-rate and commitment.

BLOUNT, Mark

Defender: 15+2 apps.
Born: Derby, 5 January 1974.
Career: Gresley Rovers, BLADES (February 1994), Peterborough United (on a non-contract basis, March 1996).
Mark Blount was not really given much of a chance at Bramall Lane and was out of League football come 1996.

BLUFF, Edgar Underwood

Inside-right: 68 apps. 16 goals
Born: Sheffield, March 1882. Died: Salisbury,July 1952.
Career: Reading (on trial, 1903), Southampton (July 1904), BLADES (September 1905), Birmingham (December 1907), St Helens Town (May 1908-April 1910).
Edgar Bluff scored on his debut for United in a 4-2 home League win over Sunderland in September 1905. A fast and dangerous forward, possessing a strong right-foot shot, he was serving with the Army Corps in the Royal Light Infantry when given a trial by Reading. He was then 'bought out' of the Army by Southampton and named as reserve for the England v. Ireland international in 1905. He netted 13 goals in 30 outings for the Saints and then made further progress after joining the Blades - although it is believed he never really settled down in Yorkshire. Bluff represented the Sheffield FA during his spell with the Blades.

BOAC TROPHY

Over a period of four weeks - from 15 May to 13 June 1965, United played Blackpool in New Zealand no fewer than 11 times. The results of those matches were (United's score given first): 3-3 (Auckland), 4-2 (Palmerston), 3-0 (Wellington), 0-3 (Masterton), 1-2 (Nelson), 2-1 (Christchurch), 1-2 (Invercargill), 3-0 (Dunedin), 2-1 (Wellington), 1-2 (Napier) & 2-1 (Auckland).
The Blades won the BOAC Trophy after gaining six victories to Blackpool's four with one game drawn.
Prior to taking part in the competition, United and Blackpool had played out a 3-3 drawn in Vancouver.

BOLAM, Robert Coltman

Outside-right: 34 apps. 2 goals
Born: Birtley, 1896. Died: 1964
Career: Birltey FC, BLADES (January 1920), Darlington (June 1922), South Shields (1923), Queen's Park Ranger's (August 1924-May 1925).
Bob Bolam scored on his League debut for the Blades from the right-wing position against West Bromwich Albion two months after joining the club. He made over 80 appearances at senior level during his career.

BOLIVIA

United were the first British professional football team to visit and play in Bolivia. They lost 3-1 in a friendly against Bolivar in La Paz on 7 June 1967. Three days later they beat Santa Cruz 3-1.

BOLTON, Joseph

Full-back: 130 apps. 6 goals
Born: Birtley, 2 February 1955.
Career: Sunderland (apprentice, June 1970m professional February 1972), Middlesbrough (July 1981), BLADES (August 1983), Matlock Town (1986).
Full-back Joe Bolton had already appeared in 332 League games (273 for Sunderland and 59 for Middlesbrough) before moving to Bramall Lane in 1983. A fine positional player, adventurous at times, he was also cool under pressure and commanding when in control. He helped the Blades win promotion from Division Three in 1984 (45 games).

33

BOLTON WANDERERS

United's playing record against the Wanderers:

Football League

Venue	P	W	D	L	F	A
Home	53	33	9	11	123	66
Away	53	8	12	33	60	116
Totals	106	41	21	44	183	182

FA Cup

Home	3	2	0	1	5	4
Away	4	2	0	2	4	16
Totals	7	4	0	3	9	20

League Cup

Home	2	0	0	2	2	4

WW2

Home	1	0	0	1	2	3
Away	1	1	0	0	4	1
Totals	2	1	0	1	6	4

Other

Away	1	0	0	1	0	1

In 1874 boys of Christ Church Sunday School, Blackburn Street, led by their master, Thomas Ogden, established a football club which sent under the name of that school and whose president was the Vicar of Christ Church. Initial membership was 6d (3p) and when the president began to lay down too many rules about the use of church premises, the club broke away and formed Bolton Wanderers in 1877, holding their earliest meetings at the Gladstone Hotel. The club turned professional in 1880, moved from their Cockle's Field ground to Pike's Lane a year later and faster gaining Football League status as one of the founder members in 1888, Bolton switched to Burnden Park in 1895, staying there until 1997 when the Reebok Stadium was built.

The Blades and the Wanderers have met in 53 League seasons so far, but the following statistics bear out the fall from grace over the years of both clubs since WW2.

Prior to the Hitler conflict they met in 32 of 43 seasons, all but one in the First Division. However, since 1946 they have opposed each other in only 21 of the 57 campaigns, with just nine taking place in the 'top flight.'

Following a 2-0 friendly win for Bolton at Bramall Lane, the first competitive match took place in on 1 February 1890 when United (after coming through the qualifying stages) opposed the Wanderers in the 2nd round of the FA Cup. United had been in existence for barely six months, while Bolton were founder members of the Football League with a good history. But surprisingly the Blades' committee agreed to switch the tie to Bolton's Pike's Lane ground for the sum of £40 with one newspaper reporter stating: "United must have taken a leave of their senses."

This proved to be an ill-judged decision as the Wanderers thrashed the hapless Blades to then tune of 13-0...still the club's worst-ever defeat in any major competition. A crowd of just 3,750 saw the rout with Jim Cassidy (5), Davie Weir (4) and Jim Brogan (3) leading the goal-rush.

The first League game took place in September 1893 (Division One) and it was the Blades who came out on top, winning 4-2 at Bramall Lane, completing the double soon afterwards with a 1-0 victory at Bolton.

United clinched their First Division title by beating Bolton 1-0 (away) on 8 April 1898. Ernie Needham playing at centre-forward, scored a quite brilliant goal in front of 19,395 spectators.

United raced to a record 7-1 home League win in 1902-03 but lost 1-0 at the Trotters' new Burnden Park ground as the Wanderers slipped into the Second Division. But the tables were turned in 1911-12 as newly-promoted Bolton waltzed to an impressive 5-0 win in the opening fixture at Bramall Lane, the legendary Joe Smith scoring twice. That reverse was avenged however as Billy Gillespie inspired the Blades to a 3-0 win in the return fixture.

The Blades have a poor record at Bolton with only one League win since 1948 (two since WW2).

On their way to winning the FA Cup in 1915, United beat Bolton 2-1 in the semi-final at Ewood Park, Jimmy Simmons and George Utley netting first half goals. But in 1922-23 it was Bolton who went through to the Final after pipping the Blades 1-0 at Old Trafford. They of course then took on and beat West Ham United 2-0 in the first Wembley Final that attracted a crowd in excess of 200,000! It could well have been United there instead (a game that got away!)

Players associated with both clubs include: Malcolm Barrass, Nathan Blake, Andy Campbell, Franz Carr, Aiden Davison, Andy Dibble (United reserve), Harold Gough, Bob Hatton, Charlie Henderson, Jim Hobson, David Holdsworth, Andy Kennedy, Gary Jones (Blades' first official loan signing), Vince Matthews, Mark Patterson, Tony Philliskirk, Martin Pike, Billy Russell and Andy Walker. Bruce Rioch played for the Blades and later managed Bolton.

BONE, James

Inside/centre-forward: 33+1 apps. 11 goals

Born: Bridge of Allan near Stirling, 22 September 1949.

Career: Fallin Boys Brigade, Bannockburn FC, Airth Castle Rovers, Partick Thistle (June 1968), Norwich City (£30,000, February 1972), BLADES (£30,000, February 1973, with Trevor Hockey moving to Carrow Road as part of the deal), Celtic (£26,000, February 1974), Arbroath (£12,000, January 1975), St Mirren (£25,000, January 1978), Heart of Midlothian (season 1982-83), Arbroath (player-manager, March 1985, finally leaving football in 1987).

Jimmy Bone was a bustling and aggressive striker, 'reckless and brave' who netted Norwich's first-ever goal in Division One. He went on to find the net over 100 times in Scottish football and won two full caps for his country (sub v. Yugoslavia in 1972 and Denmark in 1973, scoring in the latter thus helping his country qualify for the World Cup Finals in West Germany the following year) while also appearing in three Under-21 internationals.

* A racing fanatic, Bone's favourite jockey was Lester Piggott.

BOOKER, Robert

Midfielder: 109+22 apps. 14 goals

Born: Watford, 25 January 1958

Career: Bedmond Social, Brentford (professional, October 1978), BLADES (November 1988), Brentford (November 1991, retiring in May 1993), later Brighton & Hove Albion (assistant-manager).

Bob Booker was fast approaching his 31st birthday when he joined the Blades from in 1988 as a straight replacement for the injured Simon Webster. He had been at Griffin Park ten years and had made well over 275 League and Cup appearances for the Bees as a solid, resilient and dominant midfielder, strong in the tackle with a good passing technique. On leaving Bramall Lane (after twice helping the Blades gain promotion in successive season, from Divisions Three & Two in 1989 & 1990) he returned to Griffin Park and added a further 19 League appearances to his tally before retiring from first-class football in 1993.

BOOKS

Listed here are some of the many football books that have a direct reference to Sheffield United FC

* Football In Sheffield - Percy M Young (Stanley Paul 1962; Sporting Book Club 1964).
* Paul McGrath: Ooh, Aah, Paul McGrath - The Black Pearl of Inchicore (Mainstream Publishing, 1994)...McGrath's story.
* The Official Centenary History of Sheffield United FC: The First 100 Years: 1889-1989 - Denis Clarebrough (Sheffield United FC 1989).
* Sheffield United Football Club 1889-1999: A Complete Record - Denis Clarebrough & Andrew Kirkham (Sheffield United FC 1999).
* Before & After Bramall Lane (Sheffield United CC & Yorkshire Cricket in Sheffield) - Keith Farnsworth.

BOOT, Edmund

Wing-half: 48 apps.

Born: Laughton Common near Rotherham, 13 October 1915

Career: Laughton FC (1932), Denaby United (1933), Sheffield Wednesday (on trial), BLADES (trial October, professional November 1935), Huddersfield Town (March 1937, retiring in May 1953, but remaining at Leeds Road as reserve team player-coach and was appointed as the club's manager in January 1960, the fifth since WW2. He remained in office until September 1964, leaving because he had become 'disillusioned with football').

Eddie Boot who often earned glowing reports for his keenness and endeavour, was a tough, uncompromising wing-half the Blades. However, a move to Huddersfield (with his colleague Bobby Barclay) in 1937 proved successful and he appeared in the 1938 FA Cup Final (beaten by Preston North End). Boot continued to play after WW2 and was an inestimable value to the Leeds Road club and when he announced his retirement (from first-class football) in 1953, his senior appearance total with the Terriers stood at an impressive 325.

BOOTLE

United's playing record against Boston:

Football League

Venue	P	W	D	L	F	A
Home	1	1	0	0	8	3
Away	1	0	0	1	0	2
Totals	2	1	0	1	8	5

United's first-ever away game in the Football League took place on 10 September 1892 against Bootle, one of Liverpool's first football clubs which was formed in 1878 and became founder members of the Football Alliance in 1889 (twelve months after failing to win a place to the Football League).

A crowd of 3,000 at Bootle's Hawthorne Road saw the home side win that League game 2-0. However, things were different at Bramall Lane in the November when the Blades (5-0 up at the interval) raced to an 8-3 victory, Harry Hammond securing a club record five goals (later equalled by Harry Johnson).

BORBOKIS, Vassillios

Wing-back: 74 apps. 9 goals

Born: Serres, Greece, 10 February 1969

Career: Appollon FC, AEK Athens, BLADES (£900,000, July 1997), Derby County (£600,000 in a player-exchange deal involving Jonathan Hunt & Rob Kozluk, March 1999).

Right-wing-back Vas Borbokis scored on his League debut for the Blades against Sunderland on 10 August 1997. After being fined by the club for returning to Greece following injury worries (having been refused permission to do so) he was subsequently placed on the transfer list and eventually moved to Derby. Borbokis, who gained three full international cap with AEK, was a superb crosser of the ball and very useful with free-kicks.

BOSTON UNITED

United's playing record against Boston:

FA Cup

Venue	P	W	D	L	F	A
Home	1	1	0	0	5	1
Away	1	0	1	0	1	1
Totals	2	1	1	0	6	2

Boston United, first formed in 1934, and finally gaining Football League status in 2002, have played the Blades twice at senior level. After a 1-1 draw at the Lincolnshire club's York Street ground in a 2nd round FA Cup-tie in December 1982, there was only going to be one winner when the teams met for the replay at Bramall Lane - and it was the Blades who came out on top, victors by 5-1 with Alan Young netting a hat-trick, his only Cup goals for the club.

BOTTOM, Arthur Edwin
Inside/centre-forward: 28 apps. 9 goals
Born: Sheffield, 28 February 1930
Career: Sheffield YMCA, BLADES (amateur, May 1946, professional April 1947), York City (June 1954), Newcastle United (£4,500, February 1958), Chesterfield (£5,000, November 1958), Boston United (May 1960), Alfreton Town (seasons 1961-63).
After learning the 'scoring' trade with the Blades, and helping them win the Second Division title in 1953, curly-haired Arthur Bottom went on to net 105 goals in 158 senior games for York, helping them reach the FA Cup semi-final in 1955, when they were defeated by his future club Newcastle in a replay. He had made his League debut for the Blades against Stoke City in October 1948 and netted a sensational hat-trick on his first outing for the Minstermen in a 6-2 win over Wrexham. Later, in February 1957, he struck four goals in a 9-1 win over Southport. After hiss transfer to St James' Park, his ten goals in 11 matches saved the Magpies from relegation that season. Although sometimes a controversial figure on the field, Bottom was quiet and retiring off it. Without doubt he's one of York City's all-time greats.
* Bottom was a ball-boy at Bramall Lane during season 1943-4.

BOULDING, Michael Thomas
Striker: 4+3 apps. one goal
Born: Sheffield, 8 February 1975
Career: Hallam FC, Mansfield Town (professional, August 1999), Grimsby Town (August 2000), Aston Villa (on loan, July 2002), BLADES (on loan, September-October 2002), Grimsby Town (on loan, November 2002, signed permanently March 2003).
Michael Boulding, fast and direct, scored 12 goals 75 appearances for his first club, the Stags. He moved into the Premiership with Aston Villa but proved disappointing to manager Graham Taylor. He was subsequently loaned out again, this time to the Blades, scoring on his first full outing (a 4-1 home win over Wycombe Wanderers in the League Cup) having made his debut as a substitute a few days earlier against Watford (away).

BOURNEMOUTH (AFC)
United's playing record against the Cherries:
Football League

Venue	P	W	D	L	F	A
Home	5	2	2	1	8	
Away	5	3	2	0	4	1
Totals	10	5	4	1	12	6

FA Cup

Home	1	1	0	0	2	0

36

There was certainly a football club in Bournemouth as early as 1875, but the present one arose out of the remnants of the Boscombe St John's club (formed in 1890). The meeting at which Boscombe FC came into being, was held at a house in Gladstone Road in 1899. They began by playing in the Boscombe & District Junior League and utilising a ground on Castlemain Road, Pokesdown, switching to dean Court in 1910. In 1923, on gaining entry to the Football League (Division 3 South) the club changed its name to Bournemouth & Boscombe Athletic and in 1971 became known as AFC Bournemouth. The Blades first met the Cherries as recent as 1981-82 (Division 4), both games ending in goalless draws. The following season the two League fixtures again finished level, this time 2-2 at 'the Lane' and 0-0 at Dean Court.
The Blades then doubled-up in 1983-84 (winning 2-0 at home, 1-0 at Dean Court) and did likewise in 1989-90 (4-2 and 1-0), Ian Bryson scoring twice in the 4-2 win to secure promotion to the top flight. In between times, the Cherries recorded their only win, 1-0 at Bramall Lane (August 1987).
Richard Cadette, Jack Cross, George Farrow, Don Givens, Cliff Halliwell, Tom Hefferman, Jim Hutchinson, Phil Kite, Dennis Longhorn, Steve Lovell, Vince Matthews, Mark Morris, George Richardson, Nigel Spackman (also Blades manager), Charlie Wilkinson and Paul Wood are among the players who have assisted both clubs.

BOURNE, Jeffrey Albert
Winger: 30+1 apps. 11 goals
Born: Repton, 19 June 1948,
Career: Burton Albion, Derby County (June 1969), Crystal Palace (March 1977), Atlanta Chiefs (May 1978), BLADES (£35,000, September 1979), Atlanta Chiefs (May 1980),
A sturdy player, with a strong attacking flair, Jeff Bourne spent just the one season at Bramall Lane before rejoining the Chiefs after netting nine times in 49 League outings for the Rams, helping them win the First Division championship in 1975 (17 games, two goals). He scored 10 goals in 32 League appearances for Palace

BOYD, William Gillespie
Centre-forward/inside-left: 49 apps. 32 goals
Born: Cambuslang, Scotland, 27 November 1905. Died: Bristol, 14 December 1967.
Career: Regent Star (Rutherglen), Larkhall Thistle (August 1927), Clyde (June 1930), BLADES (£2,250, December 1933), Manchester United (December 1935), Workington (September 1935), Southampton (July 1936), Weymouth (August 1937-September 1939).
A former shipyard worker Bill Boyd was a small, sharp-shooting centre-forward who whose scoring record for the Blades was quite superb as it was elsewhere. He netted 205 goals in three seasons for Larkhall Thistle, bagged a further 91 in 111 Scottish League games with Clyde. He represented the Scottish League on three occasions (as a Clyde player) and was awarded two full international caps in May 1931 (v. Italy and Switzerland). In season 1933-34 Boyd finished up as top-scorer for both Clyde and the Blades and all told he netted 142 goals in 189 League games for his five major clubs.

BOYLE, Peter
Defender: 187 apps. one goal
Born: Carlingford, Co Louth 1872.
Career: Albion Rovers, Sunderland (professional, December 1896), BLADES (December 1898), Motherwell (May 1904), Clapton Orient (August-December 1905, retired).
A positively strong tackler, Peter Boyle loved a battle and it is said that he 'played the game without a care in the world.' Twice an Cup winner in 1899 and 1902, Boyle also played in the 1901 losing Final and was also capped five times by Ireland during his tin with United.
*His son, Tommy was an FA Cup winner with United in 1925.

BOYLE, Thomas W
Right-half/inside-right: 137 apps. 40 goals
Born: Sheffield, 27 February 1897.
Career: Bullcroft Main Colliery FC, BLADES (October 1921), Manchester United (March 1929), Northampton Town (player-manager, July 1930), Scarborough (manager, May 1935-37). He later became a publican, based a few miles outside Middlesbrough. Tommy Boyle, the son of Peter (above) followed in his father's footsteps by joining the Blades in 1921. A stern tackler, he remained at Bramall Lane for almost eight years. An FA Cup winner in 1925 (v. Cardiff City) he did not figure in the Blades' first team all that often during seasons 1927-28 & '28-29, hence his move to Old Trafford where he failed to hold down a first-team place.

BRADFORD, David William
Midfielder: 69+9 apps. 3 goals
Born: Manchester, 22 February 1953.
Career: Blackburn Rovers (juniors, May 1968, professional August 1971), BLADES (£10,000, July 1974), Peterborough United (on loan, October 1976), West Bromwich Albion (February 1977), Washington Diplomats/NASL (1979), Coventry City (October 1981), Tulsa Roughnecks (May 1982).
Dave Bradford was a thoughtful player with a firm belief in attacking, constructive football. A fine passer of the ball he initiated numerous attacks although his scoring record left a lot to be desired. He made 64 League appearances for Blackburn before his transfer to Bramall Lane where he before switching his allegiance to West Bromwich Albion. He failed to make the first team at The Hawthorns and later had two separate spells in America.

BRADFORD CITY
United's playing record against the Bantams:

Football League

Venue	P	W	D	L	F	A
Home	25	13	8	4	52	27
Away	25	9	5	11	40	39
Totals	50	22	13	15	92	66

FA Cup

Away	1	0	0	1	1	2

League Cup

Home	2	1	1	0	4	1
Away	2	2	0	0	3	1
Totals	4	3	1	0	7	2

WW1

Home	4	2	0	2	9	4
Away	4	2	1	1	6	4
Totals	8	4	1	3	15	

WW2

Home	1	0	1	0	2	2
Away	1	0	0	1	3	4
Totals	2	0	1	1	5	6

Yorkshire & Humberside Cup

Away	1	1	0	0	1	0

Others

Home	1	1	0	0	2	1
Away	1	1	0	0	1	0
Totals	2	2	0	0	3	1

Formed from Manningham rugby club in 1903, and immediately elected to the Football League (Division 2), Bradford City were in the top flight of English football five years later and their first meeting with the Blades in the competition took place in October of that year. It resulted in a 3-0 defeat, but later that season they turned things round by beating United 3-1 at Valley Parade, their home ground since the outset.
On a miserable rainy Monday afternoon in March 1912, the Blades recorded their biggest League win over the Bantams, beating them 7-3 at Bramall Lane with Billy Gillespie netting four times in front of 5,500 loyal supporters.
When United beat City 5-2 at Valley Parade in a second Division game in 1934-35, Scotsman Willie Boyd scored a four out of the five goals. City won the return fixture 2-1.
United's first-ever Sunday League game ended in a 2-0 defeat at Bradford in May 1983.
United registered their best League win at Bradford in 2002-03, cruising to a 5-0 victory. They later completed the double for the season with a 3-0 win at Bramall Lane.
The only FA Cup clash was in 1919-20 when City beat United, the holders of the trophy, 2-1 at Valley Parade.
The Blades and City have met each other in four different Divisions but not as yet in the Premiership.
Alf Ashmore (United reserve), Peter Beagrie, Bobby Campbell, Gordon Cowans, Aidan Davison, Steve Foley, goalkeepers Willie Foulke & Harold Gough, George Handley, Derek Hawksworth, Trevor Hockey, Tommy Hoyland, George Hutchinson, Jean-Phillipe Javary (City trialist), Alf Jeffries, Chris Kamara (also City manager), Stuart McCall, Mark Mellors, Bert Partridge, John Poole (City reserve & coach/trainer), Dean Saunders, Fred E Smith, David Staniforth, Laurens Ten Heuvel, Paul Tomlinson, Gus Uhlenbeek, Chris Wilder, Dean Windass, Curtis Woodhouse and Peter Wragg are among those who have served with both clubs.
Jack Peart played for United and manager the Bantams.

BRADFORD PARK AVENUE

United's playing record against Park Avenue:

Football League

Venue	P	W	D	L	F	A
Home	9	8	1	0	23	9
Away	9	3	2	4	14	15
Totals	18	11	3	4	37	24

FA Cup

	P	W	D	L	F	A
Home	2	2	0	0	4	1

WW1

	P	W	D	L	F	A
Home	4	3	1	0	7	3
Away	4	1	1	2	2	6
Totals	8	4	2	2	9	9

WW2

	P	W	D	L	F	A
Home	3	1	1	1	6	6
Away	3	2	0	1	6	3
Totals	5	3	1	2	12	9

Bradford's emergence as a Football League club is one of the most extraordinary in the history of the competition. In April 1907 a group of professional players belonging to the Park Avenue rugby club proposed the club converted the Association code. They had a powerful financial backer in Mr Harry Briggs who engaged the leading football stadium architect of the day, Archibald Leitch (who had designed the John Street Stand at Bramall Lane) to build a stadium alongside the Park Avenue cricket club ground which the rugby club had shared.

Bradford (Park Avenue), with outlandish confidence, applied to join the Football League for season 1907-08 but not surprisingly, had no success. Undeterred, they now approached the Southern League, at this stage the Football League's chief rivals, to take the place of Fulham who had just been elected to the Second Division of the FL. Amazingly the Southern League accepted the Yorkshire club who also entered a reserve team in the North Eastern League.

After just one season, Bradford again applied for FL status and were accepted along with Tottenham Hotspur, also from the Southern League, who as a 'non-League' side had beaten the Blades in the 1901 FA Cup Final. Now Bradford, hitherto a rugby stronghold, could boast two League clubs, City having been elected in 1903, their beginnings also via a rugby club (Manningham). For three seasons (1914-21) Bradford's two soccer teams were both in the top flight, a remarkable achievement.

The Blades first met Park Avenue in a 2nd round FA Cup-tie at Bramall Lane in 1913-14. They won 3-1 before a crowd of 51,000, George Utley scoring twice.

The next season saw the first-ever Football League meeting between the clubs, Bradford winning 2-0 at Park Avenue (thus emphasising their rapid advance) but the Blades gain revenge with a 3-2 win at 'the Lane.'

The clubs again clashed in the FA Cup and once more the Blades came out on top, winning a 3rd round tie 1-0 after extra-time on their way to a successful Final.

The last fixture took place at Park Avenue in March 1950 (Division 2) when a Fred Smith goal earned the Blades a point from a 1-1 draw.

Among the players who have served with both clubs we have: George Henson, Walter Hughes (Blades reserve), Pat Keating, Paddy Kenny and Peter Spooner.

BRADSHAW, Carl

Full-back/wide-midfielder: 148+27 apps. 13 goals
Born: Sheffield, 2 October 1968,
Career: Sheffield Wednesday (amateur, 1984, professional August 1986), Barnsley (on loan, August-September 1986), Manchester City (£50,000, September 1988), BLADES (£50,000, September 1989), Norwich City (£500,000, July 1994), Wigan Athletic (October 1997), Scunthorpe United (May 2001-May 2002), Alfreton (July 2002).
Carl Bradshaw made 175 first-class appearances for the Blades - and helped them gain promotion from Division Two in 1990 - before being sold to Norwich in what turned out to be an exceptionally profitable deal!). He helped the Latics win the Auto-Windscreen Shield at Wembley in 1999 and when he left the 'Iron' his career appearance tally in League and Cup competitions stood at almost 475 (38 goals scored). Initially a striker, he gained England Youth honours as an 'Owl' before developing into a hard-working, forceful and combative midfielder who could also play as an attacking wing-back.

BRAMALL LANE

Anyone wishing to study the history of Sheffield United must first start with the history of the ground - Bramall Lane - for the Blades are one of a handful of League clubs which were created to play at an existing ground: Chelsea, Liverpool and Plymouth Argyle made similar beginnings as did the short-lived new Brighton Tower and Thames AFC.

Bramall Lane began its sporting life as a huge cricket field, capable of hosting three matches simultaneously. In 1854 Michael Ellison, son of the Duke of Norfolk's land agent arranged the 99-year lease of eight-and-a-half acres of the Duke's property for the use by local cricket clubs. The land had the twin benefits of being flat (a rarity in Sheffield!) and sited away from the grim industrial area, which provided the Yorkshire town with its fame and wealth. Bramall Lane itself was a narrow country lane. Six cricket clubs, including Sheffield CC and The Wednesday CC, between them agreed to pay the annual rent for the whole site of £70. The first cricket match took place on 30 April 1855...and Bramall Lane soon became the sporting centre of Sheffield, used by people from all social classes and walks of life.

Selected members from each of the six cricket clubs formed a committee to run the ground, known as the Sheffield United Ground Committee - and it should be noted that the 'word' United had never been used as the name of a sporting club at this stage and simply meant 'joined together' as in 'United Kingdom.' Shares were made available at £5 each for 'proprietors' or 'shareholders' and 477 such people took up the offer. They became members of 'Sheffield United Cricket Club' although at the time no such cricket team existed. Other sports are accommodated such as athletics, bowls, cycling, hockey, lacrosse and tennis; of course footballers also made use of the fine ground, the first match taking place in 1862 between the Sheffield club (q.v) and Hallam, two of the first organised clubs to emerge from the ancient but disorganised game.

The ground was soon completely walled, enabling entrance fees to be charged (turnstiles were eventually introduced in 1872).

38

A cricket pavilion was built which encouraged the newly formed Yorkshire County Cricket Club to adopt Bramall Lane as its headquarters, with Mr J B Wostinholm, a Sheffield stockbroker, installed as secretary of the Bramall Lane Cricket ground as well as the cricket club. However, the ground was proving expense to run and other forms of revenue were sought to supplement thee meagre income derived from cricket. More football matches were played there as the number of clubs in Sheffield increased, making the town the most important football centre in the country. Wednesday FC (formed in 1867) played several games there and all local Cup competitions held their finals at Bramall Lane.

By 1875 some more land was leased from the Duke of Norfolk, upping the overall area of sporting ground to almost 12 acres with room for five cricket pitches. The fame of Bramall Lane had spread so that in 1883 an England v. Scotland International Match was hosted there, the first outside London or Glasgow. Later it would host an England v. Australia Cricket Test as well as an FA Cup Final replay (1912) and several Cup semi-finals, a unique record for a Football League ground.

Sheffield Wednesday's position in the game was rising and there were hopes that they might move into Bramall Lane permanently having played locally at Sheaf house, then Olive Grove, just a few streets away from "the Lane'.
The cricket-based committee had no love for football and hated the desecration of their sacred turf, but eventually their minds were made up when Bramall Lane was chosen as the venue for the FA Cup semi-final between Preston North End and West Bromwich Albion in 1889, the first season of the newly formed Football League. The League was proving very popular but no Yorkshire side had yet gained election. A packed crowd of 22,688, the largest semi-final attendance thus far, alerted the Committee of football's potential. Now, Charles Stokes, a member of the ground Committee, a great football man, proposed a professional club to be formed for the next season. Sheffield United (q.v) was born, in 1889.

The football ground would be laid out on the north side of the cricket 'square', opposite the cricket pavilion, the ground to be built up on three sides only, leaving the 'cricket side' open. This arrangement held until 1973 when cricket was ended at 'the Lane' after 118 years. A stand was built along the northern edge of the pitch backing on to John Street (north side) but this was totally inadequate so maestro football ground architect Archibald Leitch was hired to build a new stand able to seat 3,800 spectators with another 6,000 able to stand in the paddock.

Over the year further major changes took effect as follows:

1912	Shoreham Street (Eastern end) raised to become standing 'Spion Kop.'
1913	Terracing concreted on the 'Kop.'
1928	Terrace at Bramall Lane end (Western) extended
1935	'Kop' end had roof adding (extended in 1938).
1940	Ground damaged by bombs. Part of the John Street stand destroyed including Leitch's trademark mock-Tudor gabled press box. The 'Kop' roof was also damaged and the pitch cratered.
1948	'Kop' roof replaced.
1954	Floodlights installed for first time (switched on, March 1955). Also the John Street stand fully restored.
1958	Fifth floodlight pylon added to the top of the John Street stand.
1959	Roof over John Street stand extended to cover standing paddock.
1961	New floodlight system installed.
1961-63	Discussions took place with regards to the football club moving to a new ground at Dyche Lane, Meadowhead or moving the Yorkshire CCC to a separate ground at Bramall Lane.
1966	Bramall Lane end re-covered, with seating increased to 3,000.
1971	United promoted back to Division One; Yorkshire CCC given two years to quit.
1973	Last cricket match played at 'the Lane' - Yorkshire v. Lancashire, 7 August.
1975	South stand (with 8,000 seats) built over old cricket pitch; ground now completely enclosed on all four sides for the first time. Ground capacity now registered at 49,000 (16,000 seats).
1981	Cricket pavilion demolished, allowing dressing rooms, offices and function rooms to be moved across to the South Stand.
1991	Seats installed at the 'Kop' end.
1994	Leitch's John Street stand demolished. (New stand not built until 1996)
1996	John Street stand opened, all-seater (6,842 seats); 31 executive boxes, 325 executive seats, plus catering facilities. Ground capacity now 30,370 (all-seated).

* Clearly, the concept of a joint cricket/football stadium does not work, both sets of supporters feeling it does not suit their game. Cricket at Bramall Lane was uninspiring with its industrial back-drop and out-off-place football terracing. Football in a three-sided ground just did not seem right; for big games spectators even used the cricket pavilion, gaining only a distant view of the action. Yet the resultant ground, built without a master plan, is just another modern stadium. The old Bramall Lane was something unique; the new one is functional but has no charm. Something has been lost, perhaps never to return!

Bramall Lane Fact File
* Before 1889 'the Lane' had already staged approximately 400 football matches (at various levels), averaging around 12 per year.
* The first cricket match played there in 1855 was between The XI and The 22 (players chosen from the Broomhall, Caxton, Milton, Sheffield, Shrewsbury and Wednesday clubs).
* On 1 August 1855 the first County Cricket match was staged at "the Lane' when Sussex beat Yorkshire.
* On 29 December 1862 the first football match was staged there when Sheffield FC drew 0-0 with Hallam FC. The game was in aid of the Lancashire Distress Fund to help relieve the misery caused by the deterioration in the cotton trade as a result of the American Civil war.
* The first representative match at 'the Lane' took place on 2 December 1871 when a crowd of 2,000 saw a selected Sheffield side beat a London XI 3-1.
* In the summer of 1878, the Australian tourists played Yorkshire at cricket (over the three days almost 18,000 spectators attended).
* Soon afterwards 12,000 spectators attended the ground to watch a pre-season football practice match (a friendly) when a team clad in Blue beat the Reds 2-0. This was the first ever floodlit soccer match ever.
* A two-foot high snow barrier enclosed the Sheffield pitch when Scotland beat England 3-2 at 'the Lane' in 1883.
* Blades' goalkeeper Bill Foulke and left-half Ernest Needham were in the England side against Wales at 'the Lane' in 1897 (Needham scored in the 4-0 victory).
* Blades' right-half Harry Johnson played for England in the fourth international match at 'the Lane' (v. Scotland in 1903).

* The New John Street Stand was opened on 2 September 1895 for the First Division League game with Small Heath. A crowd of 7,000 saw the Blades win 2-0. The new throw-in law was introduced for this game as well, and the referee demonstrated the procedure to the spectators before kick-off. The well known John Street stand designed by Archibald leitch was opened in 1902 replacing the 1895 stand.
* Bramall Lane was one of 14 Football League games damaged by German bombs during WW2 - and the only one in Yorkshire.
* In 1874, an American baseball challenge match between the Boston Reds and the Philadelphia Blues was staged at Bramall Lane. Fifteen years later another exhibition baseball match was staged (March 1889). This event attracted 1,550 spectators, but unfortunately heavy rain caused the contest to be abandoned.
* Several pre-season Public Practice matches (involving United's first & second XI's) have taken place at Bramall Lane over the years.
* In April 1988 Sheffield Eagles beat Doncaster 30-14 in a Rugby League match watched by 2,397 spectators.

Full international matches at Bramall Lane
10.03.1883	England 2 Scotland 3	Att. 9,000
05.02.1887	England 7 Ireland 0	Att. 6,000
29.03.1897	England 4 Wales 0	Att. 4,900
04.04.1903	England 1 Scotland 2	Att. 32,699
20.10.1930	England 5 Ireland 1	Att. 39,064

Under-21 Internationals
27.04.1977	England 1 Scotland 0	Att. 8,934
16.04.1980	England 1 German Dem R 2	Att. 10,039
21.09.1982	England 3 West Germany 1	Att. 6,345
24.03.1984	England 2 Spain 0	Att. 11,478
13.10.1987	England 1 Turkey 1	Att. 5,854

Under-23 Internationals
7.3.1973	England 1 Czechoslovakia 0	Att. 8,003

Youth International
15.03.1972	England 4 Spain 1	Att. 4,046

Schoolboy International
06.03.1970	England 11 Ireland 0	Att. 5,200
21.04.1975	England 1 Scotland 0	Att. 10,428

Schoolboy Matches (Cup Semis & Finals)
04.04.1960	Sheffield Boys 1 Manchester Boys 3	Att. 10,000
31.03.1982	Sheffield Boys 3 Liverpool Boys 1	Att. 2,000
28.04.1982	Sheffield Boys 1 Coventry Boys 0	Att. 4,000
17.05.1984	Sheffield Boys 4 Swindon Boys 1	Att. 1,850

International Trial (England)
19.02.1881	The North 1 The South 2	Att. 3,000

Inter League
24.10.1892	North 2 Midlands 3	Att. 2,500

Representative Matches
04.02.1964	England U-23 XI 2 England Youth 2	Att. 3,496
08.03.1967	Universities AU 1 FA Amateur XI 2	Att. 2,000

FA Cup Final Replay
24.04.1912	Barnsley 1 West B Albion 0 (aet)	Att: 38,555

FA Cup Semi-finals
16.03.1889	Preston N End 1 West B Albion 0	Att. 22,688
28.02.1891	Notts County 3 Sunderland 3	Att. 22,000
11.03.1891	Notts County 2 Sunderland 0 (rep)	Att. 13,147
04.03.1893	Everton 2 Preston North End 2	Att. 20,000
16.03.1893	Everton 2 Preston N End 0 (replay)	Att. 14,000
10.03.1894	Blackburn Rovers 0 Notts County 1	Att. 20,000
20.03.1897	Aston Villa 3 Liverpool 0	Att. 30,000
19.03.1898	Nottm Forest 1 Southampton SM 1	Att. 30,000
29.03.1899	Bury 3 Nottingham Forest 2	Att. 11,200
27.03.1909	Manch Utd 1 Newcastle Utd 0	Att. 40,118
25.03.1911	Blackburn Rov 0 Bradford City 3	Att. 36,479
29.03.1913	Burnley 0 Sunderland 0	Att. 33,656
27.03.1920	Aston Villa 3 Chelsea 1	Att. 37,776
29.03.1924	Aston Villa 3 Burnley 0	Att. 54,531
27.03.1926	Manchester C 3 Manchester U 0	Att. 36,450
26.03.1938	Aston Villa 1 Preston N End 2	Att. 55,129

FA Cup 2nd & 3rd Replays/Qualifying Matches
30.10.1873	Sheffield FC 0 Shropshire WA 0	Att. 650
18.12.1880	Sheffield FC 1 Darwen 5	Att. 1,000
21.12.1881	Wednesday 2 Staveley 2	Att. 800
21.01.1882	Wednesday 3 Heeley 1	Att. 1,500
07.02.1882	Wednesday 6 Upton Park 0	Att. 3,000
04.11.1882	Wednesday 12 Spilsby 2	Att. 2,000
01.12.1883	Lockwood Bros 3 Rotherham Utd 1	Att. 1,000
13.01.1883	Wednesday 3 Nottingham Forest 2	Att. 1,000
12.02.1883	Wednesday 1 Notts County 4	Att. 3,500
03.01.1885	Wednesday 1 Nottingham Forest 2	Att. 2,000
11.12.1886	Lockwood Bros 2 Nottingham F 1	Att. 1,000
29.01.1887	Lockwood Bros 0 West B Albion 1	Att. 6,000
24.10.1888	Grimsby Town 3 Lincoln City 1	Att. 1,500
11.02.1891	Nottm Forest 5 Sunderland Albion 0	Att. 6,000
27.02.1892	Aston Villa 4 Sunderland 1	Att.25,000
04.03.1892	Everton 2 Preston North End 2	Att.26,000
16.03.1892	Everton 0 Preston N End 0 (rep)	Att.15,000
10.03.1893	Blackburn Rov 0 Notts County 1	Att.22,000
11.02.1897	Bolton Wds 3 Grimsby Town 2	Att. 8,200
10.03.1897	Aston Villa 3 Preston N End 2	Att.20,000
02.12.1897	Doncaster Rov 1 Mexborough 1	Att. 1,500
21.12.1903	Manchester Utd 1 Small Heath 1	Att. 3,000
12.02.1906	Brighton & HA 1 Middlesbrough 3	Att.11,528
28.11.1910	Gainsborough Trinity 5 Ilkeston 0	Att. 500
21.03.1912	Barnsley 3 Bradford City 2	Att.38,241
22.12.1913	Darlington 0 Port Vale 1	Att. 4,000
06.02.1922	Bradford City 0 Notts County 1	Att.29,882
21.01.1924	Halifax Town 4 Northampton T 2	Att. 6,102
07.12.1925	Bradford PA 2 Lincoln City 1	Att. 5,500
17.01.1938	Bradford City 0 Chesterfield 2	Att.21,061
21.01.1952	Gateshead 2 Ipswich Town 1	Att. 7,470

Inter Association/Representative Matches
02.12.1871	Sheffield 3 London 1	Att. 2,000*
02.03.1872	Sheffield v. London	Att.1,500+
02.11.1872	Sheffield v. London	Att. 2,000*
12.02.1873	Sheffield 2 Derbyshire 2	Att. 2,000
15.03.1873	Sheffield v. London	Att.1,000+
11.11.1873	Sheffield v. London	Att. 2,000*
04.02.1874	Sheffield v. London	Att.1,500+
14.03.1874	Sheffield 2 Glasgow 2	Att. 2,000
07.11.1874	Sheffield v. London	Att. 1,500*
29.03.1885	Sheffield v. London	Att.2,500+
20.01.1876	Sheffield 6 Birmingham 0	Att.1,000
19.02.1876	Sheffield 0 Glasgow 2	Att. 2,000
25.03.1876	Sheffield v. London	Att. 1,000*
11.11.1876	Sheffield v. London	Att. 1,000*
15.01.1877	Sheffield 7 North Wales 0	Att. 500
24.02.1877	Sheffield 14 Manchester 0	Att. 1,000
15.12.1877	Sheffield 6 Staffordshire 0	Att. 500
09.02.1878	Sheffield 2 Glasgow 4	Att. 9,000
14.12.1878	Sheffield 10 Birmingham 0	Att. 5,000
06.11.1880	Sheffield 11 Birmingham 2	Att. 3,000
11.02.1882	Sheffield 3 Glasgow 1	Att. 2,500
01.01.1883	Sheffield 4 Edinburgh 0	Att. 4,000
16.02.1884	Sheffield 1 Glasgow 2	Att. 5,000
23.01.1886	Sheffield 2 Glasgow 2	Att. 3,000
23.10.1886	Sheffield 1 Birmingham 7	Att. 4,000
28.01.1888	Sheffield 2 Glasgow 3	Att. 5,000
09.11.1889	Sheffield 1 London 0	Att. 4,000
11.01.1890	Sheffield 1 Glasgow 3	Att. 5,000
10.01.1891	Sheffield 4 Glasgow 3	Att. 9,000
06.02.1892	Sheffield 4 London 1	Att.10,000
24.10.1892	Lancs & North 2 Midlands 3	Att. 6,000

12.12.1892	Sheffield 3 Glasgow 3	Att. 12,000	20.03.1892	Sheffield Strollers 3 Wednesday W 1	Att. 4,500
21.10.1893	Sheffield 5 London 1	Att. 4,000	18.02.1895	English 3 Scottish 1	Att. 4,000
18.02.1895	Sheffield 10 London 0	Att. 4,500	17.01.1898	English 1 Scottish 1	Att. 500
07.11.1896	Sheffield 5 Glasgow 1	Att. 1,500	14.11.1898	United Res 3 Wednesday Res 1	Att. 2,000
10.12.1898	Sheffield 2 Glasgow 1	Att. 5,500	01.01.1903	United Res 0 Wednesday Res 3	Att. 7,000
16.10.1899	Sheffield 7 London 0	Att. 2,500	25.12.1903	United Res 2 Wednesday Res 2	Att.10,000
29.10.1900	Sheffield 3 Glasgow 1	Att. 4,000	26.12.1907	United Res 0 Wednesday Res 2	Att.12,000
24.10.1904	Sheffield 2 Glasgow 0	Att. 3,000	23.09.1909	Sheffield FC 1 Quick FC 3	Att. 1,000
19.10.1908	Sheffield 2 Glasgow 0	Att. 3,000	05.03.1910	United Res 1 Chesterfield 1	Att. 5,500
21.10.1912	Sheffield 1 Glasgow 1	Att. 8,000	18.02.1911	Mexborough 1 Rotherham Town 0	Att. 1,000
12.09.1921	Sheffield 1 Glasgow 1	Att. 16,000	20.03.1911	United Reserves 4 Mexborough 1	Att. 2,000
14.09.1925	Sheffield 1 Glasgow 1	Att. 18,441	10.04.1911	United Reserves 3 Wednesday Res 3	Att. 3,000
24.08.1929	Sheffield 2 Glasgow 0	Att. 12,000	14.10.1911	United Res 15 Wednesday Res 0	Att. 4,000
23.10.1933	Sheffield 3 Glasgow 4	Att. 10,000	01.05.1915	United Res 1 Wednesday Res 4	Att. 8,000
29.10.1949	Sheffield 4 Glasgow 2	Att. 22,500	03.11.1917	A Wilson XI 3 J Pennington XI 1	Att.20,000
20.11.1957	Sheffield 3 Glasgow 0	Att. 10,986	12.01.1918	United XI 3 Hadfields FC 3	Att. 3,000

* Played under Sheffield rules
\+ Played under mixed rules

14.02.1921	Sheffield Cinema/T 2 Pantomime A 2	Att.24,708

Sheffield Cup Final

10.03.1877	Heeley 3 Wednesday 4	Att. 8,000	03.12.1928	Doncaster Rov 2 Rotherham Utd 3	Att. 4,000

15.03.1940	Yorkshire XI 4 FA XI 1	Att.14,184

Charity Match

29.12.1862	Sheffield 0 Hallam 0	Att. 200	26.03.1940	English Universities 4 Army XI 2	Att. 4,569

27.08.1946	Sheffield 0 Eindhoven (Holland) 2	Att. 5,000
27.12.1952	Sheffield FC 1 Pegasus 8	Att.11,168

Other Matches/Local Cup Finals & Semi-Finals

12.02.1861	Sheffield v. Hallam	Att. 200	01.10.1956	United 7 Leeds/Wednesday XI 2	Att.17,337
29.12.1862	Sheffield v. Hallam	Att. 100	24.10.1957	Sheffield Club 2 Queen's Park 2	Att. 5,000
05.03.1867	Hallam 0 Norfolk 0	Att. 500	10.03.1958	Sheffield XI 3 International XI 4	Att.29,166
15.02.1868	Garrick 0 Wednesday 1	Att. 500	17.10.1977	United XI 1 Nottingham Forest 6	Att. 6,780
20.12.1873	Sheffield 0 Royal Engineers 4	Att. 700	17.11.1982	Sheffield FC 0 Manchester Utd 2	Att. 1,000
19.02.1878	Wednesday 1 Glasgow Rangers 2	Att. 2,000	06.05.1986	United XI 3 Sheff Wednesday 4	Att. 9.566
14.10.1878	Sheffield FA 'A' v. Sheffield FA 'B'	Att. 2,000	05.10.1986	TC's All Stars 7 Waterman's XI 5	Att.17,500
15.03.1879	Heeley 2 Wednesday 3	Att. 1,500	12.09.1988	United XI 1 Sheffield Wednesday 3	Att. 2,999
11.11.1879	Sheffield XI 4 Sheffield Zulus 5	Att. 2,000	16.03.1992	United XI 1 FF Malmo 6	Att. 3,000
21.10.1880	Wednesday 0 Queen's Park 5	Att. 2,000
12.02.1888	Wednesday XI 1 Preston N End 8	Att. 4,000
01.10.1888	Sheffield FC 1 Canadians 1	Att. 2,500
12.03.1892	Sheffield Strollers 2 Wednesday W 1	Att. 5,000

BRAWN, William Frederick

Right-winger: 14 apps. 4 goals
Born: Wellingborough, 1 August 1878. Died: London, 18 August 1932.
Career; Wellingborough White Star (June 1893), Wellingborough Principals (1894), Northampton Town (July 1895), BLADES (professional, January 1900), Aston Villa (December 1901), Middlesbrough (March 1906), Chelsea (November 1907), Brentford (August 1911), Tottenham Hotspur (WW1 guest, retired in 1915). He later ran a pub (the King's Arms) in Boston Road, Brentford while also acting as advisory-manager at Griffin Park, a position he held until his death in 1932.
Billy Brawn was one of 'the most dangerous outside-rights in the kingdom' during the early 1900s. Renowned for his speed and shooting ability, he was unusually tall for a winger (6ft 2ins) and was also weighty, tipping the scales at 13st 5lbs. He could use both feet and scored and made many goals. He gained two England caps and collected an FA Cup winners' medal with Aston Villa in 1905, later starring in Chelsea's first-ever season in Division One. He retired with over 350 League and Cup appearances to his name.

BRAYSHAW, Walter

Inside-forward; 6 apps. 3 goals
Born: Mexborough, April 1895. Died: Lincolnshire, 1935.
Career: Mexborough Rovers, Denaby United, BLADES (March 1919), Exeter City (September 1920), Denaby United (again, July 1921), Blackburn Rovers (April 1925), Southend United (January 1926), Denaby for a third time (season 1928-29).
Inside-forward Wally Brayshaw scored a hat-trick on his debut for the Blades in a Midland Group game v. Rotherham County (away) in April 1919, won 4-0. He never quite fitted the bill for League action although in later years he netted five times in 113 games for Southend.

BRAZIL, Gary Nicholas

Forward: 50+30 apps. 11 goals
Born: Tunbridge Wells, Kent, 19 September 1962.
Career: Crystal Palace (apprentice, September 1978), BLADES (professional, August 1980), Port Vale (on loan, August 1984), Mansfield Town (on loan briefly), Preston North End (£20,000, February 1985), Newcastle United (£250,000, February 1989), Fulham (on loan, September 1990, signed permanently for £110,000, November 1990) Cambridge United (on trial, August 1996), Barnet (free transfer, September 1996-May 1997), Notts County (Youth team coach, June 1998, later assistant-manager to Sam Allardyce and 'Jocky' Scott before becoming manager himself in 2001, then handing over his duties to ex-Blades star Billy Dearden, January 2002, Brazil reverting back to his role as assistant-manager).
Gary Brazil, who was not offered a contract at Selhurst Park, made more over half as many substitute appearances for the Blades than actual match starts, helping the team gain promotion from Division Three in 1984 (playing in 19 games). As an aggressive, goal-hungry forward, he did exceedingly well at Deepdale, netting 58 times in 161 League outings before moving north to Newcastle, reverting 350 miles to join Fulham in September 1990. He perhaps played his best football with the Cottagers for whom he struck 48 goals in 214 League outings.

BRELSFORD, William

Half-back: 417 apps. 2 goals
Born: Darnall, Sheffield, 1885. Died:
Sheffield, 1954.
Career: Attercliffe United, Tinsley Park,
Lodge Inn FC, Doncaster Rovers, BLADES
(April 1909), Taunton (May 1922), BLADES
(coach, 1925-40).
Bill Brelsford was an arduous half-back, a
totally reliable player who never shirked a
tackle and of whom opponents rarely got the
better in 50-50 situations. He quickly bedded
into the side forming a splendid half-back
line with Bernard Wilkinson and Albert
Sturgess. An FA Cup winner with the Blades
in 1915, Brelsford continued to play for the
club until 1922 when he moved into non-
League soccer with Taunton, later returning
to Bramall Lane as a coach.

BRENTFORD

United's playing record against the Bees:
Football League

Venue	P	W	D	L	F	A
Home	11	3	4	4	20	17
Away	11	3	2	6	15	19
Totals	22	6	6	10	35	36

League Cup

Away	1	1	0	0	4	1

Formed as a small amateur concern in 1889, Brentford were very successful in local circles, winning the championship of the West London Alliance in 1893 and a year later the Middlesex Junior Cup before lifting the London senior Amateur Cup and the Middlesex Senior Cup in 1898. Playing at the Cross Road ground, South Ealing, the club was then admitted to the Second Division of the Southern League, moving into the Football League in 1920 as original members of the Third Division, having switched to Griffin Park via Boston Park in 1904.
Brentford first opposed the Blades in League competition in 1934-35 (Division 2). The Bees won both matches: 2-1 at 'the Lane' and 3-1 at Griffin Park when a crowd of 21,017 saw the championship trophy presented to the London club.
In 1946-47 United claimed their best win over Brentford who were heading for relegation. They won 6-1 at home with Colin Collindridge, in form, scoring twice as did Jimmy Hagan.
On a very muddy, heavy and half-waterlogged pitch, a crowd of almost 21,000 saw the Bees stung 5-1 by United in a Second Division game at Bramall Lane in March 1951.
The Blades' best victory at Griffin Park is 4-1 (two goals for Tony Agana) in a Third Division encounter early in the1988-89 when they got off to a flying start to set them on their way to gain promotion.
Carl Asaba, Ian Benjamin, Graham Benstead, Marcus Bent, Bob Booker, Billy Brawn, Richard Cadette, Jack Chisholm, Glenn Cockerill, John Docherty, Charlie Field, Stewart Houston, Jean-Phillipe Javary, Francis Joseph, Chris Kamara, Scott Marshall, Bobby Reid, Wilf Rostron, Andy Scott and Tom Simons are among the players who have served with both clubs. Wally Downes and Ray Lewington both played for United and later they took over as manager at Griffin Park. Archie Clark played for the Bees and was assistant-boss and acting manager of the Blades. Jimmy Sirrel was manager at 'the Lane' and trainer/caretaker-boss at Brentford, and ex-Blades player Mick Whitham was trainer at Brentford until his death.

BRIDGEWATER, William

Inside-right: 22 apps. 9 goals
Born: Rotherham, 1866.
Career: Rotherham Town, BLADES (July 1890-May 1891), Doncaster Rovers (May 1891).
A very alert player, powerful and competitive, Billy Bridgewater played all his 22 games for the Blades in season 1890-91 when he also appeared in 23 'other'; matches and claimed a further 12 goals. It was a surprise when he left the club.

BRIGHTON & HOVE ALBION

United's playing record against the Seagulls:

Football League

Venue	P	W	D	L	F	A
Home	10	7	1	2	22	11
Away	10	2	3	5	9	13
Totals	20	9	4	7	31	24

FA Cup

Venue	P	W	D	L	F	A
Home	1	0	1	0	0	0
Away	2	1	0	1	2	2
Totals	3	1	1	1	2	2

A professional club, Brighton United, was formed in November 1897 at the Imperial Hotel, Queen's Road, but in March 1900, after less than two seasons in the Southern League, playing at The County Ground, it folded. An amateur team, Brighton & Hove Rangers was then formed by some prominent United supporters and after a season at Withdean, decided to turn semi-professional and play at The County Ground. Rangers won election to the Southern League but surprisingly, in June 1901 that club also folded. John Jackson, the former United manager, organised a meeting at the Seven Stars public house, Ship Street, on 24 June 1901 at which a new club, Brighton & Hove Albion, was formed. They took Rangers' place in the Southern League, switched to the Goldstone Ground in 1902 and gained Football League status (Division 3) in 1920.

Albion first met the Blades at The Goldstone Ground in the opening round of the FA Cup in season 1921-22, Brighton winning 1-0 to cause a major upset.

The first League meetings took place 37 years later, over the Easter period in the 1958-59 season (Division 2), the 'Seagulls' winning 2-0 at Hove and the Blades 3-1 at Bramall Lane.

There was a thrilling nine-goal contest between the clubs in United's promotion-winning campaign of 1989-90. The Blades opened up a 3-0 lead in the first-half, but Albion fought back gallantly (thanks to some slip-shod defending) and with the scores level at 4-4 with barely minutes remaining and the fans making for exits, John Francis headed home a last-gasp winner for United.

The Blades completed the 'League' double over relegated Brighton in 2002-03, winning 2-1 at home and 4-2 away.

Barry Butlin, Darren Carr, George Featherstone, Pat Gilhooley, Wally Gould, Fred Hawley, Billy Hendry, Robert Humphries (United reserve), Andy Kennedy, Ray McHale, Maurice McLafferty, Mark Mellors, Mark Morris, Dennis Mortimer, Archie Needham, Paul Rogers, Dean Saunders, Tony Towner, Mick Trusson, Chris Wilder, Paul Wood and 'Alan' Young are among the players who have assisted both clubs. Harry Haslam, Billy McEwan and Jimmy Sirrel all played for Brighton and later managed the Blades. Ex-United player Bob Booker became assistant-manager of Albion.

BRISTOL CITY

United's playing record against the Robins:

Football League

Venue	P	W	D	L	F	A
Home	15	10	3	2	36	18
Away	15	5	4	6	22	25
Totals	30	15	7	8	58	43

Play-offs

Venue	P	W	D	L	F	A
Home	1	0	1	0	1	1
Away	1	0	0	1	0	1
Totals	2	0	1	1	1	2

FA Cup

Venue	P	W	D	L	F	A
Home	2	2	0	0	5	0
Away	2	1	1	0	4	2
Totals	4	3	1	0	9	2

League Cup

Venue	P	W	D	L	F	A
Home	2	2	0	0	7	1
Away	2	0	1	1	3	4
Totals	4	2	1	1	10	5

In 1897 at a meeting held at the Albert Hall, Bedminster, Bristol City FC came into being when the Bristol South End club, formed three years earlier, decided to adopt professionalism and apply for admission to the Southern League after competing initially in the Western League. The club's first manager was Sam Hollis (ex-Arsenal) who was given £40 to buy new players. After merging with Bedminster, another leading Bristol club, City were one of the first Southern League clubs to gain entry to the Football League, elected in 1901. Three years later the Ashton Gate ground was acquired.

Bristol City first met the Blades in a 1st round FA Cup-tie in February 1904. The final score was 3-1 in favour of the Blades for whom Fred Priest scored a superb goal.

The initial League game followed on Christmas Eve 1906 (Division One) and ended in a 3-3 draw, Edgar Bluff scoring twice for the Blades at Ashton Gate, City having moved there from their St John's Lane ground two years earlier. The return fixture, played a week later, ended level at 1-1 before City went on to finish runners-up in their first season in the top flight.

The Blades' best League win over the Robins is 5-2 (in 1959-50) while they also recorded 4-0 victories in 1909-10 and 1958-59. Their best win on City soil is 4-1 (in 1957-58) when Billy Russell netted a hat-trick to avenge a 3-0 defeat at 'the Lane.'

In September 1970 United trailed 3-0 at home to City in a second Division match, bit thanks to Tony Currie's promptings the Blades fought back to grab a point from a 3-3 draw.

The teams met in the 1987-88 Third Division Play-offs, City going through to Wembley 2-1 on aggregate. At this time the Play-offs were used to decide relegation and by losing the Blades remained in the Third Division.

Ex-United stars Harry Thickett and George Hedley both became manager of City. And among the other players who have been associated with both clubs we have Wayne Allison, Archie Annan, Bill Batty, Walter 'Cocky' Bennett, Len Birks, Keith Curle, Johnny Dryden, George Hall, Gary Hamson, Fred Hawley, Paul Holland, Jamie Hoyland, Martin Kuhl, Andy Leaning, John MacPhail, Arthur Mercer, Billy Mercer, Steve Neville, Ben Shearman, Phil Starbuck, Jack Thompson, Keith Waugh and Bertie Williams. Ex-Blades player George Utley became City's trainer.

43

BRISTOL ROVERS

United's playing record against the Pirates:

Football League

Venue	P	W	D	L	F	A
Home	11	6	3	2	24	12
Away	11	0	4	7	13	25
Totals	22	6	7	9	37	37

Watney Cup

Away	1	0	1*	0	0	0

* The Blades lost 7-6 in a penalty shoot-out (after a 0-0 draw).

Bristol Rovers FC was formed at a meeting in Stapleton Road, Eastville in 1883. Initially playing under the name, Black Arabs (wearing black jerseys), the club change its name to Eastville Rovers in 1884, and after winning the Gloucestershire Senior Cup (1889) entered the Bristol & District League (1892). This eventually became the Western League. The move to Eastville Stadium (from Fishponds) took place in 1897 and a year later the name Bristol Rovers was officially recognised. For a decade, from 1986 (after a fire at Eastville) Rovers played at Bath's City Twerton Park before transferring to the Memorial Ground.

Rovers, another former Southern League club, first met the Blades in 1956-57 (Division 2). After losing 3-1 at Eastville United were then held to a 0-0 draw at 'the Lane.'

United led Rovers 2-0 in a Second Division game in November 1959 but after Billy Russell had broken his leg, the Pirates took charge and fought back to clinch a 3-2 victory.

United's best win of the six so far registered over Rovers, is 3-2, achieved twice, in 1960-61 and 1976-77.

Until 2001 Rovers enjoyed the unique record of only ever having played in the second and third sections of the Football League, but never in the top flight. They were relegated to the Third Division (the old 4th) at the end of the 2000-01 campaign.

A crowd of 19,768 packed into the Eastville Stadium to see Rovers beat the Blades 7-6 in a penalty shoot-out (after a 0-0 draw) to win the Watney Cup in August 1972.

Players who have served with both clubs include John Ball, Darren Carr, Keith Curle, Mark Foran, Francis Joseph, Phil Kite, David Staniforth, Gareth Taylor, Jamie Thomas, Alan Warboys and Steve Yates.

BROADCAST (Radio)

The first Football League game to be broadcast on radio was the Arsenal v. Sheffield United clash at Highbury on 22 January 1927. A crowd of almost 17,000 witnessed the 1-1 draw.

BRODERICK, Mortimer

Inside-right: 2 apps.
Born: Cork, 1 September 1923
Career: Cork City, BLADES (£5,000 with Pat Keating), Cork Crusaders (May 1951).
Broderick made his Football League debut for the Blades away to Grimsby Town (Division 2) in October 1950. He represented the League of Ireland prior to joining the Blades.

BROMAGE, William

Inside or outside-left: 32 apps. 5 goals
Born: Derby, 31 March 1881.
Career: Gainsborough Trinity (1901-03), Whitwick White Cross, BLADES (May 1904), Doncaster Rovers (May 1910)
Utility forward Billy Bromage was a variable player with good speed who made his Football League debut for Gainsborough Trinity in 1902.
* Two brothers - Enos and Henry - were professional goalkeepers, the former with Derby County (1888-90) and the latter with Derby County, Burton United, Leeds City & Doncaster Rovers (1899-1915). Enos' son (Enos junior) was a reserve winger with the Blades (1922) who later played for Derby, Gillingham, West Bromwich Albion, Nottingham Forest & Chester. And two more relatives - George & George E Bromage - were also footballers; the former, an outside-left, had five League outings with the Blades in 1922-23.

BROOK, Harold

Centre-forward; 289 apps. 111 goals
Born: Sheffield, 15 October 1921
Career: Woodbourn Alliance (Sheffield), Fulwood FC, BLADES
(amateur forms 1939, professional, April 1943), Leeds United
(July 1954), Lincoln City (March-May 1958) and coached the
Yorkshire League side Sheffield FC in the early 1960s.
Harold Brook suffered with injuries early in his professional
career but he overcame all that and established himself as a very
capable and confident centre-forward, clever, dexterous with
both feet, elegant in style and possessing a fine shot which
required very little back-lift. He made his debut for the Blades
in the left-back position versus Lincoln City in a North
Regional League game in September 1940 (lost 9-2). He was
quickly converted into a 'goalscorer' and skippered the Second
Division championship winning side of 1953 Leeds in 1954.
He netted 46 goals in 102 League outings during his time at
Elland Road.

BROOKS, Joseph
Left-back: 129 apps.
Born: Stalybridge, circa 1883.
Career: Stalybridge Rovers (1899), Glossop North End (August 1900), Watford (September 1901), BLADES (April1907), Watford August 1912).
Joe Brooks was a strong tacking full-back, positively sound with good pace.

BROWN, Arthur Samuel
Centre-forward: 187 apps. 104 goals
Born: Gainsborough, 6 April 1885. Died: Gainsborough, 27 June 1944.
Career: Gainsborough Church Lads' Brigade FC, Gainsborough Trinity, BLADES (£700 May1902), Sunderland (£1,600, June 1908), Fulham (October 1910), Middlesbrough (June 1912).
Arthur Brown was only 18 years, ten months and 23 days old when he played for England against Wales in February 1904. He later added a second cap to his collection v. Ireland in February 1906, scoring in a 5-0 win. He displayed all what was required of a great goalscorer - control, acceleration, shooting power, positional sense, aggression (when required) and a will to win. He made his debut for the Blades against Notts County in October 1907 and remained a regular in the side until March 1908 when, surprisingly, he demanded a transfer (without giving any real reason) and subsequently left for Sunderland for a 'world record' fee of £1,600. He netted 23 times in 55 games during his two-and-a-bit seasons on Wearside. After claiming 12 goals in 46 games for the Cottagers he switched to Middlesbrough.

BROWN, Douglas Alexander
Forward: 22+10 apps. 5 goals
Born: Poole, Dorset, 21 March 1958.
Career: Clydebank, BLADES (March 1979-May 1980).
Doug Brown spent just 14 months at Bramall Lane before ending his career in League football.

BROWN, Frederick
Inside/centre-forward: 99 apps. 20 goals
Born: Gainsborough, 28 June 1895. Died: Lincolnshire, 1960.
Career: Gainsborough Trinity (August 1913), BLADES (December 1915), Brighton & Hove Albion (May 1923), Gillingham (1924-27), Gainsborough Trinity (season 1927-28).
Fred Brown was a well-proportioned utility forward, hard to shake off the ball. He played for his local team before giving the Blades excellent service during WW1 and then scoring on his League debut against Manchester City (home) in September 1919. He netted 26 goals in almost 100 League outings for the Gills.

45

BROWN, James Grady
Goalkeeper: 203 apps.
Born: Coatbridge, 11 May 1952.
Career: Bargeddie Amateurs, Albion Rovers, Chesterfield (December 1972), BLADES (£70,000, March 1974), Detroit Express (£27,500, March 1979), Chicago Sting (1980), Washington Diplomats (1981), Cardiff City (December 1982), Kettering Town (January 1983) Chesterfield (July 1983, retired in May 1989).
A cabinet-maker by trade, Jim Brown was the first goalkeeper to score a goal in the then 14-year life of the America National Soccer League when he netted for Washington Diplomats in April 1981. He appeared in more than 200 competitive games for the Blades over a period of five years before switching to the NASL in 1979. He retired on his 37th birthday in May 1989 with 355 League appearances to his credit plus one goal, scored for Chesterfield v. Stockport County in October 1983.
He developed markedly after joining Chesterfield, excelling with close range shots, a safe handler and sometimes showing spectacular reflex actions. He was capped by Scotland against Romania in 1975 and also made four appearances for his country's Under-23 side (all as a substitute).

BROWN, Michael Robert
Midfielder: 153+5 apps* 33 goals*
Born: Hartlepool, 25 January 1977.
Career: Manchester City (apprentice, April 1993, professional September 1994), Hartlepools United (on loan, March-April 1997), Portsmouth (on loan, November-December 1999), BLADES (December 1999).
Michael Brown, who prefers the left side of midfield, scored 24 goals in 110 outings for Manchester City before transferring to Bramall Lane in 1999. An England Under-21 international (four caps gained) he was voted United's 'Player of the Year' for 2001-02 and was again in tremendous form throughout the following season when the Blades reached the semi-finals of both the Worthington Cup and FA Cup and finished third in the First Division to qualify for the Play-offs and then scoring in both legs of the semi-final (v. Nottingham Forest) to send the Blades through to a Final showdown with Wolves at The Millennium Stadium. Unfortunately he missed a penalty in the Final (his first of the season). Had he scored, the outcome, from the Blades' point of view, may well have been different (we shall never know). The driving force in midfield, he was brilliant at times, always buzzing around, wanting the ball and urging his colleagues on when the chips were down. Brown was the Blades' top-scorer with 22 goals in 2002-03 when, in fact, he had more attempts at goal (from distance) than any other player inn the First Division (73 - 42 off target). It was Brown who had the pleasure of scoring United's 200th goal in League Cup football - in the 87th minute of the 4-1 win over Wycombe Wanderers at Bramall Lane in October 2000.

BROWNING, Leonard James
Centre-forward: 74 apps. 29 goals
Born: Doncaster, 30 March 1928.
Career: Headingley Rangers, Leeds United (August 1946), BLADES (November 1951, retired in May 1953),
Following his transfer from Elland Road in 1951, Len Browning struggled with his form during his early weeks at Bramall Lane - in fact, he failed to score in any of his first ten matches. However, after breaking his duck in a 4-2 FA Cup win over West Ham in early February 1952, his performances improved ten-fold and he ended the season with eight goals to his credit in 24 outings. A Second Division championship with the Blades in 1953, Browning was struck down with tuberculosis that same year and was forced to give up the game at the age of 25. He netted 46 goals in 105 games during his time at Elland Road, playing in front of John Charles.

BRUCE, Steven Roger
Defender: 11 apps.
Born: Corbridge, Northumberland, 31 December 1960.
Career: Newcastle Boys, Northumberland County FA, Wallsend Lads' Club Gillingham (apprentice, April 1977, professional October 1978), Norwich City (£135,000,August 1984 (the transfer fee agreed to be paid in stages), Manchester United (£825,000, December 1987), Birmingham City (June 1996), BLADES (player-manager, July 1998), Huddersfield Town (manager, June 1999), Nottingham Forest (part-time coach), Wigan Athletic (manager, 20001), Crystal Palace (manager, June 2001), Birmingham City (manager, December 2001).
Steve Bruce, a former shipyard worker, started out as a strong, determined midfielder, lining up in 234 competitive games for Gillingham (and winning eight England Youth caps in the process). Then, after being successfully converted into a defender at Carrow Road, he added a further 180 appearances to his tally with the Canaries, being voted 'Man of the Match' when they won the 1985 Milk Cup Final. He was also a star performer in the Carrow Road club's Second Championship-winning campaign the following season. During his time at Old Trafford, Bruce skippered the Reds on many occasions, collecting trophies galore. Indeed, he was a key member of three Premiership, two League Cup, two FA Cup, a European Cup-winners Cup, Super Cup and two FA Charity Shield winning sides as well as claiming a handful of runners-up prizes into the bargain. It was a crying shame that he never won a full England cap, being recognised only with Youth and 'B' team honours for all the effort he put in as a solid, reliable and totally committed defender who formed a great partnership with Gary Pallister.
He joined the Board of Directors at The Alfred McAlpine Stadium, before accepting the player-manager's job at Bramall Lane, assuming at the time that money would be available for him to enter the transfer market. That wasn't to be and in effect he had to sell players before he could go out and buy new ones. Things didn't work out the way he had wished and he duly handed in his resignation in May 1999.
He guided Birmingham City into the Premiership via the Play-offs at the end of his first half-season at St Andrew's.
*In all Bruce amassed a total of 907 appearances at club level (111 goals scored). His record with Manchester United was 414 appearances and 51 goals - not bad for a defender.

BRYSON, James Ian Cook
Winger: 177+23 apps. 44 goals
Born: Kilmarnock, 26 November 1962
Career: Hurlford, Kilmarnock (part-time professional), BLADES (August 1988), Barnsley (August 1993), Preston North End (November 1993), Rochdale (July 1997), Bamber Bridge (June 1999).
A speedy Scot, always keen to take on defenders, Ian Bryson was a regular scorer for the Blades, preferring a left-sided position. Totally committed and a huge favourite with the fans, he had a powerful shoot, was a clean header of the ball and never gave less than 100 per-cent whatever the circumstances or the match. He spent five years at Bramall Lane, making exactly 200 first-team appearances and helping the team gain promotion in successive seasons (1989 & 1990) before transferring to Barnsley. After helping Preston win the 1996 Third Division championship he moved to Rochdale. During his senior career Bryson appeared in a total of 711 competitive games and 116 scored. He made 250 appearances and netted 44 goals for 'Killie'.

BUCKLEY, Patrick
Winger: 12+7 apps. 3 goals
Born: Leith, Scotland, 12 August 1946
Career: Third Lanark Wolverhampton Wanderers (February 1964), BLADES (£30,000, January 1968), Rotherham United (June 1972-May 1973).
Winger Pat Buckley, who started his career in Scotland, played in 29 League games for Wolves where it was hoped he would follow in the footsteps of three previous wingers, Norman Deeley, Johnny Hancocks and Jimmy Mullen. An out-and-out trier, he gave his all but found it hard going in the Football League.

BUDDERY, Harold
Centre-forward: 25 apps. 9 goals
Born: Sheffield, 6 October 1889. Died: 1962
Career: Doncaster Rovers (December 1912), Portsmouth (May 1913), BLADES (guest, December 1915-January 1917), Portsmouth (August 1919), Southend United (May 1921-April 1922).
Centre-forward Harry Buddery guested for the Blades during WW1 and he did well for such an inexperienced player.

BULLOCK, Darren John
Midfielder: 6 apps.
Born: Worcester, 12 February 1969.
Career: Nuneaton Borough (1989), (Huddersfield Town (professional, November 1993), Swindon Town (February 1997), Bury (February 1999), BLADES (on loan, March-April 2001), Worcester City (October 2001).
Darren Bullock, a busy, tough-tackling midfielder appeared in 156 competitive games for Huddersfield, 69 for Swindon and 63 for the Shakers before entering the Dr Martens League with Worcester in 2001.

BURGIN, Edward

Goalkeeper: 314 apps.
Born: Bradfield (Sheffield), 29 April 1927
Career: Alford Town, BLADES (April1949 after a successful trial), Doncaster Rovers (December 1957), Leeds United (March 1958), Rochdale (January 1961, retired May 1966).
Ted 'The Cat' Burgin, although rather small for a goalkeeper at 5ft 7ins, was both athletic and agile and made well over 300 senior appearances for the Blades during his eight-and-a-half years at Bramall Lane...this after writing to the club asking for a trial not stating that he was a goalkeeper - and despite collecting several fractures (mainly to his fingers). He made his Football League debut v. Swansea Town (away) in September 1949, replacing Fred White, and after a short period back in the reserves, he was first choice thereafter until Alan Hodgkinson arrived on the scene halfway through the 1956-57 season. Capped by England at 'B' team level and a Second Division championship winner with the Blades in 1953, he later made 207 League appearances for Rochdale, playing for them in the 1962 League Cup Final (v. Norwich City).

BURNLEY

United's playing record against the Clarets:

Football League

Venue	P	W	D	L	F	A
Home	48	29	15	4	92	34
Away	48	10	9	29	55	101
Totals	96	39	24	33	147	135

FA Cup

	P	W	D	L	F	A
Home	5	3	1	1	8	6
Away	5	1	2	2	8	9
Neutral	2	0	1	1	0	1
Totals	12	4	4	4	16	16

League Cup

	P	W	D	L	F	A
Home	1	1	0	0	2	0

WW2

	P	W	D	L	F	A
Home	2	1	1	0	6	2
Away	2	1	0	1	1	2
Totals	4	2	1	1	7	4

Members of the Burnley Rovers Rugby Club formed Burnley FC in 1881 and both codes were played until the name Rovers was dropped, following a meeting at the Bull Hotel in May 1882 when the club also moved to its present ground, Turf Moor.
Founder members of the Football League in 1888, Burnley first met the Blades (then of course a non-League club, in the FA Cup competition of 1889-90, United winning a 1st round tie 2-1 at 'the Lanc.' Only 2,000 spectators witnessed this momentous occasion, Scotsman W (Bill) Robertson and the mysterious 'T Wilson' (playing under an assumed name) scoring the goals.
Another famous 'knock-out' encounter saw Burnley beat the Blades 1-0 in an FA Cup-semi-final replay in 1914. The Clarets went on to lift the trophy.
United's first League game against Burnley took place in freezing conditions at Turf Moor on Christmas Day 1893. The Clarets won 4-1 with all five goals coming in the second-half. The Blades gained revenge with a 1-0 win at 'the Lane' in March.
United defeated Burnley 10-0 in January 1929 to record their biggest home win in the Football League. They scored eight times in the second-half of a rather one-sided contest in which Harry Johnson claimed four goals on his own. This came a week after Burnley had

beaten the Blades 2-1 at Turf Moor in the FA Cup.

Other notable United wins have been 6-1 in 1925-26 (Billy Gillespie & Willie Hoyland both scoring twice), 5-0 in 1913-14 (again after Burnley had won an FA Cup-tie, this time at the semi-final stage) and 5-2 in 1927-28 (Johnson grabbing another hat-trick).

In contrast Burnley beat United 5-0 in 1895-96 and likewise in 1929-30; won 6-0 in 1920-21 and 5-1 in 1962-63, while the Blades clinched their best victory at Turf Moor in 1926-27, winning 5-2 with Jimmy Shankly, brother of Bill, scoring a hat-trick.

The Blades completed the double over the Clarets in 2002-03, winning 4-2 at home and 1-0 at Turf Moor.

Tom Cowan, Gordon Cowans, John Cunningham, Johnny Dryden, Tom Egan, John Francis, Roger Hansbury, Adrian Heath (also manager of both clubs), Doug Hodgson, Tommy Hoyland, Andy McLaren, Colin Morris, Tony Philliskirk, Gareth Taylor, Des Thompson and Jimmy Yates all played for both clubs.

BURRIDGE, John

Goalkeeper: 125 apps.

Born: Workington, 3 December 1951.

Career: Workington (as an apprentice, June 1968, professional December 1969), Blackpool (£100,000, April 1971), Aston Villa (£100,000, September 1975), Southend United (on loan, January 1978), Crystal Palace (£65,000, March 1978), Queen's Park Rangers (£200,000, December 1980), Wolverhampton Wanderers (£75,000, August 1982), Derby County (on loan, September 1984), Sheffield United (£10,000, October 1984), Southampton ((£30,000, August 1987), Newcastle United (£25,000, October 1989), Hibernian (July 1991), Newcastle again (free transfer, August 1993), Scarborough (non-contract, October 1993), Lincoln City (non-contract, December 1993), Enfield (on loan, February 1994), Aberdeen (non-contract, March 1994), Barrow (non-contract, September 1994), Dumbarton (October 1994), Falkirk (November 1994), Manchester City (free transfer, December 1994), Notts County (free transfer, August 1995), Witton Albion (October 1995), Darlington (free transfer, November 1995), Grimsby Town (free transfer, December 1995), Gateshead (January 1996), Northampton Town (January 1996), player-manager of Blyth Spartans (July 1996), Scarborough (on loan, December 1996), China (goalkeeping coach, March-May 1997). Burridge also had two spells as caretaker-manager (& goalkeeping coach) of Swansea City in the mid-1990s and has acted as coach at Leeds United

As you can see, John Burridge's long and varied career took him to many different places. A fitness fanatic, he had a superb 'footballing life' and when he quit the professional game in 1997 (having joined his first club Workington 29 years earlier) he had accumulated an appearance record bettered by only one other 'keeper - Peter Shilton. Burridge played in 917 matches at senior club level (it was well over 1,000 if you include friendlies). He was past his 45th birthday when he played his last game at competitive level...for Scarborough in the Auto-Windscreen Shield game v Notts County in December 1996....giving him the honour of being the oldest player ever to appear for the Seaside club. He is also Scarborough's oldest League player (41 years, 388 days in 1993) and likewise he became the oldest-ever Darlington player, when at the age of 44 years, six days in December 1995, he lined up against Scarborough at The McCain Stadium. Besides these landmarks, the effervescent 'Budgie' Burridge is the oldest player so far to appear in the Premiership - he was aged 43 years, five months and 11 days old when he kept goal for Manchester City against QPR at Maine Road on 14 May 1995. At the time he was also listed as goalkeeping coach at Newcastle. Burridge won an Anglo-Italian Cup winners medal with Blackpool in 1970, a League Cup winners medal with Villa in 1977, a Division Two championship medal with Crystal Palace in 1979 and a Scottish Premier League Cup winners' medal with Hibs in 1991. He also helped Wolves win promotion from Division Two in 1983 and the following season was voted the Molineux club's 'Player of the Year'. He made 80 appearances for Villa and 81 for Wolves.

Some time ago, while John was still deeply involved in football, his wife said: "We've been married for 17 years. John's had 14 clubs, we've lived in six different houses and seven rented places. He's so wrapped up in football, I've heard him giving commentator Gerald Sinstadt, a TV interview in his sleep." (See also under AGE).

BURSCOUGH

United knocked Burscough (from the Lancashire Unibond League) out of the FA Cup in November 1979, beating them 3-0 at Bramall Lane in a 1st round tie before a crowd of 14,209. John Matthews, John MacPhail and Mick Speight found the net.

Burscough is a small village in Lancashire. The team, known as the 'Linnets' (their colours are green and yellow) won the FA Trophy Final of 2003 at Villa Park where the defeated Tamworth 2-1, thus becoming the first non-Conference side ever to win the trophy since its inception in 1970.

BURTON UNITED

(formerly Burton Swifts)

United's playing record against the United:

Football League

Venue	P	W	D	L	F	A
Home	1	1	0	0	3	1
Away	1	1	0	0	3	0
Totals	2	2	0	0	6	1
FA Cup						
Away	1	0	0	1	1	2
Other						
Away	1	1	0	0	1	0

A crowd of 3,500 saw United go down 2-1 to the Swifts at their Kidger's Field ground in a 2nd qualifying FA Cup-tie in October 1890, but due to the fact that the Swifts had fielded an unregistered player, they were disqualified from the competition, allowing the Blades to proceed.

After changing their name to Albion, Burton along with the Blades joined the Football League in 1892 and the first games in the competition between the two clubs both ended in wins for the Blades, 3-1 at home, 3-0 at Peel Croft. The first fixture at 'the Lane' was abandoned on 68 minutes due to fog with United 2-1 ahead.

BURTON WANDERERS

United's playing record against the Wanderers:

FA Cup

Venue	P	W	D	L	F	A
Home	1	1	0	0	1	0
Away	1	0	1	0	1	1
Totals	2	1	1	0	2	1

Midland Counties League

Home	1	0	1	0	2	2
Away	1	0	1	0	1	1
Totals	2	0	2	0	3	3

United knocked the Wanderers out of the FA Cup in the first round of the 1895-96 competition. Ernest Needham scored in both games for the Blades, including a beauty at the Wanderers' Derby Turn ground.

The Wanderers, formed in 18711, are one of the oldest club ever to have played in the Football League (1894-97).

In 1901 they amalgamated with the Swifts (q.v) to become Burton United

BURY

United's playing record against the Shakers:

Football League

Venue	P	W	D	L	F	A
Home	38	25	10	3	94	31
Away	38	13	8	17	63	70
Totals	76	38	18	20	157	101

FA Cup

Home	4	0	3	1	5	6
Away	5	2	1	2	5	7
Neutral	1	1	0	0	2	0
Totals	10	3	4	3	12	13

League Cup

Home	2	1	1	0	3	2
Away	4	0	0	4	5	12
Totals	6	1	1	4	8	14

WW2

Home	1	1	0	0	2	1
Away	1	0	1	0	2	2
Totals	2	1	1	0	4	3

Bury FC was formed mainly by members of the Bury Wesleyans and Bury Unitarians football clubs in April 1885 following successive meetings held at the Waggon & Horses and Old White Horse Hotels inn the town. After turning professional in 1885, the Shakers were elected to the Football League in 1894 and first meet the Blades in that competition at Gigg Lane in September 1895 (Division 1). The Shakers were well and truly rattled as United won 8-0, seven of their goals coming in the second-half. Harry Hammond scored five times and Tom Egan three.

United conceded five goals in the second-half of their away League game with Bury in November 1904 and lost 7-1.

United were 2-0 up on Bury in a League game at Gigg Lane in December 1926. The Shakers then stormed into a 4-2 lad before the Blades salvaged a point from a 4-3 draw.

In 1928-29 as Bury spiralled towards the Second Division, United beat them 6-1 at Bramall Lane (Harry Johnson hit a hat-trick) yet later in the season the Shakers turned the form-book upside down by winning 4-0 at Gigg Lane. In fact, Bury have been responsible for some of United's heaviest defeats in their history, notably 7-1 at Gigg Lane in 1904-05 (when England centre-forward Charlie Sagar scored four times) and 7-4 in 1925-26 when both teams were trying to come to terms with the new offside law. Shakers' future manager Norman Bullock scored a hat-trick this time. Since WW2 United can reflect on a wonderful 5-1 win on Bury soil in 1949-50 (Fred Smith was a hat-trick hero this time) and on Bonfire Night in that same season the teams fought out a 4-4 draw at 'the Lane'. A John Tudor treble helped United win 5-0 at home in 1968-69.

Just 6,499 spectators attended the United v. Bury League game at Bramall Lane in September 1935...this was to remain the lowest at the ground for more than 51 years, until March 1987). United's first-ever League Cup-tie was against Bury on 11 October 1960. A crowd of 11,551 saw the Shakers win 3-1, John Nibloe scoring for the Blades.

The Shakers knocked United out of the 1995-96 League Cup 5-4 on aggregate.

Eddie Colquhoun started his Football League career with Bury while Neil Warnock has managed both clubs. Also associated with the Blades and the Shakers (as players) we have (among others) John Ball, Tony Battersby, Dickie Bird, Darren Bullock, Ted Connor, Terry Curran, Aidan Davison, Laurent D'Jaffo, John Docherty, Arthur Eggleston, Bill Fleming, Paul Hall, Willie Hendry, Harry Hitchen, Jamie Hoyland, Jim Iley, Fred Jenkinson, Gary Kelly, Paddy Kenny, Adrian Littlejohn, Bruce Longworth, Ray McHale, Arthur Mercer, Jon Newby, Mark Patterson, Billy Peake, George Raynor (United reserve), Bobby Reid, Andy Scott, Micky Speight,

BUTLIN, Barry Desmond

Striker: 66+4 apps. 13 goals

Born: Rosliston, Derbyshire, 9 November 1949.

Career: Derby County (apprentice, April 1965, professional January 1967), Notts County (on loan, January 1969-December 1970), Luton Town (November 1972), Nottingham Forest (October 1974), Brighton & Hove Albion (on loan, September-October 1975), Reading (on loan, January-February 1977), Peterborough United (August 1977), BLADES (August 1979-May 1981).

Six-foot striker Barry Butlin struggled to get first team football with the Rams and after a lengthy loan spell with Notts County he scored 24 goals for the Hatters, obliging with a further 17 for Forest. He was not a prolific marksman as such but during his career he notched a total of 81 goals in 292 League games.

CADETTE, Richard Raymond
Striker: 31+2 apps. 7 goals
Born: Hammersmith, London, 21 March 1965
Career: Wembley (1982), Leyton Orient (August 1984) Southend United (August 1985), BLADES (£130,000, July 1987), Brentford (£80,000, July 1988), Bournemouth (on loan, March-April 1990), Falkirk (January 1992), Millwall (£135,000, October 1994, released May 1997).
A speedy, positive attacker, Richard Cadette spent just twelve months at Bramall Lane He helped Falkirk win the Scottish B& Q Cup Final in 1994 and during his time at Starks Park he netted 46 goals in 106 appearances.

CAIN, Robert
Full-back: 220 apps. 3 goals
Born: Slamannan near Glasgow, 13 February 1866.
Career: Airdrieonians (1886), Everton (June 1889), Bootle (May 1890), BLADES (May 1891), Tottenham Hotspur (May 1898), Albion Rovers (August 1899), Small Heath (October 1899, retiring in 1900...after failing to get a first team outing with the Blues).
The moustachio'd Bob Cain was a top-notch performer, strong, hard-tackling who had been a half-back with Everton but settled down at full-back with Bootle. After representing the Anglo Scots v. the Home Scots in an international trial he made his mark at Bramall Lane, having seven excellent years there during which time he made well over 200 senior appearances, gaining a League championship medal in 1898.
* Cain was sent-off in a friendly game against Woolwich Arsenal in October 1892 but was allowed to return to the field after apologising to the referee!

CALDER, William
Forward: 25 apps. 7 goals
Born: circa 1876
Career: BLADES (November 1889), Barnsley St Peter's (January 1892).
An orthodox left or right-winger, Bill Calder was a regular in the Blades' side until losing his place early in the 1891-92 season.

CALVERT, Clifford Alistair
Full-back/midfielder: 91+6 apps. 8 goals
Born: York, 21 April 1954
Career: York City (apprentice, April 1970, professional July 1972), BLADES (£38,000, September 1975), Toronto Blizzard/NASL (£40,000 deal, February 1979, which included team-mate Colin Franks).
Chris Calvert, a steady, consistent player, won England Youth international honours as a teenager. He had one excellent season at Bramall Lane, 1977-78, when he partnered John Cutbush at full-back, making 43 senior appearances.

50

CAMBRIDGE UNITED
United's playing record against Cambridge:
Football League

Venue	P	W	D	L	F	A
Home	1	0	1	0	3	3
Away	1	0	0	1	0	1
Totals	2	0	1	1	3	4
Other						
Away	1	1	0	0	1	0

Abbey United (formed in 1912) changed its name to Cambridge United in 1951 and after competing earnestly in the United Counties, Eastern and Southern Leagues (the latter from 1958), the club was elected to the Football League in 1970, following the demise of Bradford Park Avenue.
The two games between the clubs took place in 1978-79 and after a 3-3 draw at 'the Lane'
The Blades were defeated 1-0 at The Abbey Stadium in May and as a result were relegated to the Third Division where they joined their Sheffield rivals Wednesday.
Ian Benjamin, Gary Brazil, Tom Cowan, Jodie Craddock, John Francis, Ian Hamilton, Roger Hansbury, Jonathan Hunt, Jim Ryan (Cambridge player-manager), Tony Towner and Keith Waugh are among the players who have served with both the Blades and United. Jim Iley played for the Blades and was a scout for Cambridge.

CAMMACK, Stephen Richard
Forward: 25+17 apps. 5 goals
Born: Sheffield, 20 March 1954
Career: BLADES (associate schoolboy forms, apprentice June 1969, professional May 1971), Chesterfield (£11,000, January 1976), Scunthorpe United (£7,500, September, 1979), Lincoln City (£20,000, July, 1981), Scunthorpe again (£3,000 and David Hughes, March 1982), Port Vale (on loan, December 1985), Stockport County (on loan, January 1986) Scarborough (October 1986), Worksop Town (November 1986), Harworth Colliery (August 1987), Heanor Town (September 1989), Wombwell Town (player-coach, January 1991)
England Youth international (playing at Bramall Lane) Steve Cammack joined the Blades straight from school. A skilful striker on his day, he quit League football at the end of the 1986-87 season having scored 143 goals in 419 League games (104 in 245 outings for the 'Iron').

CAMPBELL, Andrew Paul
Striker: 11 apps. 3 goals
Born: Stockton-on-Tees, 18 April 1979,
Career: Middlesbrough (junior, summer 1995, professional July 1996), BLADES (on loan, December 1988-February 1989 & March-April 1989), Bolton Wanderers (on loan, March-April 2001), Cardiff City (on loan, February-March 2002, signed permanently, £950,000, April 2002.
Skilful striker Andy Campbell had two loan spells at Bramall Lane and two of his goals came in a 2-1 win over Grimsby Town. Capped by England at Youth team level and on four occasions by the Under-21's, Campbell reached the milestone of 100 League and Cup appearances with the Bluebirds at the start off the 2002-03 season.

CAMPBELL, Robert McFaul

Striker: 41+2 apps. 14 goals

Born: Belfast, 13 September 1956.

Career: Aston Villa (apprentice, June 1972, professional January 1974), Halifax Town (on loan, February 1975), Huddersfield Town (£5,000, April 1975), Sheffield United (£10,000, July 1977 - after a loan spell), Vancouver Whitecaps, NASL (June 1978), Huddersfield Town (September 1978), Halifax Town (October 1978), Brisbane City, Australia (May, 1979), Bradford City (December 1979), Derby County (£70,000, August 1983), Bradford City (on loan, September 1983, signed for £35,000, November 1983), Wigan Athletic (£25,000, October 1986-88).

Bobby Campbell was capped by Northern Ireland at Youth and senior levels and was in his country's squad for the 1982 World Cup Finals. He scored more than 200 goals in some 600 club and international matches in England and abroad and his League record was very impressive: 179 goals in 476 appearances including 121 in 274 outings in his two spells at Valley Parade and 11 in 37 for the Blades).

CAPTAINS

The following players (listed in categories in A-Z order) all captained the Blades at first team level, some much longer than others:

Pre 1900: Bob Cain, TBA Clarke, George Groves, Billy Hendry, Jack Hudson, Ernest Needham.

1900-15: Bob Benson, Ernie Needham, Albert Sturgess, George Utley, Bernard Wilkinson,

1915-39: Jock Gibson, Billy Gillespie, Harry Gooney, George Green, Harry Hooper, Tommy Johnson, Archie McPherson, Bernard Oxley, Tommy Sampy, Albert Sturgess, George Utley.

1939-60: Malcolm Barrass, Harold Brook, Jack Chisholm, Cecil Coldwell, Jimmy Hagan, Harry Hitchen, Ernie Jackson, Tommy Johnson, Harry Latham, Cliff Mason, Jack Pickering, Joe Shaw, Dick Young.

1960-80: Len Badger, Cecil Coldwell, Eddie Colquhoun, Tony Currie, Keith Eddy, Joe Shaw, Mickey Speight, Alan Woodward.

1980 to date: David Barnes, Paul Beesley, Bob Booker, Carl Bradshaw, Michael Brown, Keith Curle, Brian Gayle, Mick Henderson (team), Glyn Hodges, David Holdsworth, Stewart Houston, Vinnie Jones, Chris Kamara, Alan Kelly (club), Tony Kenworthy, Martin Kuhl, Ray Lewington, Stuart McCall, Ray McHale, Colin Morris (club), Shaun Murphy, Robert Page, Mark Patterson, Lee Sandford, Paul Stancliffe, Phil Thompson and David Tuttle.

Captain's Log

* Len Badger has been officially United's youngest first team skipper.

* Jack Hudson was officially elected as United's first-ever team captain (1889).

* Ernest 'Nudger' Needham skippered the Blades for a decade, from 1895 to 1905

CARDIFF CITY

United's playing record against the Bluebirds:

Football League

Venue	P	W	D	L	F	A
Home	27	16	4	7	58	28
Away	27	5	10	12	27	43
Totals	54	21	14	19	85	71

FA Cup

Home	2	1	0	1	5	4
Neutral	1	1	0	0	1	0
Totals	3	2	0	1	6	4

It is believed that members of both the Riverside rugby and cricket clubs formed Cardiff FC in 1899. Cardiff became a city in 1905 and three years later the South Wales & Monmouthshire FA granted permission for the club to call itself Cardiff City FC. Ninian Park was secured in 1910 and a decade later, after finishing 4th in the Southern League, the Welsh club became founder members of the new Third Division, winning promotion in their first season under skipper Fred Keenor. They then finished runners-up to Huddersfield Town in the top flight in 1921-22 and three years later lost to the Blades in the FA Cup Final before causing a major shock by beating Arsenal 1-0 in the 1927 Final.

Fred Tunstall's goal on the half-hour mark gave United that Cup Final in 1925 when 91,763 spectators paid receipts of £15,941.

In their final League game of the 1921-22 season City missed a late penalty at Birmingham in a 0-0 draw...if Davies had scored then they would have won the title!

The first two League games between the clubs (in 1921-22) finished 1-1 Ninian Park and 2-0 to Cardiff at 'the Lane'.

There was an extraordinary result on Sheffield soil on New Year's Day 1926. With the offside law still causing defenders and attackers a few problems - United hammered City 11-2 in a First Division match at Bramall Lane (the team's biggest-ever League win). Harry Johnson and David Mercer both scored hat-tricks, while the influential Billy Gillespie and Tommy Boyle scored two goals apiece.

Since WW2 the clubs have met in only 19 seasons, one of the highlights being United's win at 'the Lane' in March 1952. With the scoresheet blank at half-time in a Second Division match, the 16,398 fans certainly got good value for money after the break as United stormed to a 6-1 victory with Len Browning netting a hat-trick.

The Blades also won 6-1 at Cardiff in 1976-78 (under acting manager Cecil Coldwell) but under 6,400 fans attended this game.

The teams last met in the 4th round of the FA Cup in 1999, United winning comfortably by 4-1.

Dickie Bird, Nathan Blake, Jim Brown, Andy Campbell, Willie Carlin, Andy Dibble (Blades reserve), Jeff Eckhardt, Steve Finnieston, Roger Hansbury, Bob Hatton, Mick Henderson, Mick Hill, Ernie Marshall, Phil Kite, Tony Philliskirk, Cliff Powell, David Powell, Gil Reece, Mel Rees, Bernard Ross, Dean Saunders and Alan Warboys have all played for both clubs. Alan Cork played for United and later managed City.

CARLIN, William

Midfielder: 42 apps. 3 goals

Born: Liverpool, 6 October 1940.

Career: Liverpool Schools, Liverpool (juniors May 1955, professional May 1958), Halifax Town (£1,500, August 1962), Carlisle United (£10,000, October 1964), BLADES (£40,000, September 1967), Derby County (for a record £63,000, August 1968), Leicester City (£35,000, October 1970), Notts County (£18,000, September 1971), Cardiff City (on loan, November 1973, signed permanently December 1973, released May 1974).

Willie Carlin - a small but determined and tenacious inside-forward - played for seven different clubs in 12 seasons and all of them were involved in either promotion or relegation battles. He appeared in only one first team game for Liverpool and after their promotion from Division Two in 1962 he was transferred to Halifax who were relegated to the Fourth in 1963. He then helped Carlisle United climb up from the Third in 1965, was with Sheffield United when they dropped down to the Second Division in 1968, played for Derby County when they rose from the Second in 1969, did the same with Leicester City in 1971 and had a fifth and final promotion with Notts County who came up from the third in 1973. Carlin scored on his debut for the Blades in a 2-1 win over Newcastle at Bramall Lane on 23 September 1967. He appeared in a total of 426 League games, scoring 74 goals. He later ran a newsagent's shop near Derby before going to live in Majorca.

CARLISLE UNITED

United's playing record against the Cumbrians:

Football League

Venue	P	W	D	L	F	A
Home	9	4	3	2	11	8
Away	9	4	1	4	8	8
Totals	18	8	4	6	19	16

FA Cup

Venue	P	W	D	L	F	A
Home	1	1	0	0	3	0
Away	1	0	0	1	1	2
Totals	2	1	0	1	4	2

Carlisle United FC came into being in 1903 when the Shaddongate United and Carlisle Red Rose clubs amalgamated. After playing in the Lancashire Combination and moving from Devonshire Park to Brunton Park in 1909, United gained election to the Football League (Division 3 North) in 1928.

Earlier, in 1946-47, United cruised through a 3rd round FA Cup-tie, winning 3-0 to celebrate the first meeting between the clubs.. The following season United completed the doubled with successive 1-0 scorelines.

They then had to wait 40 years before they met the Blades in competition, doing so in 1968-69 (Division 2) when both teams won away from home with 1-0 scorelines.

After gaining promotion to the First Division, United completed another double over Carlisle in 1974-75 (2-1 & 1-0) but following relegation, the Cumbrians gained some sort of revenge with a 4-1 League win at Brunton Park in 1976-77, the Blades having registered their best win over United (3-0) earlier in the season.

The last time the clubs met was in 1985-86 when again both gained home wins (1-0 each).

Ted Ashton, Andy Barnsley, Willie Carlin, Darren Carr, Ben Clarke, Jon Cullen, Mervyn Day, Barry Hartle, Bob Hatton, Jamie Hoyland, Steven Ludlam, Tony Philliskirk, Ernie Robinson, Rob Scott, Jimmy Shankly, Ron Simpson, Paul Williams and Dick Young have all played for both the Blades and the Cumbrians. Andy Beattie managed Carlisle and was assistant-boss at Bramall Lane.

CARR, Darren John

Central defender: 22+2 apps. one goal
Born: Bristol, 4 September 1968
Career: Bristol Rovers (apprentice, September 1984, professional August 1986), Newport County (on loan, October 1987, signing permanently for £3,00, January 1988), BLADES (£8,000, March 1988), Crewe Alexandra (£35,000, September 1990), Chesterfield (£30,000, July 1993), Gillingham (£75,000, August 1998), Brighton & Hove Albion (£25,000, July 1999), Rotherham United (on loan, November 2000), Lincoln City (on loan, January 2001) Carlisle United (on loan, February 2001) Dover (August 2001), Oxford United (on trial), Rushden & Diamonds (January 2002).

At 6ft 2in tall, Darren Carr was a no-nonsense, hard-tackling centre-half, but unfortunately he struggled to hold down a first team place at Bramall Lane, making less than 25 senior appearances in two-and-a-half years.

CARR, Franz

Winger: 19 apps. 5 goals
Born: Preston, 24 September 1966.
Career: Blackburn Rovers (apprentice, April 1982, professional July 1984), Nottingham Forest (£100,000, August 1984), Sheffield Wednesday (on loan, December 1989), West Ham United (on loan, March 1991), Newcastle United (£250,000, June 1991), BLADES (£120,000, January 1993), Leicester City (£100,000, September 1994), Aston Villa (£250,000, February 1995), Reggiana/Italy (August 1996), Bolton Wanderers (on loan, October 1997), West Bromwich Albion (non-contract, February 1998, Grimsby Town (on trial, May-June 1998), later served with Runcorn.

Mercurial winger Franz Carr failed to make the grade at Ewood Park. He played over 150 games for Brian Clough, but then lost his way and he never quite fulfilled his undoubted potential at 'the Lane' only occasionally producing his seemingly rare ability. In fact, long periods in the wilderness disrupted Carr's progress.

CARR, Joseph

Left-back: 37 apps.
Born: Sheffield, April 1916. Died: Dunkirk, 1940.
Career: BLADES (amateur January 1936, professional February 1936).

After developing through the reserve team promising full-back Joe Carr made his League debut v. Blackburn Rovers in October 1937, but WW2 intervened and before he could really establish himself in the game, he was killed in the retreat from Dunkirk in 1940. He helped the Blades win the Second Division title in 1939.

CARRIGAN, Patrick

Centre-half: 35 apps.
Born: Cleland, Lanarkshire, 5 July 1898.
Career: Douglas Water Thistle FC, Leicester City (October 1923), BLADES (£1,750, March 1930), Southend United (on trial, September 1933).

Well-built defender Pat Carrigan appeared in 82 competitive matches for the Foxes and helped them win the Second Division title in 1925. He spent three seasons at Bramall Lane, having his best campaign in 1930-31 when he made 26 League and FA Cup appearances.

CAS, Marcel

Right wing-back: 3+3 apps.
Born: Breda, Holland, 30 April 1972
Career: RBC Roosendaal/Holland, Notts County (free transfer, July 2001), BLADES (signed on short term contract, January-May 2003).
Signed on a short term contract as cover for right-wing back position, experienced Dutchman Marcel Cas made his senior debut for the Blades as a substitute v. promotion-chasing Reading in February 2003 and started his first game for the club away to Wimbledon in early April. Prior to moving to Bramall Lane he appeared in over 50 games for the Magpies.

CASEY, Paul

Right-back/midfielder: 27+2 apps. 7 goals
Born: Essen, West Germany, 6 October 1961
Career: BLADES (apprentice, August 1975, professional, May 1980), Boston United (June 1982), Lincoln City (March 1988), Boston United (May 1991).
Paul Casey joined United as a teenager and did well initially before fading. However, he did play in 12 games when the Fourth Division championship was won in 1982 and six years later helped the Imps win the GM Vauxhall Conference, having earlier played for Boston in the 1985 FA Trophy Final at Wembley, gaining a runners-up medal.

CAWTHORNE, Harold

Right-back/right-half: 29 apps.
Born: Darnall, Sheffield Yorkshire, 1900. Died: 1966
Career: Dronfield Woodhouse, Huddersfield Town (October 1919), BLADES (£2,500, February 1927), Connah's Quay (May 1929).
Harold Cawthorne, signed as cover for Tom Boyle, was a hard, resilient and competitive defender, made 76 appearances for Huddersfield with whom he gained two League championship medals in 1924 and 1926 but played only twice in the middle season of the Terriers' treble-success. He spent the majority of his last 18 months of his United career playing in the reserves.

CELTIC

United's playing record against the Bhoys:

Venue	P	W	D	L	F	A
Home	4	2	1	1	4	3
Away	2	0	2	0	3	3
Totals	6	2	3	1	7	6

The first time United opposed Celtic (formed in 1888) was in a friendly on 1 September 1892 when a crowd of 4,000 at Bramall Lane saw them beat the Scottish giants 1-0, Harry Hammond the scorer.
In 1898, United (Football League champions-to-be) defeated Celtic (the Scottish champions) in 'The Championship of Great Britain' (played over two legs). See under CHAMPIONS of BRITAIN.
United's last encounter against the Glasgow club took place in October 1901 when a crowd of 4,74 attended Bramall Lane to witness the 2-2 draw in a benefit match for Blades' goalkeeper Billy Foulke.
Jimmy Bone, John Cunningham, Willie Falconer, Pat Gilhooley, Jimmy Johnstone, Olivier Tebily, Bill Toner, George Turnbull and Andy Walker all played for both clubs.
Dugald Livingstone played for Celtic and was trainer at United while former Bhoys' player and manager Lou Macari was a scout for the Blades in the 1990s.

CHAIRMEN

List of United's Chairmen in order of office:

1889-96	Michael J Ellison
1896-99	Charles Stokes
1899-1913	Charles Stokes*
1913-20	Thomas Bott*
1920	Joseph Smith*
1920-30	Walter Sissons*
1930-33	Alfred Cattell*
1933-37	George Platt*
1937-49	George Platt
1949-52	George E Marlow
1952-55	Frank Copestone
1955-57	Ernest S Atkin
1957-60	H Blacow Yates**
1960-74	Richard Wragg
1974-81	John Hassall
1981-90	Reg Brealey
1991-91	Reg Brealey/Paul Woodhouse
1992-93	Paul Woodhouse/Alan Laver (acting)/Derek Dooley
1993-94	Derek Dooley/Reg Brealey
1994-95	Reg Brealey
1995-96	Reg Brealey/Alan Laver (acting)/Mike McDonald
1996-97	Mike McDonald
1997-98	Mike McDonald+/Kevin McCabe
1998-2000	Kevin McCabe/Carlo Colombotti+
2000-02	Derek Dooley
2002-03	Derek Dooley (football)/Kevin McCabe (plc)

* Committee Chairman
** Became Club Chairman, September 1960
+ Chairman of the plc.

53

NB: At odd times the Chairmanship of the club changed during the course of a season - i.e when two names appear in the listings.
* Derek Dooley was a dynamic centre-forward whose career sadly came to an abrupt end when he fractured his leg playing for Sheffield Wednesday in a First division League game against Preston in February 1953. Gangrene set in and his leg had to be amputated. Born in Sheffield on 13 December 1929, he was an amateur with Lincoln City before signing professional forms for the Owls in 1947. He scored 63 goals on 63 games during his playing career. He returned to Hillsborough in 1962 to take charge of the development fund scheme and from January 1971 to December 1973 he was team manager. He switched loyalties in 1977 to become Commercial Manager at Bramall Lane - and he is still a dedicated 'Blade' to this day, having taken a Directorship and acted as the club's Chairman.

CHAMPIONSHIPS (Football League)
United won the Football League First Division championship in season 1897-98.
They were Second Division champions in 1952-53 & Fourth Division champions in 1981-82.
This is their complete playing record in each of those winning seasons:

Season	P	W	D	L	F	A	Pts
1897-98	30	17	8	5	56	31	42
1952-53	42	25	10	7	97	55	60
1981-82	46	27	15	4	94	41	96

(See under FOOTBALL LEAGUE).

CHAMPIONSHIP OF GREAT BRITAIN
In 1898, United (Football League champions elect) were declared Champions of Britain after beating Celtic (the Scottish League champions) in a two-legged challenge match.
The first game was played at Bramall Lane on 12 March 1898 when a crowd of 8,500 saw the Blades win 1-0 with a Ralph Gaudie goal. The return leg in Glasgow followed on 16 April when a crowd of 12,000 witnessed the 1-1 draw, Jack Almond snatching a late equaliser for the Blades to secure the win.

CHANDLER, Albert
Right-back: 80 apps.
Born: Carlisle, 15 January 1897. Died: Carlisle, 28 January 1963.
Career: Dalston Beach Reds, Carlisle Juniors, Derby County (August 1919), Newcastle United (£3,250, June 1925), BLADES (£2,625, October 1926), Northfleet (November 1929), Manchester Central (February 1930), Holmstead FC (1931), Queen of the South (season 1931-32). On his retirement he returned to Carlisle where he lived until his demise at the age of 66.
At times Bert Chandler could be brilliant, on other occasions he had the tendency to make silly mistakes - then his usually precise sliding tackle went completely wrong! In his six years with the Rams he made 183 appearances. In 1926 he was severely censored by the Blades for financial irregularities over Players' Union subs and ultimately blacklisted by the Football League as a player whose 'registration is to be refused.'
* Chandler gallantly served his country in both World Wars, commissioned in the Machine Gun Corps.

CHAPMAN, Herbert
Inside-forward: 22 apps. 2 goals
Born: Kiveton Park, Sheffield, 19 January 1878. Died: London, 6 January 1934.
Career: Kiveton Park FC, Ashton North End, Stalybridge Rovers, Rochdale (May 1897), Grimsby Town (May 1898), Swindon Town (August 1899), Sheppey United (late 1899), Worksop (May 1900), Northampton Town (May 1901), BLADES (May 1902), Notts County (£300, May 1903), Northampton (May 1904), Tottenham Hotspur (March 1905) Northampton Town for a third time (April 1907 as player-manager, a position he retained until June 1912), Leeds City (manager, June 1912-October 1919), Huddersfield Town (manager, September 1921-June 1925) and Arsenal (manager, June 1925-January 1934).
Herbert Chapman, a workmanlike inside-forward, made his senior debut for the Blades in the local derby with Wednesday in September 1902. He tried to combine playing football with working down the mines. It never really worked and after retiring he concentrated on becoming a manager, having great success in this field, especially so with Huddersfield and Arsenal, whom he guided to successive League titles, the Terriers in 1924 & 1925 and the Gunners in 1931 & 1933.. He also saw both teams lift the FA Cup (in 1922 & 1930) as well as cringing as Arsenal were beaten in the 1927 and 1932 Finals. Earlier, in 1909, he had guided Northampton to the Southern League title.
Universally acknowledged as one of the most successful and influential managers in the history of the game (up to the 1990s), Chapman changed the face of football on and off the field, although during his time at Leeds City there was an illegal payments scandal and during WW1 he worked on munitions and was not often at the club. In fact, City were thrown out of the Football League and Chapman himself was suspended for his part in the scandal. But he always strenuously denied his complicity, claiming that he had not been in office when thee illegal payments were actually made.
He was employed as an industrial manager of an oil and coke firm in Selby for a short while until his appeal was heard and upheld. At that point he worked his way back into football and in September 1921 was invited to take over the hot seat at Leeds Road.
He signed some brilliant footballers for both Huddersfield and Arsenal, including George Brown, Alex Jackson and Sam Wadsworth for the Terriers and Charlie Buchan, David Jack, Alex James and Herby Roberts for the Gunners.
Always committed to his football, he attended several matches a week, but sadly he returned from one 'cold' trip with what was initially thought to be a bad cold. Unfortunately within a few days he was in a London hospital suffering from pneumonia. He died a fortnight or so before his 56th birthday.
* Today a bust of Herbert Chapman stands in the main entrance hall at Highbury Stadium as an epitaph to one of the greatest managers of all time.

CHARITY SHIELD (SHERIFF of LONDON)
On 19 March 1898, a crowd of 19,707 saw United draw 0-0 with the famous amateur club the Corinthians in the first annual Sheriff of London Charity Shield game at the Crystal Palace. The replay took place at the same venue just over a fortnight later, on 4 April, and again the teams finished level at 1-1 in front of 7,500 spectators. Each club held the shield for six months.

CHARLES, Frederick
Inside-right: 34 apps. 6 goals
Born: Mexborough
Career: Doncaster Rovers (briefly), Mexborough Town, BLADES (March 1911), Castleford Town (1912).
Fred Charles made his League debut for Sheffield United against Middlesbrough in March 1911, but the club failed to register him in time and were fined one guinea (£1.05p) for their troubles. He assisted United in WW1.

CHARLES, Stephen
Midfielder: 144+12 apps.8 goals
Born: Sheffield, 10 May 1960,
Career: Sheffield Wednesday (amateur, 1976), BLADES (professional, January 1980), Wrexham (October 1984), Mansfield Town (£15,000, July 1987), Scunthorpe United (on loan, November 1992), Scarborough (February 1993-May 1996), Boston United, Gainsborough Trinity, Matlock Town.
After successfully finishing his student studies at Sheffield University (gaining two degrees), Steve Charles signed professional forms for the Blades as a 19 year-old to begin a long career that realised well over 600 League appearances. He represented both Sheffield Boys & England Schools at Under-15 level; was a Second Division championship winner with the Blades in 1982, helped gain promotion from Division Three in 1984, collected a Welsh Cup winners medal with Wrexham in 1986 and won two Notts County Cup winners prizes, in 1988 & 1989, and also promotion from Division Four in 1992 with Mansfield.

CHARLTON ATHLETIC
United's playing record against the Addicks:
Football League

Venue	P	W	D	L	F	A
Home	25	16	6	3	50	19
Away	25	3	7	15	24	47
Totals	50	19	13	18	74	66

FA Cup

Home	1	1	0	0	3	1
Away	2	1	1	0	1	0
Totals	3	2	1	0	4	1

League Cup

Home	2	1	1	0	1	0
Away	1	0	1	0	2	2
Totals	3	1	2	0	3	2

Charlton Athletic FC was formed in June 1905 by a group of 14 and 15 year-olds living in streets down by the River Thames in the area, which now borders the Thames Barrier. After steady progress via local Leagues and the respected Southern League the 'Addicks' gained entry to the Football League Division 3 (South) in 1921.
However the club had to wait until 1935-36 before meeting the Blades in this competition. Both games ended level: 1-1 at The Valley and 2-2 at Bramall Lane.
Charlton won 4-0 at home in 1947-48 and registered two 3-0 victories at home and away in the 1950s while the Blades eased to a couple of 5-0 home wins, in 1954-55 and again in 1958-59, 'Doc' Pace scoring four times in the latter.
When United lost 2-1 to the 'Addicks' in 1999-2000 it was their first defeat at the hands of the London club since 1957-58.
Fred Cheesemuir, Nicky Johns, Clive Mendonca, Stewart Scullion, Graham Stuart, Steve Thompson, Carl Tiler, Tony Towner, Simon Webster and Chris Wilder are among the players who have been associated with both clubs. Jim Iley was a scout for Athletic and a player with United while Mervyn Day was a United goalkeeper and later Charlton's assistant-manager.

CHEESEMUR, Frederick Harold
Inside/centre-forward: 17 apps. 2 goals
Born: Wandsworth, London, 16 January 1908. Died: 1987.
Career: Dartford, Arsenal, Charlton Athletic, Gillingham, BLADES (December 1930), Southend United (May 1934), Folkestone (1936-37).
After failing to make his mark at Highbury and Charlton, Fred Cheesemuir scored 19 goals in 55 League games for Gillingham. He did reasonably well at Bramall Lane but was never a first team regular.

CHELSEA
United's playing record against the Blues:
Premiership

Venue	P	W	D	L	F	A
Home	2	2	0	0	5	2
Away	2	1	0	1	4	4
Totals	4	3	0	1	9	6

Football League

Home	34	17	5	12	57	45
Away	34	6	10	18	37	66
Totals	68	23	15	30	94	111

FA Cup

Home	1	0	0	1	0	1
Away	3	0	0	3	0	4
Neutral	1	1	0	0	3	0
Totals	5	1	0	4	3	5

League Cup

Away	1	0	0	1	1	3

Chelsea and Sheffield United share common histories, both having been created to play in an existing stadium.

The London club entered the Football League in the year of its formation (1905) and first met the Blades in season 1907-08, when they won 3-0 at Bramall Lane but succumbed to a 4-2 defeat at Stamford Bridge, Arthur Brown scoring a hat-trick in the latter contest.

In 1915, a crowd of 49,557 (receipts £4,557) saw United beat Chelsea 3-0 in the 1915 FA Cup final. Jimmy Simmons (36 minutes), Stan Fazackerley (83) and Joe Kitchen (88) scored the goals.

United have never scored more than four goals in a League game against Chelsea. Between 1930-34 they ran up successive home wins of 4-0, 4-2, 4-1 and 4-1, while going down 5-0 at Stamford Bridge inn the latter campaign.

The Blades were level at 1-1 at half-time in their League fixture with Chelsea at Stamford Bridge in September 1961. But with Joe Shaw struggling with an injury they eventually succumbed to a 6-1 defeat. The Blades also lost 4-0 in London in 1976-77, this being thee only League game involving the clubs outside the top flight.

By losing 3-2 at Stamford Bridge on 7 May 1994 (the last day of the season) United were relegated from the Premiership after other results had gone against them!

Alan Birchenall, Nathan Blake (Chelsea junior), Billy Brawn, Tony Currie (Chelses junior), Steve Finnieston, Willie 'Fatty' Foulke, Paul Furlong, Ian 'Chico' Hamilton, Jon Harley, Stewart Houston, Vinnie Jones, Ray Lewington, Paul Parker, Terry Phelan, Derek Richardson, Nigel Spackman (also Blades manager) and Graham Stuart are among the many players who have been associated with both clubs, likewise the former Blades' manager John Harris who captained Chelsea in the 1950s, while Ian Porterfield has managed both clubs. Dave Bassett was a junior at Stamford Bridge and later Blades' manager

CHELTENHAM TOWN

Cheltenham Town played its first recorded match in 1892, They moved to their current ground at Whaddon Road in 1901, became a Football League club as recent as 1999 and over the years have played the Blades only once at senior level, losing 4-0 in a 3rd round FA Cup-tie at Bramall Lane in January 2003.

Brett Angell, Mel Eves, Nicky Marker and Tony Wagstaff -have played for both clubs.

CHESTER CITY

United's playing record against Chester:

Football League

Venue	P	W	D	L	F	A
Home	3	2	1	0	9	2
Away	3	1	1	1	4	4
Totals	6	3	2	1	13	6
Other						
Home	1	0	1	0	2	2

Formed in 1884, turning professional in 1902, Chester became a Football League club in 1931 (elected to the Third Division North). The name City was added in 1983 but sadly, after 69 years' service the club were demoted to the Conference in 2000.

Chester first encountered the Blades in the old Third Division in 1979-80, both games ending level at 1-1. Chester then recorded a famous 3-0 victory at their former Sealand Road ground a year later. United's best win is 6-1, at Bramall Lane in 1988-89 (Division 3) when both Tony Agana and Brian Deane netted hat-tricks.

Earl Barrett, Paul Beesley, Ian Benjamin, Doug Cole, Bobby Davison, Billy Dearden, Steve Ludlam, Reg Matthewson, John Ryan and Mick Speight all played for the Blades and Chester.

CHESTERFIELD (Town)

United's playing record against the Spire-ites:

Football League

Venue	P	W	D	L	F	A
Home	9	5	1	3	17	10
Away	9	2	1	6	8	12
Totals	18	7	2	9	25	22
FA Cup						
Home	1	0	1	0	1	1
Away	1	0	0	1	0	1
Totals	2	0	1	1	1	2
League Cup						
Home	1	1	0	0	3	1
WW1						
Home	1	1	0	0	4	1
Away	1	0	0	1	0	3
Totals	2	1	0	1	4	4
WW2						
Home	9	3	3	3	14	11
Away	10	3	4	3	11	14
Totals	19	6	7	6	25	25
Others						
Away	5	4	1	0	7	3

Chesterfield are fourth only to Stoke, Notts County and Nottingham Forest in age for they can trace their existence as far back as 1866, although it is fair to say that activities within the club were rather casual in their formative years. In 1891 the 'Spire-ites' won their first trophy (the Barnes Cup) and followed up a year later by winning the Sheffield Cup, Barnes Cup (again) and the Derbyshire Junior Cup.

After gaining Football League status in 1899, voted into the Second Division to replace Darwen, Chesterfield had to wait until season 1935-36 before encountering the Blades. After drawing 2-2 at Saltergate before a record crowd of 26,519 in the November, Chesterfield were torn apart at Bramall Lane to the tune of 5-0 in mid-March when Jock Dodds and Harold Barton both scored twice.

Chesterfield have recorded three League 'doubles' over the Blades (1937-38, 1979-80 & 1988-89, the last time the clubs met), while United have claimed just two over the Spire-ties, in successive seasons of 1949-50 & 1950-51.

Scores of players have served with both clubs down the years including Kevin Arnott, Alf Ashmore, Len Badger, John Barke, Frank Barlow (also Chesterfield manager), Harold Barton, Billy Beer, Arthur Bottom, Jim Brown, Steve Cammack, Darren Carr, Philip Clift, Ted Connor, Terry

Curran, Richard Cushlow (Blades reserve), Billy Dearden, Mark Dempsey, Tony Fenoughty, Dennis Finnigan, Fred Furniss (Chesterfield reserve), George Handley, Mick Henderson, Pat Holland, Jim Holmes, Kirk Jackson (United reserve), Pat Keating, Tony Kenworthy (Chesterfield trialist), Keith Kettleborough, Jeff King, Andy Leaning, Paddy McGeeney, Ray McHale, Stan Machent, Cliff Mason, John Matthews, Billy Mercer, Joe Mitchell, Bob Neave, Shane Nicholson, Bernard Oxley, Bert Parkin, Jim Pilgrim, Bill Ross, Geoff Salmons, Andy Scott, George Simpson, 'Jock' Smith, and John Tudor (Chesterfield junior). Teddy Davison was player and then manager of Chesterfield (for five years) before taking charge of United in 1932. Joe Shaw played for United and later managed the 'Spire-ites'; Neil Warnock played for Chesterfield and later became United boss; Jimmy McGuigan played for and managed Chesterfield and later joined the coaching staff at Bramall Lane and Dugald Livingstone also managed the 'Spire-ites after serving as trainer at 'the Lane' for many years.

CHESTERFIELD HOSPITAL CUP

In May 1946, United travelled to The Recreation Ground (Saltergate) where they defeated Chesterfield 1-0 to lift the local Hospital Cup. A crowd of 6,800 saw Albert Nightingale score the only goal.

CHISHOLM, Jack Richardson

Defender: 21 apps. one goal.
Born: Edmonton, North London, 9 October 1924. Died: London, August 1977.
Career: Tottenham Hotspur (junior, 1940, professional October 1942...serving as a guardsman during WW2), Brentford (October 1947), BLADES (£15,000, April 1949), Plymouth Argyle (£14,000, December 1949, retiring May 1954). He later managed Helston FC, Finchley and Romford.
After leaving Bramall Lane, the bearded Jack 'Jumbo' Chisholm - 6ft 2ins tall and 14st in weight - netted twice in 187 League and FA Cup games for Plymouth. He was an Argyle legend, being rewarded with a Testimonial in May 1955 when the Pilgrims played a combined Spurs & West Bromwich Albion side. Chisholm was also a useful cricketer, playing for Middlesex (briefly) and St Just CC. He ran the Harvest Home pub (London) and also worked in a betting shop in Edmonton. He died suddenly at the age of 52.
* The 'Chisholm Lounge' at Home Park is named after him.

CHRISTMAS DAY

The Blades have played 51 League/Wartime and friendly games on Christmas Day. Here is a summary of those fixtures

Venue	P	W	D	L	F	A
Home	33	18	12*	3	67	38
Away	18	5	1	12	17	42
Totals	51	23	13	15	84	80

* Includes one abandoned game v. Woolwich Arsenal in 1891.

Festive Lights
* United's first Christmas Day encounter was a friendly away to Lincoln City in 1889 which they lost 5-1 in front of 3,500 spectators.
* The Blades' last competitive match on 25 December was a Second Division fixture against Grimsby Town at Blundell Park in 1958. A crowd of 14,179 saw them win 2-1 with Derek Pace scoring the club's last 'festive goal.'
* 6-1 is United's biggest Christmas Day win - at home to Brentford (Division 1) in 1946, while their heaviest defeat is 6-0, at the hands of Burnley at Turf Moor (Division 1) in 1920.
* 'Jock' Dodds scored a hat-trick when United beat Swansea Town (away) on Xmas Day 1935.
* United's best home attendance on 25 December is 50,080 v. Cardiff City (Division 1) in 1923. The lowest is 2,000 for the friendly v. Woolwich Arsenal in 1891 (the game being abandoned owing to thick fog on 75 minutes with the scores level at 3-3).
* United had a run of 16 Christmas Day games without defeat from 1931-50.
* A reported record crowd of 20,263 saw United beat Wednesday 3-2 in a Central League game at Bramall Lane on 25 December 1911.
* Two former United players - John Flood and Chris Kamara - were both born on Christmas Day.

CLARKE, Benjamin

Full-back: 12 apps.
Born Dungannon, Ireland, 1911.
Career: Portadown, BLADES (April 1935), Exeter City (September 1937), Carlisle United (August 1939-May 1940). Did not figure after WW2.
Strong-kicking full-back Ben Clarke was basically a reserve at Bramall Lane. He later made 40 League appearances for the Grecians.

CLIFF, Philip Robert

Winger: 22+6 apps. 9 goals
Born: Rotherham, 20 November 1947.
Career: BLADES (juniors, April 1963, professional, November 1965), Chesterfield (February 1971-May 1973).
Yorkshireman Philip Clift made less than 30 first team appearances for the Blades during his years with the club.

COACHES/TRAINERS

Over the years there have been scores of men (some ex-players) who have been employed as a coach (at various levels) by Sheffield United. Prior to 1935 the club's 'coach' was, in fact, classified as the trainer and since 1960, a coach, besides being referred to as a trainer, has also been listed as a physiotherapist.
Here are details of United's trainer/coaches down the years:

1891-92	J Housley
1892-93	G Waller
1893-94	G Waller/S Hunt
1894-1906	G Waller/J Housley
1906-07	G Waller/J Housley/F Richards
1908-09	G Waller/J Housley/F Richards/S Waller
1909-13	G Waller/H Johnson
1913-14	G Waller/H Johnson/J Elms
1914-25	G Waller/H Johnson
1925-30	G Waller/H Johnson/W Brelsford
1930-31	T Ratcliffe/H Johnson/W Brelsford/G Waller

1931-32	W Brelsford/T Radcliff/H Johnson/W Gillespie
1932-34	W Brelsford/H Johnson
1935-35	D Steele/W Brelsford/W Eadie
1936-40	D Livingstone/W Brelsford/R Wright
1940-46	D Livingstone/R Wright
1946-48	D Livingstone/L Nightingale/R Wright
1948-49	D Livingstone/R Wright/A Egglestone
1949-50	D Livingstone/R Wright/A Egglstone/J Smith
1950-52	R Wright/A Egglestone/J Smith/E Jackson
1952-53	R Wright/E Jackson/J McCormick
1954-54	R Wright/E Jackson/H Latham
1955-56	R Wright/E Jackson/G Smith/H Latham/F White
1956-57	H Latham/F White/A Cox/R Wright
1957-59	A Cox/F White/H Latham/R Taylor
1959-60	A Cox/H Latham/F White
1960-61	A Cox/H Latham/F White/G Smith
1961-66	J Short/H Latham/F White
1966-67	J Shaw/J Short/H Latham/F White
1967-68	J Shaw/J Short/H Latham/F White/C Coldwell
1968-69	J Short/H Latham/C Coldwell/F White
1969-70	C Coldwell/F White/H Latham
1970-71	C Coldwell/W Hodgson/F White/A Hodgkinson/H Latham
1971-73	C Coldwell/A Hodgkinson/H Latham
1974-75	D Turner/C Coldwell/ A Hodgkinson
1975-76	C Coldwell/A Hodgkinson/J Short
1976-77	C Coldwell/J Short/D Turner
1977-78	D Bergara/C Coldwell/J Short/D Turner
1978-79	R Bate/O Arce/C Coldwell
1979-80	G Vowden/D Bergara/C Coldwell
1980-81	M Peters/C Coldwell/ G Vowden/D Bergara
1981-82	C Coldwell/G Lees/J Stubbs
1982-83	C Coldwell/G Lees/J Stubbs/D Finnigan
1983-84	J McSevenny/J McGuigan/J Dixon
1984-86	W McEwan, J Stubbs/J Dixon
1986-88	D Bergara/P Henson
1988-93	G Taylor/K Mincher
1993-94	G Taylor
1994-95	K Mincher/J Dungworth/W Downes/B Eastick
1995-96	W Downes/B Eastick/K Mincher/J Dungworth/V Busby
1996-97	V Busby/J Bailey/R Slade/J Dungworth/N Spackman
1997-98	W Donachie/S Thompson/J Barron/J Dungworth/R Slade/S Myles
1998-99	A Heath/J Deehan/S Thompson/J Barron/R Slade/S Myles/M Tate
1999-2000	R Slade/S Myles
2000-01	D Hodgson
2001-03	K Curle (player-coach)/K Blackwell
2003-04	K Blackwell, AS McCall (player-coach)

Coaches Clipboard

* Certain coaches/trainers ended their employment with the Blades during the course of a season, while others were appointment after the season had started, either to replace those who left or as new additions to the club's coaching staff. In the case of Jim Dixon (1980s) he was also United's physio.
* George Waller was on United's training staff for almost 39 years: from May 1892 until early in 1931...a record unequalled anywhere in the world.
* Tom Ratcliffe moved to Bramall Lane in 1930 after serving Notts County as trainer. He later returned to Meadow Lane.
* David Steele, a Scottish international wing-half with Huddersfield Town, moved to United in 1934 and was spongeman at the 1936 FA Cup Final. He later became Bradford Park Avenue's secretary-manager.
* Duggie Livingstone held the position as United first team trainer for a period 13-and-a-half years until October 1949 when he left Bramall Lane to became coach of Sparta Rotterdam (Holland). He made well over 250 appearances as a full-back for Vale of Leven, Celtic, Everton, Plymouth Argyle, Aberdeen and Tranmere Rovers (in that order). He then assisted Jersey FC before retiring in 1935 to take over as trainer at Exeter City. He also managed both the Republic of Ireland and Belgium national sides in 1951 and 1953 respectively, was manager of Newcastle United from 1954-56, Fulham from 1956-58 and Chesterfield from 1958-62. He guided Newcastle to FA Cup glory in 1955. A Scotsman, born in Alexandria near Dumbarton in February 1898, he died at Marlow, Essex in January 1981, a few weeks before his 83rd birthday. He turned down the chance to become manager at Hillsborough in 1949.
* Reg Wright was a full-back with Blackpool, Bournemouth and Chesterfield who joined United's training ranks in 1936. He actually made one appearance as a player in 1940. He was senior trainer at Bramall Lane from 1949-52, remaining with the club until 1957.
* Ernie Jackson, a former United player, resigned as trainer at Bramall Lane in August 1955... because he couldn't get on with manager Joe Mercer.
* Harry Latham looked after the first team for 14 years: 1955-69.
* George Smith, coach in 1955-56, was the former Charlton, Brentford, QPR and Ipswich Town player who later managed Crystal Palace and Portsmouth (1961-70) and was also Blades' Chief Scout in 1960-61.
* Cecil Coldwell, another ex-player, also had two spells as acting manager at Bramall Lane (1975 & 1977-78).
* Jim McGuigan had played for Hamilton Academical, Sunderland, Stockport County and Crewe Alexandra and managed Crewe, Grimsby Town, Chesterfield and Stockport before joining the coaching staff at United in November 1983, staying until 1987.

58

* Jim Dixon was said to be manager Ian Porterfield's 'eyes and ears.'
* Uruguayan Danny Bergara had played in Spain with Real Mallorca, Seville and Tenerife and became assistant-manager/coach to Harry Haslam in 1977. He was dismissed after relegation in 1981, returned in 1986 but then departed again once Dave Bassett had taken office. He also worked as England youth team coach, coached in Brunei and later managed Rochdale, Stockport County and Rotherham United.
* Geoff Taylor was also Bassett's right-hand man.
* Willie Donachie, a Scottish international, played in 438 senior games for Manchester City before becoming Joe Royle's assistant when he managed Oldham Athletic, Everton, Manchester City and Ipswich Town.
* John Deehan was a striker with Aston Villa, WBA, Norwich City, Ipswich Town, Manchester City and Barnsley. He later coached at Oakwell and Huddersfield Town, managed Norwich and Wigan Athletic and after his spell with the Blades he became coach/assistant-manager/scout under Graham Taylor at Villa Park.
* David Steele also managed Huddersfield Town (the club he played for) and Russell Slade was manager of Notts County in 1994-95.
* During 2002 & 2003 coach Kevin Blackwell, a goalkeeper with Barnet, Scarborough, Huddersfield Town, Torquay United, Notts County and Plymouth Argyle, compiled a series of videos of set-pieces/free-kicks used by every club United played against or were due to meet. Highly-rated, "...he's in the Steve McClaren class" says Blades' manager Neil Warnock.
* Blades' player-coach Stuart McCall also took over as reserve team manager at Bramall Lane in 2002-03.
* Also on the staff as Bramall Lane in 2002-03 was Andy Leaning, employed as a goalkeeping coach.

COCKERILL, Glenn
Midfielder: 69 apps. 11 goals
Born: Grimsby, 25 August 1959
Career: Ritz Café FC (Louth), Louth United, Lincoln City (November 1976), Swindon Town (record £110,000, December 1979), Lincoln City (£40,000, August 1981), BLADES (£140,000, March 1984), Southampton (£225,000, October 1985), Leyton Orient (December 1993-May 1996).
In his early days Glenn Cockerill performed as a striker but was successfully converted into a fine, workmanlike midfielder who maintained his attacking instinct. He was given few opportunities at The County Ground and returned to Sincil Bank in 1981 for a cut-down price. He did well during his eighteen-month stay at Bramall Lane, helping the Blades gain promotion at the end of his first season (10 games played). He acted as caretaker-manager at Brisbane Road prior to the appointment of Pat Holland in 1995. Cockerill appeared in more than 775 senior games as a professional (102 goals scored).
* Both his father Ron (Huddersfield Town & Grimsby Town) and brother John (Grimsby) played League football.

COCKROFT, Joseph
Wing-half: 14 apps.
Born: Barnsley, 20 June 1911. Died: Sheffield, 1964.
Career: Barnsley Schoolboys (he was in the same team as George Hunt, later of Spurs), Wombwell, Rotherham United (February 1931), Gainsborough Trinity (free transfer, June 1931), West Ham United (initially on trial in March 1933, signed full-time the following month), Dartford (during WW2), Sheffield Wednesday (September 1945), BLADES (November 1948), Wisbech Town (manager, May 1949-May 1952). On his retirement from football he went into the Licensing Victualler's Trade, later becoming a printer. Wing-half Joe Cockroft made his debut for the Blades in a League game v. Preston North End when he was almost 37 years, five months old. He missed a penalty v. Arsenal in January 1949 (lost 5-3) and scuffed another in a 0-0 draw with Huddersfield in the next match.. He made 353 League appearances all told, 251 for the Hammers whom he helped win the League War Cup at Wembley in 1940. A director of labour regulation during WW2, he was sent back to Yorkshire to do his bit for the war effort at Edgar Allen Steelworks in Sheffield, guesting for Wednesday when he could.

COLCHESTER UNITED
United's playing record against Colchester:

Football League

Venue	P	W	D	L	F	A
Home	3	2	0	1	5	2
Away	3	0	1	2	3	7
Totals	6	2	1	3	8	9

FA Cup

	P	W	D	L	F	A
Home	1	0	1	0	3	3
Away	1	1	0	0	2	0
Totals	2	1	1	0	5	3

League Cup

	P	W	D	L	F	A
Home	1	1	0	0	3	0
Away	1	1	0	0	1	0
Totals	2	2	0	0	4	0

Formed in the summer of 1937 (when members of the much older Colchester Town FC, decided to form a professional club) Colchester United, playing at Layer Road which has been in existence since 1909, made rapid progress and in 1950 were elected to the Football League (Division 3 South).
The 'U's' first opposed the Blades in the Third Division in 1979-80 and they won both matches, 1-0 at Bramall Lane and 2-1 at Layer Road.
The last two League clashed took place in 1981-82, when the Blades were declared Fourth Division champions, but not before losing 5-2 at Colchester!
In 1988-89, the Blades won a 4th round FA Cup replay 2-0 with Brian Deane scoring twice - after a thrilling 3-3 draw at Layer Road. Carl Asaba, David Barnes, Graham Benstead, Roger Hansbury, Colin Hill, Stewart Houston and Dennis Longhorn among others, have been associated with both Uniteds. Fred White played for the Blades and was a scout for Colchester.

COLDWELL, George Cecil

Full-back: 478+1 apps. 2 goals

Born: Dungworth near Sheffield, 12 January 1929

Career: Norton Woodseats, BLADES (player from September 1951-May 1967, then serving as trainer, coach, assistant-manager and also as caretaker-manager until 1983)..

Cecil Coldwell was a grand servant to Sheffield United Football Club. Indeed, he was a member of the 'staff' for 32 years. Not regarded as a quality performer on his arrival at 'the Lane' he made steady progress...in fact, it took quite some time before he established himself. He finally made his Football League debut against Southampton at The Dell in April 1952 and gained a regular place in the side during the 1953-54 season. He then went back into the reserves (having the odd first team outing) before emerging again in February 1955 and holding his position comfortably thereafter, forming a splendid full-back partnership with first Cliff Mason and then Graham Shaw. Difficult to beat on the outside, fast in recovery, he was one of the best defenders around in the late 1950's/early 60's and helped the Blades win promotion from Division Two in 1961, making 41 appearances.

COLLINDRIDGE, Colin
Outside-left: 232 apps. 95 goals
Born: Barnsley, 15 November 1920
Career: Barugh Green FC, Wolverhampton Wanderers (juniors), BLADES (professional, January 1939), Nottingham Forest (on trial, signed permanently August 1950), Coventry City (with Tommy Capel, June 1954), Bath City (May 1956).
Owing to WW2, Colin Collindridge entered League football late - he was 25 when he made his debut in the competition for the Blades v. Liverpool in August 1946 - although during the hostilities he did appear in 96 various Regional matches for United (46 goals scored), being a key member of the 1945-46 League North championship-winning team.. He helped Forest gain promotion as Third Division (South) champions in 1951. A huge favourite with the fans wherever he played, Collindridge had speed, power and skill, was direct in his play and possessed a strong shot in his left foot.

COLOURS
United's colours at the outset (1889) were, like most of the other teams in the country, rather plain looking - white shirts, blue knickers.
In 1890 the jerseys contained a narrow red stripe (on a white background) with blue knickers.
By the early 1890s the standard red and white vertical stripes came into being with the blue shorts being changed for black ones.
For the 1923-24 season the 'jersey' gave way to the shirt.
The club's traditional kit - red and white striped shirt with a pair of black shorts - has been in force for perhaps 100 years or so right now, although different designs often appear... like in 1979-81 when the tops were more red than white and in the late 1980s and again in the mid-1990s and early 2000s...when white shorts and socks were commonplace.
There have been 'V' necks, round necks, red collars, white collars, plain front, button-up neck-lines, short sleeves, long sleeves, button-up wrists - but no-one really prefers anything else than a normal, straightforward 'red and white striped shirt with a pair of black shorts and matching socks.
The second XI though, once wore red and white quartered shirts!
Numbers were first seen on the back of a shirt in 1938, squad numbers appeared for the first time in 1993-94 (on the Premiership), then disappeared, only to return in 1999.

Change Colours
In the 1920s, when obliged to change their kit, the Blades wore white shirts with a red 'V'. Then, albeit occasionally, especially during the 1930s, the team donned blue shirts, and at the odd times, played in white with red sleeves and collar.
As designs changed over the years the Blades turned out accordingly, often wearing a variety of colours from orange, all blue, diagonal stripes and canary yellow (with red trimmings).

COLQUHOUN, Edmond Peter Skiring
Defender: 428+3 apps. 23 goals
Born: Prestonpans near Edinburgh, 29 March 1945
Career: Prestonpans Primary & Prestonpans Lodge Secondary Schools, Prestonpans YMCA, Edinburgh Norton, Bury (amateur June 1961, professional, March 1962), West Bromwich Albion (£25,000, February 1967), BLADES (£27,500, October 1968), Detroit Express/NASL (seasons 1978-80), Washington Diplomats (1980, retiring in 1982).
A Scottish international (winning nine full, one Under-23 and two Youth caps) Eddie Colquhoun - who was initially a right-back - was the rock-hard skipper at the heart of the Blades' defence when promotion was won in 1971.
Strong, powerful in the air, a solid, robust tackler, he was quick over the ground and put everything he had into playing football. A real true-grit professional, it was at The Hawthorns where he switched to centre-half and he gave the Baggies good service, appearing in over 50 games before breaking his leg in an FA Cup quarter-final replay against Liverpool at Anfield. He failed to get back into the Albion team and in 1968 he left the Cup holders for Bramall Lane. Colquhoun spent ten years with the Blades before leaving to try his luck in the NASL. Currently a night-club owner, he now lives in Connisborough near Doncaster.

61

COMEBACKS
* United found themselves 3-0 and then 4-3 down to Brighton & Hove Albion in a Second Division match on 9 September 1989. They fought back to win 5-4.
* United were 3-0 up at home to Reading on 11 October 1986 before the visitors bounced back to force a draw after netting three times in a five-minute spell during the second half.
* United were 2-0 behind at Hull in a Second Division game in January 1979. Final score: Blades 3 Tigers 2.
* Trailing 3-0 away to Bristol City in September 1970, the Blades fought back to force a 3-3 draw.
* Bottom-of-the-table Fulham were 2-0 down to United in a First Division game at Bramall Lane in April 1968. They scored three times in 11 minutes to turn things round and win 3-2.
* Three-nil behind after 17 minutes against Forest in a First Division game at The City Ground on Boxing Day 1963, United hit back to earn a 3-3 draw with Mick Jones equalising in the 89th minute.
* United, 2-0 down at home to Newcastle on 27 November 1965, hit back to win 3-2 by scoring three times in the last 23 minutes, including two in the final 55 seconds!

* On 24 April 1962, the Blades were in control, 2-0 up against Manchester United with 20 minutes left of their home League game. The visitors hit back to win 3-2.

* Trailing 2-0 to Port Vale in a home Second Division game in August 1956, the Blades hit back in style to win 4-2.

* The Blades were 2-0 up but lost 3-2 to Leyton Orient in a Second Division encounter at Brisbane Road in October 1956...the first-ever League game between the clubs.

* With 25 minutes remaining of a First Division game in March 1955, United were trailing 3-0 to West Brom at The Hawthorns. The Blades stormed back to earn a point from a 3-3 draw, equalising with virtually the last kick.

* United found themselves 2-0 down and then 3-1 adrift of Barnsley in their Second Division match at Oakwell in September 1951. But a determined second-half display saw they race on to a 4-3 victory.

* An FA Cup-tie followed by a League game between United and Ipswich Town in January/February 2003 produced 12 goals. In the 4th round Cup clash at Bramall Lane saw the Blades lose a three-goal lead before grabbing victory in the last few minutes (4-3). In the League match at Portman road, United led 2-0 only to let Ipswich charge back to record a 3-2 win.

* At half-time in a League game at Bramall Lane in October 1947, Sunderland led the Blades 2-0. The final score was a 3-2 win for United, Albert Nightingale scoring the winner in the last minute after home 'keeper Jack Smith had saved Tommy Reynolds' penalty.

* United were 2-0 up in a WW2 game v. Grimsby Town in November 1942. The Mariners eventually won a thrilling end-to-end contest 4-3.

* Playing Liverpool in successive weeks in February 1942, United came back from 5-2 down to win a Football League Wartime Cup qualifying tie 7-6 on aggregate after taking the return fixture at Bramall Lane by 5-1.

* The Blades were 3-0 down to Sunderland in a League game in September 1930, but they hot back strongly to force a draw (3-3), grabbing the equaliser in the last minute.

* United were 2-0 up but lost 3-2 to Middlesbrough in an away League game in November 1922. George Elliott netted a hat-trick in the last 10 minutes for 'Boro.

* Trailing 3-0 to United with only 10 men, Chelsea hit back to force a 3-3 draw in a League game at Bramall Lane in January 1913.

* United led Sunderland 2-0 in a 1st round FA Cup-tie in January 1909 but they couldn't hold on and eventually lost the game 3-2.

* With 88 minutes played, United were trailing 4-2 to Liverpool in their FA Cup Semi-final replay in March 1899. But Fred Priest, bless his soul, netted twice to secure a 4-4 draw. The Blades eventually went through after an abandoned game and a second replay by 1-0.

* On 11 September 1897 United were 2-0 down after just five minutes in their home League game with Stoke. They hit back to win 4-3.

* Leading 3-0 after 55 minutes v. Stoke in a League game in February 1894, United had to hold on in the end for a 3-3 draw.

COMMERCIAL DEPARTMENT

Andy Daykin has been a valuable member of the Sheffield United Commercial Department for over **** years.

COMMON, Alfred

Forward: 79 apps. 24 goals
Born: Millfield, County Durham, 25 May 1880. Died: Darlington, 3 April 1946.
Career: South Hylton Juniors (1896), Jarrow (1897), Sunderland (professional, August 1900), BLADES (record £520, November 1901), Sunderland (June 1904), Middlesbrough (record £1,000, February 1905), Woolwich Arsenal (£100, August 1910), Preston North End (December 1912, retired May 1914). Moved to Darlington where, besides becoming an efficient and well-respected referee, he also enlisted as a licensee, later managing the Alma Hotel at Cockerton for 11 years until 1943).
Alf Common became the game's first £1,000 footballer when he moved from Sunderland to Middlesbrough in 1905. A jovial, loquacious footballer, he could play equally well at inside-right or centre-forward. He was aggressive, could rough it with the toughest defenders around and possessed a powerful, right-foot shot. Capped three times by England (v. Wales and Ireland in 1904 and Wales in 1906, scoring in each of his first two internationals), Common was an FA Cup winner with United 1902 and a Second Division championship winner with Preston in 1913. He scored twice for Arsenal in a 3-1 win over the Blades at Highbury in January 1912. During his career Common scored 134 goals in 419 competitive League and Cup matches.
* As a referee Common officiated a Fred Priest's benefit match between Hartlepool United and the Blades in October 1922.
* After being stripped of the captaincy by Middlesbrough in September 1907 Common was fined £10 by the club for drunkeness and violent behaviour.

CONNAUGHTON, John Patrick

Goalkeeper: 14 apps.
Born: Wigan, 23 September 1949
Career: Manchester United, Halifax Town (on loan, September 1969), Torquay United (on loan, October 1971), BLADES (£15,000, October 1972), Port Vale (May 1974), Altrincham (January 1980).
England Youth international goalkeeper John Connaughton was overshadowed by Alex Stepney and Jimmy Rimmer at Old Trafford and made only three first-team appearances for the Reds and just 14 for the Blades (in almost 18 months). However, during his career as a whole he played in almost 250 competitive games - 218 for Port Vale, being voted Vale's 'Player of the Year' in 1975. Connaughton was an FA Trophy winner with Altrincham in 1982 (beating Enfield 1-0 in the Final).

CONNOR, J Edward

Forward: 14 apps.
Born: Weaste, Liverpool, 1884. Died: Manchester, January 1955
Career: Eccles Borough/Lancashire Combination (1905), Lincoln City (amateur, November 1907), Eccles Borough (again), Walkden Central, Manchester United (professional, May 1909), Sheffield United (£750, June 1911), Bury (July 1912), Fulham (briefly), Nelson (June 1918), Exeter City (September 1919), Rochdale (July 1920), Chesterfield (October 1921), Saltney Athletic (December 1921, retiring in 1924). He later scouted for Manchester United and was for many years a member of the office staff at Old Trafford.
Able to play in any forward position, Ted Connor had an interesting, nomadic career that spanned almost 20 years. A versatile footballer, known for his sportsmanship, he appeared in more than 250 competitive games (131 in the Football League).

CONROY, Steven Harold

Goalkeeper: 135+3 apps.
Born: Chesterfield, 19 December 1956
Career: BLADES (apprentice, April 1972, professional June 1974), Rotherham United (non-contract, February 1983), Rochdale (June 1983), Rotherham United (January 1985).
Steve Conroy was a very capable goalkeeper, whose best season with the Blades came in 1978-79 when he made 41 League and six Cup appearances.

62

CONSECUTIVE LEAGUE WINS, DRAWS & LOSSES

* United won eight consecutive League games in 1893, 1903, 1958 and 1960.
* They suffered seven successive defeats in 1975 and drew six games on the bounce in 1901.
* The Blades were undefeated in 22 League games between September 1899 and January 1900 and they went 19 games without win between September 1975 and February 1976.
* United remained unbeaten in 27 home First Division games between August 1936 and November 1937.
* They had a run of ten home games without a registering a win in 1949.
* The team remained undefeated in 11 successive away matches in season 1892-93.
* The Blades failed to win a single away game in 20 attempts in a 12-month period from April 1975 to April 1976.
* And United had sequences of 11 successive home wins from April-December 1960 and six successive away victories from December 1891 to April 1892.
* United won 14 consecutive home League Cup games between 26 August 1997 and 8 January 2003. A run of 13 successive home Cup wins (both major domestic competitions) was put together between 2000-03.
(See also: FOOTBALL LEAGUE/SEQUENCES)

COOK, William

Right-back: 324 apps.
Born: Usworth near Sunderland, 2 March 1890. Died: 1974.
Career: Hebburn Argyle, BLADES (April 1912), Worksop Town (August 1927).
Bill Cook spent 15 years at Bramall Lane, amassing well over 300 senior appearances without ever scoring a goal. A two-footed crisp tackler, cool under pressure, never flustered and as sound and as solid as any defender in the game, he made his League debut - with Albert Pearson - against Bradford City (away) in September 1912 and was twice an FA Cup winner, a decade apart, in 1915 and 1925.

COOP, James Yates

Left-winger: 9 apps. one goal
Born: Horwich, 17 September 1927. Died: 1996.
Career: BLADES (May 1946), York City (July 1949-May 1951).
Jim Coop, a smart, compact outside-left, made his League debut for the Blades against Derby County (home) in November 1947 in front of almost 52,000 fans. He made only 12 League appearances for the Minstermen.

CORK, Alan Graham

Forward: 32+32 apps. 9 goals
Born: Derby, 4 March 1959
Career: Derby County (apprentice, April 1975, professional, July 1977), Lincoln City (on loan, September 1977), Wimbledon (February 1978), BLADES (March 1992), Fulham (non-contract, September 1994-May 1995). Later managed both Swansea City (during season 1997-98) and Cardiff City (October 2000-January 2002), Leicester City (assistant-manager/coach, season 2002-03).
Alan Cork's hair may have gone by the time he joined the Blades but he certainly hadn't lost his goalscoring touch. He had a wonderful career that took him all over the country.
It began at The Baseball Ground, spent 14 years with Wimbledon, helping them climb up through the Divisions and win the FA Cup in 1988. He scored 145 goals in 430 League games for the Dons (still existing records). When he hung up his boots (in May 1995) he had drawn up an excellent record: 158 goals in 521 competitive matches.

CORINTHIANS

United's playing record v. the Corinthians:

FA Cup

Venue	P	W	D	L	F	A
Home	2	2	0	0	7	2

Sheriff of London Charity Shield

Venue	P	W	D	L	F	A
Neutral	2	0	2	0	1	1

The famous Corinthians FC was formed in 1882 - in order to bring the leading amateur players of the day together in a single club. For many years the senior England team was made up of several 'Corinthian' footballers, actually provided all eleven played for the international v. Wales in 1894.
Over the years several friendly matches were played against top-line Football League clubs but only four at competitive level have been against the Blades.
In 1897-98 the teams met in the 'final' of the newly instigated Sheriff of London Shield (the forerunner to the FA and then Community Shield). A crowd of 19,707 witnessed the goalless draw at Crystal Palace and then 7,500 attended the replay the following Monday afternoon which again ended level at 1-1. As United would be crowned League champions at the end of that season, he showed the strength of the Corinthians at that time.
United came through as winners in the two FA Cup-ties involving the clubs: 5-0 in the 1st round in 1924-25 (Harry Johnson scored four goals) and 2-1 in round three in 1931-32, both fixtures taking place at Bramall Lane.

CORNER-KICKS

United were awarded 28 corner-kicks to West Ham's one during the Second Division League game at Bramall Lane on 14 October 1889 - and they still lost 2-0.
The Blades forced 20 corners during their home League game with Sunderland in September 1959. They finally scored in the very last minute of a 2-1 defeat.
United gained 18 corners to Aldershot's one in a Third Division League game at The Recreation Ground on 8 November 1988. The 'Shots' won 1-0.

63

COUNTY CUP

(Sheffield & Hallamshire Cup)

This is United's full record (first team only) in the County Cup (games against Barnsley, Doncaster Rovers, Rotherham United and Sheffield Wednesday):

Venue	P	W	D	L	F	A
Home	52	39	7	6	148	55
Away	60	24	8	28	99	107
Totals	112	63	15	34	247	162

* Three of the drawn games were decided by a penalty shoot-out and a handful of United's scheduled home games were played 'away' owing to the fact that a cricket match was being staged at Bramall Lane!

The Final Countdown

* This County Cup was first played for in 1920-21. And after beating Barnsley 3-2 in a home semi-final replay (thanks mainly to a hat-trick from Jim Plant) United went on to beat arch-rivals Wednesday 2-1 in the Final at Hillsborough in front of 21,203 fans.
* In 1923-24, after knocking out Rotherham 2-0 at home in the semi-final, United went to Hillsborough and won 2-0 to clinch the trophy for the second time.
* United's third success came in 1925-26 when once again they out-fought Wednesday in the Final, winning 3-1 at Bramall Lane before a crowd of 39,698.
* In 1929-30 the Cup once more came to Bramall Lane when the Blades beat Wednesday 2-0 at home in front of 20,000 fans.
* A year later they retained the Cup, crushing Barnsley 9-2 in the Final with Bernard Oxley scoring a hat-trick before an 8,000 crowd.
* United carried off the trophy for the sixth time in 1932-33, defeating Wednesday 4-2 in the Final at Bramall Lane when Jimmy Dunne netted all four goals before 4,000 spectators.
* There was a break of 19 years before United won the Cup outright again. This time it was in season 1951-52 when Rotherham United were beaten 2-1 in the Final before an appreciate crowd of 14,231 at Millmoor.
* When retaining the trophy in 1952-53, United ruthlessly hammered Rotherham 5-0 in the Final at Bramall Lane (att. 6,806).
* A hat-trick of triumphs followed in 1953-54 when once again Rotherham were United's victims, beaten 4-2 at Millmoor in front of 16,206 spectators.
* After losing 4-0 to Doncaster Rovers in the 1955-56 Final, United took the trophy again in 1956-57, and once more luckless Rotherham were their victims, a crowd of 9,500 seeing them beaten 3-1 at Millmoor.
* United retained the Cup with a 3-0 away victory over Sheffield Wednesday in the 1957-58 Final when the Hillsborough turnout was 21,289.
* The hat-trick was completed in 1958-59 with a another victory at Hillsborough, the Owls succumbing to a 4-1 defeat this time when the attendance was 18,221.
* And in 1959-60 the Blades made it four wins on the bounce by pipping Rotherham 2-1 in the Final at Bramall Lane when only 5,000 fans turned up.
* United's fourteenth 'County Cup' victory came in 1963-64 when they just accounted for Barnsley at Oakwell, winning a tight contest by 4-3 in front of 4,000 spectators.
* When retaining the Cup in 1964-65, the Blades defeated Doncaster Rovers 4-0 at Belle Vue with the gate reaching 11,000
* Following a Final defeat at the hands of Rotherham, United got the trophy back in 1966-67 with a 3-2 replay win over Barnsley following a 1-1 draw on the same ground. The attendances were (1) 8,903 and (2) 7,110.
* United registered one of their biggest Cup wins in 1968-69, beating Barnsley 9-0 in a semi-final replay. In the Final they were again taken to a second match before beating Doncaster Rovers (the holders) 2-0 at Bramall Lane after a 0-0 draw at Belle Vue. The home crowd was 5,612.
* After a cluster of semi-final defeats United then lost on penalties to Sheffield Wednesday in the 1973-74 Final (after a goalless draw at Hillsborough where the attendance was a useful 18,869).
* However, the Blades won a penalty shoot-out themselves in 1974-75, beating Rotherham United 4-2 from the spot (after a 0-0 draw at Bramall Lane). The attendance (on a cold October evening) was 4,154.
* Defeated in the 1975-76 and 1976-77 Finals by Wednesday and Rotherham respectively, the Blades won the 1977-78 competition when the Final was carried over to the next season. They beat Doncaster 4-1 in mid-September 1978.
* The Cup was retained in 1979-80 - the Blades winning 2-1 at Hillsborough before a crowd of 5,340.
* And then in 1981-82, the seniors won the trophy for the 21st time, edging out their neighbours Wednesday 3-2 at Bramall Lane. United's reserve side had beaten Barnsley on penalties in the semi-final (after a 0-0 draw) but it was agreed that the respective first XI's would contest the Final...and over 5,000 saw the Blades' triumph in their last 'senior' County Cup match.
NB: The trophy was shared with Wednesday in 1938-39 after a 0-0 draw at Bramall Lane in front of almost 14,000 fans.

Fact File

* United lost in the Final of 1944-45 to Wednesday, 7-3 on aggregate.
* A County Cup record crowd of 49,980 saw United beat Sheffield Wednesday 4-2 in the 1948-49 semi-final at Hillsborough. The Blades led 4-0 at half-time.
* United lost only four out of 35 County Cup games with Barnsley (all away). They won 17 and drew 10.
* Of their 20 encounters with Doncaster, the Blades won 10 and lost seven.
* Against Rotherham they were successful in 18 of their 28 matches, drawing nine and losing only three (all at home).
* United and Wednesday met 29 times: the Blades won 18, the Owls only nine with two drawn (one at each venue).

COURT CASES

* On 23 May 1994 a court case began in the High Court involving the former Aston Villa defender Paul Elliott and Welsh international and future Blades' star Dean Saunders of Aston Villa. The case referred to an incident in which Saunders (then of Liverpool) put in a supposedly dangerous tackle, effectively ending the playing career of Elliott, then a Chelsea star. The hearing lasted until the 19th June when Saunders was cleared of making a 'reckless challenge'. Elliott, however, faced a possible legal bill of £500,000. Summing up, Lord Justice Drake admitted that players should have the right to seek compensation from the courts for career-wrecking injuries as a result of foul play. However, he was satisfied in this case that Saunders made a honest attempt to play the ball.

COVENTRY CITY
(Singers FC)
United's playing record against the Sky Blues:

Premiership

Venue	P	W	D	L	F	A
Home	2	0	2	0	1	1
Away	2	1	1	0	3	1
Totals	4	1	3	0	4	2

Football League

Home	16	6	4	6	17	15
Away	16	3	5	8	22	29
Totals	32	9	9	14	39	44

FA Cup

Home	1	0	1*	0	1	1
Away	1	0	1	0	1	1
Totals	2	0	2	0	2	2

*United won 3-1 on penalties.

WW1

Home	1	1	0	0	3	1
Away	1	1	0	0	4	2
Totals	2	2	0	0	7	3

Workers of Singer's cycle factory formed Coventry City FC in 1883.

The first success came in 1891 when the Birmingham Junior Cup was won. This led, in 1894, to election to the efficient Birmingham & District League, and four years later Singers FC became Coventry City. In 1908 (having moved from their Stoke Road ground to Highfield Road in 1899) membership to the Southern League was attained and it came as quite a surprise when City gained Football League status in 1919 (Division 2)...when the League was extended from 40 to 44 clubs after WW1.

The Blades first encountered City in the competition in 1935-36 (Division 2), drawing 2-2 at Bramall Lane but losing 2-0 at Highfield Road. The Blades though gained revenge a year later, winning 3-2 at home and drawing 2-2 away.

The clubs have met in only 18 seasons including United's two Premiership campaigns and remarkably there has only been two Cup clashes - in 1997-98 - when the Blades, after a battling 1-1 draw at Highfield Road, edged through to the semi-final stage in a penalty shoot-out at Bramall Lane, goalkeeper Alan Kelly being declared the hero by saving three spot-kicks.

Ex-Blades boss Joe Mercer managed Coventry City in the 1970s while former United reserve George Raynor was also in charge at Highfield Road.

Of the players who served with both clubs we have John Ball, David Barnes, Jesse Bennett, David Bradford, Colin Collindridge, Paul Furlong, Andy Goram, George Hall, Paul Hall, Fred Hawley, Paul Heald (United reserve), Chris Marsden, Joe Mitchell, Dennis Mortimer, Peter Ndlovu, Derek Richardson, Jimmy Shankly, John Tudor, Ronnie Waldock, Keith Waugh and Paul A Williams.

* Former United goalkeeper Alan Hodgkinson was goalkeeping coach at Highfield Road (2003).

COWAN, Thomas
Full-back: 53 apps.
Born: Bellshill, Lanarkshire, 28 August 1969,
Career: Netherdale Boys Club, Clyde (July 1988), Glasgow Rangers (February 1989), BLADES (£350,000, August 1991), Stoke City (on loan, October-November 1993), Huddersfield Town (£200,000, March 1994), Burnley (£20,000, March 1999), Cambridge United (on loan February-March 2000, signed permanently, July 2000) Peterborough United (on loan, January-February 2001), York City (May 2002).
Tom Cowan - a timely tackler and long throw expert - made 50 appearances for the Blades following his 15 outings with the 'Gers. He played his best football, without doubt, with Huddersfield: 165 appearances.

COWANS, Gordon Sidney
Midfielder: 21+2 apps.
Born: Cornworth, 27 October 1958.
Career: Aston Villa (apprentice in April 1974, professional, September 1976), Bari/Italy (£500,000, July 1985), Aston Villa (£250,000, July 1988), Blackburn Rovers (£200,000, November 1991), Aston Villa (July 1993), Derby County (£80,000, February 1994), Wolverhampton Wanderers (£20,000, December 1994), BLADES (free transfer, December 1995), Bradford City (July 1996), Stockport County (March 1997), Burnley (player-coach, August 1997), Aston Villa, for a fourth time (assistant-manager/coach, May 1998).
A masterful left-sided midfielder who could ping a 40-yard pass right to the foot of a colleague with great precision Gordon Cowans helped Villa win the League Cup (1977), the First Division title (1981) and the European Cup and the European Super Cup, both in 1982. He was capped 10 times by England, and represented his country in two 'B' and five Under-21 internationals, having earlier played at Youth team level. He passed the personal milestone of 800 club appearances during season 1997-98 (75 goals scored). His record with Villa was 59 goals in a total of 529 first team outings. He was 37 years of age when he joined the Blades but one could see what a fine player he had been at his peak.

COX, Albert Edward Harrison
Full-back: 333 apps.
Born: Treeton near Rotherham,
24 June 1917.
Career: Woodhouse Mills United,
BLADES (April 1935), Halifax Town
(July 1952, retiring in May 1954).
Big-hearted full-back Albert Cox loved
the sliding tackle. He was a solid
rather than stylish performer who
gave nothing less than 100 per-
cent each and every time he took
the field. A member of United's
1939 promotion-winning side,
he made his League debut
against Blackpool in February
1936 and played straight
through until the end of the
1939-40 season before
returning in 1945-46 to
continue his service

CRADDOCK, Jody Darryl
Defender: 10 apps.
Born: Redditch, Worcs. 25 July 1975
Career: Christchurch FC (Dorset), Cambridge United (August 1993), Sunderland (£300,000, August 1997), BLADES (on loan,
August-October 1999).
Strong-tackling defender Jodie Craddock made almost 160 appearances for Cambridge United before his transfer to Sunderland where
he developed to into a very capable Premiership player.

CREWE ALEXANDRA
United's playing record against the 'Alex':
Football League

Venue	P	W	D	L	F	A
Home	7	6	1	0	15	2
Away	7	3	1	3	12	9
Totals	14	9	2	3	27	11
FA Cup						
Away	1	0	0	1	1	3

It is known that Crewe Alexandra played its first football match in 1877 (against Basford). After playing in several Leagues, including
the Football Combination and Football Alliance, along with Sheffield United, the 'Alex' or 'Railwaymen' became founder members of
the Football League Division Two in 1892.
The Blades got off to a great start by doubling-up over the 'Alex' in that first season, winning both matches with 4-0 scorelines, the
latter at Gresty Road late on in the campaign when they were vying with Small Heath (Birmingham) for the inaugural championship.
Arthur Watson scored twice in each game.
After that the clubs went their separate ways and it wasn't until 1947-48, when the 'Alex', playing in the Third Division (North)
knocked First Division United out of the FA Cup in the 3rd round, by 3-1.
Since then United have completed two more doubles, the first in 1981-82 and the second in 1998-99. They won 4-0 at home and 3-2
away in the former season, a result that clinched the Fourth Division championship title thanks' to Jeff King's last minute winner.

The scores in 1998-99 were 3-1 at 'the Lane' and 2-1 at Gresty Road.

Darren Carr, Billy Dearden, Chris Downes, Peter Duffield, Stewart Evans (United reserve), Mark Foran, John Gannon, Micky Guy, Francis Joseph, Phil Kite, Bert Lipsham, Mack, Tony Moore, Jon Newby, Terry Nicholl, Percy Oldacre, John Pemberton, Mel Rees, Oliver Tummon, Mitch Ward, Roy Warhurst and Billy Whitehurst are among the players who served with both the Blades and the 'Alex.' Jim McGuigan and Neil Warnock both played for the 'Alex' before taking to management, the latter at 'the Lane' while the former was on United's coaching staff.

CRICKET

Cricket was first played at Bramall Lane in 1855 with the first county match - Yorkshire v. Sussex - starting on 27 August of that year. When the touring Australians played Yorkshire there in a friendly in 1884 the attendance of 20,700 was a record for any cricket match in this country, perhaps the world.

The first Test Match at 'the Lane' saw England play Australia in July 1902 and the very last cricket fixture staged at the ground was the Roses match between Yorkshire and Lancashire in August 1973.

(See also under BRAMALL LANE & SHEFFIELD CRICKET CLUB).

CRICKETING-FOOTBALLERS

Jack Chisholm (Middlesex), Alonzo Drake (Yorkshire), Bill Foulke (Derbyshire), Walter Hardinge (Kent), Ted Hemsley (Worcestershire), Albert 'Tal' Lewis (Somerset), Ernest Needham (Derbyshire), Bill Ross (Nottinghamshire groundstaff), George Waller (Yorkshire) and Billy Wilkinson (Yorkshire) have all played League football (for United) as well being associated with a County cricket club. Billy Moon played once for United (in a friendly in 1891) and also for Middlesex CCC. Other footballing-cricketers who have been associated with the Blades include: Reg Baines (Rowntrees CC), Billy Dearden (Crompton CC), Andy Goram (West Bromwich Dartmouth CC), Harry Hammond (Sheffield United CC), John L Jones, Keith Kettleborough (Rotherham Town CC), Joe Kitchen (Lincolnshire), Ken Lee, Joe Lievesley (Sheffield United CC), Walter Spicer, Steve Thompson (Yorkshire Schools), George Utley, Arthur Watson, Bernard Wilkinson and Billy Wilkinson (the latter three all for Sheffield United CC).

Off The Square
* Walter Hardinge was a double international - capped by England v. Scotland at soccer in 1910 and by England against Australia at cricket in 1921.
* Andy Goram was also a double international, playing both football and cricket for Scotland.
* Jack Chisholm also played for St Just CC.
* John L Jones became a cricket coach in Leinster (Dublin) and was later groundsman at the Whitburn CC in Durham.
* George Utley was a cricket coach at Rossall School while Albert 'Tal' Lewis coached cricket in India.
* Ken Lee became a Director of Sheffield United FC.

CROOT, Frederick Richard

Outside-left: 9 apps.
Born: Rushden, Northants, 1886. Died: 1958
Career: Wellingborough, BLADES (May 1905), Leeds City (May 1907), Clydebank

Jinking, speedy left-winger Fred Croot scored 38 goals in 227 League and FA Cup appearances for the Elland Road club after failing to make an impression at Bramall Lane. He was one of the most popular players at Leeds and received the princely sum of £250 from his benefit game v. Arsenal in 1914. During WW1 he served as an Army Corporal.

CROSS, Edward E

Right-half: 25 apps.
Born: circa 1868
Career: Rotherham Town, BLADES (1890).

Teddy Cross was a wing-half who spent just the one season at Bramall Lane before moving on. He played in almost 50 first-team matches for the Blades (23 of them in non-competitive matches).

CROSS, John

Centre-forward: 46 apps. 18 goals
Born: Bury, 5 February 1927
Career: Guildford City, Bournemouth (March 1947), Northampton Town (October 1953), BLADES (£11,000, February 1954), Reading (October 1955-May 1956).

Jack Cross scored 64 goals in 137 League games for Bournemouth. A very robust player, strong with powerful right-foot shot, he did well enough at Bramall Lane but always seemed to enjoy playing in the lower Divisions.

CRYAN, Colin

Defender: 0+6 apps*
Born: Dublin, 23 March 1981
Career: BLADES (apprentice, April 1997, professional, August 1999).

Irishman Colin Cryan joined the Blades soon after leaving school and after impressing in the second XI as a powerfully built, fearless defender (having switched from his previous role in midfield) he had made only four substitute appearances in the first team before earning himself a new two-year contract, commencing in June 2002.

67

CRYSTAL PALACE

United's playing record against the Eagles:

Premier League

Venue	P	W	D	L	F	A
Home	1	0	0	1	0	1
Away	1	0	0	1	0	2
Totals	2	0	0	2	0	3
Football League						
Home	18	7	5	6	21	19
Away	18	6	5	7	18	22
Totals	36	13	10	13	39	41
Play-off Final						
Neutral	1	0	0	1	0	1
FA Cup						
Home	1	1	0	0	2	0
League Cup						
Home	1	1	0	0	3	1

There was a Crystal Palace club as early as 1861 but the present one was not 'born' until 1905. Playing at the Crystal Palace ground itself (home of many pre WW1 FA Cup Finals), the London club battled through the Southern League before gaining Football League status in 1920 as original members of the Third Division. Four years later the 'Eagles' left their Nest Ground (home since 1918) for Selhurst Park.

The Blades met Palace for the first time in the 3rd round of the FA Cup in January 1959, winning 2-0 at Bramall Lane.

The first League confrontations took place a decade later when both Second Division fixtures ended in 1-1 draws (the initial one at Selhurst Park when Tony Currie netted for the Blades while Colin Addison's penalty earned his tie a point in the return game).

A crowd of just 6,647 saw United beat Palace 1-0 (courtesy of a Colin Morris penalty) in a Second Division game in March 1987 - the lowest League crowd at Bramall Lane since September 1935.

The best of United's six League wins at 'the Lane' is 3-0, achieved in 1996-97 (Division One) when both sides were pushing for the Play-offs which they reached, only for the Eagles to gain revenge at Wembley, winning 1-0 thanks to David Hopkins' excellent strike to gain a place in the Premiership.

Paul Peschisolido scored twice in the last four minutes to earn the Blades a 3-1 League Cup victory over the Eagles in the 5th round at Bramall Lane in December 2002.

Steve Bruce and Dave Bassett have been managers of both clubs while the following have all been registered as players with the Blades and the Eagles: John Burridge, Richard Cushlow (Blades reserve), Mark Hawthorne (reserve at both clubs), Mick Hill, Glyn Hodges, Steve Kabba, Bert Menlove, Andy Morrison, Shaun Murphy, Archie Needham, John Pemberton, Terry Phelan, Gareth Taylor, David Tuttle and Carl Veart.

68

CULLEN, David Jonathan

Midfielder: 0+4 apps.
Born: Durham City, 10 January 1973.
Career: Doncaster Rovers (trainee, June 1989, professional September 1991), Spennymoor United (September 1993), Morpeth Harriers (1995), Hartlepool United (March 1997), BLADES (£250,000, January 1998), Shrewsbury Town (on loan, September 1999), Halifax Town (on loan, December 1999), Peterborough United (£35,000, March 2000-May 2002), Carlisle United (on loan, March-May 2001), Although he looked at good times (especially in the second XI) Jon Cullen failed to make any real impression at Bramall Lane.

CUNNINGHAM, John

Forward: 26 apps. 7 goals
Born: Glasgow, 1873
Career: Benburb FC, Celtic (on trial, May 1899), Burnley (November 1899), Glasgow Hibernian (December 1899), Heart of Midlothian (March 1892), Glasgow Rangers (August 1892), Preston North End (September 1893), BLADES (May 1897), Aston Villa (June 1898), Newton Heath (October 1898), Wigan County (1899-July 1901), Barrow (August 1901-May 1903).
John Cunningham was a useful footballer on his day, but could be moody. He was a Lancashire Senior Cup winner with Preston in 1895 and a League championship winner with the Blades in 1898 (when he was receiving wages of £3-a-week). He also played in Barrow's first-ever game v. Blackpool and during his career made 90 Football League appearances (17 goals).
* After making his debut for Newton Heath, the editor of the club's programme wrote: "Cunningham did not set the Ship Canal on fire, so to speak." Four months later he was suspended and place on the transfer list - having been made the scapegoat for the team's indifferent form.

CUP WINS

In season 2002-03 the Blades created a new football record by being drawn at home in each of ten Cup-ties (six in the League Cup, four in the FA Cup)...and they won them all. They defeated York City, Wycombe Wanderers, Leeds United, Sunderland, Crystal Palace and Liverpool (semi-final, 1st leg) in the Worthington Cup, and accounted for Cheltenham Town, Ipswich Town, Leeds United (again) in rounds, 3, 4, 5 & 6 the FA Cup.

CURLE, Keith

Defender: 57+4 apps one goal
Born: Bristol, 14 November 1963
Career: Bristol Rovers (apprentice, April 1980, professional, November 1981), Torquay United (November 1983), Bristol City (March 1984), Reading (£150,000, October 1987), Wimbledon (£500,000, October 1988), Manchester City (£2.5 million, August 1991), Wolverhampton Wanderers (£650,000, August 1996), BLADES (free transfer, July 2000), Mansfield Town (player-manager, June 2002).
Standing 6ft 1in tall and weighing 12st 12lb, defender Keith Curle had already amassed an excellent record of 741 club appearances by the time he joined the Blades in readiness for the 2000-01 season. Over the next two years he took his tally past the 800-mark before becoming player-manager of the Stags in the summer of 2002.
Capped three times by England at senior level and on four occasions by the 'B' team, he won the Freight Rover Trophy with Bristol City in 1986 and the Simod Cup with Reading two years later. During his second season at Bramall Lane Curle was registered as a player-coach.

CURRAN, Edward
Forward: 42+2 apps. 3 goals
Born: Hemsworth, 20 March 1955.
Career: Kinsley FC, Doncaster Rovers (trainee April 1971, professional July 1973), Nottingham Forest (£60,000, August 1975), Bury (on loan, October 1977), Derby County (£50,000, November 1977), Southampton (£60,000, August 1978), Sheffield Wednesday (£100,000, March 1979), BLADES (£100,000, August 1982), Everton (on loan, December 1982, signed permanently for £95,000, September 1983), Huddersfield Town (July 1985), Panionios/Greece (1986), Hull City (October 1986), Sunderland (November 1986), Grantham Town (mid-1987), Grimsby Town (November 1987), Chesterfield (non-contract, March-April 1988), Goole Town (player-manager, November 1989).
Soccer journeyman 'Terry' Curran would drift in and out of a game and play moderately...the next match he would perform like a world-beater...and that summed him up to a tee. He was also temperamental and occasionally produced something extra-special but was very disappointing at Bramall Lane having played splendidly for manager Jack Charlton at Wednesday! During his senior career (before slipping into non-League football in 1989) he appeared in more than 460 competitive games (412 in the Football League, scoring 72 goals).

CURRIE, Anthony William
Midfielder: 375+1 apps. 67 goals
Born: Edgware, Middlesex, 1 January 1950
Career: Childs Hill Primary & Whitefields Secondary Modern Schools (London), Hendon Boys, Queen's Park Rangers (as a junior), Chelsea (trainee), Watford (professional, September 1967), BLADES (£26,500, February 1968), Leeds United (£245,000, June 1976), Queen's Park Rangers (August 1979), Chesham United, Southend United (briefly), Torquay United (February-May 1984), Hendon, July 1984, retiring in May 1985)
Capped by England at Youth team level (against France and Eire) as a Watford player, Tony Currie also played for the England Under-23 side on nine occasions and won his only full cap against Northern Ireland in May 1972.
At school he played as a centre-half and skippered the side before changing his style and position to become an inspirational midfielder schemer who could turn a game on its end with one amazing pass or a stunning piece of artistry. He netted on his United debut against Spurs some three weeks after joining the club and quickly established himself in the first XI going on to score almost 70 goals in more than 375 appearances, and helping the Blades win promotion in 1971, before transferring to Leeds. A star player in the eyes of the press, his name often hit the headlines thus: 'Red Hot' Currie and Currie had 'em on the run...and of course he was the 'blond bombshell' of the Sheffield Blades.

(L-R) Tony Currie of Sheffield United holds off Doug Fraser of Nottingham Forest

CURTIS, John Charles
Defender: 13+3 apps
Born: Nuneaton, 3 September 1978
Career: Manchester united (trainee, August 1994, professional October 1995), Barnsley (on loan November 1999), Blackburn Rovers (£2.25 million, June 2000), BLADES (on loan, March-May 2003).
Signed as defensive cover by manager Neil Warnock in readiness for the final run-in at the end of the 2002-03 season, experienced defender John Curtis, a former England Schoolboy, Youth, 'B' and Under-21 international (16 caps gained in the alter category) had been frozen out by Rovers' boss Graeme Souness at Ewood Park but was a huge asset to the Blades as the pressure mounted. He made only 19 appearances for Manchester United 30 for Barnsley and more than 70 for Rovers. He like his colleagues was a bitterly disappointed man when the Blades lost to Wolves in the 2003 Play-off Final.

CUTBUSH, William John
Full-back: 152+3 apps. one goal
Born: Malta, 28 June 1949
Career: Kent Boys, Tottenham Hotspur (trainee, June 1964, professional, September 1966), Fulham (July 1972), BLADES (£20,000, March 1977), Wichita Wings/USA (summer 1979).
John Cutbush, who was initially a midfielder before switching to right-back, never made the Spurs' first team but went on to play in 160 League and Cup games for Fulham, appearing in the 1975 FA Cup Final defeat by West Ham. He moved to Bramall Lane on transfer deadline day in 1977 and was a first-choice selection four years before his release following relegation to the Fourth Division 1981.
* Cutbush's father Dennis was an England amateur international left-half who played for Maidstone United and the Royal Navy.

CYPRUS INTERNATIONAL SOCCER TOURNAMENT
Competing in this competition in June 1974, United played five games, their full record being:

P	W	D	L	F	A
5	3	1	1	15	3

The Blades defeated Salamas 7-0 (Alan Woodward hit a hat-trick) and Apoel 4-0 and draw 1-1 with Levski Spartak (Bulgaria) in their group matches. After defeating Hamilton Academical 3-0 in the semi-final, they lost to Levski Spartak 2-0 in the Final.

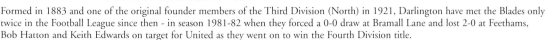

DARLINGTON

United's playing record against the Quakers:

Football League

Venue	P	W	D	L	F	A
Home	1	0	1	0	0	0
Away	1	1	0	0	2	0
Totals	2	1	1	0	2	0

FA Cup

Venue	P	W	D	L	F	A
Home	1	0	0	1	0	1

League Cup

Venue	P	W	D	L	F	A
Home	1	1	0	0	3	1
Away	2	1	1	0	3	2
Totals	3	2	1	0	6	3

Northern League

Venue	P	W	D	L	F	A
Home	2	2	0	0	12	1
Away	2	1	0	1	3	4
Totals	4	3	0	1	15	5

Formed in 1883 and one of the original founder members of the Third Division (North) in 1921, Darlington have met the Blades only twice in the Football League since then - in season 1981-82 when they forced a 0-0 draw at Bramall Lane and lost 2-0 at Feethams, Bob Hatton and Keith Edwards on target for United as they went on to win the Fourth Division title.
Earlier, season 1910-11, the Quakers riding their luck a little, surprisingly knocked United out off the FA Cup in the 1st round.
The Blades ousted the Quakers from the League Cup 5-3 on aggregate (after extra-time) in a closely fought 1st round tie in 1998-99, winning 3-1 at home after drawing 2-2 at The Feethams.
The Blades defeated Darlington 7-1 and 5-0 in successive home games n the Northern League in seasons 1891-92 and 1892-93.
Billy McEwan was manager of both clubs while Jack English played for the Blades and managed the Quakers. Ken Furphy played for Darlington and later managed the Blades. Others who have played for both clubs include Jack Almond, Bob Bolam, John Burridge, Jimmy Donnelly, Peter Duffield, Ashley Fickling, Bill Fleming, Charlie Henderson (Darlington trialist), John Hope, Cliff Mason, John Reed, Alan Roberts, Albert Trueman, Jimmy Waugh, Gordon Williams and Arthur Wharton.

DARWEN

United's playing record against Darwen:

Football League

Venue	P	W	D	L	F	A
Home	2	2	0	0	4	1
Away	2	0	1	1	4	6
Totals	4	2	1	1	8	7

Darwen (the team from the Lancashire cotton town) was formed in 1870 and were the first club to be relegated in the Football League. They played the Blades in seasons 1892-93 (Division 2 when both clubs were promoted to the top flight via the Test Match system) & 1893-94 (Division 1) and always gave a good account of themselves, twice losing at Bramall Lane (2-0 and 2-1 respectively) but winning 3-1 and then drawing 3-3 at their compact Barley Bank ground.
In 1881 Darwen reached the semi-final stage of the FA Cup.
Players who have served with both clubs include Tom Egan and Bruce Longworth.

DAVIES, David Walter

Inside-forward: 30 apps. 9 goals
Born: Treharris, Glamorgan, 1 October 1888
Career: Merthyr Town, Treharris (June 1911), Oldham Athletic (£180, May 1912), Stockport County (January 1913), BLADES (April 1913), Merthyr Town (August 1919), Treharris (August 1920-May 1921).
A Welsh international (two caps gained, both against Ireland in 1912 and 1913) David Davies netted 37 goals in a season for Treharris before joining Oldham in 1912. He made a great start to his career with the Latics, scoring in the first minute of his debut. Unfortunately he was injured soon afterwards and struggled to get back into the first team. A player with excellent ball control, his tricky, mazy runs made him a firm favourite with the fans but sadly WW1 put paid to his ambitions. He had two seasons in Welsh football before handing up his boots.

DAVIES, Frederick H

Inside-left/half-back: 29 apps. 7 goals
Born: Lancashire circa 1868.
Career: Ardwick, BLADES (August 1891-April 1894). Later emigrated to the USA.
After joining the Blades in 1891, Fred Davies played only one game in the Northern League but then did exceedingly well in the club's first Football League campaign of 1892-93, scoring five times in eight matches. Remaining at Bramall Lane until the end of the 1893-94 season he then chose to quit the game and move over to the States.

DAVIES, Joseph

Right or left winger/inside-forward: 18 apps. 7 goals
Born: Chirk, 1870. Died: Wales, 1943.
Career: Chirk, Everton (December 1888), Chirk (again), Ardwick (August 1891), BLADES (January 1894), Ardwick (November 1895), Millwall Athletic (May 1896), Reading (May 1898), Manchester City (September 1900), Stockport County (August 1901), Chirk, for a third time (May 1902, retiring in April 1906).
Versatile forward Joe Davies scored 25 goals in a total of 84 League games spread over a period of 13 years. He made over 150 appearances for his beloved Chirk.

DAVISON, Aidan John

Goalkeeper: 1+1 apps.

Born: Sedgefield, 11 May 1968

Career: Billingham Synthonia FC, Notts County (professional, March 1988), Bury (£6,000, October, 1989), Millwall (free transfer, August 1991), Bolton Wanderers (£25,000, July 1993), Hull City (on loan, November 1996), Bradford City (free, March 1997), Grimsby Town (free, July 1997), BLADES (free, August 1999, signed as cover for Simon Tracey), Bradford City again (free, January 2000).

A Northern Ireland international, capped three times at senior level and once by the 'B' team, Aidan Davison was an Auto-Windscreen Shield and Third Division promotion winner with the Mariners in 1998. Brilliant on high crosses, he made his 250th club appearance in 2002.

DAVISON, Robert

Striker: 19+8 apps. 6 goals

Born: South Shields, 17 July 1959

Career: Seaham Colliery, Huddersfield Town (£1,000, July 1980), Halifax Town (£20,000, August 1981), Derby County (£90,000, December 1982), Leeds United (£350,000, November 1987), Derby County again (on loan, September 1991), BLADES (on loan, March 1992), Leicester City (£50,000, August 1992), BLADES for a second time (free transfer, September 1993), Rotherham United (free, October 1994-May 1996), Hull City (on loan, November 1995).

Sharp-shooter Bobby Davison had a wonderfully successful career at club level. He scored 170 goals in 453 League games, having his best spells with Derby for whom he struck 91 times in 216 outings, while making a fair contribution to the Blades when partnering Brian Deane. He was Second Division championship winner with Derby in 1987 and Leeds in 1990.

De GOEY, Leendert

Midfielder: 39 apps. 5 goals

Born: Rotterdam, 29 February 1952.

Career: Sparta Rotterdam, BLADES (£125,000, August 1979), Go Ahead Eagles/Deventer (May 1980).

Efficient, hard-working Dutch midfielder Len De Goey spent only one season at Bramall Lane before returning to his home country.

DE VOGT, Wilko

Goalkeeper: 8+1 apps

Born: Breda, Holland, 17 September 1975

Career: NAC Breda, BLADES (July 2001-May 2003).

Wilko De Vogt (6ft 2ins tall, 12st 13lbs in weight) was signed as cover for Simon Tracey. He was called into action just eight times, but did well enough to get his contract renewed for a further 12 months in March 2002. Wore the 'unlucky' No 13 jersey at the 'Lane.'

DEANE, Brian Christopher

Striker: 270+3 apps. 119 goals

Born: Leeds, 7 February 1968

Career: Doncaster Rovers (juniors, April 1984, professional December 1985), BLADES (£30,000, July 1988), Leeds United (record £2.7 million, July 1993), BLADES (£1.5 million, July 1997), Benfica (£1 million, January 1998), Middlesbrough (£3.3 million, October 1998), Leicester City (£150,000, November 2001

Over a period of five years, 1993-98, striker Brian Deane was transferred between clubs for a total of a £8.5 million club with the Blades benefiting most from the sales. After his initial move to Bramall Lane in 1988, he formed a wonderful partnership with Tony Agana, scoring 106 goals over a five-year period and helping the Blades gain successive promotions from the Third to the First Division (1989 & 1990 respectively) before his departure to Elland Road - much to the disgust of the Blades' supporters and indeed, against the wishes of his manager! Capped at senior level by England on three occasions as a United player (v. New Zealand twice and Spain) he has also appeared in three 'B' internationals.

Deane had the pleasure of scoring the first goal in Premiership football - for the Blades v. Manchester United at Bramall Lane on 15 August 1992. His second in that match (from the penalty spot) set up a 2-1 win. This was the Blades' first penalty award in nearly 60 matches. He has now netted almost 220 goals in well over 680 competitive games at club level (including his spell in Portugal) and in 2003 helped Leicester regain their Premiership status at the first attempt when he formed a lethal partnership in attack with the impish Paul Dickov.

DEARDEN, William

Inside/centre-forward: 204+7 apps. 72 goals

Born: Oldham, 11 February 1944.

Career: Oldham Boys, Oldham Athletic (amateur, April 1959, professional, September 1963), Crewe Alexandra (December 1966), Chester (June 1968), BLADES (£10,000, April 1970), Chester (on loan, February 1976, signed permanently July 1976), Chesterfield (August 1977), Mansfield Town (trainer, 1979, later taking over as manager at Field Mill, July 1999-December 2001), Notts County (manager, January 2002).

A snip-of-a-signing by Blades' manager John Harris in 1970, Billy Dearden developed into one of the finest strikers in the First Division. He had a great pace and the ability to find openings in the tightest of situations and he finished well. He played fairly well with his three previous clubs (Oldham, Crewe and Chester) but had struggled at times with a cartilage injury. However, once he had taken root at 'the Lane' and following his switch from a wide position into the centre he became hot property! He was a promotion winner in 1971 (40 games played) and when he hung up his boots in 1979 he did so with the knowledge that he had scored 101 League goals in 405 appearances. He went on to give the Stags excellent service for a number of years. Dearden was also a fine club cricketer, playing for Crompton CC in the Central Lancashire League. He's a plumber and gas fitter by trade.

DEATHS

* United's Frank Levick died of pneumonia in February 1908, one month after breaking his collar-bone in a League game against Newcastle United.
* Walter 'Cocky' Bennett was killed in a colliery accident in 1908 (aged 34).
* Blades' left-winger Alf Jeffrey was 26 years of age when he died in January 1921.
* United forward Harry Hampson was 24 when he died of septicaemia in 1942.
* United player Jimmy Revill received injuries while serving his country in France during WW1. He later died in an English hospital (1917).
* United full-back Joe Carr was killed on the retreat from Dunkirk in 1940.
* United amateur John Fulford, serving with the RAF bomber command, was also killed in action during WW2.
* Former United centre-forward John Nibloe was killed in a car crash in Stourbridge in November 1964. He was only 25 years of age.
* United's reserve goalkeeper Keith Solomon died during a training session in 1981.
* Welsh international and former United midfielder/winger Trevor Hockey collapsed and died of a heart attack in April 1987, aged 43.
* Another former United player, Bob Benson, died in the dressing room after collapsing on the pitch when playing for Arsenal against Reading in a WW1 game at Highbury on 19 February 1916.
* Bury full-back Sam Wynne collapsed (and later died in the dressing room) during the first-half of a League game at Bramall Lane on 30 April 1927. The game was abandoned in the 40th minute with United 1-0 ahead. They won the 'replay' 2-0.
* In 1993 United goalkeeper Mel Rees died at the age 26 from cancer.
* Former United player Jimmy Yates committed suicide in 1922, aged 51.

DEBUTS

* Eric Houghton made his debut for Aston Villa in a Central League game against Sheffield United at Bramall Lane in 1928 and then received his first England cap on the same ground in October 1930.
* Fred Furniss made his debut for the Blades v. Everton (away) during an air-raid in May 1941. The match kicked off but it was a tense occasion as the all-clear signal was not sounded until half-time.
* It goes without saying that the eleven players used by United in the club's first games in the FA Cup, Football League, League Cup etc) were making their debuts in that specific competition, and in the first League campaign of 1892-93 the Blades gave debuts (in that competition) to 22 players. Thereafter, the highest total number of players who made their debuts in any one season, are as follows: 1895-96 (14), 1919-20 (14), 1987-88 (16), 1988-89 (14), 1995-96 (17) and 1997-98 (19). The fewest number of debutants for United in one campaign has been two, on three occasions only.
* In the club's first ever season of 1889-90 almost 50 players appeared in the senior side for the first time (all games) thus making their United debut.

DEFEATS

United's heaviest League defeat has been 10-3 away at Middlesbrough (Division 1) on 18 November 1933.
Their worst reverse in the FA Cup - 13-0 - was suffered away to Bolton Wanderers in a 2nd round tie on 1 February 1890.
In the League Cup, United's heaviest beating (goal-difference) has so far come at West Ham on 17 November 1971, the Hammers winning handsomely by 5-0.
The Blades lost 18 of their 38 League matches in 1905-06 (14 away); they succumbed to 26 defeats in 42 League matches in 1975-76 (10 at home, 16 away) and suffered 24 losses, 16 of them away (in 44 games) in 1987-88.
The Blades lost only four of their 34 League fixtures in 1899-1900 and four out of 46 in 1981-82 (all of them away).
In their first-ever League campaign of 1892-93 they were beaten only three times in 22 outings. They lost eight out of their 42 Second Division matches in 1938-39 and suffered seven defeats in 42 starts in 1970-71.

Other Heavy Defeats Suffered by United

Football League

2-9 v. Arsenal (away)	24.12.1932
1-8 v. Arsenal (away)	12.04.1930
1-7 v. Huddersfield Town (home)	12.11.1927
5-7 v. Blackburn Rovers (away)	03.03.1930
0-7 v. Tottenham Hotspur (away)	12.11.1949

FA Cup:

1-9 v. Notts County (away)	17.01.1891

League Cup

2-5 v. Stockport County (home)	24.09.1996
1-4 v. Leeds United (home)	10.10.1978

Wartime

2-9 v. Lincoln City (away)	14.09.1940
2-8 v. Sheffield Wed (away)	13.02.1943

Friendlies/Testimonials/Tours etc.

2-8 v. B'ham St George (away)	09.01.11892
0-7 v. Staveley (away)	09.11.1889
0-7 v. Grimsby Town (away)	15.02.1890

DEFENSIVE LEAGUE RECORDS

Low totals of goals conceded by the Blades' defence:

Season	Comp.	Games	Goals
1890-91	MCL	18	25
1891-92	NL	16	21
1892-93	FL2	22	19
1896-97	FL1	30	29
1899-00	FL1	34	33
1909-10	FL1	38	41
1914-15	FL1	38	41
1949-50	FL2	42	49
1958-59	FL2	42	48
1969-70	FL2	42	38
1970-71	FL2	42	39
1981-82	FL4	46	41

High totals of goals conceded by the Blades' defence:

1912-13	FL1	38	70
1925-26	FL1	42	82
1926-27	FL1	42	86
1927-28	FL1	42	86
1929-30	FL1	42	97
1933-34	FL1	42	101

In each of six successive seasons - 1925-26 to 1930-31 inclusive - United conceded 82 or more goals every campaign. During that period they played 252 League games (all in Division One) and gave away 520 goals (average 86.66 per season).

DELLAS, Traianos
Midfielder: 16+15 apps. 3 goals
Born: Thessalonika, Greece, 31 January 1976
Career: Aris Salonika, BLADES (£300,000, rising to £700,000, August 1997), AEK Athens (May 1998), AS Roma (Season 2002-03).
A 'giant' Greek Under-21 international midfielder (6ft 4ins tall), Tri Dellas's only season at 'the Lane' was hampered by injury. He later did well in his home country of Greece and also in Italy's Serie 'A'.

DEMPSEY, Mark James
Midfielder: 70+4 apps. 11 goals
Born: Manchester, 14 January 1964
Career: Manchester United (apprentice May 1978, professional January 1982), Swindon Town (on loan, January 1985), BLADES (on loan, August 1986, signed for £20,000, September 1986), Chesterfield (on loan, September 1988), Rotherham United (October 1988), Macclesfield Town (June 1991-May 1993), Gainsborough Trinity, Frickley Colliery, Burton Albion, Altrincham, Matlock Town (player-manager), Ratcliffe Borough (July 1998-2003). Also registered as a part-time coach at Old Trafford (looking after the younger players). Mark Dempsey, who was capped by the Republic of Ireland at Youth and Under-21 levels, spent two years at Bramall Lane during which time had a loan spell at Saltergate. He made his League debut for Swindon in 1985 (whilst on loan) and made just two senior appearances for the Reds (his first as a substitute in the European Cup-winners Cup v. Spartak Varna, home, in November 1983) before his move to the Blades for whom he did well in centre-field alongside Peter Beagrie, Steve Foley and Colin Morris. He had almost 150 outings in League football up to his retirement from senior League football in 1993.

DENIAL, Geoffrey
Wing-half: 11 apps.
Born: Stocksbridge, 31 January 1932.
Career: BLADES (amateur, June 1950, professional, January 1952), Oxford United (September 1956-May 1963)
After failing to establish himself in the first XI at Bramall Lane, wing-half Denial became an instrumental figure at Oxford as the Manor Ground club moved menacingly through the realms of the Southern League to reach the Football League in 1962. He appeared at left back, wing-half, inside-forward and as a striker during his seven years with the 'U's', appearing in more than 200 senior games (51 goals scored) before his release in May 1963. He played alongside Ron Atkinson on many occasions.

DERBY COUNTY
United's playing record against the Rams:

Football League

Venue	P	W	D	L	F	A
Home	44	27	7	10	79	52
Away	44	9	6	29	54	97
Totals	88	36	13	39	133	149

FA Cup

Home	1	0	0	1	0	1
Away	1	0	0	1	0	3
Neutral	4	2	2	0	7	3
Totals	6	2	2	2	7	7

WW1

Home	1	1	0	0	2	0
Away	1	0	0	1	1	2
Totals	2	1	0	1	3	2

WW2

Home	1	0	0	1	0	2
Away	2	0	0	2	4	7

Totals	3	0	0	3	4	9
Birmingham Cup						
Away	1	1	0	0	2	0
United Counties League						
Home	2	0	0	2	4	7
Away	1	0	0	1	0	2
Totals	3	0	0	3	4	9
Watney Cup						
Away	1	0	0	1	0	1

Derby County, formed by members of the Derbyshire County Cricket Club in 1884, originally played at the Racecourse ground and sported amber, chocolate and pale blue shirts. Founder members of the Football League in 1888, they moved to The Baseball ground in 1895 and stayed there until 1997 when Pryde Park became their new home.

The Blades first met the Rams in League competition in 1893-94 when they lost both First Division matches by the same score of 2-1.the following season the Rams again double-up with two 4-1 victories.
When the Blades took on Derby in a home game on 21 December 1895, the referee sent a telegram to Bramall Lane that read: 'Train delayed. Manage till I arrive.' He did arrive and the game ended all square at 1-1. United finally registered their first League win over County later that season (2-0 in March).
The Rams were 4-0 up on United in a League game at The Baseball Ground in January 1931, Jack Bowers having netted a hat-trick. The final scored was 4-3.
The Blades beat the Rams 3-1 at Bramall Lane in April 1961 to clinch promotion to the First Division.
United beat County 4-1 in the 1899 FA Cup Final at The Crystal Palace in front of 73,833 spectators (realising record receipts of £2,747). Walter 'Cocky' Bennett, Billy Beer, Jack Almond and Fred Priest scored for the Blades in the last half-hour after John Boag had given the Rams a first-half lead.
Derby were again beaten by the Blades in the semi-final of the 1901-02 competition. After successive 1-1 draws, United came through at The City Ground, Nottingham with a 1-0 victory courtesy of another Fred Priest goal.
United's best home League win over the Rams is 4-1 in 1912-13 (Joe Kitchen scored twice). They also run up two 5-3 victories at The Baseball Ground, in 1903-04 (when Arthur Brown scored twice) and in 1913-14 (when Billy Gillespie and Stan Fazackerley shared the goals).
Since WW2 (covering 57 full seasons) the clubs have met only 20 times in League action, while previously between 1895 and 1947, United lost only once at home to County in 25 matches.
The Blades played in the United Counties League in seasons 1893-94 & 1894-95. A crowd of 25,322 saw the Rams beat United 1-0 in the semi-final of the Watney Cup in August 1970.
Ex-Blades forward Colin Addison was manager of County from 1979-82 while Gary Ablett, Brett Angell, Bobby Barclay, Dickie Bird, Val Borbokis, Jeff Bourne, John Burridge, Barry Butlin, Bobby Campbell, Willie Carlin, Bert Chandler, Alan Cork, Gordon Cowans, Terry Curran, Richard Cushlow (United reserve), Bobby Davison, Stan Fazackerley, Jimmy Hagan, Glenn Hodges, Billy Hodgson, Jonathan Hunt, Alf Jeffries, Freddie Jessop, Jeff King, Rob Kozluk, Martin Kuhl, John McAlle, Colin Morris, Shane Nicholson, Paul Parker, Tom Paton, Jack Peart, Bruce Rioch, Duncan Ritchie, Dean Saunders, Paul Simpson, Fred Smith, Joe Smith, George Thompson, John Tudor (with County briefly), and Harry Wilkes are among the many players who have served with both clubs. Gerry Summers, a United player, later joined the coaching staff at County, likewise John Poole.

DERBY JUNCTION

Blades' playing record against the 'Junction':
FA Cup

Venue	P	W	D	L	F	A
Away	1	1	0	0	1	0
Midland Counties League						
Home	1	1	0	0	2	0
Away	1	1	0	0	3	1
Totals	2	2	0	0	5	1

The Blades sent the Derby side up the junction by knocking them out of the FA Cup in the 1st qualifying round of the 1890-91 tournament, TBA Clarke hitting the all-important goal (1-0) at Junction's quaint Aboretum ground. A railway team, Junction played in the well-organised Midland Counties League from 1889-93 and they met the Blades in this competition.

DERBY MIDLAND

Blades' playing record against the 'Midland':
Midland Counties League

Venue	P	W	D	L	F	A
Home	1	0	0	1	0	1
Away	1	1	0	0	5	2
Totals	2	1	0	1	5	2

Derby Midland finished next to bottom of the MC L in 1890-91, winning only five matches out of 18 - one against the Blades at Bramall Lane in late February. Earlier in the season Billy Bridgewater scored a hat-trick when United won 5-2 on Midland soil.

DERRY, Shaun Peter

Midfielder: 73+10 apps. one goal
Born: Nottingham, 6 December 1977,
Career: Notts County (apprentice, July 1994, professional April 1996), BLADES (£750,000, January 1998), Portsmouth (£300,000, March 2000).
Compact, hard-working, aggressive at times, midfielder Shaun Derry played in almost 100 League and Cup games for the Magpies before moving to Bramall Lane in 1998. He supported Nottingham Forest as a lad but chose Meadow Lane instead of The City Ground. He was a key member of Pompey's promotion-winning side of 2003, having helped Notts County on their way to lifting the Third Division title in 1998.

DEVLIN, Paul
Forward: 141+28 apps. 29 goals
Born: Birmingham, 14 April 1972
Career: Stafford Rangers, Notts County (£40,000, February 1992), Birmingham City (February 1996), BLADES (£200,000, March 1998), Notts County (on loan, October 1998), Birmingham City (on loan, February 2002, signing permanently for £200,000 in May 2002).
A smart raiding forward with good skills and a big heart, Paul Devlin made 189 appearances and scored 31 goals for Notts County before moving to the team he supported as a lad, Birmingham City. He netted 34 goals in 89 outings for Blues but following his move from St Andrew's he had to work overtime to hold down a first team place at Bramall Lane. After helping Blues gain promotion to the Premiership he rejoined the second city club on a permanent basis. Devlin, who in 1995 gained an Anglo-Italian Cup winners medal with Notts County, has now played in eight* full internationals for Scotland.

DIRECTORS
In it's early years Sheffield United Football Club was run by President/Chairman, Mr Michael J Ellison, and a Ground Committee headed by Charles Stokes.
Ellison held office until 1899 before being replaced by Lord Hawke (as President) while Stokes remained as the Committee Chairman.
It was also in the year 1899 that United became a Limited Company with the first Board of Directors being elected. And this has been so ever since.
Hawke relinquished his Presidency in 1917 and it was not until 1924 that his replacement was found, Charles Clegg accepting the role as well as acting as Chairman of the Board of Directors (Sheffield United Cricket & Football Club).
Clegg remained in office until his death in 1937, having been knighted ten years earlier.
In 1949 - after some years without a President - George Platt (later to become Life President) moved into office and was subsequently replaced in 1959 by Ernest Graham.
Then, in 1968, there was a change in the club's administration with the separate committees being dissolved.
In 1974 Dick Wragg took over as club President, holding his position until 1997 when Mike McDonald was named Chairman of the plc.
A year later Carlo Colombotti accepted the role of Chairman of the plc with Kevin McCabe becoming Chairman of the Football Club. (See under CHAIRMEN).
In 2002 film-star/actor Sean Bean was elected as a Director at Bramall Lane and along with D Dooley (Chairman), K McCabe, A Laver, M Dudley, A Bamford, S Slinn and C Steer, form the current Board of Directors at the club.

D'JAFFO, Laurent
Striker: 46+28 apps. 12 goals
Born: Aquitane, France, 5 November 1970
Career: Paris Red Star, Ayr United (October 1997), Bury (July 1998), Stockport County (£100,000, August 1999), BLADES (£100,000, February 2000), Aberdeen (season 2002-03).
A six-foot, 13st 5lbs Frenchman Laurent D'Jaffo played for a relatively unknown Paris club before joining Ayr in 1997. He netted nine goals in 43 games for the Shakers, struggled to a certain extent at Edgeley Park and then picked up a calf injury which delayed the start of his career with the Blades, although in the end he did appear in 38 matches, rarely completing 90 minutes however. The following season he was in and out of the side (mainly due to other players being injured or suspended) and when his contract expired in May 2002, he left the club, signing for the Scottish Premiership club, Aberdeen.

DOANE, Benjamin Nigel
Right-back: 20+6 apps. one goal
Born: Sheffield, 22 December 1979.
Career: BLADES (trainee, April 1996, professional, July 1998), Mansfield Town (on loan-March-April 2003).
Attacking right-back Ben Doane joined the Blades straight from school and his only goal for the club so far has been his 25-yard screamer in the League game at Crewe in March 2002 which earned a point from a 2-2 draw.

DOBSON, Samuel
Inside-forward: 37 apps. 19 goals
Born: Hutton near Preston circa 1868.
Career: Preston North End, BLADES (March 1891, retired May 1893).
Inside-forward Sammy Dobson scored five goals in eight League games for his home-town club PNE before joining the Blades in 1891. He did exceptionally well at Bramall Lane before his career came to an abrupt end following injury. He was forced to retire in the summer of 1893.

DOCHERTY, John
Outside-right: 47 apps. 13 goals
Born: Glasgow, 29 April 1940
Career: St Roch's FC, Brentford (professional, July 1959), BLADES (£6,000, March 1961), Brentford (December 1965), Reading (February 1969), Brentford again (March 1970 to May 1974).
After netting twice in 17 League games for the Bees, right-winger John Docherty made his Blades' debut in a 0-0 draw with Brighton & Hove Albion as the team headed towards promotion. He quit the game with 342 League appearances and 83 goals under his belt.

DOCHERTY, John
Inside-right/centre-forward: 21 apps. 10 goals
Born: Scotland, circa 1870
Career: Motherwell, BLADES (November 1894), Bury (November 1895).
John Docherty teamed up well with Harry Hammond and Joe Davies in the Blades' forward-line and scored his fair share of goals.

77

DODDS, Emphraim

Centre-forward: 203 apps. 128 goals

Born: Grangemouth, Stirlingshire, Scotland, 7 September 1915,

Career: Medomsley Juniors, Huddersfield Town (amateur, June 1932, professional September 1932), BLADES (free transfer, May 1934), Blackpool (£10,000, March 1939), Shamrock Rovers (1946), Everton (November 1946), Lincoln City (£6,000 October 1948). He retired in September 1950 after being expelled from the Football League in June 1950 over his role as recruiting agent for the Bogota-based Millionarios Club who were affiliated to the Colombian National League but not FIFA. He later became a successful businessman in Blackpool.

'Jock' Dodds had rare pace for such a big man. He certainly didn't lack enthusiasm and was a smart finisher, scoring more than 125 goals in a fraction over 200 games for the Blades before his move to Blackpool for family reasons in 1939. His 100th goal for United came in his 154th match...against Spurs on 12 September 1938 - some 24 hours later he was transferred to Blackpool. Ironically he had been joint top-scorer with the player he replaced at Bloomfield Road - Bob Finan - in the Second Division in 1935-36 with 34 goals. He went on to net his 200th League goal for Lincoln City with whom he ended his senior career in 1950.

He was top-scorer for the Imps in both his seasons at Sincil Bank. Dodds gained eight wartime caps for Scotland, lined up for the Blades in the 1936 FA Cup Final defeat by Arsenal (he headed against the bar towards the end of the game) and before leaving for Blackpool, he played his part in United's promotion winning campaign of 1938-39, appearing 29 games and netting 17 goals.

West Ham United's Charlie Bicknell (l) and Sheffield United's Jock Dodds (r) in action

DONCASTER ROVERS

United's playing record against Rovers:

Football League

Venue	P	W	D	L	F	A
Home	8	6	2	0	20	5
Away	8	1	4	3	7	9
Totals	16	7	6	3	27	14

FA Cup

Away	2	2	0	0	5	1

League Cup

Home	1	0	1	0	1	1
Away	1	0	0	1	1	3
Totals	2	0	1	1	2	4

WW2

Home	8	4	2	2	23	13
Away	9	3	0	6	11	21
Totals	17	7	2	8	34	34

Yorkshire & Humberside Cup

Away	1	0	1	0	0	0

Other

Home	1	1	0	0	2	1

Sheffield & Hallamshire County Shield

Home	9	8	0	1	33	11
Away	11	2	3	6	14	23
Totals	20	10	3	7	47	34

Others

Home	1	1	0	0	1	0
Away	1	0	1	0	0	0
Totals	2	1	1	0	1	0

Doncaster Rovers, formed in 1879 and a professional club since 1885, played initially at the Intake Ground before moving to the Bennetthorpe Ground in 1920 and onto Low Pasture (now Belle Vue) two years later.

Elected to the Football League (Division 2) in 1901, they twice lost their place in the competition before eventually clocking up 71 seasons overall prior to a third demotion in 1998, this time to the Conference.

The first of the eight League games between the Blades and Rovers took place on New Year's Day 1936 (Division 2) when United won 3-0, later gaining a 0-0 draw at Belle Vue.

United claimed their best win in 1956-57, Derek Hawksworth obliging with a hat-trick in a 4-0 romp at Bramall Lane. Their only triumph at Belle Vue arrived on Boxing Day 1952 when Harold Brook scored twice (as he had done in the earlier 2-2 draw) as the Blades edged towards the Second Division title.

United's two FA Cup wins came in 1937-38 (2-0 in the 3rd round) and 1988-89 (2-1 in round 2).

Jack Almond, Bill Archer, Albert Attree, Reg Baines, Bill Brelsford, Billy Bridgewater, Billy Bromage, Harry Buddery, Ted Burgin, Fred Charles, Jon Cullen, Terry Curran, Brian Deane, Alonzo Drake, Colin Grainger, Steve Hawes, Ted Hemsley, Keith Kettleborough (also Rovers manager), Mick Killourhy, Charlie Leyfield, Clive Mendonca, John Nibloe, Don Peattie, Cliff Powell, Mark Rankine, George Raynor (United reserve), Bobby Rooney, Graham Shaw, Tom Simons, George Simpson, Steve Thompson, Tyrone Thompson, Harry Wainwright, Alan Warboys, Norman Wharton, Billy Whitehurst, Paul A Williams are among the many players who have served with both clubs over the years.

DONNELLY, James
Inside/outside-right: 93 apps. 23 goals
Born: South Bank, 1879. Died: 1959.
Career: South Bank FC, Darlington St Augustine's, BLADES (November 1902), Leicester Fosse (£150, May 1907), Darlington (June 1910),

Jimmy Donnelly scored two goals on his League debut for the Blades v. Wolves in March 1903 (won 3-0). Decidedly quick with a strong-running action he averaged a goal every four games for the Blades before helping Leicester gain promotion to the First Division and then he notched the Foxes' first-ever goal in the top-flight. He was a key member of the Quakers' squad that reached the last 16 of the FA Cup in 1911 and the one that took the North-Eastern League title two years later. During his career Donnelly netted 52 goals in 163 League outings.

DOUBLES
In 1960-61 United claimed a record nine doubles in their programme of 42 League matches. They managed eight in 1981-82 when they won the Fourth Division title.

The most doubles suffered by the Blades in one single League campaign is seven in 1967-68.

United have now completed a seasonal League double over Blackburn Rovers on nine occasions - a club record.

Aston Villa with 14 have achieved the most over the Blades.

Everton have twice doubled up over the Blades with two 5-1 wins - in 1908-09 and again in 1931-32, while in 1933-34 Huddersfield Town won both League matches with 4-1 and 6-1 scorelines.

In their first season of League football (1892-93) United beat Burslem Port Vale 10-0 away and followed up with a 4-0 victory at Bramall Lane. The Blades also carved up Manchester City by 8-3 and 4-2 in 1925-26, whipped Barnsley 5-0 and 6-1 in 1956-57 and clobbered Portsmouth 5-0 and 5-1 in 1969-70.

DOWNES, Walter John
Midfielder: 8+4 apps. one goal
Born: Hammersmith, London, 9 June 1961
Career: Wimbledon (junior, July 1977, professional, January 1979), Newport County (on loan, December 1987-January 1988), BLADES (February 1988, retired in May 1988 to join the coaching staff at Bramall Lane), Brentford (manager-coach, then manager during season 2002-03).

Wally Downes appeared in 208 League games (14 goals scored) for the Dons, helping the London club climb up the ladder from the Fourth to the First Division in double-quick time. A big buddy of manager Dave Bassett, Downes retired in 1988 to join the coaching staff at 'the Lane'. He took his first managerial position with Brentford in 2002.

DRAKE, Alonzo Robson
Forward: 98 apps. 20 goals
Born: Parkgate, Rotherham, 16 April 1884
Career: Parkgate FC, Rotherham Town (on trial, 1901), Doncaster Rovers, BLADES (June 1903), Birmingham (£700, December 1907), Queen's Park Rangers (August 1908), Huddersfield Town (season 1909-10).

A hard working, dashing player said to have had bad luck with his shooting, Alonzo Drake was perhaps better known as a cricketer, playing as a professional for Yorkshire for five years: 1909-14. He appeared in 157 matches as a middle-order left-hand batsman and slow left-arm bowler. He did the double in 1913 and followed up by taking 158 wickets in the next season (average 15.30). All told he scored 4,816 runs (average 21.69) and claimed 480 wickets at 18.00 each for the Tykes. He took 100 wickets and scored 1,000 runs in a season on two occasions, with his best run return coming in 1911 when he notched 1,487 for an average of 30.97. His best bowling figures were 10-35 for Yorkshire v. Somerset. His cricketing career was cut short through poor health, leading to his sudden demise at the relatively early age of 34 in Honley, Huddersfield on 14 February, 1919

DRAPER, James
Inside-right: 13 apps. 3 goals
Born: Kimberley, (Nottingham) 1878
Career: Kimberley FC, BLADES (November 1895), Ilkeston Town (August 1897).

Jim Draper was a fairly mundane inside-forward who was given few opportunities at Bramall Lane.

DRAWS
* The Blades have been involved in one 5-5 draw in League football - at Leicester City in November 1951 (Division 2). They also drew 5-5 with an All Stars XI at Bramall Lane in October 1966 (Cecil Coldwell's testimonial match).

* So far they have also figured in six 4-4 scorelines in League action: versus Bury (1926), Sunderland (1928), Bury (1949), Southampton (1953), Walsall (1980) and Birmingham City (1996).

79

* One FA Cup match has also finished 4-4 - against Liverpool, semi-final replay in March 1899, while another testimonial/friendly with Frickley Athletic ended all square at 4-4 in 1992.
* United have drawn most League games against Blackburn Rovers - total 34. They have shared the points with Sheffield Wednesday 33 times and Manchester City 31.
* United had 12 draws out of 15 home games in 1949.
* United drew 10 of their 30 League games in 1896-97; 12 out of 34 in 1899-1900; 13 out of 38 in 1914-15; 18 out of 42 (11 at home) in 1920-21; 18 out of 42 Premiership matches in 1993-94 and 17 of their 46 Nationwide League games in 1997-98.
* Only three draws were recorded in their first season of League football of 1892-93 (22 games played). They drew just twice in 34 outings in 1904-05 and shared the points on five occasions in each of seasons 1902-03 (34 games), 1913-14 (38 matches), 1951-52 (42 fixtures) and 1969-70 (42 encounters).

DRUMMOND, John
Left-winger: 89 apps. 24 goals
Born: Edinburgh circa 1869
Career: Partick Thistle, Preston North End (August 1890), BLADES (February 1891), Liverpool (May 1894), Barnsley St Peter's (season 1895-97).
Jack Drummond was one of three players signed by the Blades from Preston North End in 1891 - the other two being Billy Hendry and Sammy Dobson. An ebullient winger, he had pace, skill, good shot and a positive approach - and his presence certainly brought a new dimension to the United team. He averaged roughly a goal every four games for the Blades, netting the crucial one that won the Test Match against Accrington at Nottingham in 1893 and so securing United's place in the First Division.
* He was related to the celebrated Preston North End player Geordie Drummond.

DRYDEN, John R
Outside-right: 19 apps. 5 goals
Born: Broomhill, Northumberland, 21 August 1908. Died: 1975.
Career: Ashington (1930), Newcastle United (£175, September 1932), Exeter City (May 1934), BLADES (May 1935), Bristol City (July 1936), Burnley (May 1938), Peterborough United (August 1939, retiring during WW2).
Dainty on his feet, quick and direct, outside-right Johnny Dryden had an interesting career that saw him score 26 goals in a total of 113 League matches. He was related to Jackie Milburn (ex-Newcastle & England) while his younger brother, James George Dryden, played briefly for Manchester City.

DUFFIELD, Peter
Striker: 47+34 apps. 20 goals
Born: Middlesbrough, 4 February 1969
Career: Middlesbrough (apprentice, June 1984, professional November 1986), BLADES (from August 1987), Halifax Town (on loan, March 1988), Rotherham United (on loan, March 1991), Blackpool (on loan, July 1992), Crewe Alexandra (on loan, January 1993), Stockport County (on loan, March 1993), Hamilton Academicals (contract, September 1993), Airdrieonians (July 1995), Raith Rovers (March 1996), Morton (November 1997), Falkirk (August 1998), Darlington (January 1999), York City (July 2000), Boston United (season 2002-03).
A busy nomadic striker, Peter Duffield, 5ft 6ins tall and weighing barely 10st 4lbs, has already suffered three broken legs during his career. His first set-back came as a Blades player against Swindon Town in an away Second Division match in December 1989. He was out of action for eight months. His other two breaks were in the same season (2001-02) with York City. Nevertheless, he bounced back each time and when the 2002-03 campaign ended his playing record was excellent - *** senior appearances and ** goals...10** coming in 186 games after leaving Bramall Lane. He was a Third Division promotion winner with the Blades in 1989.

DUGGAN CUP
In season 1932-33 and 1933-34 United played the Irish club Shamrock Rovers for the Duggan Cup.
A crowd of 20,000 saw the Blades win the first 'Final' 5-4 before drawing 1-1 in front of 10,000 spectators in the second.

DUNCAN, James
Forward: 18 apps. 3 goals
Born: Scotland, circa 1875
Career: Boys of Dundee (August 1889-May 1890),
Utility forward Jim Duncan spent nine months with the Blades during which time he occupied all five front-line positions. He played at inside-left in the club's first-ever game v. Nottingham Rangers on 7 September 1889 and his last senior appearance was on the right-wing against Rotherham Town in the replay of the Sheffield County Cup Final on 22 March 1890.

DUNDEE
Blades' playing record v. Dundee:
Others

Venue	P	W	D	L	F	A
Home	1	1	0	0	2	1
Away	1	1	0	0	1	0
Totals	2	2	0	0	3	1

These two games against Dundee (formed in 1893) were played in the Anglo-Scottish tournament 1979-80.

DUNDEE UNITED
Blades' playing record v. United:
Others

Venue	P	W	D	L	F	A
Home	1	0	1	0	0	0
Away	1	0	0	1	0	2
Totals	2	0	1	1	0	2

These two Texaco Cup matches against Dundee United (formed in 1909) took place in season 1973-74.

DUNNE, James

Centre-forward: 190 apps. 167 goals

Born: Ringsend near Dublin, 3 September 1905. Died: Dublin, 14 November 1949.

Career: Gaelic football (Dublin), Shamrock Rovers (May 1923), New Brighton (November 1925), BLADES (£500, February 1926). Arsenal (£8,250, September 1933), Southampton (£1,000, July 1936), Shamrock Rovers (June 1937); retired in May 1942 to become coach of the Bohemians club, later having a third spell with Shamrock Rovers as player-coach (1947-49).

Fair-haired Irishman Jimmy Dunne bided his time in the reserves at Bramall Lane for more than three years, and in fact, in 1927, was placed on the transfer list at £5,000...but there weren't any takers! He then exploded onto the First Division scene with 36 goals in 39 League games in 1929-30 as the Blades narrowly avoided relegation. Over the next few seasons he was virtually unstoppable, savaging defenders all over the country. Regarded as the 'ideal centre-forward' particularly strong in the air, he netted 41 times in League matches in 1930-31, followed up with another 33 the very next season and bagged 26 in 1932-33. He still holds the honour of being the last Irishman to score 30 or more League goals in three successive seasons.

When he moved to Highbury in 1933, he joined up with seven other quality forwards who were already on the Gunners' books who between them had a combined aggregate of 971 League goals. He scored 13 goals in 33 games for the Gunners before transferring to The Dell in 1936 - after failing to make Arsenal's FA Cup Final side against the Blades! Dunne was capped seven times by Ireland (all as a Blades player) and on 15 occasions by Eire (only once whilst at 'the Lane')

* Between 1967-78 Dunne's son, James junior, played League football for Torquay United and Fulham and gained one cap for Eire. His nephew Tommy Dunne was a half-back with Leicester City, Exeter City, Shrewsbury Town and Southport.

Sheffield United team group: (back row, l-r) G MacGinley, Pat Carrigan, Jack Smith, Jack Kendall, Harry Hooper, Bill Anderson, Jock Gibson; (middle row, l-r) Secretary-Manager Ted Davison, Jim Holmes, Bertie Williams, Tommy Sampy, George Hall, **Jimmy Dunne**, A Stuart, Percy Thorpe, George Green, Wilf Adey; (front row, l-r) Bernard Oxley, Harry Gooney, Bobby Barclay, Mick Killhoury, Bert Oswald, Fred Tunstall, Fred Cheesemur

EBBRELL, John Keith
Full-back: one app.
Born: Bromborough, 1 October 1969
Career: Everton (trainee, April 1985, professional, November 1986), BLADES (£1 million, March 1997, retired through injury, May 1998).
John Ebbrell was injured on his United debut versus Reading on 29th of that month and sadly he never recovered full fitness and was forced to quit top-line soccer at the age of 28. He scored 19 goals in 265 League and Cup games for the Merseysiders, was capped once by England 'B', 14 times at Under-21 level and also earned Schoolboy and Youth international honours, and in 1995 he was an FA Charity Shield winner at Wembley.

ECKHARDT, Jeffrey Edward
Defender: 87+1 apps. 2 goals
Born: Sheffield, 7 October 1965
Career: BLADES (apprentice, April 1982, professional, August 1984), Fulham (£50,000, November 1987), Stockport County (£50,000, July 1994), Cardiff City (£30,000, August 1996), Newport County (July 2001).
Strong, wholehearted and able to play at right-back, centre-half or sweeper, Jeff Eckhardt did well in the intermediate and reserve teams at Bramall Lane before establishing himself in the first XI in 1986. He moved to Craven Cottage in 1987, thus allowing Brian Smith to move into the vacant left-half (No 6) position. He went on to play in 283 competitive games for the Cottagers, and later twice helped Cardiff gain promotion to the Second. He amassed 612 senior appearances for his four 'League' clubs.

EDDY, Keith
Midfielder: 134+2 apps. 21 goals
Born: Barrow, 23 October 1944,
Career: Holker Church Old Boys (Barrow), Barrow (professional, June 1962), Watford (July 1966), BLADES (August 1972), New York Cosmos (January 1976).
Signed by Ken Furphy from his former club Watford in 1972, Keith Eddy turned out to be a splendid captain and an inspiration in centre-field for the Blades. He scored with his first kick for the club...from the spot in a penalty shoot-out against Bristol Rovers in the Watney Cup Final after coming on as a substitute. It was a huge disappointment to the club and, indeed, for all Blades' supporters when he chose to leave the English soccer scene for pastures new. Eddy helped the Hornets gain promotion to the Second Division and reach the FA Cup semi-final before becoming a 'Blade. His career in England realised more than 500 senior appearances - 482 in the Football League. He netted over 50 goals.

82

EDWARDS, Keith
Striker: 293+17 apps. 171 goals
Born: Stockton-on-Tees, 16 July 1957
Career: Stockton Boys Youth Club, BLADES (trial, August 1975, professional September 1975), Hull City (£50,000, August 1978), BLADES (£75,000 plus a further payment of £20,000 after 40 first-team appearances, September 1981), Leeds United (£125,000, August 1986), Aberdeen (September 1987), Hull City again (March 1988-September 1989), Stockport County (September 1989), Huddersfield Town (on loan, March 1990, signed permanently August 1990), Plymouth Argyle (December 1990-January 1991).
Keith Edwards, slightly built, was an intelligent, far-seeing striker, a razor-sharp opportunist. No believer in undue embroidery, he had the knack of scoring in confined spaces, was quick and tireless, could use both feet and his head, and there is no doubt that he was a first-class marksman, admired by many. He helped the Blades win the Fourth Division title in 1981 and gain promotion to the Second Division in 1984 (leading the scoring charts each time with 41 and 44 League goals respectively). He finished his senior career with exactly 300 goals to his credit in 655 appearances...a splendid return.

EGAN, Thomas William
Inside/centre-forward: 23 apps. 7 goals
Born: Chirk, Denbighshire, 1872. Died: Tibshelf, Derbyshire, November 1946.
Career: Chirk (August 1889), Fairfield/Manchester (August 1892), Ardwick (November 1893), Burnley (March 1894), Ashton North End (May 1895), BLADES (November 1895), Lincoln City (October 1896), Birdwell FC (November 1897), Altofts FC (October 1898), Darwen (June 1899), Royston United (August 1901), Stockport County (September-October 1901).
A Welsh international - capped against Scotland in 1892 - Tom Egan was described as being a ' tricky, diligent player with a good turn of speed and a fine shot at goal.'
Possessing a good, strong shot, he was a hard-working forward with a lot of drive.
He gained a Welsh Cup winners medal with Chirk in 1892, but unfortunately failed to settle down at 'the Lane'.
* Egan's two sons were both professional footballers, Doug with Derby County and Aldershot and Harry with Brighton & Hove Albion, Southend United, Aldershot and Cardiff City.

EGGLESTON, Arthur

Right-half/inside-forward: 63 apps. 9 goals
Born: Chopwell, 4 January 1910. Died: Sheffield, 1990.
Career: Spen Black & White FC, Bury (May 1930), Plymouth Argyle (July 1935), BLADES (May1937, retained until 1947 and later spent four years on United's coaching staff: 1948-52).
An alert, untiring half-back, strong in the tackle, Arthur Eggleston has already appeared in 100 League games for Bury and 45 for the Pilgrims, scoring 47 goals, before joining the Blades whom he helped win the Second Division title in 1938-39, playing in 11 games).
Unfortunately WW2 technically ended his career!

ENGLISH, John

Full-back: 73 apps.
Born: Hebburn, 13 December 1886. Died: Northhampton, January 1953.
Career: Hebburn Argyle, Wall's End Park Villa, Preston North End (May 1910), Watford (July 1912), BLADES (April 1913), Darlington (player-manager in July 1919, after refusing to re-sign for the Blades after WW1, retiring as a player in May 1921 but remained in charge at The Feethams until May 1928), Nelson (manager, June 1928), Northampton Town (manager, January 1931), Exeter City (manager, October 1935), Darlington (manager for a second spell, June 1940, retaining his position until 1944).
Jack English was a neat, intelligent and tidy full-back who came mighty close to winning full international honours for England during his time at Bramall Lane. As a player he helped United win the FA Cup in 1915, represented the Football League and gained both North-Eastern League and Third Division (North) championship medals in 1913 and 1925 respectively

EVANS, Cameron

Cameron Evans moved from Glasgow Rangers to Sheffield United in November 1968. He spent just two days at the club, played in one Central League game and then returned to Scotland because of homesickness. He eventually joined Kilmarnock.

EVANS, Robert Ernest

Left-winger: 220 apps. 339 goals
Born: Chester, 19 October 1885. Died: Chester, 28 November 1965.
Career: Saltney Ferry, Bretton FC (July 1900), Saltney Works FC (August 1902), Wrexham (May 1905), Aston Villa (March 1906), BLADES (£1,100 plus Peter Kyle, October 1908), guested for Tranmere Rovers & Sandycroft FC during WW1, Crichton's Athletic/Saltney (July 1919), Saltney Ferry, Brookhirst FC (player-manager, 1921, retired in 1925).
He subsequently worked as a welfare supervisor for Shell Mex (Ellesmere Port) and acted as trainer to the local team, Ellesmere Port Town, that included a young Joe Mercer
Bob Evans, with his long raking stride and powerful shooting, proved an excellent replacement for Bert Lipsham in United's forward-line. Initially a Welsh international (10 caps won, two goals scored) he was later honoured by England (4 appearances, one goal) after the Sheffield United secretary had delved into some paperwork and found that he had been born the 'other side' of the border in Chester. When he first played for England (v. Ireland in February 1911) one newspaper described him as being 'the best winger England and Wales ever had.' After 16 League games for Villa he was transferred to the Blades in 1908 and did an excellent job over the next seven years before WW1 disrupted his progress, collecting an FA Cup winners' medal in 1915. During the hostilities Evans (when free from working for a petroleum company) he played two games for United v Wednesday in Christmas 1918 and when peace returned in 1919 Crichton's Athletic before breaking his leg playing for Saltney Ferry. Then, as player-manager of Brookhirst FC another fractured limb enforced his retirement from the game in 1925.

Sheffield United, FA Cup winners 1914-15: (back row, l-r) secretary-manager John Nicholson, Jack English, Harold Gough, Bill Brelsford, Albert Sturgess (middle row, l-r) Bill Cook, Stan Fazackerley, George Utley, Wally Masterman, **Robert Evans** (front row, l-r) Jim Simmons, Joe Kitchen

EVER PRESENTS

Alan Woodward holds the record for most-ever campaigns for the Blades - total five. In season 1952-53 there were five ever-presents in United's ranks - a club record.
(See under APPEARANCES)

EVERTON

United's playing record against the Toffees:

Premier League

Venue	P	W	D	L	F	A
Home	2	1	1	0	1	0
Away	2	1	0	1	4	4
Totals	4	2	1	1	5	4

Football League

Home	77	25	19	13	85	64
Away	77	15	9	33	63	113
Totals	114	40	28	46	148	177

FA Cup

Home	3	3	0	0	5	1
Away	3	1	0	2	1	4
Totals	6	4	0	2	6	5

League Cup

Home	3	1	1	1	4	6
Away	1	0	0	1	0	4
Totals	4	1	1	2	4	10

WW2

Home	1	1	0	0	4	0
Away	2	0	1	1	3	4
Totals	3	1	1	1	7	4

St Domingo Church Sunday School formed a football club in the spring of 1878. Playing at Stanley Park, enthusiasm was so great that in November of that same year they decided to expand membership and changed it's name to Everton, wearing black shirts with a scarlet sash and nicknamed the 'Black watch.' Royal blue was finally adopted in 1901.

The Merseysiders moved to Goodison Park in 1892, having previously played at Priory Road (from 1882) and Anfield Road (from 1884). Founder members of the Football League in 1888, Everton celebrated their 104th season in the 'League' in 2002-03, exactly 100 of which have been spent in the top flight.

After gaining promotion to the First Division in 1893, the Blades went on to oppose the Merseysiders in 33 consecutive League campaigns up to 1930. The first meeting coincided with the Blades' first-ever match in the top flight, on 2 September 1893 at Goodison Park and resulted in an excellent 3-2 victory after being a goal down at the interval. The crowd of 15,750 was the biggest on Blades' travels that season.

United's best home League win over Everton is 5-0, recorded at Bramall Lane on 30 December 1899 (technically their last match of the 19th century).

The Merseysiders scored twice in the last three minutes of their home League game to beat United 3-1 in October 1900 and netted four times in 10 minutes during the second-half of their 5-1 home League win over the Blades in March 1923.

Since WW2 United have never scored more than two goals in a home League game against Everton, yet they registered their best win at Goodison Park on Good Friday, 1956, racing to a 4-1 victory thanks mainly to a Jack Wilkinson hat-trick, but this splendid result could not save the Blades from relegation!

United overall have conceded five goals to Everton on eight occasions (thrice at home). In 1931-32 the Toffees won both League matches 5-1 on their way to back-to-back Second and First Division championship triumphs.

A crowd of 51,745 witnessed the United v. Everton 3rd round FA Cup-tie at Bramall Lane in February 1925. Fred Tunstall's goal gave the Blades a 1-0 victory.

In April 1975, the Blades travelled to Goodison Park with Everton looking to take the First Division title. The home side went 2-0 up but plucky United fought back to win 3-2 and severely dented the Merseysider's hopes of glory. They eventually finished 4th, three points behind the champions Derby County.

Listed among the many players who served with both clubs are Gary Ablett, Brett Angell, Earl Barrett, Peter Beagrie, Bob Cain, Terry Curran, Joe Davies, Jock' Dodds, John Ebbrell, Stan Fazackerley, Harry Hammond, Adrian Heath, Don Hutchinson, David Irving, Jack Kendall, Albert 'Tal' Lewis, Charlie Leyfield, Stuart McCall, Ken McNaught, Terry Phelan, Bruce Rioch, Trevor Ross, Graham Stuart, Carl Tiler, Imre Varadi, Mitch Ward and Fred White.

Howard Kendall was a player at Everton and also managed both the Merseysiders and the Blades. Ken Furphy, Joe Mercer and Archie Clark all played for the Merseysiders and later became Blades' managers. Dugald Livingstone played for Everton and later acted as United's trainer, Mick Heaton played for Blades and became a coach at Goodison Park.

EVES, Melvyn James

Inside-forward/winger: 26+2 apps. 10 goals
Born: Wednesbury, Staffs, 10 September 1956
Career: Wolverhampton Wanderers (April 1973, professional, July 1975), Huddersfield Town (on loan, March 1984), BLADES (December 1984), Gillingham (August 1986), Mansfield Town (on loan, October 1987), Manchester City (on loan, 1988), West Bromwich Albion (on loan, 1988), Telford United (July 1989), Cheltenham Town (1993, retiring in 1994 to become a footballers' agent, one of his star recruits being the Italian Enzo Maresca, who was transferred from WBA to Juventus for £4.5 million in January 2000. Before joining the Blades in 1984, inside or outside-left Mel Eves had done splendidly at Molineux, scoring 53 goals in 214 games for Wolves whom he served for more than 11 years. He was a Second Division championship and League Cup winner in 1977 and 1980 respectively and gained three England 'B' caps (v. Singapore twice and New Zealand). He was well past his best at Bramall Lane but his experience shone through and he scored some vital goals to help keep United in the Second Division!

EXCHANGE

The Blades defeated local team Exchange 7-0 in a home Sheffield County Cup game in October 1889. Robertson (3) and Hudson (2) led the scoring in front of 1,500 spectators.

EXETER CITY

United's playing record against the Grecians:

Football League

Venue	P	W	D	L	F	A
Home	4	3	1	0	11	4
Away	4	2	1	1	7	5
Totals	8	5	2	1	18	9

Exeter City FC was formed in 1904 by the amalgamation of St Sidwell's United and Exeter United. The Grecians first played in the East Devon League and then in the Plymouth & District League, and after exhibition matches (against West Bromwich Albion and Woolwich Arsenal) the club decided to turn professional in 1908. They gained Football League status in 1920 (as members of the Third Division) and since then have always played in the lower two sections.

All eight League games against the Blades were played in the Third Division over a period of five years. The first took place at Bramall Lane in September 1979 when United won 3-1 and the last at St James' Park in March 1984 when the Blades won 2-1. The Grecians' only victory was 3-1 at home in January 1980.

Ex-Blades players Jack English and Jim Iley both managed the Grecians.

Jack Alderson, Ian Benjamin, Wally Brayshaw, Ben Clarke, Ted Connor, Johnny Dryden, Brian Gayle, Steve Lovell, Nicky Marker, David Munks, Steve Neville, Percy Oldacre, Harry Warren, Simon Webster, Steve Wigley and Jack Wilkinson all played for both clubs. And Scotsman Dugald Livingstone was a trainer with both the Blades and the Grecians.

85

West Bromwich Albion v.s Sheffield United 26th September 1972

FALCONER, William Henry
Forward/midfielder: 23+2 apps. 3 goals
Born: Aberdeen, Scotland, 5 April 1956
Career: Aberdeen (May 1982), Watford (£300,000, 1988), Middlesbrough (£305, August 1991), BLADES (£425,000, August 1993), Celtic (£375,000, June 1995), Motherwell (£200,000, January 1996), Dundee (July 1998), Clydebank (early August 2001), St Johnstone (late August 2001), Grimsby Town (March-May 2002).
Willie Falconer spent six years his home-town club (scoring six goals in 87 appearances) before joining Watford. After more than 100 games for the Hornets he was transferred to Middlesbrough and moved to Bramall Lane in 1993, having added another 50 plus appearances to his tally with 'Boro. He had two mixed seasons at Bramall Lane before returning to Scotland where he remained until 2002. Falconer, a strong, upright, purposeful midfielder, was capped by his country at Schoolboy and Youth team levels whilst at Pittodrie and was a Scottish Cup winner with Celtic in 1995.

FAMILY CONNECTIONS
The followings sets of brothers have all been associated with the Blades:

Brown - Arthur	(1902-08)	and Fred G	(1915-23)
Brelsford - Charlie	(1918)	and Bill	(1909-24)
Johnson - Harry	(1916-31)	and Tom	(1928-41)
Kelly - Alan	(1992-97)	and Gary	(2002-03)
Lilley - Harry	(1890-94)	and Bill	(1891-94)
Mercer - David	(1920-28)	and Arthur	(1926-30)
Sampy - Tommy	(1920-34)	and Billy	(1921-27)
Scott - Andy	(1992-97)	and Rob	(1993-96)
Smith - Brain	(1984-89)	and Paul	(1981-86)
Wagstaff - Tony	(1961-69)	and Barry	(1963-69)
Wilkinson - Bernard	(1899-1913)	and Billy	(1901-09)

Brotherly Love
* Both the Kelly brothers (Alan and Gary) were goalkeepers.
* Five Shankly brothers: James (Halifax Town, Coventry, Carlisle United, Sheffield United, Southend United & Barrow), Bill (Carlisle United, Preston North End and then famously Liverpool's manager), Bob (Aldershot, Barrow, Clapton Orient, Newcastle United & manager of Dundee), Sandy (Ayr United) and John (Alloa Athletic, Luton Town & Portsmouth) were all professional footballers.
* Imre Varadi's brother, Fernando, was a registered player with Fulham.
* Billy, Enos and Henry Bromage were all brothers who played professionally - Billy with Gainsborough Trinity, the Blades and Doncaster Rovers, Enos for Derby County (1888-90) and Henry, also for Derby County as well as Burton United, Leeds City and Doncaster Rovers (1899-1915). Enos' son (Enos junior) was a reserve winger with the Blades (1922) who later played for Derby, Gillingham, West Bromwich Albion, Nottingham Forest and Chester. Two other relatives, George (Derby County, Doncaster & Sheffield United) and George E (Doncaster), were also footballers.
* Brothers Alf and Tom Leafe were both associated with the Blades, Boston Town and Grimsby Town.
* Defenders Chris Short and his brother Craig Short were both at Scarborough and Notts County together (1980s). Chris joined the Blades in 1955.
* David Holdsworth (ex-United) and his brother Dean were together at the same Premiership club (Bolton Wanderers) in 2002. Earlier both had been together with Watford.
* Harry Chapman, brother of United's Herbert, scored Wednesday's goals in their 2-0 League win over the Blades in October 1910.
* Des Thompson, Blades' keeper from 1955-63, was the younger brother of George Thompson who kept goal for Chesterfield (reserves), Scunthorpe United, Preston North End, Manchester City and Carlisle United between 1947-62, collecting a runners-up medal in the 1954 FA Cup Final with PNE.
* Len Allchurch and his brother Ivor Allchurch, MBE, played together for both Swansea Town (1949-58) and Wales (debut pairing in 1955). A third brother, Sid, represented Wales as an amateur.
* John Roxburgh's brother, Andrew, played for Leicester Fosse while another brother, Walter, had trials at Filbert Street.
* Steve Jagielka, brother of United's Phil, has played for Stoke City & Shrewsbury Town.
* Ernest Milton had two footballing brothers - Albert & Arthur - both of whom were left-backs like Ernest.
* Jack Dryden's brother, James, played for Manchester City and both players were related to Jackie Milburn (ex-Newcastle United & England).
* Peter Withe's brother, Chris, was also a professional footballer, serving with Bradford City, Bury, Chester City, Mansfield Town, Newcastle United, Notts County and Shrewsbury Town, while Peter's son, Jason, was associated with West Bromwich Albion and Burnley as a reserve team player.

Keep It In The Family
* Jimmy Dunne's son, James, played for Fulham & Torquay United and gained one full cap for The Republic of Ireland. Nephew Tommy Dunne played for Exeter City, Leicester City, Shrewsbury Town and Southport.
* Two of Tom Egan's sons, Doug and Harry, were both professionals, the former with Aldershot and Derby County and the latter with Aldershot, Brighton, Cardiff City & Southend United
* Tommy Hoyland (1947-60) and his son Jamie (1990-94) both played League football for the Blades.
* Colin Morris (1982-88) and his son Lee (1997-99) also played League soccer for United.
* Steve Ludham appeared in League matches for United (1973-77) while his son Ryan, played in a handful of friendlies (1997-98).
* When managing United (1973-75), Ken Furphy and his son, Keith, both appeared in friendly matches for the Blades.
* Jimmy Hutchinson's father, Barry, played for Chesterfield, Bolton Wanderers, Derby County, Rochdale, Halifax Town and Darlington.
* Goalkeepers Alan Kelly (father & son) both played for PNE, with Alan junior moving to Bramall Lane from Deepdale in 1992.
* Chris Guthrie's son, Chris junior, played for Gateshead and Sunderland.
* The father of Blades' striker Mick Jones kept goal for Worksop Town.
* Jim Iley is Colin Grainger's brother-in-law while Grainger is the uncle of Eddie Holliday (ex-Middlesbrough).
* Charlie Henderson's father, Crosby Henderson, was a professional footballer with Birmingham, Grimsby Town, Luton Town & Newcastle United.
* Goalkeeper John Hope's son, Chris, played for Darlington, Nottingham Forest & Scunthorpe United.

* Stewart Houston's father played for St Mirren.
* United's Jack Drummond was related to Preston North End's Geordie Drummond.
* United's 1899 and 1902 FA Cup winning teams included Harry Johnson, while his two sons, Harry junior and Tommy, played in the 1925 (winning) and 1936 (losing) FA Cup Finals for the Blades. The original team of 1899 also included Peter Boyle whose son Tommy played for United in the 1925 Final as well.
* Jimmy Simmons was the nephew of United's hefty goalkeeper Billy Foulke.
* Ray McHale - the nephew of United's full-back Fred Furniss - was signed by Chesterfield manager Jim McGuigan at the age of 19 in 1969. Furniss himself had been sold by United to Chesterfield in 1955. Later McGuigan joined the coaching staff at Bramall Lane... soon after McHale had signed for United (August 1982).
* Fred Tunstall played outside-left for the Blades in the 1925 FA Cup Final win over Cardiff City. His brother-in-law, George Briggs, played outside-right for Birmingham v. West Bromwich Albion in the 1931 Final but was on the losing side.
* Trevor Ross's father, Bill, played for Arbroath, Third Lanark & Bradford City.
* Malcolm Levitt (ex-Bradford City) is Derek Hawksworth's cousin.
* Three relatives of Blades' 1988-89 forward Francis Joseph all played professional football: Leon Joseph (Spurs), Matt Joseph (Arsenal, Gillingham, Cambridge United, Leyton Orient & Ilves in France) and Roger Joseph (Brentford, Wimbledon, Millwall, WBA & Leyton Orient) all played professional football.
* Young Blades Grant Smith is the son of Gordon Smith (ex-Brighton) who should have won the FA Cup for the Hove club in 1983 (v. Manchester United).
* Malcolm Barrass, Matt, played for Manchester City & Sheffield Wednesday.
* Jimmy Hutchinson's son, Barry, played for Bolton Wanderers, Chesterfield, Derby County, Darlington, Halifax Town and Rochdale, plus a handful of non-League clubs.

FARROW, George Henry
Wing-half: 2 apps.
Born: Whitburn, 4 October 1913. Died: 1980.
Career: Stockport County (September 1931), Wolverhampton Wanderers (January 1932), Bournemouth (July 1933), Blackpool (June 1936), BLADES (January 1948, released July 1948).
George Farrow was 34 years of age when he made his League debut for United against Grimsby Town in January 1948. He made 106 League appearances for Bournemouth and 144 for Blackpool.

FAULKNER, Stephen Andrew
Defender: 18+2 apps.
Born: Sheffield, 18 December 1954.
Career: BLADES (junior, April 1970, professional, February 1972), Stockport County (on loan, March 1978), York City (May 1978), Rowntree Mackintosh FC/North-Eastern Counties League (May 1981).
Steve Faulkner, a tall central defender, made 105 appearances for York City not quite making the grade at Bramall Lane.

FAZACKERLEY, Stanley
Inside/centre-forward: 143 apps. 58 goals
Born: Preston, 3 October 1891. Died: 20 June 1946
Career: Lane End United (1906), Preston North End (professional, October 1909), Charleston FC (Boston, USA), Accrington Stanley (November 1911), Hull City (£50, August 1912), BLADES (£1,000, March 1913), Everton (record £4,000, November 1920), Wolverhampton Wanderers (November 1922), Kidderminster Harriers (season 1924-25), Derby County (August 1925, retiring on medical advice in April 1926).
Stan Fazackerley was a big name in soccer immediately before and immediately after WW1. He commanded hefty transfer fees in both eras when switching from Hull to Bramall Lane and then to Everton, the latter after insisting on a move. Tall and graceful, he was an extremely clever footballer; an adroit dribbler and dangerous anywhere near goal with his power-packed shooting and direction. He always seemed to keep a cool head and often finished in style. In the summer of 1920, Fazackerley (5ft 11ins tall, 11st 6lbs in weight) toured South Africa with the FA party, playing in two Test Matches. He helped the Blades win the FA Cup in 1915 and was in Wolves' Third Division (North) championship winning team of 1924. Fazackerley scored 114 goals in a total of 258 League appearances...his best efforts coming with the Blades.

FEATHERSTONE, George
Inside-right: 29 apps. 11 goals
Born: Middlesbrough, 1885
Career: Stockton, BLADES (February 1908), Brighton & Hove Albion (May 1909).
A variable player with good speed, George Featherstone came into the side following Arthur Brown's move to Sunderland but struggled to keep his position the following season owing to the presence of Jack Peart, Bill Batty and then Joe Kitchen.

FENOUGHTY, Thomas
Midfielder: 53+4 apps. 6 goals
Born: Rotherham, 7 June 1941.
Career: Sheffield FC, BLADES (November 1963), Chesterfield (July 1969 to May 1972).
Tom Fenoughty spent almost six years at Bramall Lane during which time he gave some solid displays in the centre of the park. He made over 100 appearances for the Spire-ites.

87

FICKLING, Ashley

Defender: 5+1 apps

Born: Sheffield, 15 November 1972

Career: BLADES (April 1989, professional, July 1991), Darlington (two loan spells, November 1992 & August 1993), Grimsby Town (March 1995), Darlington (on loan, March 1998), Scunthorpe United (July 1998), Mansfield Town (on trial), Scarborough (July 2001).

Three of Ashley Fickling's appearances for the Blades were in Cup games. A schoolboy international, highly rated, he joined the club as a youngster and battled hard to get a regular place in the side, to no effect.

FIELD, Anthony

Inside-forward: 75+5 apps. 15 goals

Born: Halifax, 6 July 1946

Career: Halifax Town (professional, July 1963), Barrow (August 1966), Southport (£5,000, March 1968), Blackburn Rovers (£20,000, October 1971), BLADES (£76,666, March 1974), New York Cosmos/NASL (February 1976).

A small, energetic and clever forward, preferring the left side, Tony Field was signed for an unusual fee from Blackburn in 1974, having already chalked up in excess of 300 senior appearances while serving with his previous clubs. He remained at Bramall Lane until joining the exodus (including team-mate Keith Eddy) over to the NASL in 1976.

(L-R) West Ham United's Kevin Lock tackles Sheffield United's Tony Field

FIELD, Charles William

Inside-forward/outside-left: 61 apps 19 goals

Born: Hanwell, Brentford, 1879.

Career: Hanwell, Royal Ordnance (Southern League), Brentford (August 1896), BLADES (May 1898), Birmingham (January 1902), Brentford (May 1906 retiring in1908).

A shade on the slight side, but a player who could hold his own, Charlie 'Oakey' Field was a prolific scorer in junior football, a record he maintained with Brentford, opening his senior career with a hat-trick from the inside-left position. Indeed, he registered four hat-tricks and a six-timer in season 1897-98 and such was his marksmanship that the bigger clubs flocked to see him in action. It was no surprise when he joined the Blades, for whom he starred as an inside-right. He was subsequently transferred to Blues with his team-mate Billy Beer, and later fought a lengthy battle against injury. He impressed observers with his pace and dribbling skills as well as his shooting. During his time at 'the Lane' Field collected an FA Cup runners-up medal in 1901 and represented a Sheffield XI against Glasgow - and he scored twice on his United debut in the 2-2 away draw with Notts County in September 1898.

FINNIESTON, Stephen James

Forward: 27 apps. 6 goals

Born: Edinburgh, 30 November 1954

Career: Weybridge Council School, Chelsea (junior, June 1969, professional November 1971), Cardiff City (on loan), BLADES (£90,000, June 1978), Addlestone FC (1981), Hatney Wintney (season 1982-83).

Scottish Youth international Steve Finnieston was an enterprising forward who netted 37 goals in 90 first-class matches for Chelsea before his move to Bramall Lane. Succecession of injuries especially with Chelsea forced him to give up competitive football, although he did play later play non-League soccer before finally hanging up his boots in 1983.

FINNIGAN, Denis Vincent
Centre-half: 29 apps.
Born: Sheffield, 23 March 1940
Career: BLADES (junior, June 1955, professional, April 1959), Chesterfield (September 1968-70).
Dennis Finnigan signed as a 'pro' at Bramall Lane after completing his National Service. A well-built defender, he remained a loyal and dedicated 'reserve' to Joe Shaw for the majority of the time (and latterly Reg Matthewson). He served the club for 13 years.

FIRSTS
* The first Football League game at Bramall Lane saw United beat Lincoln City 4-2 in the Second Division on 3 September 1892 (attendance 4,000).
* The Blades were the first team to scored 10 goals in an away Football League game - at Burslem Port Vale in December 1892 (Division 2).
* At the end of that 1892-93 season the Blades became the first team to be promoted after winning a Test match (v. Accrington).
* The first live radio broadcast of a League game featured the Blades away to Arsenal (Division 1) in January 1927.
* On 17 May 1948, the Blades played Sheffield Wednesday in a friendly in Douglas on the Isle of Man. It was the first time a match between two professional teams had ever been staged on the island and a crowd of 8,000 witnessed the 2-2 draw.
* In August 1992, United striker Brian Deane had the honour of scoring the first-ever Premiership goal v. Manchester United at Bramall Lane.

FJORTOFT, Jan-Aage
Striker: 36+6 apps. 23 goals
Born: Aalesund, Norway, 19 January 1967,
Career: Hamar FC, Lillestrom, Rapid Vienna, Swindon Town (£500,000, July 1993), Middlesbrough (£1.3 million, March 1995), BLADES (£700,000, January 1997). Barnsley (£800,000, January 1998), Eintracht Frankfurt (November 1998).
A tall, slim-looking Norwegian international striker, lacking in pace but with good control and a wonderful knack of grabbing goals (out of nothing) Jan-Aage Fjortoft drew up a splendid scoring record at Bramall Lane. He entered the German Bundesliga in 1998 having taken his tally of full caps to 72 as well as scoring 88 goals in 219 League and Cup matches for his four English clubs.

FLEMING, William
Centre-forward/inside-left: 26 apps. 6 goals
Born: 1870
Career: Darlington, BLADES (August 1893), Paisley Abercorn (May 1894), Bury (January 1896), Tottenham Hotspur (November-December 1896).
Bill Fleming had a relatively short career that ended in a surprising way. After scoring three goals in five games in the space of a month, he was then suspended by Spurs for what is believed to have been a serious crime. He left the club immediately was not heard of again!

FLO, Jostein
Striker: 79+11 apps. 22 goals
Born: Norway, 3 October 1964,
Career: Songdal FC, BLADES (£475,000, August 1993), Stromsgodset (January 1997).
Striker Jostein Flo (6ft 4ins tall and weighing almost 14st) became United's most-capped player during his time at Bramall Lane that ended early in 1997 when a problem arose over the final instalment of his transfer fee. This led to his contract being cancelled by Blades' manager Howard Kendall, and as a result Flo returned to Norway. He won 44 full caps for his country.

FLOODLIGHTS
The first recorded game of football under 'floodlights (anywhere in the world) was played on 14 October 1878 at Bramall Lane between two teams selected by the Sheffield football association. Around 12,000 spectators paid for admission but it is believed that another 6-8,000 entered the ground illegally.
The first set of major floodlights, costing around £5,000 and comprising a rack of lights on four large pylons, were erected at Bramall Lane in season 1953-54. They were officially switched on for a friendly against Rotherham United (won 2-1) on Tuesday 16 March 1954. A crowd of 17,787 saw Jack Cross and Peter Wragg score for the Blades.
A fifth pylon was added in 1958 to later to improve the lighting and three years after that a new, improved lighting system, with massive 145 foot tall pylons were installed. However, in February 1962 a severe gale damaged one of them.
Further improvements were made to the floodlighting system in the summer of 1974 (to reach the standards set by the BBC & UEFA - for televised matches) and United's League game v. Newcastle (won 2-1) was the first to receive TV coverage under the new 'lighting' on 27 August of that year.
In 1995 yet another new system was introduced to 'the Lane' - this one without any pylons.

Rays of Light
* On 8 November 1889 United were defeated 2-0 by Bolton Wanderers in a friendly played under 'Wells Lights'.
* A crowd of 5,000 witnessed the friendly played under 'electric lights' between Everton and United on Merseyside on 8 January 1890. Everton won 5-2.
* Simon Stainrod scored United's goal in the 1-1 draw with Winterton FC in a friendly on 23 October 1978 when the non-League club's floodlights were switched on for the first time.
* A crowd of 1,400 saw United beat Bourne Town 2-0 in a friendly on 4 December 1989 - in a game arranged to 'switch on' the non-League club's new floodlighting system.
* Denaby United's lights were turned on for the first time when United won 5-0 there on 23 October 1990.
* On 11 March 1991, United beat Harrogate Railways Athletic 5-1 in a friendly match arranged to switch on the lights of the non-League club. A 14 year-old schoolboy - Terry Harris - scored one of United's goals that evening.
* A crowd of around 2,000 saw Bideford Town's lights officially turned on when United beat the Devon side 3-1 on 23 March 1992.
* And a fortnight later United sent a team to Immingham to officially 'switch on' their new floodlights on 6 April 1992. This game ended 0-0 and United fielded a 14 year-old trialist (Docherty).
* When United were defeated 2-1 in a floodlit friendly by Auxerre in France in January 1991, the whole game was shown live on French TV

89

FLOOD, John Gerard
Winger: 20+6 apps. 3 goals
Born: Glasgow, 25 December 1960.
Career: BLADES (apprentice, June 1976, professional, October 1978), Airdrieonians (February 1981).
Scottish winger John Flood - five years at 'the Lane' the majority as a reserve team player.

FLYNN, John Edward
Central defender: 224+7 apps. 10 goals
Born: Workington, 20 March 1948
Career: Workington (amateur April 1963, professional, November 1967), BLADES (£5,000, July 1969), Rotherham United (£15,000, July 1978, retiring from League football in May 1980).
John Flynn served the club admirably for a decade as partner to Eddie Colquhoun at the heart of the Blades' defence. Tall and strong and blessed with all the physical requirements for his position, he was also brave, fully committed and confident in the tackle. He appeared in 38 League games for his home-town club (Workington).

FOLEY, Steven
Midfielder/winger: 68+11 apps. 18 goals
Born: Liverpool, 4 October 1962
Career: Liverpool (junior, April 1978, professional, September 1980), Fulham (on loan, December 1983), Grimsby Town (August 1984), BLADES (August 1985), Swindon Town (June 1987), Stoke City (£50,000, January 1992), Lincoln City (July 1994), Bradford City (non-contract: August-September 1995).
Tough-tackling, hard-running Steve Foley failed to make the first XI at Anfield. After a loan spell with Fulham his career took off. He went on to accumulate more than 400 senior appearances (375 in the Football League) and scored in excess of 50 goals, helping Stoke win promotion from the Second Division title and lift the Autoglass Trophy at Wembley (1993).

FA CUP (FOOTBALL ASSOCIATION CHALLENGE CUP)
United have been playing in the FA Cup since 1889 (104 seasons).

This is their full record in the competition to date (2003):

Venue	P	W	D	L	F	A
Home	148	87	33*	28	273	150
Away	150	50	36*	64	188	217
Neutral	36	13	13	10	44	35
Totals	334	150	82	102	505	402

* Two home ties & one away tie all decided on penalties.

Analysis	P	W	D	L	F	A
Competition proper	322	140	81	101	473	393
Qualifying rounds	12	10	1	1	32	9
Totals		334	150	82	102	505	402

Details of United's six Final appearances:

1899	v. Derby County	Crystal Palace	won 4-1	Att. 73,833 (recs: £2,747)
1901	v. Tottenham H	Crystal Palace	drew 2-2	Att. 114,805(recs: £3,998)
1901	v. Tottenham H (rep)	Burnden Park	lost 3-1	Att. 20.740 (recs: £1,621)
1902	v. Southampton	Crystal Palace	drew 1-1	Att. 76,914 (recs: £2,893)
1902	v. Southampton (rep)	Crystal Palace	won 2-1	Att. 36,794 (recs: £1,625)
1915	v. Chelsea	Old Trafford	won 3-0	Att. 49,577 (recs: 4,052)
1925	v. Cardiff City	Wembley	won 1-0	Att. 91,763 (recs: 15,941)
1936	v. Arsenal	Wembley	lost 1-0	Att. 93,384 (recs:£24,857)

* The Blades have played in a total of 13 semi-finals, the last in April 2003 when they were defeated 1-0 by Arsenal at Old Trafford.

Progress
* En-route to winning their first Final in 1899 the Blades knocked out Burnley 2-1 (after a 2-2 draw), Preston North End 2-1 (again after a 2-2 draw), Nottingham Forest 1-0 and Liverpool in the semi-final 1-0 (after 2-2 & 4-4 draws and one abandoned game). Nine players appeared in every game: W Beer, W Bennett, P Boyle, W Foulke, G Hedley, WH Johnson, E Needham, F Priest and H Thickett. Beer top-scored with five goals.
* Sunderland 2-1, Everton 2-0, Wolverhampton Wanderers 4-0 and Aston Villa 3-0 in a semi-final replay (after a 2-2 draw) were the Blades victims when they made progress to their second Final in 1901.Seven players appeared in all seven Cup games this season: Bennett, Foulke, Hedley, H Lipsham, T Morren, Needham and Priest. Priest top-scored with seven goals.
* In 1902, the Blades accounted for Northampton Town 2-0, Bolton Wanderers 2-1, Newcastle United 2-1 (after a 1-1 draw) and Derby County in the semi-final 1-0 (after two 1-1 draws). Boyle, A Common, Foulke, Hedley, Priest, Thickett and B Wilkinson played in all nine Cup matches this season, and Priest was top-scorer with four goals.
* In 1915 the Blades met and beat Blackpool 2-1, Liverpool 1-0, Bradford PA 1-0 (after extra-time), Oldham Athletic 3-0 (after a 0-0 draw) and Bolton Wanderers 2-1 in the semi-final. Five players - W Cook, J Kitchen, J Simmons, A Sturgess and G Utley - starred in all seven Cup games this term and Kitchen top-scored with four goals.
* Ten years later the Blades reached their fifth FA Cup Final by beating the Corinthians 5-0 (Johnson scored four times), rivals Sheffield Wednesday 3-2, Everton 1-0, West Bromwich Albion 2-0 and Southampton 2-0 in the semi-final at Chelsea. Seven players appeared in all six Cup matches this season: Cook, Gillespie, G Green, Johnson, S King and goalkeeper C Sutcliffe. Johnson was top-marksman with five goals.
* United last reached the FA Cup final in 1936 and in doing so they ousted Burnley 2-1 (after a goalless draw), Preston North End 2-0 (also after a 0-0 stalemate), Leeds United 3-1 in front of a record crowd of 68,287 at Bramall Lane), Tottenham Hotspur 3-1 and Fulham 2-1 in the semi at Molineux. Six players appeared in all eight Cup matches this season: R Barclay, H Barton, E Dodds, H Hooper, T Johnson and J Smith. 'Jock' Dodds top-scored with four goals.

Winning Reports

* 1899 - United's first Final and Steve Bloomer's last (for Derby). A record crowd of almost 74,000 attended, including Lord Rosebery who drove from Epson with his two sons, the Prime Minister Mr AJ Balfour and Lord Kinnaird. Bloomer was marshalled throughout by United's skipper Ernest 'Nudger' Needham and although the 'Rams' went in at half-time leading 1-0 goal thanks to John Boag's goal, after the interval it was one-way traffic as the Blades took control and carved through County's defence with some wonderful, attacking football. Walter Bennett, Billy Beer, Jack Almond and Fred Priest scored their goals, the first three coming in one splendid 10-minute spell when United were irresistible. This was Derby's second successive Final defeat.
United's winning team was: Foulke; Thickett, Boyle; Johnson, Morren, Needham; Bennett, Beer, Hedley, Almond, Priest.
* 1902 - After a hard-fought, hurly-burly 1-1 draw at The Crystal Palace when close on 77,000 fans saw United's Alf Common (55 minutes) and Saints' Harry Wood (88) score the goals, the replay attracted just over half of that figure and those present saw another closely-fought game, full of skill and passion, which went in favour of the Blades by 2-1. With both teams unchanged it was United who struck first through George Hedley on two minutes. There were misses at both ends over the next hour or so before Albert Brown netted an equaliser. However, with 11 minutes remaining, and the Blades looking the stronger side, Billy Barnes (in for the injured 'Cocky' Bennett) swept in the winner.
United's winning team was: Foulke; Thicket, Boyle; Johnson, Wilkinson, Needham; Barnes, Common, Hedley, Priest, Lipsham.
* 1915 - With WW1 in progress, this was billed as the 'Khaki Final' as most of the 50,000 fans packed into Old Trafford were soldiers in uniform. On a wet and gloomy afternoon, United - without broken leg victim Billy Gillespie - were by far the better team and dominated play for long periods. Jimmy Simmons deservedly opened the scoring on 36 minutes after a mis-kick by the impressive Stan Fazackerley who then made no mistake by heading a second goal with seven minutes remaining after Wally Masterman's pile-driver had bounced back off the angle of post and crossbar. Joe Kitchen wrapped things up with a third with time running out to seal a comfortable victory, thus allowing the Blades to hold on to the trophy for five years! The Earl of Derby presented the trophy to George Utley and afterwards said: "It is now the duty of everyone to join with each other and play a sterner game of football!"
The Blades' winning line-up was: HC Gough; Cook, J English; Sturgess, W Brelsford, Utley; Simmons, S Fazackerley, Kitchen, W Masterman, RE Evans.
* 1925 - With The Duke of York the guest of honour, United celebrated their first Wembley appearance by beating Cardiff City 1-0 in front of almost 92,000 fans, outside-left Fred Tunstall scoring the all-important goal after 30 minutes. He pounced after City's right-half Harry Wake had failed to clear Harold Pantling's long through ball and easily beat 'keeper Farquharson from about seven yards. Billy Gillespie was outstanding for United. Skipper Billy Gillespie was a very proud man when he collected the Cup while Tommy Boyle and Harry Johnson followed in their father's footsteps by collecting Cup winning medals.
The team-line-up was: Sutcliffe; Cook, Milton; H Pantling, King, Green; D Mercer, T Boyle, H Johnson, Gillespie, F Tunstall.

Losing Reports

* 1901 - Tottenham Hotspur became the first 'non-League' side to win the trophy since League football was introduced in 1888. The Blades fought hard and long in the first game that ended level at 2-2 in front of a massive crowd at Crystal Palace. After Fred Priest had shot United in front on 110 minutes, 'Sandy' Brown netted twice for Spurs in the 25th and 51st minutes before Walter Bennett earned a replay with the equaliser 50 seconds later. Bennett's second goal was hotly disputed by the United defenders as the linesman indicated a corner but was over-ruled by referee Kingscott! The replay, staged at Bolton, attracted a very poor crowd with many fans staying away thinking there might be a massive turnout. Both teams were unchanged and after leading through Priest's goal on 40 minutes, United had no answer to Spurs' second-half thrusts and conceded three goals in 35 minutes to end up a well-beaten outfit. John Cameron levelled things up for the Londoners on 52 minutes, Tom Smith made it 2-1 on 76 and Brown put the icing on the cake with a third three minutes from time.
United's team for this Final (both games) was: Foulke; Thickett, Boyle; Johnson, Morren, Needham; Bennett, Field, Hedley, Priest, Lipsham.
* 1936 - Arsenal, League champions three seasons running (1933-34-35) were strong favourites to win this Final. In the end they just managed it, but not after the Blades had given them a run for their money. In truth, United missed at last six clear-cut chances and should have won, 'Jock' Dodds being unlucky when his powerful header bent the crossbar on the hour mark. It was his opposite number, however, Ted Drake who grabbed the all-important and match-winning goal. The Gunners' marksman pounced on 74 minutes to decide the issue and break the hearts of the Blades' supporters in the 93,000 plus crowd. 'Wee' Alex James swung a pass out to Cliff Bastin who beat Harry Hooper and crossed hard and low into the box. Drake collected the ball, side-stepped Tom Johnson and scored with a crisp right-foot shot from 10 yards. United rallied, Dodds again struck the woodwork, but the Gunners held out to steal the Cup!
United's line-up was: Smith; H Hooper, C Wilkinson; E Jackson, Johnson, A McPherson; Barton, Barclay, Dodds, J Pickering, B Williams. The team's trainer, Bill Brelsford, had played and won in the 1915 Final while Johnson became the third member of the family to pick up a Cup medal...his dad had played in the 1899, 1901 & 1902 Finals while brother Harry had led the Blades' attack in 1925.

United's FA Cup Dosier

* First FA Cup-tie	v. Scarborough (a)	05.09.1889	won 6-1
* First FA Cup defeat	v. Bolton Wds (a)	01.02.1890	lost 0-13
* Biggest home win	v. Loughborough	08.12.1891	won 6-1
	v. Corinthians	10.01.1925	won 5-0
	v. Barrow	01.01.1956	won 5-0
* Biggest away win	v. Newcastle United	10.01.1914	won 5-0
	v. Scarborough	05.09.1889	won 6-1
* Heaviest home defeat	v. Notts County	17.01.1891	lost 9-1
* Heaviest away defeat	v. Bolton Wanderers	01.02.1890	lost 0-13
* Best unbeaten run:	14 matches	28.01.1899 to 24.02.1900	

91

Action against the Minnows

Since entering the Football League in 1892, United have been beaten in the FA Cup by the following non-League teams: Port Vale (1897-98), Tottenham Hotspur (1900-01), Swindon Town (1907-08), Darlington (1910-11) & Altrincham (1981-82).

In contrast the Blades have also met and beaten the following non-League teams in the competition: Blackpool (1892-93), Millwall Athletic (1894-95), Northampton Town (1901-02), Southampton (1901-02), Millwall (1913-14), Southend United (1919-20), the Corinthians (1924-25 & 1931-32), Worcester City (1958-59), Burscough (1979-80), Boston United (1982-83), Maidstone United (1987-88) & Rushden and Diamonds (1999-2000).

Void Matches

Two FA Cup-ties have been declared void - those against Burton Swifts (away) in 1890-91 when the hosts, despite winning 2-1, were disqualified for fielding an unregistered player, and in 1998-99 against Arsenal at Highbury when the Gunners scored what was later determined to be an 'unsporting' winner (2-1). This tie was replayed and the result was the same.

FA Cup Dosier

* For a pre-match treat prior to the 1901 Final between the Blades and Spurs, Travel Agents Thomas Cook, in conjunction with Midland Railway/Excursions Trains, arranged a tour of London with breakfast and lunch included...price 6s 6d (33p) per person.
* The 1915 FA Cup Final between United and Chelsea was billed as the 'Khaki Final'
* Bob Barclay played in two FA Cup Finals for different clubs in three seasons and was a loser in both...for the Blades v. Arsenal in 1936 and then for Huddersfield Town v. Preston North End in 1938.
* The Blades have lost three semi-finals by 1-0 scorelines: 1914 (to Burnley), 1998 (to Newcastle United) and 2003 (to Arsenal).
* United suffered their 100th defeat in FA Cup football at Preston in a 4th round tie on 26 January 2002 (losing 2-1).

FOOTBALL LEAGUE

United's full Football League record:

Div. 1	P	W	D	L	F	A
Home	1117	577	275	265	2083	1355
Away	1117	262	249	606	1320	2239
Totals	2234	839	524	871	3403	3594

Div. 1*	P	W	D	L	F	A
Home	207	107	59	41	346	213
Away	207	53	67	87	236	285
Totals	414	160	126	128	582	498

Div.2	P	W	D	L	F	A
Home	539	315	127	97	1104	551
Away	539	162	134	243	710	899
Totals	1078	477	261	340	1814	1450

Div.3	P	W	D	L	F	A
Home	115	71	24	20	230	100
Away	115	29	25	61	136	200
Totals	230	100	49	81	366	300

Div.4	P	W	D	L	F	A
Home	23	15	8	0	53	15
Away	23	12	7	4	41	26
Totals	46	27	15	4	94	41

Overall	P	W	D	L	F	A
Home	2001	1085	493	423	3816	2234
Away	2001	518	482	1001	2443	3649
Totals	4002	1603	975	1424	6259	5883

* Post 1992 (following the introduction of the Premiership)
NB - For Premiership/Test Matches/Play-offs/WW2 (1939-40) see elsewhere.

Seasons Spent in Divisions

Division 1 (pre 1992)	57
Division 1 (post 1994)	9
Division 2	26
Division 3	5
Division 4	1
Totals	98

(add the two campaigns in Premiership = 100 in 'League' football (1892-2003 inclusive).

United's results in their first season in the Football League (Div. 2) 1892-93:

Opponents	H	A
Ardwick	2-1	3-2
Bootle	8-3	0-2
Burslem Port Vale	4-0	10-0
Burton Swifts	3-1	3-0*
Crewe Alexandra	4-0	4-0
Darwen	2-0	1-3
Grimsby Town	2-0	1-0

Lincoln City	4-2	0-1	
Northwich Victoria	1-1	3-1	
Small Heath	2-0	1-1	
Walsall Town Swifts	3-0	1-1	

*The initial game with Burton Swifts (away) on 27 December 1892 was abandoned in the 68th minute through fog/darkness. United were leading 2-1 at the time; the referee arrived late and neither team wanted to play in the first place.

Full record for season 1892-93

Venue	P	W	D	L	F	A	Pts
Home	11	10	1	0	35	8	21
Away	11	6	2	3	27	11	14
Totals	22	16	3	3	62	19	35

United finished runners-up to Small Heath, missing out on the title by one point - but after beating Accrington in a Test Match 1-0 at Nottingham, the Blades were duly promoted, thus becoming the first team to achieve such a feat via the 'Test Match' system.

FOOTBALL LEAGUE CHAMPIONS

Champions (1)

United were First Division Champions in 1897-98 with this record:

Venue	P	W	D	L	F	A	Pts
Home	15	9	4	2	27	14	22
Away	15	8	4	3	29	17	20
Totals	30	17	8	5	56	31	42

The Blades, who clinched the title on 9 April with a 1-0 win at Bolton, finished five points clear of Sunderland, one of the leading clubs in the country at the time alongside Aston Villa, both having already won the championship three times each. Indeed the previous season Villa had completed the League & Cup double, emulating Preston North End's feat of 1888-89.

United's stars in a superb season were the three half-backs, gypsy Rab Howell, Tom Morren and Ernest 'Nudger' Needham, goalkeeper Bill 'Fatty' Foulke and wingers Walter 'Cocky Bennett and Fred Priest.

The team got off to a flying start and lost only one match during the first half of the campaign (2-1 at Stoke in early December) and soon afterwards both top-of-the-table games against Aston Villa (1-0 at home, 2-1 away). This gave the players a great boost and morale increased ten-fold but then came a set-back.. in front of 23,500 fans at Sunderland's cramped Newcastle Road ground on 5 March The Blades lost 3-1 to Sunderland, Rab Howell conceding two own-goals. A month ;later the return fixture was staged at Bramall Lane and although United were minus Ernest Needham (away on England duty) they avenged that defeat on Wearside with a vital 1-0 victory to edge towards the title, which was clinched soon afterwards against Bolton.

The average League attendance at Bramall Lane was 12,298 with a best of 37,389 v. Wednesday on 27 December. The lowest was just 2,500 for the visit of Derby County on the opening day of the season (1 September).

The championship team: W Fouke (29 apps), H Thicket (29), R Cain (30), R Howell (24), T Morren (26), E Needham (29), W Bennett (26), K Mckay (25), J Almond (20), J Cunningham (24), F Priest (28).

Other players: H Johnson (10), R Gaudie (6), H White (6), N Logan (5), H Howard (3), G Hedley (2), T Jenkinson (2), D Morton (2), J Blair (1), A Bradshaw (1), A French (1) & M Whitham (1).

Goalscorers: Bennett (12), Needham (8), Almond (7), Cunningham (7), McKay (5), Logan (4), Priest (4), Gaudie (2), Johnson (2), Morren (2), opponent (1), unattributed (2)...total 56.

Champions (2)

In 1952-53 United won the Second Division title, finishing two points ahead of Yorkshire rivals Huddersfield Town.

Their full record was:

Venue	P	W	D	L	F	A	Pts
Home	21	15	3	3	60	27	33
Away	21	10	7	4	37	28	27
Totals	42	25	10	7	97	55	60

Manager Reg Freeman (1st season) developed an excellent team comprising an equal sprinkling of youth and experience.

United had lost their top-flight status in 1949 (following the transfer of several quality players including Shimwell & Rickett). This was the fourth season in Division Two, having finished 3rd, 8th and 11th respectively previously, suggesting the club was on the slide!

They didn't start 1952-53 too well (winning two, losing two and drawing one of their first five matches) and come December their form was moderate with five losses behind them despite a few healthy victories ...7-2 v. Leicester City, 7-1 v. Swansea Town (the best of the season in terms of goal-difference) and 6-1 v. Lincoln City.

Jimmy Hagan, the Blades' midfield general, was pulling the strings whilst the return of Harry Latham at centre-half steadied the defence in which a young Graham Shaw at left-back was becoming a class act. All five forwards were capable of scoring and slowly but surely the results were chalked up. From New Year onwards only one match was lost (surprisingly by 3-2 at lowly Lincoln) while there was a thrilling 4-4 draw at Southampton. Nevertheless a very useful Huddersfield side matched the Blades kick-for-kick, point-for-point and it wasn't until the penultimate game of the season (at Fulham) that United clinched the title, Len Browning and Harold Brook scoring in a crucial 2-1 win.

The average League attendance at 'the Lane' was 31,027 (a fraction down on the previous season) with a best of 41,216 witnessing the 2-2 Christmas Day draw with Doncaster Rovers. The lowest was 17, 397 v. Brentford in early September.

United's heaviest defeat was a 4-0 drubbing at Bury.

The championship team: E Burgin (42 apps), F Furniss (42), G Shaw (37); J Shaw (42), H Latham (25)/H Johnson (15), H Hitchen (16)/W Toner (15); A Ringstead (42), J Hagan (37), L Browning (39), H Brook (36), D Hawksworth (42).

Other players: G Denial (9), A Bottom (6), S McNab (5), W Wood (5), G Hutchinson (3), FA Smith (3), P Wragg (1).

Goalscorers: Ringstead (22), Brook (17), Browning (17), Hagan (17), Hawksworth (10), Furniss (4), Bottom (3), G Shaw (2), McNab (1), opponents (4)...total 97.

Champions (3)

Relegated to the Fourth Division, United quickly bounced back immediately, taking the championship at the first attempt in 1981-82 with this excellent record:

Venue	P	W	D	L	F	A	Pts.
Home	23	15	8	0	53	15	53
Away	23	12	7	4	41	26	43
Totals	46	27	15	4	94	41	96

The Blades had five points to spare over second-place Bradford City at the death and the team remained unbeaten at home throughout a season for the first time since 1892-93 (almost 90 years) when promotion to the First Division was achieved.

Under the shrewd guidance of manager Ian Porterfield, the Blades played some delightful football at times, against it must be said some rather poor opposition!

Amazingly they scored only six goals in their first half-a-dozen matches - hardly what the Bramall Lane fans had hoped for. But once Bob Hatton and Keith Edwards got to know each other better, the goals began to flow and results started to appear, including a surprise 1-0 win over Arsenal in the League Cup. However, their followed another run of poor scoring (either side of Christmas) and there was a rather humiliating defeat by non-Leaguers Altrincham in the FA Cup - but all this was soon forgotten and the signing of Blackpool winger Colin Morris for £100,000 (money the club couldn't really afford) was certainly a masterful piece of business on the part of the manager. As the weeks ticked by, the team went into overdrive and powerfully carved out a path towards the title with some superb displays, including emphatic wins of 7-3 v. Northampton Town (the best of the season), 4-0 over both Stockport County and York City, 4-1 v. Torquay United and 5-1 at Halifax. United were beaten only once in their last 23 matches (a 2-1 reverse at Scunthorpe in late February). They clinched the title with a 4-0 home win over Peterborough United in the penultimate game of the season in front of the second best crowd of the season - almost 24,000. This led to a carnival atmosphere on the final Saturday away to Darlington where a huge United following boosted the Feethams attendance figure to 12,557 - the biggest there for years - as the Blades ended on a high with a 2-0 victory.

The average League attendance at 'the Lane' was 14,892...the biggest single turnout was that of 24,593 for the top-of-the-table clash with Bradford City on 30 March, the lowest 11,293 v. Colchester in mid-September.

The championship team (4-4-2): K Waugh (45 apps.); P Richardson (19+1)/J Ryan (19), A Kenworthy (45), S Houston (27)/J McPhail (26)/ J McAlle (18); P Garner (34), C Morris (23)/S Neville (22+8), J Matthews (24+1); M Trusson (44), S Charles (28+2)/J King (22+1); K Edwards (41), R Hatton (45).

Other players: P Casey (12), A Moore (4), L Tibbott (3), T Wiggan (3+2), J Broddle (1), S Conroy (1), G Brazil (0+1).

Goalscorers: Edwards (35 goals), Hatton (15), Kenworthy (15), Trusson (11), King (4), Morris (4), Neville (4), Matthews (3), Charles (1), McPhail (1), Richardson (1)...total 94.

Seasonal Choice

1892-93	Unbeaten at home, runners-up, promoted after Test Match win.
1895-96	Only one away win out of 15 (2-0 at Derby), 12th position.
1896-97	Just two away defeats, a goal-average of 42-29, runners-up.
1897-98	Champions with 42 points, gained from 17 wins & 8 draws. First time average home attendance topped five figures (12,298).
1898-99	As defending champions, United suffered 16 defeats and finished 16th
1899-00	After a titanic battle, Aston Villa (50 points) pipped United by a whisker to win the title. United - looking the likely champions in mid-April - blew their chances late on, winning only one of their final four matches while Villa won three of the last four. United dropped only four points in their first 15 matches and went on to equal the League record of 22 games without defeat. Bury ended that excellent sequence on 20 January 1900 with a 2-1 win at Gigg Lane after the Blades had been reduced to 10 men.
1900-01	Beaten 15 times in 34 games, United finished a disappointing 14th.
1902-03	No home draws, fourth position claimed.
1904-05	A total of 13 home wins, no home draws, sixth spot.
1905-06	After 17 defeats (12 away) United finished a poor 12th.
1912-13	United lost 18 matches (14 away) which saw them finish 15th.
1913-14	The average home League crowd of 21,503 was United's best at the time. The Blades finished 10th in Division One.
1919-20	After another 18 defeats (16 away) United ended up 14th.
1920-21	The Blades won only six matches (one away) yet avoided relegation to Division Two. They suffered 18 more losses, drew the other 18 games, gained 30 points to Derby's 26 and Brentford's 24, and their away victory was 6-2 at Arsenal. There was a record average League gate of 27,619.
1921-22	Finished in 11th place after 17 defeats.
1923-24	Fifth in the table after 7 wins, 7 draws and 7 defeats away from home.
1924-25	Thirteen drawn games for 14th position.
1925-26	A total of 19 wins from 42 games meant 5th position.
1927-28	As low as 13th in the Division after 17 defeats.
1929-30	United, beaten 21 times, had a goal-average of 91-96 and claimed a 5-1 victory a Old Trafford inlast game saved them.
1930-31	From a total of 18 defeats, 14 were on the road - final placing of 15th.
1931-32	United gained 20 wins, suffered 16 defeats, claimed seventh position.
1932-33	Lowest average home League attendance for 23 years (14,296) as the Blades finished 10th in table.
1933-34	Relegated in bottom spot after losing 23 matches and conceding 101 goals.
1934-35	Eleventh after 16 wins and 17 defeats (moderate season).
1935-36	Gained 20 wins, third in the table (FA Cup Final defeat).
1936-37	Only one home defeat - 1-0 to Blackburn Rovers (7th spot).
1937-38	Third in the Second Division after 22 wins.
1938-39	Runners-up & promotion after 20 wins (11 away) and 14 draws.
1946-47	Sixth in First Division following 21 wins (9 away).
1947-48	United's best-ever average home League attendance - 35,094 - despite finishing only 12th in the First Division.
1948-49	Bottom and relegated after 20 defeats.
1949-50	Collected 19 wins (10 away) and 14 draws to finish 3rd.
1951-52	18 wins, 19 defeats, 90 goals scored, a mediocre eleventh.
1952-53	Champions after 25 wins, 10 draws and 97 goals scored.
1953-54	Third from bottom after 20 defeats and 90 goals conceded.

1955-56	Relegated in bottom spot with only 33 points (21 defeats).
1957-58	Sixth in Division Two after registering 21 victories.
1958-59	A niggling third with 23 wins.
1959-60	19 wins, a 7-7-7 away record, 50 points, fourth spot.
1960-61	Runners-up & promoted with 58 points (26 wins, six draws).
1964-65	Finished 19th in the table after suffering 19 defeats.
1966-67	Won 16, lost 16, 42 points from 42 games, 10th position.
1967-68	Only 32 points (21 defeats) in 21st position - relegated.
1969-70	22 wins, only 10 goals conceded at home, sixth.
1970-71	Promoted as runners-up with 56 points (21 wins, 14 draws).
1973-74	A 7-7-7 home record, 16 defeats overall, 13th in the table.
1975-76	Bottom (22 points) after 26 defeats and conceding 82 goals.
1978-79	Relegated to Division Three in 20th spot (19 defeats).
1980-81	With 20 defeats, 40 points, 21st position, relegated to Division Four. With a figure of just 12,772, United recorded their lowest average home League crowd since 1906-07.
1981-82	Champions at the first attempt: 27 wins, unbeaten at home, 94 goals & 96 points.
1982-83	Mid-table 11th after 20 defeats
1983-84	A total of 24 wins gained, 83 points, third place and promoted.
1984-85	A season of struggle: 18 defeats, 44 points, 18th position.
1986-87	United had their lowest average League crowd for 90 years - 9,992. They finished 9th in Division 2.
1987-88	Relegated in 21st position with 46 points after 24 defeats.
1988-89	25 wins, 97 goals scored, runners-up and promotion.
1989-90	Runners-up, promotion for the second season running (24 wins, 85 pts).
1990-91	13th in Division One - 18 defeats and only 36 goals scored.
1992-93	United's first season in the Premiership; finished 13th with 52 points (18 defeats).
1993-94	Relegated from the top flight after finishing 20th (18 draws, 10 at home).
1995-95	A record of 16 wins, 14 draws and 16 defeats for 62 points and 9th spot.
1996-97	Twenty wins gained, 73 points in total, 9th position.
1997-98	Sixth in Division One after 17 draws (12 away from home).
1999-00	Failed to win any of last nine League games, slipped from 12th to 16th.
2000-01	Finished 10th in First Division after being in Play-offs in early March; 33 points behind the champions Fulham.
2001-02	Mid-table finish of 13th, never above 11th, struggled at times.
2002-03	A quite wonderful season, in both League combat and indeed in the two major Cup competitions. Perhaps the Blades' deep involvement in the latter prevented them from gaining automatic promotion. Nevertheless, a third-place finish guaranteed the Blades a place in the Play-offs where they beat Nottingham Forest (who had taken 6th spot) in the semi-final before meeting Wolves in the Final at the Millennium Stadium. Disappointingly, in front of almost 69,500 fans the Blades went down 3-0.

95

Football League Play-offs.

United have been involved in the Play-offs on four occasions - in 1987-88, 1996-97, 1997-98 and 2002-03.

In 1987-88 (the first time promotion/relegation was introduced under this system) the Blades finished third from bottom of Division Two and met Bristol City (5th in Division Three) in one of the semi-finals. The Blades were defeated 1-0 at Ashton Gate in front of a bumper 25,335 crowd before being held to a 1-1 draw at Bramall Lane (19,261), thus losing out 2-1 on aggregate and as a result being relegated.

In 1996-97 the Blades (5th in Division One) went through to the Final after knocking out Ipswich Town in the two-legged semi-final on the away goal rule after successive draws, 1-1 at home (22,312) and 2-2 away (21,467). Unfortunately, Crystal Palace destroyed United's hops of Premiership football when they won the Wembley Final 1-0 in front of 64,383 fans.

Twelve months later it was agony again for the Blades (6th in Division One) when they lost in the semi-final to Sunderland (who had finished 4th). The Wearsiders bounced back to win their home leg 2-0 in front of a bumper crowd of 40,082 after United had taken a 2-1 lead from the opening fixture at Bramall Lane (23,800).

After finished third behind Portsmouth and Leicester City in the Nationwide League First Division in 2002-03, the Blades met 6th placed Nottingham Forest in the two-legged Play-off semi-final. The first game, at The City Ground on 10 May, ended in a 1-1 draw, Michael Brown's penalty cancelling out David Johnson's opener for the home side. Forest had Michael Dawson sent-off late in the second-half for a foul on substitute Steve Kabba. The attendance was over 29,000.

The return leg at Bramall Lane five days later attracted a healthy crowd of 30,212 and what a cracking and thrilling encounter it turned out to be, as the Blades won 4-3 after extra-time. One newspaper reporter described it as 'an epic victory.' Forest led 2-0 with goals from David Johnson (30 minutes) and Andy Reid (58) but the Blades stormed back in style. Michael Brown made it 2-1 with a deflected free-kick on the hour mark before Steve Kabba smashed in a superb volley to bring the scores level in the 68th minute. More chances were created, at both ends of the field, as the game headed towards and subsequently into extra-time. And then, with eight minutes remaining 'super sub' Paul Peschisolido edged the Blades in front at 3-2 with a great individual goal and five minutes later Forest defender Des Walker headed into his own-net to make it 4-2. With the Bramall Lane supporters dancing in the stands, a Robert Page own-goal reduced the deficit to one and led to an anxious last couple of minutes but Neil Warnock's men held on to claim their place in the Final (v. Wolverhampton Wanderers) with a 5-4 aggregate victory. Phew!

The Final, at Cardiff's Millennium Stadium took place on Bank Holiday Monday, 26 May and in front of 69,473 spectators (half of them clad in red and white) the Blades were blunted 3-0 by a resilient and determined Wolves side. Neil Warnock's men simply failed to produce anything like their best form. Michael Brown missed a penalty when it was 3-0 and Paul Peschisolido had a shot blocked on the line by an arm! It was a disappointing end to aa wonderful season. But as the boss said afterwards: "We'll lick our wounds and give it everything we have next season. We'll be back."

Football League Test Match

On 22 April 1893, United met Accrington at Trent Bridge, Nottingham in a vital end-of-season Test Match. A crowd of 5,000 saw the Blades win 1-0 (Jack Drummond the scorer) and as a result promotion was gained to the First Division.

Prior to automatic promotion/relegation being introduced in 1898-99, the right to claim First Division status (or indeed, to remain in Division 2) was decided via Test Matches, whereby the bottom three teams in the top flight took on the 'champions', runners-up and the third-placed team in Division Two. Thus, at the end of the 1892-93 campaign United, who had finished runners-up to Small Heath (Birmingham) in the Second Division, met Accrington who had finished between Notts County and Newton Heath (Manchester

United) at the foot of Division One. The Blades had to work hard and long for their single goal victory over Accrington to take their place in the premier Division. The Lancashire club resigned rather than be relegated, the club folding shortly afterwards. In the two other Test Matches, Newton Heath beat Small Heath to retain their top-flight status while Darwen defeated Notts County (relegated) to clinch promotion with the Blades.

Football League Pot Pourri
* Of their 100 seasons in the Football League, the Blades spent 37 of them consecutively in the top-flight (1893-1934 inclusive).
* United have played Blackburn Rovers more times in the League football than anyone other club (138). They have also recorded more victories over the Rovers (53 with 33 coming at home) than they have any other 'League' club.
* So far Aston Villa have inflicted the most Football League defeats on the Blades (57 - with 40 coming away on Villa territory).
* United have loved playing against Blackburn against whom they have scored their highest tally of 'League' goals (222). Aston Villa (230) have scored the most against United (85 at Bramall Lane). Only two other clubs have netted over 200 - Blackburn Rovers 205 and Sunderland 206.
* United have also drawn a record 33 League games with Blackburn (20 at home).
* On 15 September 2001, when the Blades entertained Coventry City, this was their 4,000th 'League' match (including the Premiership but not the three games at the start of the ill-fated 1939-40 wartime season). Thus United became only the 15th club to attain this milestone, following (in A-Z order): Aston Villa, Blackburn Rovers, Bolton Wanderers, Burnley, Bury, Derby County, Everton, Grimsby Town, Notts County, Preston North End, Sunderland, West Bromwich Albion & Wolverhampton Wanderers.
* By the end of that 2002-03 season six more clubs had also reached that 4,000 barrier, namely Barnsley, Birmingham City, Lincoln City, Manchester City, Nottingham Forest & Sheffield Wednesday.
* United's 4,000th game in the Football League, was their home fixture v. Wolverhampton Wanderers on 26 April 2003 (a 3-3 draw); it was also their 2,000th at home with their 2,000th away coming at Preston North End a week earlier (lost 2-0).
* Of the clubs United have played at League level, they have yet to be beaten by the following: Burton United, Darlington, Glossop North End, Halifax Town, Hartlepool United, Hereford United, Northampton Town, Norwich Victoria, Peterborough United, Rochdale, Torquay United and York City.
* Of the current League clubs, the ones United have yet to meet in the competition are Boston United, Cheltenham Town, Kidderminster Harriers, Macclesfield Town, Rushden & Diamonds, Wycombe Wanderers and Yeovil Town. (ADD **** ...if REDBRIDGE)

Football League Statistics:
Most/fewest points gained in a season
96 (46 games) 1981-82 (3 pts for a win)
60 (42 games) 1952-53 (2 pts for a win)
42 (30 games) 1897-98 (2 pts for a win)
35 (22 games) 1892-93 (2 pts for a win)

31 (42 games) 1933-34 (Division 1)
22 (34 games) 1975-76 (Division 1)

Most/fewest wins in a season
27 (46 games) 1981-82 (Division 4)
26 (42 games) 1961-62 (Division 1)
25 (42 games) 1952-53 (Division 2)
16 (22 games) 1892-93 (Division 2)

6 (42 games) 1975-76 (Division 1)
6 (42 games) 1933-34 (Division 1)

Most/fewest defeats in a season
26 (42 games) 1975-76 (Division 1)
23 (42 games) 1933-34 (Division 1)

3 (22 games) 1892-93 (Division 2)
4 (34 games) 1899-1900 (Division 1)
4 (46 games) 1981-82 (Division 4)

Most/fewest draws in a season
18 (42 games) 1920-21 (Division 1)

2 (34 games) 1904-05 (Division 1)
5 (42 games) 1951-52 (Division 2)
5 (42 games) 1969-70 (Division 2)

Most/fewest goals scored in a season
102 (42 games) 1925-26 (Division 1)
97 (42 games) 1952-53 (Division 2)
62 (22 games) 1892-93 (Division 2)
33 (42 games) 1975-76 (Division 1)

Most/fewest goals conceded in a season
101 (42 games) 1933-34 (Division 1)
19 (22 games) 1892-93 (Division 2)
29 (30 games) 1896-97 (Division 1)
38 (42games) 1969-70 (Division 2)
39 (42 games) 1970-71 (Division 2)
41 (46 games) 1981-82 (Division 4)

Biggest League wins
11-2 v. Cardiff City (h) 1925-26 (Division 1)
10-0 v. B Port Vale (a) 1892-93 (Division 2)
10-0 v. Burnley (h) 1928-29 (Division 1)

Heaviest League defeats
10-3 v. Middlesbrough (a) 1933-34 (Division 1)
9-2 v. Arsenal (a) 1932-33 (Division 1)
8-1 v. Arsenal (a) 1929-30 (Division 1)
7-0 v. Tottenham H (a) 1949-50 (Division 2)
7-1 v. Huddersfield Town (h) 1927-28 (Division 1)

Highest-scoring League draw
5-5 v. Leicester City (a) 1951-52 (Division 2)

Football League Sequences
Successive wins	8	(1892-93/1903-04/1957-58/1960-61)
Successive defeats	7	(1975-76)
Successive home wins	10	(1960-61)
Successive home defeats	4	(1954-55/1964-65)
Successive away wins	6	(1892-93)
Successive away defeats	12	(1898-99)
Unbeaten matches	22	(1899-1900)
No wins (home & away)	19	(1975-76)
Undefeated home games	20	(1936-37)
Undefeated away games	10	(1899-1900/1981-82)
No Home wins	9	(1975-76)
No Away Wins	18	(1975-76)

FOOTBALL LEAGUE CUP

United entered this competition at the outset in 1960-61 and this is their full record up to and including season 2002-03:

Venue	P	W	D	L	F	A
Home	69	46	11	12	135	64
Away	63	12	15	36	74	119
Totals	132	58	26	48	209	183

League Cup Fact File

* The 'League Cup' has also been known as the Milk Cup (1981-86), the Littlewoods Cup (1986-90), the Rumbelows Cup (1990-92), the Coca-Cola Cup (1992-98) and the Worthington Cup (1998 to date).
* The knockout competition was introduced for the 1960-61 season and the Blades entered at the outset, losing 3-1 at Bury in their first-ever game (despite taking the lead on 55 seconds through John Nibloe).
* United's first win in the League Cup followed in September 1961 when they defeated Fulham 4-0 in a 1st round replay at Bramall Lane (after a 1-1 draw at Craven Cottage).
* United's best effort so far in the competition was reach the semi-final stage in 2002-03 when they were narrowly beaten 3-2 by Liverpool over two legs. After going a goal down in the first game at Bramall Lane in front of a crowd of 30,095, United stormed back to take a 2-1 lead to Anfield thanks to two Michael Tonge goals in the last quarter of an hour. However, despite a plucky performance in front of 43,837 fans on Merseyside, they finally succumbed to a Michael Owen goal in extra-time to lose the contest 3-2 on aggregate.
* United's best home win in the League Cup is 6-1 against Lincoln City in 2000.
* Their best away from Bramall Lane has been 5-1 at Stockport on 1994.
* The Blades' heaviest home defeat was in 1996, beaten 5-2 by Stockport while their heaviest on the road has come at West Ham in 1971 when they lost 5-0.
* United were knocked out of the League Cup on penalties by Grimsby Town in the 2nd round in 2002 (after a 3-3 draw).
* Their best aggregate win in the competition has been 8-4 v. Grimsby in 1982 (won 5-1 at home, drew 3-3 away).
* United won 14 home League Cup matches on the trot between 26 August 1997 and 8 January 2003. And during the period from 12 August 1997 to 21 January 2003, they played 27 League Cup matches and lost only six (two in one season: 2000-01).
* Winger Alan Woodward (32) and full-back Len Badger (30) have made most appearances in the League Cup for the Blades, while Woodward (14), Brian Deane (13) and Keith Edwards (10) have scored most goals.
* The biggest crowd to watch a League Cup game involving United is 44,061 at Arsenal in November 1971. The biggest at Bramall Lane is 39,614 v. Leeds United in October 1978.
* Michael Brown had the pleasure of scoring United's 200th goal in League Cup football - in the 87th minute of the 4-1 win over Wycombe Wanderers at Bramall Lane in October 2000.

97

FOOTBALL LEAGUE GROUP CUP

United's record in this competition:

Venue	P	W	D	L	F	A
Home	1	1	0	0	2	1
Away	2	0	1	1	1	3
Totals	3	1	1	1	3	4

United entered this competition in 1981-82. They played three matches: beating Doncaster Rovers 2-1 at home, losing 2-0 at Grimsby Town and drawing 1-1 at Chesterfield. They failed to make progress into the second phase.

FOOTBALL LEAGUE JUBILEE FUND

United met Sheffield Wednesday twice at Hillsborough in Football League Jubilee Fund matches:
20.08.1938 Wednesday 4 United 1 Att. 14,917
19.08.1939 Wednesday 2 United 4 Att. 11,450
* George Henson scored twice for the Blades in the second match.

FOOTBALL LEAGUE TROPHY

United's record in this competition is:

Venue	P	W	D	L	F	A
Home	1	0	0	1	1	3
Away	2	0	1	1	1	3
Totals	3	0	1	2	2	6

United were involved in the FLT in season 1982-83. They failed to win any of their three matches, losing 3-1 at home to Grimsby Town and 3-1 away to Lincoln City, while drawing 0-0 at Scunthorpe. They failed to qualify for the next phase.

FOOTBALLER OF THE YEAR

Future United manager Joe Mercer was voted 'Footballer of the Year' in 1949-50 after skippering Arsenal to victory in the FA Cup Final over Liverpool.
Blades' nippy striker Paul Peschisolido was voted Canada's 'Footballer of the Year' for 1996-97 when he played for both West Bromwich Albion and Fulham.

FORAN, Mark James

Defender: 11+2 apps. one goal
Born: Aldershot, 30 October 1973
Career: Millwall (juniors, June 1989, professional, November 1990), BLADES (£25,000, August 1993), Rotherham United (on loan, August 1994), Wycombe Wanderers (on loan, August 1995), Peterborough United (£40,000, February 1996), Lincoln City (on loan, January 1997), Oldham Athletic (on loan, March 1997), Crewe Alexandra (£25,000, December 1997), Bristol Rovers (August 2000), Upton Athletic/Devon (season 2002-03).
Mark Foran, at 6ft 4ins, is among the tallest players ever to don a United shirt. He never really got the opportunities to show his mettle at Bramall Lane and even after leaving the Blades he struggled to make his 'mark' with any of his other clubs, ** League appearances for Bristol Rovers being his best tally.

FORBES, Alexander Rooney

Inside-forward/wing-half: 124 apps. 17 goals
Born: Dundee, 21 January 1925
Career: Rockwell Central School (Dundee), Ashdale Boys Club, North of Scotland Schools, Dundee North End, BLADES amateur (27 September 1944), professional (2 October 1944), Arsenal (£16,000, February 1948), Leyton Orient (£3,500, August 1956-November 1957), Fulham, Gravesend (season 1958-59), Sligo Rovers (player-coach, 1960), Arsenal (coach to the juniors, September 1962), to South Africa to coach Highland Park FC, later manager of Johannesburg Rangers.
Initially a ginger-haired Scottish-born inside-forward Alex Forbes had a fair bit of skill, heaps of energy and never lacked enthusiasm. He developed into a solid, hard-working wing-half with Arsenal and went on to gain 14 caps for his country (his first five as a United player: 1947-48). He was an FA Cup and League championship winner with the Gunners in 1950 and 1953 respectively and collected a runners-up medal in the 1952 Cup Final. He made 242 senior appearances for Arsenal (20 goals).
* Forbes played ice hockey for Dundee Tigers and Scotland as a 16 year-old.

FORD, David

Inside-forward; 25+6 apps. 5 goals
Born: Sheffield, 2 March 1945
Career: Sheffield Wednesday (junior, April 1961, professional, January 1963), Newcastle United (December 1969, Jackie Sinclair moving in the opposite direction), BLADES (January 1971), Halifax Town (August 1973 to May 1976).
David Ford never quite fulfilled the promise he had shown as a teenager, although during his career he scored 42 goals in 260 League games - 31 in 122 outings with his first club, Wednesday. Ford was capped twice by England at Under-23 level whilst at Hillsborough and scored for the Owls in their 3-2 FA Cup Final defeat by Everton in 1966. He was also the first substitute used by Wednesday (v. Sunderland in October 1965). In 1971 he helped the Blades gain promotion to the First Division. After retiring from football Ford went into the heating and plumbing business in Sheffield.

FORD, Robert John

Midfielder: 164+23 apps. 7 goals
Born: Bristol, 22 September 1974
Career: Oxford United (junior, June 1990, professional, October 1992), BLADES (£400,000, November 1997-May 2002), Oxford United (season 2002-03).
Bobby Ford made 149 first-class appearances for Oxford before his transfer to Bramall Lane in 1997. An efficient, hard-working midfielder, a real fetch-and-carrier type of player, he gave the Blades excellent service for almost five years before his release in 2002.

FOREIGN TOURS/COUNTRIES/OPPOSITION

United rejected overseas tours on the grounds that Sunday games ould be expected. United finally made their first overseas tour in May/June 1936 when they visited Denmark.
Six games were played (five won, one lost) and 25 goals were scored with only 10 conceded.
Since then they have undertaken many more and over the years have visited and played in the following countries:
Algeria, Argentina, Australia, Austria, Belgium, Bolivia, Borneo, Bulgaria, Canada, Chile, China, Cyprus, Denmark, Dubai, Ecuador, Finland, France, Germany, Greece, Gibralter, Holland, Hong Kong, Israel, Italy, Kuwait, Luxembourg, Malaysia, Mexico, New Caledonian, New Zealand, Norway, Paraguay, Peru, Poland, Republic of Ireland, Spain, Sweden, Switzerland, Trinidad & Tobago, Tunisia, USA and Zambia.
* The Blades have not played 'abroad' (on foreign soil) since July 1998 when they visited Italy.

Tour Guide
* In May 1938 United were undefeated in five games on tour to Sweden in May 1938. They scored 14 goals in the process.
* In May/June 1965, United played Blackpool 12 times over in Canada and New Zealand (see under Blackpool).
* In the late 1960s the Blades played matches against teams from several South American countries, namely Argentina, Bolivia, Chile, Ecuador, Paraguay and Peru.
* When playing in Bolivia in June 1967, United became the first British professional club to visit that country.
* United have also had brief tours to the Channel Islands (Guernsey & Jersey), Scotland and Northern Ireland and also to the Isle of Man and the Isle of Wight.

Foreign Opponents
Here are some of the many big-named and respected 'foreign' teams United have played over the years, listed in A-Z order: AC Milan, ADO The Hague (Holland), Adelaide City, Ajax Amsterdam (Holland), Al Ain (Dubai), Alianza (Peru), America FC (in Mexico City), Ancona (Italy), Apoel Nicosia (Cyprus), Argentina 'B' (Buenos Aries), Atlas FC (in Mexico), Auxerre (France), AZ '67 Alkmaar (Holland), Australian Olympic XI, Barcelona (in Ecuador), Basel FC (Switzerland), Bela Vista (Brazil), Benfica (Portugal), Bolivar (in La Paz, Bolivia), Bologna (Italy), Brann SK (Norway), Brunei (national team), the Canadian Touring team, Cesena (Italy), Chilean World Cup XI (in Santiago), Dallas Americans, DOS Utrecht (Holland), DWS Amsterdam, Eintracht Frankfurt (Germany), El Ahli (Dubai), Enschede XI (Holland), Esbjerg (Sweden), Genoa (Italy), Gornik (Poland), Grazier (Austria), Groningen (Holland), Guernsey XI, Hamburger SV (Germany), Hamburg 07 (in Duisburg), Hannover 96 (Germany), Helsingborg IF (Sweden), Heracles (Holland), Hong Kong X1, Houston Dynamos, IFK Gothenburg (Sweden), IFK Norrkoping (Sweden), Israel XI Jaffa), Jersey XI, Kiev Dynamo (USSR), Lechia (Warsaw), Levski Spartak (Bulgaria), Lyn/Oslo (in Norway), Lucerne (Switzerland), Luxembourg XI, Malmo FF (Sweden), Mexican World Cup XI (in Santiago, Chile), MVV Maastricht, Nantes (France), NAC Breda (Holland), Napoli (Italy), Nuevo Leon (in Monterray, Mexico), Olympic Chaleroi (Belgium), PSV Eindhoven (Holland), Panionios (Greece), Parma Select XI (Italy), Piacenza (Italy), Peking (China), Racing Club de Lens (France), River Plate (Argentina), RC Liegeois (Belgium), SFK Lyn/Oslo (Norway), New Zealand XI, Northern NSW (Australia), FC Santa Cruz (Bolivia), Sarawak Select XI (Malaysia), Servette/Geneva (Switzerland), Seville (Spain), Schalke 04 (Germany), Sogndal IL (Norway), Sparta Amsterdam (Holland), Sparta Rotterdam (Holland), Trelleborgs FF (Sweden), Trinidad & Tobago XI, Twente Enschede (Holland), Tulsa Roughnecks (USA), Udinese (Italy), VfL Bochum (Germany), Vastra Frolunda IF (Sweden), Verona (Italy), VfL Osnabruck (W Germany), Viking Stavanger (Norway), Winterthur (Switzerland), Zambia XI.

FOREIGNERS (Overseas Born Players)

Here is an unofficial list of foreign/overseas born players who have been associated with Sheffield United at various levels (whether on trial, as a guest, on loan or as an amateur)...

Dries Boussatta (Holland), Vas Borbokis (Greece), Marcel Cas (Holland), Paul Casey (W Germany), Benoit Croissant (France), John Cutbush (Malta), Len De Goey (Holland), Wilko De Vogt (Holland), Laurent D'Jaffo (France), Tri Dellas (Thessalonika/Greece), Georgios Donis (Greece), Ebeto (Albania), Wasim El Banna (Zambia), Jan-Aage Fjortoft (Norway), Jostein Flo (Norway), Jack Gibson (USA), Davy Gijsbrechts (Belgium), Doug Hodgson (Australia), Anders Jacobsen (Norway), Jean-Phillipe Javary (France), Petr Katchouro (Belarus), Ville Lehitinen (Finland), Marcelo (Brazil), Kingsley Mbome (Yaounde), Francesco Meacci (Italy), Shaun Murphy (Australia), Roger Nilsen (Norway), Peter Ndlovu (Zimbabwe), Casper Pauckstadt (Sweden), Paul Peschisolido (Canada), Bruno Ribiero (Portugal), Alex Sabella (Argentina), Georges Santos (France), Hans Segers (Holland),Chris Short (W Germany), Axel Smeets (Karawa, Democratic Republic of Congo), Patrick Suffo (Cameroon), Frank Talia (Australia), Oliver Tebily (Ivory Coast), Laurens Ten Heuvel (Holland), Manuel Thetis (France), Gus Uhlenbeek (Surinam), Carl Veart (Australia), Pedro Verde (Argentina), Michel Vonk (Holland), Nicola Weber (France), Arthur Wharton (Accra, Ghana), Trenton Wiggan (West Indies), Jonas Wirmola (Sweden), Buba Yohanna (Yaounde).

Foreign Connection

The following United personnel have all been associated with 'foreign' clubs either as a player, manager, coach, trainer, etc. Where a player's surname is given only, he appears in the list above.

Peter Anderson, Kevin Arnott, Danny Bergara, Alan Birchenall, Borbokis, Jeff Bourne, Boussatta, David Bradford, Jim Brown, John Burridge, Viv Busby, Chris Calvert, Bobby Campbell, Franz Carr, Marcel Cas, Eddie Colquhoun, Gordon Cowans, Croissant, Terry Curran, Cutbush, Brain Deane, Dellas, D'Jaffo, Donis, De Goey, De Vogt, Keith Eddy, El Banna, Stan Fazackerley, Tony Field, Fjortoft, Flo, David Frain, Darren France, Colin Franks, Ken Furphy, Andy Goram, Chris Guthrie, Jimmy Hagan, Ian 'Chico' Hamilton, Willie Hamilton, George Handley, Roger Hansbury, Adrian Heath, Colin Hill, Trevor Hockey, Glyn Hodges, David Hodgson, Doug Hodgson, Jacobsen, Laurent D'Jaffo, Javary, Nicky Johns, Jimmy Johnstone, Francis Joseph, Katchouro, Howard Kendall, Andy Kennedy, Lehtinen, Kevin Lewis, John McGeady, Marcelo, Meacci, Ndlovu, Steve Neville, Peschisolido, Terry Phelan, Ian Porterfield, George Raynor, Trevor Ross, Sabella, Ribiero, Santos, Dean Saunders, Segers, Paddy Sloan, Smeets, Simon Stainrod, Suffo, Ten Heuvel, Thetis, John Tudor, Uhlenbeek, Robert Ullathorne, Andy Walker, Billy Whitehurst, Weber, Wirmola, Peter Withe, Paul Wood and Alan Woodward.

* See under respective player profiles for full details.

FORMATION OF CLUB

In simple terms... on Friday 22 March 1899, the Bramall Lane (Sheffield United Club) ground committee formed Sheffield United FC just six days after an FA Cup semi-final between Preston North End and West Bromwich Albion had attracted a near 23,000 crowd to Bramall Lane! The turnout for this fixture finally convinced Charles Stokes, a valuable member of the club, forming of a professional football club, utilising the facilities offered by the cricket club (at Bramall Lane) would prove successful and benefit the city of Sheffield immensely. Things developed quickly and within a matter of six months (on 7 September 1889) United played its first competitive game of football, losing 4-1 away to Notts Rangers in a friendly.

NB - United's first secretary, Mr JB Wostinholm, was also secretary of the Yorkshire CCC...perhaps unique in sport at the time (even today!).

FOULKE, William Henry

Goalkeeper: 352 apps.
Born: Dawley, Shropshire, 12 April 1874. Died: Sheffield, 1 May 1916.
Career: Alfreton, Blackwell FC, BLADES (June 1894), Chelsea (August 1905), Bradford City (April 1906, retiring November 1907).
Bill 'Fatty' Foulke was a huge man whose weight during a wonderful career rose from 13 stone to a staggering 25 stone 2 lbs, attained in his last season as a Bradford City player.
He spent 11 years at Bramall Lane before transferring to Chelsea in 1905. He was certainly the Colossus among goalkeepers, his clearances (by kicking) were quite exceptional and he could punch the ball as far as some players could kick it. A League Championship winner (1898) and twice an FA Cup winner (1899 & 1902), he also played in the 1901 Final v. Spurs and gained one full England cap v. Wales in March 1897 (won 4-0). He also scored two goals for United v. The Kaffirs (a Black African touring side) in a 7-2 friendly win at Bramall Lane in October 1899.
Besides being a fine 'keeper, Foulke was a very useful cricketers who played four times for Derbyshire in the County Championship (scoring 65 runs and taking 2-92). Sadly he died of pneumonia, aged 42.
* Some reference books have Foulke's birthplace as Blackwell, Derbyshire.

99

FOUNTAIN, John

Half-back: 36 apps.

Born: Leeds, 27 May 1932

Career: Ashley Road FC, BLADES (professional, October 1949), Swindon Town (January 1957), York City (August 1960 to April 1964).

Jack Fountain was a strong tackling, hard-working half-back who spent seven-and-a-half years as a professional at Bramall Lane during which time he averaged just five appearances per campaign. He made 152 appearances for the 'Minstermen' whom he captained several times. His career ended on a sad and sour note when he was one of the players involved in a bribery scandal that had been exposed by the Sunday People. Found guilty, he was imprisoned for 15 months.

FRAIN, David

Midfielder: 40+11 apps. 6 goals

Born: Sheffield, 11 October 1962.

Career: Rowlinson Youth Club, Dronfield United, BLADES (professional, September 1985), Rochdale (July 1988), Stockport County (£50,000, July 1989), Mansfield Town (on loan, September-October 1994); FC Seiko/Hong Kong (briefly), Stalybridge Celtic (May 1995-96).

On his day David Frain was a cultured midfielder. He had three years at Bramall Lane and all told made 279 League appearances (187 for Stockport).

FRANCIS, John Andrew

Forward: 20+33 apps. 8 goals

Born: Dewsbury, 21 November 1963,

Career: Emley, Halifax Town (on trial), Emley (again), BLADES (£10,000, September 1988), Burnley (£50,000, January 1990), Cambridge United (£95,000, August 1992), Burnley (£70,000, March 1993), Scunthorpe United (August 1996-February 1997), Halifax Town (March 1997-99).

In a 12-year career of senior football striker John Francis scored 54 goals in 321 League and Cup games. He was twice a promotion winner with the Blades in 1989 from Division Three (22 games) and 1990 from Division Two (20 outings) and two years later helped Burnley win the Fourth Division championship.

FRANKS, Colin James

Defender: 170+12 apps. 10 goals

Born: Willesden, 16 April 1951

Career: Wealdstone, Watford (professional, July 1969), BLADES (£55,555, June 1973), Toronto Blizzard (£40,000, with Chris Calvert, February 1979).

Signed by his former manager Ken Furphy, Colin Franks gave the Blades useful service for almost six years before moving into the NASL. He joined Watford in 1969 as manager Furphy strengthened his side following promotion to the Second Division. Playing alongside future Blades stars Keith Eddy and Stewart Scullion, he made 112 League appearances for the Hornets, helping them reach the FA Cup semi-final in 1970.

FRIENDLY MATCHES

It is clear to say that since 1889 United have played hundreds of friendly matches at home and abroad, against a variety of opponents, including many top-class sides.

Here are details of some of United's many 'friendly' experiences:

1889-90 - Notts Rangers (a) lost 4-1, first-ever game, 1,000 spectators saw William Robertson scored the Blades' goal. First win, 2-1 v. Heeley (h), att. 2,200. Lost 10-1 at Everton prior to Christmas while suffering other heavy defeats at Grimsby Town (7-0), Middlesbrough (6-2) and Everton again (5-2).

1890-91 - Secured three excellent home wins: 9-0 v. Sheffield FC, 7-0 v. the Casuals and 6-4 v. Heanor Town.

1891-92 - Won six of the first seven friendlies played at start of season including a 5-1 victory over Middlesbrough Ironopolis. Later beat Burnley and Mount St Mary's both by 8-1 and the Casuals 7-2 but lost 8-2 at Birmingham St George's. Jack Scott scored five goals in the win over Burnley.

1893-94 - Scored 13 goals in three friendlies in February (all won).

1896-97 - Ended season with a run of seven unbeaten friendly matches, six of them won including a 7-2 victory over Clowne in a Charity Match.

1898-99 - Only two friendlies played - a 5-2 win at Brentford in April and a 5-3 victory in a benefit Match v. the Corinthians.

1899-00 - Goalkeeper 'Fatty' Foulke scored twice for the Blades in a 7-2 win over a touring Black South African side, the Kaffirs.

1900-01 - Played two Benefit Matches v. Aston Villa - lost 5-1 away (when United's Tom Turnbull sadly broke his leg) but won 6-2 at home.

1901-02 - Played Glasgow Rangers for the first time, won 1-0 with a George Hedley goal in front of 1,600 fans at Bramall Lane.

1902-03 - United beat a West Yorkshire XI 8-5 at Bradford, Fred Priest and Herbert Chapman both scoring hat-tricks. The Blades also beat a Leeds Association XI 7-2 at the Holbeck rugby ground.

1904-05 - Drew at Tottenham Hotspur and beat both West Ham and Arsenal (also away).

1905-06 - Arthur Brown scored a double hat-trick (6 goals) in an 8-0 win at Gainsborough Trinity.

1911-12 - A crowd of 9,500 saw Billy Gillespie score twice in a 4-0 win at Birmingham.

1917-18 - United finished the season with two friendly draws against Everton (home & away).

1922-23 - A crowd of 25,000 saw the Blades lose 2-0 to Sheffield Wednesday in a benefit match at Bramall Lane.

1930-31 - The Blades crashed to a 6-0 defeat in a Charity Match against Grimsby Town at Spalding.

1931-32 - Jimmy Dunne netted five goals in a 6-1 win over Darlington in April.

1935-36 - The Blades had a successful end-of-season tour to Denmark, winning five of their six matches, including victories of 8-2 v. Aarhus and 8-4 v. Aalborg.

1937-38 - Registered four wins and two draws on a tour to Sweden in May.

1939-40 - With WW2 in full flight, United played 15 friendlies this season, losing one of them 5-0 at Huddersfield.

1944-45 - A crowd of 7,750 saw United beat a Polish XI 2-1 at Bramall Lane.

1945-46 - The Blades ended their WW2 activities with a 5-1 defeat a Combined Services XI in front of 15,000 spectators in the Olympic Stadium Berlin.

1952-53 - United toured West Germany and Holland in May and whilst over there beat VfB Lubeck 6-1.

1953-54 - Played four more games in West Germany, suffering three defeats, including a 7-3 reverse against FC Schalke 04 and a 5-1 drubbing by Karlsruhe.

1954-55 - A third successive end-f-season trip to Germany produced only one win - 1-0 over VfR Mannheim.

1955-56 - Almost 10,000 fans saw United beat Heart of Midlothian 4-2 at Bramall Lane, Peter Wragg netting twice.

1956-57 - Another tour to Germany and Holland saw United score 15 goals in five games, beating Phoenix Ludwigshafen in one of them.

1958-59 - Lost 1-0 at home to Hibernian but beat Distillery 3-1 in Ireland.

1959-60- Opened with two wins in Holland; the Blades also beat Lucerne of Switzerland 5-1 at home (Derek Pace scored twice) and another tour abroad saw Lucerne defeated again by7-0 with hot-shot Pace netting four goals on this occasion.

1960-61 - Started off by registering two good in Holland: 5-3 v. Sparta Amsterdam and 5-1 v. Volendam.

1961-62 - Played in Holland (2 wins), the USA and Canada. Played ten games in the latter two countries, recording nine wins and a draw with a goal-average of 34-7. Best win was 7-0 over Edmonton City.

1963-64 - Set the season with two fine wins in Holland, 2-1 over DOS Utrecht and 2-0 v. ADO The Hague.

1964-65 - Lost 4-0 to Sparta Rotterdam in Holland. Played in a tournament in New Zealand in May-June and met Blackpool 11 times (see under BLACKPOOL). Also won 3-2 in Hong Kong.

1965-66 - After two games in Norway, United played in stifling heat and humidity in Mexico and Santiago, Chile, participating in a tournament in the latter city as well as playing a handful of prestige friendly matches. They drew 0-0 with the Mexican World Cup XI in Mexico City and went down 2-0 to the Chilean World Cup side. They also beat AC Milan 4-0 and Seville (Spain) 4-1.

1966-67- United toured South America at the end of the season, playing games in Bolivia, Buenos Aires, Chile, Ecuador, Peru and Mexico...most of the time in very hot weather! They were the first professional side from the U.K. to play - and win - in Bolivia

1968-69 - Played three games in Italy - drawing 3-3 with Napoli and 0-0 with Bologna before beating Verona 2-0.

1969-70 - Beat De Graafchap 3-0 whilst on tour in Holland. They also drew 1-1 with VfL Bochum in West Germany.

1971-72 - Beat NAC Breda/Holland 1-0 on a pre-season tour. Ended the campaign by winning a competition in the heat of Zambia, but had Len Badger and Eddie Colquhoun sent-off during a match in Lusaka.

1973-74 - Played in a competition in Cyprus (June), lost in the Final to Levski Spartak of Bulgaria 2-0.

1974-75 - Started season with a trip to Poland; gained one win in four matches. Ended the campaign on tour in New Zealand where the temperatures were well into the 90's.

1975-76 - Played friendlies against teams from four different countries: Tunisia, France, Belgium and Holland.

1976-77 - Again there was a flurry of action early on with games against RC de Lens (France) lost 4-2, PSV Eindhoven (Holland) drew 1-1 and Olympic Charleroi (Belgium), lost 1-0.

1977-78 - Pre-season spent in sunny Devon; beat Exeter City 4-1.

1978-79 - Among the friendlies played United lost 5-0 to Servette (Switzerland) and were beaten 2-1 by the crack Argentinian side River Plate in front of 22,244 fans at Bramall Lane.

1979-80 - Beat a Select XI 9-1 at 'the Lane' in a testimonial match for Eddie Colquhoun.

1980-81 - Steve Charles scored a hat-trick in a 9-1 win over Truro City in Cornwall - this was a Memorial Fund game for young goalkeeper Keith Solomon.

1981-82 - Played pre-season games in Scotland and Sweden, registering a 4-1 win over Clyde to begin with, followed by successive 4-0 victories over Hallsta IK & Kortedala IF.

1982-83 - Contested five games in Scotland, winning four and losing one, 4-2 against Hearts at Tynecastle.

1983-84 - Lost to Motherwell early on and then toured Malaysia and China, beating Peking 2-1 in front of some 50,000 fans.

1984-85 - Four wins gained on a pre-season tour to Sweden: 17 goals scored with four from Keith Edwards in a 5-0 victory over Torp Golf.

1985-86 - A moderate pre-season with a 1-1 draw at Newcastle the best result. Later beat Guernsey 9-1 & Jersey 5-1 when visiting the Channel Islands. Goalkeeper John Burridge scored twice against Guernsey.

1986-87 - Beat Skegness Town 11-1 in early August with Tony Philliskirk and Steve Foley both scoring hat-tricks.

1987-88 - Again defeated Skegness Town in a friendly, this time by 7-0.

1988-89 - After another 8-1 success over Skegness, United won four games in Sweden including a 12-1 scoreline against Hagfors XI (a record win at first team level). Peter Duffield netted four times in this game.

1989-90 - One win, a draw and one defeat in Germany to start with - and a 2-1 home defeat by the Italian club Genoa at the end.

1990-91 - Four wins and 22 goals scored on a four-match tour of Scandinavia. Tony Agana netted two hat-tricks. Ended the season with a trip to the USA, gaining successive victories over Tulsa Renegades (2-0 & 4-1).

1991-92 - Visited Sweden and Norway in July (gaining five wins and two draws from seven matches). Played in a mini three team tournament in Sweden, with each game lasting just 20 minutes; United lost their first match in a penalty shoot-out. FF Malmo were the visitors for Paul Stancliffe's testimonial at Bramall Lane when a United XI lost 6-1. United also beat the New Zealand national side 2-1 at 'the Lane.'.

1992-93 - After a 2-0 win at Forfar Athletic, United won their next eight friendly matches including five on tour, including three big ones: 10-0 v. Ijusne AIK and 9-0 v. Bracke in Sweden and 5-0 v. Varden IL in Norway. The season ended with a 1-1 draw with Trinidad & Tobago, played at the Queen's Park Oval.

1993-94 - Out of three wins in Norway early on, United's best was a 5-1 scoreline v. Ullensalker. The Blades finished off the campaign in Australia where the weather was exceptionally hot, especially in Perth where Western Australia were beaten 2-1 in front of 13,000 fans. United also drew with the Australia Olympic side in Queensland.

1994-95 - Visited Norway and Switzerland, played seven matches, won four including a 5-1 triumph over Toggaen when John Reed hit a hat-trick. On 14 July 1994 (in Switzerland) United played Winterthur in the first-half of a friendly (1-1) and then took on Baden in the second-half (won 1-0). The Blades played in Italy late on, earning a draw but suffering two defeats.

1995-96 - Recorded five straight wins in Norway, 6-1 the best over Orkdal.

1996-97 - Undefeated in three matches in Malaysia (beat a Sarawak Select XI 3-0). Also played two games in Ireland, winning 4-0 against Glennavon and drawing 0-0 with Linfield.

1997-98 - Gained five wins out of five in Norway/Sweden. Beat the Swedish side Arjang 8-1with Petr Katchouro scoring a hat-trick. The Blades also ran up two 4-0 victories.

1998-99 - Unbeaten in three games in Italy - beat a Parma Select XI 4-0 in front of just 50 spectators! There were also low turnouts of 40 against E'Quip Romagna (1-1) and 75 v. Fiorenzuola (3-3). In August, United lost 3-1 at home to Benfica.

* Since 1999 the majority of the Blades' friendly matches have taken in place in Cornwall
(pre-season tours) whilst one testimonial game, for Dane Whitehouse, played a Bramall Lane in May 2001, saw Sheffield United beat a selected Blades All Stars XI 9-5.

101

FULHAM

United's playing record against the Cottagers:

Football League

Venue	P	W	D	L	F	A
Home	26	15	6	5	43	22
Away	26	7	6	13	35	60
Totals	52	22	12	18	78	82

FA Cup

Venue	P	W	D	L	F	A
Home	3	3	0	0	8	2
Away	1	0	1	0	1	1
Neutral	1	1	0	0	2	1
Totals	5	4	1	0	11	4

League Cup

Venue	P	W	D	L	F	A
Home	2	2	0	0	7	0
Away	1	0	1	0	1	1
Totals	3	2	1	0	8	1

Churchgoers were behind the formation of Fulham FC which started out as Fulham st Andrew's Church Sunday School FC in 1879. The team won the West London Amateur Cup in 1887 and, after adopting the name of Fulham the very next year, the championship of the West London League in its initial season of 1892-93 (when the Blades commenced life in the Football League). They have played at Craven Cottage since 1896, having had several changes of venue prior to that, including quaintly named grounds like Eel Brook Common, Purser's Cross (Roskell's Field), Half Moon in Putney and Captain James Field (New Brompton).

Fulham finally gained membership of the Football League club in 1907, and they first encountered the Blades in the competition over Easter 1935 (Division 2) when they completed the double, winning 7-2 at Craven Cottage and 2-1 at Bramall Lane. Jim Hammond netted a fourtimer for the London club in their home victory. The followed season the London club doubled-up again with 1-0 and 3-1 victories at 'the Lane' and the 'Cottage respectively.

By winning 2-1 at the 'Cottage' in April 1953, United became Second Division champions.

The Blades were well and truly blunted again in September 1957 when Roy Dwight, aided and abetted by the brilliant Johnny Haynes, scored four goals in Fulham's 6-3 win. United's best win of the 22 so far gained over Fulham in the League is 5-2 at Bramall Lane (Division 2) in 1956-57 when both Derek Hawksworth and Colin Grainer scored twice.

All of United's seven wins on Fulham soil have all been by the odd goal, the last in 1967-68 (1-0).

The Blades beat Fulham 2-1 in the 1936 FA Cup semi-final at Molineux, Don 'Dicky' Bird and Jack Pickering scoring the goals in front of more than 51,500 spectators. In January 1986, a crowd of just 7,004 witnessed a 3rd round FA Cup-tie between United and Fulham end 2-0 in favour of the Blades. This was the lowest attendance for a major Cup game at Bramall Lane since February 1895.

Ex-Blades player Jack Peart managed Fulham (1935-48), as did Ray Lewington (1986-90) while Arthur Rowley played for Fulham and managed the Blades. Billy Biggar, Gary Brazil, Arthur Brown, Viv Busby, Glenn Cockerill, Ted Connor, Alan Cork, John Cutbush, Jeff Eckhardt, Steve Foley, Alex Forbes, Chris Guthrie, Jon Harley, Charlie Hartfield, Tom Holmes, Walter Hoyland, Francis Joseph, Bert Lipsham, Ken McKay, Reg Matthewson, Paul Parker, Paul Peschisolido, Terry Phelan, Martin Pike, John Ryan, Jack Scott, Rob Scott, Tom Simons, Gus Uhlenbeek, and Alan Warboys have all played for both clubs. Dugald Livingstone managed Fulham and was United's trainer; George Utley played for United and became Fulham's trainer.

FULL MEMBERS CUP

United's record in this short-lived competition is:

Venue	P	W	D	L	F	A
Home	1	0	0	1	1	2
Away	3	1	1	1	3	3
Totals	4	1	1	2	4	5

In 1985-86, after a 1-1 draw with Leeds United at Elland Road (in front of only 2,274 fans) the Blades were knocked out by Manchester City who won 2-1 at Bramall Lane before a crowd of 3,420.

The following season, after a 2-1 win at Stoke where the turnout was almost 4,000, the Blades succumbed 1-0 to Blackburn Rovers before 2,220 supporters at Ewood Park.

FURLONG, Paul Anthony

Striker: 4 apps. 2 goals

Born: Wood Green, London, 1 October 1996.

Career: Enfield, Coventry City (£130,000, July 1991), Watford (£250,000, July 1992), Chelsea (£2.3 million, May 1994), Birmingham City (£1.5 million, July 1996), Queen's Park Rangers (on loan, August 2000) BLADES (on loan, February-March 2002), Queen's Park Rangers (on loan, July-August 2002, signing permanently, September 2002).

An FA Trophy winner with Enfield in 1988 (scoring twice in the Final replay v. Telford United), striker Paul Furlong also gained five semi-professional caps for England and then did very well in the Football League, helping Blues twice reach the First Division Play-offs. Despite suffering a few injury problems, his career record, at the end of the 2002-03 season, after he had again helped his team, QPR, win through to the Second Division Play-off Final (where they lost 1-0 to Cardiff City) was very good...over 120 goals scored in more than 280 senior appearances.

FURNISS, Frederick

Right-back: 433 apps. 18 goals
Born: Sheffield, 10 July 1922
Career: Hallam FC, BLADES (January 1943), Chesterfield (August 1955-May 1956).
A WW2 discovery by the Blades, Fred Furniss was fast in recovery, a timely tackler with an appetite for hard work. He gave the club twelve-and-a-half years excellent service, being an ever-present in the Second Division championship winning season of 1952-53 when he partnered Graham Shaw. He spent just the one season at Saltergate without ever making the first XI. He enjoyed taking penalties had poor English and he never took free kicks near to the goal.

Sheffield United's Howard Johnson (l) and Fred Furniss (r) cover as goalkeeper Ted Burgin (c) punches clear

GAGE, Kevin William

Full-back: 124+7 apps. 7 goals
Born: Chiswick, London, 21 April 1964
Career: Wimbledon (apprentice, June 1980, professional, January 1982), Aston Villa (£100,000, July 1987), BLADES (£150,000, November 1991), Preston North End (March 1996), Hull City (September 1997-May 1998).
A tigerish, hard-tackling full-back, Kevin Gage scored in all four Divisions of the Football League. An England Youth international, he became Wimbledon's youngest-ever player when he made his League debut at the age of 17 years, 15 days v. Bury (Division 4) on 2 May 1981. He was a Fourth Division championship winner two years later. After linking up with his former team-mate Glyn Hodges at Hull City, he left the League score in 1998 with more than 500 competitive appearances under his belt (36 goals scored).

GAINSBOROUGH TRINITY

Blades' playing record against Trinity:

FA Cup

Venue	P	W	D	L	F	A
Home	1	1	0	0	1	0

Midland Counties League

	P	W	D	L	F	A
Home	1	1	0	0	2	1
Away	1	0	0	1	1	4
Totals	2	1	0	1	3	5

Gainsborough trinity FC was formed in 1890 and were members of the Football League from 1896 to 1912. They are currently based in the Unibond League (Premier Division).
The Blades defeated Trinity 1-0 in a 4th qualifying FA Cup-tie on 5 December 1891, Sammy Dobson scoring he all-important goal in front of a 7,000 crowd, this after the contest had been switched from Trinity's Northolme ground to Bramall Lane.
The two MCL matches were played in season 1890-91, Will Bairstow and Gavin Crawford scoring second-half goals in the Blades' 2-1 home win after Trinity had taken the lead before the break.
Of the many players who have served with the Blades and Trinity (various levels) we have Billy Bromage, Arthur Brown, Fred Brown, George Brown, Joe Cockroft, Stewart Evans (United reserve), Bernard Harris, Charlie Howlett, Alf Jeffrey, Joe Kitchen, Harry Lilley, Wallace Masterman, John Reed, Bobby Rooney, Geoff Salmons, Ben Shearman, Des Thompson, Sam Thorpe, Oliver Tummon, Gary West, Fred White, Billy Whitehurst, Mick Whitham, Trenton Wiggan and Walter Wigmore. Neil Warnock has managed both clubs.

GALBRAITH, Dugald Thomas

Inside-right: 14 apps. 5 goals
Born: Scotland, circa 1867
Career: BLADES (August 1889-April 1890).
Scotsman Duggie Galbraith played for the Blades in their first season of 1889-90.
There were two other Scotsmen by the name of Galbraith in the game around the same period of time, between 1888-98: (a) Hugh, who served with Accrington, Bootle, Middlesbrough Ironopolis, Burnley, Luton Town & Glossop) and (b) Thomas D who was associated with Vale of Leven(1897), Sunderland and Leicester Fosse(1900). The latter may well have been the United man.

GALLACHER, Hugh Morgan

Inside/outside-left: 48 apps. 8 goals
Born: Maybole near Girvan, Ayrshire, 11 May 1870
Career: Preston North End (August 1890), BLADES (January 1893), Leicester Fosse (June 1894), Nelson (1896), New Brompton/Gillingham (1897).
Hugh Gallacher moved to Deepdale as a 20 year-old, just as North End were losing their title 'The Invincibles'. After helping them take the runners-up spot in the First Division he was transferred to United in 1893. He played in the first Sheffield League 'derby' and became noted for the eccentricity of chewing his way through an ounce of 'twist' tobacco per game - half-and-ounce per 45 minutes. One footed but nevertheless a tricky performer, he made 140 League appearances and scored 29 goals, playing perhaps his best football with PNE.

GALLIMORE, George

Outside-left: 17 apps. 2 goals
Born: Hanley, Stoke-on-Trent, 10 August 1886. Died: Stoke, 1949.
Career: Astwood Vale, East Vale FC, Stoke (August 1903), BLADES (with Albert Sturgess, June 1908), Birmingham (April 1910), Leek Town (September 1911-May 1913). He did not figure after WW1.
After joining the Blades, George Gallimore, a clever ball player (given the chance to dribble) made his senior debut for the Blades against Bury (away) in September 1908, lining up with his former Potters' colleague Albert Sturgess. He never really settled down at 'the Lane.'

GAMES PLAYED

When the curtain came down on the 2002-03 League season, United - since 1889 - had played more than 5,200 competitive matches (including all minor and major tournaments, wartime fixtures, one Test Match & the various Play-off encounters but not void games, tour and overseas friendly tournaments, local charity Cup Finals etc). They had netted close on 8,400 goals and conceded almost 7,600. This is a full breakdown of those matches:

Competition	P	W	D	L	F	A
Anglo-Italian Cup	4	1	2	1	10	8
Anglo-Scottish Cup	23	10	2	11	24	29
Associate Members Cup	4	3	0	1	6	5
Birmingham Cup	4	3	0	1	9	5
County Shield (S& HCC)	112	63	15	34	247	162
FA Cup	334	150	82	102	505	402
Football League	4002	1603	975	1424	6259	5883
Football League Cup	132	58	26	48	209	183
Football League Group Cup	3	1	1	1	3	4

Football League Trophy	3	0	1	2	2	6
Full Members Cup	4	1	1	2	4	5
London Charity Shield	2	0	2	0	1	1
Midland Counties League	18	8	3	7	32	25
Northern League	26	14	4	8	66	37
Play-offs	10	3	3	4	12	17
Premier League	84	22	28	34	96	113
Steel City Challenge Trophy	4	2	0	2	8	9
Sheffield & Derbyshire Lge.	2	0	1	1	1	2
Sherpa Van Trophy	3	0	2	1	4	5
Simod Cup	1	0	0	1	0	3
Test Match	1	1	0	0	1	0
Texaco Cup	7	1	2	4	6	12
United Counties League	13	3	5	5	15	22
Wartime (1915-19)	142	70	26	46	268	190
Wartime (1939-46)	255	117	47	91	555	453
Watney Cup	5	3	1	1	13	1
Wharncliffe Charity Cup	6	3	1	2	6	4
Yorkshire & Humber Cup	7	4	2	1	8	4
Zenith Data Systems Cup	5	2	1	2	13	8
Totals:	5216	2146	1233	1837	8383	7598

Game Talk
* The most games played by United at first team level in one single season is 69 - completed in 1961-62. They had 42 fixtures in the Football League, seven in the League Cup, six in the FA Cup, one in the County Cup and 13 friendlies.
* Owing to the Arctic weather conditions all over Britain, between 16 December 1962 and 1 March 1963 (some 11 weeks) United played only three League games (drew 0-0 at Wolves and lost 2-0 at home to West Ham) and two friendly games against Ipswich and Stoke.
* United's 1,000 game in the Football League (Divisions 1 & 2) was against West Bromwich Albion (h) on 26 April 1924, won 2-0.
* Their 1,000th game in the First Division was against Sunderland (h) on 25 January 1925 (won 2-1)...and their 4,000th in the Football League (all Divisions) followed 78 years later v. Wolverhampton Wanderers at Bramall Lane on 26 April 2003 (drew 3-3).
* A three-team tournament in Switzerland on 14 July 1994 involving United and two from the host country, FC Winterthur and Bagen saw all games of a 45-minute duration (as agreed). United drew their first 1-1 and won the second (v. Bagen) 1-0.
* One of the shortest (technically completed) matches played by United was the 35-minute each-way contest against Linthouse FC (Glasgow) in January 1891. It was agreed (before kick-off) that the friendly would be of only 70 minutes duration due to fading light.
* In 1897, United played 14 first team matches during the month of April (only two were in the League). They fulfilled 10 in 15 days during April 1958 (eight in the League) and contested nine in 17 days in April 1900 (four in the League). Over a six-week period from 18 July to 30 August 1997, the Blades competed in 14 first team matches, virtually all of them friendlies.

Two On The Same Day
United have fulfilled two first team fixtures on the same day six times.
* On 14 March 1891 the Blades beat Kilnhurst 4-1 at home in a semi-final replay of the Sheffield County Cup and also won by the same score in a friendly away to Attercliffe FC.
* A week later, on 21 March 1891, they drew 1-1 with Royal Arsenal in a friendly at The Oval and lost 2-1 at home to Doncaster Rovers in the Final of the Sheffield County Cup.
* On 18 April 1891, United played two friendlies, both away, winning 1-0 at Lincoln City and losing 3-2 at Matlock.
* On 27 February 1892 United beat Everton 2-0 in an away friendly and defeated Kilnhurst, also away, in the semi-final of the Sheffield County Cup.
* On 25 March 1895, United beat Leicester Fosse 3-2 at home in the United Counties League and also won 2-1 at Luton in a friendly.
* On 17 May 1982, a friendly at Bradford City ended 2-2 while a County Cup semi-final at Barnsley also finished level at 0-0.

GANNON, John Spencer
Midfielder: 196+13 apps. 8 goals
Born: Wimbledon, 18 December 1966
Career: Wimbledon (junior, April 1982, professional, December 1984), Crewe Alexandra (on loan, December 1986) BLADES (February 1989), Middlesbrough (on loan, November-December 1993), Oldham Athletic (£20,000, March 1996-May 1997), Mansfield Town (assistant-manager, season 2002-03).
John Gannon was a skilful player with a sweet left-foot, who was always seeking to open the game up from his midfield role, although at times his passing was rather average. Signed by his former boss Dave Bassett during Blades' promotion year of 1989 (playing in the last 16 games), twelve months later he was also key member of the team that rose up from Division Two. He went on to appear in well over 200 first-class matches before moving to Oldham in 1996. He drifted out of top-line football in 1997 with almost 250 competitive appearances under his belt. In 2002 he became assistant-manager to another ex-Blades player, Keith Curle, at Field Mill.

GARBETT, Terence Graham
Midfielder: 31+9 apps.
Born: Lanchester, 9 September 1945
Career: Stockton (1961), Middlesbrough (professional, August 1963), Watford (August 1966), Blackburn Rovers (September 1971), BLADES (£30,000, February 1974), New York Cosmos (February 1976).
Signed by his former boss Ken Furphy in 1974, midfielder Terry Garbett had earlier made exactly 200 League appearances for Watford whom helped reach the 1970 FA Cup semi-final. With several more Football League players (from various clubs) he opted for a change in scenery and entered the NASL in 1976.

105

GARDNER, Charles Richard

Inside-forward: 12 apps. one goal
Born: Birmingham, 22 December 1912. Died: 1997
Career: Evesham, Birmingham (amateur, September 1932), Notts County (professional, May 1933), Stourbridge (January 1935), Manchester United (May 1935), BLADES (£1,400, May 1937-May 1939).
A year after helping Manchester United win the Second Division title, Dick Gardner joined the Blades but only stayed at Bramall Lane for a season, being unable to hold down a regular first team place.

GARNER, Paul

Left-back: 297+4 apps. 11 goals
Born: Doncaster, 1 December 1955,
Career: Huddersfield Town (apprentice, April 1971, professional, December 1972), BLADES (£59,555, November 1975), Gillingham (on loan, September 1983), Mansfield Town (September 1984, retired through injury, May 1989).
England Youth international Paul Garner was with Huddersfield when they were relegated from Division Two in 1973 and from the Third Division in 1975. He then joined the Blades who were subsequently demoted three times - from the First Division in 1976, from the Second in 1979 and from the Third in 1981. Eventually, after five relegation campaigns, Garner's luck changed and he went on to help the Blades win the Fourth Division title in 1982 and climb out of the Third Division in 1984.
He retired through injury having appeared in well over 450 League games for his four clubs. Garner then became an insurance agent, based in Sheffield before buying his own milk round in Renishaw. As a Mansfield player he helped the Stags gain promotion from Division Four in 1986, win the Freight Rover Trophy in 1987 and lift the Notts County Cup two years later.

Sheffield United squad 1978-79: (back row, l-r) Coach Cec Coldwell, Tony Kenworthy, **Paul Garner**, Craig Renwick, Colin Franks, Jim Brown, Steve Conroy, Steve Finnieston, Simon Stainrod, Mike Guy, Andy Keeley; (front row, l-r) John Cutbush, Gary Hamson, Cliff Calvert, Assistant Manager Danny Bergara, Manager Harry Haslam, Alan Woodward, Mick Speight, Alex Sabella

GATE RECEIPTS

This is how the gate receipts record has been broken at Bramall Lane (since 1889):

£325,000*	United v. Liverpool	LCSF/1	07.01.2002
£298,364	United v. Coventry City F	AC Rd 6 rep	17.03.1998
£262,292	United v. Manchester Utd	FAC Rd 5	14.02.1993
£171,095	United v. Manchester Utd	FAC Rd 6	11.03.1990
£67,806	United v. Newcastle Utd	FLC Rd 2	27.09.1988
£65,092	United v. Sheffield Wed	Div 3	05.04.1980
£37,501	United v. Arsenal	FAC Rd 3	07.01.1978
£33,001	United v. Newcastle Utd	FAC Rd 3	08.01.1977
£11,582	United v. Cardiff City	Div 2	27.04.1971
£8,530	United v. Sheffield Wed	FAC Rd 6	12.03.1960
£4,961	Aston Villa v. Chelsea	FAC S/F	27.03.1920
£5,290	Manch Utd v. Newcastle U	FAC S/F	27.03.1909
£2,525	England v. Scotland	International	04.04.1903
£1,183	United v. Wednesday	FAC Rd 2	10.02.1900
£962	United v. Wednesday	Div 1	27.12.1897
£912	Aston Villa v. Liverpool	FAC S/F	20.03.1897
£867	Aston Villa v. Sunderland	FAC S/F	27.02.1892
£667	PNE v. West B Albion	FAC S/F	16.03.1889

* Approximate/unconfirmed figure.

Money Talk

Receipts of £4,783 from the United v. Aston Villa (League Cup North semi-final) in April 1944, that of £3,981 from the United v. Sunderland FA Cup-tie in January 1926 and the £3,741 which was banked from the United v. West Bromwich Albion FA Cup-tie in March 1925, were all 'club' records at the time.

GATESHEAD

Formed in 1899 as South Shields, the club has had an interesting life. It was elected to the Football League in 1919 (Division 2), were playing in the Third Division (North) come 1928, changed its name to Gateshead two years later and survived, just about (with Newcastle and Sunderland breathing down the neck) until 1960 when they failed with their re-election bid (replaced by FA Cup giant-killers Peterborough United from the Midland League who at the time were managed by former Blades player, Jimmy Hagan).

United have met Gateshead just once, beating them 1-0 in a 4th round FA Cup-tie at Bramall Lane in January 1951...and it was Hagan who scored the only goal of a tight contest.

GAUDIE, Ralph

Forward: 6 apps. 2 goals

Born: Guisborough, February 1876.

Career: South Bank FC (August 1895), Sheffield Saracens (1896), BLADES (April 1897), Aston Villa (August 1898), Woolwich Arsenal (October 1899), Manchester United (August 1903), Darlaston (May 1904), Stourbridge (1906, retired 1908).

Ralph Gaudie could play as a left-half or inside-forward and he did reasonably well. Whilst recovering from illness he worked as a newspaper reporter on The Germiston Times in South Africa before returning to Arsenal in October 1900. He helped the Blades win the First Division championship in 1898, netting twice on his League debut against Notts County (away). He scored 24 goals in 50 senior games for the Gunners.

* Gaudie may well have had a second Christian name as the Aston Villa records list him as Richard R.

GAYLE, Brian Wilbert

Defender: 135+2 apps. 11 goals

Born: Kingston, Jamaica, 6 March 1965

Career: Wimbledon (apprentice, June 1981, professional November 1982), Manchester City (£325,000, July 1988), Ipswich Town (£700,000, January 1990), BLADES (£750,000, September 1991), Exeter City (August 1996), Rotherham United (October 1996), Bristol Rovers (free, March 1997), Shrewsbury Town (free, December 1997), Telford United (seasons 1999-2003).

A record buy in 1990, defender Brian Gayle was a determined and combative captain for the Blades. A rock-solid performer, he made 100 appearances for the Dons, 66 for Manchester City and 62 for Ipswich. He underwent four separate operations on his right knee in the space of 15 months before leaving Bramall Lane in 1996.

GERMANY

Sheffield United played their first game in Germany on 16 May 1946 - losing 5-1 in Berlin to a BOAR Select XI in a friendly. The attendance was 15,000.

GIBRALTER INTERNATIONAL SOCCER FESTIVAL

United took part in this Festival in May 1976. They beat Lincoln City 6-5 on penalties (after a 2-2 draw in normal playing time) before losing 4-1 to Wolverhampton Wanderers in the Final in front of 5,500 spectators.

GIBSON, John Rutherford

Right/left-back: 80 apps.

Born: Philadelphia, USA, 23 March 1898. Died: Luton, July 1974.

Career: Netherbyrne FC, Blantyre Celtic, Sunderland (November 1920), Hull City (May 1922), BLADES (£3,000, March 1929), Luton Town (May 1933, retired June 1934). Later employed by Vauxhall Motors (Luton) as an inspector (1936-64).

A fine, well-built defender, 'Jock' Gibson was signed from Hull City for £3,000 in March 1929. He never really played with real confidence at 'the Lane' despite having two lengthy spells in the first XI between December 1929 and December 1930.

* Gibson left the States at the age of two, moving to Sheffield with his family. When he was 13, the Gibson family moved north to Hamilton, Lanarkshire.

GIBSON, Sidney

Right-winger: 118 apps. 29 goals

Born: Walgrave near Wellingborough, Northants, 20 May 1899. Died: 1938

Career: Kettering Town, Nottingham Forest (May 1921), BLADES (£5,000, September 1928, retired through injury, May 1932).

Sid Gibson, a decidedly quick and direct winger, made a slow start to his career at Bramall Lane, struggling due mainly to health problems. Then, once into his stride he went on to play in well over 100 first-class matches for the Blades, having one of his finest afternoon's at Old Trafford in April 1930 when Manchester United where whipped 5-1 in a vital relegation battle. His career was ended after suffering a knee injury v. Derby County in January 1932.

* Some reference books have Gibson's Christian name spelt as Sydney.

GILHOOLEY, Patrick

Forward: 15 apps. 3 goals

Born: Draffan, Lanarkshire, Scotland, 6 July 1876. Died: Sussex, 20 February 1907.

Career: Vale of Avon Juveniles (1892), Larkhall Thistle (1894), Cambuslang Hibernian (1895), Celtic (August 1896), BLADES (May 1900), Tottenham Hotspur (September 1901), Brighton & Hove Albion (April 1904-May 1905).

Principally a winger, Pat Gilhooley also enjoyed playing as an inside-forward. Either side of a moderate spell at Bramall Lane, he netted 20 goals in 50 games for Celtic and 8 in 61 for Spurs He represented the Scottish League v. the Football League in April 1819

GILLESPIE, William

Inside/centre-forward: 563 apps. 181 goals
Born: Kerrykeel, County Londonderry, Ireland, 5 August 1891.
Died: Bexley (Kent), 1981.
Career: Derry Institute (1907), Derry Celtic (1908), Leeds City (May 1910), BLADES (£500, December 1911), Derry City (August 1931), BLADES (November 1931, as senior trainer/coach to May 1932).

Billy Gillespie scored on his Blades' debut in the 2-2 draw with Newcastle United a week after joining the club. A most gifted, scheming, attacking forward, he was also a shrewd captain and for a time Blades' most capped player, spending most of his 21 years at Bramall Lane thrilling the United supporters with his tremendous forward play.

Gillespie broke a leg in the last minute of United's opening League game of the 1914-15 season, away at Sunderland (lost 3-2) and was out of action until September 1915...by that time WW1 was in progress and United had won the FA Cup (he later won a Cup medal in 1925). He scored 19 goals in 60 appearances during the hostilities, and was raring to go when League football resumed in 1919. In 1931 Gillespie went back to play a few games in Ireland but soon returned to Bramall Lane where he stayed for another year, acting as a senior trainer/coach. He was capped 25 times at full international level (seven by Ireland and 18 by Northern Ireland).

GILLINGHAM

(formerly New Brompton)
United's playing record against the Gills:

Football League

Venue	P	W	D	L	F	A
Home	8	3	2	3	15	9
Away	8	2	2	4	10	16
Totals	16	5	4	7	25	25

Formed initially as New Brompton FC in 1893 (taking over The Priestfield Stadium immediately) the club changed its name to Gillingham in 1913 and gained entry into the Football League seven years later (Division Three). However, the 'Gills' went out in 1938 before returning in 1950.

They met the Blades for the first time in November 1979 (Division Three), losing 4-0 at Bramall Lane. But they reversed matters later with a smart 3-0 victory at The Priestfield Stadium.

Ten goals were scored in the two League games between the clubs in 1983-84, United again winning 4-0 at home but losing 4-2 away. After gaining promotion to the First Division, the 'Gills' recorded their best win over United in 2000-01 (4-2 at home). In 2002-03 both League meetings ended in draws.

Archie Clark managed both clubs while Ex-Blades wing-half Gerry Summers was manager of Gillingham during the early 1980s.

Carl Asaba, Fred Brown, Steve Bruce (also Blades manager), Darren Carr, Fred Cheesemuir, Mel Eves, Hugh Gallacher, Paul Garner, Francis Joseph, Andy Kennedy, Phil Kite, Mark Morris, Terry Nicholl, 'Iffy' Onuora, Mike Trusson, Gary West, Ronnie Waldock are among the many players who've served with the Blades and the Gills. Harry Haslam was manager of the Blades and coach at Gillingham.

GIVENS, Daniel Joseph

Forward: 12 apps. 3 goals
Born: Limerick, 9 August 1949
Career: Dublin Rangers (season 1964-65), Manchester United (apprentice, June 1965 professional December 1966), Luton Town (April 1970), Queen's Park Rangers (£40,000, July 1972), Birmingham City (£165,000, August 1978), AFC Bournemouth (on loan, March-April 1980), BLADES (March 1981), Neuchatel Xamax/Switzerland (June 1981, retired in May 1987); later returned as Youth team coach with the Swiss club (June 1993), taking over as team manager in November 1993, before acting as assistant-manager (to 2001). On moving back to the Republic of Ireland he was subsequently appointed manager of the Eire Under-21 side.

'Don' Givens, the son of a champion hurdler, followed the well-trodden path from Ireland to Old Trafford. He suffered badly from homesickness early on in his career but decided to stay in England where he developed into a fine goalscorer, going on to partner Malcolm Macdonald at Luton. He won the first of his 56 caps for the Republic of Ireland against Denmark in May 1969, whilst still a member of Manchester United's reserve side and did not make his League debut until three months later. It was the first of 408 in the competition, 113 goals scored, 76 of them coming in 242 games for QPR. With his very last kick in the Football League - for the Blades against Walsall in May 1981 - he missed a penalty that sent United down to the Fourth Division. He was plagued by hip injuries whilst with Blues and, indeed, it was an arthritic hip that eventually led to his retirement. He helped Neuchatel Xamax win the Swiss League championship in 1987 and his total of 19 international goals was a record at the time and since bettered by Frank Stapleton and Niall Quinn.

GLOSSOP

(North End)

United's playing record against Glossop:

Football League

Venue	P	W	D	L	F	A
Home	1	1	0	0	4	0
Away	1	0	1	0	2	2
Totals	2	1	1	0	6	2

The smallest town to have housed a Football League club playing in the 'top flight' and formed as Glossop North End in 1877, the Derbyshire club gained entry into the Football League in 1898 and had just one season in the First Division (1899-1900) when they opposed the Blades for the only time at competitive level so far. They distinguished themselves at their North Road ground when holding out for a 2-2 draw in early December but lost heavily by 4-0 at Bramall Lane as united finished runners-up to Aston Villa in the championship, while luckless Glossop were relegated after gaining only four points away from home. They remained in the League (Division 2) until 1915.

Joe Brooks, Archie Needham and Bill Ross all played for both clubs.

GLOVER, Dean Victor

Defender: 5 apps.

Born: West Bromwich, 29 December 1963

Career: Kings Norton Schools, West Midlands Boys, Aston Villa (apprentice June 1980, professional December 1981), BLADES (on loan, October-November 1986), Middlesbrough (June 1987), Port Vale (for a record fee of £200,000, February 1989; retired from League football in May 1988); Newcastle Town (manager, 1988-91), Port Vale (coach).

A very fine defender, Dean Glover made 39 appearances for Villa, over 50 for Middlesbrough and 430 for Port Vale, helping the latter win the Autoglass Trophy in 1993 and promotion to Division Two the following year.

GOALKEEPERS

* Goalkeepers first appeared in different coloured jerseys (to the rest of the team) in season 1909-10.

* Willie Foulke (2 goals) v. The Kaffirs in a friendly in October 1899, John Burridge (2) v. Guernsey XI in May 1986 and Paul Tomlinson (one v. Dallas Americans in May 1985) are goalkeepers who have scored while playing in United's first XI.

* Foulke was keeping goal when he scored his brace while Burridge and Tomlinson both appeared as outfield players.

* Winger Alan Woodward went in goal in the 11th minute of United's League game v. Leeds at Bramall Lane in November 1967. He played exceptionally well as did his defenders as the Blades won 1-0. Woodward also spent two-and-half hours (covering five matches) between the posts and conceded just one goal v. Manchester City in October 1973.

* United 'keeper John Hope kept seven clean-sheets in successive matches between 20 March and 17 April 1971.

* Goalkeeper Carl Muggleton's only first team appearance for United was as a substitute, an outfield player, sent on in the 88th minute against Reading (away) in a First Division game on 27 April 1996 (won 3-0).

* Defender Albert Sturgess deputised in goal for United for well over 300 minutes during his time at the club. He let in only eight goals, including three at West Brom in March 1922. He actually took over as goalie on seven occasions.

* Goalkeeper Paddy Kenny appeared in all but one of United's *** competitive games in the 2002-03 season. Alan Hodgkinson played in 56 out of 69 first-team games in 1961-62 (including 53 out of a total of 55 in League, FA Cup and League Cup).

GOAL-NETS

Goal-nets were used for the first time in a United game on 10 October 1891 when South Bank FC visited Bramall Lane for a Northern League game. The Blades won 6-0.

Goal-nets were first invented and patented by JA Brodie of Liverpool in 1890. The first important game in which nets were used with the North v. South challenge match at Nottingham (Trent Bridge) and they were also used in the 1891 FA Cup Final.

Sheffield United v.s Derby County Match ticket, March 15th 1902

GOALS & GOALSCORERS

**Champion Football League scorers
(qualification: 75 goals)**
201 Harry Johnson
158 Alan Woodward
143 Jimmy Dunne
143 Keith Edwards
140 Derek Pace
129 Fred Tunstall
127 Billy Gillespie
117 Jimmy Hagan
113 'Jock' Dodds
105 Joe Kitchen
102 Jack Pickering
101 Alf Ringstead
100 Arthur Brown

**FA Cup marksmen:
(qualification: 12 goals)**
20 Harry Johnson
18 Derek Pace
18 Fred Priest
15 Billy Russell
12 Ernest Needham

**League Cup sharp-shooters
(qualification: 10 goals)**
14 Alan Woodward
13 Brian Deane
10 Keith Edwards

**All Competitions (including wartime)
(qualification: 100 goals)**
252 Harry Johnson
193 Alan Woodward
191 Jack Pickering
175 Derek Pace
171 Keith Edwards
169 Joe Kitchen
167 Jimmy Dunne
161 Billy Gillespie
51 Jimmy Hagan
135 Fred Tunstall
128 'Jock' Dodds
119 Brian Deane
111 Harold Brook
109 Alf Ringstead
104 Arthur Brown
103 Derek Hawksworth

For United's leading wartime scorers, see under WARTIME FOOTBALL

Goal-Talk
* United's first goalscorer was William Robertson against Notts Rangers in an away friendly on 7 September 1889 (lost 4-1).
* The club's first 'home' scorer was Billy Mosforth against Grimsby Town, also in a friendly, on 30 September 1889.
* Jimmy Dunne's record of scoring 30 or more goals in three successive seasons of top-flight football for United (1929-32) has now stood for over 70 years. He was top-scorer for the club a spell four seasons on the trot (1929-33).
* Only three other players have scored 30 or more League goals in a season for the Blades: 'Jock' Dodds 33 (in 1935-36), Keith Edwards, twice with 35 (1981-82) & 33 (1983-84) and Harry Johnson, also twice, with 33 (1927-28) & 31 (1928-29).
* Harry Hammond was United's leading scorer in three of the club's first League football (missing out in 1893-94).
* Arthur Brown topped United's scoring charts five years running: 1903-08. He amassed 92 League goals during that time.
* Harry Johnson was the Blades' leading marksman no fewer than eight times in nine seasons during the 1920s, finishing second to Tommy Boyle in 1924-25. He netted a total of 186 League goals between 1920 and 1929.
* Derek Pace fell one season short of Johnson's record - top-scoring seven years in succession: 1957-1964. He claimed a total of 130 League goals in that time.
* Alan Woodward set a club record for a winger when he headed United's scoring charts seven times between 1968 and 1978.
* Keith Edwards finished up as top-dog in United's goalscoring lists on four occasions in the 1980s while Brian Deane followed him by taking top-spot three years running 1989-92, and then headed the charts again in the first season of Premiership football. When he returned to 'the Lane' in 1997-98 Deane once gain finished up as leading scorer.
* Jimmy Dunne scored at least one goal in each of 12 successive First Division matches between 24 October 1931 (v. Grimsby Town) and 1 January 1932 (v. Blackburn Rovers). He claimed 19 in all.
* Fans following United home and away in 1925-26 were never short of goals as 17 were scored in successive matches in December/January of that season as the Blades drew 2-2 at Everton and the beat Cardiff City 11-2.
* And during the month of January 1928 United's three League fixtures produced 22 goals, including a 6-4 home win over Arsenal.
* United set off like a house on fire at the start of the 1956-57 season by scoring 21 goals in their first five League games (all of which were won).
* In November 1949 supporters witnessed 15 goals in two successive games...a 4-4 draw with Bury and a 7-0 defeat at Tottenham.
* The most League goals scored in a season of 'English' football by an Irishman is 41 - Jimmy Dunne's tally for the Blades in 1930-31.
* On 6 May 1939, Harold Hampson scored for United after just 10 seconds v. Spurs (Division 2) at Bramall Lane. At the time this was said to have been the third-fastest goal recorded in League football (behind George James' 5-second strike for West Bromwich Albion v. Nottingham Forest in December 1924 and Swansea Town's full-back Sid Lawrence's own-goal after just six seconds against Sheffield United on 13 November 1937 - although some references have this 'goal' down as being scored in 3/4 seconds impossible as three players touched the ball before it entered the net).
* Ronnie Simpson then beat Hampson's record by netting for the Blades eight seconds into the away League game at Burnley on 26 October 1963. United won 2-1.
* Another eight-second hero was Bill Hodgson, against DWS Amsterdam on tour in Holland in August 1961 (won 5-0).
* Keith Edwards netted a total of 11 goals in eight consecutive matches for the Blades between 19 March and 12 April 1977.
* Bob Hatton netted his 200th career League goal for the Blades against Tranmere Rovers (home) on 7 November 1981 to set up a 2-0 win.
* The Blades scored eight goals in the second-half of their home League game with Burnley in January 1929 (won 10-0). The referee for this game was Stanley Rous, later President of FIFA.
* United conceded four goals in each half of their First Division League game at Arsenal in April 1930 (lost 8-1).
* The Blades let in six goals in their Northern Section away game at Sunderland in August 1941 to lose 7-1.
* The Blades also conceded five second-half goals at Grimsby in a Northern Section game in November 1941 and lost again by 7-1.
* In September 1947, another second-half collapse saw United give away five goals at Portsmouth where they eventually lost 6-0 (Division 1).
* Stan Fazackerley scored in eight consecutive League games for the Blades between March-April 1914 (netting nine in total).
* In October 1899 v. Wolves in a League game at Bramall Lane, Peter Boyle scored one of the longest goals on record by a United player - finding the net from fully 55 yards in a 5-2 win.
* United failed to score a first-half goal in 24 of their 42 League matches in 1973-74 - eight in succession during March & April.

* The Blades did not score a single goal in any of six consecutive Premiership games played during December 1993. There were three 0-0 draws and three defeats.
* They had done likewise in February 1976 - being goalless in five League games and one FA Cup-tie.
* United failed to find the net of five successive First Division matches in February/March 1922 (four defeats, one draw).
* During November and December 1931, five League games involving the Blades produced 35 goals: the scorelines were 4-2, 3-4, 5-4, 3-5 and 4-1. And 23 goals were scored in four successive League games in December/January 1921-22.
* The Blades netted 32 in four tour games in Sweden in August 1988.
* Eight goals were scored (seven by the Blades) in the second-half of their friendly at Skegness Town in July 1988. The final score was 8-1.
* Nine goals were registered after half-time of United's tour game against Hagfors XI (Sweden) in August 1988. Leading 4-0 at the break, the Blades won 12-1.
* The Blades netted four times in the first eight minutes of their home League game v. Newcastle United in January 1955. They went on to win 6-2.
* United's defence conceded five goals in three successive games in January 1978 - losing 5-0 at Arsenal in the FA Cup, and 5-1 to Bolton and 5-1 to Sunderland in the League.
* When United lost 6-1 in a First Division game at Bolton in December 1948, all seven goals were scored in the second-half.
* Three years later - in September 1951 - seven goals came in the second-half of United's home League clash with rivals Sheffield Wednesday. At half-time the Blades led 2-1 before going on to clinch the points with a 7-3 victory.
* When United drew 5-5 with Leicester at Filbert Street in November 1951 (Division 2), seven goals came in the first-half with the home side claiming four of them (4-3).
* All seven goals in United's 6-1 home League win over Cardiff City in March 1952, arrived in the second-half.
* Six goals were scored (3-3) in the first 45 minutes of United's League Division 2 encounter at Southampton in March 1953. The final score was 4-4.
* After holding Spurs at 0-0 in a First Division game at White Hart Lane in March 1955, United capitulated after the interval and lost 5-0.
* Leading 1-0 at half-time, United went on to beat Rotherham 6-1 at Millmoor in a Second Division match in March 1958.
* Chelsea and United were locked together at 1-1 at half-time in a First Division match at Stamford Bridge; the Londoners took charge and went on to win 6-1.
* After a goalless first-half at Fratton Park in September 1970, United controlled the proceedings after the break and went on to beat Portsmouth 5-1.
* The scoresheet was blank when the half-time whistle sounded in the United-Birmingham City League game at Bramall Lane in January 1985. The second 45 minutes produced seven goals as the Blades were beaten 4-3.
* There was a second-half goal-rush during United's friendly away to Skegness Town in August 1986. Leading 3-0 at the break, the Blades carved out an 11-1 win as nine more goals flew into the nets.
* The most League goals scored by United in any one season is 102 in 1925-26 (Division One); the most conceded has been 101 in 42 First Division matches in 1933-34. They gave away 97 in 1929-30.
* Ace marksman Ian Rush scored 381 goals at club level and a further 28 for Wales.
* Rush's fellow countryman Dean Saunders scored 264 goals as a club player and 22 for Wales.
* In 2002-03, Michael Brown became the first United player since Colin Morris in 1983-84 to score over 20 goals in a season of competitive matches.
* United's 500th goal in the FA Cup was scored by defender Phil Jagielka v. Ipswich Town (home) on 25 January 2003.
  (For other high-scoring games see under HALF-TIME SCORES).

Own-Goals
* Sid Lawrence, the Swansea Town full-back, put the ball past his own goalkeeper with only the third or fourth kick of the Second Division game against the Blades at the Vetch Field on 13 November 1937. George Lowrie kicked-off, passing the ball to his inside-partner who in turn gave it to Lawrence who knocked it into the net...perhaps five seconds at least after the start of the game (see above).
* Paul Garner conceded two own-goals in the first 15 minutes of United's 4-1 friendly defeat at Wolves on 27 May 1976.
* Joe Shaw's own-goal in a 2-1 win at Villa Park in September 1962, was one of the best United 'keeper Alan Hodgkinson ever saw!
* David Holdsworth scored for both teams when United lost 2-1 in a First Division match at Swindon in February 1997. In the next game v. Norwich City, he conceded another own-goal as the Blades lost 3-2.

GOONEY, William Harry
Wing-half: 148 apps. 2 goals
Born: Sheffield, 8 October 1910. Died: 1978
Career: Norton Woodseats, BLADES (1930), Plymouth Argyle (June 1935), Luton Town (March 1936-May 1938).
Did not feature after WW2.
An England Schoolboy international, Harry Gooney gave the Blades' five years excellent service as a skilfull half-back.

GORAM, Andrew Lewis
Goalkeeper: 9 apps.
Born: Bury, 13 April 1964.
Career: West Bromwich Albion (apprentice June 1980), Oldham Athletic (professional, August 1981), Hibernian (£325,000, October 1987), Glasgow Rangers (£1 million, June 1991), Notts County (free transfer, September 1998), BLADES (free, September 1998), Motherwell (free, January 1999), Manchester United (£100,000, March 2001), Coventry City (free, June 2001), Oldham Athletic (free, March 2002), Queen of the South (June 2002); coaching in Brazil (2003).
Goalkeeper Andy Goram - who was released by West Bromwich Albion boss Ron Atkinson without ever breaking into the first team at The Hawthorns - did superbly well at Boundary Park, making 215 appearances for the Latics. He followed up with a further 162 for Hibs and 261 for Rangers, helping the 'Gers win five Premiership titles, two League Cup and three Scottish FA Cup Finals. He also established himself in the Scottish national side and went on to gain a total of 43 caps, plus one at Under-21 level. With his career drawing to a close, he had a brief spell at Bramall Lane in 1998. Ex-Manchester United player Gordon Strachan signed him for relegated Coventry, and early in the 2001-02 season Goran took his total of senior appearances at club and international level to past the 750 mark.
* He is one of the very few sportsmen to have represented his country at both international football and cricket.

111

GOUGH, Harold

Goalkeeper: 335 apps.
Born: Chesterfield, 31 December 1890. Died: 1970.
Career: Spital Olympic, Bradford City (July 1910), Castleford Town (August 1911), BLADES (April 1913), Castleford (January 1925), Harrogate Town (October 1926), Oldham Athletic (February 1927), Bolton Wanderers (December 1927), Torquay United (June 1928, retiring through injury, May 1930).
Goalkeeper, Harold Gough broke his contract with United by taking licensed premises (against the club's rules) and therefore returned to his former club (Castleford) in 1925. He took over from Ted Hufton in the Blades' goal and two years later collected an FA Cup winners' medals after a fine display against Chelsea.

GOULDING, Stephen

Full-back: 46 apps.
Born: Mexborough, 21 January 1954
Career: BLADES (junior, April 1970, professional May 1971, retired through injury, July 1976).
Right-back Steve Goulding was forced to retire at the age of 22. He had been at Bramall Lane for six years and had his best season in the first XI in 1972-73, making 24 appearances.

GRAINGER, Colin

Left-winger: 98 apps. 27 goals
Born: Havercroft, near Wakefield, Yorkshire, 10 June 1933.
Career: Rye Hill Junior & South Hindley Secondary Modern Schools, South Elmsall FC, Wrexham (groundstaff, 1949, professional February 1951), BLADES (£5,000, June 1953), Sunderland (£12,000, February 1957), Leeds United (£25,000, July 1960), Port Vale (£6,000, October 1961), Doncaster Rovers (free transfer, August 1964), Macclesfield Town (free, May 1966, released November 1966 after series of injuries). Took employment in Harrogate and became a professional singer, later a Director of Halewood Vinters Wine & Spirits, now residing in Skelmanthorpe.
Colin Grainger was a sprightly outside-left, mobile and aggressive who had a fine career Indeed, he favoured more clubs with his talents than most of his fellow England players from the same period. He was capped seven times by his country (1956 & 1957).
* Grainger is Jim Iley's brother-in-law and the uncle of Eddie Holliday (ex-Middlesbrough).

GREEN, George Henry

Left-half/left-back: 438 apps. 10 goals
Born: Leamington Spa, 2 May 1901. Died: Warwickshire, 1980
Career: Leamington Town, Nuneaton Borough, BLADES (£400, July 1923), Leamington Town (July 1934-36).
George Green always looked calm and collected and was a model of consistency. Believing in the vigorous approach, though by no means a mere spoiler, he was a fine tackler and accurate passer of the ball, completing a fine triangle on the United left with Billy Gillespie and Fred Tunstall. Rewarding to watch for his sheer 'Englishness' he skippered the Blades during his last years at the club. Capped eight times by England between (1925-28) he gained an FA Cup winners medal in 1925.

112

Sheffield United, FA Cup winners 1924-25: (back row, l-r) secretary-manager John Nicholson, Harry Pantling, Seth King, Bill Cook, Charles Sutcliffe, Ernest Milton, **George Green** (middle row, l-r) Thomas Boyle, Harry Johnson, Billy Gillespie (front row, l-r) Dave Mercer, Fred Tunstall

GRIMSBY TOWN

United's playing record against the Mariners:

Football League

Venue	P	W	D	L	F	A
Home	25	16	5	4	55	30
Away	25	15	3	7	39	30
Totals	50	31	8	11	94	60

FA Cup

Home	2	1	1	0	5	1
Away	3	1	0	2	2	4
Totals	5	2	1	2	7	5

League Cup

Home	2	2	0	0	7	2
Away	3	0	2*	1	6	8
Totals	5	2	2	1	13	10

WW1

Home	5	4	1	0	19	5
Away	5	1	2	2	4	6
Totals	10	5	3	2	23	11

WW2

Home	11	7	4	0	37	13
Away	12+	3	1	8	21	31
Totals	23	10	5	8	58	44

Others

Home	1	0	0	1	1	3
Away	3	1	0	2	2	8
Totals	4	1	0	3	3	11

* United won one game on penalties
+Four games played at Scunthorpe.

Grimsby Pelham FC - as they were first known - came into being at a meeting held at the Wellington Arms in September 1878. A year later Pelham became Town and after spells at Clee Park and Abbey Park, the Mariners moved into their present home in Cleethorpes (namely Blundell Park). Grimsby gained Football League status at the same time as the Blades and during season 2002-03, the two clubs, who they played against each other initially, in 1892-93, met in the Second Division.

The venue for the first clash was Bramall Lane, on 26 September 1892. United won 2-0, Ernest Needham scoring one of the goals. The return fixture also went in favour of the Blades who won 1-0 at Abbey Park.

This though was not the first time the teams had met on a football pitch. That event took place in the 3rd qualifying round of the FA Cup the previous season when United won 2-1 on Grimsby soil.

In 1939 the teams met again in the FA Cup and this time the Mariners came out on top, winning a replay 1-0 at Blundell Park (after a 0-0 draw). They were eventually knocked out at the semi-final stage 5-0 by Wolves.

In 1982-83, with United clinging onto a 5-4 aggregate 2nd round League Cup lead over the Mariners, Keith Edwards came off the subs' bench to score a hat-trick to earn his side a 5-1 win on the night and an 8-4 final scoreline (over the two legs).

During the home League game with Grimsby on 29 September 1984, a 'goal' scored Glenn Cockerill was disallowed by the referee (and linesman) who thought the ball had hit the outside of the netting when in fact it had bounced back into play from the stanchion inside the goal. United lost 3-2.

The Blades doubled up over relegated Grimsby in 2002-03, winning 2-1 at home and 4-1 away.

The half-time score in a WW2 game between United and Grimsby in January 1943 was 0-0. The Blades then swept into a 5-0 lead before the Mariners scored three times in the last six minutes to reduce the deficit to 5-3.

The Mariners beat the Blades on penalties to go through to the 3rd round of the League Cup in 2001-02. The 2nd round clash at Blundell Park had finished 3-3 after extra-time.

Kingsley Black, Michael Boulding, John Burridge, Franz Carr (Town trialist), Herbert Chapman, Terry Curran, Aidan Davison, Tony Daws, Willie Falconer, Ashley Fickling, Steve Foley, Edward Grant, Wilson Greenwood, Ian Hamilton, Charlie Henderson, Jim Hobson, Ernest Jackson, John L Jones, Steve Kabba, Dicky Leafe, Clive Mendonca, Hugh Morris, Bill Ross, Georges Santos, Fred E Smith and Mick Speight are all listed as having played for both clubs. Jim McGuigan managed the mariners and was assistant-boss/coach at Bramall Lane.

GROUNDS

* United have only had ONE home ground - Bramall Lane - and indeed, they have played over 2,000 League games there, along with more than 1,500 'other' matches.
* United have played competitive football matches on more than 150 different grounds since 1889.
* On Saturday 5 and Monday 7 April 2003, United played successive AWAY Football League games on the SAME ground (Selhurst Park) against Crystal Palace (drew 2-2) and Wimbledon (lost 1-0) respectively.
* Trevor Hockey played on all 92 Football League club grounds during his professional career.
(See also under BRAMALL LANE & WEMBLEY).

GROUNDSMEN

Harry Wright was employed as head groundsman at Bramall Lane from 1866 until 1892 (26 years).
Jack Ulyett took over until 1905 and for the next 15 years (until 1920) Reg Merry looked after the turf.
Fred Keen came next - acting as head groundsman until 1949 (29 years). He was followed, in turn, by Tom Parkin (1950-64), Reg Barker (1964-75), David Robins (1975-83), Frank Holland (1983-88), Glenn Northcliff (1988 to date).
* Kelly Barrowclough is head groundsman at United's training ground (2003).

113

GROVES, George J
Utility: 20 apps.
Born: Nottingham, 19 October 1868. Died: 1941
Career: Sheffield FC, BLADES (September 1889 to May 1894).
The versatile George Groves, who could play in several outfield positions, spent five seasons as a reserve at Bramall Lane before being released. An amateur player who assisted several clubs including Captain of Royal Arsenal.

GROVES, James Albert
Full-back: 65 apps.
Born: South Bank near Middlesbrough, July 1883. Died: circa 1955.
Career: South Bank, Lincoln City (June 1903), BLADES (April 1904), Middlesbrough (August 1907), Wingate Albion (seasons 1910-12).
Light-weight defender Bert Groves could occupy both full-back positions, playing with keenness and vigour, although at times he was a shade reckless with his lunging tackles. He left Bramall Lane because it was agreed that someone faster and more robust would perform better. In his prime he featured in an England international trial - the North v. the South in 1905 - and came close to winning a full cap.

GUEST PLAYERS
During the two World Wars, United (like virtually every other team in the country) utilised players from other clubs as guests to boost their line-up. Here are details of the players who assisted the Blades:
WW1 - CH Brelsford (Wednesday), H Buddery (Portsmouth), TE Cawley (Leeds City), W Chapman (Barnsley), J Godfrey (Nottingham Forest), E Hall (South Shields), GA Handley (Bradford City/RFC), AR Leafe (West Ham Utd), JT Mitchell (Luton Town), A Pace (Hull City), W Petter (Ecclesfield Utd), Corporal G Philip (Sunderland), JS Poole (Nottingham Forest), BW Shearman (WBA), O Tummon (Oldham Athletic), Capt R Whiting (Arsenal), A Wilkinson (Rotherham County) and H Wrightson (a United supporter).
WW2 - WH Archer (Grantham), R Barclay (Huddersfield Town), E Boot (Huddersfield Town), G Bradley (Leicester City), L Butcher (RAF), A Calverley (Huddersfield Town), J Chafer (amateur), G Dewis (Leicester City), KJ Gadsby (Leeds United), D Grainger (Southport), F Jenkinson (Bury), Johnstone (Glasgow Rangers), H Knott (Hull City), D Kuhnel (Aldershot), GE Laking (Middlesbrough), E Marshall (Cardiff City), J Milburn (Newcastle Utd), W Millership (Sheffield Wednesday), E Nettleton (York City), CJ Poole (Mansfield Town), L Scott (Arsenal), H Shepherd (Rotherham Utd), J Smith (Plymouth Argyle), FC Steele (Stoke City), HM Swift (Sheffield Wednesday) and W Whitaker (Chesterfield).

Other guest players:
G Aizlewood (Sheffield FC), A Attree (Doncaster Rovers), G Bakewell (Derby County) and W Beardshaw (Sheffield FC) all in 1889; C Burridge (Sheffield FC) 1893, AE Dashper (Crouch EV) 1894, M Dickens (Blackburn Rovers) 1991, Ebeto (Albania) 1994, Fox (Scots Guards) 1893, D Francis 1992, G McGahey 1894, W Moon (Old Westminsters) 1890, W Robertson (Newcastle W) 1889, Thompson (Ackworth College) 1894 and Thorpe & Whitaker (Ecclesfield FC) 1889.
A total of 14 guest players were utilised in season 1944-45 as against none at all in 1943-44.

GUTHRIE, Christopher William
Centre/inside-forward: 77+2 apps. 23 goals
Born: Dilston near Hexham 7 September 1953
Career: Newcastle United (apprentice, December 1970, professional January 1971), Southend United (£10,000, November 1972), BLADES (£90,000, May 1975), Swindon Town (£22,500, July 1977), Fulham (£65,000, September 1978), Millwall (£100,000, February 1980-March 1982); Witney Town (player-manager, July 1982), Roda JC/Holland (November 1982), Willem I/Holland (December 1982), Helmond Sport CF/Holland (1983), FC Seiko/Hong Kong (February 1984), Blyth Spartans (April 1985), Racing White/Holland (September 1985), Ashington (Commercial Manager, 1987), Newcastle United (kit manager, 1989-Octoiber 1993), also coaching youngsters in the Teeside area.
Chris Guthrie played for England at both schoolboy and youth team levels and was a regular scorer in Newcastle's second and third teams but failed to establish himself in the League side (owing to the form of Malcolm Macdonald and John Tudor). After moving from St James' Park he netted 40 times in 118 games for Southend, did at Bramall Lane, carried on his good form at Fulham but injuries ruined his League career at Millwall and, indeed, he retired for a short time before returning as a regular performer in Holland.
* His son, Chris junior, played for Sunderland and Gateshead.

GUY, Michael James
Midfielder: 16+7 apps. 3 goals
Born: Limavady, Northern Ireland, 4 February 1953
Career: Coleraine (1974), BLADES (March 1978), Crewe Alexandra (September 1979 to May 1981).
An aggressive Irishman, Micky Guy was as keen as mustard out on the park but lacked that extra touch of finesse that is required at a higher level. He played in 55 League games for the 'Alex.'

HAGAN, James

Inside-forward: 442 apps.151 goals
Born: Washington, County Durham, 21 January 1917.
Died: Sheffield, 27 February 1998
Career: Washington Schools,Usworth Colliery, Liverpool (amateur, January 1932), Derby County (amateur May 1933, professional June 1936), BLADES (£2,925, November 1938, retired March 1958), Peterborough United (manager, August 1958-October 1962), West Bromwich Albion (manager April 1963-May 1967), Manchester City (scout, season 1967-68), then out of football; Benfica (coach/manager/trainer, March 1970). After quitting the game he became a driving instructor in Sutton Coldfield.

An England schoolboy international
(v. Scotland and Wales in 1932),
Jimmy Hagan, was an inside-forward for the discerning supporter. Quiet, unobtrusive and unselfish but a master with the ball, he was able to create chances out of nothing for his colleagues and scored regularly himself, often after a mazy, penetrative dribble. He helped the Blades win the Second Division title, in 1953, and was capped once by England at senior level (v. Denmark in 1948) while also starring 16 Wartime/Victory internationals (1939-46), scoring 13 goals. Hagan was over 39 years of age when he played his last game for the Blades in 1957.
* Sheffield Wednesday offered a record fee of £32,500 for Hagan in 1950 but Haga rejected the move.

HALF-TIME SCORELINES

Here are some of the many high-scoring first-half scorelines involving United with final score of the game indicated in brackets:

08.01.1890	Everton 5 United 0	Friendly	(5-2)
01.02.1890	Bolton Wds 5 United 0	FAC	(13-0)
15,12.1891	Mount St M 0 United 6	Friendly	(1-8)
26.11.1892	United 5 Bootle 0	Division 2	(8-3)
10.12.1892	B Port Vale 0 United 5	Division 2	(0-10)
15.04.1895	United 5 Bolton Wds 0	Division 1	(5-0)
26.12.1904	United 5 Stoke 1	Division 1	(5-2)
22.12.1917	Barnsley 1 United 5	WMS	(3-6)
17.02.1923	United 6 Birmingham 0	Division 1	(7-1)
08.03.1924	United 5 Tottenham 1	Division 1	(6-2)
01.01.1926	United 5 Cardiff City 1	Division 1	(11-2)
09.05.1931	United 5 Barnsley 0	CCF	(9-2)
18.11.1933	Middlesbro' 6 United 2	Division 1	(10-3)
21.12.1935	United 5 Hull City 0	Division 2	(7-0)
28.05.1936	Aarhus 0 United 5	Friendly	(2-8)
31.05.1936	Aalborg 3 United 5	Friendly	(4-8)
19.09.1940	Lincoln City 5 United 1	WNR	(9-2)
13.02.1943	Sheff Wed 6 United 1	LCNQ	(8-2)
27.01.1945	United 6 Lincoln City 1	LWCQ	(10-2)
12.11.1949	Tottenham H 5 United 0	Division 2	(7-0)
01.01.1955	United 5 Newcastle U 2	Division 1	(6-2)
24.08.1959	United 5 Hull City 0	Division 2	(6-0)
11.08.1960	Sparta Amstd 0 United 5	Friendly	(3-5)
27.11.1971	United 4 Ipswich T 0	Division 1	(7-0)
04.09.1973	United 4 Arsenal 0	Division 1	(5-0)
04.03.1980	United 4 Select XI 0	Testimonial	(9-1)
22.03.1981	Truro City 0 United 5	Memorial	(1-9)
03.08.1988	Hagfors XI 0 United 4	Friendly	(1-12)
24.07.1989	TSV Havelse 0 United 5	Friendly	(0-6)
29.07.1995	Orkdal 0 United 5	Friendly	(1-6)

* There have been several more 4-0 as well as several 4-1 half-time scorelines.

Interval Gossip
There was no half-time break during the United-Arsenal League game at Bramall Lane on 24 January 1925...due to a late kick-off and fading light. The Blades won 2-1.

HALIFAX TOWN

United's playing record against the Shaymen:

Football League

Venue	P	W	D	L	F	A
Home	1	0	1	0	2	2
Away	1	1	0	0	5	1
Totals	2	1	1	0	7	3

League Cup

	P	W	D	L	F	A
Home	1	1	0	0	4	2

WW2

	P	W	D	L	F	A
Home	2	1	0	1	4	3
Away	2	1	1	0	5	3
Totals	4	2	1	1	9	6

Yorkshire & Humberside Cup

	P	W	D	L	F	A
Away	1	0	0	1	0	1
Neutral	1	1	0	0	1	0
Totals	2	1	0	1	1	1

Others

	P	W	D	L	F	A
Away	1	0	0	1	0	1
Neutral	1	1	0	0	1	0
Totals	2	1	0	1	1	1

Mr A E Jones (who wrote under the nom de plume 'Old Sport' in the Halifax Evening Courier) was responsible the formation of Halifax Town FC, after he had arranged a public meeting at the Saddle Hotel in April 1911. The townsfolk heartily approved his suggestion and Dr A H Muir was appointed its first president with Joe McClelland as secretary. Playing initially at Sandhall, and then Exley, The Shay became 'home' in 1921 when the club was one of thee original members of the Football League Division 3 (North). Until losing their League status in 2001, the 'Shaymen' had played all their football in the two lowest Divisions.
The two League games against the Blades took place in 1981-82 (Division 4), the first at Bramall Lane, the second at The Shay - and Tony Kenworthy netted in both fixtures. The League Cup encounter, was staged in September 1975 when Chris Guthrie scored a hat-trick for the rampant Blades.
Ex-Blades players Harry Hooper, Chris Wilder and Peter Wragg all became Halifax Town managers.
Wayne Allison, Reg Baines, Russell Black, Bobby Campbell, Willie Carlin, John Connaughton, Albert Cox, Jon Cullen, Bobby Davison, Peter Duffield, Tony Field, David Ford, John Francis, Jim Gannon (United reserve), George Hutchinson, Richard Lucas, Ray McHale, Arthur Mercer, Harry Mills, Percy Oldacre, Walter Rickett, Jim Shankly, Tom Simons, Grant Smith, David Staniforth and Fred Tunstall are among the many players who've served with both clubs.

HALL, George William E
Left-half: 23 apps.
Born: Worksop, 5 September 1912. Died: Worksop, 1989.
Career: Worksop Town, BLADES (April 1932), Coventry City (May 1935), Newport County (March 1936), Bristol City (September 1937-May 1939). Did not play competitive football after WW2.
A competent player, who was basically a reserve at Bramall Lane, George Hall made only 70 League and Cup appearances during his professional career

HALL, Paul Anthony
Forward: 1+3 apps. one goal
Born: Manchester, 3 July 1972.
Career: Torquay United (trainee, July 1988, professional, July 1990), Portsmouth (£70,000, March 1993), Coventry City (£300,000, August 1998), Bury (on loan, February 1999), BLADES (on loan, December 1999), West Bromwich Albion (on loan, February 2000), Walsall (free transfer, March 2000), Rushden & Diamonds (free, October 2001).
Jamaican international and World Cup star Paul Hall (36 caps won to date) has played energetically throughout his career, producing some excellent displays, mainly as a wide midfielder. He had 111 outings for Torquay, 217 for Pompey (42 goals) and 63 for Walsall and reached the personal milestone of 450 club appearances (League & Cup) in 2002. A year later he helped Rushden & Diamonds win the Third Division title (ahead of Hartlepool United)..

HALLIWELL, Jonathan Clifford
Left-half/inside-forward: 27 apps.
Born: Darnall, Sheffield, 20 May 1898. Died: 1984.
Career: Darnall Old Boys, BLADES (April 1920), Bournemouth (June 1926, retiring in May 1932).
Cliff Halliwell played most of his football in the reserves during his seven-year stay at Bramall Lane, but then appeared in 217 League games for the Cherries, scoring two goals before injuries caught up with him in 1932.

HAMILTON, Ian Michael
Midfielder: 68+8 apps. 15 goals
Born: Streatham, London, 31 October 1950
Career: Stratham & London schools, Chelsea (amateur, April 1966, professional January 1968), Southend United (£5,000, September 1968), Aston Villa (£40,000, June 1969), BLADES (July 1976). Minnesota Kicks/NASL (May 1978), Rotherham United (Football in the Community officer, mid 1980s)
'Chico' Hamilton did well with every club he served. Capped by England at Youth team level, he had a terrific left foot and did some sterling work in centre-field, netting 65 goals in a career total of 308 League games. He played for Villa in the 1971 & 1975 League Cup Finals, gaining a winners' medal in the latter and helped the Midlanders win the Third Division title in 1972 and gain promotion from the Second Division in 1975. He was also the youngest ever Chelsea player when making his debut for the London club in March 1967 at the age of 16 years, four month, 18 days.

HAMILTON, Ian Richard
Midfielder: 48+10 apps. 4 goals
Born: Stevenage, Herts, 14 December 1967
Career: Southampton (apprentice, April 1984, professional, December 1985), Cambridge United (March 1988), Scunthorpe United (December 1988), West Bromwich Albion (£160,000, June 1992), BLADES (March 1998), Grimsby Town (on loan, November 1999), Notts County (August 2000), Lincoln City (free transfer, November 2001), Woking (September 2002)
With well over 470 senior appearances under his belt, Ian Hamilton was a vastly experienced campaigner when he joined the Blades from West Brom in 1992. At his best, he enjoyed driving forward from his midfield position and scored some excellent goals. He failed to get a single first team outing with Saints, helped Scunthorpe reach the Play-off Final in 1992 and a year later was in the Baggies promotion-winning side from Division Two.

HAMILTON, William Murdock
Midfielder: 92 apps. 21 goals
Born: Airdrie, 16 February 1938. Died: Canada, April 1976.
Career: Drumpelliers Amateurs (Coatbridge), BLADES (professional, February 1956), Middlesbrough (£12,000, February 1961), Heart of Midlothian (£5,000, June 1962), Hibernian (£6,000, October 1963), Aston Villa (£25,000, August 1965), Heart of Midlothian (August 1967), South African football (May 1969-April 1970), Ross County (July 1970), Hamilton Academical (October 1970-May 1972).
Willie Hamilton possessed wonderful ball control and always caught the eye out on the field. A Scottish international inside-forward (capped against Finland in 1965) he made his debut for the Blades against Coventry City (a) in a friendly in November 1956 and scored in a 6-0 win. His League bow followed in February 1957 v. Blackburn. He won his only club honour while domiciled in Edinburgh when Hearts lifted the Scottish League Cup in 1963, although he did play a big part in helping the Blades gain promotion to the top flight two years earlier. He also made two appearances for the Scottish League. His career was marred by injury and illness and died at a relatively young age

HAMMOND, Walter Henry
Centre-forward: 170 apps. 69 goals
Born: Chorlton near Bolton, August 1868. Died: Bolton, December 1921.
Career: Edghill FC, Everton (briefly, March 1890 - one League game at left-back), BLADES (June 1891), New Brighton Tower (May 1897), Leicester Fosse (May 1900-April 1901).
An honest performer with fair speed, some class and a bit of cleverness, Harry Hammond was the first Blades' player to be sent-off in a League game, dismissed for fighting during a 4-0 win at Crewe Alexandra in April 1893. He so incensed the crowd that a panicky flight from the 'Alex' ground seemed the wisest option to him. He was eventually tracked won by a couple of his team-mates hiding on Crewe railway station still wearing his kit.
He received a fine but no ban for his misdemeanour. Soon after moving to Leicester he was hospitalised with typhoid fever and when he finally regained full fitness some five months later, the Foxes were in the middle of an 11-match run without a win.

117

HAMPSON, Harold

Inside/centre-forward: 61 apps. 19 goals
Born: Little Hulton, 8 June 1918. Died: 1942.
Career: Walkden Methodists, Everton (briefly, in 1935), Walkden Methodists, Southport (August 1936), BLADES (£2,250, Southport, July 1938)
A hard-working, persistent forward, Harold Hampson starred in United's promotion winning side in the last full League campaign before WW2 and was, in fact, one of the first footballers to be called up to serve in the forces. Hampson scored 13 goals in 31 League games for the Southport prior to becoming a 'Blade.' He sadly died of septicaemia.

HAMSON, Gary

Midfielder: 123+1 apps. 9 goals
Born: Sandiacre, 24 August 1959.
Career: BLADES (apprentice, August 1976, professional, November 1976), Leeds United (£140,000, July 1979), Bristol City (July 1986), Port Vale (£5,000, December 1986, retired March 1988, appointed Youth team coach, August 1988-July 1989). Later worked as a builder.
On 30 October 1976, left-sided midfielder Gary Hamson made his Football League debut for the Blades against Cardiff City at the age of 17 years, 2 months, 6 days. He went on to appear in 292 games in that competition, scoring 16 goals. An all-round footballer, who tackled well, passed with precision and occasionally delivered a telling shot, Hamson's best season with the Blades came in 1977-78 when partnering Ian Hamilton in the engine-room
*Hamson is only Blades' teenager so far to appear in 100 League games.

HANDLEY, George Albert

Outside-left: 16 'other' apps. 3 goals
Born: Totley, Sheffield, January qtr, 1886. Died: 1952
Career: Sheffield Schools, Hallam FC, Chesterfield (January 1904), Bradford City (October 1906), Southampton (May 1911), Goole Town (player-manager, April 1912), Bradford City (December 1913), Royal Flying Corps (WW1), Barrow (briefly), Bradford City (May 1919), Bruhl FC (player/coach, 1920), St Gallen/Switzerland (coach, April 1922).
A WW1 guest from Bradford City, outside-left George Handley made 16 appearances for the Blades in the 1918-19 season, partnering Bill Masterman the majority of the time. As a teenager he played for Sheffield Schools against London Schools.

HARDINGE, Harold Thomas William

Inside-left: 154 apps. 46 goals
Born: Greenwich, London, 25 February 1886.
Career: Eltham FC, Tonbridge, Maidstone United, Newcastle United (May 1905), Sheffield United (£350, December 1907), Woolwich Arsenal (£500, June 1913, retiring in May 1921). Later becoming assistant-coach at Tottenham Hotspur (1935-36).
"Walter" Hardinge was a polished and scheming inside-left). Capped by England in 1910, he was an enigmatic man and player, consistent only in his inconsistency, he spent far too much time languishing in the reserves yet still managed a fair striking record for the Blades (approximately a goal every three-and-half games).
He also played County cricket for Kent between 1902-33, appearing in 623 first-class matches, scoring 33,519 runs (including 75 centuries) in 1,021 innings for an average of 36.51, passing the 1,000 run mark in season 18 times. His best score was 263 not out v. Gloucestershire in 1928. He also took 371 wickets (average 26.48) with a best of 7-64 and snapped up 297 catches. He helped Kent win the championship three times (1909, 190 & 1913) and in 1915 was voted 'Wisden Cricketer of the Year.' He played in one Test Match v. Australia at Headingly in 1921, thus making him a double-international.
Hardinge served as a Chief Petty Officer with the Royal Navy Air Force during WW1 and for many years after retiring from cricket, was employed by the sports goods firm, John Wisden & Co. He died in Cambridge on 8 May 1965

HARLEY, Jonathan

Left-back: 10+1 apps. one goal
Born: Maidstone, Kent, 26 September 1979.
Career: Chelsea (trainee, April 1996, professional March 1997), Wimbledon (on loan, October 2000), Fulham (£3.5 million, August 2001), BLADES (on loan, November-December 2002)
England Youth and Under-23 international Jon Harley spent a month at Bramall Lane on loan from Fulham when injuries affected Neil Warnock's squad. He scored one goal, a real beauty, in a 2-0 win at Reading in mid-December 2002. He was an FA Cup winner with Chelsea in 2000.

HARRIS, Bernard

Full-back: 46 apps.
Born: Sheffield, 14 March 1901.
Career: Gainsborough Trinity (1919), Rotherham County (September 1922), BLADES (May 1923), Luton Town (October 1928), Queen's Park Rangers (July 1929), Llanelli (briefly), Swindon Town (July 1933), Margate (1935).
Full-back BernARD Harris made well over 200 senior appearances during his career (178 in the Football League). Initially signed as cover for Messrs Cook and Milton, he made his Blades debut against Cardiff City in September 1924 and appeared in 27 League games in 1926-27 before moving to Kenilworth Road after Bert Chandler had bedded himself in the right-back position.

HARROP, James

Centre-half: 14 apps.
Born: Heeley, Sheffield, May 1884. Died: 1958.
Career: Heeley County School, Sheffield Wednesday (amateur, 1904), Denaby United (1906), Rotherham Town (August 1907), Liverpool (January 1908), Aston Villa (£600, June 1912), BLADES (£1,500, March 1921-May 1922).
The son of a Yorkshire farmer, Jimmy Harrop was a cool, methodical defender, crafty at times with a clever brain and his presence at the heart of the Villa defence went a long way to winning the FA Cup in 1913. He made 171 appearances for the Birmingham club before moving back his roots to sign for the Blades when approaching his 37th birthday. He twice represented the Football League side, appeared in two international trials for England but had the misfortune (as team captain) to miss Villa's 1920 FA Cup Final triumph through injury. During WW1 Harrop worked as an agricultural implement manufacturer.

HARTFIELD, Charles Joseph
Full-back/midfielder: 52+13 apps. one goal
Born: Lambeth, London, 4 September 1971.
Career: Arsenal (YTS, September 1987, professional September 1989), BLADES (August 1991), Fulham (on loan, February 1997), Swansea City (November 1997), Telford United (June 1999).
After failing to make the first team at Highbury, England Youth international Charlie Hartfield spent six years at Bramall Lane, starting off as a left-back before maturing into a central midfielder and set-piece specialist. Injuries disrupted his game in the last two seasons.

HARTLE, Barry
Outside-left/left-back/midfielder: 117 apps. 21 goals
Born: Salford near Manchester, 8 August 1939.
Career: Junior football, Watford (professional, August 1956), BLADES (£2750, June 1960), Carlisle United (£14,000, July 1966), Stockport County (£2,000, September 1967), Oldham Athletic (June 1970), Southport (July 1971), Macclesfield Town (July 1972), Buxton (season 1974-75), Witton Albion (season 1975-76), Hyde United (briefly, August-October 1976).
Originally a winger, Barry Hartle developed into a very capable, hard-working midfielder who could also play as an attacking left-back. He made 307 League appearances during his career.

HARTLEPOOL UNITED
United's playing record against the 'Pool:

Football League

Venue	P	W	D	L	F	A
Home	1	0	1	0	1	1
Away	1	1	0	0	3	2
Totals	2	1	1	0	4	3

FA Cup

Home	1	1	0	0	1	0

League Cup

Home	1	1	0	0	2	0
Away	1	0	1	0	2	2
Totals	2	1	1	0	4	2

The inspiration for the launching of Hartlepool United FC followed the success of West Hartlepool FC (in existence since 1881) who won the FA Amateur Cup in 1905. Three years later a new professional concern was founded (Hartlepool United) who entered the North-eastern League and immediately won the Durham Senior Cup in successive seasons, gaining entry to the Football League, as original members of Division Three, in 1921.
The two League games came in United's Fourth Division championship winning season of 1981-82. The 'Pool played well above themselves to earn a point at 'the Lane' at a time when United were leading the table, and they fought hard and long in the return fixture at Victoria Park in March before going down to the odd goal in five.
The Blades knocked Hartlepool out of the FA Cup with a 1-0 home win in 1992-93, Alan Cork poaching the all-important goal to earn his side a money-spinning 5th round tie against Manchester United.
The League Cup games were played in the 1st round in 1988-89, The Blades winning 4-2 on aggregate.
Ex-Blades stars Viv Busby, John MacPhail (as player-boss) and Fred Priest all managed Hartlepool, while Neil Warnock played for the 'Pool and managed the Blades. Jon Cullen, Harry Hooper, John Hope, Don Hutchinson, Richard Lucas, Frank Talia, Alf Tootill and Paul Williams are other players who have served with both clubs.

HATTON, Robert John
Striker: 114+4 apps. 43 goals
Born: Hull, 10 April, 1947
Career: Wath Wanderers (June 1962), Wolverhampton Wanderers (apprentice, June 1963, professional November 1964), Bolton Wanderers (March 1967), Northampton Town (October 1968), Carlisle United (July 1969), Birmingham City (October 1971), Blackpool (July 1976), Luton Town (July 1978), BLADES (July 1980), Cardiff City (December 1982). Retired from League football in May 1983. Later assisted Lodge Cotterill FC (Birmingham Sunday club). He was later employed by an insurance company and has also worked on a local Birmingham radio (as a matchday summariser).
Bob Hatton was a nomadic striker who could score goals from any angle, with either foot and with his head, in all Divisions, from almost any distance. He netted 217 times in 620 League appearances, including 34 in 95 outings for the Blades, playing in 45 of the 46 games when the Fourth Division title was won in 1982. A well-built player who preferred to occupy a slot on the left side of the field, he helped Blues' gain promotion from the Second Division in 1971-72. Lacking the glamour of several star players alongside him (Trevor Francis among them) he was often the unsung hero but his unselfish work and clinical finishing made him a vital member of all the side.

HAT-TRICKS
* Harry Johnson scored a record 20 hat-tricks for the Blades (18 League, 2 FA Cup).
* Jimmy Dunne claimed six trebles in one season (1930-31)...also a record.
* The first player to score a hat-trick for the Blades was W (Bill) Robertson v. Exchange FC (home) in a Sheffield County Cup game on 19 October 1889 (won 7-2).
* Harry Hammond followed up with United's first 'League' treble against Lincoln City (home) on 3 September 1892 (the club's initial game in the competition).
* Brian Deane and Tony Agana both hit trebles in United's 6-1 home League win over Chester City (Division 3) on 17 September 1988. This was the first 'double' hat-trick event by Blades' players since 1 January 1926 when Harry Johnson and David Mercer both scored three-timers in an 11-2 home win over Cardiff City (Division 1).
* In wartime football, the 'double hat-trick achievement was done four times - by Joe Kitchen (4 goals) and Stan Fazackerley (3) v. Barnsley in January 1919; by Jack Pickering (4) and Colin Collindridge (3) v. Notts County in December 1939; by Harold Barton and Charlie Thompson v. Lincoln City in December 1941 and by Albert Nightingale and Walter Rickett v. Lincoln City in January 1945.

119

* Two hat-tricks were also scored by United players in the following friendly/tour matches: David Frain and Paul Smith v. Guernsey XI (May 1986), Tony Philliskirk and Steve Foley v. Skegness Town (August 1986) and Tony Agana and Peter Duffield v. Vassunda (August 1988).
* Billy Russell hit a hat-trick in 18 minutes for the Blades v. Newcastle United in an away 6th round FA Cup-tie in March 1961.
* Jimmy Dunne scored a hat-trick of headers for the Blades in a 3-1 home League win over Portsmouth in September 1930.
* Two years later Dunne headed four goals for United in their 4-2 County Cup win over Sheffield Wednesday in October 1932.
* Harry Johnson scored a second-half hat-trick in 18 minutes for the Blades v. Wednesday in a 5th round FA Cup replay on 22 February 1928 a crowd of 59,447. This was the first treble by a player in a Sheffield League or Cup derby.
* Brian Deane netted two hat-trick in the space of four days in January 1993 v. Burnley in the FA Cup and Ipswich Town in the Premiership.
* The only player to score six goals (two hat-tricks!) for United has been Arthur Brown in a friendly against Gainsborough Trinity (away) in September 1906.
* Two players have scored five goals in a League game for the Blades - Harry Hammond v. Bootle in November 1892 and Harry Johnson v. West Ham United in December 1927. Jack Stone (v. Mansfield Town in December 1942), Jimmy Dunne (v. Darlington, April 1932) and Adrian Littlejohn (v. Ljusne AIK, July 1992) all notched a fivetimer in 'other' matches.
* Harry Johnson (United) and Charlie Buchan (Sunderland) scored hat-tricks in Blades' 5-3 League win at Roker Park in April 1923.
* Carl Asaba scored the Blades' only hat-trick in 2002-03... in the League game v Brighton & Hove Albion (away). His treble included two penalties.

HAWKSWORTH, Derek Marshall

Outside-left: 286 apps. 103 goals
Born: Bradford, 16 July 1927
Career: Bradford Park Avenue (amateur), Huddersfield Town (amateur), RAF, Bradford City (professional, October 1948), BLADES (£12,000, December 1950), Huddersfield Town (in part-exchange for Ronnie Simpson, plus £6,000, May 1958), Lincoln City (£3,000, February 1960), Bradford City (£3,000, January 1961), Nelson (July 1962-May 1964). He ran a newsagents ship after quitting football.

Derek Hawksworth scored on his League debut for the Blades against Blackburn Rovers (a) in December 1950 (won 2-0). A predominantly right-footed player who preferred the left-wing berth, he was a strong, fast and deliberate raider who was a regular scorer during his six-and-a-half years at Bramall Lane, helping the Blades win the second Division championship in 1952-53 when he was an ever-present. During his career Hawksworth appeared in 485 League games and scored 144 goals. He played for England 'B' against France 'B' in 1952. He is a cousin of Malcolm Levitt (ex-Bradford City)

Sheffield United's Derek Hawksworth (r) tries to poke the ball past West Ham United goalkeeper Ernie Gregory (l)

HAWLEY, Frederick
Centre-half: 104 apps. one goal
Born: Derby, 28 July 1890.
Career: Derby Midland, Shelton United, Leys Recreationalists, Ripley Town, BLADES (January 1913), Coventry City (August 1919), Birmingham City (January 1920), Swindon Town (May 1920), Bristol City (March 1923), Brighton & Hove Albion (June 1925), Queen's Park Rangers (May 1926), Loughborough Corinthians (April 1928). Retired in May 1929. Guested for Derby County, Notts County, Birmingham City & Nottingham Forest during WW1.
Before the 1914-18 conflict Fred Hawley, a powerfully-built defender, was a First Division regular with the Blades but he took some time to settle down after the hostilities were over. Neither of his Midlands clubs received much service from him but he did give a good account of himself with each of his Southern League clubs until the end of his long career.

HEATON, James Michael
Left-back: 39+3 apps.
Born: Sheffield, 15 January 1947. Died: 11 April 1995.
Career: BLADES (apprentice, June 1962, professional November 1964), Blackburn Rovers (£7,000, October 1971, retired May 1977 to open a Sports shop). Later appointed reserve team coach at Ewood Park and then senior coach under manager Howard Kendall at Blackburn and Everton; becoming Community Officer at Blackburn; then Workington Town (manager, 1989), Manchester City (assistant-manager to Kendall).
Mick Heaton, small and agile, with a never-say-die attitude, was an ebullient character, who spent long periods in United's Central League side before being lured away by Ken Furphy. He went on to establish himself at Ewood Park, skippering Rovers and making 19877 appearances for the Lancashire club before suffering a serious knee injury which, despite a brave attempt to regain full fitness, forced him into early retirement (as a player) in 1977. When he teamed up with ex-Blades boss Kendall at Blackburn, it was the start of along and successful partnership that moved on to Everton. However, after achieving championship, European and FA Cup glory at Goodison Park Kendall left to take charge of Athletic Bilbao but because of the strict ruling regarding the employment of non-Basques, Heaton was not allowed to join him in Spain. After failing to get a managerial post himself, Heaton returned to Blackburn in n 1988 to run the Community Programme at Ewood Park and later managed Workington (of the HFS Loans League) before teaming up again with Kendall at Maine Road. He sadly died in a road accident at the age of 48.

HEDLEY, George Albert
Centre-forward: 155 apps. 39 goals
Born: South Bank near Middlesbrough, 3 May 1876. Died: Bristol, 16 August 1942.
Career: South Bank, BLADES (1896, professional in May 1898), Southampton (May 1903) Wolverhampton Wanderers (May 1906, retiring in April 1913). On quitting football he was appointed manager of Bristol City, retaining the position until May 1915. After WW1 he became a licensee in Bristol (1918-41), returning to Wolverhampton to take on a boarding house.
George Hedley made his League debut for Sheffield United in hail, sleet and snow against West Bromwich Albion in March 1898. He spent a total of six years at Bramall Lane, during which time he gained two FA Cup winners' medals (1899 & 1902) and also played in the 1901 Final v. Spurs. Strong, robust and fearless, he was very much an advocate of the open game (a belief he even pleaded in a newspaper article in 1909) and simply loved playing knockout football, helping Wolves win the FA Cup in 1908 when he scored in a 3-1 victory over Newcastle United. He was also a Southern League championship winner with Saints in 1904.
Hedley wore the same pair of boots for eight seasons, finally discarding a pair with 17 patches on them in 1908.

HEELEY FC
(Sheffield)
United beat their near neighbours Heeley 1-0 in the 2nd qualifying round of the FA Cup in October 1889...after agreeing for the tie to be switched to Bramall Lane A crowd of 3,000 saw the game decided by an own-goal, scored by Dick Stokes.
Earlier, a competitive friendly between the two teams (in mid-September 1889) had seen the Blades win 2-1, while later in the season United again triumphed 1-0 in a County Cup game at 'the Lane.'

HEFFERMAN, Thomas Patrick
Right-back: 98 apps. 5 goals
Born: Dublin, 30 April 1955
Career: Dunleary Celtic, Tottenham Hotspur (professional, October 1977), Bournemouth (May 1979), BLADES (£20,000, August 1983), Bournemouth (June 1985-May 1988).
Big, strong and resilient, Tom Hefferman did not possess great speed, but often produced some finely judged interventions and a lot of clean kicking. He made 217 League appearances during his two spells at Dean Court...but failed to get a first team outing with Spurs. He played in 42 games when the Blades gained promotion from Division Three in 1984.

HEIGHT
Tallest
United's 1920s centre-half Jimmy McCourt at 6ft 1ins is possibly one of the tallest player to serve the Blades.
United's goalkeeper Bill 'Fatty' Foulke was 6ft 2ins tall (and during his career weighed anything between 15 and 25 stone). He used to wear a jersey three times ordinary size.
Other players at 6ft 2ins or over who have served with United include Alan Kelly (1992-99), Charlie Bell (1964-68), Brian Deane (1988-93/97-98), Tri Dellas (1997-98), Stewart Evans (1980-82), Steve Faulkner (1972-78), strikers Jan-Aage Fjortoft (1997-98) and Jostein Flo (1993-96) and defenders Mark Foran (1993-96) and Michel Vonk (1995-98).
Perhaps the tallest player ever to oppose United is Kevin Francis, the giant striker who, at 6ft 7ins in height, scored for Birmingham City against the Blades in December 1995 (Division 1).

Shortest
John 'Tiny' Smith was only 5ft 2ins tall and made his senior debut for the Blades in October 1944 as a guest from Plymouth Argyle.
Other small players who have donned United's colours include Billy Mosforth (1889-90) and Alf Jeffrey (1919-20) both of whom measured 5ft 3ins, while Scottish wing-wizard Jimmy Johnston was 5ft 4ins.
Since WW2 United have had several 'small' players on their books, among them 1950s winger Fred 'Jock' Smith (at 5ft 5ins), plus Mickey Ash, Pat Buckley, Willie Carlin, Franz Carr, John Docherty, Nick Henry, Trevor Hockey, Billy Hodgson, George Jones, Colin Morris, Paul Peschisolido, Walter Rickett, Willie Smith, Dennis Thompson and Mark Todd.
United's 1897-98 half-back line of Rab Howell (5ft 5 1/4ins), Tommy Morren (5ft 5 1/4) and Ernest Needham (5ft 5ins), all

121

internationals and recipients of an FA Cup winners' medal - was by far the smallest in the country.

* One of the shortest (smallest) players ever to line up against United has Tommy Magee of West Bromwich Albion (1920s/30s) who was a fraction over 5ft 2ins tall. Around the same era, there was also Syd Tufnell of Blackpool who was a shade bigger than Magee.

* One of the smallest goalkeepers ever to play in a full international for England is Sheffield Wednesday's Teddy Davison (1920s) who were both 5ft 7ins tall. And the coincidental twist attached to them is that Davison signed Hodgkinson for the Blades when he was manager at Bramall Lane.

HEMSLEY, Edward John Orton

Left-back: 292+1 apps. 10 goals

Born: Stoke-on-Trent, 1 September 1943

Career: Bridgnorth Grammar School, Shrewsbury Town (juniors, April 1958, professional July 1961), BLADES (£27,500, August 1968), Doncaster Rovers (July 1977-May 1979). After ending his soccer career Hemsley became a turf accountant, based in Dronfield, near the White Swan pub.

Signed for the Blades by his previous manager Arthur Rowley, Ted Hemsley took Mick Heaton's place at left-back in United's first team. He was a tough-tackling defender with a heart of gold, very difficult to pass especially on the outside, who gave absolutely everything he had out on the field, making almost 300 senior appearances for the club to add to the 250 plus he made for the 'Shrews.' He helped the Blades win promotion in 1971 (40 games played).

* Hemsley played home and away games at Bramall Lane - as a Sheffield United footballer and Worcestershire cricketer (v. Yorkshire).

Ted Hemsley (Sheffield United), battles against Trevor Francis (Birmingham City)

HENDERSON, Charles John

Inside/centre-forward: 14 apps. 4 goals

Born: Durham, April 1870. Died: circa 1933.

Career: South Bank FC, Darlington (on trial, 1886), Grimsby Town (April 1892), Leith Athletic (February 1893), Bolton Wanderers (August 1894), Wolverhampton Wanderers (£20, April 1895), BLADES (August 1896-May 1897), Dundee Harp (August 1897), Edinburgh Thistle (September 1899), Grimsby Town (April 1902-February 1903).

Top-scorer for Bolton in 1894-85 and an FA Cup finalist with Wolves the following season, the moustachio'd, fair-haired Charlie Henderson played mainly as an inside-forward, having plenty of attacking flair and possessing a strong right-foot shot. He was quite fearless at times and was often involved in scuffles with his opponents.

* His son, Crosby Henderson (born in May 1895) played for Newcastle United, Birmingham, Grimsby and Luton Town.

HENDERSON, Michael Robert

Right-back/midfielder: 87+2 apps.

Born: Gosforth, near Newcastle, 31 March 1956

Career: Sunderland (apprentice, June 1972, professional March 1974), Watford (£140,000, November 1979), Cardiff City (March 1982), BLADES (August 1982), Chesterfield (January 1985, retired May 1989, later on coaching staff at Saltergate for a number of years).

Mick Henderson made 92 appearances for Sunderland 64 for Watford and 11 for Cardiff before joining the Blades in 1982. A positive player, showing a fair amount of aggression when required, he did well at Bramall Lane for two-and-half seasons (helping United gain promotion from Division Three in 1984) before moving to Chesterfield with whom he won a Fourth Division championship medal in 1985.

122

HENDRY, William Henry

Centre-forward/centre-half: 121 apps. 3 goals
Born: Dundee, June 1864. Died: 1901
Career: Dundee & Invergowrie Schools, DunbLane Thistle, Dundee Wanderers, West Bromwich Albion (August 1888), Stoke (March 1889), Kidderminster Harriers (briefly), Preston North End (January 1890), BLADES (February 1891). Dundee (May 1895), Bury (1896), Brighton United (1898), Watford (August 1899, retiring through poor health in March 1900).
Billy Hendry captained United for four years, from 1891-95, and was instrumental in the rise of the club around that time, being a star player in the promotion-winning side of 1893. Initially a centre-forward he was the first WBA player to receive a suspension following his involvement in an on-field brawl with the Bolton left-back Ernie Siddons in November 1888 for which he received a four-week ban. He switched to the centre-half position at Deepdale. Hendry's qualities were his headwork and wholehearted endeavour. He was a cool, calculated performer who enjoyed driving forward, given the chance.

HENRY, Nicholas Ian

Midfielder: 17+4 apps.
Born: Liverpool, 21 February 1969
Career: Oldham Athletic (trainee, June 1985, professional July 1987), BLADES (£50,000, with Doug Hodgson as part of the deal, February 1997) Walsall (free transfer, March 1999), Tranmere Rovers (free July 1999), Scarborough (July 2002).
Nick Henry was a Second Division championship winner with Oldham Athletic 1991 and he also played for the Latics in the losing League Cup Final of 1990 and in the Premiership. A keen-tackling, totally committed and energetic midfielder he 333 senior appearances during his 12 years at Boundary Park and in 2002-03 he reached the personal milestone of 400 League games.
Henry was involved in a serious car crash in 2000 and soon afterwards was diagnosed as suffering from a blood disorder which drained his energy during matches.

HENSON, George Horace

Centre-forward: 17 apps. 7 goals
Born: Stoney Stratford, Buckinghamshire, 25 November 1911. Died 1988.
Career: Stoney Stratford FC, Wolverton FC, Northampton Town (amateur, July 1932, professional January 1933), Mexborough (1934), Wolverhampton Wanderers (August 1935), Bradford Park Avenue (July 1937), BLADES (£2,600, March 1939-April 1940).
He did not play League football after WW2.
Signed to replace 'Jock' Dodds, George Henson had already scored over 60 goals in more than 130 League games before moving to Bramall Lane. He still had the technique up front but unfortunately WW2 ended his career like it did many other footballers. He did however play local soccer until 1950.

HEREFORD UNITED

United's playing record against the Bulls:
Football League

Venue	P	W	D	L	F	A
Home	2	0	2	0	3	3
Away	2	0	2	0	3	3
Totals	4	0	4	0	6	6

Formed in 1924 and members of the Southern League for many years, Hereford United gain admission to the Football League (Division 4) in 1972, remaining in the competition for 25 years before being replaced by Macclesfield Town.
United's only meetings with the famous FA Cup giant-killers, who lost their League status in 1997 (after 25 seasons in the competition) came in 1976-77 (Division 2) and 1981-82 (Division 4)...and amazingly all four ended in draws (1-1 and 2-2 at Bramall Lane and 2-2 and 1-1 at Edgar Street in that order). Plucky Hereford were battling to avoid relegation in 1977 while the Blades were charging towards the championship in 1982.
Former Blades' player Colin Addison played for and managed the 'Bulls' during their great Cup years of the early 1970s. Tony Agana, Alan Birchenall, Garry Jones. Ken Mallender, Cliff Powell, Phil Starbuck and Charlie Thompson. John Barnwell played for the Blades and was coach at Hereford.

HETHERSTON, Peter

Winger: 11 apps.
Born: Bellshill, Scotland, 6 November 1964
Career: Falkirk, Watford (July 1987), BLADES (February 1988), Falkirk (May 1988-May 1992).
Winger Peter Hetherston never really made an impact in the Football League although he did well with Falkirk for whom he made well over 100 senior appearances.

HIGH-SCORING GAMES

(see also under GOALS & WINS)
The most goals scored in a game involving United game (to date) is 13..

Here are the details of all Blade' high-scoring games:
Football League
11-2 v. Cardiff City (h)	January 1926
3-10 v. Middlesbrough (a)	November 1934

FA Cup
0-13 v. Bolton Wanderers (a)	February 1890

Friendlies
12-1 v. Hagfors XI/Sweden (a)	July 1988
8-5 v. West Yorkshire XI (a)	September 1903.

123

Blades' Goal Rush

In August 1986, Skegness Town were thrashed 11-1 and when touring Sweden in July 1988, United beat a Hagfor XI 11-0.
United have also won two League games by scores of 10-0 v. Burslem Port Vale (a) in December 1892 and v. Burnley (h) in January 1929. They whipped Lincoln City 10-2 in a home WW2 game in January 1945; lost 9-2 to the Imps in September 1940 (WW2) and succumbed to an 8-2 defeat at Sheffield Wednesday in February 1943 (WW2).
On tour in Denmark in 1936 United ran up scores of 8-4 v. Aalborg and 8-2 v. Aarhus, and in July 1992 they defeated Ljusne 10-0 in another friendly in Sweden. In November 1980 United beat a Select XI 8-4 in a testimonial match at Bramall Lane.
A League game between the Blades and Leicester City ended 5-5 in November 1951, while two more League games in 1925-26, at Bury (lost 7-4) in September and at home to Manchester City (won 8-3) in October, both produced 11 goals. There have been several other 10-goal matches. (See also under WINS).

HILL, Colin Frederick
Central defender: 96+8 apps. one goal
Born: Uxbridge, Middlesex, 12 November 1963
Career: Arsenal (apprentice, April 1980, professional, August 1981), CS Maritimo /Portugal (June 1986), Colchester United (free transfer, October 1987), BLADES (£85,000, August 1989), Leicester City (£200,000, March 1992), FC Trelleborg/Sweden (May 1997), Northampton Town (November 1997, retired June 1999).
When Colin Hill was sold to Leicester City in 1992, 1/6th of his transfer fee went to Colchester United in respect of a sell-on agreement made when he was secured from the Layer Road club. A solid, highly competitive defender and a Northern Ireland international (capped 26 times) he became the first Northampton player to gain honours at senior level for 30 years when he represented his country in 1998. He was a promotion winner (from Division Two) with the Blades in 1990 and a League Cup winner with Leicester in 1997. He retired with a total in excess of 550 senior appearances to his name, 479 with his five English clubs

HILL, Michael Richard
Centre-forward: 42+2 apps. 12 goals
Born: Hereford, 3 December 1947
Career: Cardiff City (briefly, 1963), Bethesda Athletic (March 1965), BLADES (September 1965), Ipswich Town (October 1969), Crystal Palace (December 1973-February 1976); South African football.
Welsh international striker Mick Hill (two caps won v. Czechoslovakia and Romania, 1972) netted 33 goals in a total of 148 League appearances made over a period of 11 years.
Six feet tall and weighing almost 12st, he was skilful on the ground and during the 1970-71 season the BBC's 'Match of the Day' cameras enthused on a wonderful individual goal he scored for Ipswich against Liverpool when he left three or four defenders in his wake following a mazy run from the halfway line.
On his release by Cardiff he became a clerk in Hereford but signed for Bethesda, after being persuaded to continue playing again by his father! He made his debut for the Blades as a 'sub' against Sunderland at Bramall Lane in October 1966 and struck his first League goal towards the end of that season in a 2-2 draw at Leicester, following up with another in his first Sheffield derby. His contract was cancelled at Selhurst Park and almost immediately he went over to South Africa. He qualified to play for the Principality on the basis of his father's birthplace.

HILL, Robert
Centre-forward: 68 apps. 21 goals
Born: Scotland, circa 1868.
Career: Linfield, BLADES, Ardwick/Manchester City (November 1895-May 1897).
A Scotsman who started his career in Ireland, Bob Hill was a fine marksman who averaged a goal every three matches throughout his career. There were perhaps too many players of a similar bent at Bramall Lane - hence his departure.

HILL, Walter
Right-back/half-back: 25 apps.
Born: Sheffield circa 1870
Career: Grimethorpe FC, BLADES (September 1891-May 1896).
Wally Hill made his mark by playing exceedingly well for the Blades in the 1892 Sheffield County Cup victory over Wednesday Wanderers, helping set up one of the goals for Jack Scott. He made his League debut v. Bootle in September 1892 but was never regarded as a first-team regular, just a valuable and reliable reserve. He drifted into obscurity after leaving Bramall Lane.

HITCHEN, Harold
Right-half: 172 apps. 15 goals
Born: Liverpool, 22 October 1922. Died: 1993.
Career: Formby FC, New Brighton (September 1946), BLADES (£4,000, May 1948), Bury (May 1953-April 1954).
Harry Hitchen was a powerfully-built wing-half who possessed a fearsome tackle. He skippered the Blades for a short while before losing his place during the 1952-53 promotion-winning campaign when the likes of Geoff Denial, Bill Toner, Joe Shaw and even Harold Brook were all competing for a middle-line position.

HOBSON, James
Outside-right: 15 apps. 2 goals
Born: Ecclesfield, 1886.
Career: Rotherham (1902), Worksop Town (1904), BLADES (April 1907), New Brompton (May 1909), Grimsby Town (1910), Bolton Wanderers (season 1911-12).
Despite playing competitive football for 10 years, Jim Hobson only played League soccer for the Blades. He was a capable reserve to George Thompson and Jack Lang during his two years at Bramall Lane.

HOBSON, Walter
Centre-half: 14 apps. one goal
Born: Sheffield, circa 1867
Career: Owlerton FC, BLADES (September 1889-May 1890), Owlerton FC.
Centre-half Walter Hobson made 41 appearances in all games for the Blades in his only season with the club. He played splendidly in the club's first-ever FA Cup-tie against Scarborough in October 1889 and scored his only competitive goal in a 6-0 victory over Attercliffe in the Sheffield County Cup in January 1890. He was eventually replaced at the heart of the defence by Rab Howell.

HOCKEY, Trevor
Winger/midfielder: 82 apps. 4 goals
Born: Keighley, Yorkshire, 1 May 1943. Died: Keighley, 2 April 1987.
Career: Played both codes of rugby as well as football at school; West Riding Under-19s, Keighley Central YC, Bradford City (amateur, June 1958, professional May 1960), Nottingham Forest (£15,000, November 1961), Newcastle United (£25,000, November 1963), Birmingham City (£22,500, November 1965), Sheffield United (£40,000, January 1971), Norwich City (February 1973), Aston Villa (£38,000, June 1973), Bradford City (June 1974), San Jose Earthquakes & Los Angeles Quick Silver (summer 1975), Athlone Town (player-manager, March 1976), San Diego Jaws (NASL, April 1976), Stalybridge Celtic (manager, August 1977). Later coached the British Army soldiers' children's soccer team on the Rhine and attempted to start a soccer School at Keighley rugby club.
Yet another of football's journeyman, Trevor Hockey's professional career spanned almost 16 years during which time he amassed well over 600 senior appearances (24 for Aston Villa, one goal scored) and played on all 92 League grounds that were being used when he was in action...all this after his rugby exploits at school. Hockey won nine full caps for Wales (via parentage qualification) and a Second Division championship medal with Newcastle (1965). A real gritty performer, he added drive and determination, conviction and aggression to the midfield, he helped the Blades gain promotion to the First Division in 1971 (playing in 17 matches). Sadly Hockey died of a heart attack whilst taking part in a 5-a-side tournament in his home-town of Keighley in 1987.
* In 1976, at the age of 25, Hockey became the youngest player to appear in a competitive game on every Football League ground.

HODGES, Glyn Peter
Forward/midfielder: 134+37 apps. 22 goals
Born: Streatham, London, 30 April 1963
Career: Wimbledon (apprentice, June 1979, professional, February 1981), Newcastle United (£300,000, July 1987), Watford (£300,000, October 1987), Crystal Palace (£410,000, June 19990), BLADES (on loan, January 1991, signed permanently, April 1991), Derby County (February 1996), Sin Tao/Hong Kong (May 1996), Hull City (August 1997), Nottingham Forest (February 1998), Scarborough (non-contract, January 1999, retired February 1999); later Barnsley (coach & caretaker-manager, 2002-03).
Glyn Hodges had the knack of scoring vital goals...but at times was frustrating and enigmatic, yet also a delight to watch! A Welsh international, capped 13 times at senior level between 1984-90 (two goals scored) having earlier represented his country in three Youth matches and also the Under-21 side (five outings), he was a regular performer in the Dons; side that leapt to from the Fourth to the First Division in during the 1980s, making a major contribution in 1983-84 with 15 goals in 42 Third Division matches. In fact, he played for the London club in all four Divisions. After leaving Plough Lane he was voted Watford's 'Player of the Year' in 1989 and scored on his first three matches for the Blades. When he hung up his boots in 1998 - after almost 20 years as a player - his record was excellent: 106 goals in 631 club and international matches.

HODGKINSON, Alan
Goalkeeper: 675 apps.
Born: Laughton, Rotherham, 16 October 1936,
Career: Laughton Council & Dinnington Secondary Modern Schools, Thurscroft Youth Club, Worksop Town, BLADES (amateur, January 1953, professional, September 1953), retired May 1971); became assistant-trainer/coach/scout at Bramall Lane, also a scout for Manchester United and later goalkeeping coach at Coventry City (2002-03).
Alan Hodgkinson guarded the Blades' goal for a prodigious period, maintaining an exceptionally high standard throughout. Indeed, after taking over from Ted Burgin, he remained first-choice between the posts for 15 years (1957-71 inclusive) before handing over hiss gloves to John Hope. Heavy in build, sound and courageous in performance, he was not a huge fellow but certainly did the job in hand. He twice helped the Blades win promotion from Division Two (1961 & 1971) and reach the FA Cup semi-finals in 1961 and a decade later he was again in goal when promotion was attained once more to the top flight. He gained five full England caps, lining up against Scotland, the Republic of Ireland (twice) and Denmark in 1957 and Wales in 1960, conceding five goals, one in each game. He was unlucky not to go to the 1958 World Cup finals in Sweden (Bolton's Eddie Hopkinson & Burnley's Colin McDonald being preferred instead).
* 'Hodgy' was one of the few players to keep a programme from every game he played in. He now has a pretty good collection!

125

HODGSON, Douglas John

Defender: 30+8 apps. one goal

Born: Frankston, Australia, 27 February 1969

Career: Heidelberg/Australia, BLADES (£30,000 with Carl Veart, July 1994), Plymouth Argyle (on loan, August-September 1995), Burnley (on loan, October 1996), Oldham Athletic (February 1997), Northampton Town (£20,000, October 1998, retired, December 1999).

Hard-tackling Aussie defender Doug Hodgson, 6ft 2ins tall and 13st 10lbs in weight, simply hated to lose and was booked numerous times and received his fair share of injuries during his career in England. He played as an emergency striker or Oldham. When he called it a day in 1998 he had made exactly 100 appearances in 'English' League and Cup football.

HODGSON, William

Inside-forward: 183 apps. 37 goals

Born: Glasgow, 9 July 1935.

Career: St Johnstone (professional, May 1954), Guildford City (on loan), BLADES (£3,250, May 1957), Leicester City (September 1963), Derby County (June 1965), Rotherham United (September 1967), York City (December 1967-May 1970); later employed as a coach at both Bramall Lane and Bootham Crescent.

A diminutive, enthusiastic, lively and seemingly tireless utility forward, Billy Hodgson played for the Blades and later gaining a League Cup winners medal with the Foxes (1965) after collecting a loser's tankard the year before. He made well over 400 appearances (383 in the Football League) for his five 'English' clubs.

HOLDSWORTH, David Gary

Defender: 118 apps. 7 goals

Born: Walthamstow, 8 November 1968

Career: Watford (apprentice June 1985, professional November 1986), BLADES (£450,000, October 1996), Birmingham City (£1.2 million, March 1999), Walsall (on loan, January-March 2002), Bolton Wanderers (free transfer, September 2002).

Capped by England at Youth and Under-21 levels, David Holdsworth made almost 300 appearances for Watford and after leaving Bramall Lane made over 100 more for Blues and a handful for Walsall before teaming up with his twin brother, Dean, at The Reebok Stadium. Impressive during his time at Vicarage Road, he always gives 100 per-cent on the field, and his wholehearted displays made him a form favourite with the supporters wherever he played.

HOLLAND, Paul

Midfielder: 13+7 apps. 2 goals

Born: Lincoln, 8 July 1973

Career: Kesteven Schools, Lincolnshire schools, Carre's GS Sleaford, Mansfield Town (associated schoolboy forms, August 1987, apprentice July 1989, professional July 1991), BLADES (£250,000, rising to £350,000 after an agreed number of appearances, June 1995), Chesterfield (£150,000, January 1996), Bristol City (£200,000, September 1999, retied March 2002).

A creative midfielder who added a touch of bite to the centre of the park, Paul Holland gained four England Under-21 caps and also represented his country at both Schoolboy and Youth team levels. When he quit top-class football in 2002, his appearance tally (in League and Cup action) stood at 375 (47 goals). He helped Mansfield win promotion from Division Four in 1992 and was s elected in the PFA Annual Third Division side in 1995 after bouncing back quicker than expected following medial ligament surgery. Blades boss Dave Bassett flew over to France to secure Holland's signature after he had starred for the England Under-21 side against Brazil in the Toulon Tournament.

HOLMES, James

Centre/left-half: 135 apps.

Born: Skelmersdale, 27 December 1908. Died: 1971.

Career: Liverpool (1926), Wigan Borough (August 1928), Prescot Cables FC (July 1929), Chesterfield (August 1930), BLADES, West Ham United (September 1936), Reading (March 1937-September 1941). He did not play after WW22.

A powerfully built 'pivot' Jimmy Holmes was a player who enjoyed a battle and at times suffered the wrath of the referee and occasionally his manager! After a poor display in a County Cup semi-final v. Doncaster Rovers in 1934, Jimmy Holmes was suspended for two weeks but on his day he was a totally committed footballer who enjoyed a reasonably fine career (at various levels). He appeared in almost 40 WW2 games for Reading.

HOLMES, J Thomas

Outside-right: 14 apps. one goal

Born: Chesterfield, 1880

Career: Sheffield Brunswick, BLADES (October 1991), Fulham (1904), Southern United, Fulham (June 1906), Tunbridge Wells Rangers (May 1909).

Not a regular performer with the Blades orFulham, Tom Holmes made his League debut against Derby County in October 1901, having had his first outing at senior level in a benefit match v. Celtic five days earlier. He was reserve to Walter 'Cocky' Bennett.

HOME FROM HOME

* The Blades - on completion of the 2002-03 campaign and having met 97 different clubs - completed their 100th League season, thus joining the select band of 17 League 'centurians'.

* United's record is relatively rare in that all their 2,043 home League/Premiership matches have been played at one ground - Bramall Lane. Of the other '16' in the '100' club, only Burnley (Turf Moor) and Preston North End (Deepdale) have played all their home matches at the same venue.

* During the 1940-41 wartime season, after bomb damage had rendered Bramall Lane unsafe, five home Cup matches were played at Hillsborough and one at Millmoor (Rotherham).

* United have only twice remained unbeaten at home throughout a League season:

* In 1892-93 (Div. 2) playing 11 matches 10 wins, one draw) and in 1981-82 (Div. 4), playing 23 matches (15 wins, 8 draws). They lost once in 1899-1900, 1936-37 & 1970-71.

* The Blades lost only eight of 84 home League games played during the last four seasons prior to WW2 (1935-39).

* The most matches won at home in a League season has been 16, achieved on seven separate occasions, thus:
>From 21 matches: in 1936-37, 1958-59, 1960-61 & 1969-70 (all in Div. 2).
>From 23 matches: in 1982-83 & 1988-89 (in Div. 3) & 1997-98 (in the new Div. 1).
* Their best season in the top flight was in 1925-26 - 15 wins and three draws from 21 matches.
* United lost a record 10 of their 21 home First Division League games in seasons 1967-68 & 1975-76.
* United won 14 consecutive home League Cup games between 26 August 1997 and 8 January 2003. And a run of 13 successive home Cup wins (both major domestic competitions) was put together between 2000-03.
* The Blades drew 11 out of 21 home games in 1920-21 (Div. 1) and 10 in both 1949-50 (Div. 2) and 1993-94 (Premiership).
* The most goals scored at home by the Blades in a complete League season is 72 in 21 matches in 1925-26 (Div. 1)...the first season of the new (and present day) offside law. During this campaign they also recorded their biggest home League win - beating Cardiff City 11-2.
* The Blades' biggest home League defeat has been 7-1, at the hands of Huddersfield Town on 12 November 1927. Their two heaviest Cup reverses at 'the Lane' have been 4-1 against Leeds United on 10 October 1978 and 5-2 top Stockport County on 24 September 1996, both in the League Cup.
* United's 1,000th home League game took place on 26 March 1955 when they were held to a 2-2 draw by Huddersfield Town in a Yorkshire derby.
* The 2,000th home League/Premiership match followed more than 47 years later, on 2 September 2002, and it was also against Yorkshire rivals, this Bradford City, and again the scoreline finished level at 2-2.
* United's 2,000th 'Football League' home game was against Wolverhampton Wanderers on 26 April 2003 (a 3-3 draw). This was also the Blades' 4,000th 'League' game.
 (See also under FOOTBALL LEAGUE/SEQUENCES).

HOOPER, Harry Reed
Right-back: 307 apps. 12 goals
Born: Burnley, 16 December 1910. Died: 1970.
Career: Nelson Trades FC (1926), Nelson (August 1928), BLADES (February 1930), Hartlepool United (July 1947-May 1950).
Harry Hooper skippered United against Arsenal in the 1936 FA Cup Final and helped the team gain promotion from the Second Division three years later. A very effective full-back, stylish to a degree, he relied on a highly developed positional sense and was a clean kicker of the ball which he used to great effect when taking penalties. Hooper broke his right leg in a 5-1 defeat at Wolves in October 1932 and was out of action until February 1933. On retiring in 1950 Hooper had well over 350 senior appearances under his belt.

127

HOPE, John William March
Goalkeeper: 71 apps.
Born: Shildon, County Durham, 30 March 1949
Career: Darlington (professional, May 1967), Newcastle United (£8,000, March 1969), BLADES (exchange deal involving John Tudor, January 1971), Preston North End (on loan, season 1973-74), Hartlepool United (July 1975), Stockton (coach, October 1980), Wingate FC (manager, July 1986), Whitby Town (October 1988), Willington (manager, June 1989), Hartlepool United (assistant-coach, January 1991), Darlington (coach, 1992-93).
Reserve to Irish international Willie McFaul at Newcastle, John Hope was substitute for the Geordies in the 1969 Inter Cities Fairs Cup Final v. Ujpesti Dozsa. Tall, strong and ideally built for a goalkeeper, he found a regular spot in the Blades' line-up despite suffering a number of knee operations. He was a member of the Blades 1971 promotion-winning side (playing in 17 games).
* His son, Chris, played for Darlington, Nottingham Forest and Scunthorpe United.

HOUSTON, Stewart Mackie
Left-back: 121+1 apps. one goal
Born: Dunoon, Argyll, 20 August 1949
Career: Port Glasgow Rangers, Chelsea (1967), Brentford (£17,000, 1972), Manchester United (£55,000, December 1973), BLADES (July 1980), Colchester United (player-coach, 1983), Plymouth Argyle (coach), Arsenal (assistant-manager, 1990), Queen's Park Rangers (manager, 1996-97), Tottenham Hotspur (assistant-manager/coach, 1998-2000), Walsall (assistant-manager, briefly, August-September 2002), Queen's Park Rangers (scout).
Consistent full-back Stewart Houston was signed by manager Tommy Docherty twice - first for Chelsea and then Manchester United. A player who loved to over-lap, he often acted as an extra attacker for the Reds with whom he won a Second Division championship in 1975 and appeared in the FA Cup Final defeat by Southampton twelve months later. Unfortunately he missed the 1977 Final through injury, his place being taken by Arthur Albiston who then generously offered Houston his winners' medal after the game! He made 250 appearances for Manchester United. In 1982 Houston won a Fourth Division Championship medal with the Blades at a time when he career was winding down. Capped by Scotland in 1976, he also represented his country in two Under-23 internationals and was assistant to manager George Graham at Highbury. Houston's father played League football for St Mirren.

HOWARD, Henry
Wing-half: 61 apps. 22 goals
Born: Rotherham 1871.
Career: Yorkshire local football, Rotherham Town (on trial, 1893), Sheffield Wednesday (on trial, 1894), BLADES (May 1895), Birmingham (April 1902), Wisbech Town (August 1906-May 1907).
Harry Howard was a solidly built, defensively minded player who always seemed to promise more than he achieved. He made his League debut for the Blades against Sunderland (home) in April 1898, replacing Ernie Needham who was on England duty.
After leaving Bramall Lane he appeared in 51 matches for Blues.

HOWELL, Rabbi
Half-back: 240 apps. 11 goals
Born: Wincobank, Sheffield, 12 October 1869. Died: 1937
Career: Ecclesfield, Rotherham Swifts, BLADES (£250, June 1890), Liverpool (April 1898), Preston North End (June 1901, retired September 1903 through injury).
Rab Howell was the first blooded gypsy to play League football and represent England at full international level. He was born in a caravan, the son of a local tinker and although a shade on the small size (under 5ft 6ins tall) he was very effective with loads of stamina and quick over short distances. He was a key member of the Blades' League championship winning side of 1898 but was transferred from the club after disciplinary problems. He was eventually forced to retire in 1903 after breaking his leg playing for Preston against Burnley. When he was carried off the pitch at Deepdale, so upset were his colleagues and supporters that a collection was made there and then. It raised almost £29. Howell represented his country (England) twice: against Ireland in March 1895 (scored once in a 9-0 win) and Scotland in April 1899.

HOWITT, Robert Gibb
Inside-forward; 98 apps. 33 goals
Born: Glasgow, 15 July 1929
Career: Partick Thistle, BLADES (£8,000, July 1955), Stoke City (April 1958, retired through injury, May 1963); later manager of Motherwell.
A Scottish League representative (with Partick) Bobby Howitt was a workmanlike forward with an eye for goal. He averaged a goal every three games for the Blades before going on to help the Potters win the Second Division title in 1963 when he played as a wing-half sometimes behind Stanley Matthews.
* He was signed by United on the recommendation of a scout...manager Joe Mercer had never seen him play.

HOWLETT, Charles Henry
Goalkeeper: 112 apps.
Born: Lincolnshire, circa 1865. Died: 1906.
Career: Gainsborough Trinity, BLADES (August 1889), Gainsborough Trinity (May 1894-95).
Charlie Howlett was United's first goalkeeper - and he wore spectacles, making him the scapegoat for many defeats when suffered in wet or muddy conditions! Indeed, he stood between the posts when the Blades lost 13-0 to Bolton Wanderers in a 2nd round FA Cup-tie in February 1890. In the days when centre-forwards and their colleagues used to barge into keepers, Howlett was very wary and nervous at times when under pressure but nevertheless he still managed to appear in well over a century of games for the Blades whom he served from for four seasons.
* Howlett was a very good musician who enjoyed playing the banjo.

HOYLAND, Jamie William
Midfielder: 90+22 apps. 9 goals
Born: Sheffield, 23 January 1966
Career: Manchester City (apprentice, June 1982, profession al November 1983), Bury (July 1986), BLADES (record £250,000, July 1990), Bristol City (on loan, March 1994), Burnley (£130,000, October 1994), Carlisle United (on loan, November 1997), Scarborough (free transfer, player/coach, August 1998-May 1999).
A strong-running midfielder (and occasional solid defender) with good power in the air, Jamie Hoyland made 205 first-class appearances for Bury and later played in 105 games for Burnley. An England Youth international he followed his father into the Blades' first XI and did very well for four years before moving to Turf Moor. He was voted Scarborough's 'Player of the Year' in 1999.
* His father, Tommy (q.v) played also played Bradford City.

HOYLAND, Thomas
Wing-half: 209 apps. 18 goals
Born: Sheffield, 14 June 1932
Career: BLADES (juniors, July 1947, professional, October 1949), Bradford City (October 1961-May 1963).
Tommy Hoyland scored on his debut for the Blades when occupying the right-wing position. But it was at wing-half where he played his best football, being first to the ball, tackling with great effect and he was quick as well.
* Son Jamie (q.v) followed his father into the Blades' team.

HOYLAND, Walter
Inside-left: 27 apps. 4 goals
Born: Sheffield, 14 August 1901. Died: 1985.
Career: BLADES (professional January 1920), Fulham (£500, March 1927), Boston (July 1928), Loughborough Corinthians (June 1929), Peterborough & Fletton United (August 1930), Mansfield Town (June 1932-May 1933).
Walter Hoyland spent seven seasons as a dedicated reserve at Bramall Lane. He netted four times in 22 League games for Fulham in a little over a year, but had to wait until 1932 before entering the competition again, this time with the Stags (23 outings, 9 goals).

HUDDERSFIELD TOWN

United's playing record against the Terriers:

Football League

Venue	P	W	D	L	F	A
Home	42	12	15	15	56	62
Away	42	10	14	18	46	62
Totals	84	22	29	33	102	124

FA Cup

	P	W	D	L	F	A
Home	2	1	1	0	3	1
Away	5	1	2	2	4	6
Neutral	4	0	2	2	3	5
Totals	11	2	5	4	10	12

WW1

	P	W	D	L	F	A
Home	4	4	0	0	12	2
Away	4	0	1	3	4	8
Totals	8	4	1	3	16	10

WW2

	P	W	D	L	F	A
Home	4	3	0	1	10	6
Away	3	1	0	2	5	7
Totals	7	4	0	3	15	13

Formed deep in the heart of Rugby League country at the Albert Hotel in 1908 and elected to the Football League in 1910 (after competing in the North-Eastern League), Huddersfield Town were threatened with extinction in 1919, but somehow survived and quickly won three successive League titles in succession under the leadership of former Blades' player Herbert Chapman (1924-26) as well as winning the FA Cup Final (1922) after finishing runners-up two years earlier and taking second place again in 1928.

United's first senior game with the 'Terriers' was a 1st round FA Cup-tie in 1913. But the game at Leeds Road was abandoned through snow with 15 minutes remaining and United 2-1 up. Unfortunately, the replay the following Wednesday afternoon went Town's way by 3-1.

The first League encounter followed just after Christmas, 1920. It ended level at 1-1, Billy Gillespie scoring for the Blades at Bramall Lane. The 'Terriers' won the return fixture 1-0.

As Huddersfield dominated League football during the mid-1920s, United were on the wrong end of some thrashings, notably a 7-1 reverse at Leeds Road in November 1927 (when they conceded six goals in the second-half) and a 6-1 drubbing on the same ground the following season.

In fact, United won only one home League game out of 14 between 1920-34, with the rampant 'Terriers' doubling-up no fewer than five times in all and winning a total of 17 matches, nine at 'the Lane'.

By beating Huddersfield 1-0 at Leeds Road in April 1928, the Blades saved themselves from relegation and at the same time destroyed Town's hopes of completing the League and FA Cup double.

Immediately after WW2 the teams played out four draws in the first six League games before United's fortunes changed as they produced far better results between 1952 and 1961. When they beat Town 3-1 in March 1956 it was their first home League triumph over the Terriers since 1929 and in seasons 1955-56, 1956-57, 1959-60 and 1960-61 they completed the double (recording their best-ever away win, 4-1, in November 1956) ...although they did crash to a 6-3 defeat at 'the Lane' in season 1953-54 when the 'Terriers' finished a creditable third behind Wolves and West Brom in the First Division table. During the late 160s/early '70s things were fairly even out on the pitch and to a certain extent during the 1980s, but United did manage an impressive 5-1 triumph in 1988-89 (when both sides were based in the Third Division). And by beating Huddersfield 2-1 (away) in May 1988, the Blades earned a place in the Play-offs; alas they were defeated over two legs by Bristol City.

Huddersfield beat United 1-0 in a second replay of the 1928 FA Cup semi-final at Maine Road (after 2-2 and 0-0 draws at Old Trafford and Goodison Park). The 'Terriers' also won FA Cup-ties in 1930 and 1957, while United replied with wins in 1946 (over two legs) and 1989.

Ex-Blades player, Eddie Boot, managed the Terriers in the early 1960s, while Neil Warnock and Steve Bruce have managed both clubs. Andy Beattie managed the Terriers and was later assistant-boss at 'the Lane.' John Deehan, Mick Whitham and Peter Withe were all associated with both clubs (coach/trainers) while David Steele managed the Terriers before becoming Blades' trainer. Lou Macari managed Huddersfield and later became a scout for the Blades.

Wayne Allison, Graham Bailey, Bob Barclay, Darren Bullock, Bobby Campbell, Harold Cawthorne, Tom Cowan, Terry Curran, Bobby Davison, Andy Dibble (United reserve), Jock Dodds (Town reserve), Alonzo Drake, Keith Edwards, Mel Eves, Paul Garner, Derek Hawksworth, Ian Holmes, George Hutchinson, Fred Jenkinson, Tony Kenworthy (Town trialist), Seth King, Rob Kozluk, Kevin Lewis, Chris Marsden, Colin Morris, Andy Morrison, Peter Ndlovu, Albert Nightingale, 'Iffy' Onuora, George Richardson, Jack Robinson, Chris Short, Ron Simpson, Phil Starbuck, Rob Ullathorne, Roy Warhurst (Town amateur) and Simon Webster are among the many players to have donned the respective striped shirts of the Blades and Town.

HUDSON, Jack

Left-half: 16 apps. 3 goals
Born: circa 1865
Career: Wednesday, BLADES (September 1889 to May 1891).
Jack Hudson, a well-built, competitive wing-half, played in the Blades' first-ever game against Nottingham Rangers in September 1889. He was a regular during that season but faded after that.

HUDSON, William A

Outside-right: one app.
Born: Swansea, 10 March 1928
Career: Pembroke Borough, Manchester City (on trial), Leeds United (May 1951), BLADES (May 1952), Mansfield Town (free transfer, May 1954-May 1955).
Welsh amateur international Billy Hudson made his debut for the Blades in front of almost 50,000 fans at Chelsea in September 1953 (won 2-1). An average player he figured in only 11 League games throughout his career.

129

HUFTON, Arthur Edward

Goalkeeper: 28 apps.

Born: Southwell, Notts, 25 November 1893. Died: Swansea, 2 February 1967

Career: Atlas & Norfolk Works FC, BLADES (April 1912), West Ham United (guest during WW1, then signed for £350, May 1919), Watford (June 1932). From 1934 he was employed by a car company in London's West End, retaining the job for many years while also working part-time behind the scenes at Upton Park.

After producing some excellent performances for the Blades at the end of the 1912-13 season, goalkeeper Ted Hufton broke his nose in a trial match before the start of the next campaign and lost his place in the team to Harry Gough (the man he had replaced). During the war he was wounded serving in the Coldstream Guards and whilst recuperating he played as a guest for West Ham, eventually signing for the Hammers to replace Joe Hughes and played in the London club's first-ever Football League game against Lincoln City in August 1919. Hufton endured the batterings that were a goalkeeper's lot in the 1920s and helped the Hammers gain promotion to the top flight and played in the first Wembley FA Cup Final of 1923. Between May 1923 and May 1929 he made more appearances for England than any of the 15 goalkeepers his country used and but for injuries he would surely have won more than his six caps. Something of a penalty-king, Hufton saved 11 out of 18 spot-kicks fired at him in two seasons. He was almost 40 when he left Upton Park, having appeared in 401 League and Cup games

HULL CITY

United's playing record against the Tigers:

Football League

Venue	P	W	D	L	F	A
Home	20	11	6	3	51	20
Away	20	6	9	5	28	27
Totals	40	17	15	8	79	47
FA Cup						
Home	1	1	0	0	2	0
Away	1	0	1	0	1	1
Totals	2	1	1	0	3	1
League Cup						
Home	1	1	0	0	3	1
Away	2	0	0	2	0	3
Totals	3	1	0	2	3	4
WW1						
Home	5	3	1	1	9	2
Away	5	1	2	2	8	11
Totals	10	4	3	3	17	13
WW2						
Home	1	1	0	0	3	1
Away	1	0	0	1	0	1
Totals	2	1	0	1	3	2
Others						
Away	5	2	0	3	4	4

Hull City FC was formed in 1904...by a group of brave men who certainly gambled with a soccer team based deep in the heart of Rugby League territory. Indeed, the footballers used the rugby ground (The Boulevard) during its first season before gaining Football League status in Division Two and switching to Anlaby Road, staying there until 1946 when they switched to Boothferry Park (although they had spent the last two WW2 season back at The Boulevard). In 2002 the 'Tigers' moved to a another new ground, The Kingston Communications Stadium (initial capacity 24,500).

Although they have never played in the top-flight of English football, Hull have spent 50 seasons in the Second Division - only Barnsley and Leicester City have played more times at this level.

The 'Tigers' first met the Blades on 8 December 1934 (Division 2) when they won 4-3 at Bramall Lane (a surprising result at the time). United, though, gained revenge by winning 3-0 at Anlaby Road later in the campaign and the following season, courtesy of a Jack Pickering hat-trick, they whipped Hull 7-0 at home, thus driving more nails into the Tigers' relegation coffin.

At the end of the 1949-50 United and Wednesday (with a game in hand) were neck and neck vying for promotion from Division Two. The Blades' won their last match against Hull (at home) by 5-0 (Harold Brook scoring twice), and with the Owls drawing 2-2 with West Ham, United therefore had one point advantage but a slightly inferior goal-average, 68.49 to Wednesday's 67.48. Wednesday's final match was against the champions Spurs. A 0-0 draw would see them through...and that's precisely what they achieved!

The Blades led the Tigers 4-0 after 24 minutes of their home Second Division game in August 1959. The final score was 6-0.

The last two League meetings, in 1989-90, both finished goalless.

Th first FA Cup-tie between the clubs took place in 1982-83, when the Blades won a 1st round replay 2-0 (after a 1-1 draw at Boothferry Park).

The initial League Cup contest had taken place in 1975-76 when the Tigers won a 3rd round contest by 2-0. United, though, had to wait seven years before gaining revenge with an aggregate 3-2 win in round one in 1982-83.

Gary Ablett, Chris Bettney, Terry Curran, Aidan Davison, Bobby Davison, Keith Edwards, Stan Fazackerley, Kevin Gage, Jack Gibson, Glyn Hodges, Joe Kitchen, Brian Marwood, David Mercer, Jack Pears, George Richardson, Jack Robinson, Jack Sheen, Jack Smith, Jock Smith, Gerry Summers, Alan Warboys, Billy Whitehurst, Dean Windass and Bill Wood are among the many players who have assisted both clubs.

HUNT, Jonathan Richard

Midfielder: 25+9 apps. 2 goals

Born: Camden, London, 2 November 1971

Career: Barnet (juniors, 1986, professional September 1989), Southend United (July 1993), Birmingham City (£50,000, September 1994), Derby County (£500,000, May 1997), BLADES (on loan, August 1998), Ipswich Town (on loan, October 1998), BLADES (£25,000, March 1999), Cambridge United (on loan, March 2000), Wimbledon (free transfer, September 2000-May 2001), non-League football.

A double winner with Birmingham in 1995 (Second Division championship & Auto-Windscreen Shield victory) midfielder Jonathan Hunt could play wide on either flank and was also something of a dead-ball specialist. He had made well over 200 first-class appearances when he joined the Blades on loan and when he entered non-League football in 2001 his career tally stood at 305 (37 goals).

HUTCHISON, George Henry

Outside-right or left/inside-forward: 84 apps. 11 goals
Born: Allerton Bywater near Castleford, Yorkshire, 31 October 1929.
Career: Huddersfield Town (amateur, May 1945, professional January 1947), BLADES (March 1948), Tottenham Hotspur (June 1953), Guildford (July 1954), Leeds United (August 1955), Halifax Town (July 1956), Bradford City (July-November 1958).
A fast, nimble winger, George Hutchison contested the right-wing berth with Denis Thompson at Bramall Lane, while also playing in other forward positions before moving to Spurs following the emergence of Alf Ringstead.

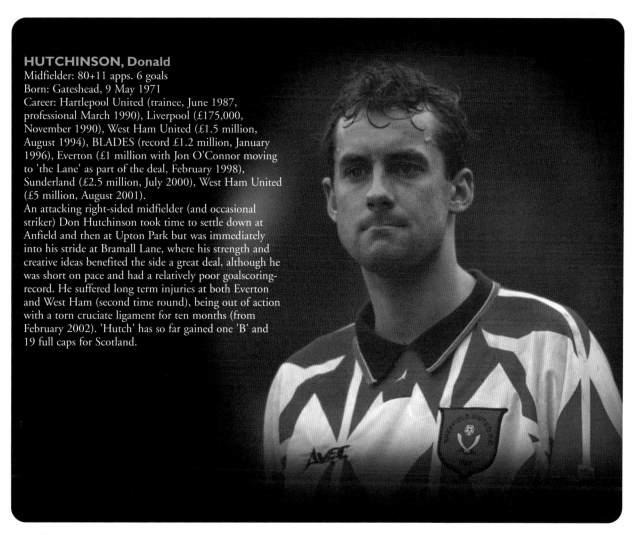

HUTCHINSON, Donald

Midfielder: 80+11 apps. 6 goals
Born: Gateshead, 9 May 1971
Career: Hartlepool United (trainee, June 1987, professional March 1990), Liverpool (£175,000, November 1990), West Ham United (£1.5 million, August 1994), BLADES (record £1.2 million, January 1996), Everton (£1 million with Jon O'Connor moving to 'the Lane' as part of the deal, February 1998), Sunderland (£2.5 million, July 2000), West Ham United (£5 million, August 2001).
An attacking right-sided midfielder (and occasional striker) Don Hutchison took time to settle down at Anfield and then at Upton Park but was immediately into his stride at Bramall Lane, where his strength and creative ideas benefited the side a great deal, although he was short on pace and had a relatively poor goalscoring-record. He suffered long term injuries at both Everton and West Ham (second time round), being out of action with a torn cruciate ligament for ten months (from February 2002). 'Hutch' has so far gained one 'B' and 19 full caps for Scotland.

131

HUTCHINSON, James Arthur

Inside-forward: 15 apps. 9 goals
Born: Sheffield, 28 December 1915.
Career: Aqueduct FC (Sheffield), BLADES (professional, November 1937), Royal Navy (WW2), Lincoln City (guest), Bournemouth (June 1946), Lincoln City (November 1946), Oldham Athletic (February 1949), Denaby United (August 1950-May 1952).
Strong, fast off the mark, difficult to knock off the ball, Jimmy Hutchinson made his first-team debut for the Blades against his future club Lincoln City in a WW2 game in November 1939. A sharp-shooter, he had a fine scoring record throughout his career, and was leading marksman with 32 goals when helping the Imps win the third Division (North) championship in 1948. He lost his place at Sincil Bank to ex-Blades star Jock Dodds.
* His son, Barry, played for Bolton, Chesterfield, Derby County, Darlington, Halifax Town and Rochdale, plus a handful of non-League clubs.

ILEY, James

Wing-half: 112 apps. 13 goals

Born: South Kirby, Yorkshire, 15 December 1935

Career: Moorthorpe St Joseph's Boys Club, Pontefract FC, BLADES (juniors, March 1951, professional June 1953), Tottenham Hotspur (£16,000, August 1957), Nottingham Forest (£16,000, August 1959), Newcastle United (£17,000, September 1962), Peterborough United (player-manager, January 1969-September 1972), Cambridge United (scout, October 1972-March 1963), Barnsley (manager, April 1973), Blackburn Rovers (manager, April 1978), Luton Town (scout, October 1978), Bury (manager, July 1980-February 1984), Exeter City (manager, June 1984-April 1985), Charlton Athletic (scout), Luton Town (scout).

An England Under-23 international (one cap) and Football League representative, Jim Iley, a former colliery lad at Frickley pit before turning professional, made his League debut for the Blades as a 17 year-old. He quickly began to be noticed and earned a move to White Hart Lane where he won his England honour. He failed to settle in London and opted to move back north, joining Forest in 1959 when manager Billy Walker was rebuilding his team following FA Cup glory. He did well at The City Ground and then became the cornerstone of Newcastle's Second Division promotion-winning side in 1965. The always seemingly balding Iley was regarded as 'the complete player', possessing good control, versatility, tremendous shooting power (mainly right-footed), consistency and a team-man's attitude. He skippered most of the clubs he played for and during a wonderful career accumulated more than 600 appearances (545 in the Football League) and scored over 35 goals. Iley took over as player-manager of Posh following the resignation of Norman Rigby and later had a turbulent 172 days in charge at Ewood Park. Later after leaving football, he resided in Bolton and ran an Italian restaurant in Chorley.

* Iley's brother-in-law is the ex-Blades winger Colin Grainger.

INJURIES & ILLNESS

United players who were forced to quit the game through injury in the year indicated, include: John Barnwell (1971), Ernest Blackwell (1925), Len Browning (1954), Martin Dickinson (1981), Sammy Dobson (1893), Wally Downes (1989), John Ebbrell (1997), Steve Finnieston (1980), Sid Gibson (1932), Steve Goulding (1977), Billy Hendry (1895), Bruce Longworth (1926), John McGeady (1977), Ken McNaught (1986), Jim Platt (1924), Brian Smith (1989), John Spencer (1960), Les Tibbott (1983), David White (1998), Dane Whitehouse (2000) and Julian Winter (1990).

Treatment Table
* Around 25 fans were injured during an FA Cup-tie with Burnley at Bramall Lane in March 1962 after railings collapsed. A crowd of 57,000 saw the Clarets win 1-0.
* Several fans were injured when a retaining wall collapsed at Millmoor during United's League game with Rotherham on 6 October 1979. It was due to fighting between rival supporters. The Blades won 2-1.
* Goalkeeper Tom McAlister broke a leg in the 31st minute of United's League game v. Manchester City in October 1977. Alan Woodward took over but the Blades lost 2-1.
* Frank Levick broke a collar-bone, playing for United against Newcastle on 1 January 1908 and had scored. He was taken to hospital where he died a month later, aged 21. (See under Deaths).

INTERNATIONAL BLADES

Here are details of Sheffield united players who gained representative honours at various levels whilst serving with the club (numbers in brackets indicate caps won):

Senior Caps

Australia	S Murphy (22*), C Veart (2)
Belarus	P Katchouro (7)
Canada	P Peschisolido (2*)
England	R Barclay (3), W Bennett (2), R Benson (1), AS Brown (2), A Common (2), AW Currie (7), BC Deane (3), RE Evans (4), WJ Foulke (1), HC Gough (1), C Grainger (6), GH Green (8), J Hagan (1), HTW Hardinge (1), GA Hedley (1), A Hodgkinson (5), R Howell (1), WH Johnson (6), MD Jones (2), HE Lilley (1), HB Lipsham (1), V Matthews (1), DW Mercer (2), T Morren (1), E Needham (16), HH Pantling (1), J Pickering (1), AE Priest (1), GL Shaw (5), A Sturgess (2), H Thickett (2), FE Tunstall (7), M Whitham (1), B Wilkinson (1).
Greece	V Borborkis (3)
Ireland	P Doyle (5), J Dunne (7)
Ivory Coast	O Tebily (2)
Northern Ireland	CF Hill (6)
Norway	J Flo (3), R Nilsen (3)
Republic of Ireland	J Dunne (1), W Gillespie (25), AT Kelly (22), A Ringstead (20)
Scotland	JG Brown (1), AR Forbes (5), E Colquhoun (9)
Wales	L Allchurch (4), NA Blake (5), J Davies (3), RE Evans (4), T Hockey (4), G Hodges (5), WR John (3), JL Jones (9), H Morris (1), R Page (7*), D Powell (10), GI Reece (16), DM Saunders (5)

* Still adding to tally as United players

Wartime (1915-19)

England:	J English (1), HC Gough (1)

Wartime (1939-46)

England:	J Hagan (14)

Victory Internationals (1945-46)

England:	J Hagan (2)

FA Overseas Tours

To South Africa (1910)
> R Benson, J Lievesley, A Sturgess

To South Africa (1920)
> DW Mercer, SN Fazackerley

To Canada (1926)
> DW Mercer, J Waugh

To Canada (1950)
> J Hagan

To Australia (1951)
> F Burgin, J Hagan, J Shaw

'B' Internationals
England:
> E Burgin, BC Deane, J Hagan, DW Hawksworth, M Speight, WR Quinn

Northern Ireland:
> DP Shiels (1)

Under-23 Internationals
England:
> L Badger (13), AJ Birchenall (4), AW Currie (13), A Hodgkinson (7), MD Jones (9), B Shaw (2), GL Shaw (5)

Northern Ireland:

MK Todd (2)

Scotland:

JG Brown (2)

Greece

T Dellas (2)

Under-21 Internationals
England:

PS Beagrie (2), WR Quinn (2), L Morris (1), C Woodhouse (3)

Football League Representative Honours:
L Badger, R Benson, A Common, W Cook, AW Currie, J English, WJ Foulke, C Grainger, GH Green, J Hagan, H Hammond, GA Hedley, A Hodgkinson, I Iley, H Johnson, WH Johnson, J Lievesley, HB Lipsham, DW Mercer, T Morren, E Needham, J Pickering, GL Shaw, J Shaw, H Thickett, F Tunstall, A Woodward.

Amateur Internationals
England:

W Russell (4)

Scotland:

J Roxburgh (1)

Sheffield & Yorkshire County XI

E Bluff (1)

Capped before and/or after playing for United.
Here is an unofficial list of players who represented their country at senior level either (a) before joining the Blades or (b) after leaving Bramall Lane. Wartime guests have not been included, neither have players who were released by the club, having had trials or had been registered on schoolboy forms:

Australia: C Veart
Belarus   P Katchouro
Cameroon   P Suffo
England: A Common, K Curle, AW Currie, C Grainger, MD Jones, B Marwood, P Parker, M Peters, EA Sandford,
                P Thompson, D White, P Withe
Ivory Coast   O Tebily
Northern Ireland: K Black, CF Hill, P Sloan, PA Williams
Norway   J Flo, R Nilsen
Republic of Ireland: D Givens, A Kelly, D Kelly, P McGrath, T Phelan, JW Sloan
Scotland: AR Forbes, S Houston, D Hutchinson, J Johnstone, S McCall, B Rioch, A Walker
Wales: L Allchurch, NA Blake, AG Dibble, TE Egan, RE Evans, M Hill, T Hockey, G Hodges, WR John, JL Jones,
                V Jones, H Morris, R Page, D Powell, GI Reece, I Rush, D Saunders, G Taylor, B Williams
Zimbabwe   P Ndlovu
England (Amateur) J Roxburgh

The following future or ex-United players/personnel all gained representative honours at various levels during WW2 (including Victory internationals: 1945-46):
Scotland: E Dodds

United managers who played at international level:
Joe Mercer and Martin Peters (England) & John Harris (Scotland WW2). Assistant/caretaker-boss Danny Bergara was capped by Uruguay, while Blades' assistant-manager Andy Beattie represented Scotland.

International Talk Back
* The first two United players to win full international honours were Harry Lilley and Mick Whitham, who were both capped by England on the same day, 5 March 1892, in separate games: Lilley versus Wales and Whitham v. Ireland.
* Robert Ernest Evans played for Wales against England and England against Wales in the early 1900s. He also played for both countries against Scotland and Ireland. Evans, was by birth, an Englishman (from Chester) and played for the Blades between 1908-19
* Ernest Needham won his first cap in April 1894 v. Scotland in Glasgow.
* No less than nine international players were in United's side against Liverpool in November 1903 (eight English and one Irish). The other two - Brown and Common - later went on to win full caps.
* Billy Gillespie scored two unique goals for Ireland against England in 1913 - the first went in off England's right-back Bob Crompton and the other off his Bramall Lane team-mate and left-back colleague Bob Benson who was making his international debut.
* United had six international strikers on their books in 1998 - Brian Deane (England), Dean Saunders (Wales), Jan-Aage Fjortoft (Norway), Gareth Taylor (Wales), Andy Walker (Scotland) and Petr Katchouro (Belarus).
* Jimmy Hagan scored 12 goals for England during WW2 (1941-46). Crowds of 103,000 and 133,000 saw him play against the Scots at Hampden Park in April 1943 & April 1944 respectively.
* Jock Dodds (ex-United centre-forward) scored a hat-trick in Scotland's 5-2 win over England at Hampden Park in April 1942.
* A crowd of 133,000
* Towards the end of the 1903-04 season, United's team was frequently made up of ten Englishmen and one Irishman (Peter Boyle). In 1902 the team had 9 internationals, by 1904 there were 8 internationals and 3 were later capped.
* Steve Cammack played for England Youth v. Spain at Bramall Lane on 15 March 1972

IPSWICH TOWN

United's playing record against the 'Tractormen':

Premier League

Venue	P	W	D	L	F	A
Home	2	1	1	0	4	1
Away	2	0	1	1	2	3
Totals	4	1	2	1	6	4

Football League

Home	21	9	6	6	35	24
Away	21	3	8	10	16	30
Totals	42	12	14	16	51	54

Play-offs

Home	1	0	1	0	1	1
Away	1	0	1*	0	2	2
Totals	2	0	2	0	3	3

FA Cup

Home	2	2	0	0	5	3
Away	2	0	1	1	3	4
Totals	4	2	1	1	8	7

* Qualified for the Final on away goal rule.

Ipswich Town FC was formed at a meeting held at the Town Hall as far back as 1878 when Mr T C Cobbold, MP, was appointed President. Originally it was called the Ipswich Association FC, to distinguish it from the older Ipswich FC, which had played rugby. These two units amalgamated in 1888, adopted Portman Road as its new ground (from Brook's Hall) and the 'handling' code was officially dropped in 1893

Elected to the Football League in 1938, over the next 24 years Ipswich Town won the Third Division (South) title twice (in 1954 & 1957), the Second Division championship in 1961 and the League crown a year later.

They first faced the Blades in the Football League in 1957-558 (Division 2) drawing 1-1 at 'the Lane' and winning 1-0 at Portman Road. The following season United recorded their first win, 2-0 at home.

United played their first ever League game on a Saturday night against Ipswich (at Portman Rod) on 26 March 1960. A crowd of 19,048 saw them lose 2-0.

United's biggest win over the so-called 'Tractormen' is 7-0, achieved at Bramall Lane in 1971-72 when hot-shot Alan Woodward scored four times.

Bit United have an abysmal record on Ipswich soil...only three wins in 25 starts (all in the League - their first coming in 1960-61 and the last in 1974-75, both by 1-0). The latter gave them their only 'double

The Blades were 2-1 up with two minutes remaining of their 3rd round FA Cup-tie at Portman Road in January 1974. They lost 3-2! A cracking 4th round FA Cup-tie between the teams at Bramall Lane in January 2003 went in favour of the Blades by 4-3. After trailing 3-0, Ipswich fought back to level the scores only for Paul Peschisolido to grab a last-ditch winner for United. Phil Jagielka scored the Blades' 500th FA Cup goal in this game.

In 1996-97 the clubs meet in the end-of-season First Division Play-off semi-final - and it was United who came out on top, drawing 1-1 at home and 2-2 away (despite having 'keeper Alan Kelly hobbling around, injured) to qualify to meet Crystal Palace at Wembley for a place in the Premiership. Alas, David Hopkins' well-struck shot in the dying minutes gave the 'Eagles' a 1-0 victory.

David Barnes, Marcus Bent, Brian Gayle, Mick Hill, Jonathan Hunt, Les Tibbott and Gus Uhlenbeek are among the players who have served with Ipswich as well as the Blades. John Deehan (Town player, United coach etc.) was also associated with both clubs, likewise Bill Anderson (United player, Town scout).

IRISH CONNECTIONS

United's record against Irish clubs:

P	W	D	L	F	A
13	8	3	2	36	21

The Blades have played against seven 'Irish' clubs - Belfast Celtic (1933-34), Bohemians (1902-03), Derry City (1932-33), Distillery (1902-03 & 1958-59), Glenavon (1993-94 & 1996-87), Linfield Athletic (1894-95 & 1996-97) and Shamrock Rovers (1932-33 & 1933-34).

United's first game (a friendly) against an Irish side took place on 5 November 1894 when a crowd of 1,500 saw plenty of fireworks as the Blades carved out a win 5-0 at Bramall Lane.

In the early 1930s United played Shamrock Rovers for the Duggan Cup. They beat Rovers 5-4 in Ireland in April 1933 and the following season, after a 1-1 draw at the same venue (September 1933), they won 6-4 in Dublin in April 1934.

Irish Blarney

* Initially Paul McGrath won a record 83 caps for the Republic of Ireland before his tally was bettered by another former Villa player, Tony Cascarino, with 88. McGrath is also Villa's most capped player with 51 international appearances, beating the previous record-holder, Peter McParland (with 33).

* Jimmy Dunne (born in Ringsend, Ireland in 1905) scored 167 goals for United (1926-33) and is the last Irishman to net over 30 League goals in successive seasons.

* Don Givens was appointed manager of the Republic of Ireland Under-21 side in 2001.

JACKSON, Ernest

Wing-half: 400 apps. 19 goals

Born: Sheffield, 11 June 1914. Died: Sheffield, 1996.

Career: Sheffield Wednesday (junior, August 1929), Grimsby Town (on trial, 1930), Atlas & Norfolk FC, BLADES (June 1932), Boston United (May 1949), BLADES (coach, 1950-55).

A home grown wing-half who fought his way into United's 1936 FA Cup Final side via the 'A' team, Ernest Jackson was one of the few players to serve the club before, during and after WW2, helping the Blades gained promotion in 1939. A very useful performer who would surely have gained international honours if it hadn't been for WW2, he was strong in the tackle, had a terrific engine and gave the Blades excellent service, making his League debut against Wolverhampton Wanderers in February 1933. He returned to Bramall Lane as a coach in 1950 and when he quit football, several people within the club were bitterly disappointed. He played in Wednesday's reserve side at the age of 15.

JACOBSEN, Anders
Defender: 8+5 apps.
Born: Norway, 18 April 1968
Career: IK Start (Norway), BLADES (December 1998), Stoke City (free transfer, August 1999), Notts County (free, September 2000), Skeid/Oslo (July 2001).
A cultured and thoughtful central defender, Anders Jacobsen found it hard going at times with the Blades but he battled on and after leaving Bramall Lane made 54 appearances for the Potters, helping them win the Auto-Windscreen Shield in 2000.

JAGIELKA, Philip Nikodern
Full-back/midfielder: 77+23 apps* 5 goals*
Born: Manchester, 17 August 1982
Career: BLADES (apprentice, July 1998, professional May 2000).
An England Youth international at Under-18 & 20 levels, the hard-working, athletic Phil Jagielka made excellent progress during the 2001-02 season and the following year was quite outstanding as the Blades reached the semi-finals of both the Worthington Cup and FA Cup competitions as well as reaching the First Division Play-off Final (v. Wolverhampton Wanderers - his 100th senior appearance for the club). He signed a new contract for the club in the summer of 2003...soon after he had been voted the club's 'Young Player of the Year.'
* His brother, Steve, initially with Stoke City, now plays for Shrewsbury Town.

137

JAVARY, Jean-Phillipe
Midfielder: 8+6 apps* one goal*
Born: Montpellier, France, 10 January 1978
Career: ASOA Valence, RCD Espanyol, Montpellier, Raith Rovers (January 2000), Brentford (free transfer, August 2000), Plymouth Argyle (non-contract, February 2001), Partick Thistle (October 2001), Raith Rovers (November 2001), Bradford City (on trial), BLADES (March 2002).
A former French Youth international, Jean-Phillipe Javary - a combative midfielder - made 12 appearances in Scottish League football and he also failed to impress with either Brentford or Plymouth. Earlier in his career he had over 100 games with his French and Spanish clubs.

JEFFREY, Alfred Howard
Outside-left: 4 apps. 2 goals
Born: Sheffield, 4 March 1895. Died: January 1921
Career: Trinity Wesleyans FC, BLADES (August 1919 until his death),
Reserve left-winger Alf Jeffrey scored twice on his League debut for the Blades v. West Bromwich Albion (the ultimate champions that season) at The Hawthorns in February 1920. Sadly he died at the age of 25 and later his father claimed that his death was due to injuries received playing football.

JEFFRIES, Alfred
Winger: 51 apps. 10 goals
Born: Bishop Auckland, 21 September 1914.
Career: Norwich City (August 1934), Bradford City (May 1935), Derby County (February, 1937), BLADES (£3,200, June 1939-April 1943). Did not figure after WW2.
Alf Jeffries was a talented winger, whose opportunities were limited at Norwich and Derby before WW2 put paid to his career at Bramall Lane. He scored 12 goals in 59 games for Bradford.

JENKINSON, Frederick
Full-back: 62 'other' apps
Born: Chapeltown, 1910
Career: Chapeltown, Intake WMC, BLADES (on trial August 1928), Huddersfield Town (professional, October 1928), Intake WMC, Stockport County (July 1931-38), Bury (August 1939-May 1945), BLADES (WW2 guest: March 1940 to April 1943)
After an unsuccessful trail at Bramall Lane and no first team outings with Huddersfield. Full-back Fred Jenkinson was disillusioned with football before being brought back into the game by Stockport for whom he appeared in 295 first-class matches as a resilient, tough-tackling full-back. He guested for the Blades in more than 60 matches during WW2.

138

JESSOP, Frederick Samuel
Left-back/half-back: 31 apps. one goal
Born: Barrow Hill, Derbyshire, 7 February 1907. Died: 1979
Career: Staveley Works FC, Derby County (amateur January 1926, professional March 1926), BLADES (December 1937), Atherstone Town (season 1946-47).
Essentially a wing-half, Freddie Jessop could fill in at full-back and also as an inside-forward...a utility player who was regularly summoned to fill a gap somewhere in the team. He broke his leg playing for Derby in 1932 and struggled to regain full fitness. He was past his best when he joined the Blades but was totally committed when called into action at right-half during the Second Division championship season of 1938-39.

JOHN, William Ronald
Goalkeeper: 31 apps.
Born: Briton Ferry, nr Neath, 29 January 1911. Died: Port Talbot, 12 July 1973.
Career: Neath Road Council School, Briton Ferry Schoolboys, Briton Ferry Athletic, Swansea Town (amateur, February 1927), Walsall (professional, May 1928), Stoke City (£400, April 1932), Preston North End (£500, June 1934), BLADES (£1,250, December 1934), Manchester United (£600, June 1936), Newport County (May 1937), Swansea Town (July 1937); guested for Blackburn Rovers, Bolton Wanderers, Burnley and Southport during WW2. He retired in 1945 to become a hotel manager in South Wales.
Goalkeeper 'Roy' John - who started his playing career as a full-back - had already made over 150 appearances before joining the Blades and was also an established Welsh international (with nine caps already won), later taking his tally up to 14, three coming as a 'Blade.' He also represented his country against England in a red cross international in November 1939 and played for a Welsh XI v. RAF in 1942...having helped Stoke win the Second Division title ten years earlier.
* One pen-portrait described John as being 'a dashing and darting goalkeeper - a gay cavalier who laughs fortune in the face.'

JOHNSON, Charles
Left-back: 74 apps.
Born: North Shields, 29 April 1884. Died: circa 1955.
Career: Willington Athletic, BLADES (March 1905), South Shields (1910) Jarrow Caledonias (player manager, close of season 1910) South Shields (1913- 1915).
Charlie Johnson made his League debut for the Blades against Everton in February 1906, partnering Bob Benson at full-back. Strongly built, resourceful and confident in his kicking, he held his position until November 1908 when he was replaced by Joe Brooks. After that Johnson was virtually a reserve at Bramall Lane where he remained until the outbreak of WW1.

JOHNSON, Harry

Centre-forward: 395 apps. 252 goals

Born: Ecclesfield, Sheffield, 4 January 1899. Died: Sheffield, May 1981.

Career: Ecclesfield FC (1914), BLADES (January 1916...served in Army during WW1), Mansfield Town (£500, July 1931-May 1936)

Harry Johnson was a brilliant goalscoring centre-forward, full of enthusiasm, incredibly fast over the ground and difficult to mark, although he did have the tendency to miss quite a few 'sitters'. He scored a record number of goals - more than 250 in just under 400 senior appearances - for the Blades whom he served for over 15 years, from 1916-31. He netted a fivetimer when West Ham were whipped 6-2 in a League game on Boxing Day 1927, thus equalling the club record of most goals in a game, held at the time by Harry Hammond, who had achieved that feat back in 1892.

He also scored on his League debut v. Blackburn Rovers (home) in October 1919, having obliged with his first goal for the club in a Midland Section wartime game v. Grimsby Town in September 1916. During the hostilities Johnson - who always carried a smile on his face, no matter what the circumstances - enlisted in the Army and was involved in the Battle of Verdun in 1918. On leaving the forces after the armistice, he was re-engaged by the Blades and immediately established himself in the side, having his best seasons by far in 1927-28 and 1928-29 when he scored 43 and 31 goals respectively. An FA Cup winner in 1925, he surprisingly never gained a full England cap, although when at his peak, there was an awful lot of competition for that spot. He did, however, earn a Football League call up (along with Dixie Dean) and celebrated by scoring a hat-trick in a 9-1 win over the Irish League at St James' Park, Newcastle in September 1927 when amazingly all his side's nine goals came in a 41-minute spell in the first-half, Dean outdoing him by claiming four! The son of Harry senior, Johnson was always a part-time footballer and carried on his job as an analyst chemist at Hadfield's Steelworks in Sheffield until he retired in 1963, always maintaining that if he had become a full-time professional he would have lost his appetite for the game. After leaving Bramall Lane he added another 104 goals in 163 appearances to his overall set of statistics and helping the Stags win the Bass Charity Vase in 1935. He hung up his boots with an aggregate League record of 476 outings and 309 goals - one every 1.5 games for 17 seasons with two-thirds of them coming in the First Division.

* His father, Harry senior (q.v) was twice an FA Cup winner with United (1899 & 1902) while his brother Tom, a centre-half, was on the losing side in the 1926 FA Cup Final v. Arsenal.

The Johnsons were a truly remarkable footballing family.

JOHNSON, Howard

Centre-half/centre-forward: 107 apps. one goal

Born: Sheffield, 17 July 1925

Career: Norton Woodseats, BLADES (March 1951), York City (August 1957, retiring May 1958) Denaby United.

Howard Johnson, was a part-time professional, a rock-solid defender, powerful in the tackle who was a registered player at Bramall Lane for six years. He played his last four games for the Blades as a centre-forward, scoring his only goal for the club in his final match - a 2-1 FA Cup defeat at Huddersfield in January 1957. He helped the club win the Second Division title in 1953.

139

JOHNSON, Thomas
Centre/left-half/left-back: 257 apps.
Born: Ecclesfield, 4 May 1911. Died: Sheffield, August 1983
Career: Ecclesfield United, BLADES (amateur, July 1927, professional May 1929), Lincoln City (March 1946, retiring, December 1948). Later worked as United's scout in the Yorkshire area (from February 1949) while also employed as an electrical engineer in Sheffield
Tom Johnson's displays at the heart of the defence were a feature of United's strength in the mid-to late 1930s and early '40s. Younger brother of Harry (q.v) and another son of William Harry (q.v) he joined the Blades from his local club and made his League debut for against Bolton Wanderers in March 1930 when he replaced the injured George Green. Slow to develop, he made intermittent appearances over the next four seasons before establishing himself as the 'stopper' in the side during the 1934-35 campaign, going on to win an FA Cup medal in 1936 and then leading the side to promotion in 1938-39. He stayed at Bramall Lane until 1946 and retired two years later after helping Lincoln win the Third Division (North) championship.

Fulham's Ronnie Rooke (r) cuts back inside Sheffield United's Tom Johnson (l)

JOHNSON, William Harry
Half-back: 275 apps. 7 goals
Born: Ecclesfield, Sheffield, March 1876. Died: Sheffield, 1940.
Career: Atlas & Norfolk FC, BLADES (August 1895, retired April 1909, taking a position as trainer at Bramall Lane until 1934), 'Harry' Johnson was a tremendously hard-working player, totally committed, a 90-minute grafter who served United as a player for 13 years during which time he filled all three half-back positions. A player with an attacking bent, he possessed a strong, right-foot shot, could centre exceedingly well when given the time and space, and was quick in recovery. He made his first team debut at centre-half in a friendly against Corinthians in December 1995, following up with his first League game v. Preston North End at Bramall Lane in October 1897 and at the end of that season collected a League championship medal (making 10 appearances), following up with two FA Cup winners' prizes in 1899 & 1902, as well as earning six full England caps, gained between 1900-03. Johnson, who was badly injured at Sunderland in January 1906 and took quite a while to regain full fitness, announced his retirement as a player in 1909. He remained on the club's training staff until 1934, thus giving the Blades a total of 39 years service. * Father of Harry Johnson junior (q.v) and Thomas Johnson (q.v).

JOHNSTONE, James Connelly
Outside-right: 13 apps. 2 goals
Born: Viewpark, Uddington, Lanarkshire, 30 September 1944
Career: Viewpark FC, Celtic (April 1961, professional October 1961), Blantyre Celtic (for development, season 1961-62), San Jose Earthquakes/NASL (June 1975), BLADES (November 1975), Dundee (June 1977), Shelbourne/Ireland (November 1977), Elgin City (season 1978-79), Blantyre Celtic (re-instated as a 'junior' July 1980, retired May 1981).
Flame-haired, midget right-winger Jimmy Johnstone, just 5ft 4ins tall, made a romantic rise from being a Parkhead ball boy in the late 1950s to a famous Celtic star a few years later. He had a few ups and downs with authority, but at his peak, he was a superb entertainer, his jinking, carving, menacing runs down the flank (and inside) bemused opponents, their physical advantages proving no obstacle at times. Johnstone played in 515 first-class games for Celtic and scored 130 goals. He gained a winners medal for victories in the 1967 European Cup Final, nine successive Scottish League championships (1966-74), five Scottish Cup Finals (1967-1969-1971-1972 & 1974) and five Scottish League Cup Finals (1966. 1967, 1969, 1970 & 1975). He collected runners-up prizes in the European Cup (1970), Scottish Cup (1966, 1970 & 1973) and League Cup (1965, 1971, 1972, 1973 & 1974). Johnstone also won 23 full caps for his country (1965-75), made four appearances for the Scottish League and played in two Under-23 internationals.
He was 31 when he joined the Blades and although he occasionally produced some exciting skills, unfortunately drink, gambling and a few other problems, led to his quick departure. When at his brilliant best, north of the border, Johnstone was described by one journalist as the 'flying flea.'

JONES, George Henry
Outside-right/left: 184 apps. 59 goals
Born: Sheffield. 27 November 1918. Died: Yorkshire, 1995.
Career: Woodburn Alliance, BLADES (November 1935), Barnsley (February 1951, retiring, May 1952).
Two-footed winger George Jones was quick, had good control and possessed a pretty useful shot. Unfortunately illness affected his game from time to time and he missed quite a few games during the late 1940s. He helped United gain promotion from the Second Division in 1938-39, appearing in 21 matches and scoring four goals, two of them vital.

JONES, Glyn
Centre/inside-forward: 31 apps. 4 goals
Born: Dalton, Rotherham, 8 April 1936
Career: Schoolboy football, Rotherham United (amateur, 1951), BLADES (amateur August 1953, professional June 1954), Rotherham United (December 1957), Mansfield Town (July 1959), Heanor Town (June 1961).
Although a useful footballer, the only club Glyn Jones was able to hold down a regular first team position was Mansfield Town (18 goals in 45 appearances in two seasons).
He was capped by England at both Schoolboy and Youth levels.

JONES, John Leonard
Centre-half/left-half/outside-right: 37 apps. 6 goals
Born: Rhuddlan, near Rhyl, 1866. Died: Sunderland, 24 November 1931
Career: Rhuddlan (1882), Bootle (1888), Stockton (1891), Grimsby Town (May 1893), BLADES (May 1894), Tottenham Hotspur (May 1897...with McKay and Cain), Worcester City (July 1905, retired May 1906). Thereafter continued to be involved in sport, initially playing in exhibition matches on a synthetic surface at London's Olympia, later coaching cricket in Leinster (Ireland) in 1907 and in Durban, South Africa in 1909. He was then groundsman at Whitburn CC in Durham for a few years from March 1923. In later life he worked as a pattern-maker in Sunderland. A Welsh international (21 caps won between March 1895 and March 1904) Jack Jones also represented the Southern League v. London FA in 1898 and Sheffield v. Glasgow in 1896. He skippered Spurs to the Southern League title in 1900 and FA Cup victory a year later when the Blades were beaten in a replay. Described as being a 'most capable half, very speedy on the ball, supports his front men well and generally plays a judicious game' he was certainly skilful and wholehearted and was undoubtedly a fine tactician who combined splendidly with his forwards. Jones was also a fine cricketer, and coached both cricket and soccer at Rugby School when his duties with Spurs allowed. He died from head injuries after falling down a stairway at his place of work
* Jones was the first Spurs player to win full international honours (v. Ireland in 1898),

JONES, Michael David
Centre-forward: 172 apps. 76 goals
Born: Worksop, 24 April 1945
Career: Priory Secondary School (Worksop), Worksop & Rotherham Boys, Dinnington Miners' Welfare FC, BLADES (professional, November 1962), Leeds United (£100,000, September 1967, retired through injury, October 1975).
Later ran a sports shop in Leeds.
As a youngster Mick Jones once netted 14 goals in a game for his school. He never looked back...and after joining the Blades as a 17 year-old he continued to hit the target, with England Under-23 honours quickly bestowed on him, with two full caps following soon afterwards against West Germany and Sweden on tour in 1965. Having the traditional virtues of a old-fashioned centre-forward, he was quite a handful for defenders to cope with and his move to Elland Road (when he became Leeds' first £100,000 player) shocked the Blades' supporters. He formed a deadly strike-partnership with Allan Clarke (he was the bludgeon with Clarke acting as the rapier) and went on to rattle in 111 goals in 309 games for Leeds, whom he helped win the Fairs Cup in 1968 and 1971, the League championship in 1969 and the FA Cup in 1972, while also gaining an FA Cup runners-up medal in 1970. A serious knee injury ended Jones' career in 1975. Leeds' manager Don Revie described Jones as being: 'The complete team player who made a tremendous contribution to the team's success' while his strike-partner Allan Clarke said: 'People tended to overlook the work of Mick out on the field. He never cribbed; he just got on with job, quietly and efficiently, making those diagonal runs and drawing defenders out of position, allowing his colleagues the space they required to drive in on goal."
* Jones' father kept goal for Worksop Town.

JONES, Philip Howard
Midfielder: 33+3 apps. one goal
Born: Middlesbrough, 12 September 1961
Career: BLADES (apprentice, April 1977, professional June 1979), Boston United (May 1981).
Phil Jones had one good season of first team football with the Blades, making 20 appearances at competitive level in 1980-81 before his release following relegation to the Fourth Division.

JONES, Vincent Peter
Midfielder/defender: 41 apps. 2 goals
Born: Watford, 5 January 1965
Career: Wealdstone, Wimbledon (£10,000, November 1986), Leeds United (£650,000, June 1989), BLADES (record £650,000, September 1990), Chelsea (record £575,000, August 1991), Wimbledon (£700,000, September 1992), Queen's Park Rangers (£500,000, March-March 1999).
Tough, resilient, a great motivator on the field, Vinny Jones hated to lose a football match. As well as his never-say-die approach, he was also known for his intimidatory style and was often in trouble with officialdom...he was sent-off over a dozen times during his career. Controversial he may have been, but he certainly made opponents jump around on the field and at times if his colleagues were not pulling their weight, they too got a kick up the backside from the effervescent Mr. Jones. An FA Cup winner with Wimbledon in 1988 and a key member of Chelsea's Second Division championship winning side of 1990, Jones went on to gain nine full caps for Wales (1995-97) and when he finally hung up his boots (in 1999) he had amassed an exceptionally fine record of 486 senior appearances at club and international level (40 goals scored). He played in more than 320 games in his two spells with the Dons whom he skippered several times.
* Millionaire Jones is now a successful film star (his first movie was Lock, Stock and Two Smoking Barrels) and greyhound owner, who once had his own television game and chat show.

141

JOSEPH, Francis
8+12 apps. 4 goals
Born: Kilburn, London, 6 March 1960
Career: Hillingdon Borough (1978), Wimbledon (£1,000, November 1980), Brentford (£40,000, July 1982), Wimbledon (on loan, March 1987), Reading (£20,000, July 1987), Bristol Rovers (on loan, January 1988), Aldershot (on loan, March 1988), BLADES (free transfer, July 1988), Gillingham (free, March 1989), Crewe Alexandra (free, December 1989), Fulham (free, August 1990), Racing Ghent (Belgium), Barnet (non-contract, October-December 1991).
Nomadic footballer Francis Joseph spent 14 years as a professional during which time he served with 12 different clubs. His best spell came at Brentford (55 goals in 135 League outings) and he hit 15 goals in a total of 59 games for the Dons. He was a member of the Blades' 1989 promotion-winning team in 1989 (13 appearances).
* Three of Joseph's relatives - Leon Joseph (Spurs), Matt Joseph (Arsenal, Gillingham, Cambridge United, Leyton Orient and FC Ilves in France) and Roger Joseph (Brentford, Wimbledon, Millwall, WBA & Leyton Orient) - all played professional football.

142

Sneffield United v.s Manchester United, 26th December 1964

KABBA, Steven
Striker: 25+8 apps* 11 goals*
Born: Lambeth, London, 7 March 1981
Career: Crystal Palace (trainee, June 1997, professional June 1999), Luton Town (on loan, March 2002), Grimsby Town (on loan, September-October 2002), BLADES (£250,000, November 2002).
Unable to get into the Palace side (he was the fifth striker in line at Selhurst Park) Steve Kabba had a loan spell at Kenilworth Road (to keep him active) before manager Neil Warnock acquired him to bolster up the Blades' strike-force. His goals (v. Leeds United) shot the Blades into the semi-finals of the 2003 FA Cup. He also played his part in helping United reach the First Division Play-off Final that same season (v. Wolverhampton Wanderers). In May 2003 kabba was named in the Sierra Leone national team squad.

KAMARA, Christopher
Defender/midfielder: 22+3 apps.
Born: Middlesbrough, 25 December 1957
Career: Portsmouth (apprentice, April 1974, professional December 1975), Swindon Town (£20,000, August 1977), Portsmouth (£50,000, August 1981), Brentford (£20,000, October 1981), Swindon Town (£14,500, August 1985), Stoke City (£27,500, July 1988), Leeds United (£150,000, January 1990), Luton Town (£150,000, November 1991), BLADES (on loan, November 1992), Middlesbrough (on loan), February 1993), BLADES (free transfer, July 1993), Bradford City (free, July 1994, then player/coach, briefly, retired as player May 1995, then manager at Valley Parade, November 1995-December 1997), Stoke City (manager, January-March 1998). Now a football reporter/summariser for Sky Sport.
A leader to the last, Chris Kamara was a strong, purposeful footballer who always enjoyed a battle and a challenge. He was never found wanting and during his career amassed well over 770 senior appearances, helping Swindon win the Fourth Division title in 1986 and Leeds the Second Division prize in 1990. Unfortunately he was not a success as a manager.

KATCHOURO, Petr
Striker: 63+57 apps. 23 goals.
Born: Urss, Belarus, 2 August 1972
Career: Dinamo Minsk, BLADES (two-week trial, then signed for £650,000, July 1996), Chengdu Wuniu/China (March 2000).
After his big-money move from Dinamo Minsk, and a few outings in friendly matches, Belarusian international Petr Katchouro made his Blades League debut on the opening day of the campaign as a substitute in a 1-0 defeat at Reading. He had a very good first season, scoring 14 goals in 48 competitive matches and being voted the club's 'Player of the Year.' After that he lost his way a bit, may well have moved to QPR or PAOK Salonika, but stuck it out and although troubled by injuries from time to time, he managed to net some vital goals and set up plenty more for his colleagues. Capped 25 times by his country, Katchouro holds the Blades' record for most substitute appearances (57 at competitive level).
*Katchouro almost missed the start of the 1996-97 campaign because of problems over his work permit. Thankfully, a local MP intervened, sorted things out and he was able to commence the programme with the rest of his team-mates.

KAY, Alexander
Full-back: 6 apps.
Born: Scotland, circa 1875
Career: Partick Thistle (1897), BLADES (May 1901), West Ham United (August 1903).
Alex Kay was recruited as cover for full-backs Peter Boyle and Harry Thickett and was given only six outings in Blades' League side, one of them as an emergency centre-forward in a 4-0 defeat at Notts County in March 1902. He did not figure in the Hammers' first XI.

KEATING, Patrick Joseph
Outside-left: 3 apps.
Born: Cork, 17 September 1930
Career: Cork City, BLADES (signed with P.O'Sullivan in February 1950) Wisbech Town (May 1951), Bradford Park Avenue (September 1953), Chesterfield (October 1953-May 1957).
Pat Keating made his Football League debut for the Blades against Cardiff City (away) in November 1950. He looked out of place at a higher level of and after just three matches moved to Wisbech Town. He later returned to the Football League and after a couple of months at Bradford went on to score over 20 goals in almost 100 games for Chesterfield.

KEELEY, Andrew James
Defender: 34 apps. one goal
Born: Basildon, Essex, 16 September 1956
Career: Tottenham Hotspur (apprentice, April 1973, professional, January 1974), BLADES (December 1977), Scunthorpe United (July 1981-May 1983).
Big, strong defender, who had six League outings with Spurs, Andrew Keeley was one of the many players to leave the club following relegation to the Fourth Division in 1981.

143

KELLY, Alan Thomas

Goalkeeper: 252+3 apps.

Born: Preston, 11 August 1968

Career: Preston North End (apprentice, July 1984, professional September 1985), , BLADES (£200,000, July 1992), Blackburn Rovers (£675,000, July 1999), Stockport County (on loan, April 2001), Birmingham City (on loan, August 2001).

Goalkeeper Alan Kelly followed his father (Alan senior) into the League side at Deepdale and went on to appear in 164 first team games before transferring to Bramall Lane in 1992.

He took over between the posts (eventually) from Simon Tracey and made well over 250 appearances for the Blades before moving into the Premiership with Blackburn.

Capped at Youth and Under-23 sides by the Republic of Ireland he went on to gain a total of 34 full caps for his country as a superb shot-stopper, courageous and consistent to the last. He was voted as the First Division's top 'keeper in the PFA team in 1996 ...after he had skippered United, one of the first in his position to achieve that feat.

* Alan's brother, Gary (q.v.) played in one League game for the Blades at the end of the 2002-03 season.

KELLY, David Thomas

Striker: 26+14 apps. 8 goals

Born: Birmingham, 25 November 1965

Career: West Bromwich Albion (associate schoolboy forms, 1980), Wolverhampton wanderers (on trial, 1981), Southampton (on trial, 1982), Alvechurch, Walsall (December 1983), West Ham United (£600,000, August 1988), Leicester City (£300,000, March 1990), Newcastle United (£250,000, December 1991), Wolverhampton Wanderers (£750,000, June 1993), Sunderland (£1 million, September 1995), Tranmere Rovers (£350,000, August 1997), BLADES (free transfer, July 2000), Motherwell (free, July 2001), Stoke City (on trial, December 2001), Mansfield Town (free, January 2002).

During the later 1980s/early '90s David Kelly was rated as one of the finest marksmen anywhere in the Football League. When he moved to Bramall Lane he had already notched 233 goals (in 672 club appearances) while gaining 26 full caps for the Republic of Ireland as well as representing his country in two 'B', one Under-23 and three Under-21 internationals ...and he had helped Newcastle win the First Division title (1993).

On his day he was sharp, alert and had the great knack of being in the right place at the right time. A defender's worst nightmare, Kelly reached the milestone of 600 League appearances in 2002.

KELLY, Gary Alexander

Goalkeeper: one app.

Born: Preston, 3 August 1966.

Career: Newcastle United (apprentice, August 1982, professional June 1984), Blackpool (on loan, October-November 1988), Bury (££60,000, October 1989), Oldham Athletic (£10,000, August 1996), BLADES (March 2003, released May 2003). Signed as extra cover for another former Gigg Lane favourite Paddy Kenny, experienced goalkeeper Gary Kelly was called up for just one first team appearance in 2002-03, taking over between the posts for the final League game of the season at Watford. Prior to his arrival at Bramall Lane, Kelly had represented the Republic of Ireland in eight Under-21 internationals as well as appearing in one game for both the Under-23 side and 'B' team. He was also an FA Youth Cup winner with Newcastle in 1985 and when he left the Blades, his career appearance record stood at more than 625 competitive games (over 520 coming in the Football League). He was on the bench for United's 2003 Play-off Final v. Wolves.

* He is the older brother of Alan Kelly (q.v), the former Preston North End and Blackburn goalkeeper who spent seven years with the Blades (1992-97).

KEMP, Samuel Patrick

Outside-right: 17 apps. one goal

Born: Stockton-on-Tees, 29 August 1932

Career: Whitby Town, Sunderland (March 1952), BLADES (February 1957), Mansfield Town (£2,000, May 1958), Gateshead (October 1958-May 1959). Sammy Kemp was an out-and-out right-winger, fast but lacking the ability to make the grade as a First Division player. He made only 33 League appearances during his career.

KENDALL, John William
Goalkeeper: 91 apps.
Born: Broughton, near Brigg, Lancashire, 9 October 1905. Died: 1963.
Career: Broughton Rangers (North Lindsey League), Lincoln City (March 1922), Everton (£1,250, April 1924), Preston North End (£1,000, May 1927), Lincoln City (£750, July 1928), BLADES (£1,125, March 1930), Peterborough United (July 1934-May 1938).
When he arrived at Bramall Lane, goalkeeper Jack Kendall had 140 League games to his credit and he quickly made his mark with the Blades, adding a further 80 top that total during his four-year stay with the club. Described (in the late 1920s) as "...a cool, fearless player with a keen eye who possesses an enormous reach" his career was badly affected by injury at both Goodison Park and Deepdale. As a teenager he had worked on Lord Yarborough's estate at Broughton and became a goalie by accident when his junior team's first choice 'keeper failed to turn up.

KENNEDY, Andrew John
Centre-forward: 8+1 apps. one goal
Born: Stirling, 8 October 1964
Career: Sauchie Athletic, Glasgow Rangers (professional, October 1982), Seiko FC/Hong Kong (on loan), Birmingham City (£50,000, March 1985), BLADES (on loan, March 1987), Blackburn Rovers (£50,000, June 1988), Watford (£60,000, August 1990), Bolton Wanderers (on loan, October 1991), Brighton & Hove Albion (September 1992), Gillingham (non-contract, September 1994 to March 1995).
A hard-working player, always willing to take on defenders, Andy Kennedy (a former Scottish Youth international) helped Blues' win promotion from Division Two in 1983. In the long term, however, the faults in his technique (a poor first-touch and tendency to lie too wide) became obvious and he was latterly utilised mainly as substitute in the hope that his pace would unsettle tiring defences. During his League career (north and south of the border) he scored 58 goals in 229 appearances.

KENNY, Patrick Joseph
Goalkeeper: 59 apps*
Born: Halifax, 17 May 1978
Career: Bradford Park Avenue (1995), Bury (£10,000, August 1998), BLADES (on loan initially, August 2002, signed September 2002 for an undisclosed fee).
At 6ft 1in tall and 14st 6lbs in weight, Paddy Kenny was one of the sturdiest goalkeepers outside the premiership when he joined the Blades after making 150 appearances for Bury. In his last season at Gigg Lane he had been sent-off twice (after clumsy challenges) and had also saved three penalties, and was sold to United when the Shakers hit financial problems. He had an excellent first season at Bramall Lane, missing only one game out of a possible 60 as the Blades reached two major Cup semi-finals and the First Division Play-off Final (v. Wolves). Indeed, during the Nationwide First Division campaign, he was on the field for more than 4,050 minutes (45 games), participated in over 4,350 minutes of 'League' football including the three Play-off matches...and well over 5,400 minutes in all competitions. And sadly at the end he had nothing to show for his efforts! Kenny was voted Blades' 2003 'Player of the Year.'

KENWORTHY, Anthony David
Central defender: 350+7 apps. 39 goals
Born: Leeds, 30 October 1958
Career: BLADES (apprentice, September 1974, professional July 1976), Mansfield Town (on loan, March-April 1986, signed permanently May 1986), Huddersfield Town (on trial, August 1990), Chesterfield (on trial, March 1991), Ashfield United (December 1993), Oakham United (July 1994-96).
Tony Kenworthy was a redoubtable player for the Blades. An England Youth international, he spent twelve seasons as a professional at Bramall Lane, helping the team win the Fourth Division championship in 1982 (45 games played) and gain promotion two years later (only playing in eight games). As a 'Stag' he gained promotion from the Fourth Division in 1986, collected a Freight Rover Trophy winners' medal in 1987 and was a Notts County Cup winner on three occasions: 1987-88-89.
* When having trial with Huddersfield, Kenworthy was convicted of a motoring offence and sentenced to six months imprisonment. He was released in March 1991

KETTLEBOROUGH, Keith Frank
Inside-forward/midfielder: 183 apps. 24 goals
Born: Rotherham, 29 June 1935
Career: Rotherham YMCA, Rotherham United (December 1955), BLADES (£15,000, December 1960), Newcastle United (£22,500, December 1965), Doncaster Rovers (£12,000, player-manager, December 1966), Chesterfield (£6,000, November 1967), Matlock Town (player-coach, August 1969-71).
A hard-working player with a tremendous engine and receding hairline, Keith Kettleborough was twice called up for England training in 1965 and 1966. He appeared in a total of 404 League matches (39 goals scored) during his career.
As well as being a fine footballer he was also a very useful cricketer, being an efficient run-maker for Rotherham Town CC. He now lives in the village of Wickersley near Rotherham having owned a dairy before becoming a sports coach and clerk of works at Birkdale Preparatory School in Sheffield.

KIDDERMINSTER HARRIERS
As yet the Blades have not met the Harriers (formed in September 1886 and a Football League club since 2001) in major competition. However, the did complete the double over the Aggborough club in the Midland Counties League in season 1890-91 before 'Kidder' resigned, their results being expunged from the record books.
Players who have served with both clubs include: Stan Fazackerley, Billy Hendry and Alec Stacey.

KILLOURHY, Michael
Inside-forward: 31 apps. 6 goals
Born: New Springs, Wigan, 19 February 1911. Died: Southport, November 2002.
Career: Coldstream Guards, Wigan Borough (September 1928), BLADES (November 1931), Doncaster Rovers (record fee of £750, February 1936-April 1942), Coldstream Guards (during WW2), Denaby United (1946-48), Goole Town. Later became a schoolmaster in Doncaster and was also a golfer of county class.
A forward, hard to shake off the ball, Mike Killourhy covered for Messrs Barclay, Dodds and Pickering during his four-year stay at Bramall Lane. A Football League debutant for Wigan v. Rochdale in February 1931, he went on to make 107 appearances in the competition, 63 for Doncaster, whom he twice helped into second place in the third Division (North) in the two seasons before WW2 (1938 & 1939). He netted 39 goals.

KING, Jeffrey
Midfielder: 41+2 apps. 5 goals
Born: Fauldhouse, 9 November 1953
Career: Fauldhouse United, Albion Rovers (1970), Derby County (£7,000, April 1974), Notts County (on loan, January 1976), Portsmouth (on loan, March 1976), Walsall (November 1977), Sheffield Wednesday (August 1978), BLADES (January 1982), Chesterfield (non-contract, October 1983), Stafford Rangers (November 1983), Altrincham (February 1984), Burton Albion (August 1984), Kettering Town (November 1984 to May 1985).
A fiery midfield player Jeff King produced some of his best football in Sheffield, making 68 appearances for the Owls and 43 for the Blades. He was also involved in two promotions, with Wednesday in 1979-80 and United as Fourth Division champions in 1981-82.

KING, Seth
Centre-half: 119 apps.
Born: Penistone, 14 February 1897. Died: Leigh, 8 February 1958
Career: Penistone, Huddersfield Town (as an amateur), Penistone, BLADES (November 1920), Oldham Athletic (£400, May 1929, retired from League football through injury, February 1932, Denaby United (season 1932-34).
Seth King was aenergetic, robust and had the ability to pass came later venturing forward, given the opportunity. An accurate passer of the ball, sometimes picking out a colleague 50 yards away, he played exceptionally well in the 1925 FA Cup final victory over Cardiff City and remained at Bramall Lane until 1929 when he was transferred, perhaps surprisingly, to Oldham. He made almost 100 appearances for the Latics, his experience and influence being invaluable to the younger players at Boundary Park, being an ever-present ion his first two seasons there. When retiring from League football in 1932, he immediately took over a public house in Sheffield.

KITCHEN, Joseph Ernest

Centre/inside-forward/outside-right: 342 apps. 169 goals

Born: Brigg, Lincolnshire, 1890. Died: Lincolnshire, 2 April 1962

Career: Gainsborough Trinity, BLADES (March 1908), Rotherham County August 1920), BLADES (December 1920), Hull City (September 1921), Scunthorpe United (August 1923), Gainsborough Trinity (September 1924), Shirebrook (September-November 1925).

Joe Kitchen's exciting and penetrating solo bursts made him a great favourite with the Blades' supporters. He was the dressing room comedian and always tried to boost morale in the camp when things were at a rather low ebb. He made his debut in United's red and white stripes against Manchester City (Division 1) a few days after joining. A versatile performer, he scored United's final goal in their 1915 FA Cup Final win over Chelsea and was called up for two Victory internationals in 1919 but injury forced him out of both matches. He remained at Bramall Lane until 1920 when he moved to Rotherham, returning to United for a second spell four months later. Kitchen also starred on the cricket field for Lincolnshire, scoring two centuries.

Sheffield United, FA Cup winners 1914-15: (back row, l-r) secretary-manager John Nicholson, Jack English, Harold Gough, Bill Brelsford, Albert Sturgess (middle row, l-r) Bill Cook, Stan Fazackerley, George Utley, Wally Masterman, Robert Evans (front row, l-r) Jim Simmons, **Joe Kitchen**

KITE, Philip David

Goalkeeper: 18 apps.

Born: Bristol, 26 October 1962

Career: Bristol Rovers (apprentice, June 1978, professional October 1980), Tottenham Hotspur (on loan, January 1984), Southampton (£50,000, August 1984), Middlesbrough (on loan, March 1986), Gillingham (February 1987), Bournemouth (£20,000, August 1989), BLADES (£25,000, August 1990), Mansfield Town (on loan, November 1991), Plymouth Argyle (on loan, September 1992), Rotherham United (on loan, October 1992), Crewe Alexandra (on loan November 1992), Stockport County (on loan, March 1993), Cardiff City (free transfer, July 1993), Bristol City (free, August 1994), Bristol Rovers (free, August 1996, later appointed the club's official physiotherapist).

Goalkeeper Phil Kite (6ft 1in, 14st 7lbs) began and ended his playing days with Bristol Rovers. He played for different five clubs during the 1992-93 season and all told served with 14 while making a total of 238 League appearances in 16 years as a professional.

An England Schoolboy and Youth international, he was recruited following an injury to Simon Tracey at Bramall Lane but then after Tracey had regained full fitness, went back into the reserves (and on loan at various locations) before leaving in 1993.

KOZLUK, Robert
Defender: 118+13 apps*, one goal*
Born: Mansfield, 5 August 1977
Career: Derby County (apprentice, April 1994, professional, February 1996), BLADES (in a £600,000 package deal involving Vassilios Borbokis and Jonathan Hunt, March 1999), Huddersfield Town (on loan, September-October 2000).
An England Under-21 international (2 caps gained) Rob Kozluk made 16 appearances in the Premiership with Derby before moving to Bramall Lane. Able to play at full-back (either side), he is quick, has good anticipation and links up well when going forward. He suffered a serious knee injury at Maine Road in October 2001 and was out of action for quite some time before returning to help the Blades reach two major Cup semi-finals and the First Division Play-off Final in 2002-03 (v. Wolves).

KUHL, Martin
Midfielder/defender: 42 apps. 4 goals
Born; Frimley, 10 January 1965
Career: Schools, Birmingham City (apprentice, June 1981, professional January 1983), BLADES (player-exchange deal involving Steve Wigley, March 1987), Watford (rated at £300,000 in player-exchange deal with Tony Agana and Peter Hetherston, February 1988), Portsmouth (£125,000, September 1988), Derby County (£650,000, September 1992), Notts County (on loan, September 1994), Bristol City (£300,000 December 1994), Farnborough Town (August 1997), Weymouth (August 2002)
Martin Kuhl was an enthusiastic, hard-working player who took time to settle in at St Andrew's before going on to make over 130 appearances for Blues. His adaptability led to him appearing in all ten outfield positions during his career but his best proved to be a midfield where he did well for the Blades in his relatively short stay at Bramall Lane. During senior career Kuhl - who helped Blues gain promotion in 1985 - amassed a fine record of 564 League and Cup appearances and 50 goals

KYLE, Peter
Inside-right: 10 apps. 4 goals
Born: RutherGlenn, Glasgow, September 1880. Died: Scotland, 1957.
Career: Glasgow & District Schools, Glasgow Parkhead (1896), Partick Thistle, Clyde (trialist), Liverpool (July 1899), Leicester Fosse (May 1900), Wellingborough, West Ham United (November 1902), Kettering Town, Heart of Midlothian (trialist), Larkhall Thistle (February 1904), Port Glasgow Athletic (July 1904), Tottenham Hotspur (July 1905), Woolwich Arsenal (April 1906), Aston Villa (March 1908), BLADES (October 1908), Royal Albert (July 1909), Watford (November 1909-February 1910). Returned to Scotland before the Great War.
Peter Kyle, with his smartly waxed moustache and black hair, was a dangerous centre-forward with an eye for goal. He had a nomadic career in the game, travelling all over Britain. He may have participated at various levels with 17 different clubs and made well over 200 League and Cup appearances, scoring more than 40 goals. Kyle could be somewhat temperamental at times and was suspended by Spurs for breach of club rules in March 1906 (he never played for the London club again). A Scottish international trialist, his last game for Arsenal was against Aston Villa - next month he moved from the Gunners to Villa Park! He scored 19 goals in 41 games for Spurs, netted 22 in 60 for Arsenal, played only played times for Villa (after failing to settle in Birmingham) and then bagged a couple of goals on his League debut for the Blades against Manchester United in October 1908.
* There is no firm evidence that this Peter Kyle did assist all the clubs listed above as there was another Scottish-born player bearing the same name and description around at the same time (possibly related). However, I have listed all the clubs who did have a Peter Kyle (Forward) registered with them between 1896 and 1910.

LAKE, Michael Charles

Midfielder: 27+19 apps. 5 goals

Born: Denton, 16 November 1966

Career: Macclesfield Town, BLADES (£40,000, October 1989), Wrexham (£60,000, November 1992-May 1995).

Midfielder Michael Lake broke his leg against Ipswich Town on 13 January 1990 and was out of action for nine months. Soon after his return he was sold to Wrexham for whom he played in 58 League games before moving into non-League soccer in 1995.

LANG, John

Outside-right: 105 apps. 13 goals

Born: Kilbirnie, Ayrshire, 16 August 1882. Died: 1934.

Career: Co-operative United FC (Glasgow), Govan FC, Barnsley (July 1902), BLADES (February 1903), Leicester Fosse (£75, September 1909), Denaby United (August 1910).

The right-wing partner to Jimmy Donnelly for several of his early seasons at Bramall Lane, John Lang, fast and tricky given the space, was near to winning full international honours for Scotland when he appeared for the Anglo Scots against Home Scots in March 1905, having earlier gained Junior caps as a teenager north of the border.

* The cheque for £75 paid by Leicester for Lang in 1909 bounced on first presentation.

LATHAM, Harry

Left-back/centre-half: 427 apps. one goal

Born: Sheffield, 9 January 1921. Died: Sheffield, 1983.

Career: BLADES (groundstaff, October 1937, professional October 1938, retired May 1953, then joined club's coaching staff, remaining in office until 1974).

A stout defender (able to play as a full-back), Harry Latham lacked style but was, on the whole, was a fine 'stopper' centre-half who did the basic things well, clearing his lines efficiency without any fuss or bother. He could also bring a few smiles to a dull dressing room. After turning professional in 1938, Latham had to wait until August 1946 before making his League debut against Liverpool (due of course to WW2). During the hostilities he actually appeared in well over 200 games for the Blades - so he was an experienced campaigner when peacetime football returned. He skippered the team in the early 1950s and on his retirement in 1953 (after gaining a Second Division championship medal) he joined the club's coaching/training staff, going on to give the Blades 38 years service.

* Latham's son, Stuart, was a registered player with Sheffield Wednesday.

Arsenal's Jimmy Logie (r) shoots, watched by Sheffield United's Harold Latham (l) and Ted Shimwell (c)

LEAFE, Alfred Richard

Outside-right/inside-forward: 32 apps. 16 goals

Born: Boston, Lincolnshire, 1891. Died: 9 May 1964

Career: Boston Town (1907), Grimsby Town (amateur, May 1909), Boston Town (May 1910), BLADES (November 1911), West Ham United (May 1913, retired April 1922).

Dicky Leafe made only one League appearance for the Mariners before returning to Boston. He then returned to League action with the Blades and scored eight goals in 12 Division One matches in his first-part season at Bramall Lane, proof of both promise and opportunism but he never quite sustained that form although in later years, after putting on a bit of weight, he made things difficult for his opponents as a West Ham player (scoring seven goals in 32 outings).

* Alf's elder brother, Tom Leafe, also played for Boston Town and Grimsby Town.

LEANING, Andrew John

Goalkeeper: 25 apps.

Born: Howden near Goole, 18 May 1963

Career: Rowntree Mackintosh FC, York City (professional, June 1985), BLADES (May 1987), Bristol City (on loan, September 1988, signed for £12,000, November 1988), Lincoln City (March 1994), Dundee (free transfer, July 1996), Chesterfield (free, October 1996, later player/goalkeeper-coach at Saltergate before retiring through injury, January 2000).

When goalkeeper Andy Leaning retired at the age of 36 (after suffering a ruptured muscle in his leg) he had appeared in 280 competitive matches. Standing 6ft 1in tall and weighing 14s 7lbs, he was in brilliant form for Lincoln in the mid-1990s before suffering a nasty back injury. A competent and brave 'keeper on his day, he made 86 appearances for the Minstermen, 89 for Bristol City (where he spent an awful lot of time in the 2nd XI) and 51 for the Imps. He coached ex-Blade Billy Mercer at Saltergate.

LEEDS CITY

Blades' playing record against City:

WW1

Venue	P	W	D	L	F	A
Home	4	3	1	0	9	4
Away	4	1	0	3	4	8
Totals	8	4	1	3	13	12

Leeds City came into being in season 1904-05, playing its first season in the West Yorkshire League before gaining Football League status at the end of that campaign (Division 2). The club - playing initially at the Wellington Road ground, Hunslet - lasted for only 14 years before losing its status. In 1919, when the League programme resumed in earnest following the conflict of WW1, City made a decent enough start, gaining 10 points from their first eight games. But then the club was suspended and eventually expelled after an astonishing scandal involving alleged illegal payments to players during the war. Port Vale took over their fixtures for the remainder of that season.

United's superstar Billy Gillespie started his Football League career with Leeds City (1910). Fred Croot and goalkeeper Charlie Sutcliffe are two other Blades' players who also assisted City while Herbert Chapman, a former United player, later became manager at Leeds.

LEEDS UNITED

United's playing record against United:

Premier League

Venue	P	W	D	L	F	A
Home	2	1	1	0	4	3
Away	2	0	0	2	2	5
Totals	4	1	1	2	6	8
Football League						
Home	30	12	10	8	45	41
Away	30	6	9	15	30	57
Totals	60	18	19	23	75	98
FA Cup						
Home	2	2	0	0	4	1
Away	1	0	0	1	0	1
Totals	3	2	0	1	4	2
League Cup						
Home	3	2	0	1	4	5
WW2						
Home	3	3	0	0	15	3
Away	5	1	0	4	5	10
Totals	8	4	0	4	20	13
Others						
Away	2	0	1	1	1	4

Immediately the Leeds City club (founded in 1904) was wound up by the FA in October 1919, following allegations of illegal payments to players, a meeting was called by a Leeds solicitor, Mr Alf Masser, at which Leeds United FC was formed. The club quickly moved into Elland Road, joined the Midland League and played its first game within a month. In the summer of 1920 Leeds were elected to the Football League (Division 2), taking the place of Lincoln City. They first met the Blades some four years later after gaining promotion, both fixtures ending all-square at 1-1.

Honours were fairly even on the field during the period 1924-34 (United gaining their first win on Leeds' soil in 1933) but after a lapse and the hostilities of WW2 had ended, battle recommenced in 1946-47 when the Blades carved out an exciting 6-2 win at 'the Lane', four of the forwards scoring except Albert Nightingale who was later to join Leeds!

The Blades beat Leeds 1-0 in a home First Division match in November 1967 despite having Alan Woodward in goal for 81 minutes. Twice the Blades have conceded five goals in a League game to Leeds...in 1974-75 at Elland Road (lost 5-1) and 1987-88, also away, (lost 5-0). Their best win on Leeds' territory is 3-0, in 1952-53 when the Blades were well on their way to winning the Second Division title.

One of the earliest kick-off times in United's history - 11am - was at Elland Road for a Second Division game on 28 September 1985. A crowd of 15,622 saw two Blades' players sent-off (Steve Foley and Ray Lewington) as the teams shared the points after a hard-fought 1-1 draw.

United have lost their last six League/Premiership games at Elland Road (1987-94), conceding 20 goals.

The teams have met just three times in the FA Cup - in the 5th round in 1936 when a record Bramall Lane crowd of 68,287 saw the Blades win 3-1 in a match marred by thick fog, on their way to the Final against Arsenal; in the 6th round in 1968 when Leeds edged home 1-0 at Elland Road and at the quarter-final stage in March 2003 when Steve Kabba's goal earned the Blades a courageous 1-0 victory. This was, in fact, the Blades' 150th win in the FA Cup.

The three League Cup clashes took place in 1970-71 (when the Blades won 1-0 in round 2), in 1978-79 (when Leeds triumphed 4-1 at the 'Lane' in round three) and in 2002-03 (when once again the Blades took the honours, winning another 3rd round-tie 2-1 at 'the Lane'). In the latter contest, the Blades, 1-0 down, seemed to be going out of the competition despite all their brave efforts. Then, with the 90 minutes already up, Phil Jagielka cracked home a sensational 30-yarder to bring the scores level and with extra-time looming, Zimbabwean international Peter Ndlovu sent the home crowd wild when he forced in the winner after Paul Peschisolido had done the spadework. This was, in fact, United's 150th win in the FA Cup.

The Blades' last Football League game before WW2 (played in September 1939) ended in a 1-0 win at Leeds.

Tony Agana, Paul Beesley, Harold Brook, Len Browning, Ted Burgin, Tony Currie, Bobby Davison, Mervyn Day, Brian Deane, Martin Dickinson, Keith Edwards, Colin Grainger, Gary Hamson, Billy Hudson, George Hutchinson, Mick Jones, Vinnie Jones, Chris Kamara, Cliff Mason, Albert Nightingale, John Pemberton, Terry Phelan, Bruno Ribiero, Ian Rush, Alex Sabella, Alec Stacey, Imre Varadi, Norman Wharton, David White and Charlie Wilkinson are just some of the many players who have served with both clubs down the years. Others associated with both the Blades and Leeds include Ian Porterfield (Elland Road trialist, Blades manager), John Burridge (Blades 'keeper, Leeds coach) and Fred White (United player, Leeds scout).

LEICESTER CITY (FOSSE)

United's playing record against the Foxes:

Football League

Venue	P	W	D	L	F	A
Home	37	15	12	10	69	51
Away	37	9	16	12	50	63
Totals	74	24	28	22	119	114

FA Cup

	P	W	D	L	F	A
Home	3	3	0	0	6	2
Away	1	0	0	1	0	3
Neutral	3	0	2	1	0	2
Totals	7	3	2	2	6	7

League Cup

	P	W	D	L	F	A
Away	1	0	0	1	0	2

WW1

	P	W	D	L	F	A
Home	4	3	0	1	9	3
Away	4	2	1	1	10	7
Totals	8	5	1	2	19	10

United Counties League

	P	W	D	L	F	A
Home	1	1	0	0	3	2

Formed in a house on the Roman Fosse Way in 1884 by a group of young footballers who were mostly former pupils of Wyggeston School, Leicester Fosse played initially on Victoria Park. In 1887 they took a ground on Belgrave Road, moved back to Victoria Park in 1888 and onto Filbert Street in 1891 where they were to stay until 2002 when the club switched to the new all-seater Walker Stadium. City gained election to the Football League in 1894, reached the top-flight for the first time in 1908 and changed its name to Leicester City in 1919.

The first meeting between themselves and the Blades was in the FA Cup of 1899-1900 when the Fosse went down 1-0 at 'the Lane' in the opening round.

The first League clash followed on 24 October 1908, Fosse playing out a 1-1 draw at Filbert Street after Bob Evans had given United the lead before half-time.

United's best League win over City is 7-1, achieved at 'the Lane' in season 1929-30 when Irishman Jimmy Dunne scored four times and missed another three! The following week Dunne netted the winner as the Blades won the return fixture 2-1.

Bobby Liddle netted all his side's goals when Leicester beat the Blades 4-0 at Filbert Street in August 1933.

In November 1951 United played out their only 5-5 draw in League football, haring the spoils with Leicester at Filbert Street (Division 2). A crowd of 33,775 saw the doing-dong battle and Jimmy Hagan was outstanding for the Blades. This is how the scoring went (City's score first): 0-1, 1-1, 2-1, 2-2, 2-3, 3-3, 3-4 (half-time), 3-5, 4-5 and then 5-5.

In 1989-90 United grabbed their best win at Filbert Street, clipping the Foxes' tails to the tune of 5-2 to clinch promotion to the First Division. Tony Agana scored twice.

In season 2002-03, the Blades held City to a 0-0 draw at their new Walker Stadium and then thanks to a brace from Carl Asaba (his vital second coming in the dying minutes after City's Callum Davidson had been sent-off) won the return fixture over Easter by 2-1 to confirm their place in the Play-off zone.

After two hard fought contests at Elland Road and The City Ground (Nottingham), both of which ended goalless, Leicester beat promotion-chasing United in the 1961 FA Cup semi-final 2nd replay at St Andrew's by 2-0. Two penalties were missed in the match - Graham Shaw firing wide with the Blades' effort. City lost in the Final to double-winners Spurs 2-0.

The Blades' beat the Fosse in the United Counties League in season 1894-95.

Alan Birchenall, Brian Deane, Willie Carlin, Pat Carrigan, Franz Carr, Bobby Davison, Jimmy Donnelly, Hugh Gallacher, Harry Hammond, Colin Hill, Billy Hodgson, David Kelly, Peter Kyle, John Lang, Albert 'Tal' Lewis, Fred Milnes, Shane Nicholson, John Roxburgh, Geoff Salmons, Steve Thompson, Albert Trueman, Rob Ullathorne and Alan Young are some of the players who have served with both clubs.

Dave Bassett has managed at both Sheffield United and Leicester City while Arthur Rowley was a goalscorer with the Foxes and manager at Bramall Lane; both Alan Cork and Gerry Summers were players with the Blades and later coaches at Filbert Street, Cork also acting as the Foxes' assistant-manager.

LEVICK, Frank

Inside-right: 18 apps. 5 goals
Born: Eckington, 1882. Died: February 1908
Career: Sheffield Wednesday (August 1904), Rotherham Town (1906), BLADES (May 1907).

Sadly, Frank Levick died of pneumonia in hospital in 1908, aged only 21. He fractured his collar-bone playing in a League game against Newcastle at Bramall Lane on New Year's Day of that year and was taken to hospital. His injury was treated and set but he was taken ill and never recovered. He had failed to make much of an impression with the owls or Rotherham but looked a good signing by the Blades before tragedy struck.

LEWINGTON, Raymond

Midfielder: 43 apps.
Born: Lambeth, London, 7 September 1956
Career: Chelsea (associate school 1971, apprentice, April 1973, professional February 1974), Vancouver Whitecaps (£40,000, February 1979), Wimbledon (on loan, September 1979), Fulham (£50,000, March 1980), BLADES (£40,000, July 1985), Fulham (£20,000, player-manager, July 1986-May 1990), Watford (manager, July 2002).

An ever-present in Chelsea's Second Division promotion-winning side in 1976-77, Ray Lewington lacked the necessary pace to make his mark in the top flight and was no part of manager Danny Blanchflower's long-term plans at Stamford Bridge. Transferred into the NASL after 92 games for the London club, he later did well with Fulham and to a certain extent with the Blades, making 276 appearances for the Cottagers in his two spells there, while doing a good job as manager as well (1986-90). He then returned to management with the Hornets and in 2002-03 took them into the FA Cup semi-finals where they were defeated 2-1 by Premiership side Southampton at Villa Park.

151

LEWIS, Albert Edward Talbot
Goalkeeper/full-back: 17 apps.
Born: Bedminster, 20 January 1877. Died: Redland, Bristol 22 February 1956
Career: Bedminster (January 1896), Bristol City (May 1897), Everton (briefly in 1898), Bristol City (1899), Walsall (May 1901), BLADES (May 1902), Sunderland (with Alf Common, May 1904), Luton Town (July 1905), Leicester City (August 1906), Bristol City (October 1907). Later coached cricket in India
The tall, athletic and versatile Albert 'Tal' Lewis kept goal. After two moderate spells with Bristol City and 32 games for the Saddlers, he made his senior debut for United against Liverpool (at home) in November 1902 when he deputised for goalkeeper Bill Foulke in a 2-0 win. In need of regular first team football, he tried his luck at Sunderland but after making only four appearances he quickly moved to Luton and then onto Leicester before ending his career back at Ashton Gate. He was also a fine all-round Somerset cricketer (1899-1914) and amassed 7,745 runs in 210 matches for an average of 21.45. His highest score was 201 not-out in a championship match v. Kent at Taunton in 1909. His bowling average was 23.16 (522 wickets taken, 12,091 runs conceded) with 8-103 his best return. He also claimed 106 catches.

LEWIS, Kevin
Right: 79 apps. 29 goals
Born: Ellesmere Port, Cheshire, 19 September 1940
Career: BLADES (juniors 1954, amateur September 1955, professional October 1957), Liverpool (record £13,000, June 1960), Huddersfield Town (£18,000, August 1963-May 1965), Port Elizabeth FC/South Africa (July 1965-66).
Although tall, thin and rather lightweight, England Youth international Kevin Lewis was a useful forward, two-footed with a strong shot, who made his Central League debut for the Blades eight days before his 16th birthday. After leaving Bramall Lane he played at centre-forward for Liverpool and ended his career with 75 goals in a total of 180 League games.

LEYFIELD, Charles
Winger: 40 apps. 13 goals
Born: Chester, 30 October 1911. Died: 1982
Career: Chester junior football, Everton (April 1930), BLADES (£2,500, May 1937), Doncaster Rovers (November 1938).
A sturdy, two-footed winger, Charlie Leyfield was a useful asset to the Blades' forward-line, making his debut on the left against Nottingham Forest on the opening day of the 1937-38 season. He had a handful of games on the opposite flank before holding down the left-wing berth until late March. With Frank Joyner and George Jones challenging for his position, Leyfield was allowed to leave the club for Belle Vue.

LEYTON ORIENT (also Clapton Orient & Orient)
United's playing record against Orient:
Football League

Venue	P	W	D	L	F	A
Home	12	6	1	5	26	18
Away	12	4	4	4	17	19
Totals	24	10	5	9	43	37

Formed originally in 1881 by members of the Homerton Theological College as the Glyn Cricket & Football Club, changing later to Eagle FC, and then Orient (in 1888), Leyton Orient were elected to the Football League in 1905 (as Clapton Orient) and after playing at Millfields Road, moved to Brisbane Road in 1937, adopting their current title in 1946, although for a 21-year period (1966-87) only the name Orient was used.
The Blades played the 'O's' for the first time at League level in October 1956 (Division 2) when they were beaten at home 3-2, later winning the return fixture by 2-1.
Orient, in fact, won their first four League matches at Bramall Lane before the Blades finally broke their duck with a 4-1 triumph in 1960-61. They also won in London that season to complete their only double so far.
The last time the clubs met was in 1983-84 when United won 6-3 at home (after being 3-2 down) but lost 2-0 at Brisbane Road. Paul Beesley, Peter Boyle, Richard Cadette, Glenn Cockerill (also Orient manager), Mervyn Day, Alex Forbes, Paul Heald (United reserve), Bert Menlove, Mel Rees, Tom Simons, Chris Wilder are among the players who have been registered with both clubs. Harry Haslam was an Orient player and later Blades' manager.

LIEVESLEY, Joseph
Goalkeeper: 288 apps.
Born: Staveley, Derbyshire, 25 July 1883. Died: New Rossington (Doncaster), 18 October 1941.
Career: Poolsbrook FC, BLADES (May 1903). Woolwich Arsenal (June 1913, retired 1916).
A safe, re-assuring goalkeeper, never flashy but reliable with a safe pair of hands, Joe Lievesley served United for nine years. He took over from Bill Foulke as the Blades' last line of defence, retaining the position, virtually unchallenged, until John Mitchell arrived on the scene in 1911. He toured South Africa with the FA party in June 1910, playing in all three matches (all won). In his time at Highbury, he played in 79 competitive matches and gained a Norwich Hospital Cup winners medal in 1914 and a London Challenge Cup runners-up medal twelve months later.
* He preferred to spell his name Leivesley (reversing the 'i' & 'e').

LILLEY, Edward Henry
Left-back: 65 apps.
Born: Staveley, Derbyshire, circa 1870
Career: Staveley, BLADES (June 1890), Gainsborough Trinity (August 1894, retired March 1895 through injury).
Harry Lilley was one of the first Sheffield United player to win full international honours when he was capped by England against Wales at Wrexham on 5 March 1892 (starring in a 2-0 win). Able to occupy both full-back positions, he was deservedly a favourite figure at Bramall Lane, possessing a good, clean kick while displaying immense vitality. He spent four years with United before transferring to Gainsborough, retiring soon afterwards through injury.

LILLEY, John William
Goalkeeper: 30 apps.
Born: Staveley, circa 1872
Career: Staveley, BLADES (November 1891), Rotherham Town (August 1894).
An older brother of Harold E (q.v) Will Lilley also played for his local junior club before joining United. He made his debut in the Northern League, away at Newcastle East End in December 1891, but following the emergence of Bill Foulke, moved to Rotherham three years later.

LINCOLN CITY

United's playing record against the Imps:

Football League

Venue	P	W	D	L	F	A
Home	9	7	1	1	27	8
Away	9	3	1	5	14	16
Totals	18	10	2	6	41	24

FA Cup

Home	3	3	0	2	8	2
Away	2	1	1	0	4	0
Totals	5	4	1	0	12	2

League Cup

Home	1	1	0	0	6	1
Away	1	0	0	1	0	1
Totals	2	1	0	1	6	2

WW1

Home	5	5	0	0	28	3
Away	5	2	1	2	8	10
Totals	10	7	1	2	36	13

WW2

Home	5	4	1	0	29	7
Away	5	1	1	3	5	15
Totals	10	5	2	3	34	22

Midland Counties League

Home	1	1	0	0	2	1
Away	1	0	0	1	1	2
Totals	2	1	0	1	3	3

Others

Away	2	0	1	1	4	7
Neutral	1	0	1	0	2	2
Totals	3	0	2	1	6	9

The original Lincoln Football Club was established in the 1806s and was one of the first to be affiliated to the Football Association. Early matches were played against the famous Sheffield Club (q.v) and later became known as Lincoln Lindum. The present organisation was formed at a public meeting held at The Monson Arms Hotel in June 1884. In its third season City won the Lincolnshire Cup, became founder members of the Midland League in 1889 (being that competition's first winners) and then, like the Blades, were one of the founder members of the newly formed Second Division in 1892.
The first League game between the clubs took place on 3 September 1892 when a crowd of 4,000 saw Harry Hammond score a hat-trick in Blades' win 4-2 (after a late start). The Imps won the return fixture 1-0...and it was to be another 60 years before the teams came face to face in the League again - United winning 6-1 at Bramall Lane but losing 3-2 at Sincil Bank in 1952-53.
Bill Egerton scored five goals in Lincoln's 7-3 win over the Blades in a WW1 game in September 1915.
The Blades scored 34 goals in 10 WW2 games against the Imps, beating them 10-2 at 'the Lane' in January 1945, having lost 9-2 at Sincil Bank in September 1940. United also won 9-0 at home in December 1941.
United beat Lincoln 6-1 in a home Second Division game in December 1958 after scoring four goals in a nine-minute spell.
The first-ever competitive meeting occurred a year before the initial League clash, United winning 4-1 in a 2nd qualifying round of the FA Cup in 1891. There have since been four other encounters in this competition and the Blades have won three of them including a 4-0 romp at Lincoln in a 3rd round tie in January 1964.
When the Imps visited Bramall Lane for a 1st round, 1st leg League Cup encounter in August 2000, Marcus Bent netted a hat-trick for the Blades in their emphatic 6-1 win.
A crowd of just 1,379 attended the 2nd leg at Sincil Bank the following month - the lowest audience the Blades have ever played to in this competition.
Several players have been associated with both clubs over the years, including Harry Barton, Tony Battersby, Bill Batty, Salvatore Bibbo (Blades reserve), Harold Brook, John Burridge, Steve Cammack, Darren Carr, Paul Casey, Glenn Cockerill, Ted Connor, Richard Cooper, Alan Cork, Tony Daws, Matt Dickens, 'Jock' Dodds, Tom Egan, Steve Foley, Mark Foran, Dennis Gratton, Bert Groves, Ian Hamilton, John Harrison, Derek Hawksworth, Jim Hutchinson, Tom Johnson, Jack Kendall, Andy Leaning, Richard Lucas, Barry Matthews, Shane Nicholson, George Richardson, Alan Roberts, Ernie Robertson, Bobby Rooney, Bill Ross, Alf Settle, Paul Smith, Steve Thompson (also manager of both clubs), Mitch Ward, Walter Webster, Gary West, Fred White, Chris Wilder and Dick Young.
Bill Anderson was a reserve team player with the Blades and later managed the Imps while City players Billy Archer and George Nelson served the Blades as guests during wartime football. And Derek Dooley was an amateur player with Lincoln.

153

LIPSHAM, Herbert Broughall

Outside-left: 259 apps. 34 goals
Born: Chester, 29 April 1878. Died: Toronto, 1932
Career: St Oswald's (a local church team), Chester, Crewe Alexandra (June 1898), BLADES (February 1900), Fulham (April 1908), Millwall (May 1910, then player-manager August 1911, retiring as a player in May 1913, remaining as manager until 1919); worked in an 'advisory capacity' for 12 months at The Den (August 1919-July 1920), West Norwood (coach, August 1920); Northfleet (manager, July 1922-May 1923). He emigrated to Canada in the summer of 1923. Bert Lipsham was an enthusiastic, wholly dedicated left-winger, speedy with a redoubtable shot but perhaps lacking finesse with his crosses, most of which it is said, were delivered far 'too strongly' across the face of goal. He gained a Cheshire Cup winners' medal with Crewe and also represented Cheshire County before joining the Blades. He quickly settled in his stride, making his Football League debut on 3 March against one of the strongest teams around, Aston Villa. After collecting a runners-up medal when United lost to Spurs in the 1901 FA Cup Final replay, Lipsham duly picked up a winners' prize a year later when the Blades beat Southampton. He gained one England cap and twice represented the Football League, both times against the Irish League. He partnered Reg Foster of the Corinthians in a 0-0 draw with Wales at Wrexham in his full international in March 1902 (Ernie Needham played behind him). Unfortunately he had a poor match and was never considered again (at senior level). Lipsham, having made well over 250 first-class appearances for the Blades, joined Fulham in 1908, switching to Millwall two years later. After playing for the Southern League against both the Football League and Irish League in his first season with the Lions, he was appointed the London club's first player-manager, reluctantly hanging up his boots in 1913 (soon after helping Millwall win the Kent Senior Shield). He retained his managerial status until 1919 and remained in football until 1923 when, with his family, he chose to emigrate to Canada. Sadly whilst over there he was dogged by misfortune, losing his right hand in a timber-yard accident in Toronto dying of a heart attack at his place of work in 1932.

LITTLEJOHN, Adrian Sylvester

Forward/midfielder: 55+30 apps. 14 goals
Born: Wolverhampton, 26 September 1970
Career: West Bromwich Albion (apprentice, April 1987), Walsall (professional May 1989), BLADES (free transfer, September 1991), Plymouth Argyle (£100,000, September 1995), Oldham Athletic (free transfer, March 1998), Bury (£75,000, November 1998), BLADES (free, October 2001, released December 2001), Port Vale (January 2003).
An England Youth international at The Hawthorns (despite not appearing in Albion' first team) Adrian Littlejohn made a name for himself at Walsall, having 54 senior outings before his transfer to Bramall Lane. A naturally gifted footballer, with pace, skill and strong shot, he continued his form with the Blades with whom he stayed for four seasons. Thereafter he made 134 appearances for the Pilgrims (32 goals), 23 for the Latics and 112 for the Shakers before returning to 'the Lane' for a second spell.

LIVERPOOL

United's playing record against the Merseysiders:

Premier League

Venue	P	W	D	L	F	A
Home	2	1	1	0	1	0
Away	2	1	0	1	3	3
Totals	4	2	1	1	4	3

Football League

Venue	P	W	D	L	F	A
Home	56	26	13	17	90	61
Away	56	8	12	36	58	123
Totals	116	34	25	53	148	184

FA Cup

Venue	P	W	D	L	F	A
Home	2	1	1	0	2	1
Away	2	1	0	1	2	2
Neutral	3	1	2	0	7	6
Totals	7	3	3	1	11	9

League Cup

Venue	P	W	D	L	F	A
Home	3	2	1	0	3	1
Away	3	0	0	3	0	9
Totals	6	2	1	3	3	10

WW2

Venue	P	W	D	L	F	A
Home	3	3	0	0	10	3
Away	2	1	0	1	5	5
Totals	5	4	0	1	15	8

Liverpool's origins are similar to Sheffield United's inasmuch that both clubs were 'created' to play at an existing ground. However,

Anfield, so long synonymous with Liverpool FC's glory days, started life as the home of Everton in 1884, but eight years later the 'Toffeemen' had a dispute with the landlord and as a result decided to decamp across Stanley Park at Goodison Park. At that juncture the landlord chose to create his own club - Liverpool - and in 1893 (twelve months after the Blades had gained membership to the Football League) the Merseysiders were elected to the Second Division, immediately winning promotion as champions (unbeaten) to join United in the top flight for the 1894-95 campaign.

The first League match between the clubs took place at Anfield on 6 October 1894. It ended in a 2-2 draw, as did the return clash at Bramall Lane two months later.

United have won only nine of their 58 League/Premiership matches at Anfield, their best being their first, 4-0 in 1897-98 when Neil Logan scored twice.

Between 1903 and 1922 United failed to win any of 15 League games at Anfield and between 1953 and 1965 they lost nine on the trot. Their last win on Liverpool soil came in the Premiership in 1993-94 when they upset the form book by recording a 2-1 victory.

Dick Forshaw scored four times in Liverpool's 4-1 League win over the Blades in October 1924.

In 1899 the Blades beat Liverpool in the FA Cup semi-final, Fred Priest's goal giving them a 1-0 victory at Derby after two draws (2-2 at Nottingham and 4-4 at Bolton, plus an abandonment due to spectators encroaching onto the Fallowfield pitch in Manchester with the Merseysiders 1-0 up). Three Liverpool players were later suspended for their rough and tough behaviour in the final game. This was the first time the clubs had met in this competition.

Liverpool beat United 3-2 on aggregate in the semi-final of the 2000-03 League Cup. After winning 2-1 at Bramall Lane in the first leg before a crowd of 30,095, the battling Blades went down 2-0 after extra-time in the return clash at Anfield.

A two-legged Football League Wartime Cup qualifying tie played in February 1942, finished United 7 Liverpool 6 on aggregate (the Blades coming back from 5-2 down to win the second leg at Bramall Lane by 5-1).

At the start of the ill-fated 1939-40 League season the Blades beat Liverpool 2-1 at Bramall Lane.

Internationals Rab Howell, Don Hutchinson, Ian Rush, Phil Thompson (also Liverpool caretaker-boss) and Dean Saunders have served with both clubs along with Gary Ablett, Harry Barton, Frank Becton, Willie Carlin, Jack Drummond; Steve Foley and Walter Hughes (Reds' reserves); Jimmy Harrop, Walter Hughes (Blades reserve), Peter Kyle, Kevin Lewis, Archie McPherson, Billy Mercer, Jack Pears ('Pool amateur), Bert Pearson and Nigel Spackman (also Blades manager), Blades' star Jimmy Hagan was an amateur with Liverpool.

LOAN PLAYERS

Here details of the players signed on loan by United over the years, listed in A-Z order with the season in brackets:
Gary Ablett 1995-96, Brett Angell 1995-96, Earl Barrett 1997-98, Graham Benstead 1987-88, Kingsley Black 1994-95, Michael Boulding 2002-03, Darren Bullock 2000-01, Viv Busby 1979-80, Andy Campbell (two separate spells) 1998-99 & 1999-2000, Bobby Campbell 1977-78, John Curtis (2002-03), Bobby Davison 1991-92, Mervyn Day 1991-92, Mark Dempsey* 1986-87, Andy Dibble 1997-98, Richard Edghill 2002-03, Scott Fitzgerald 1995-96, Paul Furlong 2001-02, Kevin Gage* 1991-92, John Gannon* 1988-89, Dean Glover 1986-87, Des Hamilton 1998-99, Roger Hansbury 1987-88, Jon Harley 2002-03, Glyn Hodges* 1990-91, Jon Hunt 1998-99, David Irving 1975-76, Gary Jones 1974-75, Chris Kamara 1992-93, Andy Kennedy 1986-87, Paddy Kenny* 2002-03, David Lee 1997-98, Dennis Longhorn 1976-77, Steve Lovell 2001-02, Scott Marshall 1994-95, Jon-Paul McGovern 2002-03, Alan McLeary 1992-93, Billy Mercer* 1994-95, Tommy Mooney 2002-03, John Moore 1988-89, Andy Morrison 2000-01, Dennis Mortimer 1984-85, Carl Muggleton 1995-96, Jon Newby 2000-01, Alex Notman 1999-2000, Paul Peschisolido* 2000-01, Terry Poole 1979-80, Wayne Quinn 2002-03, Mark Rankine 2002-03, Bruce Rioch 1978-79, Trevor Ross* 1982-83, Ian Rush 1997-98, Vaughan Ryan 1988-89, Geoff Salmons 1977-78, Andy Sayer 1990-91, Hans Segers 1987-88, Paul Simpson 1996-97, Manuel Thetis 2000-01, James Thomas 2000-01, Phil Thompson 1984-85, Tony Towner 1982-83, Michael Twiss 1998-99, Nicolas Weber 2000-01, Simon Webster* 1987-88, Paul Williams 1987-88, Stuart Wilson 1999-2000 and Dean Windass* 2002-03.
* Player was signed on a permanent basis after his loan spell.

Fact
Not including wartime 'guests' and players who appeared in off friendly/testimonial matches etc, Gary Jones, secured from Bolton Wanderers in 1974, was United's first 'loan' signing when the Football League officially endorsed the arrangement.

LOCAL DERBIES

The first 'Sheffield' derby contested by the Blades' was a friendly against Heeley (away) on 14 September 1889. A crowd of 2,200 saw the Blades win 2-1 with Duncan and Mack the scorers.

The first competitive derby followed soon afterwards when the Blades beat Heeley 1-0 in an FA Cup 2nd qualifying round encounter at Bramall Lane, Stokes conceding an own-goal to give United a 1-0 victory in front of 3,000 spectators.

The first derby against Sheffield FC took place on 28 October 1889. Again it was away and this time the scoreline finished level at 1-1.

In the Football League, the Blades and Wednesday first did battle on 16 October 1893 (Division 1) when a crowd of 27,000 assembled inside 'the Lane' to witness the 1-1 draw.

(See also under SHEFFIELD WEDNESDAY).

LOCOMOTIV

A 1936 LNER B-class locomotive number 2849 was named Sheffield United. It was taken out of service in 1959 and scrapped a year or so later.

LOGAN, Neil

Centre-half/centre-forward: 6 apps. 4 goals
Born: Burnbank, Scotland, circa 1874
Career: Blantyre, RutherGlenn Glenncairn FC, BLADES (November 1897), Swindon Town (April 1898), Blackburn Rovers (August 1902), Swindon Town (February 1903).
Versatile Scotsman Neil Logan played his first five games for the Blades in the centre-forward position, scoring four goals (twice against both Liverpool and Bolton in successive home matches in the space of three days). His later outing for the club was at centre-half in a 2-0 defeat by West Brom. He played at left-half, inside-right and centre-half for Blackburn (22 League games) and went on to make over 100 appearances in the Southern League for Swindon.

155

LONG EATON RANGERS
United's playing record against the Rangers:
Midland Counties League

Venue	P	W	D	L	F	A
Home	1	0	0	1	0	1
Away	1	1	0	0	3	2
Totals	2	1	0	1	3	3

The two MCL games between the Blades and Rangers were played in season 1890-91, Arthur Watson scoring twice in his side's 3-2 away win.

LONG SERVICE
The following have served Sheffield United for more than 20 years:

39 years (1895-1934)	Harry Johnson snr (player/coach/trainer)
39 years (1892-1931)	George Waller (player/trainer)
38 years (1935-73)	Harry Latham (player/coach/trainer)
33 years (1899-1932)	John Nicholson (secretary)
33 years (1937-50/'52-72)	Fred White (player/reserve team manager/coach/scout)
32 years (1951-83)	Cecil Coldwell (player/coach/acting-manager)
30 years (1891-1931)*	Ernie 'Nudger' Needham (player, staff, scout)
29 years (1920-49)	Fred Keen (groundsman)
26 years (1977 to date)	Derek Dooley (Commercial/Director/Chairman etc)
24 years (1889-1913)	Charles Stokes (committee member/Chairman)
23 years (1953-76)	Alan Hodgkinson (player/coach)
22 years (1926-48)	Jack Pickering (player)
22 years (1945-67)	Joe Shaw (player/coach)
21 years (1911-32)	Billy Gillespie (player/coach)
20 years (1932-52)	Teddy Dawson (secretary/manager)
20 years (1938-58)	Jimmy Hagan (player)
20 years (1952-72)	Arnold Newton (secretary)

* Worked behind the scenes at Bramall Lane.

Other long serving personnel at the club include players Jack Smith (19 years each), Len Badger, Fred Tunstall & Alan Woodward, plus Andy Daykin (over 18 years as Commercial/General Manager), John Harris (17 years as manager/General Manager/Senior Executive).

156

LONGHORN, Dennis
Midfielder: 41+3 apps. one goal
Born: Southampton, 12 September 1950
Career: Bournemouth & Boscombe Athletic (apprentice, April 1966, professional August 1968), Mansfield Town (£5,000, December 1971), Sunderland (£31,000, plus John Latham and an extra £20,000 after set number of appearances, February 1974), BLADES (on loan, October 1976, signed for £25,000 November 1976), Aldershot (£20,000, February 1978), Colchester United (May 1980), Halstead FC/Essex (manager: 1989-90).
Hard-working midfielder Dennis Longhorn was the first signing made by Mansfield manager Danny Williams. He developed well at Field Mill and attracted the attention of Sunderland boss Bob Stokoe who paid a 'hefty' fee for his transfer in 1974. Longhorn made 93 League appearances for the Stags and 40 for Sunderland before spending 18 months at Bramall Lane. He went on to take his career appearance tally in League football to 326

LONGWORTH, Bruce
Right-half: 14 apps. one goal
Born: Lanchester, 1898. Died: 1955
Career: Hopley's All Blacks, Bolton Wanderers (July 1919), BLADES (£2,300, October 1924), Bury (February 1926), Darwen (August 1927, retired October 1927).
Bruce Longworth was an aggressive player who made 82 appearances in five years for Bolton before his move to Bramall Lane for what was at the time, a fairly big fee. Unfortunately dogged by injuries and after brief spells with Bury and Darwen he was forced to retire through injury.

LOUGHBOROUGH (Town)
In December 1890 United surged through into the 1st round proper of the FA Cup by beating Loughborough 6-1 at home after the Leicestershire club deciding to waive the right to stage the tie at their relatively small Athletic ground, switching it to 'the Lane' instead. Bill Robertson (2) and Arthur Watson both scored twice in front of 2,800 spectators.
'Boro were elected to the Football League in 1895, staying in the Second Division until 1900, having had to apply for re-election on three occasions during that time.
Bill Mellor was a player with both clubs.

LOVELL, Stephen William Henry
Striker: 3+2 apps. One goal
Born: Amersham, 6 December 1980
Career: AFC Bournemouth (trainee, April 1997, professional July 1999), Portsmouth (£250,000, August 1999), Exeter City (on loan, March 2000), BLADES (on loan, March-April 2002).
Two-footed striker signed on loan at the end of the 2001-02 season, Steve Lovell had failed to find the net in eight outings for the Cherries before his surprising big-money transfer to Fratton Park.

LOWE, David
Outside-right: 3 apps.
Born: Dudley, circa 1899.
Career: Tividale White Star (Dudley), Cradley Heath (1918), BLADES (April 1922), Cradley Town (February 1923), Old Hill Wanderers (1925).
Outside-right Davey Lowe found the rise from local football in the heart of the Black County into the First Division far too difficult and although at times he did well in the second XI, he returned to Cradley after barely 18 months at 'the Lane.' He made his League debut (in place of David Mercer) on the right-wing in front of 40,000 fans at Everton in April 1922 (1-1) and then played in that season's County Cup semi-final replay defeat by Barnsley.

LUCAS, Richard
Full-back: 10+3 apps.
Born: Chapeltown, 22 September 1970
Career: BLADES (YTS, April 1987, professional July 1989), Preston North End (£40,000, December 1992), Lincoln City (on loan, October 1994), Scarborough (free transfer, July 1995), Hartlepool United (free, March 1997), Halifax Town (free, August 1998), Boston United (June 2000).
Compact defender, who prefers the full-back berth and strong with his left-foot, the versatile Richard Lucas - whose attitude and commitment on the pitch can never be faulted - failed to establish himself in the first team at Bramall Lane but later reached the personal milestone of 300 competitive appearances in the year 2000 with Boston.

LUDLAM, Steven John
Midfielder: 33+2 apps. one goal
Born: Chesterfield, 18 October 1955
Career: BLADES, Carlisle United (£16,200, May 1977), Chester City (July 1980-May 1983).
An unyielding footballer, strong in his performance, Steve Ludlam appeared in over 100 games for both Carlisle and Chester after leaving Bramall Lane.

LUTON TOWN

United's playing record against the Hatters:

Football League

Venue	P	W	D	L	F	A
Home	17	8	6	3	27	23
Away	17	6	2	9	24	29
Totals	34	14	8	12	51	52

FA Cup

Home	2	1	0	1	5	3

League Cup

Home	3	2	0	1	6	2
Away	1	0	0	1	1	3
Totals	4	2	0	2	7	5

Formed inside Luton Town Hall in April 1885, by an amalgamation of two leading local clubs, Luton Town Wanderers (who had already featured in the FA Cup) and Excelsior (a works team), Luton Town FC turned professional in 1890 and joined the Football League in 1897 (Division 2), the same year they moved to their Dunstable Road ground from Dallow Lane, transferring to Kenilworth Road (their current home) in 1905.
Unfortunately after just one season in the 'League' they went out, returning 22 years later (in 1920) when they became members of the newly-formed Third Division.
It was not until season 1937-338 that the Blades first met the Hatters in the competition and when they did it was United who came out on top, winning 2-0 at home and 3-2 away to complete the first of three doubles over the Kenilworth Road outfit.
United's best wins (of the 14 so far registered in the League) have been 4-1 at home in 1977-78 when Simon Stainrod scored twice, and 6-3 away in 1994-95 (in the 'new' Division 1) when Kevin Gage and Carl Veart claimed two goals apiece.
When the Blades defeated the Hatters 2-1 in March 1991, it completed an unbeaten sequence of nine games (eight won, one drawn) and as a result they went on to avoid relegation comfortably.
There were four different scorers when the Blades beat Luton 4-0 in a 3rd round FA Cup-tie at Bramall Lane in January 1992.
Harry Haslam managed both the Blades and the Hatters. Bruce Rioch started his League career at Kenilworth Road while Peter Anderson, Billy Barnes, Ian Benjamin, Alan Birchenall, Kingsley Black, Viv Busby, Barry Butlin, Viv Busby, Mervyn Day, Andy Dibble (United reserve), Jim Draper, Jock Gibson, Don Givens, Bill Gooney, Bertie Harris, Bob Hatton, Steve Kabba, Chris Kamara, Albert 'Tal' Lewis, Joe Lievesley, John Ryan and Imre Varadi have also represented both clubs. Also associated: Archie Clark (Luton player, Blades assisant manager) and Danny Begara (United coach/caretaker-manager, Town scout).

157

MACCLESFIELD (Town)
A Football League club since 1997, and playing at Moss Rose, the 'Silkmen' (Macclesfield's nickname) met the Blades at competitive level September 2003 at the Football League Cup.
Players who have served with both clubs include Barry Hartle, Mark Dempsey, Colin Grainger, Michael Lake, Billy Peake, Tony Philliskirk, Jim Plant and Paul Smith.

MACHENT, Stanley Charles
Wing-half/inside-forward: 115 apps. 19 goals
Born: Chesterfield: 23 March 1921
Career: BLADES (professional October 1938), Chesterfield (November 1947-May 1949).
Compact footballer Stan Machent joined United as a 17 year-old and was nurtured through the intermediate and reserve teams during the first seven months of his professional career and was all set to play in Blades' League side when WW2 arrived and disrupted his progress. Although he made almost 100 appearances for the seniors during the conflict he had to wait until August 1946 before making his League debut in a 1-0 home defeat by Liverpool. With Ernie Jackson and Alex Forbes manning the wing-half positions and Jimmy Hagan, Harold Brook and Albert Nightingale the main inside-forwards, Machent moved to pastures new by joining Chesterfield in 1947.

MACK, S
Defender: 15 apps.
Born: circa 1869
Career: Nottingham Rangers (1887), BLADES (September 1889), Crewe Alexandra (May 1890).
A versatile defender, able to play in any half-back position as well as left-back (even as a forward in an emergency) Mack lined up in United's first-ever game against his former club in September 1889. He spent juts the one season at Bramall Lane before leaving for Crewe Alexandra.

MACKENZIE, Ian Stanley
Defender: 53+3 apps. 3 goals
Born: Rotherham, 27 September 1950
Career: BLADES (apprentice September 1966, professional September 1968), Southend United (on loan, March 1975), Mansfield Town (July 1975 to May 1978).
A reliable defender, strong in his approach, Ian Mackenzie was mainly a reserve team player at Bramall Lane who later made over 70 first-class appearances for the Stags helping them win the Third Division championship in 1977.

MacPHAIL, John
Central defender: 169 apps. 9 goals
Born: Dundee, 7 December 1955
Career: St Columbus FC (Dundee), Dundee (1972, professional December 1973), BLADES (£30,000, January 1979), York City (on loan, February 1982, signed permanently, May 1982), Bristol City (£14,000, July 1986), Sunderland (£23,000, July 1987), Hartlepool United (free, September 1990, manager August 1993 to September 1994, retired as a player, March 1995).
Rugged defender John MacPhail made 84 appearances for Dundee before moving into the Football League in a vain attempt to help the Blades stave off relegation in 1979. Unfortunately his presence failed to prevent demotion but over the next few years he was a great competitor despite suffering relegation again in 1981...and not getting on too well with manager Ian Porterfield! After doing his part in setting the Blades up for a Fourth Division championship triumph he departed to York City for whom he appeared in 173 first-class matches, following up with 37 for Bristol City, 153 for Sunderland and 189 for Hartlepool before leaving The Victoria Ground after an unhappy alliance with new manager David McCreery. He gained a second 4th Division championship medal with York in 1984 and a Third Division winners medal with Sunderland in 1988. MacPhail is said to have been one of the finest centre-halves ever to play for the Minstermen, being voted 'Clubman of the Year' in 1984 and 1985.
* MacPhail is the oldest player to appear in a League game for Hartlepool - aged 39 years, 93 days v. Wigan Athletic on 28 February 1995.

McALISTER, Thomas Gerald
Goalkeeper: 78 apps.
Born: Clydebank, Scotland, 10 December 1952
Career: BLADES (apprentice, November 1969, professional May 1970), Rotherham United (January 1976), Blackpool (July 1979), Swindon Town (May 1980).
Goalkeeper Tom McAlister made well over 250 senior appearances during his 10 year-year professional career. Highly thought of when he joined the club, he replaced John Hope in the Blades' side in 1971 and was first choice until October 1973 when sadly he broke his leg playing against Manchester City. He was out of action for quite a long time. Regarded as a penalty-saving expert, he later gave Rotherham three-and-half years service during which time he played in 159 League matches.

McALLE, John Edward
Defender: 24 apps.
Born: Liverpool, 31 January 1950
Career: Wolverhampton Wanderers (apprentice, July 1965, professional February 1967), BLADES (£10,000, August 1981), Derby County (April 1982-May 1984), Harrisons FC (seasons 1984-86). Later head groundsman at the Merryhill Shopping complex at Brierley Hill near Dudley before starting his own landscape business.
Defender John McAlle was 31 years of age when he joined the Blades, having made 508 senior appearances for Wolves. He did not establish himself in the first XI at Molineux until 1970 but over the next decade he produced some wonderful displays at the heart of the Wanderers' defence, helping the Black Country club win the Texaco Cup in 1971, reach the UEFA Cup Final a year later (beaten by Spurs), triumph in the 1974 League Cup Final (v. Manchester City) and win the Second Division championship in 1977. After fracturing his right leg during an FA Cup-tie with Watford in February 1980 he failed to get back into the Wolves side on regaining full fitness and opted for a move to Bramall Lane. Although managing only 18 games, he played well alongside John MacPhail in 1981-82 when the Blades won the Fourth Division title. He quit Derby after the Rams had suffered relegation and he had fallen out with new manager Peter Taylor.

McCALL, Andrew Stuart Murray
Midfielder: 43+3 apps*
Born: Leeds, 19 June 1964
Career: Bradford City (apprentice, June 1980, professional, June 1982), Everton (£850,000, June 1988), Glasgow Rangers (£1.2 million, August 1991), Bradford City (free transfer, June 1998), BLADES (free, June 2002, later appointed player-coach, later reserve team manager whilst still an active player).
A snip-of-a-singing by Blades manager Neil Warnock, when he stepped foot inside Bramall Lane in the summer of 2002, flame-haired midfielder Stuart McCall had already appeared in 859 League and Cup games (in England & Scotland) and had netted 84 goals...and he had 40 full and two Scottish under-21 caps to his credit. He had helped Bradford win the Third Division title in 1985, Rangers clinch five Scottish League titles, two Scottish Cups and three League Cups and had scored twice, to no avail, in the 1989 FA Cup Final for Everton. A tremendous driving force and splendid motivator, he added drive and commitment to the Blades' midfield and was certainly an inspirational performer as the Blades reached two major Cup semi-finals and the First Division Play-offs in 2002-03...although injury ruled him out of the two semi-final legs, he did come on as a second-half substitute in the Final showdown with Wolves at Cardiff's Millennium Stadium, but walked off with his team-mates as a loser.
* Stuart's father, Andy McCall, played for Blackpool, Leeds United, Halifax Town and West Bromwich Albion and was inside Valley Parade the day of the fire disaster in May 1985 watching his son in action against Lincoln City.

McCARTHY, Michael
Goalkeeper: 9 apps.
Born: Cork, 22 December 1913. Died: 1973.
Career: Shamrock Rovers, BLADES (August 1934), Brideville FC (January 1935).
Republic of Ireland international goalkeeper Mick McCarthy (capped once v. Holland in 1932) had done very well in his home country with Shamrock Rovers but failed to grasp the chance of making his name in the First Division and spent only a few months at Bramall Lane before returning to Ireland. In 1933-34 the Blades had used four different 'keepers - Kendall, Smith & Wilkes - and a replacement was required but McCarthy didn't quite fit the bill.

McCORMICK, James
Right-half: 23 apps. one goal
Born: Rotherham, 24 August 1883
Career: Attercliffe, BLADES (May 1904), Plymouth Argyle (July 1907), BLADES (May 1910), Plymouth Argyle (December 1910-May 1920).
A tall, upright footballer, Jimmy McCormick struggled to come to terms with the rigours of professional League football with the Blades, an at times was caught out defensively. Nevertheless he certainly enjoyed his time in South Devon, amassing 276 appearances and scoring 22 goals in his two spells with Plymouth Argyle who he helped win the Southern League championship in 1913 and gain entry into the Football League as a result of the team's performances during the pre WW1 era.

McCOURT, James
Centre-half: 66 apps. 4 goals
Born: Bellshill, Scotland, 8 September 1896
Career: Bedlay Juniors, Third Lanark, BLADES (£2,350, February 1921), Manchester City (August 1924) Dykehead FC (May 1925).
Centre-half Jimmy McCourt a tall thoughtful, intelligent player who fed his forwards well. He made his debut for the Blades against Derby County (away) a few days after signing and remained as first team pivot until October 1922 when Jimmy Waugh replaced him.

McGEADY, John T
Winger: 18+5 apps.
Born: Glasgow, 17 April 1958
Career: Third Lanark, BLADES (June 1974), California Surf/NASL (summer of 1978), Newport County (October 1978, retired in May 1979).
Initially signed as a 'promising young reserve' to Alan Woodward, John McGeady made his senior debut for the Blades' on the right-wing in the County Cup Final against Sheffield Wednesday in October 1975; his League bow followed v. Middlesbrough on Boxing Day and his best run in the first team came between January and March 1976 before he suffered a complicated fracture off the leg at Blackpool in mid-November 1976. He never really got back on track and made only two appearances for Newport following a spell in America.

McGEENEY, Patrick Michael
Full-back/midfielder: 19+1 apps.
Born: Sheffield, 31 October 1966
Career: BLADES (apprentice, April 1983, professional, October 1984), Rochdale (on loan, November 1986), Chesterfield (August 1987-May 1989).
Paddy McGeeney spent four years at Bramall Lane. He went on to appear in 45 leagues approximately for the Spire-ites. He made his debut for the Blades at left-back in the semi-final of the Associate Members' Cup v. Hull City in May 1984 with his League baptism following in March 19875 v. Leeds United when he occupied the No.4 slot.

McGOVERN, Jon-Paul
Forward/midfielder: 14+4 apps. 3 goals
Born: Glasgow, 3 October 1980
Career: Celtic, BLADES (on loan, August 2002 to February 2003), Celtic.
Right-sided midfielder Jon-Paul McGovern made his League debut for the Blades in the second game of the 2002-03 season as a substitute v. Portsmouth and scored his first goal in the third match, to earn a point from a 1-1 draw at home to Walsall. He did well initially but was not considered for first team action after Christmas.

159

McGRATH, Paul
Defender: 14 apps.
Born: Ealing, London, 4 December 1959.
Career: St Patrick's Athletic (Dublin), Manchester United (£30,000, April 1982), Aston Villa (£450,000, August 1989), Derby County (£100,000, October 1996), BLADES (free transfer, August 1997, retired May 1998).
Although born in London, Paul McGrath moved to Ireland with his parents as a youngster and he was 22 years of age when Ron Atkinson signed him for Manchester United. A tall, commanding central defender, well built, he was cool, controlled and steady under pressure and went on to play in almost 200 first-class games during his seven years at Old Trafford (16 goals scored), gaining an FA Cup winners medal in 1985. Despite his dodgy knees, McGrath continued to do the business for Aston Villa and he certainly paid back the near half-a-million pound transfer fee (with interest)! He helped Villa beat his old club United in the 1994 League Cup Final and added a second League Cup medal to his collection in 1996 (v Leeds). As his career continued, so his performances got better and better! He went on win 83 full international caps for the Republic of Eire and starred in 323 senior games for Villa before moving to Derby County in 1996. After 14 games for the Blades, he duly ended a wonderful career with a 648 appearances under his belt at club and international levels.
* McGrath's testimonial match in 1995 when Villa beat Birmingham City 2-0 in front of realised gate receipts of almost £99,000.

McGREGOR, William
Born: Perthshire, Scotland, 1847. Died: Birmingham, 1911.
If it hadn't been for Scotsman William McGregor, there wouldn't be a Football League. He moved to Birmingham in 1870 and purchased a drapery business in Summer Lane, Aston. Not really interested in football (he played it once but didn't like it) but was lucky to get involved with Aston Villa, initially as an organiser and administrator before becoming a Director.
One winter's evening in 1886, when during a conversation with his friend Joe Tillotson, it came to light that several clubs in the North of England were contemplating forming a soccer League modelled on the American baseball system. This left McGregor thinking and a few days later he mentioned the matter to two of his Villa colleagues, Fergus Johnstone and Josuah Margoschis, both of whom were enthusiastic about the idea. Things developed quickly and after a handful of meetings with various members of other clubs, by early March 1888 McGregor knew he had gained enough support to set the ball rolling and form a competition whereby by teams would form a League and play against each other at home and away on a seasonal basis.
On 22 March 1888 McGregor called a meeting at Anderton's Hotel in London. The clubs represented were Aston Villa, Derby County, Notts County, Stoke City, Wolverhampton Wanderers and West Bromwich Albion from the Midlands but only Blackburn Rovers and Burnley from the North of the country.
However, a month later, on 17 April 1888 at the Royal Hotel, Manchester, representatives from 15 clubs were present, the others being Accrington, Bolton Wanderers, Everton, Halliwell, Nottingham Forest, Preston North End and Sheffield Wednesday. Halliwell, Forest and Wednesday were not accepted because of the difficulty in arranging fixtures but the others were, and on that day the Football League was formed, the original 12 members agreeing to an annual subscription of £2. 2s (£2.10).
McGregor had done a wonderful job and the soccer lovers throughout the world can be proud of what the Scotsman accomplished all those years ago.

McGUIRE, James
Wing-half: 64 apps. one goal
Born: Wallsend-on-Tyne, 10 December 1883.
Career: North Shields Athletic (1900), Barnsley (May 1903), North Shields (August 1905), BLADES (with George Thompson, August 1906), North Shields (October 1913).
A small but conscientious wing-half, Jimmy McGuire had an excellent first season at Bramall Lane before losing his way.

McHALE, Raymond
Midfielder/forward: 90+2 apps. 33 goals
Born: Sheffield, 12 August 1950
Career: Hillsborough Boys Club, Chesterfield (professional, August 1970), Halifax Town (October 1974), Swindon Town (September 1976), Brighton & Hove Albion (May 1980), Barnsley (Match 1981), BLADES (August 1982), Bury (on loan, February 1983), Swansea City (January 1985), Rochdale (non-contract, August 1986), Scarborough (non-contract, December 1986-March 1987).
A totally committed, hard-working midfielder who after a rather disappointing start to his career at Bramall Lane, Ray McHale played a big part in helping the Blades gain promotion in 1984 (42 outings). During a fine career he amassed almost 600 League appearances, scoring 87 goals. His best spells came at Chesterfield and Swindon.

McKAY, Kenneth
Inside-right: 28 apps. 5 apps.
Born: Scotland, circa 1872.
Career: Hamilton Academical, BLADES (1897), Tottenham Hotspur (May 1898), Thames Ironworks/West Ham United (May 1899), Fulham (January 1901-May1902)
Diminutive Scottish inside-forward Ken McKay spent a little over a year at Bramall Lane before leaving to join Spurs. Despite his short stay he certainly played his part in setting the Blades on the road for their League title success that season, and it was a considerable surprise when he left the club for White Hart Lane. He averaged a goal every two games for Spurs (25 in 53 outings) before moving across London to join the Hammers. He later helped the Cottagers win the Second Division of the Southern League in 1902. He represented the United League against the Thames & Medway League as a Spurs player in 1898 (scoring twice).

McLAFFERTY, Maurice
Full-back: 19 apps.
Born: Glasgow, 7 August 1922
Career: St Mirren, BLADES (August 1951), Brighton & Hove Albion (July 1952-May 1953).
Scottish-born defender Maurice McLafferty failed to settle in Sheffield and spent one season at Bramall Lane, sharing the left-back position with Albert Cox. He made 21 League appearances for Brighton.

McLAREN, Andrew
Inside-forward: 34 apps. 4 goals
Born: Larkhall, Scotland, 24 January 1922. Died: 1996.
Career: Larkhall Thistle, Preston North End (professional, February 1939), Burnley (December 1948), BLADES (£12,000, March1949), Barrow (February 1951). Bradford PA, Southport. Rochdale, Fleetwood.
Six months after joining United Andy McLaren broke his leg playing against Chesterfield (away) and was out of action until April 1950. He regained full fitness but after a decent run in the first team during the opening months of the 1950-51 season he was transferred to Barrow for whom he scored 52 goals in 152 League appearances.

McNAB, Samuel
Winger/inside-forward: 14 apps. 5 goals
Born: Glasgow, 20 October 1926. Died: 1995
Career: Dalry Thistle, BLADES (January 1952), York City (May 1954-June1956).
Basically a second team player at Bramall Lane, Sam McNab helped the Blades win the County Cup in his first season at the club when he appeared on the right-wing. He also occupied the left flank and inside-left positions before moving to Bootham Crescent where he lined up in the same forward-line as Arthur Bottom.

McNAUGHT, Kenneth
Centre-half: 41 apps. 6 goals
Born: Kirkcaldy, Fife, 11th January 1955.
Career: Everton (junior, July 1970, professional, May 1972), Aston Villa (£200,000, July 1977), West Bromwich Albion (£125,000, August 1983), Manchester City (on loan, December 1984-January 1985), BLADES (£10,000, July 1985, retired in May 1986), Dunfermline Athletic (coach), Swansea City (assistant-manager), Vale of Earn FC (manager).
Ken McNaught, who gained both youth and amateur honours for Scotland as a teenager. had 65 outings for Everton before becoming the back-bone of Aston Villa's defence, helping the Midland club win the League championship, European Cup and Super Cup in the early 1980s. After 260 outings for Villa he made his West Brom debut at Villa Park and added another 100 games to his tally with The Hawthorns club before switching to Bramall Lane after a loan spell at Maine Road. He had one solid season with the Blades and on his retirement in 1986 he was appointed coach at Dunfermline Athletic, later holding the position of assistant-boss at Swansea. He now works at the 'pro's shop at the famous Gleneagles golf course in Scotland.
* Ken McNaught's father, Willie, was a full Scottish international.

McPHERSON, Archibald
Wing-half/inside-forward: 68 apps. one goal
Born: Alva, Clackmannanshire, 10 February 1910. Died: 1969.
Career: Bathgate, Glasgow Rangers (March 1928), Liverpool (November 1929), BLADES (£1,895, December 1934), Falkirk (June 1937), Alloa Athletic (manager, 1945-47).
Scotsman Archie McPherson played for the Blades in the 1936 FA Cup Final defeat by Arsenal. At Anfield he played as an inside-forward, and one reporter described him as being "an accurate purveyor...and also a fine manipulator and excellent controller of the ball." Those qualities were still his hallmark after he was converted into a half-back.

MAIDSTONE UNITED
United knocked the non-League side out in the 3rd round of the 1987-88 FA Cup competition. The Blades just held on for a 1-0 victory, thanks to Mark Dempsey's 51st minute goal, scored in front of 8,907 hardy spectators.
Formed in 1897, Maidstone eventually reached the Southern League in 1971 and later spent four seasons in the Football League before being declared bankrupt in 1992 and were forced to resign just a few weeks into that season. Thus the club liquidated after 95 years of steady progress.
Harold Hardinge, Nicky Johns and John Ryan were associated with both clubs.

MALLENDER, Kenneth
Defender: 169+2 apps. 4 goals
Born: Thrybergh near Rotherham, 10 December 1943
Career: BLADES (amateur April 1959, professional February 1961), Norwich City (£38,500, October 1968), Hereford United (player-coach, July 1971-May 1973).
A strong-tackling performer who read the game well, Ken Mallender was a vital member of United's successful Northern Intermediate side before making his League debut against Blackpool in April 1962. After some excellent displays in the Blades defence, he lost his place to Eddie Colquhoun and, in fact, wasn't one of manager Arthur Rowley's favourite players. He eventually left Bramall Lane for Carrow Road. He still resides in Hereford.

161

MANAGERS (of Sheffield United Football Club)

(For career details of managers, see under individual entries).

List of the Blades' managers down the years:

Name	Term of Office
John B Wostinholm*	May 1889-May 1899
John Nicholson*	May 1899-April 1932
JE 'Teddy' Davison*	June 1932-August 1952
Reg Freeman	August 1952-August 1955
Joe Mercer, OBE	August 1955-December 1958
Archie Clark**	December 1958-April 1959
Johnny Harris+	April 1959-July 1968
Arthur Rowley	July 1968-August 1969
John Harris	August 1969-December 1973
Ken Furphy	December 1973-October 1975
Cecil Coldwell	October 1975 (15 days)
Jimmy Sirrel	October 1975-September 1977
Cecil Coldwell**	September 1977-January 1978
Harry Haslam	January 1978-January 1981
Martin Peters, MBE	January-May 1981
Ian Porterfield	June 1981-January 1986
Billy McEwan***	March 1986-January 1988
Danny Bergara**	January 1988 (19 days)
Dave Bassett	January 1988-December 1995
Howard Kendall	December 1995-June 1997
Nigel Spackman**	June 1997-March 1998
Steve Thompson**	March-July 1998
Steve Bruce	July 1998-May 1999
Adrian Heath	June-December 1999
Neil Warnock	December 1999 to date

* Acted as secretary-manager

** Appointed acting/caretaker-manager (Spackman: June-August 1977)

*** Acting manager from January-March 1986

+ Continued as General Manager until 1970

NB - For detailed pen picture biographies of United's managers, see under individual write-ups.

162

Manager's Fact File (A-Z order);

* John Beckett Wostinholm, a local man, was part of the 'committee' elected to run the football club in its early years. He was the 'man in charge' and was assisted by Henry Hebert Stones, with trainers Jack Houseley and George Waller, plus a handful of players including Jack Hudson, Billy Hendry and Ernest Needham also adding and abetting. Wostinholm was in office for ten years.

* John Nicholson was appointed secretary-manager of Sheffield United FC in 1899. He was also the secretary of the Attercliffe Football Club and assistant-secretary of the Sheffield & Hallamshire FA. Although technically a manager, his position within the club was that of secretary, feeding on all the information that was passed to him via the committee. Nicholson was a very knowledgeable man, and was well in tune as to what was going on in the footballing world. Occasionally during his reign in office he acted as the club's honorary treasurer and was also President of the Midland League. He was a key member of the Sheffield Football Association and was President of the Yorkshire Cricket Council League. He died in 1932 following a road accident.

League record as United's manager (with committee)

P	W	D	L
1336	533	309	594

* John Edward 'Teddy' Davison, 20 years in office (to 1952) was born in Gateshead on 2 September 1877. He was a goalkeeper with Wednesday (1908-26), Mansfield Town ((player-manager with Mifa1926-27) and Chesterfield (manager, 1927-32) before taking over the reins at Bramall Lane. He took the Blades to the 1936 FA Cup Final and guided the team back into the First Division - and he also signed some star players including Jimmy Hagan. On leaving the Blades he returned to take charge of Chesterfield (to 1958). He died in Wortley near Sheffield in February 1971.

League record as United's manager

P	W	D	L
546	226	129	191

* Reginald 'Reg' Vincent Freeman, born in New Brighton on 20 December 1897, was a full-back with Northern Nomads (1919-20), Oldham Athletic (1920-23), Middlesbrough (1923-30) and Rotherham United (1930-34, taking over as manager at Millmoor until 1952). He guided Rotherham to promotion from Division Two in 1951 and saw the Blades win the Second Division title in at the end of his first season in charge. He died in the village of Wickersley in 4 August 1955 whilst still in charge at 'the Lane.'

League record as United's manager:

P	W	D	L
126	53	28	45

* Joseph 'Joe' Mercer, OBE, was a great wing-half who starred for Everton (1931-46), Arsenal (1946-54) and England (winning five full & 27 wartime caps). He was a League championship winner three times, the first with Everton in 1939 and then twice more with Arsenal in 1948 & 1953. As captain, he duly collected the FA Cup after Arsenal's 2-0 win over Liverpool in 1950 and then earned a runners-up prize two years later. He was voted 'Footballer of the Year' in 1950. As a manager he guided Manchester City to the League title, League Cup, FA Cup & European-Cup-winners Cup glory in successive years: 1968-71 inclusive. He was awarded the OBE in 1976 and a year later was placed in charge of the England team. Mercer was born in Ellesmere Port, Cheshire on 9 August 1914 and died on his 76th birthday in 1990.

League record as United's manager:

P	W	D	L
149	63	32	54

* Archibald 'Archie' Clark was born in Maidstone, Kent on 4 April 1902 and died in Sheffield on 14 January 1967. He played at centre-half for Brentford (1927), Arsenal (season 1927-28), Luton Town (1928-31), Everton (1931-36) and Tranmere Rovers (1936-39) before taking over as manager of Gillingham where he stayed until moving to Bramall Lane as Mercer's assistant (he played with Joe at Goodison Park). He was Football League championship winner in 1932 and later five prizes to Gillingham including two Southern League titles (1947 & 1949). When Mercer left Clark held the position of caretaker-manager at 'the Lane' until John Harris took over.
League record as United's manager:

P	W	D	L
20	13	2	5

* John Harris was the first man to have two spells in charge at 'the Lane' covering a total of 15 years. He was born in Glasgow on 30 June 1917 and died in Sheffield on 24 July 1988. A full-back or centre-half with Swindon Town, Swansea Town, Tottenham Hotspur (1939) and Wolves (during WW2) he moved to Chelsea for £8,000 in 1945 and after acting as player-manager of Chester (1956-59) he was appointed boss of the Blades, holding office initially until 1969, then serving as general manager before having his second spell from 1969 to 1973. He was later Chief Scout for Sheffield Wednesday (late 1970s). A Wartime international for Scotland (v. England in 1945), he helped Wolves reach two League North Cup Finals (losing in 1944, winning in 1945) and he skippered the Chelsea side that clinched their first League title in 1955 and as a manager was twice a promotion-winner with the Blades (1961 & 1971, as runners-up in Division 2). He produced and signed many great players for the Blades, Trevor Hockey, Stewart Scullion and Billy Dearden (for a bargain £10,000) among them.
League record as United's manager:

P	W	D	L
567	234	138	195

* Arthur George Rowley scored more League goals (434) than any other footballer between 1946 and 1965, during which time he played as an inside or centre-forward for West Bromwich Albion, Fulham, Leicester City and Shrewsbury Town (as player-manager). He helped both Albion and Fulham (as champions) gain promotion to the First Division in 1949, twice came up from Division Two with Leicester (1954 & 1957) and then won promotion yet again with Shrewsbury Town in 1959 and Southend United in 1982, the latter as manager, having taken over at Roots Hall in 1970 following his departure from Bramall Lane. He was remained as manager at Gay Meadow until 1968, later taking charge of Telford United and Oswestry Town. An England 'B' international, he also represented the Football League. Rowley was born in Wolverhampton on 21 April 1926 and died in Shrewsbury on 18 December 2002.
League record as United's manager:

P	W	D	L
42	16	11	15

* Kenneth Furphy, born in Stockton-on-Tees on 28 March 1931, was a wing-half with Everton, Runcorn and Darlington before becoming player-coach at the Feethams in the late 1950s. He served as player-manager at both Workington and Watford before taking charge of Blackburn Rovers in 1971, holding office for two years. After his near two-year spell at 'the Lane' he coached three clubs in the NASL, New York Cosmos, Detroit Express and Washington Diplomats (up to 1981) and following a coaching post in Bermuda, he returned to America to manage Cleveland Force (his last position in football). A Fourth Division championship winner in 1964 (with Workington) and a Third Division winner in 1969 (with Watford), he also won the Super Bowl in 1977 with Detroit. Furphy later worked for BBC Radio Devon.
League record as United's manager:

P	W	D	L
78	27	22	29

* Cecil Coldwell, a former player, also had two spells as United's manager (see under Coldwell, Cecil).
League record as United's manager:

P	W	D	L
23	11	5	7

* James 'Jimmy' Sirrel is a Scotsman, born in Glasgow on 2 February 1922, who played for Celtic (1945-49), Bradford PA (1949-51), Brighton & Hove Albion (1951-54) and Aldershot (1954, later trainer to 1967) before becoming trainer/acting manager of Brentford (retaining his position until 1969). He then took charge of Notts County (1969-75) and after leaving Bramall Lane he had a second spell in charge at Meadow Lane (1977-87) before working as a part-time scout for Derby County. Sirrel, football mad, won promotion from all three Divisions (4 to 3 to 2) in 1971, 1973 and 1981 respectively.
League record as United's manager:

P	W	D	L
78	20	22	36

* Harold 'Harry' Haslam was born in Manchester on 30 July 1921 and died on 10 September 1986. A full-back with Manchester United (WW2), Rochdale (as an amateur), Oldham Athletic, Brighton & Hove Albion, Leyton Orient, Guildford City and Hastings United (the latter as player-manager), he was then in charge of Eastbourne United, coached at Gillingham, managed both Barry Town and Tonbridge, scouted for Fulham and Luton Town, becoming the Hatters manager in 1972 and remaining at Kenilworth Road until 1978 when he switched his duties to Bramall Lane, taking over as public Relations Officer for a short while in 1981, the year he also worked as an England scout. Haslam's only club honour was to gain promotion as manager with Luton in 1974.
League record as United's manager:

P	W	D	L
134	46	30	58

* Martin Peters, MBE, London-born, and an England World Cup hero in 1966, spent just over four months as manager at Bramall Lane (See under PETERS, Martin Stanford).
League record as United's manager:

P	W	D	L
16	3	6	7

163

* John 'Ian' Porterfield was born in Dunfermline on 11 February 1946 and was a midfielder with Leeds United (on trial), Hearts and Glasgow Rangers (as a junior), Raith Rovers (to 1967), Sunderland for a decade (to 1977) and Sheffield Wednesday (as player/player-coach) before managing Rotherham United (1980-81). He spent almost five years in charge at Bramall Lane, leaving the Blades for a two years spell as boss of Aberdeen (1986-88), later assistant-manager of Chelsea (1989), then manager of Reading (1989-91) and Chelsea (1991-93) before coaching in Zimbabwe, Saudi Arabia and Zambia. An FA Cup winner with Sunderland in 1973 when his goal beat Leeds United, he later gained a Third Division championship medal with Rotherham (1981), took the Blades to the Fourth Division title a year later and in 1988 lifted the Scottish League Cup as boss of Aberdeen.
League record as United's manager:

P	W	D	L
213	94	55	64

* William 'Billy' J M McEwan, born in Clelland on 29 June 1951, was a midfielder with Hibernian, Blackpool, Brighton & Hove Albion, Chesterfield, Mansfield Town, Peterborough United and Rotherham United before spending three-and-a-half years at Bramall Lane (initially as coach from September 1984, then acting manager from March 1986 and manager after that). He returned to Millmoor as manager (1988-91), winning the Fourth Division championship in 1989.
League record as United's manager:

P	W	D	L
84	28	23	33

* Daniel 'Danny' Albert Bergara was born in Uruguay in 1943 and played in midfield for racing Club Montevideo, Real Mallorca, Seville and Tenerife before retiring to become coach at Luton Town (1973). Between 1978-81 he was assistant-manager at Bramall Lane and after a spell as England Youth team coach he took a similar position in Brunei, returning to England as coach of Sheffield FC in 1984, acting as coach/assistant-manager and caretaker-manager for 19 days (in January, 1988) of the Blades prior to his appointment as manager of Rochdale (season 1988-89), later holding the same position with Stockport County (1989-95). A Uruguayan Youth international, he twice won the Spanish Second Division title with Mallorca in 1965 and Seville in 1969, guided Stockport to promotion from Division Four in 1991 and to Auto-Windscreen runners-up in 1992 and 1993.
League record as United's manager:

P	W	D	L
1	1	0	0

David 'Harry' Bassett was a wartime baby, born in Watford 4 September 1944. He was a midfielder with Watford Juniors, Chelsea Juniors, Walton & Hersham and Wimbledon before becoming coach at Plough Lane in 1979, then manager 1981-87. Briefly in 1984 he took charge of Crystal Palace, managed his home town club Watford during season 1987-88 and then took charge at Bramall Lane until 1995, later managing Palace (again, 1996-97), Nottingham Forest (1997-98), Barnsley (1999-2000) and Leicester City (2001-02, becoming Director of Football at The Walker Stadium for season 2002-03). An England Amateur international, Bassett was an FA Amateur Cup winner with Walton & Hersham (1973), won three Southern League titles with the Dons (1975, 1976 & 1977), was a promotion winner in 1981, 1983 (as Division 4 champions), 1984 and 1986 with the same club and achieved two more promotions, 1989 and 1990 with the Blades.
League record as United's manager:

P	W	D	L
338	127	87	124

* Howard Kendall was born in Ryton-on-Tyne on 22 May 1946. His career started, effectively as a Ryton & District Schoolboy player and thereafter he settled own to become a quality midfielder with Preston North End (from 1961), Everton (1967-74)), Birmingham City (signed in a deal involving Bob Latchford), Stoke City (1977-79), Blackburn Rovers (player-manager, 1979-81), Everton (manager, 1981-87), Athletic Bilbao/Spain (manager, 1987-89), Manchester City (manager, 1989-90), Everton (manager 1990-93), Xanthi/Greece (manager, 1994), Notts County (manager, 1995) and Sheffield United (manager: 1995-97), Everton (manager 1997-98), Jerez/Spain (manager, 1998), Greece (manager, 1999-2001). He was twice an FA Cup runner-up, with PNE in 1964 (becoming the youngest player at that time to appear in the Final, aged 17 years, 345 days v. West Ham) and Everton in 1968. He then helped the Merseysiders win the League title in 1970 (as a player) and then, as a manager, took Blackburn to the Third Division championship (1980) before doing great things back at Goodison Park, leading Everton to the League title again (1985 & 1987), to FA Cup glory in 1984, (runners-up in 1985), to European Cup-winners Cup success in 1985, and three FA Charity Shield triumphs in 1984, 1985 & 1986 (shared). He also gained Schoolboy, Youth and six England Under-23 caps and played for the Football League XI. On 8 May 1981 he became the youngest manager ever appointed by Everton (aged 34 years, 351 days), was voted 'Manager of the Year' in 1985. He amassed a total of 613 senior appearances and scored 65 goals.
League record as United's manager:

P	W	D	L
71	31	24	16

* Nigel Spackman was manager at Bramall Lane for eight months before handing over the chair to Steve Thompson in 1998 (See under SPACKMAN, Nigel).
League record as United's manager:
P   W   D   L
34   5   13   6

* 'Steve' Thompson was in the 'hot seat' at thee Lane for three months at the end of the 1997098 season - after Spackman's departure and Steve Bruce's arrival (See under THOMPSON, Steven Paul).
League record as United's manager:
P   W   D   L
12   4   4   4

* 'Steve Bruce' was eleven months in charge of the Blades: season 1998-99. (See under BRUCE, Stephen Roger)
League record as United's manager:
P   W   D   L
46   18   13   15

* Adrian Paul Heath was born in Stoke-on-Trent on 11 January 1981. A sprightly forward, always on the lookout for goals, he had a decent career, playing in turn, for Stoke City (1979-82), Everton (1982-89), Espanyol/Spain (1989), Aston Villa (1989-90), Manchester City (1990-92), Stoke City (1992), Burnley (1992), Sheffield United (as a player/assistant-manager, December 1995-March 1996), Burnley (non-contract, March 1996, later manager in season 1996-97), Everton (player-coach, season 1997-98), Sunderland (coach/scout season 1998-99), Sheffield United (manager for seven months in 1999), Sunderland (scout, 2000). An England 'B' and Under-21 international (capped eight times at the latter level) Heath scored 120 goals in a total of 535 League games over a period of 18 years. He made just five substitute appearances for the Blades (four in the League, one in the FA Cup).
League record as United's manager:
P   W   D   L
21   4   6   11

* Neil Warnock was born in Sheffield on 1 December 1948. A forward in his playing days, he assisted Chesterfield (1968-69), Rotherham United (1969-71), Hartlepool United (1971-72), Scunthorpe United (1972-75), Aldershot (1975-76), Barnsley (1976-78), York City (1978), Crewe Alexandra (1978-79) and Burton Albion (1979-80) before becoming manager of Gainsborough Trinity (1980). The following year he was place in charge of his former club, Burton Albion and for three years, 1986-89, managed Scarborough prior to taking the hot seat at Notts County (1989-93). He next acted as a consultant at Torquay United (early in 1993, having a spell in charge before the end of that season) and then bossed at Huddersfield Town (1993-95), Plymouth Argyle (1995-97), Oldham Athletic (1997-98) and Bury (1998-99) prior to his engagement with the Blades in December 1999. And what a great job he's done since then, leading the club into two major Cup semi-finals and to third spot in the First Division table in season 2002-03 and ultimately the Play-off Final. Earlier in his career (albeit only as a manager) he won the GM Vauxhall Conference with Scarborough (1987), gained successive promotions from Divisions Three and Two with Notts County (1990 & 1991) and he also lifted Huddersfield Town into Division One and Plymouth Argyle into Division 2 (in 11996 and 1997 respectively)...He's now regarded as a 'Play-off' specialist' despite the disappointment of seeing his Blades side lose 3-0 to Wolves in the First Division 'Final' of 2003.
League record as United's manager (not including Play-offs):
P   W   D   L
163 66   46   51

165

Assistant-Managers

Among the men who, down the years, have acted as assistant-manager at Bramall Lane, we have: Archie Clark (to Harris) Andy Beattie (to John Harris, 1967-68), Danny Bergara (to Haslam), Kevin Blackwell (to Warnock), Viv Busby, Cecil Coldwell (to Sirrel), John Deehan (to Steve Bruce), Adrian Heath (to Thompson, briefly), John McSevenny (to Porterfield), Martin Peters (to Haslam), John Short (to Johnny Harris), Nigel Spackman (to Kendall), Geoff Taylor (to Bassett) and Kevin Blackwell (to Warnock).

Ex-United players (all levels) who went on to become a League club manager (including roles as player-manager, part-time manager and/or caretaker-manager) in world soccer:

Colin Addison	Cardiff City, Hereford Utd, Swansea City
Bill Anderson	Lincoln City
Peter Anderson	Millwall
Jack Barke	Mansfield Town
Frank Barlow	Chesterfield, Scunthorpe United
John Barnwell	Hereford Utd, Northampton Town, Notts County, Walsall, Wolves
Billy Beer	Birmingham
Jimmy Bone	Arbroath
Eddie Boot	Huddersfield Town
Tommy Boyle	Northampton Town
Gary Brazil	Notts County (two spells)
Steve Bruce	Birmingham City, Crystal Palace, Huddersfield T, Wigan Athletic
John Burridge	Swansea City
Viv Busby	Hartlepool United
Herbert Chapman	Arsenal, Huddersfield Town
Cecil Coldwell	Sheffield United
Glenn Cockerill	Leyton Orient
Alan Cork	Cardiff City, Swansea City
Keith Curle	Mansfield Town
Teddy Davison	Sheffield United
Mervyn Day	Carlisle United
Billy Dearden	Mansfield Town, Notts County
Wally Downes	Brentford
Jack English	Darlington, Nelson, Northampton Town, Exeter City
Alex Forbes	Johannesburg Rangers
Don Givens	Xamax Neuchatel (Switzerland)
Jimmy Hagan	Benfica, FC Oporto, Peterborough Utd, Sporting Lisbon, West Bromwich Albion
Adrian Heath	Burnley
George Hedley	Bristol City
Trevor Hockey	Athlone Town
Glyn Hodges	Barnsley
Harry Hooper	Halifax Town
Stewart Houston	Queen's Park Rangers
Bobby Howitt	Motherwell
Jim Iley	Barnsley, Blackburn Rovers, Bury, Exeter City
Chris Kamara	Bradford City, Stoke City
Keith Kettleborough	Doncaster Rovers
Ray Lewington	Brentford, Fulham, Watford
Alan McLeary	Millwall (joint)
John McPhail	Hartlepool United
Archie McPherson	Alloa Athletic
Jack Peart	Bradford City, Fulham, Rochdale
Martin Peters	Sheffield United
Jack Poole	Mansfield Town
Fred Priest	Hartlepool United
George Raynor	Coventry City, Doncaster Rovers, Juventus, Lazio
Bruce Rioch	Arsenal, Bolton Wanderers, Middlesbrough, Millwall, Norwich City, Torquay United, Wigan Athletic
John Ryan	Cambridge United
Dean Saunders	Derby County
Joe Shaw	Chesterfield
Paul Simpson	Rochdale
Nigel Spackman	Barnsley, Sheffield United
Mick Speight	Chester City
Simon Stainrod	Ayr United, Dundee, Falkirk
Gerry Summers	Gillingham, Oxford United
Harry Thickett	Bristol City
Phil Thompson	Liverpool
Steve Thompson	Doncaster Rovers, Lincoln City, Sheffield Utd, Southend United
Sam Thorpe	Buxton
Bill Toner	Dumbarton
Chris Wilder	Halifax Town
Peter Withe	Wimbledon, Thailand National team
Peter Wragg	Halifax Town
Dick Young	Carlisle United

NB - Messrs Addison, Barnwell, Hagan, Rioch and Withe also coached/managed abroad, while Raynor (a United reserve team player) also manager/coach the Swedish national team as well as coaching other clubs abroad.

Managerial Chit-Chat
* Future United boss Joe Mercer was the first man to manage a League Cup-winning side (Aston Villa in 1961). Mercer was the first 'manager' to play for United, appearing in two friendly games against Reading in November 1955 and the Royal Signals side the following month.
* As managers, Ken Furphy (1975), Martin Peters (19081), Ian Porterfield (1985), Billy McEwan (1986) and Dave Bassett (1992) also donned the red and white stripes of United in various non-competitive matches.
* Phil Thompson acted as caretaker-manager at Liverpool when Gerard Houllier was off duty though illness (2001-02).
* In 2002, ex-United player-manager Steve Bruce took Birmingham City back into the top flight of English football for the first time in 16 years - after being in charge at St Andrew's for just six months.
* United assistant-boss in 1999, Adrian Heath, made five substitute appearances for the Blades during the second-half of the 1995-96 season. He also played for Stoke City (2 spells), Everton, Aston Villa, Espanyol (Spain), Manchester City and Burnley (2 spells) while also managing the Turf Moor club. An England 'B' and Under-21 international (8 caps gained in the latter category) he scored 120 goals 534 League games covering a period of 18 years (1979-97).
* Joe Mercer was caretaker-manager of England in 1977.

Non-League Bosses
Here are some of the many Blades' players (not listed as major League club managers) who, after quitting the major soccer scene, went into management at non-League level: Malcolm Barrass (Wigan Athletic*), Alan Birchenall (Trowbridge Town), Jack Chisholm (Finchley, Helston FC, Romford), Joe Cockroft (Wisbech Town), Terry Curran (Goole Town), RE (Bob) Evans (Brookhirst FC), Dean Glover (Newcastle Town), Chris Guthrie (Witney Town), George Handley (Goole Town), Mick Heaton (Workington Town), John Hope (Wingate, Willington FC), Bert Lipsham (Millwall (Athletic*, Northfleet), Dennis Longhorn (Halstead FC, Essex), Ken McNaught (Vale of Earn FC, Scotland), Vince Matthews (Oswestry Town, Shrewsbury Town*), Dennis Mortimer (Redditch United), Derek Pace (Walsall Wood), Tom Phillipson (Bilston United), David Powell (Bridgend Police FC), Bill Punton (Diss Town, Yarmouth Town), George Richardson (Bangor City), Paul Richardson (Gloucester City, Fairfield), Sam Thorpe (Buxton), John Tudor (South Shields), Fred Tunstall (Boston United), Imre Varadi (Matlock Town, Stalybridge Celtic) & Billy Whitehurst (Frickley Colliery).
* Then a non-League club.

MANCHESTER CITY (also Ardwick)

United's playing record against City:

Premier League

Venue	P	W	D	L	F	A
Home	2	0	1	1	1	2
Away	2	0	1	1	0	2
Totals	4	0	2	2	1	4

Football League

	P	W	D	L	F	A
Home	52	20	17	15	92	80
Away	52	13	12	27	74	102
Totals	104	33	29	42	166	182

FA Cup

	P	W	D	L	F	A
Home	3	2	1	0	6	1
Away	1	0	1	0	0	0
Neutral	1	1	0	0	1	0
Totals	5	3	2	0	7	1

League Cup

	P	W	D	L	F	A
Away	1	0	0	1	2	4

WW2

	P	W	D	L	F	A
Home	1	0	0	1	2	3
Away	1	0	0	1	1	2
Totals	2	0	0	2	3	5

Others

	P	W	D	L	F	A
Home	4	2	0	2	8	8
Away	2	0	0	2	1	4
Totals	6	2	0	4	9	12

Manchester City were formed as a Limited Company in 1894 after their predecessors, Ardwick, had been forced into bankruptcy. However, many historians, including myself, like to trace the club's history back to 1880 when St Mark's Church, West Gorton, added a football section to its cricket club. The two amalgamated with Gorton Athletic in 1884 to become Gorton FC and because of a change of ground, subsequently took the name Ardwick in 1887.
Manchester City are listed amongst United's oldest League opponents, both clubs having been founder members of the Second Division in 1892 (when of course City were known as 'Ardwick').
Both fixtures in that inaugural campaign took place in March 1893. The first at Hyde Road (City's ground from 1887 to 1923 when they moved to Maine Road) ended in a 3-2 win for the Blades who then completed the double with a 2-1 home victory (Ernest Needham scoring both goals).
The next two meetings followed in 1899 when the Manchester club was now called City. And again the Blades double dup with scores of 3-0 and 2-1.
After United's Fred Tunstall had missed a first-half penalty, City went to town and scored five times in the second period to whip the Blades 5-0 at Maine Road in a League game in September 1924 - Roberts netted a hat-trick.
Harry Johnson scored four times as United went 8-0 up on City in a home League game in October 1925 (the first season of the new offside law). They faded late on as the visitors reduced the scoreline to 8-3. This is United's best win to date over the 'Blues' but only 8,250 fans enjoyed the party. The return fixture, played a week later, ended in a 4-2 win for United.
Overall United have a poor record at Maine Road, having won there only three times since WW2. In fact, they lost nine League games in successive dating back to 1933 while their heaviest defeat there has been 6-0, as recent as 1999-2000.
Yet between 1905 and 1911 the Blades recorded five successive wins including their best-ever in the series, 4-0 in October 1910...a scoreline they repeated in 1930-31 when Jimmy Dunne claimed a hat-trick.
Two goals were scored in the first 80 seconds of United's League game with City at Maine Road in August 1954. City led 4-1 at half-time and went on to win 5-2.

167

The Blades were 2-0 down at half-time against City in February 1972 (Division 1). Trevor Hockey broke his leg but the team fought back to earn a point from a 3-3 draw.

After United had been beaten 6-0 at Maine Road by a rampant City in August 1999 they slipped to the bottom of the First Division.

United beat City 2-0 in a 4th round FA Cup-tie in January 1939 having played 80 minutes with only 10 men following an injury to Jackson.

In season 1988-89 the Blades beat City 4-1 at Maine Road in a 3rd round League Cup-tie.

In 2000-03 both clubs celebrated their 100th season of League football.

In 1951 the Blades had two forwards named Fred Smith. Centre-forward FE ('Big Fred') was signed in 1947 whilst FA (Jack or 'Little' Fred) had recently arrived from Hull City. Manchester City's secretary arrived at Bramall Lane under instructions to sign 'Fred' Smith...and legend has it that he went away with the wrong player - at least that's what City fans have always believed!

Both Howard Kendall and Joe Mercer managed the Blades and City.

Earl Barrett, Peter Beagrie, Paul Beesley, Carl Bradshaw, Michael Brown, John Burridge, Keith Curle, Joe Davies, Andy Dibble (United reserve), Richard Edghill, Mel Eves, Brian Gayle, Adrian Heath, Bob Hill, Jamie Hoyland, Billy Hudson, Jim McCourt, Ken McNaught, Hugh Morris, Andy Morrison, Ferry Phelan, John Ryan, Paul Simpson, Fred E Smith, Gareth Taylor, Simon Tracey, George Utley, Imre Varadi, Michel Vonk, Roy Warhurst, David White and Jimmy Yates are among the players who have represented both clubs. Mike Heaton was a United player and assistant-boss at Maine Road, Willie Donachie and John Deehan have been associated with both clubs and ex-Blades inside-forward Jimmy Hagan became a scout for City.

MANCHESTER UNITED (also Newton Heath)

United's playing record against the Reds:

Premiership

Venue	P	W	D	L	F	A
Home	2	1	0	1	2	4
Away	2	0	0	2	1	5
Totals	4	1	0	3	3	9

Football League

Home	41	21	9	11	74	49
Away	41	11	6	24	47	83
Totals	42	32	15	35	121	132

FA Cup

Home	4	1	0	3	2	5

WW2

Home	3	1	0	2	4	6
Away	3	1	1	1	5	6
Totals	6	2	1	3	9	12

When Newton Heath (formed in 1878) went bankrupt in 1902, Manchester United came into being, playing at Bank Street (Clayton), switching to Old Trafford in 1910.

Newton Heath, in fact, was founded by a dining room committee of the carriage and wagon works of the Lancashire & Yorkshire Railway Company and registered initially as Newton Heath L & YR Cricket & Football Club. They won the Manchester Cup in 1886 and as Newton Heath gained entry to the Football League with the Blades in 1892, although taking up positions in different Divisions, the Heathens going straight into the top flight. Therefore, it wasn't until the next season (1893-94) after the Blades had gained promotion, that they first met in the competition. And it was the team from Sheffield who came out on top, winning both games, 3-1 at Bramall Lane and 2-0 at Bank Street.

Newton Heath became Manchester United in 1902. The team moved to Old Trafford eight years later and the Blades became the second team to visit there, losing 1-0 on 5 March 1910 in front of 40,000 spectators (filling half the ground which was built to house 80,000).

The Blades' best home League win over United is 6-1 - achieved twice, in 1911-12 (when Dicky Leafe scored a hat-trick) and in 1928-29 when Harry Johnson netted three times.

Amazingly the Blades also beat United 5-1 at Old Trafford in May 1930 to save themselves from relegation to the Second Division. One of the Blades' finest wins (albeit a modest scoreline of 2-1) came at Bramall Lane in January 1948 when Manchester United fielded what was to be their FA Cup-winning side (except for the goalkeeper). After just seven minutes play, Jack Smith, the Blades' 'keeper was taken off injured. Winger Colin Collindridge took over between the posts (no 'subs' in these days) and from that point on it seemed as if Manchester United, who were dominating the play, would cruise to a comfortable victory. They took the lead through Jack Rowley and the writing was on the wall for the Blades but then amazingly George Jones scored twice before the interval to put the Blades in front. And although the visitors bombarded Collindridge's goal after that, they couldn't equalise and reserve Ernie Jackson.

The Blades led 2-0 at Old Trafford in a First Division match in May 1949 but they fell away at lost 3-2.

Brian Deane had the pleasure of scoring the first-ever goal in the Premiership, for the Blades in their 2-1 win over United at Bramall Lane on 15 August 1992 in front of more than 28,000 fans.

The four FA Cup-ties between the two clubs all took place between 1990 and 1995 9all at Bramall Lane), The Reds won a 6th round encounter by 1-0 in March 1990 to set things off. In 1992-93, however, the Blades caused an upset by winning a 5th round tie 2-1 (after trailing to a Ryan Giggs goal) and even surviving a late Steve Bruce penalty.

Among the many players who have served with both clubs down the years we have Willie Boyd, Tom Boyle, John Connaughton, Ted Connor, John Cunningham, John Curtis, Mark Dempsey, Dick Gardner, Don Givens, Andy Goram, Wilson Greenwood, Stewart Houston, Roy John, Jim Leighton (on loan at 'the Lane'), Paul McGrath, Fred Milnes, Alex Notman, Paul Parker, Jack Peden, Charlie Roberts (Blades trialist), Paddy Sloan (also Blades Chief Scout), Mark Todd, Michael Twiss and Enoch West.

Steve Bruce played for United and later managed the Blades while Lane players Harold Brook, Jock Dodds & George Farrow all guested for the Reds in wartime football, as did Harry Haslam and Arthur Rowley who later became Blades' managers. Alan Hodgkinson was a scout for the Old Trafford club while Lou Macari worked in the same capacity for the Blades, likewise another ex-United player Dick Duckworth.

MANSFIELD TOWN

United's playing record against the Stags:

Football League

Venue	P	W	D	L	F	A
Home	4	3	0	1	8	3
Away	4	2	2	0	7	5
Totals	8	5	2	1	15	8

FA Cup

Home	2	1	1	0	2	1
Away	3	0	1	2	3	5
Totals	5	1	2	2	5	6

WW2

Home	5	3	1	1	17	8
Away	5	1	1	3	9	14
Totals	10	4	2	4	26	22

Other

Home	1	1	0	0	1	0

Formed as Mansfield Wesleyans in 1897, the club took the title Mansfield Wesley in 1906 before becoming Mansfield Town in 1910...after the Mansfield Wesleyan Chapel trustees demanded that club change it's name as 'it has no longer had any connection with either the chapel or school.' The new club (Mansfield Town) participated in the Notts & Derby District League, then the Central Alliance before gaining membership of the Football League in 1931.

In 1979-80 the Blades doubled up with wins of 1-0 (h) and 4-3 (a) and they ran up another sound victory when winning a home Fourth Division game by 4-1 in 1981-82.

The Stags' only win over United was a surprise - a 2-1 scoreline at Bramall Lane in April 1989 when the Blades were pushing for promotion from Division Three.

After a 0-0 draw at Bramall Lane, a then record attendance at Field Mill - 20,374 (recs. £1,750) - saw the Stags beat the Blades 2-1 in a 4th round FA Cup replay in January 1951. Jack Fountain made his senior debut for the Blades. This was of course the first-ever meeting between the clubs.

The Blades first met the Stags in the League in season 1977-78 (Division 2). After a 1-1 draw at Field Mill United won the return fixture at Bramall Lane 2-0.

Another FA Cup-tie in 1968-69 resulted in a 2-1 victory for Mansfield in round 3 as they surged on towards the quarter-finals. Twenty years later the Blades gained their only Cup victory over the Field Mill side, winning a 1st round replay 2-1 at 'the Lane.'

Teddy Davison managed both the Blades and Mansfield; Jack Barke (WW1), Jack Poole (WW1) and Billy Dearden were all United players and later Stags' bosses; and Keith Curle, after leaving United became player-manager at Field Mill, assisted by ex-Blade John Gannon.

Of the many other players who served with both clubs down the years we have Gary Brazil, Michael Boulding, Steve Charles, Graeme Crawford, Ben Doane, Mel Eves, Ashley Fickling, David Frain, Paul Garner, Paul Holland, Walter Hoyland, Billy Hudson, Harry Johnson, Glyn Jones, David Kelly, Sam Kemp, Tony Kenworthy, Phil Kite, Dennis Longhorn, Ian Mackenzie, John Matthews, 'Iffy' Onuora, George Raynor (Blades reserve), John Reed, Alf Ringstead, Mark Todd and Imre Varadi.

MARCELO (Marcelo Cipriano Dos Santos)

Striker: 61+22 apps. 32 goals
Born: Niteroi, Brazil, 11 October 1969
Career: Benfica, Deportivo Alaves, BLADES (£400,000, October 1997), Birmingham City (£500,000, October 1999), Walsall (free transfer, February 2002).

A keen, enthusiastic, bustling striker, Marcelo was good in the air and at times caused problems for the bigger defenders on the ground. He had an excellent scoring record with the Blades, did a good job with Blues and then helped Walsall stave off relegation at the end of season 2001-02.

MARKER, Nicholas Robert Thomas

Defender/midfielder: 78+1 apps. 5 goals
Born: Budleigh Salterton, Devon, 3 May 1965
Career: Exeter City (apprentice, June 1981, professional May 1983), Plymouth Argyle (October 1987), Blackburn Rovers (September 1992), BLADES (£450,000, July 1997), Cheltenham Town (briefly, 1999), Tiverton Town (January 2000).

Nicky Marker was a gritty, determined, hard-working midfielder who at times dictated play very well, breaking up attacks with some timely inceptions before releasing a telling pass to his front men. He made 233 appearances for Plymouth and now lives in the Devon city.

MARSDEN, Christopher
Midfielder: 15+3 apps. one goal
Born: Sheffield, 3 January 1969
Career: BLADES (apprentice June 1985, professional January 1987), Huddersfield Town (July 1988), Coventry City (on loan, November 1993), Wolverhampton Wanderers (£250,000, January 1994), Notts County (£250,000, November 1994), Stockport County (£70,000, January 1996), Birmingham City (£500,000, October 1995), Southampton (£800,000, February 1998).
Midfielder Chris Marsden, with his shaven-head, developed into a no-nonsense competitor after leaving Bramall Lane. Referred to as 'the engine-room workhorse' he reached the personal milestone of 400 senior appearances during 2002. He was signed by his former Stockport boss Dave Jones for Southampton. He scored on his League debut for the Blades v. Blackburn Rovers (home) in August 1987 (won 3-1). He helped Saints reach the FA Cup v. Arsenal in 2003.

MARSHALL, Ernest
Wing-half: 16 apps.
Born: Dinnington, 23 May 1918. Died: 1983
Career: BLADES (professional, May 1935), Cardiff City (May 1939-47). Guested for Tottenham Hotspur during WW2.
Reserve wing-half Ernie Marshall spent four seasons at Bramall Lane during which time he managed only 13 first-team appearances. His career was obviously blighted by WW2 when he served in the armed forces. He played in the three void League games for Cardiff before the hostilities and in just one match in 1946 before leaving Ninian Park..

MARSHALL, Scott Roderick
Defender: 17 apps.
Born: Edinburgh, 1 May 1973
Career: Arsenal (YTS, June 1989, professional March 1991), Rotherham United (December 1993), BLADES (on loan, August-November 1994), Southampton (free transfer, August 1998), Brentford (£250,000, October 1999-May 2001).
Scott Marshall, a Scottish Youth and Under-21 international (five caps gained in the latter category) was signed on loan by the Blades at the start of the 1994-95 League season when a handful of players were injured including Paul Beesley. He suffered with hamstring and knee injuries during his time at The Dell and Griffin Park.

MARWOOD, Brian
Forward/winger: 17+10 apps. 3 goals
Born: Seaham Harbour, County Durham, 5 February 1960
Career: North-east Junior football, Seaham Secondary school, Hull City (apprentice, June 1976, professional, February 1978), Sheffield Wednesday (£115,000, August 1984), Arsenal (£600,000, March 1988), BLADES (£300,000, September 1990), Middlesbrough (October 1991), Swindon Town (non-contract, March 1993), Barnet (August 1993, retired January 1994). Later worked as a PFA representative and Sky Sport summariser.
Brian Marwood, capped once by England as an Arsenal player v. Saudi Arabia in 1989, was an incisive little player who always gave a good account of himself no matter what the circumstances or the opposition. He made 397 League appearances for his seven clubs and netted 98 goals. He helped the Gunners win the First Division championship and Mercantile Centenary Trophy in 1989.

MASON, Clifford Ernest
Left-back/forward: 109 apps. 2 goals
Born: York, 27 November 1929
Career: Sunderland (professional, January 1950), Darlington (July 1952), BLADES (£6,500, August 1955), Leeds United (March 1962), Scunthorpe United (February 1964), Chesterfield (July 1964-January 1965).
Signed initially as cover for Graham Shaw, Cliff Mason was not the fastest of defenders but he made up for his lack of pace with some splendid first-time tackling and excellent positional sense. He was used as an outside-right during the Blades promotion-campaign in 1960-61. He made 252 League appearances during his career.

MASTERMAN, Wallace
Inside-left: 92 apps. 32 goals
Born: Newcastle, 29 January 1888. Died: 1965
Career: Stockton FC, Gainsborough Trinity (May 1910), BLADES (June 1914), Stoke (January-May 1920).
Wallace Masterman was both hardworking and effective at inside-left during the 1914-15 season after taking over Billy Gillespie's role. He played very well in the Blades' FA Cup Final victory over Chelsea before WW1 disrupted his career, although he did appear in almost 50 games for the club during the hostilities. He was a reserve during his half-season with Stoke.

MATLOCK (TOWN)
The Derbyshire club were dismissed from the FA Cup in a 3rd qualifying round by United in November 1890. A crowd of 2,000 saw Bernard Shaw score twice in a 3-0 win at Bramall Lane.
In season 1895-96, Matlock finished bottom of the Midland Counties League, losing all 28 matches and conceding 130 goals.

MATTHEWS, John Barry
Outside-left: 15 apps. 3 goals
Born: Sheffield, 18 January 1926. Died: 1995.
Career: Birmingham University, BLADES (amateur, October 1943-December 1945), Lincoln City (amateur, October 1949), Corby Town (July 1952), Peterborough United (May 1953), Corby Town (June 1954), Spalding United (June 1955-May 1956).
A WW2 player with the Blades, Barry Matthews remained an amateur throughout his playing career. He was a draughtsman in a local Sheffield factory having been a student at the university.

MATTHEWS, John Melvin

Midfielder: 121+5 apps. 18 goals

Born: Camden Town, London, 1 November 1955

Career: Arsenal (apprentice, April 1972, professional August 1973), BLADES (£90,000, August 1978), Mansfield Town (August 1982), Chesterfield (free transfer, August 1984), Plymouth Argyle (free, August 1985), Torquay United (free, July 1989), Dorchester Town (July 1990-May 1991).

John Matthews was a long-striding, purposeful wing-half who, given the opportunity, could release a stunning right-foot shot. Perhaps a shade on the slow side, he refused to take that vital penalty against Walsall at the of the 1980-81 campaign, allowing Don Givens to step up, miss it and send the Blades down! Matthews helped the Blades take the Fourth Division title in 1981-82, the Stags win the Fourth Division championship in 1984-85 and Plymouth gain promotion from Division Three a year later.

MATTHEWS, Vincent

Centre-half: 141 apps. 3 goals

Born: Aylesbury, Bucks, 15 January 1896. Died: Oxford, 15 November 1950.

Career: St Frideswide FC (Aylesbury), Oxford City, Bournemouth & Boscombe Athletic (May 1920), Bolton Wanderers (January 1923), Tranmere Rovers (May 1925), BLADES (£2,300, July 1927), Shamrock Rovers (May 1931), Shrewsbury Town (June 1935), Oswestry Town (July 1936). He returned to Oxford in 1944 where he worked for Morris Motors at Cowley while also coaching locally and playing the odd game for the works football team.

Vince Matthews was a powerfully built centre-half who was something of a late developer, being rated as one of the best pivots in the game around the late 1920s. He made full use of his height and weight (6ft 1ins, 13st 4 lbs) and was essentially described as being a 'rugged performer'. He gained two England caps, lining up against France in Paris and Belgium in Antwerp in May 1928 when he had his club colleague George Green alongside him in the half-back line. He spent four years at Bramall Lane and was still involved in the game he enjoyed when he died at the age of 54.

MATTHEWSON, Reginald

Defender: 173+3 apps. 5 goals

Born: Sheffield, 6 August 1939.

Career: Sheffield Boys, BLADES (juniors, August 1955, professional August 1958), Fulham (£30,000, February 1968), Chester City (January 1973-May 1976, then coach), Bangor City (player-coach, seasons 1978-80), Shrewsbury Town (assistant-manager/coach, season 1980-81), Wrexham (coach, 1981-82). He left football to take up an operative job at Ellesmere Port.

Reg Matthewson was a reliable, compact, stern defender who took over initially from Gerry Summers, then moved into the middle in place of Joe Shaw before an injury let in Ken Mallender. He made his Blades League debut against his future club at Craven Cottage in March 1962 and was given the run-around by Maurice Cook who scored a hat-trick in his side's 5-2 win. He went on to play in 174 games for Fulham, helping them gain promotion from the Third Division in 1971.

171

MEDAL WINNERS

During his playing career, Scottish international winger Jimmy Johnstone gained 29 club medals with Celtic (20 were winners' prizes, nine runners-up).

Ian Rush collected a total of 28 medals with Liverpool (17 winners, 11 runners-up), while Rush's Anfield club colleague, Phil Thompson, gained 18 winners medals and four runners-up prizes during his career with the Merseysiders. Both Rush's and Thompson's tallies including Charity Shield victories.

MELLOR, William

Left-back/right-half: 6 apps.

Born: Lancashire circa 1868

Career: Heywood Central, BLADES (June 1892), Sheffield Wednesday (June 1893), Loughborough Town (May 1895-May 1896).

A reserve defender throughout his League career, Bill Mellor made just one appearance for the Owls and three for Loughborough.

MELLORS, Mark

Goalkeeper: one app.

Born: Basford, Notts, 30 April 1890. Died: 1961

Career: Carrington FC, Nottingham Forest (on trial, May 1900), Bulwell United, Notts County (September 1902), Brighton & Hove Albion (1904), BLADES (August 1906), Bradford City (March 1909, retired May 1918).

Reserve goalkeeper Mark Mellors made his League debut for the Blades against Arsenal in February 1908, deputising for Joe Lievesley. He later appeared in 82 competitive games for Bradford.

MENDONCA, Clive Paul

Forward: 13+15 apps. 5 goals
Born: Islington, London, 9 September 1968
Career: BLADES (apprentice, June 1984, professional September 1986), Doncaster Rovers (on loan, February 1988), Rotherham United (£35,000, March 1988), BLADES (£114,000, July 1991), Grimsby Town (on loan, January 1992, signed permanently for £85,000, August 1992), Charlton Athletic (£700,000, May 1997, retired through injury May 2001).
Clive Mendonca was a consistent goalscorer for the Blades junior team but failed to do the business when promoted to the first XI...and he even struggled to find his form when he returned for second spell at 'the Lane.' But elsewhere he found the net regularly, scoring 31 goals in 102 games for the Millermen, 66 in 187 outings for the Mariners and 45 in 96 appearances for Charlton, who he helped win the First Division championship in 2000, having earlier been a key member of the Addicks side that reached the Premiership via the Play-offs in 1998.

MENLOVE, Bertram

Centre-forward/inside-left: 81 apps. 41 goals
Born: St Albans, 8 December 1892. Died: 1970
Career: Barnet Alston FC, Aston Villa (briefly, 1919), Crystal Palace (May 1920), BLADES (£2,000, March 1922), Boston Town (March 1926), Aldershot (1927), Worksop Town (on trial), Bangor City (1928), Clapton Orient (August 1929), Coleraine (season 1930-31).
Bertie Menlove was a thoughtful, calculating player who was signed as cover for Harry Johnson whom he eventually partnered up front before struggling with injuries.

MERCER, Arthur Stanley

Inside-right: 39 apps. 15 goals
Born: St Helens, 1903. Died: 1994.
Career: Parr St Peter's FC, Wigan Borough (May 1921), Bury (1925), BLADES (October 1926), Rhyl Athletic (December 1927), Connah's Quay, Bristol City (1930), Chester (1931), Halifax Town (1932), Dartford (1934), Rhyl Athletic (1936).
Arthur Mercer had notched 20 goals in 50 League games for his two previous clubs before joining the Blades.
Mercer made 133 League appearances and scored 34 goals after leaving Bramall Lane.
* Brother of David William Mercer (q.v) and uncle to Arthur jnr (ex-Torquay United: 1946-49), he and his brother were regular right-wing partners for the Blades during the 1926-27 season.

MERCER, David William

Outside/inside-right: 250 apps. 22 goals
Born: St Helens, 20 March 1893.
Died: Torquay, 4 June 1950.
Career: Prescot Athletic (Liverpool County Combination), Skelmersdale, Hull City (January 1914), BLADES (record £4,250, December 1920), Shirebrook (July 1928), Torquay United (May 1929, announcing his retirement in May 1930).
David Mercer was a mercurial inside-right who twinkled in the colours of both Hull City and Sheffield United. His craft and cleverness at times was superb and many defenders were bamboozled as he skipped past them to send over teasing crosses. He won his spurs as an out-and-out winger during WW1 when his dazzling footwork was seen to best advantage. Indeed, he made over 200 consecutive appearances for the Tigers over a four-year period commencing with his debut on 18 April 1914 and ending on 2 April 1920. In one fixture - played in early January 1919 - he scored all of the Tigers' six goals against the Blades before the match was abandoned due to fading light after 70 minutes play.
He obviously impressed the Blades - and after maintaining his form he duly moved from Anlaby Road (Hull) to Bramall Lane in 1920...just six months after touring South Africa with the FA (playing in one game against the South African National XI). He quickly became a firm favourite with the Blades' fans, despite showing an initial lack of confidence at a higher level. However, his form improved dramatically when partnered by Tommy Sampy and he went on to gain two full caps for England, appearing against Ireland in October 1922 and Belgium in March 1923, scoring in the latter match that ended in a 6-1 win. Two years later he celebrated again, this time with an FA Cup winners medal after helping United beat Cardiff City at Wembley. After retiring he lived and worked in Torquay until his death in 1950.
* Brother of Arthur Mercer, whom he partnered at Bramall Lane and father of Arthur junior who played for Torquay United from 1946-49.

MERCER, William

Goalkeeper: 4 apps.

Born: Liverpool, 22 May 1969

Career: Liverpool (apprentice, June 1985, professional August 1987), Rotherham United (February 1989), BLADES (£75,000, October 1994), Chesterfield (£93,000, September 1995), Bristol City (£300,000, October 1999, later coach at Ashton Gate).

Groomed at Anfield (as understudy to Bruce Grobbelaar) Billy Mercer made 138 senior appearances for Rotherham before becoming reserve to at Bramall Lane. He later played in another 174 games for Chesterfield (whom he captained several times) prior to linking up with Bristol City where he was voted 'Player of the Season' in 2000.

MIDDLESBROUGH

United's playing record against 'Boro:

Premier League

Venue	P	W	D	L	F	A
Home	1	1	0	0	2	0
Away	1	0	0	1	0	2
Totals	2	1	0	1	2	2

Football League

Home	44	24	10	10	74	43
Away	44	13	9	22	55	92
Totals	88	37	19	32	129	137

FA Cup

Home	1	1	0	0	3	0
Away	1	0	1	0	1	1
Totals	2	1	1	0	4	1

Northern League

Home	2	1	0	1	3	4
Away	2	1	0	1	3	3
Totals	4	2	0	2	6	7

WW2

Home	1	0	0	1	2	7
Away	1	1	0	0	4	3
Totals	2	1	0	1	6	10

Other

Home	1	0	0	1	0	1

Middlesbrough, formed in 1875 by members of the town's cricket club at a meeting in a gymnasium of the Albert Park Hotel, twice lifted the FA Amateur Cup before gaining entry to the Second Division of the Football League in 1899, winning promotion to the top flight in 1902 behind the champions West Bromwich Albion.

Their first League game against United took place at Linthorpe Road in November 1902, the Blades winning 2-0, but later in the season 'Boro gained revenge with a 3-1 victory at 'the Lane.'

United's best League win over 'Boro was in 1921-22 when, thanks to a Harry Johnson treble, they cruised home 6-1 at 'the Lane.' Two years previously Joe Kitchen had bagged a hat-trick in a 5-1 win, also at 'the Lane.'

United - after taking an early lead - crashed to an embarrassing 10-3 defeat at Middlesbrough on 18 November 1933 - their heaviest League defeat in terms of goals conceded.

Mick Fenton scored five goals in Middlesbrough's 7-2 victory over the Blades at Bramall Lane in January 1946 (WW2).

Although 'Boro gained automatic promotion in 1997-98 (losing just twice at home) the Blades were the only team to take all six points off the Teesiders, winning 2-1 at The Riverside Stadium in October and 1-0 at Bramall Lane in April as they pressed for a Play-off spot.

The clubs have been paired together just once in the FA Cup, United winning a 2nd round tie 3-0 (after a replay) in 1922-23.

Bruce Rioch played for the Blades and managed Middlesbrough while Reg Freeman played for 'Boro and managed United.

Jack Alderson, Peter Beagrie, Joe Bolton, Billy Brawn, Arthur Brown, Andy Campbell, the country's first £1,000 footballer Alf Common, Brian Deane, Andy Dibble (United reserve), Peter Duffield, Willie Falconer, George Featherstone, Jan-Aage Fjortoft, John Gannon, Dean Glover, Bert Groves, Willie Hamilton, George Hedley (with South Bank), Chris Kamara, Phil Kite, Brian Marwood, Tom Morren, Fred Priest, Alan Roberts, John Tudor ('Boro reserve), Ronnie Waldock, George Waller, Dean Windass all served with both clubs as players.

MIDDLESBROUGH IRONOPOLIS

Blades' playing record against Ironopolis:

North League

Venue	P	W	D	L	F	A
Home	2	0	2	0	2	2
Away	2	0	0	2	1	3
Totals	4	0	2	2	3	5

A League club for a short time, Ironopolis were defeated by United 5-1 in a friendly match in September 1891. This was the first game in which linesmen were used instead of umpires.

After that there were four games played in the Northern League with Ironopolis coming out on top overall.

Tom Morren and Alex Wallace played for both clubs.

MIDLAND COUNTIES LEAGUE

United participated in the MCL in season 1890-91. They finished 5th with this record:

P	W	D	L	F	A	Pts
18	8	3	7	32	25	19

United completed the double over Kidderminster Harriers before they resigned from the League; their results being expunged, They also beat Warwick County at home, but this club failed to complete its programme.

United's biggest MCL win of the eight achieved was 5-0 at home to Staveley in April 1891. They also beat Derby Midland 5-2 away. Their heaviest defeat, 4-1, was suffered at Gainsborough Trinity in early November. They also lost 3-1 at Burslem Port Vale.

Billy Bridgewater registered nine goals to finish up as top-scorer.

MILLS, Henry

Centre-forward: 3 apps. 2 goals

Born: Bishop Auckland, County Durham, 23 July 1922

Career: Consett, BLADES (professional, June 1946), Rotherham United (March 1948), Tunbridge Wells (May 1948), Rochdale (April 1951), Halifax Town (August 1952-April 1953).

Reserve centre-forward Harry Mills scored on his Football League debut for the Blades v. Sunderland (away) in March 1947 and netted again in his second match at Bolton. However, he failed to establish himself in the side and moved to Millmoor in 1948.

MILLWALL (Athletic)

United's playing record against the Lions:

Football League

Venue	P	W	D	L	F	A
Home	18	10	3	5	32	22
Away	18	5	3	10	16	26
Totals	36	15	6	15	48	48

FA Cup

Home	1	1	0	0	3	1
Away	1	1	0	0	4	0
Totals	2	2	0	0	7	1

League Cup

Away	1	0	0		2	3

Formed in 1885 by employees of a jam and marmalade factory in West Ferry Road called Morton & Co, Millwall Rovers had its first headquarters in the Islanders Pub in Tooke Street, Millwall. The first trophy won was London's East End Cup in 1887. Two years later the name Rovers was replaced by Athletic and in 1985 the club became known as Millwall (Football & Athletic Company).

Playing at The Den (Cold Blow Lane, their home since 1910) Millwall did exceedingly well in the Southern League before gaining entry to the Football League in 1920. But it wasn't until mid-October 1937 that the 'Lions' first met the Blades in this competition. United, eager to regain their top flight status, won 2-1 at Bramall Lane but they weren't so lucky in London, losing the return fixture 4-0 down Cold Blow Lane!

United's best win of the 14 so far recorded against the Lions at League level is 5-2 in a Second Division fixture in 1977-78 (Bobby Campbell scored twice).

United have not avoided defeat on Millwall territory since 1983.

The teams first opposed each other in the FA Cup in February 1895 when United won a 1st round tie 3-1. The second meeting took place in February 1914 when this time the Blades carved out a 4-0 third round victory in London.

Millwall's current home (occupied since 1993) is The New Den, on Zampa Rod, Bermondsey, SE16.

Herbert Lipsham, an ex-United player, was Millwall's first 'professional and full-time manager; Bruce Rioch also played for the Blades and managed the Lions, likewise Alan McLeary (Lions joint-manager). Other Blades' players who also served with the Lions include Jack Almond, Peter Anderson (also Lions manager), Mark Beard, Kingsley Black, Richard Cadette, Joe Davies, Aidan Davison, Scott Fitzgerald, Mark Foran, Chris Guthrie, Robert Humphries (United reserve), Nicky Johns, Hugh Morris, Colin Rawson, Jock Smith, Tony Towner, Dave Tuttle, Carl Veart and Mike Whelan.

MILNES, Frederick Houghton

Full-back: 12 apps.

Born: Wortley, 26 January 1878.

Career: Sheffield Wycliffe FC, Sheffield FC (from 1896), BLADES (four separate spells as an amateur, March-April 1903, November 1903, April-October 1904 & March 1905), West Ham United (October 1904), Tottenham Hotspur (March 1905), Manchester United (March 1906), Leicester Fosse (February 1907), Pilgrims FC (April-August 1907), Reading (briefly), Ilford (July 1908), Norwich City (September 1908, retired May 1909).

Fred Milnes was a classy amateur international full-back whose primary allegiance was to the long-established Sheffield club for whom he scored a vital penalty in their 1904 FA Amateur Cup Final victory. However, he was always willing to lend his assistance on a non-contract basis to almost any senior club who asked, turning down many others because of prior commitments. He toured Canada and the USA with the Pilgrims (an amateur combination) in 1907.

MILTON, Ernest

Left-back: 271 apps. 44 goals

Born: Kimberworth, 7 August 1897. Died: Sheffield, 1984

Career: Parkgate Christ Church FC, BLADES (January 1917, retired May 1927),

Fair-haired Ernest Milton joined the Blades towards the end of WW1 after playing local football for a church side. He spent more than nine years at Bramall Lane before an ankle injury ended his career in 1926. An FA Cup winner in 1925, Milton was a steady defender, full of energy whose distribution was not brilliant.

* Two of Ernest Milton's brothers were also left-backs: Albert with Barnsley, Sunderland and Swindon Town and Alfred with Rotherham County, Coventry City and Gillingham.

MITCHELL, Joseph Thomas
Goalkeeper: 44 apps.
Born: Darnall, 1 January 1886. Died: 1964
Career: Darnall Congregationalists FC, Thorpe Hesley FC, BLADES (April1908), Luton Town (February 1913), South Shields (1919), Coventry City (February 1920), Chesterfield (December 1920), Barnsley (season 1922-23).
Signed initially as reserve to Joe Lievesley, goalkeeper Joe Mitchell made only a handful of senior appearances in his first two years at 'the Lane' but always performed well, and did even better during a prolonged run in the side following an injury to Lievesley (1912-13).

MONTGOMERY, Nicholas Anthony
Midfielder: 50+33 apps* 3 goals*
Born: Leeds, 28 October 1981
Career: BLADES (trainee, July 1998, professional July 2000).
Nick Montgomery had a tremendous 2002-03 season as the Blades' competitive, hard-working box-to-box midfielder. Full of energy, he was a great companion to Michael Brown in the engine-room as the Blades reached two major Cup semi-finals and the First Division Play-offs. He is currently lying second in the list of United players with most substitute appearances (behind Petr Katchoura whose overall and final tally for the Blades was 57)

MOONEY, Thomas John
Midfielder: 4+2 apps. one goal
Born: Billingham, 11 August 1971
Career: Aston Villa (trainee, July 1987, professional November 1989), Scarborough (free transfer, August 1990), Southend United (£100,000, July 1993), Watford (March 1994), Birmingham City (free transfer, July 2001), Stoke City (on loan, September-December 2002), BLADES (on loan, February-March 2003). He was released from St Andrew's in May 2003.
A hard-running, hard-working industrious midfielder, Tommy Mooney certainly adds impetus and competitiveness to a team. He failed to get into Villa's first XI, but thereafter netted 40 goals in 129 games for Scarborough, five in 21 for Southend, 65 in 288 games for the Hornets and 15 in 38 for Blues whom he helped gain promotion to the Premiership in 2002 before his brief association with the Potters. His only for the Blades came in the 2-0 win over Walsall in the round of the in February 2003, a fortnight after his debut v. Millwall in the League.

MOORE, Anthony Peter
Full-back: 33 apps.
Born: Wolverhampton, 19 September 1957
Career: Burton Albion, BLADES (July 1979), Crewe Alexandra (August 1982), Worksop Town (March 1983), Rochdale (non-contract, October 1984).
A defender, Tony Moore played at right-back in place of John Cutbush when called into the Blades' first XI. He had four outings during the 1981-82 Fourth Division championship season of 1981-82.

MOREMONT, Ralph
Centre-half: 2 apps.
Born: Sheffield, 24 September 1924. Died: 1982.
Career: Hampton's Sports FC, BLADES (professional September 1946), Chester (May 1950), Rochdale (August-November 1955).
A reserve defender, surprisingly Ralph Moremont made his Football League debut for the Blades at centre-forward against Grimsby Town in an away Second Division match in February 1950, helping his side win 3-1. He scored 19 goals in 121 Third Division North games for Chester.

MORREN, Thomas
Centre-half: 190 apps. 6 goals
Born: Middlesbrough, 1875. Died: 31 January 1929
Career: Middlesbrough Vulcan, Middlesbrough Ironopolis, Middlesbrough,, BLADES (November 1895); retiring in May 1904, he took over a newsagents' shop the Hunters Bar area of Sheffield which he ran until his death in 1929 after a short illness.
Tommy Morren was Middlesbrough's centre-half when they won the Amateur Cup in 1895 and four years later he lined up in the same position for Sheffield United when they lifted the FA Cup. He also appeared for the Blades in the 1901 FA Cup Final defeat by Spurs and was a League championship winner at Bramall Lane in 1898.
He was all set to sign for Reading and, in fact, was on his way down to there when he was somehow persuaded to get off the train, discuss terms and sign for the Blades in 1895. Morren was only just over 5ft 5ins tall - one of the smallest defenders of his era - but despite his size he was mighty effective, always in the thick of the action and generally gave some sterling displays for the Blades. On the debit side, however, he was criticised at times for straying out of position although it could not be denied that he was a rare worrier to the opposition when he did drive forward from his defensive duties.
He made his first team debut for the Blades in a friendly against the Corinthians on 27 December 1895 when he lined up alongside Ernie Needham.

175

MORRIS, Colin

Winger: 280+7 apps. 84 goals
Born: Blyth, 22 August 1953
Career: Burnley (apprentice, August 1969,
professional August 1971), Southend United
(January 1977), Blackpool (December 1979),
BLADES (£100,000, February 1982),
Scarborough (July 1988-May 1989).
A very skilful two-footed winger, a huge
favourite with the Bramall Lane faithful, Colin
Morris took, scored and missed more penalties
than any other United player in the club's
history...and he never shirked responsibility
when a spot-kick was awarded. With a bit
more eagerness and commitment he could well
have been a class performer. He made only 11
appearances during his eight years at Turf Moor
but quickly made up for lost time by scoring
30 goals in 156 League & Cup outings for the
Shrimpers. His career realised a total of 582
competitive appearances and 149 goals. He
helped the Blades win the Fourth Division title
in 1982. Prior to Michael Brown's tally in
2003, Morris had been the last United midfield
player to score over 20 goals in a season, doing
so in 1985-86.

MORRIS, Hugh

Inside-forward/winger: 41 apps. 9 goals
Born: Chirk, 1872. Died: Chirk, 20 September1897.
Career: Chirk (July 1889), Ardwick (May 1891), BLADES (December 1893), Manchester City (November 1895), Grimsby Town
(May 1896), Millwall Athletic (May 1897 until his demise).
Welsh international Hugh Morris was an industrious little forward with one reporter describing him as 'an exceedingly clever player'
when performing for Chirk, while another said that he had the tendency to 'pass to and fro when a well aimed shot was needed.' He
was a Welsh Cup winner in 1890 before making his League debut with Ardwick in 1892. He had two useful seasons at Bramall Lane
before returning to Manchester. He died of tuberculosis at the young age of 25.

MORRIS, Lee

Forward: 16+18 apps. 8 goals
Born: Blackpool, 30 April 1980
Career: BLADES (apprentice, June 1996, professional, December 1997), Derby County (£1.8 million, June 1999), Huddersfield Town
(on loan, March-April 2001).
England Youth and Under-21 international Lee Morris,son of Colin Morris, a left-sided striker who can also operate as an attacking
midfielder, struggled to make an impact due to injuries at Bramall Lane but after a slow start at Derby, he developed into a very useful
player with the ability to ghost past defenders. He scored on his debut for Huddersfield.

MORRIS, Mark John

Defender: 66+3 apps. 4 goals
Born: Carshalton, Surrey, 26 September 1962.
Career: Wimbledon (apprentice, June 1978, professional September 1980), Aldershot (on loan, September 1985), Watford (July 1987),
BLADES (£175,000, July 1989), Bournemouth (£95,000, July 1991), Gillingham (on loan, September 1996), Brighton & Hove
Albion (October 1996), Hastings United (December 1997), Dorchester Town (February 1999-2003).
Central defender Mark Morris - a Fourth Division championship winner in 1983 - made 168 League appearances for the Dons and
194 for the Cherries, amassing a total of in the competition all told for his seven clubs (23 goals scored). Strong, enthusiastic and a
hard-tackler, he took over from Brian Smith in the Blades' line-up following promotion to the First Division in 1989.

MORRISON, Andrew Charles

Centre-half: 3+1 apps.
Born: Inverness, 30 July 1970
Career: Plymouth Argyle (apprentice, July 1986, professional July 1988), Blackburn Rovers (£500,000, August 1993), Blackpool
(£245,000, December 1994), Huddersfield town (£500,000, July 1996), Manchester City (£80,000, October 1998), Blackpool (on
loan, September 2000), Crystal Palace (on loan, October 2000), BLADES (on loan, March-April 2001). Forced to retire with a serious
knee injury, March 2002.
Andy Morrison (6ft tall and 14st 8lbs in weight) was a solid, uncompromising central defender who was resolute, particularly strong in
the air and a great motivator. He accumulated 310 senior appearances and scored 18 goals during his 16-year career.

MORRISON, Owen
Midfielder: 3+5 apps.
Born: Londonderry, Northern Ireland, 8 December 1981
Career Sheffield Wednesday (apprentice, April 1998, professional January 1999), BLADES (signed on short-term contract, February-March 2003)
Capped by his country at Schoolboy, Youth and Under-21 levels, left-sided midfielder Owen Morrison - very popular with the Owls' supporters - joined the Blades, on loan, after a rather disappointing 18 months at Hillsborough during which time he was badly affected by injury.

MORTIMER, Dennis George
Midfielder: 7 apps.
Born: Liverpool, 5 April 1952.
Career: Kirby Boys, Coventry City (apprentice July 1967, professional September 1969), Aston Villa (£175,000 December 1975), BLADES (on loan, December 1984), Brighton & Hove Albion (August 1985), Birmingham City (August 1986), Kettering Town (non-contract, August 1987), Redditch United (player-manager, late 1987-October 1988), West Bromwich Albion (casual reserve team player & Community Officer, August 1989, Youth-team manager 1992, assistant-manager June 1993 to October 1994), Aston Villa (Academy/Youth team coach, late 1990s).
An excellent midfield player with drive, determination, loads of skill and the will to win, Dennis Mortimer first shot to prominence with Coventry when his hair was so long that the fans called him Doris! After moving to Villa Park he became a vital member of Ron Saunders' side which won the League Cup in 1977, the Football League championship in 1981 and both the European Cup and Super Cup in 1982, making more than 400 appearances for the Birmingham-based club (36 goals) Capped by England six times as a youth player, 'Morty' also played in three 'B' & six Under-23 internationals and in 1971 he toured Australia with the FA party.

MOSFORTH, William
Outside-left: 9 apps. 4 goals
Born: Sheffield, 1868. Died: 1929
Career: BLADES (September 1889-May 1890).
Blades' first left-winger who played in the club's opening fixture against Nottingham Rangers on 7 September 1889. He made 28 appearances for the first XI in his only season at 'the Lane' (nine at competitive level). He was replaced in the team by Arthur Watson.

MUNKS, David
Defender: 124+5 apps. 2 goals
Born: Sheffield, 29 April 1947
Career: Sheffield Boys & Yorkshire Schools, BLADES (apprentice, June 1962, professional, April 1964), Portsmouth (May 1969), Swindon Town (December 1973), Exeter City (December 1974-May 1976).
An England Youth international (capped against Belgium, Spain and Scotland in 1965), David Munks had an excellent career, appearing in more than 300 League & Cup games for his four clubs. After recovering from a broken leg suffered against Highbury in November 1965, he went on to give the Blades excellent service before doing likewise at Fratton Park

177

MURPHY, Shaun Peter
Centre-half: 181+1 apps* 12 goals*
Born: Sydney, Australia, 5 November 1970
Career: Perth Italia, Notts County (September 1992), West Bromwich Albion (£500,000, December 1996), BLADES (free transfer, July 1999), Crystal Palace (on loan, February-May 2002).
Honoured by Australia at Youth & Under-23 levels, the raven-haired Shaun Murphy went on to gain more than 20 full caps for his country as a bold, resilient and reliable centre-half who formed a great partnership alongside Robert Page at the heart of the Blades' defence, the pair playing particularly well for most of the 2002-03 when the Blades reached two Cup semi-finals and finished third in the First Division. Unfortunately he missed all three Play-off games owing to his wife's illness. Prior to moving to Bramall Lane, Murphy had made 135 appearances for Notts County and 78 for WBA.

NAMES

Shortest

The player with the shortest name (including his Christian name) to have served with the Blades at senior level is Henry Orr (8 letters) in 1958-64.

Other short-named players include Michael ASH (1960-65), Marcelle CAS (2002-03), Albert EH COX (1935), Mervyn Richard DAY (1991), Geoffrey DEY (1980), Jostein FLO (1993-95), Michael James GUY (1978-79), David John LEE (1997), Kenneth LEE (1942) and Reginald PYE (1917).

There was a player named (Christian name not known) FOX registered with the club in 1893

Longest

The player with the longest surname to have served the club is

Keith Frank KETTLEBOROUGH (13 letters). Adding on his two Christian names, his overall name contains 23 letters.

Charles William WEATHERSPOON (26 letters) played in one Football League games to the Blades in 1951.

Name Game

* Mark Hooper played for Sheffield Wednesday v. WBA in the 1935 FA Cup Final and Harry Hooper (no relation) played for United v. Arsenal in the Final a year later.

* Smith and Jones were aliases for two Scottish players used by the Blades in a friendly against Rotherham Town in November 1889.

* Over the course of time a total of ten players with the surname of Smith have appeared for the Blades in senior League and/or competitive matches. There have been over 20 represent the club at all levels. In contrast there have been 10 players named Jones and eleven with the name of Thompson.

* Two players with a double-barrelled surname have served with United: Dr James Brown-Sim in 1908 and Donald S Watt-Smith 1939.

NEAVE, Robert A

Centre-half: 11 apps.

Born: Lochee, Scotland, 23 May 1894. Died: 1951

Career: Glasgow Perthshire, BLADES (April 1912), Chesterfield (March 1913), Rochdale (1914-15), Kilmarnock (1919-20), Johnstone FC (Perth), Helensburgh (1923-24).

A 5'6"or 5'7" defender, signed as cover by the Blades for the 1912-13 season, Bob Neave failed to bed in at Bramall Lane, nor indeed with his two other Football League clubs and after WW1 returned to his native Scotland.

NDLOVU, Peter

Forward: 99+16 apps* 20 goals*

Born: Bulawayo, Zimbabwe, 25 February 1973

Career: Highlanders FC/Zimbabwe (1989), Coventry City (£10,000, August 1991), Birmingham City (£1.6 million, July 1997), Huddersfield Town (on loan, December 2000), BLADES (free transfer, February 2001).

A Zimbabwean international (16 full caps gained, Peter Ndlovu did very well at Highfield Road, scoring 41 goals 197 senior appearances before moving to St Andrew's in 1997. During his three years with Blues he enjoyed playing wide on the left (and even the right). He has always given defenders plenty to think about with his electrifying pace, ball skills and work-rate although injuries have interrupted his game over at times. He had an excellent 2002-03 season as the Blades qualified for two Cup semi-finals and reached the First Division Play-off Final v. Wolves which sadly ended in defeat. His skill down the flank certainly caused plenty of experienced defenders to work overtime in trying to contain him.

NEEDHAM, Archibald

Inside-forward: 16 apps. 6 goals

Born: Sheffield, August 1881. Died: Sussex, 1950

Career: Sheffield Schools, BLADES (August 1901), Crystal Palace (July 1905), Glossop North End (June 1909), Wolverhampton Wanderers (August 1910), Brighton & Hove Albion (July 1911-May 1915). Did not re-appear after WW1.

A forceful player with strong right-foot shot, Archie Needham played alongside his brother Jack at Molineux (season 1910-11). He spent four years at Bramall Lane, during which time he never really commanded a regular position in the side despite his enthusiasm. He scored 12 goals in 31 League games for Glossop and six in 32 for Wolves. He was no relation to Ernest Needham (q.v).

NEEDHAM, Ernest

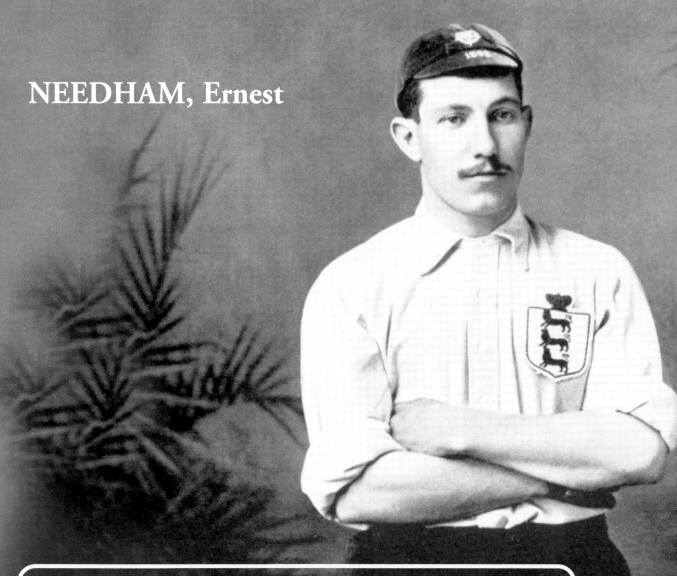

Left-half: 554 apps. 65 goals

Born: Newbold Moor, Chesterfield, 21 January 1873. Died: Staveley (Derbyshire), 8 March 1936.

Career: Staveley Wanderers, Staveley FC, BLADES (April 1891, retiring in April 1913 after 22 years dedicated service on the field). He later did much work behind the scenes for United and also scouted for the club (on a part-time basis).

Ernest 'Nudger' Needham made his Football League debut for the Blades in November 1920, in a 2-0 win over Notts County. He quickly made his mark and remained as United's left-half for 20 years, earning the title 'The Prince of Half-backs.' He was also a very useful cricketer, scoring 6,375 runs (including seven 100s) for Derbyshire between 1901-12. For eight years (from April 1894 to March 1902) he was a regular on the international scene, winning 16 full caps (six against Scotland), scoring three goals (all v. Wales)...and was the first United player to captain his country. He also appeared in six Inter-League games as well as gaining First Division championship and two FA Cup winners' medals (in 1898, 1899 & 1902 respectively) while also appearing in the 1901 Final against Spurs. Short and solid, he had great endurance and combined stamina and pace with pluck and determination. His advice was simple: 'Keep your eye on your opponent, but keep him outside.' One of United's greatest-ever players due to his achievements.

* In 1973, on the 100th anniversary of Needham's birth, an article in the Sheffield Morning Telegraph said this about the great man: 'Needham was acknowledged far and wide as a very special footballer...Praise was heaped upon him at a time when superlatives (like the Welfare State) were unthought of, long before the personality cult came in, and in an age when sporting journalists used adjectives as sparingly as a miser spends his pennies...It took an extraordinary man to inspire a flood of unrestrained praise, and Needham was an extraordinary man...He was modest off the field and a warrior on it; a gritty performer...Needham, a 30 bob-a-week only in 1891 when he signed, later he was paid £4 a week (plus bonuses) footballer, he didn't drink and for many years he was projected as thee ideal model for any young man with sporting ambitions...He was an unusual man, a sterling character with the sportsman's essential urge to win...But he was a thinker, too, and actually wrote a book on football, though typically, in it he said little about his own remarkable talents."

NELSON

The Blades never encountered Nelson at competitive level.
Players who served with both clubs include Ted Connor, Hugh Gallacher, Derek Hawksworth, Harry Hooper, Bernie Radford and Jack Smith. Jack English played for the Blades and later managed Nelson.

NELSON, George

Inside-forward: 24 'other' apps.
Born: Mexborough, Yorkshire, 5 February 1925
Career: Sheffield Wednesday (amateur, 1942), Denaby Rovers, BLADES (August 1943), Dundee (WW2 guest, 1945-46), Lincoln City (September 1946-May 1948).
A WW2 player at Bramall Lane, George Nelson rejected a professional contract with both the Blades and Dundee. He served in the Royal Navy during the war. His only League game was for Lincoln against Brighton in November 1946.

NEUTRAL GROUNDS

The Blades have played several major competitive and, indeed, foreign/tour and friendly matches on a neutral ground. Here is a list of some of them:

Date	Opposition	Competition	Venue	Result
12.03.1889	Casuals	Fr	The Oval	lost 1-0
17.03.1890	Staveley	WCC SF	Chesterfield	won 2-1
22.03.1890	Rotherham Town	SCC F/r	Rotherham Swifts	lost 1-0
21.03.1891	Royal Arsenal	Fr	The Oval	drew 1-1
31.10.1891	Casuals	Fr	The Oval	lost 3-0
27.02.1892	Kilnhurst	SCC SF	Carbrook	won 4-0
31.03.1892	Attercliffe	WCC	The Grove	won 2-0
10.11.1892	Casuals	Fr	Leyton	won 2-1
09.02.1893	Grimsby Town	CM	Hull	won 2-0
22.04.1893	Accrington	Test Match	Trent Bridge	won 1-0
24.03.1894	Corinthians	Fr	Queen's Club	lost 4-1
12.04.1894	Casuals	Fr	Leyton	won 3-0
23.03.1895	Corinthians	Fr	Leyton	won 2-1
18.01.1896	Old Carthusians	Fr	Crystal Palace	won 2-0
21.03.1896	Corinthians	Fr	Queen's Club	won 4-0
25.03.1896	Devon XI	Fr	Plymouth	won 4-1
25.04.1896	Walsall	LMC	Perry Barr	lost 1-0
22.09.1986	Notts County	Fr	Fartown (Hudd'fld)	lost 1-0
28.11.1896	Corinthians	Fr	Queen's Club	drew 0-0
27.04.1897	Sheppey Utd	Fr	Sheerness	won 4-1
30.04.1897	Comb Suffolk XI	Fr	Lowestoft	won 4-1
27.11.1897	Corinthians	Fr	Queen's Club	lost 2-0
19.03.1898	Corinthians	SL Shield	Crystal Palace	drew 0-0
04.04.1898	Corinthians	SLS replay	Crystal Palace	drew 1-1
18.03.1899	Liverpool	FAC SF	The City Ground	drew 2-2
23.03.1899	Liverpool	FAC SF rep	Burnden Park	drew 4-4
27.03.1899	Liverpool	FAC SF 2 rep	Fallowfield	Abandoned
30.03.1899	Liverpool	FAC SF 2 rep	Baseball Ground	won 1-0
15.04.1899	Derby County	FAC Final	Crystal Palace	won 4-1
16.04.1900	Corinthians	Fr	Crystal Palace	won 4-0
11.04.1901	South Wales XI	Fr	Cardiff	won 2-0
06.04.1901	Aston Villa	FAC SF	The City Ground	drew 2-2
11.04.1901	Aston Villa	FAC SF rep	Derby	won 3-0
20.04.1901	Tottenham Hotspur	FAC Final	Crystal Palace	drew 2-2
27.04.1901	Tottenham Hotspur	FAC Final rep	Burnden Park	lost 3-1
15.03.1902	Derby County	FAC SF	The Hawthorns	drew 1-1
20.03.1902	Derby County	FAC SF rep	Molineux	drew 1-1
27.03.1902	Derby County	FAC SF 2 rep	The City Ground	won 1-0
19.04.1902	Southampton	FAC Final	Crystal Palace	drew 1-1
26.04.1902	Southampton	FAC Final rep	Crystal Palace	won 2-1
06.04.1903	West Yorks XI	Fr	Valley Parade	won 8-5
29.04.1903	Leeds Assoc XI	Fr	Holbeck Rugby C	won 7-2
16.04.1914	Manchester City	FAC Rd 4,2 r	Villa Park	won 1-0
28.03.1914	Burnley	FAC SF	Old Trafford	drew 0-0
01.04.1914	Burnley	FAC SF rep	Goodison Park	lost 1-0
27.03.1915	Bolton Wds	FAC SF	Ewood Park	won 2-1
24.04.1915	Chelsea	FAC Final	Old Trafford	won 3-0
17.03.1921	Barnsley	CCS SF rep	Hillsborough	won 3-2
22.01.1923	Nottingham Forest	FAC Rd 1,2 r	Meadow Lane	drew 1-1
25.01.1923	Nottingham Forest	FAC Rd 1,3 r	Hillsborough	won 1-0
24.03.1923	Bolton Wanderers	FAC SF	Old Trafford	lost 1-0
28.03.1925	Southampton	FAC SF	Stamford Bridge	won 2-0
25.04.1925	Cardiff City	FAC Final	Wembley	won 1-0
24.03.1928	Huddersfield Town	FAC SF	Old Trafford	drew 2-2
26.03.1928	Huddersfield Town	FAC SF rep	Goodison Park	drew 0-0
02.04.1928	Huddersfield Town	FAC SF 2 rep	Maine Road	lost 1-0
28.04.1931	Grimsby Town	Fr	Spalding	lost 6-0
21.03.1936	Fulham	FAC SF	Molineux	won 2-1

25.04.1936	Arsenal	FAC Final	Wembley	lost 1-0
26.12.1942	Grimsby Town	WW2	Scunthorpe	drew 3-3
17.05.1948	Sheffield Wed	Fr	Douglas IOM	drew 2-2
24.11.1948	Western Command	Fr	Whittingham B	won 3-0
18.03.1961	Leicester City	FAC SF	Elland Road	drew 0-0
23.03.1961	Leicester City	FAC SF rep	The City Ground	drew 0-0
27.03.1961	Leicester City	FAC SF 2 rep	St Andrew's	lost 2-0
15.01.1962	Bury	FAC Rd 3, 3r	Hillsborough	won 2-0
03.04.1993	Sheffield Wed	FAC SF	Wembley	lost 1-2
26.05.1997	Crystal Palace	Div 1 P/O Final	Wembley	lost 1-0
05.04.1998	Newcastle United	FAC SF	Old Trafford	lost 1-0
13.04.2003	Arsenal	FAC SF	Old Trafford	lost 1-0
26.05.2003	Wolverhampton Wds	Div 1 P/O Final	Millennium Stadium	lost 3-0

NB: Certain League games (including fixtures against Bradford City at the Odsal Stadium, Charlton Athletic at Selhurst Park, Manchester United at Maine Road, QPR, Wimbledon etc) were played on grounds shared by the clubs named. During WW2 United also used Hillsborough for some home games, while several tour matches were also played on various neutral grounds, depending on the circumstances.

The two friendlies against Western Command were played at the Army barracks in Lichfield. Also, during the WW2 period following bomb damage to Bramall Lane, United played home games at Millmoor.

NEVILLE, Steven Francis
Winger/forward: 54+11 apps. 7 goals
Born: Walthamstow, London, 18 September 1957
Career: Southampton (on trial, April 1973, apprentice, August 1973, professional September 1975), Exeter City (September 1978), BLADES (£70,000, October 1980), Exeter City (October 1982), Bristol City (November 1984), Exeter City (July 1988, player-coach July 1989-May 1991), South China FC/Hong Kong (August 1991-92).
Steve Neville played his part in helping the Blades win the Fourth Division championship in 1982 but found it much harder the following year. A skilful, darting forward, he did very well during his three spells at St James' Park, scoring 88 goals in a total of 305 League games for the Grecians.

NEW BRIGHTON
New Brighton FC, founded in August 1921 - two months after a meeting had been held at Egerton Street School - took over the interests and fixtures of South Liverpool AFC.
The Merseysiders were members of the Football League from 1923 to 1951 when they were replaced by Workington - after failing to gain re-election to the Third Division (North).
The only competitive game between New Brighton and the Blades was a 3rd round FA Cup-tie at Bramall Lane in January 1949 when over 28,000 spectators saw George Jones score a hat-trick in United's 5-2 victory....this after the visitors had gone in at half-time with a 2-1 lead.
Among the handful of players who have assisted both clubs are Jimmy Dunne and Harry Hitchen.

NEWBY, Jonathan Philip Robert
Utility forward: 3+10 apps.
Born: Warrington, 28 November 1978
Career: Liverpool (juniors, June 1995, professional, May 1997), Crewe Alexandra (on loan, March 2000), BLADES (on loan, August-November 2000), Bury (£100,000, February 2001).
An FA Youth Cup winner with Liverpool in 1996, Jon Newby made four 'sub' appearances during his time at Anfield (playing once in the Premiership). A player with a high work-rate, he gained experience at born Gresty Road and Bramall Lane before becoming a key player at Gigg Lane. He was voted the fans and the players' 'Player of the Year' in 2001-02 after an ever-present campaign with the Shakers.

181

NEWCASTLE EAST END

Blades' playing record against East End:

Northern League

Venue	P	W	D	L	F	A
Home	1	1	0	0	3	0
Away	1	1	0	0	2	1
Totals	2	2	0	0	5	1

The Blades played Newcastle East End in season 1891-92 before the Tyneside club became known as Newcastle United. United's five goals against East End were shared by five different players.

NEWCASTLE UNITED

United's playing record against the Magpies:

Premier League

Venue	P	W	D	L	F	A
Home	1	1	0	0	2	0
Away	1	0	0	1	0	4
Totals	2	1	0	1	2	4
Football League						
Home	51	32	13	6	96	48
Away	51	9	13	29	53	103
Totals	102	41	26	35	149	151
FA Cup						
Home	3	1	1	1	2	3
Away	6	2	1	3	11	11
Neutral	1	0	0	1	0	1
Totals	10	3	2	5	13	15
League Cup						
Home	3	2	1	0	7	2
Away	2	1	0	1	2	2
Totals	5	3	1	1	9	4
Northern League						
Home	1	1	0	0	5	1
Away	1	0	1	0	1	1
Totals	2	1	1	0	6	2
WW2						
Home	4	3	0	1	9	0
Away	4	1	0	3	7	14
Totals	8	4	0	4	16	14
Other						
Home	1	0	0	1	0	1

Round the time the Blades began their Football League career (1892) events were occurring at Newcastle which would have a profound effect on English soccer. The two major clubs on Tyneside were Newcastle East End and Newcastle West End. The latter club, after going through a bad period, decided to pack in, offering their St James' park ground to their local rivals. East End gratefully accepted the offer and agreed to move homes, almost immediately adopted the name Newcastle United. Within a year the club had been elected to the Second Division. And the rest as they say, is history.

Newcastle's first promotion came in 1898 (runners-up to Burnley) and from then until 1939 they spent 37 consecutive seasons playing League football against the Blades, aided by the extraordinary coincidence of both clubs being relegated together in 1934, enabling the sequence to continue until the outbreak of WW2.

United's run of 37 consecutive seasons against Newcastle is equalled only by the sequences against Aston Villa (q.v), Blackburn Rovers (q.v) and Sunderland (q.v) all of which ran from 1893 to 1934.

In September 1898, the two United's played against each other for the first time at League level, a crowd of 6,000 witnessing a 2-2 draw at Bramall Lane. Later in the season the Blades won 2-1 at St James' Park.

The initial FA Cup clash had taken place five years earlier, when the Magpies won a home 1st round tie 2-0.

Since those opening 37 season sequences, the two clubs have meet in only 15 of the 57 post WW2 League campaigns. The Blades have lost six out of 52 home matches but have won nine times at St James' Park. Only seven seasons have been out of the top flight.

The Blades' biggest win in the sequence was a 6-2 victory on New Year's Day 1955 (Division 1). They scored four times in the first eight minutes.

The Blades ran in two successive 5-1 home wins in Division two in the mid-1930s during a run of five consecutive victories. On the other hand the Blades lost eight consecutive matches at St James' Park between 1930 and 1938, culminating in successive 4-0 and 6-0 defeats. Their best win over the Magpies in the North-east came in 1929-30 when they recorded an excellent 5-3 victory, Jimmy Dunne scoring a hat-trick.

By failing to beat Newcastle at home (0-0) in the penultimate League game of the 1948-49 season, the Blades were relegated to the Second Division. The last 'League' game between the clubs was in the Premiership in 1993-94. The Blades won 2-0 at home thanks to a brace from Nathan Blake. Earlier in the season they had crashed 4-0 on Tyneside.

A hat-trick in the first 18 minutes by Billy Russell enabled the Blades to beat United 3-1 at St James' Park in a 6th round FA Cup-tie in 1961.

When the Magpies were beaten 5-0 at home by the Blades in a 1st round FA Cup-tie in January 1914, they finished the game with only eight men. Jimmy Simmons scored twice.

A crowd of 53,452 saw the Magpies beat the Blades in the 1998 FA Cup semi-final showdown at Old Trafford by a single goal, scored by Alan Shearer after an hour's play.

United lost 6-0 at Newcastle in a League North game in August 1945 - after a four-hour train journey from Sheffield!

The following are among the many players who served with both clubs: Jack Alderson, Bob Benson, Arthur Bottom, Gary Brazil, John Burridge, Viv Busby, Franz Carr, Bert Chandler, Johnny Dryden, David Ford, Chris Guthrie, Walter Hardinge, Trevor Hockey, Glyn

Hodges, John Hope, Jim Iley, David Kelly, Gary Kelly, Keith Kettleborough, Bert Partridge, Jack Peart, Tom Phillipson, Bill Punton, Wayne Quinn, Ian Rush, Peter Spooner, George Thompson, John Tudor, Rob Ullathorne (Newcastle trialist), Imre Varadi, Andy Walker, Billy Whitehurst and Peter Withe. Dugald Livingstone was manager of Newcastle and trainer of the Blades.

NEWCASTLE WEST END

Blades' playing record against West End:

Northern League

Venue	P	W	D	L	F	A
Home	1	1	0	0	5	1
Away	1	0	0	1	3	4
Totals	2	1	0	1	8	5

The Blades played West End in season 1891-92 prior to the Tyneside club folding.

A crowd of 3,000 saw the game at Bramall Lane in December when Sammy Dobson netted twice for the Blades. Arthur Watson notched two goals in the return fixture.

NEWPORT COUNTY

United's playing record against County:

Football League

Venue	P	W	D	L	F	A
Home	3	3	0	0	6	0
Away	3	1	0	2	3	7
Totals	6	4	0	2	9	7

FA Cup

Venue	P	W	D	L	F	A
Home	1	1	0	0	2	0
Away	1	1	0	0	4	1
Totals	2	2	0	0	6	1

Formed as a professional club in 1912, Newport County enjoyed 60 seasons of League football before losing their status in 1988.

In season 1946-47 County lost 29 of their 42 Second Division matches and conceded 133 goals including a 13-0 defeat at Newcastle.

All six League meetings with the Blades were confined to the Third Division in the early 1980s. United won all three home fixtures by 2-0, while County recorded 4-0 and 3-1 victories at Somerton Park before losing the last match 2-0.

The Blades dumped County out of the FA Cup in successive seasons of 3rd round action, beating them 2-0 at Bramall Lane. January 1952 and 4-1 at Somerton Park twelve months later.

Colin Addison played for United and twice managed Newport, while Welsh internationals Roy John and Gil Reece have played for both clubs along with Darren Carr, Wally Downes, Jeff Eckhardt, Paul Hall, John McGeady and Irish cap Paul A Williams.

NIBLOE, John Alistair

Centre-forward: 29 apps. 7 goals

Born: Sheffield, 1 June 1939. Died: Stourbridge, 12 November, 1964

Career: BLADES (junior, June 1956, professional August 1958), Stoke City (£3,000, October 1961), Doncaster Rovers (£5,000, October 1962), Stockport County (July 1964 until his death).

John Nibloe scored United's first-ever goal in the League Cup - obliging after just 55 seconds of at Bury on 11 October 1960. This was also the Blades' first game in the competition (lost 3-1). A durable striker with an eye for goal, he was part of United's Second Division promotion-winning side of 1961. Sadly his career lasted only eight years before he was killed in car crash in the Black Country at the age of 25.

NICHOLL, Terence John

Midfielder: 16+11 apps. one goal

Born: Wilmslow, Cheshire, 16 September 1952

Career: Crewe Alexandra (apprentice, April 1969, professional February 1972), BLADES (March 1973), Southend United (May 1975), Gillingham (October 1976-May 1981).

A hardly midfielder, Terry Nicholl never really established himself in the Blades' first XI after doing very well at Gresty Road. He regained his form at Roots Hall and later scored 11 goals in 184 League games for the Gills.

NICHOLSON, Shane Michael

Full-back: 22+4 apps. 3 goals

Born: Newark, Notts, 3 June 1970

Career: Lincoln City (schoolboy forms July 1984, trainec, June 1986, professional July 1988), Derby County (£100,000, April 1992), West Bromwich Albion (£150,000, February 1996), Chesterfield (free transfer, August 1998), Stockport County (free, June 1999), BLADES (free, July 2001), Tranmere Rovers (July 2002).

Shane Nicholson became Lincoln's youngest post-WW2 debutant when he appeared against Burnley in November 1986 at the age of 16 years and 172 days. He developed into a fine attacking left full-back who could also man midfield if required and played in 158 first-class games for the imps, helping them win the GM Vauxhall Conference in 1988. He made 87 appearances for the Rams and 60 for West Brom before being sacked by after admitting to being a frequent user of amphetamines for which he received a three-month suspension and had to undergo a period of rehabilitation. He added a further 25 outings to his tally with Chesterfield and 80 for Stockport prior to spending a season at Bramall Lane.

183

NICKNAMES

Every player to a certain degree has had a nickname attached to him...here are a few of those associated with United stars:

Wayne 'Chief' Allison
Walter 'Cocky' Bennett
Don 'Dickie' Bird
Ted 'The Cat' Burgin
John 'Budgie' Burridge
Gordon 'Sid' Cowans
Edward 'Terry' Curran
Jimmy 'Snowy' Dunne
Bill 'Fatty'/'Little Willie' Foulke
Colin 'The Singing Winger' Grainger
Ian 'Chico' Hamilton
Harry 'Wally' Hardinge
Don 'Hutch' Hutchinson
William Ronald 'Roy' John

David 'Ned' Kelly
Dennis 'Morty' Mortimer
Ernest 'Nudger' Needham
Jimmy 'Old Aeroplane Legs' Revill
FA 'Little Fred' Smith
FE 'Big Fred' Smith
Jack 'Smiler' Smith
Joe 'Aeroplane' Smith
John 'Tiny' Smith
Paul 'Tommo' Tomlinson
Albert 'Alf' Tootill
Albert 'Nigger' Trueman
Alan 'Woody' Woodward
Alexander 'Alan' Young

* The club (first XI) has also had various nicknames, thus: the 'Cutlers', the 'Laneites', the 'Blades' and 'United'. The reserves have been dubbed the 'Stiffs.'

NIGHTINGALE, Albert

Inside-forward: 225 apps. 88 goals
Born: Thryburgh near Rotherham, 10 November 1923
Career: Thurcroft FC, BLADES (June 1941), Huddersfield Town (March 1948), Blackburn Rovers (October 1951), Leeds United (£10,000, October 1952). He retired in May 1957 after failing to recover from a bad knee injury, suffered against Everton on the opening day of the 1956-57 season.

A busy, hard-working inside-forward with splendid close control, allied to craft and skill, Albert Nightingale could also be subtle and aggressive and was able to wriggle his way past defenders in the tightest of situations before firing in a powerful shot or clipping a short, decisive pass to one of his colleagues. He made his name during WW2 and after the hostilities continued to perform well, scoring 14 goals in 62 League games for the Blades before asking to go on the transfer list. He then netted 20 times in 119 League matches for Huddersfield (after a 'barter deal' had took him to Leeds Road), five in 35 for Blackburn and 48 in 130 for Leeds where he teamed up with John Charles. He had twice slipped through Leeds' grasp earlier in his career.

NILSEN, Roger

Defender: 177+13 apps.
Born: Tromso, Norway, 8 August 1969
Career: Viking Stavanger, BLADES (£550,000, November 1993), Tottenham Hotspur (free transfer, March 1999), Grazer AK/Austria (June 1999).
A fine Norwegian defender (31 full caps gained for his country) Roger Nilsen was able to play at left-back or centre-half. He was generally a very consistent performer if he made it mistake it was often punished! A precise kicker, good in the air he surprisingly never scored a single goal in his 190 games for the Blades despite going forward for several set-pierces.

NON-LEAGUE OPPOSITION

(See also under FA CUP)
* Striker Peter Withe served with two ex-Football League clubs (then non-League clubs) early in his career: Barrow & Southport.

NORTHAMPTON TOWN

United's playing record against the Cobblers:

Football League

Venue	P	W	D	L	F	A
Home	3	2	1	0	13	5
Away	3	3	0	0	5	2
Totals	6	5	1	0	18	7

FA Cup

Venue	P	W	D	L	F	A
Away	1	1	0	0	2	0

League Cup

Venue	P	W	D	L	F	A
Home	1	1	0	0	2	1
Away	1	1	0	0	1	0
Totals	2	2	0	0	3	1

184

Both United and Town share a unique distinction, having played for much of their histories at a county cricket ground, Northampton occupying the County Ground for almost 100 years, from 1897 until 1994 when they moved to Sixfields.

They club was formed by a group of sports-minded teachers connected with the Northampton & District Elementary Schools' Association. Entering the Midland League in 1897 the club lost £765 in its first year, achieving Southern League status in 1901 and joining the Football League in 1920 as original members of the Third Division.

The 'Cobblers' first meet the Blades in season 1965-66 after amazingly climbing the ladder into the top flight, having been members of the Football League for just 45 years. The Blades won 1-0 at The County Ground in front of 17,300 fans (courtesy of a rare Ken Mallender goal) but were then held at 2-2 in the return fixture with Mick Jones scoring twice.

In their Fourth Division championship-winning season of 1981-82, the Blades, as part of a 19-match unbeaten run, hammered luckless Northampton 7-3 at Bramall Lane with Keith Edwards hitting a hat-trick.

The first-ever competitive game between the clubs saw the Cobblers, then a non-League side, lose 2-0 to the Blades in a 1st round FA Cup-tie in 1901-02.

The two League Cup clashes took place in 1990-91, the Blades winning a 2nd round tie 3-1 on aggregate.

John Barnwell, Tommy Boyle and Jack English all played for the Blades and later managed Northampton.

Tony Battersby, Ian Benjamin, Jesse Bennett, Billy Brawn, John Burridge, Herbert Chapman, Jack Cross, Bob Hatton, George Henson, Colin Hill, Doug Hodgson Bert Partridge, Bernie Radford, Ernie Robinson, Rob Scott and Chris Wilder also played for the Blades and the Cobblers.

NORTHERN LEAGUE

United played in the Northern League in seasons 1891-92 and 1892-93. They finished a creditable third both times with these set of statistics:

Season	P	W	D	L	F	A	Pt
1891-92	16	10	2	4	48	21	22
1892-93	10	4	2	4	18	16	10
Totals	26	14	4	8	66	37	32

In 1891-92 the Blades recorded three excellent home wins of 7-1 v. Darlington in September 6-0 v. South Bank on October and 6-0 v. Stockton in December. Their heaviest defeat was 3-0 at Middlesborough (h) in November while they also went down 4-3 at Newcastle West End in March.

United completed the double over both Newcastle clubs, East End and West End, as well as South Bank and Sunderland Albion.

The following season (when they were also playing in the Football League for the first time) they beat Newcastle East End 5-1 (home) in September and Darlington 5-0 (home) in December. They crashed to a 5-0 defeat at Stockton in January. However, only one double was achieved this time... over Darlington. Harry Hammond scored a total of 13 Northern League goals for the Blades (ten coming in 1891-92).

NORTHWICH VICTORIA

United's playing record against the 'Vics':

Football League

Venue	P	W	D	L	F	A
Home	1	0	1	0	1	1
Away	1	1	0	0	3	1
Totals	2	1	1	0	4	2

Two of the founder members of the Second Division in 1892-93, the Blades just got the better of the 'Vics' in the two League games played that season. A crowd of 3,000 saw Ernest Needham salvage a point in the 1-1 draw in January while 2,250 fans attended the Drill Field for the return fixture in which Rab Howell, Harry Hammond and Jack Drummond netted for the Blades.

The 'Vic's (now members of the Nationwide Conference) still use the Drill Field which is believed to be one of the longest disputed by Hallam FC of Sheffield c. 1860 surviving football ground in history.

NORWICH CITY

United's playing record against the Canaries:

Premier League

Venue	P	W	D	L	F	A
Home	2	0	0	2	1	3
Away	2	1	0	1	2	2
Totals	4	1	0	3	3	5

Football League

Venue	P	W	D	L	F	A
Home	23	13	6	4	36	22
Away	23	4	9	10	26	39
Totals	46	17	15	14	62	61

FA Cup

Venue	P	W	D	L	F	A
Home	2	1	1	0	4	2
Away	3	0	0	3	4	7
Totals	5	1	1	3	8	9

League Cup

Venue	P	W	D	L	F	A
Home	1	0	1	0	2	2
Away	1	0	0	1	1	2
Totals	2	0	1	1	3	4

Norwich City FC was formed in 1902, largely through the initiative of two local schoolmasters who called a meeting at the Criterion Café. However, members of the club were shocked by an FA Commission, which, in 1904, declared the club professional and ejected them from the FA Amateur Cup. This set-back only strengthened their determination. Mew officials were appointed and a professional club was officially established at a meeting held at the Agriculture Hall in March 1905.

Elected to the Football League via the Southern League in 1920, the Canaries first met the Blades in season 1934-35 (Division 2). After the Canaries had recorded a 3-1 win at their quaintly named ground, The Nest on Rosary Road, the teams fought out a 1-1 draw at Bramall Lane.

185

United's best win of the 18 so far registered in all competitions, is 4-0 at home in 1938-39 (Division 2) while their heaviest defeats have been 5-2 at home and 4-0 away in 1985-86 when United ran away with the Second Division title.

United, it must be said, have a poor record at Carrow Road (City's home since 1935). They have gained just five wins there, two before WW2 (1-0 and 2-1), in 1975-76 (3-1), in the Premiership in 1993-94 (1-0) and the last in 2002-03 (3-2).

A full-house at Carrow Road (38,000) saw Norwich beat United 3-2 in a 6th round FA Cup replay.

Third Division City had already knocked out three First Division sides, Manchester United, Cardiff City and Tottenham Hotspur, and after Billy Russell had given the Blades a first half lead at Bramall Lane it looked as if the Canaries' brilliant run was coming to an end. But backed by 10,000 supporters they stormed forward after the break and with goalkeeper Nethercott injured, Johnny Crossan equalised late on to earn a replay. It was a tension-packed night in Norfolk for the replay as City became only the second Third Division team to reach the semi-final stage.

Three years later, goals by Keith Kettleborough, Russell and 'Doc' Pace saw United gain some revenge with a 3-1 victory in the 5th round tie 3-1 at Bramall Lane.

The two League Cup matches were played in 1974-75 when United went out in the 4th round after a replay.

Bruce Rioch played for the Blades and later managed the Canaries, while Steve Bruce played for both clubs as well as managing the Blades, likewise Martin Peters.

Graham Benstead, Keith Bannister (Blades reserve), Jim Bone, Carl Bradshaw, Viv Busby, Roger Hansbury, Trevor Hockey, Alf Jeffries, Ken Mallender, Fred Milnes, Alex Notman, Jack Peart, Paul Peschisolido, Bill Punton, John Ryan, Tom Simons, Paddy Sloan, Albert Sturgess, -Simon Tracey, Rob Ullathorne and Norman Wharton are some of the other players who have served with both clubs. Also associated: John Deehan (City player & United coach etc).

NOTMAN, Alexander McKeachie

Forward: 7+3 apps. 3 goals
Born: Edinburgh, 10 December 1979
Career: Manchester United (trainee, April 1986, professional December 1996), Aberdeen (on loan, February 1999), BLADES (on loan, January-March 2000), Norwich City (£250,000, November 2000).

A Scottish international, capped at School and Youth levels before appearing in Under-21 matches, Alex Notman made one substitute appearance for Manchester United and two for Aberdeen before having a loan spell at Bramall Lane. He later partnered Iwan Roberts in the Norwich attack and helped the Canaries reach the First Division Play-off Final in 2002.

NOTTINGHAM FOREST

United's playing record against Forest:

Premier League

Venue	P	W	D	L	F	A
Home	1	0	1	0	0	0
Away	1	1	0	0	2	0
Totals	2	1	1	0	2	0

Football League

Venue	P	W	D	L	F	A
Home	44	20	8	16	64	61
Away	44	11	12	21	51	77
Totals	88	31	20	37	115	138

Play-offs

Venue	P	W	D	L	F	A
Home	1	1	0	0	4	3
Away	1	0	1	0	1	1
Totals	2	1	1	0	5	4

FA Cup

Venue	P	W	D	L	F	A
Home	5	3	1	1	8	3
Away	5	2	1	2	7	7
Neutral	2	1	1	0	2	1
Totals	12	6	3	3	17	11

United Counties League

Venue	P	W	D	L	F	A
Home	2	0	1	1	2	6
Away	2	1	0	1	2	3
Totals	4	1	1	2	4	9

WW1

Venue	P	W	D	L	F	A
Home	4	1	1	2	5	7
Away	4	1	1	2	2	5
Totals	8	2	2	4	7	12

WW2

Venue	P	W	D	L	F	A
Home	5	3	2	0	10	4
Away	5	1	2	2	9	13
Totals	10	4	4	2	19	17

One of the world's oldest clubs, formed at a meeting in the Clinton Arms in 1865, Nottingham Forest (known originally as Forest Football Club) surprisingly were not one of the founder members of the Football League. Indeed, they did not gain entry into the competition until 1892 (along with United) going straight into the top flight, having won the Football Alliance the previous season. Therefore, they too, celebrated 100 years of League football in 2002-03.

The first time the Blades met Forest on the pitch was in a friendly at Bramall Lane in November 1889; United won 2-0 before 500 spectators. In March Forest won a re-match on their own ground by 2-1 before a crowd of 2,500.

Several more friendlies took place before the clubs did battle against each other in the Football League, Forest winning 2-0 at 'the Lane' and being held to a 1-1 draw at the Town Ground in 1893-94 (Division 1).

During this same season both clubs opposed each other in the United Counties League, United losing 3-1 away and drawing 0-0 at home. From 1893 the teams met in 17 consecutive seasons of top-flight football. United's best win in this sequence was 4-0 at home in 1904-05.

A 4-0 defeat at the hands of Forest on 31 March 1900 cost United the League championship - they finished runners-up to Aston Villa by just two points: 50-48.

Forest's record at Bramall Lane is pretty useful, unbeaten in 24 of their 43 matches, registering 16 wins and eight draws. (Only Aston Villa and Liverpool with 17 wins each, have better records).

A crowd of over 28,000 saw Forest win 4-0 at Bramall Lane in April 1957 to clinch promotion to the First Division, while in 1976-77 they whipped the Blades 6-1 at The City Ground to record their biggest win so far.

The Blades put nine goals past Brian Clough's in 1991-92, winning 4-2 at home and 5-2 away.

However, League meetings since WW2 have been sporadic, with only 20 taking place in 57 seasons, with the seven in the First Division between 1961-68 the only measure of continuity.

Forest failed to score in either of the two Premiership matches in 1992-93, drawing 0-0 at 'the Lane' and losing 2-0 at The City Ground, a defeat that signalled the Reds' departure to the Nationwide League.

United met Forest in the 2003 League Division One two-legged Play-off semi-final. There was a crowd of 29,064 at The City Ground for the first leg on 10 May where Michael Brown's penalty cancelled out an opening goal by David Johnson and Forest had defender Michael Dawson sent-off for a foul tackle on Steve Kabba. The return fixture at Bramall Lane five days later attracted a crowd of just over 30,000 and what a thrilling contest it turned out to be! Forest led 2-0 after 58 minutes, but Forest stormed back with a deflected free-kick from Michael Brown and a stunning volley from Steve Kabba to level things up halfway through the second-half. It was tense, it was hectic and it was certainly nerve-racking as the game went into extra-time. Then, with eight minutes remaining, up popped United's 'super sub' Paul Peschisolido to put the Blades in front. The cheering hadn't died down before veteran defender Des Walker headed into his own net to make it 4-2. A Robert Page own-goal a minute or so from the end made it a close finish but the Blades held on to clinch a 5-4 aggregate victory and a place in the Play-off Final against Wolverhampton Wanderers at Cardiff's Millennium Stadium. What a night...and a delighted and joyous Neil Warnock confirmed that it was "...the greatest highlight of my career."

FA Cup meetings between the teams have been frequent, with nine seasons of knockout action taking place (only Burnley and Wolves with eight campaigns, are approaching that number against the Blades). So far United have won six ties to Forest's three. The most drawn out fixture, and indeed, the only one to require a replay, took place in 1922-23 and lasted seven hours before the Blades finally edged through to the 2nd round with a 1-0 victory at the fourth attempt at Hillsborough.

United beat Forest (the FA Cup holders) 3-0 in a 4th round tie at The City Ground in January 1960, Derek Pace netting a hat-trick.

The Blades were beaten 6-2 at home by Forest in a United Counties League game in 1894-95.

Dave Bassett has managed both clubs while Colin Addison, Bill Anderson, John Barnwell, Kingsley Black, Barry Butlin, Franz Carr, Colin Collindridge, Terry Curran, Sid Gibson, Trevor Hockey, Glyn Hodges, Jim Iley, Mark Mellors, Jack Poole (Blades WW1), Colin Rawson Dean Saunders, Hans Segers, Ben Shearman, Jack Smith, Phil Starbuck, Carl Tiler, John Tudor (Forest trialist), Steve Wigley and Peter Withe are among the many players who have served with both the Blades and Forest. Steve Bruce was player-manager of the Blades and also a part-time coach with Forest while Andy Beattie managed Forest before becoming assistant-boss of United.

NOTTS COUNTY

United's playing record against the Magpies:

Football League

Venue	P	W	D	L	F	A
Home	34	23	4	7	70	33
Away	34	15	5	14	55	55
Totals	68	38	9	21	125	88

FA Cup

Home	3	1	1	1	6	11
Away	2	2	0	0	7	5
Totals	5	3	1	1	13	16

United Counties League

Away	1	0	1	0	0	0

Others

Home	2	0	1*	1	7	8
Away	1	1	0	0	1	0
Totals	2	1	0	1	5	5

WW1

Home	4	1	2	1	9	5
Away	4	1	0	3	8	10
Totals	8	2	2	4	17	15

WW2

Home	4	4	0	0	20	4
Away	4	0	1	3	2	7
Totals	8	4	1	3	22	11

Watney Cup

Away	1	1	0	0	3	0

* County won 2-1 on penalties after a 3-3 draw.

Sheffield and Nottingham played a massive part in the early organisation of football in the 19th century, their two associations to the forefront in the codification of the game, both influencing the Football Association in its formative years. Notts County became part of this tradition in 1862. Certainly one of the world's oldest clubs, County, in fact, commenced operations at a meeting at Cremorne Gardens (Nottingham) in November 1862 with Messrs W Arkwright and Chas Deakin selecting the first team.

Founder members of the Football League in 1888, County have now played more League matches than any other club (4,250 at the end of the 2002-03 season). And like United they too once performed on a cricket ground (Trent Bridge) which they occupied from 1883 to 1910 when they switched to Meadow Lane.

County first met United in serious match action in the 1st qualifying round of the FA Cup in season 1890-91 and they quickly showed how good they were, despite going behind, with a comprehensive 9-1 victory at Bramall Lane - which still remains as United's biggest home defeat in any major competition.

The initial League encounters took place in 1897-98 (Division 1), the Blades winning 3-1 at Nottingham on New Year's Day but losing 1-0 at Bramall Lane six weeks later.

On two occasions United have won seven successive home League matches against County: 1900-07 and 1912-35, and during the period 1951-85 the Blades ran up a sequence of eight successive home victories with 5-1 their best (in 1978-79) when Mick Speight scored twice. The Blades won 5-1 at Trent Bridge in 1904-05 to register their best away win.

After United had defeated County 3-2 in a home League game in March 1909, the referee reported both teams 'for weakness.'

Jim Iley took four penalties for United in the two League games against the Magpies in 1956-57. He scored twice from the spot in a 5-1 home win in October but then missed two spot-kicks in the 2-2 draw at Meadow Lane in February.

With seven minutes left on the clock, United were 3-1 down at Meadow Lane in a 3rd Round FA Cup replay with Notts County on 23 January 1999. But with Wayne Quinn sent-off, the ten men stormed back, scored twice late on to take the game into extra-time and then the Brazilian Marcelo stepped up to grab a dramatic winner in the fourth minute of injury-time.

As yet the Blades have still be drawn against either of the two Nottingham clubs in the League Cup.

Over 14,400 fans saw the Blades beat County 3-0 in a Watney Cup-tie in July 1972

Howard Kendall, Jimmy Sirrel, Steve Thompson and Neil Warnock have all managed both clubs, while John Barnwell, Gary Brazil and Billy Dearden all played for United and later managed County. Andy Beattie was professional advisor and general manager of County and assistant-boss of United. Colin Addison was a Blades player and later County's assistant-manager while Jack Poole played for United in WW1 and later became County's trainer.

Tony Agana, Tony Battersby, Ian Benjamin, Alan Birchenall, John Burridge, Barry Butlin, Willie Carlin, Aidan Davison, Herbert Chapman, Tony Daws, Shaun Derry, Paul Devlin, Jim Gannon (Blades reserve), Dick Gardner, Andy Goram, Ian Hamilton, Anders Jacobsen, Jeff King, Martin Kuhl, Chris Marsden, Mark Mellors, Shaun Murphy, Derek Pace, Jack Peart, Ernie Robertson, Paul Rogers, Bill Ross, Chris Short, John Tudor (County junior), Harry Warren, Chris Wilder and Alan Young are among the other players who have also served with both clubs.

NUMBERING OF PLAYERS

Although numbers were first sewed onto the backs of the players' jerseys for the 1933 FA Cup Final (when they ran from 1-22) it was not until 1939 (passed at the Football League's AGM by 24 votes to 20) that numbers first appeared on club jerseys, United producing them for their Football League Jubilee Fund game against Sheffield Wednesday at Hillsborough in August 1939.

1985-86 Official Brochure

OFFSIDE RULE

The current offside rule was introduced for the 1925-26 season and United opened with a 2-2 away draw at Everton in the first match on 29 August.

United's 42 League games that season produced 184 goals (102 scored, 82 conceded). Among the many high-scoring games were the following - wins of 11-2 v. Cardiff City, 8-3 v. Manchester City, 6-1 v. Burnley and 4-3 v. Newcastle United, and defeats of 6-1 at Sunderland and 7-4 at Bury. United failed to score in only five matches.

OGDEN, Alan

Full-back: 9+7 apps.
Born: Rotherham, 15 April 1954
Career: BLADES (apprentice, June 1969, professional May 1971), York City (September 1974-April 1975).
Reserve full-back Alan Ogden had a relatively short League career, making just 19 appearances in the competition for his two clubs.

OLDACRE, Percy

Centre-forward: 8 apps. 5 goals
Born: Stoke-on-Trent, 25 October 1892. Died: Stoke-on-Trent, 26 January 1970
Career: Stoke (briefly, 1910), Sheffield Wednesday (guest, WW1), Exeter City (September 1919), Castleford Town (May 1920), BLADES (March 1921), Halifax Town (August 1923), Crewe Alexandra (1924), Shrewsbury Town (1925) Port Vale (£150, August 1926), Hurst FC (player-coach, May 1927).
Bold and keen, centre-forward Percy Oldacre made his Football League debut for the Blades against Liverpool (away) in September 1921. He had a good scoring record at Bramall Lane but failed to hold down his position in the side and moved to Halifax Town after two years' service. He netted 12 goals in 26 League games for Crewe.

OLDHAM ATHLETIC

United's playing record against the Latics:

Premier League

Venue	P	W	D	L	F	A
Home	2	2	0	0	4	1
Away	2	0	2	0	2	2
Totals	4	2	2	0	6	3

Football League

Home	22	17	3	2	43	19
Away	22	8	4	10	33	39
Totals	44	25	7	12	76	58

FA Cup

Home	1	1	0	0	3	0
Away	1	0	1	0	0	0
Totals	2	1	1	0	3	0

Others

Home	1	1	0	0	7	2
Away	3	1	0	2	3	7
Totals	4	2	0	2	10	9

In 1895 John Garland, the landlord of the Feathersall and Junction Hotel, decided to form a football team - Pine Villa. Four years later, Oldham County came into being but quickly went out of business, the liquidators persuading Pine Villa to take over their ground (on Sheepfoot Lane) and change their name to Oldham Athletic.

Elected to the Football League Division Two in 1907 (the year they also moved into Boundary Park) the Latics first met the Blades in League battle in season 1910-11 (Division 1), winning both games - 2-1 at home on Boxing Day and 3-1 away on Easter Monday as they went on to finish runners-up to Manchester City.

Then, in 1914-15, they came mighty close to winning the League championship again! After an excellent season when they defeated United 3-0 at 'the Lane' but lost 3-0 at home, the Latics lost their last match to Liverpool and duly handed the title to Everton on the same day that the Blades beat Chelsea in the FA Cup Final. Coincidentally United had beaten Oldham 3-0 in a 4th round replay, on their way to the Final.

United's biggest League win of the 25 so far recorded over the Latics is 5-1, at Boundary Park in November 1985 when they scored five times in 24 minutes either side of half-time. Their best home win is 4-0 in 1911-12 when left-winger Bob Evans scored twice.

The Latics' biggest win is 5-0 at Bramall Lane in 1987-88. Blades' manager Billy McEwan resigned soon after the game, but they were still relegated under Dave Bassett.

Neil Warnock has managed both the Blades and the Latics...while Harry Haslam played for the Latics and managed United.

Earl Barrett, David Davies, Billy Dearden, Mick Faulkner (United reserve), Mark Foran, John Gannon, Andy Goram, Barry Gordine (United reserve), Harry Gough, Barry Hartle, Nick Henry, Doug Hodgson, Jimmy Hutchinson, David Irving, Gary Kelly, Seth King, Adrian Littlejohn, Jack Pears, Tony Philliskirk, Eddie Shimwell, Simon Stainrod, Phil Starbuck, Oliver Tummon, Michel Vonk, Roy Warhurst, Simon Webster and Alan Young have all played for both clubs.

ONES THAT GOT AWAY!

Here are some of the many players who, after leaving Bramall Lane, made a name for themselves elsewhere:

Ian Benjamin	(481 League appearances for various clubs)
Eddie Boot	(325 first-class games for Huddersfield)
Arthur Bottom	(108 League goals, 92 for York City)
Gary Brazil	(123 goals in 450+ League appearances, various clubs)
Julian Broddle	(235 League games, 149 for Scunthorpe)
Steve Cammack	(110 goals in 245 League games for Scunthorpe)
Bobby Campbell	(158 goals in close on 450 League appearances)
Graeme Crawford	(426 League appearances in goal, 235 for York)
Tony Daws	(256 League appearances: 1987-97; 183 for Scunthorpe)

189

John Docherty	(over 300 senior games: 1965-74; 158 for Brentford)
Jeff Eckhardt	(over 525 League & Cup appearances: 1987-2001)
Stewart Evans	(almost 400 League appearances: 1982-94)
Steve Foley	(275 League appearances: 1987-96; 151 for Swindon)
Alex Forbes	(229 League appearances & Scottish caps: 1948-58)
John Francis	(well over 200 League games: 1990-97)
Jim Gannon	(almost 500 League & Cup games, 480 for Stockport, 1990-2000).
Walter Gould	(288 League appearances for York & Brighton, 1961-68)
Paul Heald	(over 250 League & Cup appearances, 219 for Orient, 1988-2003)
Ian Holmes	(51 goals in 232 League outings; 30 in 159 for York: 1973-80).
Jim Iley	(446 League appearances: 1957-73; 232 for Newcastle)
Mick Jones	(77 goals in 219 League games for Leeds United: 1967-74)
Ted Hufton	(401 first-class games for West Ham plus England honours).
Steve Ludlam	(over 100 games for both Carlisle & Chester: 1977-83).
Terry Nicholl	(234 League games: 1975-81; 184 for Gillingham).
Rob Scott	(250 appearances, 1995-2003, over 150 for Rotherham)
Paul Smith	(276 League appearances after United: 1986-95; 232 for Lincoln)
Imre Varadi	(174 goals in 490 games after moving from 'the Lane' in 1979)
Roy Warhurst	(312 League appearances: 1950-61; 213 for Birmingham City).
Peter Wragg	(83 goals in 337 League games from 1956 after United in 1956)

ONUORA, Ifem

Forward: 8 apps* one goal*
Born: Glasgow, 28 July 1967
Career: Bradford University, Huddersfield Town (professional, July 1998), Mansfield Town (£30,000, July 1994), Gillingham (£25,000, August 1996), Swindon Town (£120,000, March 1998), Gillingham (£125,000, January 2000), BLADES (July 2002).
'Iffy' Onuora, at 6ft 1ins tall and almost 14st in weight, is the perfect foil for any striker and over the years he's scored and made his fair share of goals. He netted 40 in 211 games for Huddersfield, grabbed eight in 30 for the Stags (including a hat-trick in just seven minutes during a 6-1 home League win over Lincoln City in March 19945), notched 55 in 170 outings in his two spells with the Gills and secured another 25 in 80 games for Swindon. Owing to a frustrating injury problem (suffered in September) he did not figure all that often in Blades' successful 2002-03 campaign, making only eight first team appearances and scoring one goal, the winner in the League game at Burnley in late August (1-0).

ORR, Henry

Wing-half: 14 apps. one goal
Born: Lisburn, Northern Ireland, 31 October 1936.
Career: Distillery (£9,000 with Dennis Shiels, October 1958), Peterborough United (July 1964-May 1967).
A stout, able half-back with good positional sense, Harry Orr was used as a reserve at Bramall Lane, replacing Gerry Summers in most of his matches. He made over 50 senior appearances for Posh.

OSWALD, Robert Raymond Broome

Inside/outside-left: 115 apps. 24 goals
Born: Bo'ness, Scotland, 20 December 1904. Died: 1961
Career: Bo'ness, Reading, BLADES (£4,000, July 1930), Southend United (August 1934-May 1937).
Signed as cover for Fred Tunstall, Bob Oswald made nine League appearances in his first season at 'the Lane' before establishing himself on the left-wing in 1931-32 when he partnered Jack Pickering. Fast and direct, he was outstanding the following year but after relegation was suffered at the end of the 1933-34 campaign he was transferred to Southend.

OVERSEAS TOURS/OPPOSITION
(See under FRIENDLIES & TOURS)

OXFORD UNITED
United's playing record against United:
Football League

Venue	P	W	D	L	F	A
Home	12	8	1	3	25	13
Away	12	3	4	5	13	21
Totals	24	11	5	8	38	34

League Cup

Away	1	0	0	1	1	3

A Football League club for barely 40 years (elected in place of Accrington Stanley in 1962) Oxford United came to prominence as Headington United (formed in 1893). They played in the Southern League, pulling off several giant-killing acts in the FA Cup with Ron Atkinson as their skipper.

However, 'Big Ron' had left for pastures new when the two Uniteds first met in the Football League in season 1968-69 (Division 2), Oxford completing the double with first a 2-1 win at Bramall Lane and then a last-match 1-0 victory at their Manor Ground where they played from 1925 until 2002.

The Blades registered a 5-1 win at 'the Lane' in 1969-70 (Alan Woodward scoring twice) while also claiming a 4-2 victory at The Manor Ground in 1997-98.

The only League Cup meeting so far took place in 1986-97 when Oxford won a 3rd round tie 3-1.

Ex-Blades wing-half Gerry Summers managed Oxford from 1969-75 while Darren Carr (Oxford trialist), Jeff Denial, Bobby Ford, Dean Saunders, Andy Scott, Paul Simpson, Imre Varadi, Billy Whitehurst and Dean Windass are among the players who have served with both clubs. Fred White played for the Blades and was an Oxford scout.

OXLEY, Bernard
Utility forward: 129 apps. 14 goals
Born: Whitwell, 16 June 1907. Died: 1975
Career: Whitwell Old Boys, Chesterfield (April 1925), BLADES (May 1928), Sheffield Wednesday (April 1934), Plymouth Argyle (September 1935), Stockport County (April 1937), Worksop Town (seasons: 1938). Did not play after WW2.
Able to play in most front-line positions but preferring either the outside-right berth, Bernie Oxley gave the Blades good value during his five-and-a-half years at Bramall Lane. He missed only four League games in 1931-32 and was generally a very competent performer.
He went on to score four times in 14 League outings for the Owls and later netted 10 goals in his 68 matches for Stockport.

Sheffield United v.s West Bromich Albion August 28th 1971

P

PACE, Derek John
Centre-forward: 302 apps. 175 goals
Born: Essington near Wolverhampton, 11 March 1932.
Died: 1989.
Career: Bloxwich Strollers, Aston Villa (professional,
September 1949), BLADES (December 1957), Notts
County (December 1964), Walsall (July 1966, retired
May 1967), Walsall Wood (manager, 1968-70).
Centre-forward 'Doc' Pace was 'discovered' by the former
Aston Villa defender George Cummings. He went on to
amass a fine scoring record during his time at Villa Park,
netting 42 goals in 107 appearances before transferring to
the Blades on Boxing Day 1957 (signed by future Villa
manager Joe Mercer). One of United's most successful
and popular strikers of the post WW2 period, he
possessed exquisite timing, was brave and finished
expertly, using both feet and his head despite not being
the tallest of centre-forwards. He spent seven years at
Bramall Lane, adding 175 more goals to his tally in a little
over 300 games after scoring on his debut in a 4-2 home
win over Blackburn Rovers in a Second Division game.
He then served with Notts County and Walsall before
announcing his retirement through injury in 1967. Pace
represented the Army v Ireland during his National
Service in the RAMC and he also played in the 1961 FA
Cup semi-final for the Blades whom he helped gain
promotion to the First Division in that same season
(playing in all 42 matches).

(L-R) Chelsea's Peter Bonetti and Tommy Docherty combine to foil Sheffield United's Doc Pace

PAGE, Robert John
Centre-half: 47+1 apps*
Born: Llwynpia, South Wales, 3 September 1974
Career: Watford (trainee, July 1990, professional, April 1993), BLADES (on loan, August 2000, signed for £350,000, October 2000). Welsh international at Schoolboy, Youth, Under-21 (six caps) and senior levels (30* appearances), Robert Page was discarded by the new regime at Watford (after helping the Hornets reach the Premiership in 1999) but quickly made his mark at Bramall Lane, forming a splendid central defensive partnership with first Keith Curle and then the Aussie Shaun Murphy. Perhaps lacking in pace, he nevertheless is a strong tackler, good in the air, reads the game well and above all has wonderful anticipation. After being voted the supporters' 'Player of the Year' he immediately followed up with a wonderfully consistent 2002-03 campaign when the Blades reached two Cup semi-finals and the First Division Play-off Final, although he did increase the heart beat of a few thousand Blades' supporters with his late own-goal in the 5-4 aggregate semi-final victory over Nottingham Forest! Sadly it wasn't a happy day at his national venue as the Blades lost 3-0 to Wolves in the Final.

PANTLING, Herbert Harold
Right-half: 368 apps. 2 goals
Born: Leighton Buzzard, Bedfordshire, 16 May 1891. Died: Sheffield, 22 December 1952.
Career: Watford (amateur, April 1908, professional, June 1911), BLADES (April 1914), Rotherham United (May 1926), Heanor Town (November 1927, retired May 1929). Worked as a licensee in Sheffield until his death at the age of 61.
Harold Pantling, sturdily built, had a reputation of being a 'hard man' and indeed, was the first United player to be sent-off twice in the same season (1917-18). A strong, aggressive and sometimes ruthless defender, who could deliver long and short passes to a tee, he very rarely produced a poor performance. An FA Cup winner with the Blades in 1925, he was capped once by England against Ireland in Belfast in October 1923, playing behind his team-mate Fred Tunstall in a 2-1 defeat. Pantling joined Watford as an amateur, turned professional at the age of 20 and moved to Bramall Lane in 1914. Over the next 12 years he amassed a fine with the Blades before leaving to join Rotherham.

PARKER, Paul Andrew
Full-back/defender: 7+3 apps.
Born: West Ham, London, 4 April 1964
Career: Essex & Havering Schools, Fulham (apprentice, June 1980, professional April 1982), Queen's Park Rangers (£300,000, June 1987), Manchester United (£2 million, August 1991), Derby County (free transfer, August 1996), BLADES (November 1996), Fulham (non-contract, January 1997), Chelsea (March 1997), Heybridge Swifts (June 1998), Farnborough Town (player-coach, season 1999-2000), Chelmsford Town (assistant-manager/coach, season 2000-01).
Right-back Paul Parker made over 180 appearances for Fulham and 160 for QPR before joining Manchester United for he added a further 146 games to his tally. An adaptable, compact footballer, with exceptional positional sense, he enjoyed bringing the ball out of defence and setting up an attack rather than giving it a huge kick downfield, hoping to find a colleague. He represented England at four different levels during a fine career, winning eight Under-21, three 'B' & 19 senior caps following his appearances for the Youth team. He was a League Cup winner in 1992, a Premiership winner in 1993 and 1994, also an FA Cup winner in the latter year as well as helping United win the Charity Shield in 1993. He ended his senior career with more than 530 club and international appearances under his belt.

PARKER, William E
Wing-half: 83 apps. 3 goals
Born: Sheffield, 5 April 1880. Died: 1940
Career: Malin Bridge FC (Sheffield), BLADES (March 1899-May 1909). He later became a Director of the club.
Bill Parker made his Football League debut for the Blades against Manchester City in March 1902, having played in five friendly matches prior to that. A dedicated clubman, he was called into action only periodically over the next six seasons before having his best campaign in the first XI in his last year with the club (24 League outings).

PARKIN, Herbert Buttery
Full-back: 96 apps. one goal
Born: Sheffield, 10 April 1920. Died: 1992.
Career: BLADES (April 1942), Chesterfield (August 1951-May 1953).
Bert Parkin broke his right left five inches above the knee playing for the Blades against Nottingham Forest (away) in September 1944. The WW2 game was held up for 20 minutes while first-aid men and the club's trainers treated him. After regaining full fitness Parkin continued playing for United until 1951, later adding 55 League outings to his tally with Chesterfield.

PARTRIDGE, Albert Edward
Winger/right-back: 103 apps. 22 goals
Born: Birmingham, 13 February 1901. Died: Shipley, 11 November 1966.
Career: Newcastle United (August 1921), Redditch Town (February 1922), BLADES (August 1923), Bradford City (May 1929), Northampton Town (August 1933-May 1934).
Bert Partridge had a fine turn of speed but was described as a bit of a 'hit and miss' winger who also played a few games at right-back for the Blades during the second-half of the 1928-29 season. He scored on his League debut for United v. Manchester City (h) in September 1923 (won 3-0).

PATON, Thomas Henry
Centre-forward/inside-right: 21 apps. 4 goals
Born: Larkhall, Scotland, circa 1878
Career: Glasgow Rangers, Derby County (May 1904), BLADES (March 1906), St Mirren (February 1907).
A very useful and effective striker north of the border, Tom Paton found it hard to come to grips with League football in England, scoring only four times for both the Rams and the Blades.

PATTERSON, Mark Andrew
Midfielder: 84+2 apps. 4 goals
Born: Darwen, 24 May 1965
Career: Blackburn Rovers (apprentice, June 1981, professional May 1983), Preston North End (£20,000, June 1988), Bury (£10,000, February 1990), Bolton Wanderers (£65,000, January 1991), BLADES (£300,000, December 1995), Southend United (on loan, March-April 1997), Bury (£125,000, December 1997), Blackpool (on loan, December 1998), Southend United (free transfer, March 1999), Leigh RMI (player-coach, May 1999).
A left-sided midfielder, who grafted throughout the 90-minutes, Mark Patterson was described as being a 'real battler', the favourite with the fans' but a player who at times could be sloppy with his passes. A Full Members' Cup winner with Blackburn in 1987, Patterson quit League football in the summer of 1999 with 588 senior appearances to his credit (73 goals).

PEAKE, William Edward
Half-back/inside-right: 27 apps. 6 goals
Born: Bolton, 1889.
Career: Eccles Borough, BLADES (January 1910), Bury (May 1913), Newcross FC (1921), Macclesfield FC (1921-22), Manchester North End (1922-24).
A Schoolmaster, Billy Peake made his League debut for the Blades v. Bolton Wanderers in January 1910. He was regarded as a reserve during his four years at Bramall Lane but never let the side down when called into the first team. He scored 35 goals in 168 League games for Bury and must be regarded as a player who escaped from United's nest.

PEARS, John
Outside-left: 16 apps. 4 goals
Born: Ormskirk, 23 February 1907.
Career: Westhead St James' FC, Skelmersdale United (July 1926), Burscough Rangers (December 1926), Liverpool (amateur, August 1927), Rotherham United (professional, August 1928), Accrington Stanley (May 1929), Oldham Athletic (July 1930), Preston North End (March 1934), BLADES (£1,500, November 1934), Swansea Town (£350, August 1935), Hull City (£100, June 1937), Mossley (August 1938).
Seemingly a smart acquisition from Preston, Jack Pears scored twice on his League debut for the Blades against Newcastle United in November 1934 (won 5-1). But after that initial flourish he struggled with his form and left Bramall Lane for the Vetch Field at the start of the next season. Early in his career Pears was described by in the Topical Times as being a 'remarkable opportunist with a left foot shot that a mule might envy'. Indeed, he had scored well for his four previous clubs (including 34 in 92 League games for the Latics) but somehow lost his way after leaving Deepdale.

PEARSON, Albert Victor
Outside-left: 6 apps.
Born: Tynemouth, County Durham, 30 August 1892. Died: Manchester, 24 January 1975.
Career: Hebburn Argyle, BLADES (July 1912), Port Vale (May 1914), Liverpool (March 1919), Port Vale (June 1921), LLanelli (May 1922), Rochdale (June 1923), Stockport County (November 1925), Ashton National FC (June 1929).
Bert Pearson - regarded as a an inside forward at the lane although not a prolific goalscorer - made his Football League debut for the Blades (with Bill Cook) against Bradford City in September 1912. His best spell if his career came at Rochdale (12 goals in 53 games) although he did net four goals in 44 League outings for Liverpool and six in 69 games for Stockport.

PEART, John George
Centre-forward: 28 apps. 7 goals
Born: South Shields, 3 October 1888. Died: Paddington, London, 3 September 1948.
Career: South Shields Adelaide FC (August 1905), BLADES (May 1907), Stoke (July 1901), Newcastle United (£600, March 1912), Notts County (February 1913), Rochdale (WW1 guest), Birmingham (November 1919), Derby County (January 1920), Ebbw Vale (as player-manager, August 1920), Port Vale (as a player, January 1922), Norwich City (July 1922), Rochdale (as player-manager, March 1923, retiring as a player in May 1924), Bradford City (manager, July 1930), Fulham (manager from May 1935 to his demise in 1948).
A Second Division championship winner with Notts County in 1914, Jack Peart represented the Football League XI once and the Southern League XI on three occasions during his varied career. One of the great travellers in the world of football, he was a fine opportunist goalscorer, although this facet of his game was only just emerging at Bramall Lane. He had a reputation for being 'the most injured man in football'. He proved to be a reasonably successful manager, taking Fulham to an FA Cup semi-final.

PEATTIE, Donald Simpson
Forward: 4+2 apps. 2 goals
Born: York, 5 April 1963
Career: Gretna, BLADES (August 1984), Doncaster Rovers (on loan, January-April 1986, later signed permanently).
A reserve team player at 'the Lane' Don Peattie only made a handful of first team appearances before dropping down the ladder.

PEMBERTON, John Matthews
Full-back/defender: 76+1 apps.
Born: Oldham, 18 November 1964
Career: Chadderton, Rochdale (non-contract, September 1984), Chadderton (November 1984), Crewe Alexandra (£1,000, March 1985), Crystal Palace (£80,000, March 1988), BLADES (£300,000, July 1990), Leeds United (£250,000, November 1993), Crewe Alexandra (free transfer, August 1997),
Attacking full-back John Pemberton was certainly quick over the ground. He tackled with belief and was strong in recovery. He made 139 senior appearances in his two spells at Gresty Road and played in 389 League & Cup games all told (three goals scored).

PENALTY KICK
* The penalty kick was introduced to League and Cup football in England in September 1891.
* The first to be awarded in a United game went to Sunderland Albion in a Northern League encounter on Wearside on 12 September 1891. The kick was successfully converted and Albion went on to win the game 4-3. However, after the game the referee consulted with his linesman and between them agreed that the 'foul' had taken place outside the 'offence zone' and as a result the goal was scrubbed

194

out, leaving the final scoreline as 4-2.
* The first penalty awarded to United came in the Northern League game v. Middlesbrough (away) on 17 October 1891. Jack Scott missed from the spot but the Blades still won 2-1.
* Ernest Needham became the first United player to score from the spot, doing so against Blackburn Rovers (won 3-2) in March 1894 (Division 1).
* Charlie Howlett was the first United goalkeeper to save a penalty - in the local derby against Wednesday in an away League game in November 1893 (won 2-1).
* On 2 May 1981, United were awarded a penalty in the 87th minute of their vital end-of-season League Division Two game at home to Walsall who themselves (via Don Penn) had netted from the spot just a few minutes earlier to take the lead (1-0). Don Givens stepped forward to take the crucial kick...he missed and as a result the Blades were relegated while the Saddlers stayed up!
* United were awarded three penalties in their friendly match against the Polish XI in March 1945. Two were missed in a 2-1 victory.
* Three penalties were missed in United's League game v. Bradford Park Avenue in April 1915 - two by the visitors. The Blades won 3-2.
* Blades' forward Bob Benson was the first to score twice from the spot in the same match - in a 7-3 home League win over Bradford City in March 1912.
* Later Colin Morris scored two penalties in the same match on four separate occasions; while Fred Furniss, Peter Duffield and Harry Barton each achieved the feat twice.
* A trio of United players - Fred Tunstall (v. Notts County, December 1924), Harold Hampson (v. Rotherham United, November 1941) and Jim Iley (in the space of four minutes v. Notts County, February 1957) - have missed two penalties in a game for the Blades.
* Ernie Needham had three attempts at scoring a penalty for United v. Sunderland in a League game in December 1898. He netted with his last kick in a 3-0 win. He was the first United player to score and miss from 12-yards in the same match.
* United's goalkeeper 'Fatty' Foulke saved a penalty in successive matches in 1894-95 v. WBA (League) and Corinthians (friendly). And then in February and March 1901 he saved spot-kicks in successive FA Cup-ties v. Sunderland (won 2-1) and v. Wolves (won 4-0).
* Keeper Joe Lievesley saved two penalties when United beat Manchester City 2-1 in a home League game in March 1906. He stopped another two in successive League games v. Aston Villa and Manchester United on 14/15 April 1911.
* Two United players - Bill Brelsford and Jimmy Simmons - both missed from the spot in the same Midland Section wartime game v. Hull City (h) in November 1915. United still won 3-0.
* Nine penalties were awarded to United during the 1922-23 season (six were missed, two of them by Jimmy McCourt).
* Harold Pantling took over in goal (from the injured Gough) after just 15 minutes of United's League game at Manchester City in August 1923 - and with his first touch of the ball he saved a penalty. The Blades still lost 2-1.
* Fred Tunstall missed two spot-kicks in successive matches v. Aston Villa (lost 3-2) and Leicester City (lost 4-1) in February 1929.
* Joe Cockroft did likewise in January 1949, missing from the 12-yard spot against Arsenal and Huddersfield Town in successive First Division matches.
* Harold Barton missed three penalties in 1942-43 - versus Grimsby Town (at home & away) and against Barnsley at Oakwell.
* Joe Kitchen could and should have had a hat-trick when United beat Liverpool 4-2 in a home League game in December 1909 - but somehow he missed from the penalty spot.
* Both sides missed from the spot in the FA Cup-tie between United and Wednesday in February 1898. The Owls won 4-1.
* Ernie Needham took two penalties for United against PNE in an FA Cup 2nd round replay in February 1899 - he scored one and missed one as the Blades won 2-1.
* United players between them missed five penalties during the 1922-23 season - all in the first 16 matches.
* United defender Harry Latham conceded two penalties in a WW2 game v. Derby County in March 1945. One was scored, one missed (saved by 'keeper Hewitt) as the Rams won 3-2.
* Three penalties were awarded in the Bolton Wanderers v. United League Division One game at Burnden Park in April 1947. Alex Forbes missed from the spot for the Blades, Lol Hamlett did likewise for the Wanderers but John Roberts scored to help the home side win 3-2.
* On a snowbound pitch, Johnny Hancocks netted two penalties for Wolves in their 4-3 defeat of United in a 4th round FA Cup replay at Bramall Lane in February 1950. Harold Brook scored from the spot for the Blades.
* Three penalties were awarded in the United-Grimsby Town Second Division game at Bramall Lane in March 1951. Fred Furniss scored for the Blades; Mackenzie missed one and scored one for the Mariners as United won 4-2.
* Furniss was at it again in December 1953. When the Blades (2-1 up) were awarded a penalty in the closing minutes of their home League game with Portsmouth, he picked the ball up but couldn't find the spot! The pitch was a morass of sticky mud, which had covered the 12-yard spot. The referee called out the groundsman who painted the mark on the pitch, thus allowing Furniss to place the ball down before cracking it into the net to seal victory.
* Prior to missing two penalties in an away League game at Notts County (see above) Jim Iley scored two for the Blades against the Magpies in a 5-1 Second Division win at Bramall Lane in October 1956.
* United were awarded 13 penalties in all games during 1956-57.
* United 'keeper Keith Waugh saved two penalties in the Pennine Radio Cup match against Bradford City on 17 May 1982. The game ended 2-2 before United won 4-3 on penalties.
* United 'keeper Graham Benstead stopped two penalties in successive League games v. Northampton Town and Brentford in September 1988. He saved another v. Fulham in the November and dived to keep out a fourth v. Wigan in March 1989. All four games were won.
* One other United 'keeper - Jack Alderson - also saved four penalties in the League in a season (1927-28), while John Burridge saved four in 1985-86, one of them in a friendly.
* Alan Hodgkinson saved a penalty in the 1961 FA Cup semi-final replay with Leicester City at St Andrew's and Graham Shaw missed one. The Blades lost 2-0.
* Goalkeeper Paul Tomlinson, on his League debut for United, saved a penalty v. Southend United in November 1983 (won 5-0).
* Colin Morris missed three times from spot in season 1985-86 - but scored on 10 other occasions, including two against Wimbledon (h) in a 4- 0 win in the August and two more against Seville in a friendly in Match. Earlier, Morris missed two spot-kicks in December 1983 v. Newport County (away) and Bolton (home). He also netted one when completing a hat-trick in the game with Bolton which the Blades won 5-0. In 1986-87 he took six penalties and had a 50% success rate.
* All told Morris took a total of 60 penalties in all games for the Blades. He missed 12 of them. In the Football League alone his record

195

was 35 conversions from 47 taken. Fred Tunstall scored 32 (out of 40) in League matches and was probably the Blades' most consistent penalty-taker, missing only once from the spot in 17 attempts during one excellent spell.

* Tony Currie missed twice from the spot in successive League games in February 1971 v. Luton Town and Charlton. Thankfully the Blades won both matches.

* In (January 1981) John Ryan also missed two penalties in successive matches against Portsmouth and Gillingham - and this time both games ended in 1-0 defeats.

* There were three penalties in the two League games between the Blades and Manchester United in season 1962-63 - Ronnie Simpson missed one and scored one for the Blades while Bobby Charlton scored for the Reds.

* United goalkeeper Tom McAlister saved three penalties during the club's Zambian tour in May 1972 (two in one match).

* Ian Bryson and Carl Bradshaw both missed penalties when United beat Bournemouth 2-0 in a Second Division game in January 1990.

* The following goalkeepers saved penalties on their League debut for the Blades - Bill Foulke (v. WBA, September 1894), Andy Leaning (v. Bournemouth, August 1987) and Mervyn Day (v. Wimbledon, May 1992).

* In all games (League, Cup, friendlies etc - but not including shoot-outs) United have been awarded well over 650 penalties of which around 450 have been converted. They have netted 127 in League football alone (out of 204).

* Jack Smith saved the most penalties for United - 10 in the League, 11 in total.

* Michael Brown missed his first penalty of the season in the Play-off Final v. Wolves at Cardiff's Millennium Stadium in May 2003. The Blades were 3-0 down at the time.

Penalty Shoot-Outs
Over the years United have been involved in 13 penalty shoot-outs, as follows:

(1) United lost 7-6 in a penalty shoot-out to Bristol Rovers in the semi-final of the 1972 Watney Cup at Eastville. Ted Hemsley missed with his kick.

(2) After drawing 0-0 with Sheffield Wednesday in the County Cup Final at Hillsborough in January 1974, John Flynn and Eddie Colquhoun both missed from the spot as the Owls won the penalty shoot-out 4-3.

(3) A friendly in Algiers in May 1974 against an Algerian XI finished level at 0-0 before United won the shoot-out 4-3. Blades' 'keeper Jim Brown saved two spot-kicks.

(4) United won the County Cup Final in October 1974 by beating Rotherham United 4-2 in a shoot-out after a goalless draw at Bramall Lane. Brown again saved from the spot.

(5) In May 1976, during a tournament in Gibralter, United beat Lincoln City 6-5 from 'the spot' in the semi-final (after a 2-2 draw).

(6) The Blades won the County Cup Final in May 1982 after defeating Barnsley 5-4 on penalties at Oakwell after a 0-0 draw.

(7) The Pennine Radio Cup clash (with Bradford City at Valley Parade in May 1982 went to penalties - United winning 4-3 (after a 2-2 draw). United 'keeper Keith Waugh saved two kicks.

(8) In a mini tournament in Sweden in July 1991 (with games of 20 minutes duration), United were eliminated after losing 4-2 on penalties to Varbergs (after a 0-0 draw).

(9) A Zenith Data Systems Cup, 2nd round encounter with Notts County in October 1991 went to penalties (after a 3-3 draw). The Magpies won 2-1 after Dane Whitehouse, Jamie Hoyland, Clive Mendonca and John Gannon had all missed for the Blades.

(10) In March 1993, after drawing 1-1 (aet) with Blackburn Rovers in a 6th round FA Cup replay, United's players held their nerve to win the penalty shoot-out 5-3, Alan Kelly saving from Jason Wilcox to help clinch the tie.

(11) United beat Coventry City 3-1 on penalties to win an FA Cup quarter final replay in March 1998. Roger Nilsen, Bobby Ford and Wayne Quinn netted from the spot while Blades' goalkeeper Alan Kelly was undoubtedly the hero of the hour, saving efforts from three Sky Blues players.

(12) United almost come a cropper to non-League opposition after they had been held to a 1-1 draw (aet) by Rushden & Diamonds in a 3rd round FA Cup replay at Bramall Lane in January 2000. Somehow the Blades eased through 6-5 via the penalty shoot-out.

(13) United were knocked out of the Worthington League Cup by Grimsby Town in the 2nd round in September 2001. After a 3-3 draw (aet) the Mariners went through by winning 4-2 from the 'spot.'

PESCHISOLIDO, Paulo Pasquale
Striker: 31+30 apps* 16 goals*
Born: Scarborough Ontario, Canada, 25 May 1971.
Career: Toronto Blizzard/NASL, Kansas City Comets/NASL (1990-91), Toronto Blizzard/NASL, Birmingham City (£25,000, November 1992), Stoke City (£400,000 in a player-exchange deal involving David Regis, August 1994), West Bromwich Albion (£600,000, July 1996), Fulham (£1.1 million, October 1997), Queen's Park Rangers (on loan, November 2000), BLADES (on loan, January 2001), Norwich City (on loan, March 2001), BLADES (signed for £150,000, July 2001).

Canadian international Paul Peschisolido (45* full & 11 Under-23 caps to his credit plus nine Olympic Games appearances) is an exciting, all-action, industrious utility forward, eager inside the penalty area. He certainly made a big impact at St Andrew's and likewise at Stoke and later at West Bromwich Albion, although he did not have such an impact at Fulham or QPR. He was used sparingly, sometimes with lethal effect as a second-half (even late) substitute it must be said by Blades' manager Neil Warnock during the 2002-03 season, having been dogged by injury prior to that. As a 'sub' he helped the Blades reach the Play-offs (scoring a vital goal in the semis v. Nottingham Forest) and then came on in the Final defeat by Wolves. In 1990 the impish 'Pesch' was voted the USA Major Indoor Soccer League's 'Newcomer of the Year' and helped Fulham win the Second Division championship in 1999. He is married to Blues' Managing-Director Karren Brady.

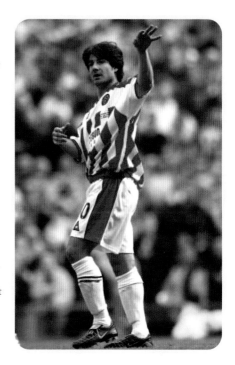

PETERBOROUGH UNITED

United's playing record against Posh:

Football League

Venue	P	W	D	L	F	A
Home	1	1	0	0	4	0
Away	1	1	0	0	4	0
Totals	2	2	0	0	8	0

FA Cup

Venue	P	W	D	L	F	A
Away	1	1	0	0	3	1

League Cup

Venue	P	W	D	L	F	A
Home	1	1	0	0	1	0
Away	1	0	1	0	2	2
Totals	2	1	1	0	3	2

Watney Cup

Venue	P	W	D	L	F	A
Away	1	1	0	0	4	0

The old Peterborough & Fletton United FC, founded in 1925, was suspended by the FA during season 1932-33 and disbanded. Local enthusiasts, determined to carry on, formed a new professional club, Peterborough United, in 1934 and entered the Midland League the following year. They won five successive titles (1955-60) and were undefeated in 1958-59 when they also reached the 3rd round of the FA Cup and won the Northamptonshire Senior Cup, the Maunsell Cup and finished runners-up in the East Anglia Cup.

Elected to the Football League in place of Gateshead in 1960, 'Posh' quickly got into their stride and ran away with the Fourth Division title in their first season in the competition with Terry Bly scoring 52 goals out of a record 134.

The following season United knocked them out of the FA Cup, winning a 4th round tie 3-1 at London Road, Billy Russell (2) and 'Doc' Pace on target. The only League meetings between the clubs took place in 1981-82 (Division 4) and it was the Blades' who grabbed the glory with two 4-0 wins, Keith Edwards scoring twice in each game.

Over 9,200 fans saw the Blades beat Peterboro' 4-0 at London Road in the semi-final of the Watney Cup in August 1972.

Ex-United players Jimmy Hagan and John Barnwell have both managed Peterborough (Hagan being in charge when 'Posh' first entered the Football League in 1960). Players: Ian Benjamin, Mark Blount, David Bradford, Barry Butlin, Tom Cowan, Jon Cullen, Johnny Dryden, Mark Foran, Walter Hoyland, Jack Kendall, Barry Matthews, Harry Orr, Tony Philliskirk, Martin Pike, Colin Rawson, Paddy Shiels, Paddy Sloan, John Turley, Dave Tuttle and Keith Waugh as well as Jim Iley (as Posh player-manager) are among the others who have assisted both clubs.

PETERS, Martin, MBE

Midfielder: 27+1 apps. 4 goals

Born: Plaistow, East London, 8 November 1943.

Career: Dagenham & Essex Schools, London Boys, West Ham United (apprentice, May 1959, professional November 1960), Tottenham Hotspur (£200,000 player-exchange deal, March 1970), Norwich City (March 1975), BLADES (£25,000, player-coach, August 1980, player-manager January-June 1981), Gorleston Town (season 1981-82). Later Director of Tottenham Hotspur FC (appointed 1998).

England's 'other' goal hero in the 1966 World Cup Final, Martin Peters had represented his country in six schoolboy internationals before joining West Ham in 1959. He quickly added Youth caps to his tally (1960-62) and after scoring 100 goals in 364 League and Cup appearances for the Hammers and gaining a European Cup-winners Cup in 1965, he switched to Spurs in a swap-deal involving Jimmy Greaves. Twice a League Cup winner with Spurs in 1971 & 1973, he also gained a UEFA Cup winners' medal in 1974 and netted 76 times in 260 competitive outings for the London club before moving to Norwich in 1975. A goal-hungry midfielder who was 'ten years ahead of his time' according to Alf Ramsey, Peters hit 241 goals in 909 games at club level (over 1,000 all games), giving the Blades one relegated season while also taking over as team boss from Harry Haslam. He scored 20 goals for England in 67 full internationals (1966-76). Peters later joined his colleague Geoff Hurst in the motor insurance business. He was awarded the MBE in 1978.

PHELAN, Terence Michael

Full-back: 9 apps.

Born: Manchester, 16 March 1967

Career: Leeds United (apprentice, June 1983, professional August 1984), Swansea City (free transfer, July 1986), Wimbledon (£100,000, July 1987), Manchester City (£2.5 million, August 1992), Chelsea (£900,000, November 1995), Everton (£850,000, January 1997), Crystal Palace (on loan, October 1999), Fulham (free, February 2000), BLADES (free, August 2001), Charleston Battery/USA (November 2001).

A Republic of Ireland international left-back (capped 41 times at senior level as well as appearing in 'B', Under-23, Under-21 and Youth team matches), Terry Phelan joined the Blades on a three-month contract as cover for injuries and suspensions. Although not fully match-fit his experience went a long way in helping the team come through a difficult period. An FA Cup winner with Wimbledon in 1988, he appeared in 491 club games (including 198 for the Dons and 122 for Manchester City) before moving over to the States in the autumn of 2001.

PHILIP, George C

Centre-forward: 10 'other' apps. 2 goals

Born: Newport-on-Tay near Dundee, circa 1890

Career: Dundee, Sunderland (April 1914), Dundee, BLADES (WW1 guest: September-December 1918).

George Philip guested for the Blades during the Great War. Earlier he had scored 22 goals in only 38 senior games for Sunderland for whom, he made his League debut against United in September 1914.

197

PHILLIPSON, William Thomas
Centre-forward: 61 apps. 27 goals
Born: Ryton-on-Tyne, 31 October 1898. Died: Wolverhampton, 19 November 1965.
Career: Scotswood FC (May 1914), Army Service (WW1), Newcastle United (£500, December 1919), Swindon Town (£500, May 1921), Wolverhampton Wanderers (£1,000, December 1923), BLADES (£2,600, March 1928), Bilston United (player-manager, July 1930), Walsall (August 1931-May 1932).
Just after signing from Wolves, Tom Phillipson scored on his League debut for the Blades v. Middlesbrough (h) in a 4-1 win. A big, broad-shouldered centre-forward, noted for his first-time shooting, he loved to race after the ball and was never afraid to mix it with the hefty defenders of his day. He once scored 14 goals (out of 15) in one schoolboy game and netted 10 in the next. After gaining two England schoolboy caps, he served as an Army sergeant in Russia during WW1 but never really got a chance at Newcastle with so many potential stars around at the same time. He netted 24 goals in 87 League outings with Swindon and then notched 111 in 159 games for Wolves, helping them win the third Division (North) in 1924 and set a club record of 37 goals in senior games in 1925-26. It was a shock to the Molineux faithful when he left to join the Blades in 1928, but although nearing his 30th birthday he still produced the goods and when he quit League soccer in 1930 he had amassed an exceptionally fine record of 159 goals in 301 appearances. On retiring Phillipson concentrated on his business interests in Wolverhampton and went into local politics. In the spring of 1938 he was elected Mayor of the Town and in 1947 watched Dennis Westcott beat his scoring record for Wolves.

PHILLISKIRK, Anthony
Forward: 74+21 apps. 22 goals
Born: Sunderland, 10 February 1965
Career: BLADES (apprentice, April 1981, professional August 1983), Rotherham United (on loan, October 1986), Oldham Athletic (£25,000, July 1988), Preston North End (£30,000, February 1989), Bolton Wanderers (£50,000, June 1989), Peterborough United (£85,000, October 1992), Burnley (£80,000, January 1994), Carlisle United (on loan, October 1995), Cardiff City (£60,000, December 1995), Macclesfield Town (on loan, February 1998), Oldham Athletic (August 1998).
An England Schoolboy international, striker Tony Philliskirk developed into both a maker and taker of chances who scored consistently well throughout his career having made his League debut for the Blades against Brentford in October 1983 and netted his first goal for the club in a 1-0 win at Plymouth Argyle later in the month. He helped the Blades win promotion from Division Three that season.

PHYSIOTHERAPISTS
1962-81	Geoff Goodall
1981-86	Jim Dixon
1986-87	Ian Bailey
1988-94	Derek French
1994-96	Derek French/Denis Circuit
1996-97	Denis Circuit
1997-98	Denis Circuit/Dennis Pettitt/Stuart Paveley
1998-99	Dennis Pettitt/Stuart Paveley
1999-2000	Dennis Pettitt
2000-03	Dennis Pettitt/Nigel Cox

(See also under COACHES & TRAINERS)

Physio's Report:
Jim Dixon was also United's trainer/physio in the mid-1980s and in the cases of Messrs Circuit (1997) and Paveley (1998) they both left the club during that year.
Dean Riddle was United's fitness Consultant in 2002-03.

PICKERING, John
Inside/centre-forward: 561 apps. 191 goals
Born: Mortomley near Barnsley, 18 December 1908. Died: Bournemouth, 1977.
Career: Barnsley Grammar School, Mortomley St Saviour's, BLADES (May 1926, retired May 1948).
'Jack' Pickering was a stylish, cultured inside-forward with powerful shot who many thought would develop into an international-class player while others feared his temperament which was so often betrayed in a lack of urgency. He did play for England nevertheless, versus Scotland in Glasgow in April 1933 and also represented the Football League, but it was at club level where he performed best, appearing for the Blades v. Arsenal in the 1936 FA Cup Final. Among the handful of players who assisted the club before, during and after WW2, he eventually retired in 1948. He broke his leg in the local derby with Sheffield Wednesday in March 1939 and was out of the team for six weeks, but still collected his Second Division championship medal. He netted 102 League and 79 wartime goals for the Blades. A qualified accountant, Pickering, later ran a hotel in Bournemouth.

PIKE, Martin Russell
Full-back: 160+4 apps. 5 goals
Born: South Shields, 21 October 1964
Career: West Bromwich Albion (apprentice, June 1981, professional October 1982), Peterborough United (August 1983), BLADES (August 1986), Tranmere Rovers (on loan, November 1989), Bolton Wanderers (on loan, December 1989), Fulham (£60,000, February 1990), Rotherham United (August 1994-May 1996).
A totally committed full-back, as keen as mustard who loved to venture forward, given the chance, Martin Pike was very popular with the supporters (despite a few shortcomings) and generally gave a good account of himself out on the park. He failed to break into the first XI at West Brom, made 126 League appearances for Posh, and 190 for Fulham whom he helped gain promotion from Division Three in 1992 (missing only one game).

PILGRIM, James Edward
Full-back: 15 apps.
Born: Holmes Chapel, 1879.
Career: Rotherham Swifts, BLADES (October 1896), Chesterfield (July 1899), Rotherham Town (season 1901-02).
Able to play in either full-back position, Jim Pilgrim stepped in for the injured Peter Boyle to partner Harry Thicket during the first half of the 1898-99 season. He made 54 League appearances for Chesterfield.

PLANT, James
Left-half/full-back: 70 apps. 5 goals
Born: Whitwell, circa 1895
Career: Whitwell Old Boys, BLADES (November 1919), Macclesfield (1926).
The versatile Jim Plant made his League debut for the Blades in the 0-0 draw with Derby County in February 1920 when he replaced George Utley. A strong, crisp tackler, his best season at Bramall Lane was in 1922-23 when he made 44 senior appearances in the half-back line along with Jimmy Waugh and Harry Pantling. He lost his place to George Green.

PLAYER OF THE YEAR (Award)
The Sheffield United Supporters' Club started its annual 'Player of the Year' awards in 1966-67 and the first recipient of the trophy was goalkeeper Alan Hodgkinson. Since then the following have all won the star prize: Ken Mallender (1968), Dave Powell (1969), Alan Woodward (on four occasions, in 1970, '74, '76 & '78), Tony Currie (1971), Trevor Hockey (1972), Ted Hemsley (1973), Keith Edwards (twice, 1977 & '84), Jim Brown (1975), Tony Kenworthy (twice, 1979 & '80), Bob Hatton (1981), Mike Trusson (twice, 1982 & '83), Glenn Cockerill (1985), Paul Stancliffe (twice, 1986 & '88), Peter Beagrie (1987), Tony Agana (1989) and Simon Tracey (twice, 1990 & '92), Brian Deane (1991), Paul Beesley (1993), Carl Bradshaw (1994), Kevin Gage (1995), Alan Kelly (1996), Petr Katchouro (1997) Nicky Marker (1998), Curtis Woodhouse (1999), Paul Devlin (2000), Shaun Murphy (2001), Michael Brown (2002) and goalkeeper Paddy Kenny (2003).

PLAYERS
* A record number of players (57) were used in senior matches by United during the course of season 1997-98 (44 in the League). There were a record number of injuries as well!
* The 100th player to appear in a Football League game for United was Herbert Chapman, on the opening day of the 1902-03 season against Wednesday at home, lost 3-2.
* In September 1950 both right-backs scored twice in the same Second Division match when the Blades beat West Ham 5-3 at Upton Park. Hammers' No2 Ernie Devlin conceded two own-goals while Fred Furness netted twice from the penalty spot for the Blades.
* United were unchanged for nine successive matches in November & December 1923.
* United played with only 10 throughout their Midland Counties League game v. Long Eaton Rangers on 28 March 1891 - but still won 3-2. Cross and Lilley both missed their trains and the trainer, Jack Houseley played at right-back.

PLYMOUTH ARGYLE
United's playing record against the Pilgrims:

Football League

Venue	P	W	D	L	F	A
Home	17	11	4	2	29	8
Away	17	3	4	10	9	25
Totals	34	14	8	12	38	33

League Cup

	P	W	D	L	F	A
Away	1	0	0	1	1	2

Formed initially as the Argyle Football Club in the Borough Arms (a coffee house on Bedford Street, Plymouth) in September 1886 by pupils from both State and Private Schools, Plymouth Argyle became a professional body in 1903 and after doing superbly well in the Southern League, finally gained Football League status in 1920 as founder members of the Third Division.
Having suffered the agony of finishing runners-up in the Third Division (South) six seasons running (1921-27) they finally gained promotion in 1930 before opposing the Blades for the first time in the competition in 1934-35 (Division 2), winning both matches, 2-1 at 'the Lane' and 2-0 in Devon.
United's best win over the Pilgrims is 5-0, achieved courtesy of an Arthur Bottom hat-trick, at Bramall Lane in 1952-53, the season they crashed to a 5-2 defeat at Home Park, and in January 1960, 'Doc' Pace netted twice in a 4-0 home win.
The Blades have won only three times at Plymouth - the last in 1983-84 (1-0) when the Pilgrims reached the semi-final stage of the FA Cup.
The Pilgrims' only other League win at Bramall Lane was in 1938 (also 1-0).
Despite Alan Birchenall giving United the lead, they lost 2-1 to Argyle in a 2nd round League Cup-tie at Home Park in 1964.
Neil Warnock has managed both the Blades and the Pilgrims. United's ace striker Keith Edwards also played for Argyle as did Walter Bennett, Len Birks, Julian Broddle, Jack Chisholm, Arthur Eggleston, Stewart Evans (Blades reserve), Bill Gooney, Doug Hodgson, Phil Kite, Adrian Littlejohn, Jimmy McCormick, Nicky Marker, John Matthews, Andy Morrison, Bernie Oxley, Grant Smith, Phil Starbuck, Alf Tootill, Mike Trusson and Ronnie Waldock among others. Stewart Houston played for the Blades and was coach at Argyle.

POINTS
(See also: FOOTBALL LEAGUE)
The most points gained by United in a complete season of League football has been 96 (out of a possible 138) in 1981-82 (Division 4).
Despite not being founder members of the Football League, United became only the fifth team (behind Aston Villa, Sunderland, Everton and Blackburn Rovers) to reach the milestone of 1,000 points.

199

POOLE, John Smith
Centre-half/left-half: 25 'other' apps. one goal
Born: Kirkby-in-Ashfield, Derbyshire, March 1892. Died: 12 March 1967
Career: Codnor YC, Sutton Junction, Nottingham Forest (season 1914-15), Army service (stationed in Sunderland), BLADES (WW1 guest: January 1916-March 1917, Sunderland (May 1919), Bradford City (May 1924, reserve team player-coach, August 1927, first team trainer August 1930), Mansfield Town (trainer-manager, May 1938-October 1944), Notts County (trainer, September 1944), Derby County (trainer, 1946-56), Sutton Town (Central Alliance, trainer/coach, August 1956-May 1957).
Owing to WW1, Jack Poole was 27 years of age when he finally made his Football League debut for Sunderland against Aston Villa in August 1919. He played in the same team as Charlie Buchan at Roker Park and made over 150 appearances for the Wearsiders before moving to Bradford in 1924. He went on to play in another 101 games for the Bantams before becoming player-manager of Mansfield in 1938, a position held for six years.

PORTSMOUTH
United's playing record against Pompey:
Football League

Venue	P	W	D	L	F	A
Home	33	24	3	6	72	33
Away	33	11	6	16	47	59
Totals	66	35	9	22	119	92

FA Cup

Venue	P	W	D	L	F	A
Home	1	1	0	0	3	0
Away	2	0	0	2	1	4
Totals	3	1	0	2	4	4

League Cup

Venue	P	W	D	L	F	A
Home	1	1	0	0	1	0

It all happened in 1898...Alderman J E Pink and five other local business and professional men agreed to purchase some ground close to Goldsmith Avenue for £4,950 which they developed into Fratton Park in record-breaking time. A team of 'professional' footballers was signed up by manager Frank Brettell to form Portsmouth FC and entry was gained to the Southern League, the first match taking place in September 1899.
After winning the Southern League title in 1919-20, Pompey were elected to the Football League, playing initially in the Third Division. And, in fact, they had the honour of being the first club to start out in that Division and go on to reach the FA Cup Final, doing so in 1934, and they were also the first to win the trophy in 1939.
It was not until January 1928 that the Blades met Pompey for the first time in a League game, the Fratton Park side having become the first team from the original Third Division members to reach the top flight. The venue was Bramall Lane and in front of 23,282 fans United won 3-1. Pompey, though, gained revenge later in the season with a 4-1 home victory.
Between 1928 and 1933 Pompey held the upper hand, winning four times at both Sheffield and at Fratton Park
In the four seasons immediately after WW2, Pompey were regarded as one of the country's finest teams, winning the League title in successive seasons (1949 & 1950) and during that period they whipped the Blades 6-0 at Fratton Park (September 1947)
Soon afterwards winger Peter Harris scored four goals in Pompey's 6-2 home League win over United in October 1954.
The Blades won home games by 5-2 in May 1955 and 5-0 in October 1969 (when Gil Reece netted a hat-trick), and they also triumphed twice away with 5-1 scorelines, in August 1969 and in September 1970, Alan Woodward obliging with a treble in the latter game. Meanwhile Graham Shaw scored with a 50-yarder in a 3-1 home win over Pompey in September 1960.United have lost just two home matches against Pompey since WW2, the last in 1955. United's last win at Fratton Park was in 1996 (2-1).
In the Second Division match between the teams in 1986-87, four players were sent-off including United's Peter Beagrie. Paul Mariner scored the only goal, putting the ball past his own 'keeper to hand the Blades victory.
Dave Bassett's first game in charge of United was the 2-1defeat in the 4th round of the FA Cup at Portsmouth on 1 February 1988 - after Tony Philliskirk had given the Blades a 19-second lead
In 2002-03, with Pompey heading the First Division (on their way to the Premiership) United inflicted upon them a rare Fratton Park defeat, winning 2-1 with goals by Peter Ndlovu and Michael Brown whose netted with a stunning strike late on.
Brett Angell, Michael Brown, Harry Buddery, Shaun Derry, Paul Hall, Chris Kamara, Jeff King, Martin Kuhl, Steve Lovell, David Munks, Trevor Ross, Lee Sandford, Carl Tiler, Bob Widdowson, Steve Wigley and Paul Wood are among the players who have served with both clubs.

PORT VALE (Burslem)
United's playing record against the Valiants:
Football League

Venue	P	W	D	L	F	A
Home	14	10	3	1	33	11
Away	14	7	5	2	34	15
Totals	28	17	8	3	67	26

FA Cup

Venue	P	W	D	L	F	A
Home	1	0	1	0	1	1
Away	2	1	0	1	3	3
Totals	3	1	1	1	4	4

Midland Counties League

Venue	P	W	D	L	F	A
Home	1	0	1	0	1	1
Away	1	0	0	1	1	3
Totals	2	0	1	1	2	4

Formed in 1876 as Port Vale, the club adopted the 'prefix' Burslem in 1884 upon moving to that part of the Potteries. The team duly took its place in the newly-formed Second Division in 1892 alongside the Blades and ten other clubs. But slipped out of the League after four seasons only to return in 1898, remaining until 1907. Two years later they dropped the name 'Burslem' before securing a ground at Hanley in 1913. Six years later, in 1919, following the compulsory disbanding of Leeds City for allegations of illegal

200

payments (never proven), Vale re-entered the Football League, filling the vacant place in Division Two.

Their first League game against the Blades took place on 10 December 1892 and it turned out to be quite a sensational afternoon as United landed a handsome and record-breaking 10-0 victory at the Athletic Ground, Cobridge. There was a strong wind blowing and the pitch was covered by four inches of snow. With barely 500 hardy spectators present, United went 3-0 up after 10 minutes and led 5-0 at half-time. Harry Hammond scored four times during the course of the match. In winning by that margin, the Blades became the first and remain the only team to have claimed 10 goals in away League game.

A week later United won 4-0 at Bramall Lane to rub more salt into the 'Valiants' wounds.

The clubs did not face each other again until 1934-35 when the Vale exacted some revenge by winning 2-0 at home on the opening Saturday.

Their only victory on Blades' soil (3-1) came in 1999-2000 when they were fighting a losing battling against relegation from Division One.

The clubs have so far met twice in the FA Cup...Vale winning a 1st round replay by 2-1 after extra-time in 1897-98. With the scores level at 1-1, United's giant goalkeeper Bill Foulke frequently ventured upfield to try and force the winner. He was caught out as Vale counter-attacked and snatched the deciding goal themselves. The Blades later claimed a 2-1 victory in a 4th round home tie in 1962-63.

Archie Annan, Paul Beesley, Marcus Bent, Len Birks, Gary Brazil, Steve Cammack, John Connaughton, Dean Glover, Colin Grainger, Gary Hamson, Adrian Littlejohn, Percy Oldacre, Bert Pearson, Jack Peart, Paul Smith, Gareth Taylor, Percy Thorpe, Michael Twiss, Harry Wainwright, Gary West and Jack Wilkinson are listed among the players who served with both clubs.

POWELL, Clifford George

Defender: 14+3 apps.

Born: Watford, 21 February 1968

Career: Watford (apprentice, April 1984, professional February 1986), Hereford United (on loan, December 1987), BLADES (March 1988), Doncaster Rovers (on loan, March 1989), Cardiff City (on loan, November 1989); retired, June 1989 through injury.

Reserve defender Cliff Powell made his senior debut for the Blades as a second-half substitute in a 5-0 defeat at Leeds United soon after joining the club. He played in just 22 League games during his career.

POWELL, David

Defender/midfielder: 100 apps. 2 goals

Born: Dolgarrog, Caernarfonshire, 15 October 1944.

Career: Gwydyn Rovers, Wrexham (groundstaff January 1962, professional, May 1963), BLADES (£40,000, September 1968), Cardiff City (with Gil Reece, September 1972, retired, May 1974). In 1975 he became a police officer, based in Bridgend, and later trained police recruits as well as managing the local force's football team.

A Welsh international, capped 11 times at senior level (ten as a United player) and on four occasions by the Under-23s, the versatile David Powell, slim and stylish, was a fine defender, quick in recovery. A hard but fair tackler, deliberate in his actions, he was always involved in the action. Unfortunately injuries ruined his career. He appeared in 134 League games for Wrexham and 36 for Cardiff. He helped the Blades win promotion to the First Division in 1971, was a Welsh Cup winner with Cardiff in 1973 and a finalist two years later.

PREMIER LEAGUE

United played in the Premiership (Premier League) for the first time in season 1992-93 when they finished in 14th position. The following season the Blades were relegated.

This is their full record of Premiership football:

Venue	P	W	D	L	F	A	Pts
Home	42	16	16	10	57	42	64
Away	42	6	12	24	39	71	30
Totals	84	22	28	34	96	113	94

Premiership Facts:

* United's first game in the Premiership was against Manchester United at Bramall Lane on 15 August 1992. A crowd of 28,070 saw them win 2-1. Brian Deane had the pleasure of scoring both United's goals and at the same time netted the first in the competition itself.

* Four days later United suffered their first defeat, beaten 2-1 by Liverpool at Anfield...Deane again on target.

* United's first PL draw was a 2-2 stalemate at home to Wimbledon on 25 August.

* Their first home defeat was against Aston Villa (2-0) on 29 August and their first away win was claimed at Chelsea (2-1) on 31 October 1992 (Deane again a scorer).

* United's biggest home crowd for a PL game is 30,044 v. Sheffield Wednesday on 23 October 1993. Away from home it is 41,949 at Old Trafford v. Manchester United on 18 August 1993.

* The lowest at Bramall Lane is 13,646 v. West Ham United 28 March 1994 and the lowest away, just 3,979 v. Wimbledon at Plough Lane on 20 February 1993.

* Deane (14) and Adrian Littlejohn (11) scored most PL goals for the Blades while Carl Bradshaw (72) appeared in most PL matches.

201

PRESTON NORTH END

United's playing record against the Shakers:

Football League

Venue	P	W	D	L	F	A
Home	40	27	7	6	81	40
Away	40	8	11	21	43	75
Totals	80	35	18	27	124	115

FA Cup

Home	2	2	0	0	4	1
Away	3	0	2	1	3	4
Totals	5	2	2	1	7	5

League Cup

Home	1	1	0	0	2	0
Away	1	0	0	1	0	3
Totals	2	1	0	1	2	3

WW2

Home	1	1	0	0	2	0
Away	3	0	1	2	3	9
Totals	4	1	1	2	5	9

Preston North End (founded in 1881 by players keen to get away from the rugby code and other sports which had been preferred by the original north End Cricket & Rugby Club, formed in 1863) were one of the leading clubs in the country during the 1880s. They were also one of the first to embrace professionalism, originally illegally, signing players from Scotland and finding them jobs on the Preston area.

The early game in England was chiefly one of dribbling and rushing, but north of the border Queen's Park pioneered the passing game. The Scottish 'professors' coached their Preston team-mates in the art of passing the ball and this gave North End a distinct advantage over their local counterparts. Although it was neighbours Blackburn Rovers and Blackburn Olympic who took the honours in the FA Cup, Preston soon starting to sweep all before them (they walloped Hyde 26-0 in an FA Cup-tie in 1887) and became the first team to complete the League and Cup double when the former was instituted in 1888-89, North End remaining unbeaten all season.

By the time the Blades entered the Football League in 1892, the passing game was being widely practised and North End had lost a lot of their early advantage.

Th first League game between United and PNE took place in November 1893 and 3,250 fans witnessed a 1-1 draw. Later in the season United lost 3-0 at Deepdale.

Over the years the two clubs have fought out some fine battles, United enjoying an unbeaten home record from 1897 until WW2, embracing 19 matches, 16 won.

Since the 1950s, Preston's fortunes have slumped until recently with only six seasons in opposition before the end of the century. United's best victories took place in consecutive seasons - in 1909-10 they won 5-1 at home, and a year later triumphed 5-0, Joe Kitchen scoring twice in each game. In 1954-55 North End had a rare 5-0 win at 'the Lane' as United lost 10 of their opening 13 League matches, conceding 38 goals in the process. United recovered bravely to finish in mid-table.

United can claim four victories at Deepdale, the last (2-0) coming as far back as 1955-56, the season they finished bottom of the First Division.

In the FA Cup, the clubs have been paired only three times. In 1899 and 1936 United won at Bramall Lane (after draws at Deepdale) and remarkably each time the Blades went on to reach the Final, beating Derby, in the first but losing to Arsenal in the second. In 2002 the clubs were drawn at Deepdale, North End winning 2-0 after Peter Ndlovu ha\d given the Blades the lead.

North End knocked the Blades out of the League Cup in 1999-2000, winning a 2nd round tie 3-2 on aggregate.

Robert Atkins, Frank Becton, Gary Brazil, Ian Bryson, Alf Common, John Cunningham, Jack Drummond, Sammy Dobson, Jack English, Stan Fazackerley, Kevin Gage, Hugh Gallacher, Billy Hendry, John Hope, Rab Howell, Roy John, Alan Kelly, Jack Kendall, Richard Lucas, Andy McLaren, Mark Patterson, Jack Pears, Tony Philliskirk, Joe Walton, Arthur Wharton, Norman Wharton and Paul A Williams are among the players who have served with both clubs. Howard Kendall played for North and managed the Blades and Andy Beattie was a player with Preston and assistant-manager of United.

Sheffield United team group: (back row, l-r) Secretary John Nicholson, Director Smith, Harry Johnson, Albert Groves, Joe Lievesley, Bob Benson, Trainer Waller, Director Tomlinson (middle row, l-r) Jimmy Donnelly, Arthur Brown, Ernest Needham, Alonzo Drake, **Fred Priest**, Bert Lipsham (front row, l-r) Johnny Lang, Bernard Wilkinson.

PRIEST, Alfred Ernest

Inside & outside-left/full-back: 248 apps. 86 goals
Born: Darlington, 1875. Died: Hartlepool, 5 May 1922.
Career: South Bank, BLADES (July 1896), South Bank (December 1905), Middlesbrough (September 1906, retired in 1907 when he became trainer at Ayresome Park), Hartlepool United (manager, August 1908-May 1912). Thereafter ran a pub in Hartlepool for ten years until his death in 1922.
Fred Priest was a 'prober' of defences, a glutton for work who developed a useful scoring record for the Blades and always did well in international matches. He made his name as an outside-left but was switched inside to let in Bert Lipsham, being able to bring the best of his winger with his clever, decisive and thoughtful prompting. A League Championship winner in 1898, followed by two FA Cup Final triumphs in 1899 and 1902, Priest also played in the 1901 Final.

PROFESSIONALISM

Professionalism in football was first seen as long ago as 1879 when Blackburn Rovers and Darwen recruited players from Scotland and paid them wages. Over the next year or so Bolton and Preston North End followed suit.
But it wasn't until 20 July 1885 that professionalism was finally accepted into English soccer...an important step in the history of the game.
Immediately it meant that the teams attracting fair attendances, Sheffield United among them, could sign star players and reward them with payment for their efforts! However, there were restrictions initially...which stated that no player could play in an FA Cup game before he had resided in the local area for at least two years!

PROFESSIONAL FOOTBALLERS' ASSOCIATION (PFA)

The first attempt to form a Player's Union was made in October 1893. It failed.
However, six years later, in July 1899, a Union (named The National Union of Association Players) was formed but quickly became defunct due to lack of support.
The PFA (Players' Union) came into being on 2 December 1907 and was recognised as a Trade Union on 10 March 1908 when it was registered as Football Players' and Trainers' Union.
Later that year (August) the FA gave it's official approval but surprisingly withdrew in March 1909.
But then, in August 1909 - after players had threatened to strike - the FA and Union got back on track and since then their 'Union/PFA' has done tremendous things for thee game, especially the players. The title 'PFA' was officially adopted in August 1958.
* Players associated with Sheffield United and also with the PFA include Brian Marwood.

PROGRAMMES

Sheffield United FC began producing its own matchday programme in 1897-98.
Prior to that team cards/sheets (similar to postcards) were issued and sold at important matches.
Those first full programmes comprised eight pages but were quickly enlarged to 16-page publications and proved exceptionally good value for money. Photographs started to appear just before WW1.
Unfortunately the club secretary John Nicholson showed very little interest in the programme and during the 1920s it was not half as good, although in 1930 it was increased to 20 pages.
After Nicholson's tragic death (in a road accident in 1932) the programme picked up again and a two-colour cover came into being in 1935.
During WW2 the programme reverted to a single sheet (sometimes taking in four pages) and after the hostilities, with the government placing a restriction order on paper, the Blades' programme, like most club productions up and down the country, was of a rather poor quality.
An eight-page programme (priced at 3d) re-appeared in 1952 and a year later photographs returned to lighten up the blandness.
The United programme remained practically unaltered for the next 15 years of so with the 'Football League Review' being inserted in the mid-1960s.

203

Come 1969, more photographs appeared in the programme and in 1970-71 the 16-page edition (now titled "the Lane' Line Up' and referred to in the main as the matchday magazine, costing one shilling/5p) often featured a large action shot on the front, a double-page spread of statistics inside and the team line-ups on the outside back cover.

A multi-coloured front adorned the 24-page programme in the mid-1970s (price: 15p) and full colour printing came into operation in 1980, giving the programme a glossy feel to it - and the cover price rose accordingly.

It cost the supporter 50p in 1984; the price had doubled by 1990 and then it went up to £2 before the turn of the century.

A football club's programme acts as an almanac and as an avid collector of programmes myself, I know full well that a full set makes very interesting and can prove to be a huge investment.

There are hundreds of supporters up and down the country who collect programmes from the matches they attend; others collect them for one club only; others tend to start their collecting from the day they began watching/supporting a team. It's an interesting hobby - but mighty expensive these days, especially if you attempt to seek out those golden oldies.

PROMOTION

United have so far gained promotion on nine separate occasions.

Season	Promoted To	Notes
1892-93	Division 1	Beat Accrington in Test Match
1938-39	Division 1	Back 'up' after five seasons
1952-53	Division 1	Champions of Division 2
1960-61	Division 1	Runners-up to Ipswich Town
1970-71	Division 1	Runners-up to Leicester City
1981-82	Division 3	Champions of Division 4
1983-84	Division 2	3rd in Div. 3 behind Oxford & Wimbledon
1988-89	Division 2	Runners-up to Wolverhampton Wds
1989-90	Division 1	Runners-up to Leeds United

NB: 1992 Founder Members of the 'new' Premiership

In 1983-84 United were involved in a great promotion battle with Hull City, finally pipping the Tigers for a place in the top flight on goal-difference.

In 1949-50 the Blades failed to overcome their arch-rivals Sheffield Wednesday in a tremendous Second Division promotion race by just 0.008 of a goal. (See also: FOOTBALL LEAGUE)

PUBLIC LIMITED COMPANY

Sheffield United Football Club officially became a Limited Company (club) in August 1899 - only the second club in the country to take such a standing - Small Heath (Birmingham City) were the first in July 1888. In August 1997 United were registered as a plc with Mike McDonald the first chairman.

PUBLIC PRACTICE MATCHES

>From 1889 until 1958 - with the odd exception - public practices matches were staged at Bramall Lane prior to the start of each season. The games usually featured the Stripes (first team players) against the Whites (reserves) and the gate receipts were usually divided among local charities.

In 1948 the Whites were battered 8-0 and in 1957 they crashed 9-1. The biggest reported attendance for a practice match is 9,000, in August 1925 (the FA Cup was on show).

PUBLICANS

Several footballers become licensees whether looking after a pub or hotel. Here are a few who went into the licensing trade after removing their boots!

Len Allchurch, Bill Beer, Tom Boyle, Billy Brawn, Alf Common, George Hedley, 'Roy' John, Seth King, Harold Pantling, Jack Pickering, Fred Priest, Bill Ross, Eddie Shimwell and Harry Thickett.

* Joe Cockroft went into the licensing victualler's trade.

PUNTON, William Hamilton

Outside-left: 21 apps. 3 goals

Born: Glennkindrie, East Lothian, 9 May 1934

Career: Bredalbane FC, Portadown (August 1953), Newcastle United (£6,000, February 1954), Southend United (player-exchange involving John McGuigan, July 1958), Norwich City (July 1959), BLADES (£7,500, November 1966), Scunthorpe United (January 1968), Yarmouth Town (player-coach, June 1969, later manager, May 1974-April 1990), Diss Town (manager, May 1990-May 1995). He also worked for the Norfolk County Council for a number of years.

An orthodox left-winger, who at times could bemuse his marking full-back, Bill Punton made 23 League appearances for Newcastle over a period of four years. After a season at Roots Hall he then gave Norwich splendid service, scoring 29 goals in 256 games and helping them win the 1962 League Cup Final (when he scored twice in the Final v. Rochdale) before assisting the Blades. He brought local success to both Yarmouth and Diss, and in the case of the latter club, to national recognition in the FA Vase in 1994.

QUEEN'S PARK RANGERS

United's playing record against QPR:

Premier League

Venue	P	W	D	L	F	A
Home	2	0	1	1	2	3
Away	2	0	0	2	3	5
Totals	4	0	1	3	5	8

Football League

Venue	P	W	D	L	F	A
Home	15	4	10	1	17	11
Away	15	4	3	8	19	23
Totals	30	8	13	9	36	34

FA Cup

Venue	P	W	D	L	F	A
Away	1	1	0	0	1	0

There is an element of doubt regarding the exact date Queen's Park Rangers Football Club was formed. Some say 1885, others 1886, even 1887...whatever the year, it is certain that it came about when Christ Church Rangers and St Jude's Institute amalgamated. After playing in the Southern League for many seasons, enjoying some success, QPR were elected to the Football League in 1920. However, they languished in the Third Division/South until rising to the Second in 1948 ...and it was another 20 years before they gained promotion to the top flight.

The Blades and Rangers, in fact, have met only in 17 seasons, nine of which have been since 1990. And the 34 'League' games have produced 14 draws, 11 in Sheffield.

The first League fixtures took place in 1949-50, Rangers forcing a 1-1 draw at Bramall Lane in October, while the Blades won 3-1 at Loftus Road in February, all the goals coming in a 4-minute spell after half-time, with Harold Brook netting twice.

United scored twice in the last 90 seconds to earn a 2-2 draw at QPR in a Second Division game in March 1971, Ted Hemsley netting a last-ditch penalty to save a point.

Rangers had the better of the exchanges in the four Premiership games

United beat QPR in the 4th round of the FA Cup in 1923, Tommy Sampy's goal taking them through to the semi-finals.

Since their formation in 1886, Rangers have changed their ground no fewer than 15 times; non have been named Queen's Park but the London club has played League matches at The White City and, indeed, at Wormwood Scrubs!

Tony Currie was a star performer with both the Blades and QPR.

Stewart Houston played for the Blades and later managed Rangers.

Players who served with both clubs include Billy Barnes, goalkeepers Graham Benstead and John Burridge, Bob Bolam, Tony Currie, Alonzo Drake, Paul Furlong, Don Givens, Bernie Harris, Fred Hawley, Nicky Johns, Vinnie Jones, Paul Parker, Paul Peschisolido, Derek Richardson, Jack Sheen, Tom Simons, Nigel Spackman, Simon Stainrod, Gareth Taylor and Steve Yates. Bruce Rioch played for the Blades and was later assistant-manager of QPR.

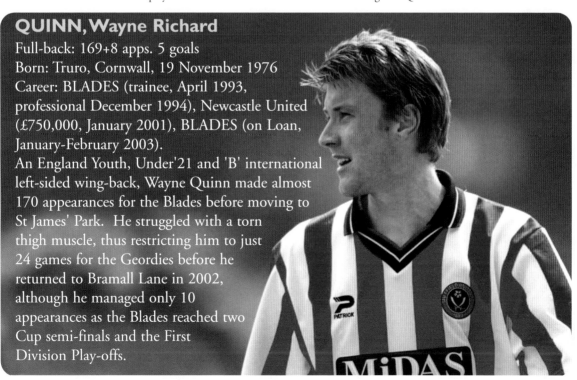

QUINN, Wayne Richard

Full-back: 169+8 apps. 5 goals
Born: Truro, Cornwall, 19 November 1976
Career: BLADES (trainee, April 1993, professional December 1994), Newcastle United (£750,000, January 2001), BLADES (on Loan, January-February 2003).

An England Youth, Under'21 and 'B' international left-sided wing-back, Wayne Quinn made almost 170 appearances for the Blades before moving to St James' Park. He struggled with a torn thigh muscle, thus restricting him to just 24 games for the Geordies before he returned to Bramall Lane in 2002, although he managed only 10 appearances as the Blades reached two Cup semi-finals and the First Division Play-offs.

206

Left: Sheffield United v.s Tottenham Hotspur Dec 27th 1965
Right: Programme October 20th 1930

RADFORD, Bernard

Centre-forward/inside-left: 22 apps. 7 goals
Born: West Melton, 1907.
Career: Darfield FC, Nelson (1927), BLADES (May 1929), Northampton Town (June 1931-July 1932).
A utility forward, Bernie Radford was signed by the Blades after scoring 41 goals in 55 League games for Nelsen. He did well initially at Bramall Lane (six goals in his first 15 games) but then got bogged down, hence his move to Northampton.

RANKINE, Simon Mark

Utility: 8+1 apps.
Born: Doncaster, 30 September 1969
Career: Doncaster Boys, Doncaster Rovers (trainee, April 1987, professional, July 1988), Wolverhampton Wanderers (£70,000, January 1992), Preston North End (£100,000, September 1996), BLADES (on loan, March-May 2003).
The versatile Mark Rankine appeared in almost 200 games for his home-town club Doncaster before joining Wolves in 1992. A strong, forceful player, who prefers the right-back or right-half berths, he lost his place to Jamie Smith at Molineux, hence his transfer to Deepdale (having played in 167 games for the Wanderers). He was in North End's Second Division promotion-winning team in 1999 and was a key member of the Lillywhites' line-up as they reached the 2001 First Division Play-off Final where they lost to their Lancashire neighbours Bolton Wanderers.
Signed by manager Neil Warnock to strengthen the squad for the final push towards promotion, he made his debut in a 2-2 draw at Crystal Palace in April 2003. His presence certainly made a huge impact in the two Play-offs semi-final encounters with Nottingham Forest and then he lined up in the Final against his former club, Wolves, sadly ending up on the losing side.

RAWSON, Albert Noble

Inside-right/centre-forward: 20 apps. 8 goals
Born: West Melton, October 1900. Died: 1949
Career: Darnall Old Boys, BLADES (professional, May 1919), Birmingham (February 1923), Barnsley (July 1924-May 1925). After retiring worked for a coal-mining concern in Yorkshire.
Albert Rawson was a reserve at Bramall Lane where he struggled to get into the first XI owing to the form of Messrs Gillespie, Fazackerley and Kitchen. He scored eight vital goals to help Blues avoid relegation to the Second Division in 1923.

RAWSON, Colin

Wing-half: 76 apps. one goal
Born: Langwith, Derbyshire, 12 November 1926.
Career: Shirebrook FC, Welbeck Colliery, Nottingham Forest (September 1944), Peterborough United/Midland League (August 1947), Rotherham United (July 1948), BLADES (March 1953), Millwall (October 1955), Torquay United (July 1959), Taunton Town (player-coach, season 1961-62).
After failing to gain a place in Forest's first team, wing-half Colin Rawson went on to make well over 450 appearances at senior level (427 in the Football League, including 159 for Millwall and 111 for Rotherham) before dropping down to a lower level in 1961. A clever, stylish performer, he added guile and class to the team and spent two-and-a-half years at Bramall Lane during which time he put in many useful performances. He had been a Third Division (North) championship winner with Rotherham in 1950-51, skippered the Lions for four seasons before moving to Devon, quickly helping Torquay gain promotion to the Third Division in 1960. Rawson was one of the few players to appear in all six Divisions of the Football League (1,2,3, 4, 3rd South & 3rd North).

RAYNOR, George S

Born: Wombwell, South Yorkshire, 13 January 1907.
Career: Elsecar Bible Class, Mexborough Athletic (on trial), Wombwell (July 1932), BLADES (reserves, season 1930-31 - he played in one senior game v. Sheffield Wednesday in the County Cup of 1931), Mansfield Town (July 1932), Rotherham United (August 1933), Bury (February 1935), Aldershot (July 1939, assistant-trainer from 1945 after guesting for Bournemouth, Bury, Charlton Athletic, Crystal Palace and Hull City during WW2), Iraq (coach, briefly), AIK Sweden (coach, season 1946-47), Sweden national team coach (1947-49), Roma (coach, 1951), SS Lazio (coach, 1953), Coventry City (coach, June 1955, manager January-June 1956, coach, June-August 1956), Lincolnshire schools (coach, August-December 1956), Sweden national coach (December 1956-May 1957), Skegness Town (July 1960, also working as a stores manager at Butlin's), Doncaster Rovers (May 1967-December 1968), later coach at AIK Stockholm and Atviaaberg (Sweden). He was acclaimed Knight of the Order of Vasa (Sweden).
As a player George Raynor was a clever right-winger who escaped the grips of United. He guided Sweden to the gold medal in the 1948 Olympic Games Soccer Final and to the third place in 1958 World Cup as well as finishing third in the 1950 World Cup and likewise in the 1952 Olympics. Also during the 1950s he did well in Italy's Serie 'A' with Juventus and Lazio; and was earning £5-a-week as boss of Skegness Town. He played alongside United's Jimmy Hagan in Aldershot's team during WW2.

READING

United's playing record against the Royals:
Football League

Venue	P	W	D	L	F	A
Home	11	6	4	1	21	9
Away	11	4	0	7	11	12
Totals	22	10	4	8	32	21

FA Cup

Home	1	1	0	0	1	0

Formed in 1871 at a public meeting held at the Bridge Street Rooms, Reading entered the FA Cup as early as 1877 when they amalgamated with Reading Hornets. The club was further strengthened in 1889 when Early FC joined them and in 1897 the first major trophy was won - the Berks & Bucks Cup.
One of the founder members of the Third Division in 1920, Reading - originally dubbed the 'Biscuitmen' - have as yet never tasted top-flight football. And it was not until 1979-80 that they first met the Blades in League action. Goals by Mick Speight and Barry Butlin gave the Blades a 2-0 win at 'the Lane' while the return fixture at Elm Park ended in a 2-1 victory for Reading.
United's first away win was registered at the sixth attempt in 1988-89 (3-1) and the last in 2002-03 (by 2-0)...their first at the impressive Madejski Stadium, the Royals' fifth ground.
The only clash in the FA Cup-tie was a 5th round tie in 1998 when Lee Sandford's goal gave the Blades a 1-0 win...on their way to the semi-finals.

Ian Porterfield managed both the Blades and Reading.
Carl Asaba, Salvatore Bibbo (United reserve), Edgar Bluff, Barry Butlin, Jack Cross, Keith Curle, Joe Davies, John Docherty, Jimmy Holmes, Francis Joseph, Fred Milnes, Bert Oswald, Bill Ross, Lee Sandford, Grant Smith, Percy Thorpe and the Wagstaff brothers, Barry and Tony, and Billy Whitehurst are among the players who have served with both clubs.

REECE, Gilbert Ivor
Inside-forward/winger: 225+16 apps. 67 goals
Born: Cardiff, 2 July 1942
Career: St Patrick's FC (Cardiff), Cardiff City (as a junior July 1960), Ton Pentre (on loan, September 1961), Pembroke United (briefly), Pembroke Borough (June 1962), Newport County (professional, June 1963), BLADES (£10,000, April 1965), Cardiff City (with David Powell, September 1972), Swansea City (July 1976), Barry Town (season 1977-78).

Fast and clever and not easily knocked off the ball, Gil Reece was a welcome addition to the United forward-line when brought in to replace Len Allchurch (sold to Stockport County). He had his leg broken at Blackpool in November 1966 and was absent from first team duty until April 1967. Did came back strongly and did very well the following season. Honoured by his country as a schoolboy, he became a Welsh international, gaining 29 caps at senior level between 1965-75 (the first 16 as a United player). In fact, he won his first cap against England (October 1965) just two years after giving up plumbing! Reece helped the Blades win promotion in 1971 (playing in 27 games) and was twice a Welsh Cup winner with Cardiff (in 1973 & 1974).

REED, John Paul
Winger: 23+4 apps 3 goals
Born: Rotherham, 27 August 1972
Career: BLADES (YTS, August 1988, professional July 1990), Scarborough (on loan, January 1991 & September 1991), Darlington (on loan, March 1993), Mansfield Town (on loan, September 1993), Blackpool (free transfer, July 1997), Ethnikos/Greece (August 1998), Bury (briefly), Gainsborough Trinity (September 1999), Leek Town, Gainsborough Trinity (2002-03).
Basically regarded as a reserve winger wherever he played, John Reed only made 61 League appearances over a period of six years (May 1992-May 1998).

REES, Melvyn John
Goalkeeper: 8 apps.
Born: Cardiff, 25 January 1967. Died: May 1993
Career: Cardiff City (YTS, April 1983, professional September 1984), Watford (July 1987), Crewe Alexandra (on loan, August-September 1989), Leyton Orient (on loan, January 1990), West Bromwich Albion (September 1990), BLADES (£25,000, March 1992).
One of the youngest players ever to appear in all four Divisions of the Football League, goalkeeper Mel Rees (a Welsh Youth international) was first reserve to Simon Tracey at Bramall Lane but when called into action often produced a wonderful display. An injury forced him to withdraw from the Welsh squad and soon afterwards he was taken ill (prior to the start of the 1992-93 season). Sadly, after lengthy hospital treatment, Rees died from cancer at the age of 26.

REID, Robert
Outside-left: 36 apps. 10 goals
Born: Hamilton, Lanarkshire, 19 February 1911. Died: Scotland, 1987.
Career: Fernigar Violet (1929), Hamilton Academical (August 1931). Brentford (January 1936), BLADES (record fee of £5,500, February 1939), Bury (November 1946). Later appointed trainer at Airdrieonians (to March 1965) before serving as physiotherapist at Hamilton Academical.
A quick-moving winger with plenty of tricks to show his opponents, Bobby Reid had an exceptionally good scoring record at Griffin Park, netting 33 times in 103 League games for the Bees. Unfortunately, after helping the Blades gain promotion to the First Division, WW2 disrupted his progress at Bramall Lane and after the hostilities he was transferred to Gigg Lane. Prior to joining Brentford, Reid had represented Hamilton Schools. He was capped twice for his country against England and Northern Ireland in 1938, and he also made two appearances for the Scottish League as well as helping Hamilton reach the Scottish Cup Final in 1935. He was also the Blade's record signing in 1939.

RELEGATION
United have suffered relegation on nine occasions, as follows:

Season	Down To	Notes
1933-34	Division 2	Bottom, relegated with Newcastle Utd
1948-49	Division 2	22nd and last, relegated with Preston NE
1955-56	Division 2	The wooden-spoon again, down with Huddersfield
1967-68	Division 2	21st position, Fulham below them
1975-76	Division 2	Bottom, demoted with Burnley & Wolves
1978-79	Division 3	20th, down with Millwall & Blackburn
1980-81	Division 4	21st, down with Colchester, Blackpool & Hull
1987-88	Division 3	21st again, Reading & Huddersfield below them
1993-94	Division 1	20th in Premiership, down with Oldham & Swindon

United suffered three relegations in five years (1976-81, playing in all four Divisions of the Football League in double-quick time.
(See also: FOOTBALL LEAGUE & PREMIERSHIP)

RENWICK, Craig
Defender: 9+1 apps.
Born: Lanark, 22 September 1958
Career: East Stirling, BLADES (April 1978-November1980).
Reserve defender Craig Renwick spent one season at Bramall Lane before leaving the English soccer scene.

RESERVES
* United first played a scratch or reserve XI in 1890, playing a series of friendly matches.
* In 1891-92 United's second string played in the Hallamshire League as Sheffield Strollers and they took the championship at the first attempt.
* In 1894-95 the Blades' second team was registered as Sheffield United reserves, going on to win both the Sheffield Association League title and the Wharncliffe Cup in 1896-97, following up by becoming champions of the West Yorkshire League in 1897-98.
* For the 1898-99 season United second XI entered the Midland League. They were declared champions four times in seven years: in 1901, 1904, 1905 & 1907 and were also winners of the Wharncliffe Charity League in 1904.
* When the Midland League was dissolved in 1915, United played in the Midland Combination League (albeit briefly) before WW1 halted proceedings.
* In 1921-22 the Blades gained entry to the Central League and lifted the championship at the first time of asking, taking the runners-up spot in 1923. Their record in 1921 (when they finished four points ahead of Manchester City) was:

P	W	D	L	F	A	Pts
42	24	8	10	67	36	56

* In 1928-29 the second XI participated in the Midlands Mid-week League and between 1929-31 played in the competitive Yorkshire Mid-week League.
* The outbreak of WW2 halted second XI football for a short time before United entered a team in the Sheffield Association League: 1941-45.
* Central League action commenced in 1945-46 but it wasn't until 1965-66 that United lifted the championship trophy for the first time, finishing five points ahead of Stoke City, with this record:

P	W	D	L	F	A	Pts
42	25	12	5	97	49	62

* The Central League became known as the Pontins League in 1990-91 and two more Divisions were formed soon afterwards.
* United were relegated (from Division 1) in 1996 with Wolves, Notts County & West Bromwich Albion and they went down again the following season (with Blackpool) when the Premiership Division was introduced.
* In 1998 United's 2nd XI lifted the Pontins League Cup.
* In 2000-01 the Pontins League became the Avon Insurance League and United's second-string were the first winners, pipping Wrexham by three points with this record:

P	W	D	L	F	A	Pts
22	13	2	7	34	20	41

* The Blades also won the Avon Insurance League Cup in 2001, beating Stoke City in the Final.
* In season 2002-03 the Blades' second XI won the Avon Insurance League Premier Division title (ahead of Walsall) with this record:

P	W	D	L	F	A	Pts
20	11	4	5	36	19	37

* What is believed to be a record crowd of 20,263 attended the United v. Wednesday second XI game at Bramall Lane on 25 December 1911. The Blades won 5-1.
* Over the years United's reserve side has run up some big scores, among them: 13-0 v. Leeds Albion (friendly: October 1891); 11-0 v. Barnsley St Peter's (Sheffield Cup: January 1894); 1-0 v. Notts County (Midland League: November 1905); 15-0 v. Sheffield Club (Wharncliffe Charity Cup: October 1911) & 9-1 v. Stoke City (Central League: March 1957).
* In that 15-0 win over Sheffield Club, Fred Groves and Bert Cook both netted fivetimers...Groves surprisingly never appeared for the first team.
* In February 1978 United's second XI lost 10-0 away to Aston Villa in the Central League - Allan Evans, later to become a Scottish international centre-half, scored six goals from the centre-forward position!
* Jim Shankly (the second of five famous brothers including Bill) scored 39 goals for United's second XI and four in the Football League during season 1926-27. He was deemed 'too slow' for regular first team duty.

REVILL, James W
Outside-left: 71 apps. 4 goals
Born: Sutton-in-Ashfield, circa 1889. Died: 1917.
Career: Tibshelf FC, BLADES (April 1910).
Jimmy Revill - nicknamed 'old aeroplane legs' by the Bramall Lane supporters -
was severely wounded in France during 1915-16 and died later in an English hospital (1917). Quick over 20-30 yards, he competed with limitless enthusiasm but owing to the continuing form of Bob Evans, his first team outings were limited to a certain extent - and then war broke out! He made his League debut v. Woolwich Arsenal in September of the following year, having his best season in 1913-14 when he scored three times in 37 League and Cup games.

RIBIERO, Bruno
Midfielder: 16+14 apps. one goal
Born: Setubal, Portugal, 22 October 1975
Career: Vitoria Setubal, Leeds United, BLADES (£500,000, October 1999), Uniao Leira/Portugal (on loan, November 2000-May 2001, signed permanently July 2001.).
An Adrian Heath signing from Elland Road, Bruno Ribiero failed to deliver the goods at Bramall Lane. He was certainly a firm favourite with the supporters but never really looked the part during his stay with the Blades. He scored six goals in 52 games for Leeds.

RICHARDSON, Brian

Wing-half: 336 apps. 9 goals

Born: Sheffield, 5 October 1934

Career: BLADES (professional, December 1954), Swindon Town (January 1966), Rochdale (July 1966-April 1967).

A very consistent performer, resolute to the last, Brian Richardson was a tremendous asset to the team, his workmanlike displays in centre-field being admired by many. Quick and a hard but a confident tackler, he gave the Blades fifteen years excellent service and was part of that wonderful middle-line comprising himself, Joe Shaw and Gerry Summers during the late 1950s/early '60s. He made his debut for the club on tour in Germany in May 1955 and his first appearance in the League side followed seven months later v. Luton Town. He missed only one game when the Blades gained promotion to the First Division in 1961.

RICHARDSON, Derek

Goalkeeper: 55 apps.

Born: Hackney, London, 13 July 1956

Career: Chelsea (apprentice, July 1972, professional February 1974), Queen's Park Rangers (April 1976), BLADES (£50,000, December 1979), Coventry City (March-May 1982).

An England Youth and semi-professional goalkeeper, Derek Richardson failed to make the first XI at Stamford Bridge and played n 31 League games for QPR before moving to Bramall Lane halfway through the 1979-80 season (to take over from the injured Steve Conroy). He never made Coventry's League side either!

RICHARDSON, George

Forward: 37 apps. 9 goals

Born: Worksop, 12 December 1912. Died: 1968

Career: Manton Colliery, Manton Athletic (1932), Huddersfield Town (April 1933), BLADES (May1934), Hull City (November 1938), Ransome & Marles FC/Newark Works side (WW2 guest), Bangor City (player-manager, July 1948).

A useful 'attacker' George Richardson averaged a goal every four games for the Blades and one in two for the Tigers (15 in 36) before entering management.

RICHARDSON, George William Richard

Left-half: 14 apps.

Born: Gainsborough, 1899. Died: November 1963

Career: Gainsborough Wednesday, Lincoln City (February 1920), BLADES (£1,225, December 1921), Bournemouth & Boscombe Athletic (£200, July 1924), Boston Town.

(June 1925, remaining there for several seasons).

After developing his game with Lincoln, the Blades paid a large fee for wing-half George Richardson but he saw very little League action at 'the Lane' or indeed with Bournemouth before eventually moving back into non-League football with Boston.

RICHARDSON, Paul

Midfielder: 44+1 apps. 3 goals

Born: Shirebrook, Notts, 25 October 1949

Career: Nottingham Forest (apprentice August 1965, professional August 1967), Chester (October 1976), Stoke City (£50,000, June 1977), BLADES (£25,000, August 1981), Blackpool (on loan, January 1983), Swindon Town (July 1983), Swansea City (non-contract, September-December 1984). Retired from first-class football in January 1985; became manager of Gloucester City (1985-87) and then Fairford FC (Gloucester) while also working for British telecom.

Tall and stylish midfielder Paul Richardson had an excellent career in top-class football, making 437 League appearances and scoring 32 goals. An England Youth international, he made his First Division debut for Forest as a substitute in a 2-1 defeat at Southampton in September 1967 and played his last game sixteen-and-a-half years later for Swansea v. Plymouth Argyle in December 1984. In between times, after giving Forest supreme service for some eleven years, he scored the vital goal (against Notts County) on the last day of the 1978-79 season to clinch promotion to the First Division for Stoke City and then did a pretty sound job at Bramall Lane, helping the Blades win the Fourth Division championship (1982).

RICKETT, Walter

Winger: 276 apps. 74 goals

Born: Sheffield, 20 March 1917. Died: 1991.

Career: Aqueduct FC (Sheffield), BLADES (May 1939), Blackpool (January 1948), Sheffield Wednesday (£6,000, October 1949), Rotherham United (September 1952), Halifax Town (August 1953, retiring, April 1954).

Walter Rickett (5ft 6ins tall) was a lively but sturdy two-footed winger who possessed strong attacking flair and was mighty dangerous when he decided to cut inside his opponents and head for goal. As tough as they come, he was a real bundle of energy, always on the go, and this facet was amply demonstrated during WW2 football when he appeared in more than 200 matches for the Blades, scoring almost 60 goals including one on his home debut against Sheffield Wednesday in March 1940 (won 4-3, East Midland Division). After a decade with the Blades he moved to Blackpool and played in the 1948 season FA Cup Final defeat by Manchester United before transferring to Hillsborough. Capped by England 'B' v. Switzerland 'B' in 1950, two years later Rickett helped the Owls win the Second Division title.

RIDGE, Roy

Full-back: 14 apps.

Born: Ecclesfield, 21 October 1934

Career: Ecclesfield FC, BLADES (November 1951), Rochdale (August 1964-May 1966).

Reserve full-back Roy Ridge was a professional with United for almost 13 years, during which time he appeared in only 11 League matches, nine in one season (1953-54). After leaving Bramall Lane he spent two seasons with Rochdale and played in 84 out of a possible 92 League games.

RINGSTEAD, Alfred

Outside-right: 271 apps. 109 goals
Born: Dublin, 14 October 1927
Career: Trials with Everton (amateur, 1944), Northwich
Victoria (1946, professional 1948), BLADES (£2,850,
November 1950), Mansfield Town (July 1959), Frickley
Colliery (August 1960).
Alf Ringstead made his League debut at the age of 23 and to
celebrate the occasion he scored with a diving header for the
Blades against Second Division leaders Coventry City in
December 1950 (won 2-0). Able to use both feet, he was
quick, decisive, could head a ball hard and true and had the
ability to 'lose' his opponent at a vital stage in open play and
as a result scored some mightily important goals. A Republic of
Ireland international (capped 20 times between 1951-59)
Ringstead was an ever-present when the Blades won the
Second Division championship in 1952.

Charlton Athletic's Derek Ufton (r) watches as Sheffield United's Alf Ringstead (l) fails to get a touch to a cross

RIOCH, Bruce David
Midfielder: 8 apps. One goal
Born: Aldershot, 6 September 1947.
Career: Stapsley High School, Dynamos Boys Club, Cambridge & District & London Borough Schools, Luton Town (apprentice, July 1963, professional September 1964), Aston Villa (£100,000, with brother Neil, July 1969), Derby County (£200,000, February 1974), Everton (£180,000, December 1976), Derby County (£150,000, November 1977), Birmingham City (on loan, December 1978), BLADES (on loan, March 1979), Seattle Sounders/NASL (March 1980) Torquay United (October 1980, player-manager July 1982 to January 1984); Seattle Sounders/NASL (coach, July1985 to January 1986), Middlesbrough (assistant-manager, February 1986, manager March 1986 to March 1990), Millwall (manager April 1990 to March 1992), Bolton Wanderers (manager May 1992 to May 1995), Arsenal (manager, June 1995 to August 1996), Queen's Park Rangers (assistant-manager/coach, September 1996 to May 1997), Norwich City (manager, June 1998 to April 2000), Wigan Athletic (manager, July 2000 to February 2001). Applied, unsuccessfully, for other managerial/coaching jobs afterwards.
Bruce Rioch, a string-running, hard-shooting midfielder, had the distinction of being the first English-born player ever to captain Scotland. Born the son of a Scottish sergeant major, he went on to win 24 full caps and he accumulated in excess of 600 League and Cup appearances at club level. He helped Derby win the First Division title in 1975 and as a manager guided Middlesbrough to promotion from Division Three to Division One in 1987 & 1988; steered Bolton to promotion to the First Division in 1993 into the Premiership in 1995.
His brother Daniel (Neil) also played for Luton and Villa, as well as York City, Northampton and Plymouth

RITCHIE, Duncan
Winger: 13 apps. one goal
Born: Scotland, circa 1887
Career: Dumbarton, Raith Rovers, BLADES (August 1912), Derby County (Jul 1913-April 1914). Did not feature after WW1.
A player who preferred the left-flank, Duncan Ritchie seemed out of his depth in the English First Division. He only made two appearances for the Rams in their relegation campaign.

ROBERTS, Alan
Outside-right: 46+6 apps. 2 goals
Born: Newcastle-upon-Tyne, 8 December 1964
Career: Middlesbrough (apprentice, April 1981, professional December 1982), Darlington (September 1985), BLADES (£16,000, July 1988), Lincoln City (£63,000, October 1989, retired through injury November 1990).
Alan Roberts was a highly skilful winger who made 32 League appearances for Middlesbrough and 119 for Darlington before trying his luck at Bramall Lane. He played some good football for the Blades, helping them gain promotion from Division Three in 1989 before losing his place and eventually moving to Sincil Bank for a record fee paid by the Imps. Unfortunately they never got their money's worth as Roberts was forced to quit the game through injury after just one season.

ROBERTSON, W
Centre-forward: 38 apps. 14 goals
Born: Dundee, circa 1875
Career: Dundee Strathclyde, BLADES (August 1889).
W Robertson (probably named Bill) was a brave and robust centre-forward who scored United's first goal in the club's first-ever match against Nottingham Rangers in September 1889. He also claimed the Blades' first hat-trick, in a Sheffield County Cup game against Exchange FC on 19 October 1889 (won 7-0) and had the ill-luck to became the first United player to be sent-off when dismissed against Rotherham Town, in the Sheffield County Cup Final replay on 22 March 1890. Robertson did not miss a single first team game from that initial outing v Notts Rangers until the final fixture of the season. He received a testimonial against the Blades in April 1891.

ROBINS, Arthur
Outside-right: 11 apps.
Born: Northampton, 1888. Died: 1924
Career: Raunds St Peters FC, BLADES (February 1909), Castleford Town (May 1910).
Acting as cover for first John Lang and then Joe Walton, Archie Robins was an efficient replacement when called into action.

ROBINSON, Ernest George
Right-back/right-half: 18 apps.
Born: Shiney Row, County Durham, 21 January 1910. Died: Vancouver, March 1991.
Career: Houghton Colliery, York City, Notts County (1929), Nelson (June 1930), Northampton Town (March 1931), Tunbridge Wells Rangers (October 1931), Barnsley (August 1932), BLADES (£500, May 1933), Carlisle United (£175, August 1934), Lincoln City (August 1935-September 1939), in Holland (as trainer/coach post-war, ending up with FC Enschede). Emigrated to Canada in 1985 when he died six years later.
Ernie Robertson was a dependable and enthusiastic defender, who was described by a Carlisle pundit in 1934 as being a 'sturdy, good tackler with strong kick aided by real direction.' He made 169 League appearances in total (including 38 for Carlisle and 64 for Lincoln).

ROBINSON, John
Outside-right: 4 apps.
Born: Leeds, 1 April 1913. Died: 1989.
Career: Huddersfield Town (professional, 1936), BLADES (May1936) Hull City (1939). Did not re-appear after WW2.
Recruited as a reserve by the Blades, Jack Robinson made his League debut in a 0-0 draw with Aston Villa in April 1938. He failed to get any first team calls from Huddersfield or Hull.

ROCHDALE
United's playing record against the 'Dale:
Football League

Venue	P	W	D	L	F	A
Home	1	1	0	0	3	1
Away	1	1	0	0	1	0
Totals	2	2	0	0	4	1

Formed in 1907 (after the earlier Rochdale Town club had gone out of business) Rochdale immediately joined the Manchester League before graduating to the Lancashire Combination and gaining Football League status in 1921, when they became one of the original members of the newly-formed Third Division (North).

Now in their 75th season, Rochdale have spent 39 out of 45 seasons in the bottom sector, a 'record' bettered only by Hartlepool United (41) and Darlington (40).

The only League games between the Blades and the 'Dale took place in 1981-82 (Division 4). At Spotland in the January, Keith Edwards' goal gave United a 1-0 victory and in May, two more goals by Edwards and another from Bob Hatton earned a 3-1 win to clinch automatic promotion, with the title itself following 11 days later.

Ex-Blades forward Jack Peart was Rochdale's manager from 1923-30. Danny Bergara who was associated with the Blades during the 1980s, was manager at Spotland in 1988-89 while Harry Haslam was an amateur with the 'Dale and later boss at Bramall Lane.

Eric Barber (United reserve), Billy Biggar, Ian Bryson, Ted Burgin, Herbert Chapman, Ted Connor, Steve Conroy, Simon Copeland (United reserve), Graeme Crawford, Matt Dickins (United reserve), David Frain, Wilson Greenwood, Paddy McGeeney, Ray McHale, Harry Mills, Tony Moore, Ralph Moremont, Bob Neave, Bert Pearson, John Pemberton, Brian Richardson, Roy Ridge, Billy Russell, Paul Simpson ('Dale player-manager), Tony Towner, George Underwood, Walter Webster, Paul A Williams and Alan Young are among the players who have served with both clubs.

ROGERS, Paul Anthony

Midfielder: 133+6 apps. 11 goals
Born: Portsmouth, 21 March 1965
Career: Sutton United, BLADES (£50,000, January 1992), Notts County (in an exchange deal involving Chris Short, December 1995), Wigan Athletic (on loan, December 1996, signed permanently for £50,000, March 1997), Brighton & Hove Albion (July 1999-May 2003; then appointed Commercial manager at the club)

Capped six times at semi-professional by England (as a Sutton player) Paul Rogers developed into a hard-working, gritty, determined midfielder with the Blades, and after losing his place in 1995 and following a change of management at Bramall Lane he moved to pastures new. He helped Notts County reach the Second Division Play-off Final in 1996 and a year later gained a Third Division championship winning medal with Wigan, adding a Auto-Windscreen Shield winners; prize to his collection in 1999, following up with a second Third Division medal with Brighton in 2001, quickly followed by a Division Two winners; medal in 2002. He went on to amass in excess of 400 League and Cup appearances during his career.

ROONEY, Robert M

Inside-left/winger: 16 apps. 3 goals
Born: Cowie, Stirlingshire, 8 July 1938
Career: Clydebank (1956), BLADES (£300, June 1958), Doncaster Rovers (£5,000, October 1962), Lincoln City (player exchange involving Albert Broadbent, January 1963), Cambridge City (July 1964), Gainsborough Trinity (May 1965), Spalding United (December 1967-May 1968).

Bobby Rooney's entire career realised only 48 League appearances (seven goals). He was virtually a reserve at every club he served, having 28 of his games with the Imps.

ROSS, Trevor William

Midfielder: 8 apps.
Born: Ashton-under-Lyne, 16 January 1957
Career: Hartshead school, Lancashire schools, Arsenal (schoolboy forms, April 1970, apprentice, May 1972, professional, June 1974), Everton (£170,000, November 1977), Portsmouth (on loan, October 1982), BLADES (on loan, December 1982), AEK Athens (June 1983), BLADES (January 1984), Bury (August 1984-May 1987), Altrincham (season 1987-88).

Trevor Ross, a hard-working, reliable midfielder, had already made over 200 League and Cup appearances before having his first spell at Bramall Lane. An England schoolboy international (8 caps), he went on to play in one Under-21 international for Scotland (parentage qualification) and

* His father William Ross senior played for Third Lanark, Arbroath and Bradford City.

ROSS, William

Outside-left: 24 apps. 3 goals
Born: Kiveton Park, Sheffield, 1874.
Career: Kiveton Park, Chesterfield (April 1894), BLADES (July 1895), Lincoln City (November 1897), Gravesend United (August 1898), Reading (1899), Notts County (May 1900), Grimsby Town (June 1904), Glossop North End (May 1905 to April 1908). Later worked in the hotel trade in Derbyshire. In 1914 he attempted to get onto the Board at Glossop, but fell foul of the FA's then ban on former professionals becoming directors. He was also a useful cricketer and in 1902 was a member of the groundstaff at Trent Bridge (Notts).

Bill Ross was a consistent performer throughout his career, although he travelled around quite a bit in search of first team football. His best years were spent with Notts County for whom he scored 28 goals in 110 League games, following up later with seven in 32 for Grimsby and 21 in 51 for Glossop.

ROSS, William Bernard

Outside-right: 3 apps. one goal
Born: Swansea, 8 November 1924
Career: Towey United, Cardiff City (1944), BLADES (£4,000, May 1948), Southport (August 1949-May 1951).

Bernie Ross made his League debut for the Blades against Derby County (a) on 28 August 1948 but after that he struggled to get into the first team and after spending just over a season at Bramall Lane, he switched his allegiance to Southport (then members of the Third Division North) for whom he played over 50 senior matches.

213

ROSTRON, John Wilfred
Full-back/winger: 35+6 apps. 3 goals
Born: Sunderland, 29 September 1956
Career: St Thomas Aquintas school (Sunderland), Arsenal (amateur 1971, apprentice, August 1972, professional October 1973), Sunderland (£40,000, July 1977), Watford (£150,000, October 1979), Sheffield Wednesday (free transfer, January 1989), BLADES (free, September 1989), Brentford (free, January 1991-May 1993).
Initially a left-winger and an England schoolboy international in that position, Wilf Rostron was eventually converted into a fine attacking left-back who had an excellent career that spanned 20 years, helping the Blades gain promotion from Division Two in 1990. In that time he amassed over 600 senior appearances (495 in the Football League) and scored more than 50 goals.

ROTHERHAM UNITED (also County & Town)
United's playing record against the Millermen:

Football League

Venue	P	W	D	L	F	A
Home	12	7	1	4	21	19
Away	12	7	3	2	24	12
Totals	24	14	4	6	45	31

FA Cup

	P	W	D	L	F	A
Home	1	1	0	0	2	1
Away	1	0	1	0	2	2
Totals	2	1	1	0	4	3

League Cup

	P	W	D	L	F	A
Home	2	1	1	0	6	2
Away	2	1	0	1	3	2
Totals	4	2	1	1	9	4

WW1

	P	W	D	L	F	A
Home	7	6	0	1	15	5
Away	7	5	0	2	13	5
Totals	14	11	0	3	28	10

WW2

	P	W	D	L	F	A
Home	11	6	2	3	32	15
Away	11	6	3	2	29	18
Totals	22	12	5	5	61	33

Yorkshire & Humberside Cup

	P	W	D	L	F	A
Home	1	0	1	0	1	1

Sheffield & Hallamshire County Cup

	P	W	D	L	F	A
Home	16	11	2*	3	41	15
Away	12	7	0	5	23	16
Totals	28	18	2	8	64	31

Midland Counties League

	P	W	D	L	F	A
Home	1	1	0	0	3	0
Away	1	0	0	1	0	1
Totals	2	1	0	1	3	1

Others

	P	W	D	L	F	A
Home	1	0	1	0	1	1
Away	1	1	0	0	1	0
Totals	2	1	1	0	2	1

* Blades won 4-2 on penalties after a 0-0 draw in the Final in October 1974.

The Yorkshire side has a complex club history. Initially called Rotherham Town (formed in 1870) and playing at their Red House Ground, they gained entry to the Football League in 1893, staying for only three seasons before failing to win re-election in 1896. Twice winners of the Midland League prior to 1893, they eventually returned there.
Another team in Rotherham, originally called Thornhill United (formed in 1877) became Rotherham County in 1905, playing at Millmoor from 1907, having also participated in the Midland League (1903-04). Immediately after WW1 (in 1919) when the Football League expanded its membership from 40 to 44 clubs, Rotherham County was voted in. Four years later, the two Rotherham clubs (Town and County) amalgamated to become 'Rotherham United.'
The Blades against Rotherham County but met 'Town' in the FA Cup in December 1889, winning a 4th qualifying round replay 2-1 following a 2-2 draw at the Red House Ground (having led 2-0 at half-time).
The first meetings League against Rotherham United took place in season 1951-52 (Division 2).
The Blades won 1-0 at 'the Lane' (thanks to Harold Brook's goal;) but went down 3-1 at Millmoor before a bumper crowd of 25,137. Later that year (in mid-December 1952) a record attendance of 25,170 at the same ground saw United win 2-0.
Their three astonishing matches between the clubs in the 1950s. The Blades opened their 1956-57 League programme with a comprehensive 4-0 win at Millmoor (wingers Alf Ringstead and Colin Grainger sharing the goals) and then just before Christmas Rotherham came to Bramall Lane and ripped United apart to the tune of 7-2. A year later it was Rotherham 1 United 6 at Millmoor (Kevin Lewis and 'Doc' both netting twice).
United were 2-0 up on Rotherham in their home Second Division game in October 1959. The Millers fought back to win 3-2, netting the clinching goal in the 89th minute.
The Blades have not lost a League game against Rotherham since 1981, completing their fifth double in 2002-03 with a 1-0 victory at home and 2-1 win at Millmoor.
When the Millers beat the Blades 7-2 in a WW2 game in January 1944, their centre-forward Wally Ardron scored four goals.
And in the Sheffield & Hallamshire County Cup, which begun in 1920, the teams have met each other on 28 occasions, clashing in six Finals with the Blades winning four of them.
Taking into consideration the close proximity of the two clubs, there have been several players who have worn the colours of both United and the Millermen over the years, among them Kevin Arnott, Andy Barnsley, Harry Barton, Billy Bridgewater, Pat Buckley,

Darren Carr, Philip Clift, Joe Cockroft, Steve Conroy, Albert Cox, Teddy Cross, Bobby Davison, Mark Dempsey, Alonzo Drake (Rotherham trialist), Peter Duffield, Stewart Evans (Blades reserve), John Flynn, Mark Foran, Bernie Harris, Jimmy Harrop, Jim Hobson, Billy Hodgson, Harry Howard (Rotherham trialist), Glyn Jones, Keith Kettleborough, Joe Kitchen, Phil Kite, Frank Levick, Bill Lilley, Tom McAlister, Scott Marshall, Clive Mendonca, Billy Mercer, Harry Mills, Harold Pantling, Jack Pears, Tony Philliskirk, Martin Pike, Jim Pilgrim, Colin Rawson, George Raynor (Blades reserve), Walter Rickett, Rob Scott, Ben Shearman, George Simpson, Walter Spicer, Paul Stancliffe, Charlie Sutcliffe, Harry Thickett, Mark Todd, Tony Towner, Mike Trusson, Imre Varadi, Barry Wagstaff, Arthur Watson, Chris Wilder, Bernard Wilkinson, Alf Wilson, Curtis Woodhouse and Peter Wragg.

Danny Bergara, Reg Freeman, Billy McEwan and Ian Porterfield have all managed both the Blades and Rotherham. Neil Warnock played for the Millermen and managed the Blades; ex-Blades midfielder Ian Hamilton became Football in the Community Officer at Millmoor and former Blades player Mick Whitham was a trainer at Rotherham.

ROXBURGH, John A

Outside-left: 5 apps. 2 goals
Born: Granton, Edinburgh, 10 November 1901.
Career: Edinburgh Emmett, Rugby Town, Leicester Fosse/City (June 1920), Aston Villa (October 1922), Stoke (February 1924), BLADES (August 1925), Sheffield FC (1925-28).

John Roxburgh was selected for an England amateur international before his birthplace was confirmed! A jinking left-winger, full of vim and vigour, he made his League debut for Leicester at the age of 18 (v West Ham United) and went on to score three goals in 50 senior games for the Foxes before moving to Villa Park. He had a useful 'half-season' with Villa, replacing Billy Kirton in the main, scoring twice on his debut against his future club Stoke. He netted twice on his debut for the Blades v. Leeds United in November 1925 but managed only four more outings as his career slowly ground to a halt.

* John's brother, Andrew Roxburgh, also played professional football for Leicester City and they appeared in the same side together during their time at Filbert Street (1920-21). A third Roxburgh sibling, Walter, had trials with Leicester in 1921.

NB: Some reference books have his name spelt Roxborough.

RUGBY

The first Rugby match staged at Bramall Lane saw Yorkshire beaten 33-13 by the touring Australians on 25 September 1911. The attendance was 2,247.

Since then only spasmodic oval ball action has been witnessed at United's home with Sheffield Eagles playing their first Rugby League game there in 1988 against Doncaster.

RUSH, Ian James

Striker: 4 apps.
Born: St Asaph, Denbighshire, 20 October 1961
Career: Deeside Primary & Flintshire Comprehensive schools (as pupil & player), Chester (apprentice, August 1977, professional September 1979), Liverpool (£300,000, April 1980), Juventus (sold for a record fee of £3.2 million, June 1986, transfer effective from August 1987), Liverpool (on loan, season 1986-87), Liverpool (re-signed for a British record fee of £2.8 million, August 1988), Leeds United (May 1996), Newcastle United (August 1997), BLADES (on loan February-March 1998), Wrexham (free transfer, August 1998-retired July 1999). Later appointed 'strikers' coach at Anfield (2002).

Ian Rush, the brilliant Welsh international striker, who was on loan at Bramall Lane for four weeks in 1998, had a wonderful career that spanned 22 years. In that time he achieved great success, especially with Liverpool, with whom he gained 17 winners' medals...for five Football League championships (1982, '83, '84, '86 & '90); five League Cups (1981, '82, '83, '84 & '95), three FA Cups (1986, '89 & '92), the European Cup (1984) and two Charity Shields (1982 & '89) and the Screen Sport Super Cup. He also collected 11 runners-up prizes. He also gained 73 full caps for his country (67 with Liverpool), earning two more at Under-21 level as well as playing in schoolboy internationals and representing the Football League v. the Italian League in 1991. He scored a total of 381 goals in 816 club matches (including his record with Juventus). He netted 346 times in 659 outings for Liverpool, 40 in season 1983-84. Only England World Cup star Roger Hunt netted more goals for the Merseysiders. Rush also netted 19 goals for Wales and 18 for Juventus (four in one Italian Cup-tie against Pescari).

RUSHDEN & DIAMONDS

United's playing record against the Diamonds:

FA Cup

Venue	P	W	D	L	F	A
Home	1	0	1	0	1	1
Away	1	0	1*	0	1	1
Totals	2	0	2	0	2	2

* Won 6-5 on penalties.

In 1992 Rushden Town amalgamated with Irthlingborough Diamonds to form Rushden & Diamonds. Playing at Nene Park, they came through the Southern League (Midland Division), then the Southern League (Premier Division) to reach the Conference in 1996, gaining entry to the Football League in 2001 under manager Brian Talbot. They qualified for the Play-offs (in sixth place) at the end of their first season (beaten by Cheltenham Town in the Final).

The Blades were so very nearly bundled out of the FA Cup by then non-League Diamonds in the 3rd round in December 1999. After a hard-fought 1-1 draw at Bramall Lane, United were again held by the Conference side at Nene Park, being pegged back in extra-time before somehow squeezing through on penalties. But honours on the night went to the gallant little Northants club for a terrific effort. Graham Benstead, Darren Carr and Paul Hall are among the players who have served with both clubs.

215

RUSSELL, William
Inside-forward: 174 apps. 73 goals
Born: Hounslow, 7 July 1935
Career: Rhyl, BLADES (August1957),
Bolton Wanderers (March 1963-May
1965), Rochdale (July 1966-May
1968).
Billy Russell, who arrived at Bramall
Lane as an unknown footballer from
the Welsh League, developed into a
fast and direct inside-forward who
went on to score his fair share of goals
for the Blades, helping them win
promotion from Division Two in 1961
(missing only one game). An amateur
international (capped four times by
England before he turned professional)
Russell spent two rather unhappy
injury-plagued years at Bolton before
having a spell out of the game, finally
rounding off his career at Rochdale.

(L-R) Chelsea goalkeeper Peter Bonetti saves at the feet of Sheffield United's Bill Russell

RYAN, John Gilbert
Utility: 71 apps. 22 goals
Born: Lewisham, 20 July 1947
Career: Maidstone United, Arsenal (October 1964), Fulham (July 1965), Luton Town (July 1969), Norwich City (£60,000, August 1976), Seattle Sounders/NASL (£70,000, March 1979), BLADES (£70,000, September 1980), Manchester City (January 1982, then youth team coach until July 1983), Stockport County (non-contract, August 1983), Chester City (non-contract, player-coach, September 1983), Cambridge United (player-manager/coach, January 1984-January 1985), Maidstone United (player-coach, 1985-86, then assistant-manager, 1986-90), Sittingbourne (manager, season 1991-192).
The versatile John Ryan (who started his career as an inside-forward but was successfully converted into a defender) could and would play in any position! He was a dogged performer, possessing a powerful shot (mainly in his right foot) and was pretty useful from the penalty spot, although he did miss two vital kicks for the Blades in successive League matches against Portsmouth and Gillingham in January 1981 when both matches ended in a 1-0 defeat...as the Blades slipped towards the relegation trap-door. He made well over 500 League appearances during his career including 266 for Luton and 116 for Norwich. He twice helped Luton gain promotion, from Division Three in 1970 and Division Two in 1974, both times as runners-up). And he helped the Blades on their way to winning the Fourth Division title in 1982 (playing in 19 games).

Left: Arsenal v.s Sheffield United, April 25th 1936
Right: Under 21 International at Bramall Lane April 27th 1977.

SABELLA, Alejandro
Inside-forward: 88 apps. 10 goals
Born: Argentina, 5 November 1954
Career: River Plate (Argentina), BLADES (£160,000, July 1978), Leeds United (for a record fee of £400,000, June 1980), Estudiantes (January 1982-May 1987).
Alex Sabella could control a ball on a sixpence, but he failed to establish himself on the English scene and at times could be so frustrating to watch. He certainly didn't like the physical challenges of the burly defenders who marked him. After returning to his native country he went on to play in eight full internationals for Argentina (1983-84), taking over the position vacated by Ossie Ardiles.

SALMONS, Geoffrey
Midfielder: 207+12 apps. 10 goals
Born: Mexborough, 14 January 1948
Career: BLADES (juniors, April 1963, professional, February 1966), Stoke City (£165,000, July 1974), BLADES (on loan, September 1977), Leicester City (October 1977), Chesterfield (August 1978), Gainsborough Trinity (June 1982-84).
A fine attacking player, predominantly left-footed, Geoff Salmons worked overtime in the Blades' engine-room and was always a willing worker from the first to the last whistle of every game he played in. He created more goals than he scored but his work-rate could not be faulted. He played exceedingly well alongside Tony Currie in the Blades' midfield, helping the team gain promotion (behind his future club Leicester City) to the First Division in 1971. Salmons made 409 League appearances in total (including 185 for the Blades, 118 for Stoke and 120 for Chesterfield).

SAMPY, Thomas
Inside or centre-forward/right-half: 483 apps. 33 goals
Born: Backworth near Newcastle-upon-Tyne, 14 March 1899.
Died: Yorkshire, 1978.
Career: Seaton Delaval, Chopwell Institute, BLADES (November 1920), Barnsley (May 1934)

A dynamic and sometimes quite an aggressive player, Tommy Sampy scored on his League debut for the Blades against Blackburn Rovers in February 1921 when he played at inside-left in place of Billy Gillespie. He established himself in the first team during the 1921-22 season but after some enterprising displays he lost his form and was, perhaps surprisingly, left out of United's 1925 FA Cup-winning side. After 15 seasons with the Blades he left Bramall Lane for Oakwell and afterwards said that they were 'wasted years' of his life!
* His brother, William Albert Sampy (q.v) also played for the Blades, Swansea Town and Waterford.

SAMPY, William Albert
Full-back: 37 apps.
Born: Backworth, 21 January 1901. Died: Coventry, 1973.
Career: Chopwell Institute, BLADES (April 1921), Swansea Town (May 1927), Waterford (seasons 1930-32).
Strong-limbed, tough tackling full-back Billy Sampy was and began his footballing career playing in the same team as his brother Thomas (q.v). After Tommy had made his debut, Billy quickly followed suit, having his first outing for the Blades against Hartlepools in a benefit match in October 1922, playing in defence with his brother in attack.
Sampy the younger remained with United until 1926 when he was transferred to Swansea. He made over 40 senior appearances for the Welsh club before ending his career in Ireland.

SANDFORD, Edward Albert
Inside-forward/wing-half: 5 apps. one goal
Born: Handsworth, Birmingham, 22 October 1910. Died:1995
Career: Wattville Road School, Tantany Athletic, Overend Wesley, Birmingham Carriage Works, Smethwick Highfield, West Bromwich Albion (professional, October 1929), BLADES (£1,500, March 1939), Morris Commercial FC (1940-43); West Bromwich Albion (coach, 1950s, then scout 1961-67).
Teddy Sandford played in two FA Cup Finals for the Baggies, gaining a winners' medal in 1931 (v. Birmingham) and a loser's prize in 1935 (v. Sheffield Wednesday, when he scored in a 4-2 defeat). In fact, in 1931, he was one of the youngest players ever to collect a Cup winners medal, aged 20 years, 176 days. He started out as an goalscoring inside-forward, but was converted into a splendidly effective centre-half at The Hawthorns. He netted 75 goals in 317 appearances for Albion and was capped once by England v. Wales in 1932. He was well past his best when he joined the Blades, although WW2 did intervene.

SANDFORD, Lee Robert
Defender: 173+12 apps. 5 goals
Born: Basingstoke, 22 April 1968
Career: Portsmouth (apprentice, June 1984, professional December 1985), Stoke City (£140,000, December 1989), BLADES (£500,000, July 1996), Reading (on loan, September 1997), Stockport County (on loan, October 2001), Woking (August 2002).
Able to play as a left-back, central-half or sweeper, Lee Sandford was an utterly reliable performer, strong in every department of defensive play with an excellent sense of anticipation. An England Youth international, he made well over 400 senior appearances before moving to Bramall Lane - 90 for Pompey and 324 for the Potters, helping the latter club win the Autoglass Trophy and the Second Division championship in 1992 & 1993 respectively.

218

SANTOS, Georges
Midfielder: 40+28 apps. 6 goals
Born: Marseille, France, 15 August 1970
Career: Toulon (France), Tranmere Rovers (July 1998), West Bromwich Albion (£25,000, March 2000), BLADES (free transfer, July 2000, released May 2002), Grimsby Town (December 2002).
A strong, effective ball-winner, Georges Santos always plays with a sense of urgency and perhaps this was his downfall at times! His rapid sending-off against his former club West Brom in March 2002 (he had been on the pitch for just two minutes as a substitute) marked the end of his career at Bramall Lane.

SAUNDERS, Dean Nicholas
Striker: 54+1 apps. 22 goals
Born: Swansea, 21 June 1964
Career: Swansea City (apprentice, professional June 1982), Cardiff City (on loan, March 1985), Brighton & Hove Albion (free transfer, August 1985), Oxford United (£60,000, March 1987), Derby County (£1 million, October 1988), Liverpool (£2.9 million, July 1991), Aston Villa (£2.3 million, September 1992), Galatasary (£2.35 million, July 1995), Nottingham Forest (£1.5 million, July 1996), BLADES (free transfer, December 1997), Benfica (£500,000, December 1998), Bradford City (free transfer, August 1999, retired July 2001), Derby County (coach, 2002, caretaker-manager May 2003).
One of the game's most prolific marksmen, Dean Saunders struck his first goal in League football for Swansea against Oldham Athletic in March 1984. Seven years later he is still finding the back of the net! A positive, all-action, unselfish 'centre-forward' who simply knows where the 'goal' is, he scored in every season from his debut at competitive level in 1983-84 until 2001-02 - and when he hung up his shooting boots at the end of that latter campaign, his record in club and international football was very impressive indeed - 805 appearances and 276 goals! Saunders also holds the Welsh international record for being the most capped outfield player (75 gained between 1986-2001), two more than Peter Nicholas and three more than Mark Hughes but now Gary Speed is closing him down fast! Surprisingly Saunders has only won two club medals, the first with Liverpool in the FA Cup in 1992 and his second with Villa in the League Cup in 1994 when he scored twice in the 3-1 win over Manchester United.
His best performances on the whole have come with Derby (131 senior appearances & 57 goals) and Villa (144 outings & 49 goals)...but wherever he played he gave his all and during his time at Bramall Lane the fans certainly enjoyed what they saw from a top-class striker.
Saunders scored one of the cheekiest goals on record for United against Port Vale at Bramall Lane on 28 March 1998. The ball was going out for a throw-in with both Saunders and the Vale 'keeper chasing after it from different angles. The 'goalie' (Tomlinson) gave up and turned round to head back towards his area. But the quick-thinking Saunders picked the ball up, threw it against the back of Tomlinson, collected the rebound and clipped in a wonderful goal to clinch a 2-0 win. Following the sacking manager John Gregory in May 2003, Saunders who had returned to the club as a part-time coach, was given the role as caretaker-boss of the Rams.
* In May 1994, a court case commenced in the High Court (London) involving former Villa defender Paul Elliott (Chelsea) and Saunders (then with Villa). It revolved round a tackle by Saunders (playing for Liverpool) on Elliott that effectively ended his playing career. (See Court Cases) Saunders was also arrested for disorderly behaviour in April 1993 after an incident in an Essex night club.

SAVAGE, Harry
Outside-left: 10 apps.
Born: Frodsham, 1897.
Career: Crewe Alexandra (August 1919), BLADES (July 1920), Watford (season 1921-22).
Signed to replace Oliver Tummon on the Blades' left-wing, Harry Savage made a positive start by then faded...before leaving the club following the emergence of Fred Tunstall.

SCARBOROUGH
United' playing record against 'Boro:

FA Cup

Venue	P	W	D	L	F	A
Home	1	1	0	0	6	1

Yorkshire & Humberside Cup

	P	W	D	L	F	A
Away	1	1	0	0	3	1
Neutral	1	1	0	0	2	1
Totals	2	2	0	0	5	2

Scarborough FC began, like United, from a cricket background when members of the town's cricket club formed a football section in 1879, playing at the North Marine Road cricket ground. After years of minor League football, the 'Boro eventually gained Football League status in 1987 (as Conference champions) but lost their place 12 years later when they returned to the Conference.
The Blades' emphatic 6-1 victory over Scarborough was, in fact, their first-ever FA Cup match, a 1st qualifying round encounter on 5 October 1889...long before Scarborough became a League club. A 'very good' crowd saw Dugald Galbraith (2), Donald Fraser (2), Billy Mosforth and Bill Robertson score the goals, with Galbraith having the pleasure of claiming the Blades' first goal in the competition.
Reg Baines, Jeff Birch (Blades reserve), John Burridge, Steve Cammack, Steve Charles, Tony Daws, Chris Downes, Ashley Fickling, Matt Foreman (United reserve), Glyn Hodges, Jamie Hoyland, Richard Lucas, Ray McHale, Tommy Mooney, Colin Morris, John Reed, Rob Scott, Chris Short, Mark Todd are among the players who have assisted the Blades and 'Boro.
Neil Warnock managed both clubs, Tommy Boyle played for the Blades and managed 'Boro.

SCORELINES
United's most frequent scoreline (win or lose) is 1-0 - with this result being recorded more than 600 times in major competitive action (League, FAC & LC). The Blades have also played out over 500 1-1 draws.
>From 1889 to date United's first XI has so far registered 62 different scorelines (from 0-0 through to 0-13).

SCOTT, Andrew

Left-back/forward: 49+38 apps. 12 goals
Born: Epsom, 2 August 1972
Career: Sutton United, BLADES (£50,000, December 1992), Brentford (£95,000, November 1997), Chesterfield (on loan, October 1996), Bury (on loan, March 1997), Oxford United (£75,000, January 2001).
Initially a left-back, Andy Scott was successfully converted into a striker who did very well in difficult circumstances during his time at Bramall Lane. A Third Division championship winner with the Blades in 1993, he went on to score 35 goals in 136 games for the Bees.
NB: Brother Rob (q.v) was also a professional footballer.

SCOTT, Jack

Centre-forward: 22 apps. 11 goals
Born: Scotland, circa 1870
Career: Leith Athletic, BLADES (September 1891), Gainsborough (December1992).
Jack Scott had the misfortune to miss the first penalty awarded to United - in a 2-1 Northern League win at Middlesbrough in October 1891. His scoring record was superb.

SCOTT, Robert

Forward/defender: 4+6 apps. one goal
Born: Epsom, 15 August 1973
Career: Sutton United, BLADES (£25,000, August 1993), Scarborough (on loan, March 1995), Northampton Town (on loan, November 1995), Fulham (£40,000, January 1996), Carlisle United (on loan, August 1998), Rotherham United (£50,000, November 1998).
As a forward (mainly playing on the wing) Rob Scott found it tough to get first team football at Bramall Lane but after leaving for Fulham he certainly made up for lost ground after converting into a versatile defender. He made close on 100 appearances for the Cottagers and has now amassed in excess of 150 for Rotherham. Perhaps another player who escaped from the United net!

SCOTTISH CONNECTION

United have played the following Scottish clubs at first team level:
Ayr United, Celtic, Clyde, Dundee, Dundee United, Dunfermline Athletic, East Stirling, Falkirk, Forfar Athletic, Glasgow Rangers, Greta FC, Hamilton Academical, Heart of Midlothian, Hibernian, Kilmarnock, Leith Athletic, Linthouse FC, Motherwell, Queen of the South, Raith Rovers, St Mirren, Third Lanark and Victoria United.
United also played Berwick Rangers (technically an English club playing in the Scottish League) in 1982-83 (won 2-1).
Including the Berwick game, United's playing record against Scottish clubs is impressive:

P	W	D	L	F	A
50	25	12	13	69	62

Tartan Talk

* United's first opponents from north of the border were Linthouse FC (Glasgow) who visited Bramall Lane for a friendly in January 1891. The Blades won 2-1 in front of 1,250 spectators.
* United's best win of the 25 so far recorded against Scottish opposition, is away to Clyde in July 1981. They also won 4-2 at Raith Rovers in January 1895, 4-2 at home to Hearts in February 1956 and 4-3 away to Dunfermline in October 1959. The Blades lost 4-1 at Third Lanark in March 1895.
* United beat Celtic (over two legs) to win the Championship of Britain in 1897-98 (see under CELTIC & appropriate section).

SCOUTS

Among the men who have acted as a scout for the Blades we have ex-players Alan Hodgkinson, Tom Johnson (late 1940s/50s), Ernie Needham, Paddy Sloan and Fred White. The latter also scouted for Birmingham City, Blackburn Rovers, Colchester United, Leeds United and Oxford United.
Others employed in a scouting capacity at 'the Lane' include Lou Macari (ex-Manchester United and Celtic player), George C Smith (1960-61), John Short (mid-1970s) and latterly Kevin Randell.
Macari was also employed as a scout by the Blades (under manager Steve Bruce) likewise Dick Duckworth (also ex-Manchester United). The following were all associated with Sheffield United FC and scouted for other clubs (listed): Bill Anderson (Arsenal, Ipswich Town), Danny Bergara (Luton Town), Ted Connor (Manchester United), John Deehan (Aston Villa), Jimmy Hagan (Manchester City), Johnny Harris (Sheffield Wednesday), Harry Haslam (Fulham Luton Town & England), Adrian Heath (Sunderland), Alan Hodgkinson (Manchester United), Jim Iley (Cambridge United, Charlton Athletic, Luton Town), Teddy Sandford (West Bromwich Albion), Jimmy Sirrel (Derby County) and Gerry Summers (Derby County, Southampton).

SCULLION, Stewart McNab Adam

Winger: 67+4 apps. 7 goals
Born: Bo'ness, Scotland, 18 April 1946
Career: Chesham United, Charlton Athletic (March 1965), Watford (February 1966), BLADES (May 1971), Watford (£15,000, December 1973-May 1976).
Able to use both feet effectively, winger Stewart Scullion was a brainy winger, quick over the ground, who did well when the Blades returned to the top flight in 1970-71. During his two spells at Vicarage Road he netted 49 goals in 312 League games, helping the Hornets win the third Division championship in 1969 and reach the semi-final of the FA Cup in 1970

SCUNTHORPE UNITED

United's playing record against the Iron:

Football League

Venue	P	W	D	L	F	A
Home	5	5	0	0	14	5
Away	5	1	3	1	7	6
Totals	10	6	3	1	21	11
Others						
Away	2	1	1	0	3	2

It is thought that in 1899 (possibly early 1900), Brumby Hall FC (playing at the Old Showground) consolidated their position in local football by amalgamating with several other clubs and changing its name to Scunthorpe United. In 1910, after joining forces with North Lindsey United, it became known as Scunthorpe and Lindsey United, Lindsey being dropped in 1958.

The 'Iron' as they became known over the years, gained entry to the Football League in 1950 (after service in the Midland League) when it was agreed to increase membership from 88 clubs to 92. Third Division (North) champions eight years later, they duly won promotion to the Second Division and in the 1958-59 season met the Blades for the first time at Bramall Lane in the October. Four-nil down at thee interval (due to Alf Ringstead's splendid hat-trick) they reduced the deficit by one in the second-half. The following March the Blades completed the double with a 3-1 win at the Old Showground.

Although the Blades have won all five League matches at home (encompassing fixtures in three different Divisions) that initial 'double' remains their only one over the 'Iron.'

The Lincolnshire club's only victory over United came in 1981-82 - and it was a rare defeat for the Fourth Division champions who went down 2-1.

Neil Warnock played for Scunthorpe and managed the Blades while Frank Barlow played for the Blades and managed the 'Iron' (1984-87). Players who have served the two Uniteds over the years include Gary Ablett ('Iron' trialist), Brian Arblaster (Blades reserve), Michael Ash, John Barke, Peter Beagrie, Ernie Blackwell, Carl Bradshaw, Julian Broddle, Steve Cammack, Steve Charles, Graeme Crawford, Tony Daws; Geoff Dey, Gerald Dodds & Tom Evans (Blades reserves); Ashley Fickling, John Francis, Ian Hamilton, Kirk Jackson (Blades reserve),Andy Keeley, Joe Kitchen, Cliff Mason, Bill Punton, Brian Smith, Jack Thompson, Fred Tunstall, George Underwood, Imre Varadi, Harry Wainwright, Ronnie Waldock and Walter Webster.

SEASONS

Longest

The longest season so far in United's history spanned 10 months and three weeks 11 months in 1974-75.
Here at the full details of the longest campaigns:

10 months 21 days	1974-75	17 July to 7 June
10 months 15 days	1946-47	31 August to 14 June
10 months 11 days	1968-69	27 July to 7 June
10 months 9 days	1966-67	6 August to 15 June
10 months 4 days	1964-65	12 August to 16 June
10 months 0 days	1961-62	9 August to 9 June

Seasonal Review

The earliest United have commenced their Football League programme was on 9 August 1969.

Their first competitive match at the start of a campaign came when they played Notts County (away) in the Watney Cup on 29 July 1972.

United's earliest 'seasonal' start of any kind was a friendly, on tour in Switzerland, on 14 July 1994 v. Winterthur/Baden FC (see under FRIENDLIES).

The latest date United have fulfilled a League game was on 14 June 1947 v. Stoke City at Bramall Lane, United won 2-1.

United's all-time 'late' end-of-season match was played on 18 June 1966 against Ascuncion (in Paraguay) at the end of their South American tour.

SECRETARIES

Here is a list of the Sheffield United club secretaries:

1889-92	John Beckitt Wostinholm
1892-93	A George Winnell*/Wostinholm
1893-99	Wostinholm
1899-1932	John Nicholson
1932-52	JE 'Teddy' Davison
1952-72	Arnold Newton
1972-73	Newton/Keith Walker
1973-78	Walker
1978-83	Richard 'Dick' Chester
1983-88	Geoff Smith
1988-89	Smith/David Capper
1989-2001	Capper
2001	John Howarth

* George Winnell took the secretary's chair in September 1892 and held it until November 1893, though John Wostinholm remained secretary of the County Cricket Club.

Secretary's Note-pad

* Although John Wostinholm was basically United's manager/secretary for ten years from 1889-99 when the club was run by a committee. He was assisted for some considerable time by Henry Herbert Stones who dealt with most matters appertaining to the football side of the club.

* Howard Hawley was assistant-secretary to Teddy Davison for practically 20 years.

* Nicholson (who spent almost 33 years in office) was sadly killed in a road accident on his way to watch United play a League game at Villa Park on 23 April 1932. The players were stunned and lost the match 5-0.

SEGERS, Johannes

Goalkeeper: 11 apps.
Born: Eindhoven, Holland, 30 October 1961
Career: PSV Eindhoven (November 1977, professional October 1978), Nottingham Forest (£50,000, August 1984), Stoke City (on loan, February 1987), BLADES (on loan, November 1987), Dunfermline Athletic (on loan, March 1988), Wimbledon (£180,000, September 1988), Wolverhampton Wanderers (free transfer, August 1996), Tottenham Hotspur (free transfer, August 1998, later appointed goalkeeping coach at White Hart Lane).

221

Hans Segers did well between the posts for the Blades, after being brought in on loan following an injury to Andy Leaning. He appeared in 322 senior games for the Dons and when he retired in 2000, he had accumulated in some 600 League and Cup appearances for his eight club, including PSV.
* In the summer of 1997 Segers was found not guilty in the footballers' bribe case (with Bruce Grobbelaar, John Fashanu and a Malaysian businessman).

SENDINGS-OFF

* The first United player to be sent-off is thought to have been Robertson, in the Sheffield Challenge Cup Final replay v. Rotherham in March 1890.

Here is a near-complete list of United players who have been sent-off at first team level:

W Robertson	v. Rotherham Town (a)	SCCF replay	22.03.1890
R Cain	v. Woolwich Arsenal (a)	Friendly	20.10.1892
H Hammond	v. Crewe Alexandra (h)	Division 2	12.04.1893
R Hill	v. West B Albion (h)	Division 1	28.10.1893
W Gillespie	v. Lincoln City (h)	WW1 MS	04.12.1915
W Brelsford	v. Wednesday (h)	WW1 MS	15.01.1916
H Pantling	v. Huddersfield T (h)	WW1 MS	24.11.1917
H Pantling	v. Leeds City (a)	WW1 MS	09.03.1918
H Pantling	v. Bolton Wds (a)	Division 1	19.03.1921
W Gillespie	v. Bolton Wds (a)	Division 1	05.05.1928
H Hooper	v. Doncaster Rovers (a)	CCSF/1	02.05.1934
E Dodds	v. Swansea Town (a)	Division 2	25.02.1937
E Dodds	v. Sandviken (a)	Friendly	18.05.1938
J Hagan	v. Swansea Town (h)	Division 2	20.12.1952
T Hoyland	v. Huddersfield T (h)	FAC Rd 3/R	07.01.1957
D Pace	v. Grimsby Town (h)	Division 2	27.12.1958
W Gould	v. Rotherham Utd (a)	Division 2	15.04.1959
L Badger	v. Leeds United (a)	Division 1	31.10.1964
K Kettleborough	v. Aston Villa (h)	FAC Rd 4	30.01.1965
B Shaw	v. Atlas FC/Mexico (a)	Friendly	19.05.1966
K Mallender	v. Manchester C (a)	Division 1	06.05.1967
L Badger	v. Zambia XI (a)	Friendly	07.05.1972
E Colquhoun	v. Zambia XI (a)	Friendly	07.05.1972
A Currie	v. Peterborough U (a)	WC S/F	02.08.1972
A Currie	v. Everton (a)	Division 1	17.03.1973
M Speight	v. Stoke City (h)	Division 1	16.02.1974
S Goulding	v. Algerian XI (a)	Friendly	03.05.1974
L Badger	v. Stoke City (a)	Division 1	05.10.1974
E Colquhoun	v. Norwich City (h)	LC Rd 4	12.11.1974
E Hemsley	v. Heracles (a)	Friendly	27.07.1975
L Badger	v. Birmingham C (a)	Division 1	04.10.1975
R Campbell	v. Oldham Athletic (a)	Division 2	17.12.1977
J Flynn	v. Oldham Athletic (a)	Division 2	17.12.1977
A Woodward	v. Burnley (a)	Division 2	11.03.1978
A Keeley	v. Burnley (a)	Division 2	11.03.1978
A Kenworthy	v. Orient (a)	Division 2	11.11.1978
M Guy	v. Brighton HA (a)	Division 2	17.03.1978
J Cutbush	v. Colchester U (a)	Division 3	21.08.1079
M Speight	v. Brentford (a)	Division 3	22.10.1979
J Matthews	v. Exeter City (a)	Division 3	12.01.1980
M Trusson	v. Fulham (a)	Division 3	26.12.1980
M Trusson	v. Altrincham (a)	FAC Rd 1/R	23.11.1981
P Richardson	v. Halifax Town (a)	Division 4	02.01.1982
S Neville	v. Scunthorpe Utd (a)	Division 4	20.02.1982
P Garner	v. Portsmouth (a)	Division 3	28.08.1982
R Atkins	v. Grimsby Town (a)	LC Rd 2/1	12.10.1982
P Richardson	v. Exeter City (a)	Division 3	23.10.1982
M Henderson	v. Southend Utd (a)	Division 3	26.03.1983
M Henderson	v. Walsall (a)	Division 3	06.09.1983
J Bolton	v. Oldham Ath (a)	Division 2	08.09.1984
G Cockerill	v. Oldham Ath (a)	Division 2	08.09.1984
S Foley	v. Leeds United (a)	Division 2	28.09.1985
R Lewington	v. Leeds United (a)	Division 2	28.09.1985
K McNaught	v. Wimbledon (a)	Division 2	21.12.1985
P Withe	v. Wimbledon (a)	Division 2	21.12.1985
P Beagrie	v. Portsmouth (h)	Division 2	13.12.1986
S Foley	v. Derby County (h)	Division 2	25.04.1987
C Wilder	v. Millwall (a)	Division 2	28.12.1987
W Downes	v. Leeds United (a)	Division 2	19.03.1988
P Williams	v. Ipswich Town (h)	Division 1	26.03.1988
W Downes	v. Bradford City (h)	Division 1	04.03.1988
B Deane	v. Notts County (a)	Division 3	26.12.1988
P Stancliffe	v. Chesterfield (h)	Division 3	02.01.1989

R Booker	v. Wrexham (a)	Division 3	17.01.1989
G Benstead	v. Wrexham (a)	Division 3	17.01.1989
M Pike	v. TSV Friesen (a)	Friendly	25.07.1989
D Barnes	v. Tottenham H (a)	Division 1	20.10.1990
V Jones	v. Manchester C (a)	Division 1	19.01.1991
J Gannon	v. Sunderland (a)	Division 1	09.03.1991
D Whitehouse	v. Frolunda (a)	Friendly	04.08.1991
C Hartfield	v. Oldham Athletic (a)	Division 1	07.09.1991
P Beesley	v. Oldham Athletic (a)	Division 1	07.09.1991
B Gayle	v. West Ham Utd (a)	Division 1	02.12.1991
B Gayle	v. Forfar Athletic (a)	Friendly	21.07.1991
S Tracey	v. Tottenham Hot (a)	Premiership	02.09.1992
C Bradshaw	v. Coventry City (h)	Premiership	28.11.1992
A Littlejohn	v. Burnley (a)	FAC Rd 3	02.01.1993
G Hodges	v. Sheffield Wed (a)	Premiership	21.04.1993
T Cowan	v. Kongsvinger (a)	Friendly	29.07.1993
A Littlejohn	v. Blackpool (a)	LC Rd 2/1	21.09.1993
D Tuttle	v. Southampton (a)	Premiership	02.10.1993
C Bradshaw	v. Blackburn Rovers (h)	Premiership	15.01.1994
A Cork	v. Blackburn Rovers (h)	Premiership	15.01.1994
S Tracey	v. Oldham Athletic (a)	Premiership	03.05.1994
N Blake	v. Udinese (h)	Anglo-Italian	24.08.1994
G Hodges	v. Udinese (h)	Anglo-Italian	24.08.1994
C Hartfield	v. Udinese (h)	Anglo-Italian	24.08.1994
D Bassett*	v. Udinese (h)	Anglo-Italian	24.08.1994
J Flo	v. Notts County (a)	Division 1	27.08.1994
B Gayle	v. Sunderland (h)	Division 1	13.09.1994
N Blake	v. West B Albion (h)	Division 1	10.12.1994
P Beesley	v. Middlesbrough (h)	Division 1	26.12.1994
C Hartfield	v. Manchester Utd (h)	FAC Rd 3	09.01.1995
K Gage	v. Bristol City (a)	Division 1	21.01.1995
D Tuttle	v. Sunderland (a)	Division 1	01.04.1995
G Hodges	v. Barnsley (a)	Division 1	29.04.1995
B Gayle	v. Oldham Athletic (a)	Division 1	28.08.1995
D Whitehouse	v. Ipswich Town (h)	Division 1	30.09.1995
N Blake	v. Southend United (a)	Division 1	14.10.1995
M Vonk	v. Tranmere Rovers (a)	Division 1	13.01.1996
G Taylor	v. Wolverhampton W (a)	Division 1	21.09.1996
N Henry	v. Huddersfield Town (a)	Division 1	31.03.1997
N Henry	v. Ipswich Town (a)	P/O SF 2/L	14.05.1997
M Vonk	v. Norwich City (a)	Division 1	06.12.1997
C Short	v. Ipswich Town (a)	FAC Rd 4	24.01.1998
S Tracey	v. Portsmouth (a)	Division 1	31.01.1998
P Devlin	v. E'Quip Romagna (a)	Friendly	23.07.1998
I Hamilton	v. Birmingham C (h)	Division 1	22.08.1998
L Sandford	v. Bolton Wanderers (a)	Division 1	29.08.1998
I Hamilton	v. Crystal Palace (a)	Division 1	27.09.1998
R Nilsen	v. Tranmere Rovers (h)	Division 1	07.11.1998
P Katchouro	v. Queen's Park Rgs (a)	Division 1	21.11.1998
N Henry	v. Bristol City (a)	Division 1	05.12.1998
W Quinn	v. Notts County (a)	FAC Rd 3/R	23.01.1999
R Kozluk	v. Wolverhampton W (h)	Division 1	05.04.1999
R Kozluk	v. Ipswich Town (a)	Division 1	09.05.1999
A Smeets	v. Portsmouth (a)	Division 1	07.08.1999
S Tracey	v. Manchester C (a)	Division 1	21.08.1999
D Gysbrechts	v. West B Albion (a)	Division 1	27.11.1999
S Murphy	v. Fulham (a)	Division 1	15.04.2000
P Devlin	v. Preston North E (a)	Division 1	19.08.2000
M Brown	v. Birmingham C (a)	Division 1	09.09.2000
M Bent	v. Norwich City (a)	Division 1	21.10.2000
R Ford	v. Southampton (a)	FAC Rd 3	06.01.2001
R Ullathorne	v. West B Albion (a)	Division 1	20.01.2001
C Asaba	v. Norwich City (h)	Division 1	29.09.2001
B Doane	v. Walsall (a)	Division 1	24.11.2001
S Nicholson	v. West B Albion (a)	Division 1	08.12.2001
P Devlin	v. Wolverhampton W (a)	Division 1	29.12.2001
S Tracey	v. West B Albion (h)	Division 1	16.03.2002
G Santos	v. West B Albion (h)	Division 1	16.03.2002
P Suffo	v. West B Albion (h)	Division 1	16.03.2002
I Onuora	v. Norwich City (a)	Division 1	07.09.2002
S Jagielka	v. Watford (h)	Division 1	28.09.2002
J Harley	v. Walsall (a)	Division 1	26.12.2002
W Quinn	v. Norwich City (h)	Division 1	22.02.2003
P Ndlovu	v. Norwich City (h)	Division 1	22.02.2003

* Bassett was United's manager at the time.

223

Early Baths

* Harold Pantling was the first United player to be sent-off twice in the same season (1917-18).
* Bob Cain was sent-off during United's friendly with Woolwich Arsenal in October 1892, but was allowed back onto the field after apologising to the referee.
* Two Sheffield Wednesday players - Ambrose Langley and Jack Pryce - were sent-off during the second-half of an ill-tempered 2nd round FA Cup replay against the Blades on 19 February 1900. United won 2-0 in front of almost 23,000 spectators.
* Four players and a manager were sent-off during the United v. Udinese Anglo-Italian Cup game at Bramall Lane in August 1994. Besides three Blades' men, Nathan Blake, Glenn Hodges and Charlie Hartfield, Udinese's Kozminski also saw red while United's manager Dave Bassett was 'sent-off' after protesting from the touchline!
* Four players were sent-off during the United v. Portsmouth Second Division game at Bramall Lane in December 1986 - Peter Beagrie (United)   plus three from Pompey. Paul Mariner's own-goal gave the Blades a 1-0 victory.
* Goalkeeper Graham Benstead was sent-off after the final whistle of United's League game at Wrexham in 1989. Hunter of Wrexham was also dismissed in this match.
* Paul Garner was the first United player dismissed for a professional foul - receiving instant dismissal (a straight red card) v. Portsmouth at Fratton Park in August 1982.
* After his sending-off at Ipswich in the second leg of the 1997 Play-off Semi-final, Nick Henry missed the Final v. Crystal Palace at Wembley.
* When United's Harry Hammond was sent-off against Crewe Alexandra (with Alex's Sproston) he had to flee the ground in a hurry to get away   from irate supporters. The Second Division game ended in a 4-0 win for the Blades.
* Adrian Littlejohn was sent-off with future United player Adrian Heath in the Cup-tie at Burnley in 1993.
* On 19 January 1991, United's hard-man Vinnie Jones was booked after just five seconds of a First Division match at Maine Road for a tackle on Manchester city's player-manager Peter Reid. He was later booked for a second-time (again for a foul on Reid) and was subsequently sent-off.
* Wally Downes was sent-off twice in his first six games for United - v. Leeds (away) and Bradford City (home) in March/April 1988.
* Georges Santos, playing for Tranmere Rovers, was sent-off against United (his future club) in August 1999 (Division 1).
* Three United players saw 'red' during the First Division game with West Bromwich Albion at Bramall Lane in March 2002 - goalkeeper Simon Tracey (early on) and substitutes George Santos and Patrick Suffo, who went off in the space of two second-half minutes.

SETTLE, Alfred

Left-half: 138 apps. 3 goals
Born: Barugh Green, 17 September 1912. Died: 1988
Career: Grantham Rovers, BLADES (January 1935), Lincoln City (February 1946-April 1946).
After making his League debut for the Blades against Hull City in April 1936, Alf Settle, a strong, stocky, well-built wing-half with an aggressive nature, Alf Settle had to wait until September 1937 before his next outing. He gained a regular place in the side during that season and was an ever-present in 1938-39 when promotion was gained to the First Division. An ankle injury (suffered in October 1942) ended effectively ended his career although he did attempt an aborted comeback with the Imps after the hostilities (12 appearances).

SHAMROCK ROVERS

Blades' playing record against Rovers:

Duggan Cup

Venue	P	W	D	L	F	A
Home	1	1	0	0	6	4
Away	3	2	1	0	10	5
Totals	4	3	1	0	16	9

United met Shamrock Rovers, one of the more famous clubs in Ireland, four times in the Duggan Cup, playing twice in 1933 (won 5-4 and drew 1-1, both away) and twice in 1934 (won 6-4 at home and 4-0 away).
Jimmy Dunne scored a hat-trick in the 5-4 victory which attracted a 20,000 crowd, and Jock Dodds in the 4-0 triumph.
Shamrock Rovers have won their domestic League championship 15 times and the FIA Cup 24 times.

SHANKLY, James

Centre-forward: 8 apps. 4 goals
Born: Glennbuck, Scotland, 19 June 1902. Died: 1972
Career: Glennbuck Cherrypickers (1919), Guildford United (1921), Halifax Town (August 1924), Nuneaton Town (briefly), Coventry City (February 1926), Carlisle United (August 1926), BLADES (December 1926), Southend United (May 1928), Barrow (season 1933-34), Carlisle United (1936-38).
Jimmy Shankly scored on his League debut for the Blades v. Newcastle United (h) in February 1927 (won 2-1). Signed from Carlisle United as cover for Harry Johnson, he was certainly a useful reserve who went on to 97 goals in 147 League games for Southend and 47 in 78 for Barrow before returning to Carlisle.
* Brothers Bill (ex-Carlisle United, Preston North End and then famously Liverpool's manager), Bob (Aldershot, Barrow, Clapton Orient, Newcastle United & manager of Dundee), Sandy (ex-Ayr United) and John (Alloa Athletic, Luton Town & Portsmouth) were all professional footballers.

SHARES

In 1899, when Sheffield United Football Club became a Limited Company, supporters/businessmen etc, who had initially purchased £5 shares in the Cricket/Football Club, were allowed to exchange them for £20 original (new) shares. The value of these shares has risen steadily over the years - and each share is now valued at around £5,000.

SHAW, Bernard

Full-back: 161+1 apps. 33 goals

Born: Sheffield, 14 March 1945

Career: BLADES (amateur, June 1960, professional October 1962), Wolverhampton Wanderers (July 1969), Sheffield Wednesday (June 1973-May 1976).

An England Youth international who partnered fellow 'Blade' Len Badger at this level for both club and country, Bernard Shaw was also chosen to represent his country's Under-23 side. He played alongside his elder brother Graham in three senior games for the Blades but health problems interfered badly with his career at Bramall Lane, although it was also said that he had the 'wrong attitude' to become a first-class player. He went on to play in 156 games for Wolves, gaining a UEFA Cup runners-up medal in 1972, and later added another 113 appearances to his tally with the Owls before his release in 1976 following their demotion to the Third Division.

SHAW, Graham Laurence

Full-back: 498 apps. 15 goals

Born: Sheffield, 9 July 1934

Career: BLADES (juniors 1950, then Army service, professional, July 1951), Doncaster Rovers (September 1967-May 1968).

Although he always seemed to line up at left-back, Graham Shaw often preferred to use his right foot. A smart, confident tackler, he was an excellent positional player who chose to use the ball to advantage rather than giving it a mighty thump downfield and hoping for the best. He made his League debut for the Blades as a 17 year-old in the Sheffield derby at Hillsborough in January 1952 when a crowd of over 65,000 saw the Owls oiled and feathered 3-1. Shaw loved his long-range shooting and during his career he scored some cracking goals from well outside the area. One of his best was the 40-yarder he netted against Arsenal in a home First Division match in April 1955 (1-1). He helped the Blades win the Second Division championship in 1953 and regain their top-flight status in 1961.

* United manager Joe Mercer wanted to sell Shaw to Stoke City but the defender refused to go.

225

SHAW, Joseph

Half-back: 714 apps. 8 goals

Born: Murton, County Durham, 23 June 1928

Career: Upton Colliery FC, BLADES (March 1945, retired May 1966, then coach at Bramall Lane until October 1967) Manager, York City and Chesterfield.

Joe Shaw - one of the Blades' finest-ever players - made his senior debut for the club against Huddersfield Town (home) in April 1945 (WW2). His next first team appearance came three years later in August 1948 and his last in February 1966 v. West Ham United. He started out as an inside-forward but was successfully converted into a wonderful wing-half before settling down at centre-half despite not being all that tall. He could read a game superbly, his anticipation was second to none, and he formed part of that great United middle-line of the later 1950s/early '60s with Brian Richardson and Gerry Summers playing either side of him. Twice member of Second Division promotion-winning sides in 1953 (as champions) and 1961 (as runners-up), he had many fine games in United's colours...and one suspects that if he'd played for a more fashionable club he would certainly have gained full international honours for England. Two of Shaw's eight goals for the Blades were brilliant efforts, both struck from distance, and both came in United's 4-4 Second Division draw with Bury in November 1949.

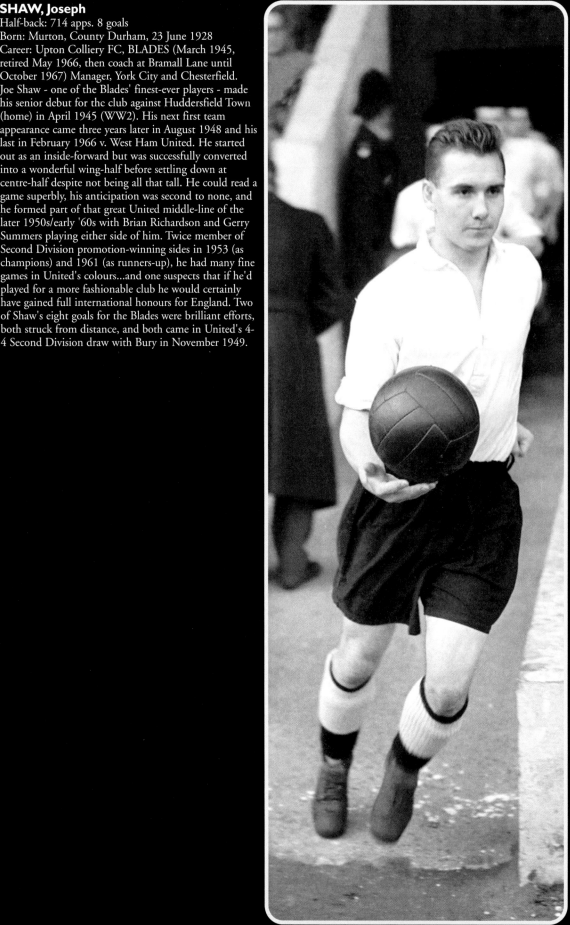

SHEARMAN, Benjamin W

Inside/outside-left: 75 'other' apps. 12 goals
Born: Lincoln, June 1884. Died: October 1958
Career: St Mary's Council School (Lincoln), Sheffield & District Schools, Attercliffe High Hazels, Worksop Town, Rotherham Town (seasons 1907-09), Bristol City (August 1909), West Bromwich Albion (£100, June 1911), BLADES (WW1 guest: September 1915-May 1918), Nottingham Forest (£250, July 1919), Gainsborough Trinity (August 1920), Norton Woodseats (trainer-coach, August 1922 until his retirement in 1938).
Ben Shearman was an elusive left-winger, quick of the mark, who delivered strikingly accurate deep crosses, whether hit high or low from the touchline. He gained an FA Cup runners-up medal with WBA in 1912, represented the Football League on two occasions (1911) and during his career played in over 250 senior matches, 143 for WBA. He was a vital member of the Blades' front-line during WW1.

SHEEN, John

Inside-forward: 47 apps. 7 goals
Born: Airdrie, Scotland, 30 August 1920. Died: 1997.
Career: Airdrie Schoolboy football, Ballieston Juniors (1935-36), BLADES (September 1937), Linfield (WW2 guest: 1940-42), Hull City (July 1946), Shrewsbury Town (August 1947).
Jock Sheen, strong , played made all of his appearances for the Blades during WW2. He won the both the Irish Cup and the Irish League title with Linfield in 1941 & 1942 and skippered Hull for part of the 1946-47 season.

SHEFFIELD FC

United accounted for the Sheffield Club 3-0 in a home 3rd qualifying FA Cup-tie in November 1889. A crowd of 2,000 saw Donald Fraser, James Duncan and an 'own-goal' hit the target.
The Sheffield Club was formed in 1857 by members of the Sheffield Cricket Club, by now playing at the new Bramall Lane ground. The committee comprised good, upright Sheffield citizens, future captains of industry, merchants, solicitors, technologists, intellectuals and academics who brought their intelligence to bear of the rules of the game.
Unlike cricket, where the MCC code allowed all players to perform using the same laws, football had no equivalent. So, having studied the laws obtained from a number of public schools, they rejected them all and produced their own. The 'Sheffield Rules 'became widely used by many clubs in the North of England, which is more than can be said of the Football Association's first laws issued in 1863.
Although the Sheffield club was not invited to the FA's inaugural meeting, the committee had many critical comments and constructive suggestions to make regarding their draft laws.
Sheffield FC rejected the use of hands as well as 'hacking' and tripping. The FA's version of the game varied little from Rugby - the ball could be handled, even caught, the player calling 'mark' to win a free-kick; touchdowns behind the opponents' line earned a kick at goal; throw-ins were to be at right-angles to the touchline; the goal-posts had no crossbar; players were deemed offside if they were ahead of the ball; hacking and tripping by players was allowed and passing was not encouraged while dribbling was.
Sheffield FC wanted a game to be distinctly different from Rugby...no handling, no tripping. The Sheffield secretary in his letter to the FA described their game as 'more appropriate to wrestling.'
Eventually this correspondence led to matches between Sheffield and London with further exchange of ideas. By 1867, a Sheffield FA had been created, representing 26 clubs from the Sheffield district. Needless to say the Sheffield club itself played a great part in this organisation. Sheffield v. London matches were now being arranged on a regular basis, three or four a year, the FA laws gradually changing, accommodating outside interests, notably Sheffield's!
Sheffield FC and the Association can lay claim to banning handling, tripping and hacking and the introduction of the crossbar, the corner-kick, the six-yard goal-kick, the indirect free-kick and the use of two umpires to control the game. And they probably introduced the art of heading the ball rather than catching it as previously had been the case.
As the influence of the FA Cup spread, so did thee revised FA laws, football being now distinctly different to rugby. Sheffield can be proud of its part in the creation of the world's favourite sport.
Sheffield FC remained an amateur organisation, but as the Sheffield FA got swallowed up into the FA itself, its influence waned. After Sheffield FC had met United in the FA Cup in 1889 (see above) the following year they lost 13-0 to Rotherham Town...and there is nor record of them having entered the competition since.
In its prime the Sheffield club provided players to the first England teams of the 1870s. Th club laid claim to being the first (and therefore senior) Association Football Club in the world, thus its place is secure in the history of the game.

SHEFFIELD CHALLENGE CUP

United first competed in this competition in season 1889-90. They reached the Final after knocking out Exchange FC 7-0, Heeley 1-0, Attercliffe 6-0 and Staveley 2-0 (all at home). Rotherham then lifted the trophy by winning the Final replay 1-0 (after a 0-0 draw).
In 1890-91, after ousting Attercliffe 7-1 and Kilnhurst 4-1 in a replay (after a 3-3 draw), they were defeated 2-1 by Doncaster Rovers in the Final. All four matches were played at Bramall Lane.
The following season, after successive 4-0 wins over Doncaster Rovers (home) and Kilnhurst (away) the United reserve team (under the name of Sheffield Strollers) lifted the trophy with a 2-1 win over Sheffeild Wednesday reserves team in the Final at Bramall Lane (5,000 crowd).

SHEFFIELD & DERBY LEAGUE (SDL)

In season 1896-97, United's reserves competed in the Sheffield & Derby League, but for the two local derbies against rivals Wednesday, the first team played, drawing 0-0 at home and losing 2-1 away.

SHEFFIELD UNITED CRICKET CLUB

It would not be proper for any work on Sheffield United FC to be published without mention of the cricket club which was associated with Bramall Lane from 1854 (long before it became a football ground) to 1973 when the ground was converted to a football-only stadium.
The history of Bramall Lane (q.v) shows that Michael J Ellison, the son of the Duke of Norfolk's land agent, a cricket fanatic, arranged for the site to be rented for £70 per annum on a 99 year lease. Six cricket clubs jumped at the chance to utilise this near-perfect cricket field, away from the industrial gloom of the town and virtually flat, a rarity in Sheffield!
These clubs were the Sheffield Club, Wednesday, Broomhall, Milton, Caxton and Shrewsbury who would divide payment of the rent between them. A committee was formed to run the ground on behalf of the clubs, known as Sheffield United Cricket Club. This was, however, a 'club without a team', but when a football club was mooted in 1889, it naturally took the name 'Sheffield United.'
By 1864 the ground was the head-quarters of the Yorkshire County Cricket Club with Joseph Beckett Wostinholm (q.v) a partner in a

227

firm of stockbrokers and estate agents, installed as secretary of the Ground Committee, Sheffield United Cricket club as well as Yorkshire CCC. In 1892, the Cricket Club at least became a team, playing of course at Bramall Lane itself, and by 1899 'Sheffield United Cricket & Football Club Ltd' was created. Michael J Ellison, himself, was named President, with JB Wostinholm secretary. Sheffield United CC enjoyed its best playing period between the wars, regularly winning the Yorkshire Council Championship. Bramall Lane was a coaching 'academy' for young cricketers with a winter shed, despite Yorkshire having left to take up residency at Leeds, but with Sheffield still used as a regular venue for county matches.

However, after WW2, cricket gradually declined in popularity, whilst football enjoyed a boom period. When the club had started in the 19th century, cricket was 'king'. The footballers accepted this, grudgingly, despite the revenue that the game raised.

Now the cricketers were blatantly subsidised by the football section, which resented this drain on its resources.

By 1970 the writing was on the wall and eventually the cricket club was asked to leave; and the last county match played at Bramall Lane was, symbolically the 'Roses' match of August 1973.

The Cricket Club was given a derisory £15,000 'golden hand-shake' and decamped to the totally unsatisfactory ground at Dore as Sheffield United (1973) Cricket Club. Whereas previously the cricketers had enjoyed the administration facilities of a county ground, now they had to do everything themselves. For a time it looked as though the club would die.

Subsequently, in 1982, they obtained the old Firth Vickers Ground at Bawtry Road, hopeful that the county would share it as a county ground, but Yorkshire CCC plumped for Abbeydale Park as its new home in Sheffield.

Over the years Bawtry Road has been built up considerably and today the United CC is a thriving organisation with an indoor school, turning out four sides very weekend during the season.

In the early days, several Sheffield United footballers turned out for the cricket team, notably Ernest 'Nudger' Needham, George Waller, Arthur Watson, Harry Hammond, Bernard Wilkinson, Billy Wilkinson, Jack Jones, Alonzo Drake, Joe Lievesley and Joe Kitchen.

In later years Sheffield United CC produced Fred Trueman and Devon Malcolm, two of England's finest fast bowlers.

SHEFFIELD WEDNESDAY (WEDNESDAY until 1929)

United's playing record against the Owls:

Premier League

Venue	P	W	D	L	F	A
Home	2	0	2	0	2	2
Away	2	0	1	1	2	4
Totals	4	0	3	1	4	6

Football League

Home	50	23	17	10	79	52
Away	50	16	13	21	62	75
Totals	100	39	30	31	141	127

FA Cup

Home	4	2	1	2	9	9
Away	4	1	2	0	4	2
Neutral	1	0	0	1	1	2
Totals	9	3	3	3	14	13

League Cup

Home	1	0	1	0	1	1
Away	2	0	0	2	1	4
Totals	3	0	1	2	2	5

United Counties League

Home	2	1	1	0	2	0
Away	2	0	2	0	2	2
Totals	4	1	3	0	4	2

WW1

Home	8	4	2	2	11	11
Away	8	2	2	4	8	13
Totals	16	6	4	6	19	24

WW2

Home	12	5	4	3+	19	14
Away	11	4	1	6+	19	30
Totals	23	9	5	9	38	44

Sheffield & Hallamshire County Cup

Home	12	9	1	2	28	14
Away	17	9	1*	7	32	27
Totals	29	18	2	9	60	41

Steel City Challenge Cup

Home	2	1	0	1	5	4
Away	2	1	0	1	3	5
Totals	4	2	0	2	8	9

Others

Home	10	3	3	4	15	17
Away	13	4	2	7	12	22
Totals	23	7	5	11	27	39

* Blades lost 4-3 on penalties after a 0-0 draw in the 1974 Final

+ The two games played in May 1945 also counted both SSC & League North.

Sheffield Wednesday, like United, had their origins in a cricket club. The Wednesday CC was formed in 1825, adding a football section in 1867. Bramall Lane had been Sheffield's centre of sport since its opening in 1855 when six cricket clubs agreed to use the new ground, Wednesday being amongst them.

Wednesday's first football ground was Highfield. The club moved to Myrtle Road in 1869, switched to Sheaf House in 1877 before arriving at their first 'proper ground' at Olive Grove, a couple of streets away from Bramall Lane, in 1887. It was the close proximity of a professional club Bramall Lane (now regarded as the major football arena outside London) that persuaded the committee to form their own football club (Sheffield United).

Olive Grove lease ran out, so a purpose-built ground at Owlerton (leading to the adoption of the nickname 'The Owls' despite the difference of pronunciation - the 'Owl' in Owlerton rhyming with 'roll') was built in 1899; in 1912 the ground was renamed 'Hillsborough.'

Although United's inaugural season saw them play 57 friendly and Cup matches, strangely Wednesday were not amongst them. They became Blades' opponents for the first time December 1890. The corresponding fixture the following season attracted almost 23,000 spectators and this time Wednesday were crushed to the tune of 5-0.

Both clubs were elected to the Football League in 1892, Wednesday going straight into Division One, United into Division Two. So the first meeting in the 'League' had to wait until Monday, 16 October 1893 when the teams fought out a 1-1 draw at Bramall Lane. A crowd of 27,000 saw Robert Hill volley the Blades into an early lead only for Fred Spiksley to equalise on 12 minutes. This encounter became over-heated and the referee stopped proceedings at one point to lecture both teams. Wednesday were the happier team, however, as they played with only 10 men for a fair proportion of the second half after tough-nut Harry Davis had been knocked unconscious!

The return game, which was also played on a Monday in November, resulted in a win for United by 2-1, Jack Drummond and Harry Hammond the scorers.

Thus began a series of competitive matches comprising 22 seasons, lasting until 1920, and although Wednesday were relegated in 1899, they did meet the Blades in the FA Cup during that campaign. In fact, the 2nd round tie in February 1900 was abandoned due to heavy snow after 53 minutes with the scoresheet blank. The 'replay' also ended level at 1-1 before United won an ill-tempered 'third' game at Owlerton by 2-0 (their first victory there). Second-half goals by Needham (a 50th minute penalty...after Ambrose Langley had fouled George Hedley) and Billy Beer settled the issue after two Wednesday players - Jack Pryce (for a terrible tackle on Hedley) and Langley (for ending Walter 'Cock' Bennett's interest in the game) - were both sent-off by strict referee Jack Lewis of Blackburn.

Regrettably both teams have experienced bad times, Wednesday playing in Division three, the Blades in Division Four. And over the years they have met each other in only 52 out of a possible 100 League seasons.

Since WW2 the clubs have opposed each other only 20 times in 57 seasons of League action.

United's last League game on Wednesday's ground when it was called Owlerton was on 26 October 1912. They lost 1-0 in front of 17,000 fans.

United played the Owls four times in succession during March/April 1919. They won 2-0 and 1-0 in Midland Group matches and lost 1-0 and won 1-0 in two friendly encounters.

When the Blades were beaten 5-0 at home by Wednesday in a wartime game in March 1918
, Ted Glennon scored four times of the Owls' goals, while United hit the woodwork on five occasions in the second-half. The attendance was 15,000.

Harry Johnson netted the first hat-trick in a competitive Sheffield derby, for the Blades in their 4-1 victory in a 4th round FA Cup replay in 1928.

Ten goals were scored in the Second Division derby at Bramall Lane in September 1951, as United recorded their best-ever win over the Owls, crushing them 7-3 in front of 51,075 fans. The Owls went ahead after just 90 seconds when Keith Thomas netted with a superb diving header (his only goal for Wednesday). The Blades soon equalised through Alf Ringstead and the classy Harold Brook made it 2-1 on 20 minutes. A penalty save by Wednesday 'keeper Dave McIntosh from Fred Furniss kept the visitors in the game and when Dennis Woodhead levelled things up on the hour it looked as if the Owls might get a result. At this juncture however, the Blades sharpened up and went to town, scoring five goals in the last 30 minutes, Derek Hawksworth (2), Fred A Smith and Brook and Ringstead again, all finding the net. Despite this hammering the Owls still finished up as Second Division champions, inspired by Derek Dooley who scored 46 goals in only 30 games.

The return fixture drew a record League crowd for a Sheffield derby - 66,384 - to Hillsborough in January 1952. And United completed the 'double' by winning 3-1 with Ringstead netting twice. Graham Shaw (aged 17) made his debut for the Blades.

United's best League win on Wednesday soil has been 3-1, registered on no less than five occasions, the last in 1991-92.

United's worst days have been a 5-2 defeat at Hillsborough in 1928-29 and a depressing 4-0 collapse in the Third Division in 1979-80 when Wednesday gained promotion.

When the Blades completed a 'League' double over Wednesday in 1961-62 (1-0 at home and 2-1 away) 'Doc' Pace scored all three goals.

The 200th derby (all competitions including friendlies) between the Blades and the Owls ended all square at 2-2 on 24 September 1966 in front of 42,730 fans at Hillsborough. United led 2-0 in the First Division encounter but struggled in the second-half with injuries.

Honours were even (one win each) in 2002-03 by the Owls suffered most, being relegated to the Nationwide League Division Three.

The clubs have met six times in the FA Cup (United winning the first three in 1900, 1925 and 1928). When the Blades lifted the trophy in 1925, they knocked the Owls out in the second round, coming back from 2-0 down to win 3-2.

The last three Cup clashes have all been post WW2 (in 1954, 1960 and 1993) and they have gone in favour of the Owls, who beat Blades 2-1 in front of 75,364 spectators in the semi-final at Wembley in the latter year. The 6th round tie at 'the Lane' in March 1960 attracted a crowd of 59,692, the biggest at the ground since 1938 (this was due to the erection of a temporary stand, which housed 3,200 fans on the cricket side).

Two of the four United Counties League games (those played in 1893-94) ended in 1-1 draws.

Included among the many players who have served with both (at various levels) are: Earl Barrett, Harold Barton, Harold Bell, Ernest Blackwell, Joe Booth, Carl Bradshaw, Charles Brelsford, Harold Buddery, Franz Carr, Tom Cawley, Alf Calverley, George Cole, Terry Curran, Bob Curry, David Ford, Sidney Ford, Ken Gadsy, Joe Godfrey, Jimmy Harrop, Paul Heald, Jack Hudson, Tom Johnson, Jeff King, George Laking, Brian Marwood, Billy Mellors, Walter Millership, Owen Morrison, Billy Mosforth, Percy Oldacre, Bernard Oxley, Harry Pratt, Albert Price, Neil Ramsbottom, Walter Rickett, Wilf Rostron, Harold Salt, Bernard Shaw, Jack Smith, Simon Stainrod, Hugh Swift, Charles Taylor, Stan Taylor, Oliver Tummon, George Underwood, Imre Varadi, George Waller, Alan Warboys, Fred White & Dean Windass.

Stuart Latham, the son of former Blades player Harry Latham, was registered with Wednesday. Former United skipper George Utley became trainer at Hillsborough and, of course, there's centre-forward Derek Dooley who scored 63 goals in 63 League and Cup games for the Owls before he sadly broke his leg playing against Preston in February 1953. He later became deeply associated with the Blades!

229

SHERIFF OF LONDON CHARITY SHIELD

In 1897-98, United (the Football League champions elect) met the famous amateur side, the Corinthians at The Crystal Palace. A crowd of 19,707 witnessed a 0-0 draw. The replay at the same venue attracted a crowd of 7,500 and again the scoreline finished level at 1-1. The trophy was shared.

SHERPA VAN TROPHY

United's record in the SVT;

Venue	P	W	D	L	F	A
Home	1	0	1	0	2	2
Away	2	0	0	2	1	3
Totals	3	0	1	2	3	5

United participated in this sponsored competition in 1988-89. They lost their opening game 1-0 at Wrexham (in front a meagre crowd of 1,510) and after a 2-2 home draw with Chesterfield, they met Wrexham again (in the second phase) only to lose 2-1 at The Racecourse Ground.

SHIELS, Dennis Patrick

Utility forward: 35 apps. 10 goals
Born: Belfast, 24 August 1938
Career: Distillery, BLADES (October 1958), Peterborough United (July 1964), Notts County (July 1965-April 1966).
A Northern Ireland 'B' international, Shiels joined the Blades with his colleague Orr. A lively player, he made his League debut against Fulham soon after arriving at 'the Lane' and netted five times in 18 Second Division matches 1959-60 but only made three appearances when promotion was gained the following year.

SHIMWELL, Edward

Full-back: 51 apps. one goal
Born: Matlock, Derbyshire, 27 February 1920. Died: 1988
Career: Wirksworth FC, BLADES, Blackpool (£7,500, December, 1946), Oldham Athletic (free transfer, May 1957), Burton Albion (player-coach, July 1958, retired December 1958). Later became a licensee in Matlock.
Transferred to Blackpool after breaking his contract with the Blades by occasionally working in a pub owned by his mother-in-law, Eddie Shimwell went on to play in three FA Cup Finals for Blackpool...v. Manchester United in 1948, Newcastle in 1951 and Bolton in 1953. He scored a penalty in the 4-2 defeat in 1948 and in doing so became the first full-back ever to find the net in a Wembley showdown. After receiving another losers' medal, he successfully gained a winners' prize in 1953 when Stanley Matthews shone in front of him down the right-wing. Shimwell also played for England against Sweden in Stockholm in May 1949. A strong-kicking, powerfully built full-back, with a crunching shoulder-charge when delivered right, he always looked comfortable on the ball and seemed to have ample time to deliver a pass to a colleague. He used his weight effectively, and his sliding tackle was often delivered to perfection. It was a bad move on the part of the United management to let him go! He made 324 appearances for the Seasiders (seven goals scored). A dislocated shoulder brought about a premature end to his Blackpool days although he did play on elsewhere, but not so effectively.
* Shimwell once scored a goal from fully 60 yards for Blackpool against Chester in a 4th round FA Cup-tie in January 1948.

SHIRT SPONSORS

United players had a company name across the front of their shirts was in 1979-80 In 1983-84, Simons took over the mantle; for the next decade (1985-95) Laver's name was showing and from 1995 and thereafter the sponsors have been 'Wards' (Vaux), then Midas Games before the Chinese Soft Drinks manufacturer DeSun took over the mantle for the 2002-03 season.
* The first time a match was sponsored at Bramall Lane was on 22 March 1975 when Sheffield United beat West Ham 3-2 in League Division One game.

SHORT, Christian Mark

Defender: 51+6 apps.
Born: Munster, Germany, 9 May 1970.
Career: Pickering Town FC, Scarborough (July 1988), Notts County (£100,000, September 1990), Huddersfield Town (on loan, December 1994), BLADES (in player-exchange deal involving Paul Rogers, December 1995), Stoke City (free transfer, July 1998, retired August 2000).
Sidelined through injury for almost two years (from November 1996 to August 1998) Chris Short never really gained full match fitness and was forced to quit the game in 2000 after making more than 270 senior appearances at club level. On his day he was a very professional, confident and resilient full-back who had one excellent season at 'the Lane', that of 1996-97 when he had 33 outings in the first XI.
* His brother Craig Short played for Scarborough, Notts County, Derby County and Everton and is now with Premiership side Blackburn Rovers.

SHREWSBURY TOWN

United's playing record against the Shrews
Football League

Venue	P	W	D	L	F	A
Home	4	0	2	2	2	4
Away	4	0	1	3	4	9
Totals	8	0	3	5	6	13

League Cup

Venue	P	W	D	L	F	A
Home	2	1	1	0	5	2
Away	2	1	0	1	4	2
Totals	4	2	1	1	9	4

Although there was a football team, in Shrewsbury much earlier, the present-day club was formed in 1886 and won the Welsh Cup as early as 1891 and spent several seasons in the Birmingham & District and Midland Leagues before being elected to the Football League in 1950, along with Scunthorpe United (q.v).

It was not until 1983-84 that the teams met for the first time at competitive level, the Blades winning a closely-fought 2nd round League Cup-tie 4-3 on aggregate.

The first League encounters followed the very next season. United drew 3-3 at Gay Meadow in the November but surprisingly lost 1-0 at Bramall Lane at the end of April.

United's 2-0 League win at Shrewsbury on Tuesday 17 November 1987 was witnessed by just 22,555 spectators. Only one other match (away to Colchester United, Division Three, in 1980-81) has attracted a lower gate - 2,439 - since WW2.

United beat the 'Shrews' 6-0 on aggregate (thanks to two 3-0 victories) in the 1st round of the League Cup in 1999-2000.

Arthur Rowley played for and managed the 'Shrews' and was in charge at 'the Lane' in 1968-69 while Vince Matthews played for the Blades and became player-manager of the 'Shrews.' Jim Coop, Jon Cullen, Ted Hemsley, Percy Oldacre and Jock Sheen served with both clubs as player and ex-Blade Reg Matthewson was assistant-manager/coach at Gay Meadow.

SIMMONS, James

Inside-forward/outside-right: 301 apps. 67 goals
Born: Blackwell circa 1888
Career: Blackwell Colliery, BLADES (November 1908), West Ham United (August 1920, retired May 1922).

A nephew of United's goalkeeper Billy Foulke, Jimmy Simmons was a talented, two-footed utility forward, slightly built with a big heart who suffered his fair share of injuries during a useful career. He made his League debut for the Blades against Middlesbrough in April 1909 and was a regular in the side from that point on, later scoring United's first goal in the 1915 FA Cup Final victory over Chelsea. Simmons remained at Bramall Lane until 1920 when he moved to West Ham. He was forced to retire through injury at the age of 34, a year before the Hammers reached their first FA Cup Final.

SIMOD CUP

United's played just one game in this competition - losing 3-0 to Leeds United at Elland Road on 25 November 1987. The attendance was 4,426.

SIMONS, Henry Thomas

Inside/centre-forward: 10 apps. 2 goals
Born: Clapton, 1887. Died: 1956
Career: Peel Institute FC (1903), Clapton Orient (March 1906), Leyton (October 1906), Tufnell Park (1907), Doncaster Rovers (1908), BLADES (September 1910), Halifax Town (August1912), Merthyr Town (1912), Brentford (1913), Fulham (June 1914), Queen's Park Rangers (November 1914), Norwich City (September 1920), Margate (November 1920-April 1922).

Tom Simons scored on his League debut for United in a 4-0 home win over Manchester City in October 1920. He was a lively forward but something of journeyman as his career indicates. He never really settled down with any of his major clubs, spending most of his career in the Southern League.

231

SIMPSON, George R

Full-back: 12 apps.
Born: Chesterfield, 1876. Died: Chesterfield, 1955
Career: Sheepbridge FC, BLADES (September 1897), Doncaster Rovers (August 1900), Chesterfield (1903), Rotherham Town (May 1905 - 06).

A reserve full-back, George Simpson made his senior debut for the Blades in a 1st round FA Cup-tie against Burslem Port Vale in January 1898. He went on to score twice in 64 League games for Doncaster.

SIMPSON, Paul David

Forward: 2+4 apps.
Born: Carlisle, 26 July 1966
Career: Manchester City (trainee, July 1982, professional August 1983), Oxford United (£200,000, October 1988), Derby County (£500,000, February 1992), BLADES (on loan, December 1996), Wolverhampton Wanderers (£75,000, October 1997), Walsall (two loan spells: September-October 1998 & December 1998-January 1999), Blackpool (free transfer, August 2000), Rochdale (free, March 2002, appointed player-manager May 2002, resigned May 2003).

In his prime Paul Simpson (only 5ft 6ins tall) was an excellent left-footed utility forward, fast and tricky with a cracking shot. He gained five England Under-21 caps (having earlier represented his country at youth team level). He reached the milestone of 600 League appearances in 2002, the same year he helped Blackpool win the LDV Vans Trophy at The Millennium Stadium and Rochdale reach the Third Division Play-offs.

SIMPSON, Ronald

Utility-forward: 239 apps. 47 goals
Born: Carlisle, 25 February 1934
Career: Holme Head Works FC, Huddersfield Town (amateur, August 1960, professional February 1951), BLADES (in player-exchange deal involving Derek Hawksworth plus £6,000, May 1958), Carlisle United (December 1964-May 1966), Queen of the South (season 1966-67).

Ronnie Simpson was a cracking player who had pace, good skills and a powerful shot. He could play in any forward position but preferred the left-wing where he formed a fine partnership at 'the Lane' with Billy Hodgson, helping the Blades win promotion from the Second Division in 1961 when he missed only two games. He later gained a Third Division championship medal with Carlisle (1965). He scored 26 goals in 118 games for Huddersfield.

SLOAN, Josuah Walter
Inside-forward/wing-half: 13 apps. 2 goals
Born: Lurgan, Ireland, 30 April 1921. Died: 1993.
Career: Glenavon, Manchester United (September 1937), Tranmere Rovers (May 1939), Arsenal (May 1946), BLADES (February 1948), AC Milan (£7,000, June 1948), Turin (briefly), Udinese (1949), Brescia (1950), Norwich City (December 1951-March 1952), Peterborough United, Rabat FC/Malta (coach), Lockheed Leamington (January 1956), Bath City (coach, May 1956), Juventus FC of Melbourne, Australia (coach, 1963-64), later Chairman of the National Association of Soccer Coaches.
Capped twice by the Republic of Ireland (1946) and once by Northern Ireland (1947), Paddy Sloan, despite being associated with Manchester United and Tranmere prior to WW2, did not make his League debut until August 1946 when he lined up at inside-right for Arsenal against Wolves in 6-1 First Division defeat at Molineux. After leaving Highbury he never really made his mark anywhere else although he did flourish occasionally in Italy. He later became a highly-respected coach.

SMEETS, Axel
Midfielder: 4+4 apps.
Born: Karawa, Democratic Republic of Conga, 12 April 1974.
Career: AA Ghent (Belgium), BLADES (free transfer, July 1999-June 2000).
Axel Smeets was one of Adrian Heath's first signings for the Blades. He found the transition to English football difficult and after just one season at the 'Lane, during which time he was sent-off for two yellow cards, he was released June 2000).

SMITH, Brian
Defender: 103+6 apps.
Born: Sheffield, 27 October 1966
Career: BLADES (apprentice, August 1982, professional October 1984), Scunthorpe United (on loan, March 1987); retired in 1989 through injury.
A member of United's 1989 Third Division promotion-winning side (35 games played) Brian Smith was sound defender with a good, reliable and committed attitude. Unfortunately his career was cut short through injury.

SMITH, Frederick Adamson
Inside-forward; 44 apps. 11 goals
Born: Aberdeen, 14 February 1926
Career: Hall Russell's FC (Aberdeen), Royal Navy (three years service), Aberdeen (August 1948), Hull City (October 1949), BLADES (£4,000, April 1951), Millwall (January 1953), Chesterfield (July 1956-January 1957).
'Jock' Smith, also known as 'Little Fred' to the fans, was both hard working and constructive. He scored a goal every four games for the Blades before moving south to Millwall in 1953, ending his career with Chesterfield (season 1956-57).

SMITH, Frederick Edward
Inside/centre-forward: 63 apps. 23 goals
Born: Spondon, Derby, 7 May 1926
Career: Draycott FC, Derby County (June 1947), BLADES (March 1948, player-exchange deal involving Richard Cushlow), Manchester City (£6,000, May 1952), Grimsby Town (£4,000, September 1952), Bradford City (July 1954, in exchange for Ron Harbertson), Frickley Colliery (December 1954-May 1956).
Fred Smith - simply known as 'Big Fred' to the fans - was a six-foot inside or centre-forward who was doing well with the Blades until struck down by injury. He went on to net 24 goals in 50 League games for Grimsby.

SMITH, Grant Gordon
Midfielder: 4+10 apps*
Born: Irvine, Scotland, 5 May 1980
Career: Wycombe Wanderers, Reading (free transfer, August 1998), Heart of Midlothian (free, March 1999), Livingston (free, July 2000), Clydebank (free, December 2000), BLADES (free, July 2000), Halifax Town (on loan, September-November 2001), Plymouth Argyle (on loan, March-May 2003).
Son of Gordon Smith, who played for Brighton & Hove Albion v. Manchester United in the 1983 FA Cup Final and also Glasgow Rangers, left-sided midfielder Grant Smith played in just over 20 games north of the border before joining United two months before his 20th birthday.

SMITH, John Clayton
Goalkeeper: 498 apps.
Born: Stocksbridge, 15 September 1910. Died: 1986
Career: Worksop Town, BLADES (October 1930, retired May 1949, later recalled for first team duty).
Jack 'Smiler' Smith was a very capable goalkeeper who joined United as a 20 year-old and played in the 1936 FA Cup Final (v. Arsenal), also helping the Blades win promotion from the Second Division in 1939 (playing in all 42 games). After breaking his wrist in 1934, his career was placed in jeopardy, but thankfully, the injury healed and he continued to perform superbly well between the posts, being fearless, acrobatic, a safe-handler and above all calm under pressure, always giving encouragement to the defenders in front of him. He was so near to an England call-up but had the likes of first Harry Hibbs of Birmingham and then Everton's Ted Sagar and Vic Woodley of Chelsea barring his way. Smith officially announced his retirement at the end of the 1948-49 season but was recalled for two games during September 1949 before Ted Burgin took over.

SMITH, John
Inside/centre-forward: 13 apps. 6 goals
Born: Wardley, near Newcastle, 15 September 1886. Killed in action, 1916.
Career: Hebburn Argyle, Hull City (June 1905), BLADES (November 1910), Nottingham Forest (£450, March 1911), Nelson (August 1911), York City (season 1912-13).
Jack Smith made his debut for United against Middlesbrough in November 1910.
He had been a great figure in Hull City's early League campaigns, a prolific and noted marksman who headed the Second Division list in 1907-08 with 30 goals - gaining representative honours with the Football League (v. the Scottish League) for his efforts. He went on to net a total of 91 goals in 156 senior appearances for the Tigers, managed only half-a-dozen for the Blades.

232

SMITH, Joseph

Full-back: 50 apps.

Born: Sutton-on-Trent, 1907.

Career: Kiveton Park, BLADES (April 1909), South Shields (May 1913), Derby County (season 1914-15).

Joe 'aeroplane' Smith was a fearless and at times rather a reckless full-back his best season came in 1911-12 at 'the Lane' when he playe in 26 League and FA Cup matches, mainly at right-back as partner to Bob Benson.

SMITH, Paul Michael

Outside-right/full-back: 33+7 apps. one goal

Born: Rotherham, 9 November 1964.

Career: BLADES (apprentice, April 1981, professional November 1982), Stockport County (on loan, August 1985), Port Vale (£10,000, July 1986), Lincoln City (record fee of £48,000, September 1987), Macclesfield Town (on trial, season 1995-96).

A fast -raiding right-winger, Paul Smith became a consistent performer after leaving Bramall Lane and during his career scored 40 goals in 319 League games. He was converted into a full-back by United.

SOUTH BANK

Blades' playing record against South Bank:

Northern League

Venue	P	W	D	L	F	A
Home	1	1	0	0	6	0
Away	1	1	0	0	5	0
Totals	2	2	0	0	11	0

The Blades played South Bank in the Northern League in season 1891-92 and goal nets were used for the first time when United won their home game 6-0 on 10 October 1891. A crowd of 2,500 saw Harry Hammond score a hat-trick.

SOUTHAMPTON

United's playing record against the Saints

Premier League

Venue	P	W	D	L	F	A
Home	2	1	1	0	2	0
Away	2	0	1	1	5	6
Totals	4	1	2	1	7	6
Football League						
Home	19	13	3	3	53	24
Away	19	5	6	8	26	34
Totals	38	18	9	11	79	58
FA Cup						
Away	2	0	0	2	0	2
Neutral	3	2	1	0	5	2
Totals	5	2	1	2	5	4

Southampton FC of today was formed in 1885 as Southampton St Mary's, largely by players from the Deanery club, which had been established by school teachers in 1880.

Most of the club's early players were, at the time, associated with St Mary's Church.

In 1894, and by now a professional outfit, Saints became founder members of the Southern League, where they were to remain until 1920 (when the gained election to the Football League), having dropped 'St Mary's' from their title in 1897.

In 1900 Saints became the first non-League club to reach the FA Cup final (since the introduction of the Football League in 1888) and two years later United met them for the first time, in the 1902 Cup Final at The Crystal Palace. After a 1-1 draw in front of a crowd of 76,914 (recs. £2,893) the Blades triumphed 2-1 in a replay at the same venue when this time the turnout was much lower, 33,068 (recs. £1,625). Alf Common (55 minutes) gave the Blades the lead in the first game only for Harry Wood to equalise with just a couple of minutes remaining. George Hedley got the Blades off to a flier in the replay, netting on two minutes. Brown equalised with 20 minutes remaining but Billy Barnes (who had replaced Billy Bennett, injured in the first match) nipped in to grab the winner for United on 79. The Guests of Honour at the replay was Duc do Mandos (the Spanish Ambassador) and Sir Spencer Ponsonby Fane.

United's 100th FA Cup match was their third meeting with Saints - in the semi-final of the FA Cup at Stamford Bridge in March 1925. A crowd of 65,754 saw the Blades win 2-0 with goals from Tom Parker (o.g) and Fred Tunstall.

Ten years later (in season 1934-35) the clubs met for the first time in the Football League (Division 2) and it was United who came out on top, drawing 1-1 at The Dell and then winning 6-1 at Bramall Lane with Jock Dodds scoring four times. The Dell remained Saints' home until 2001 when hey moved to the Friends' Provident St Mary's Stadium on Britannia Road.

The final match of the 1938-39 season saw United at The Dell needing to win to gain promotion back to the First Division. However, Saints' defence performed heroically, denying the Blades time and again; a 2-1 defeat meant that Manchester United were promoted instead (on goal-average).

Saints attained top-flight status in 1966-67 and their first encounter at this level also went United's way, 3-2 at The Dell in October when Mick Jones netted twice. Alan Woodward did likewise in Blades' 2-0 home win later inn the season.

Much earlier, in 1952-53, the two Second Division games produced 16 goals. Jimmy Hagan claimed a hat-trick when United won 5-3 at 'the Lane' and full-back Graham Shaw was on target twice in the resounding 4-4 draw at The Dell.

In Premiership action during the early 1990, the honours were even, one win apiece and two draws.

Since WW2 United have lost two FA Cup-ties at Southampton, 1963 and 2001, both by 1-0.

Bob Benson, Edgar Bluff, Bill Boyd, John Burridge, Glenn Cockerill, Terry Curran, Jimmy Dunne, Ian Hamilton (Saints reserve), George Handley, George Hedley, David Kelly (Saints trialist), Phil Kite, Chris Marsden, Scott Marshall, Steve Neville, Gareth Taylor (Saints trainee), Albert Trueman, Chris Wilder, Charlie Wilkinson and Jimmy Yates are among the players who have assisted both clubs. Gerry Summers played for the Blades and later scouted for Saints.

233

SOUTHEND UNITED

United's playing record against the Shrimpers:

Football League

Venue	P	W	D	L	F	A
Home	7	5	0	2	16	3
Away	7	2	0	5	10	13
Totals	14	7	0	7	26	16

FA Cup

Home	1	1	0	0	3	0
Away	2	2	0	0	6	1
Totals	3	3	0	0	9	1

Formed in 1906 as a professional club and with Bob Jack as secretary-manager, Southend United immediately found a place in the Southern League where the remained until gaining Football League status in 1920.

It was, however, not until the 1979-80 season that they first met the Blades in this competition, losing 2-0 at Bramall Lane (when Paul Garner and John Matthews found the net) but taking revenge at roots Hall later in the season with a 2-1 victory.

Surprisingly there has not been a single draw in any of the 14 League fixtures played so far.

The Blades first met Southend when they were a non-League club, beating them 3-0 at Bramall Lane in the 1st round of the FA Cup in January 1920, the match having been switched from the 'Shrimpers' ground at Prittewell. Stan Fazackerley (2) and Ernie Milton (after his penalty had been saved) scored the goals in front of more than 40,000 spectators.

Arthur Rowley and Steve Thompson have managed both clubs while Brett Angell, Billy Barnes, Tony Battersby, Mark Beard, Ian Benjamin, Percy Beaumont, Dickie Bird, Wally Brayshaw, Harry Buddery, John Burridge, Richard Cadette, Pat Carrigan, Fred Cheesemuir, Tony Currie, Chris Guthrie, 'Chico' Hamilton, Mick Harmston, Jonathan Hunt, Ian Mackenzie, Tommy Mooney, Colin Morris, Terry Nicholl, Bert Oswald, Mark Patterson, Bill Punton, Jimmy Shankly and Dennis Thompson all played for the Blades and the Shrimpers (among others).

SOUTHPORT

The Blades have yet to meet Southport in a major competition.

Players who have served with both clubs include: Tony Field, Harold Hampson, Barry Hartle, Walter Hughes (Blades reserve), Roy John (Southport WW2), Bernie Ross, Sam Thorpe and Peter Withe.

SPACKMAN, Nigel James

Midfielder: 23+ 4 apps.

Born: Romsey, near Eastleigh, Hampshire, 2 December 1960.

Career: Andover FC, Bournemouth (May 1980), Chelsea (£40,000, June 1983), Liverpool (£400,000, February 1987), Queen's Park Rangers (£500,000, February 1989), Glasgow Rangers (£500,000, November 1990), Chelsea (£485,000, September 1982), BLADES (July 1996 as assistant-manager & player-coach, later acting manager August 1997-March 1998). Left club in the summer of 1998, later worked as soccer summariser on Sky Sport TV.

Signed by Howard Kendall in the summer of 1996, midfielder Nigel Spackman had already a vastly experienced professional prior to moving to Bramall Lane. He had entered competitive League football in 1980 and four years later helped Chelsea win the Second Division title, following up with a Full Members Cup triumph with Chelsea and then a League championship victory with Liverpool in 1988. North of the border he gained three Premiership and both Scottish League and Scottish Cup winners' medals with Rangers (making 124 appearances for the Ibrox Park club) During a fine career Spackman scored 27 goals in almost 650 senior appearances (430 in the Football League). As Blades' manager (for some eight months) he had no money to spend on new players and was knocked back with injuries ruled out two key members of his team. He also had to sell Carl Tiler, Mitch Ward, Brian Deane, Jan-Aage Fjortoft and Don Hutchinson to make ends meet, causing friction and uneasiness within the camp and with the supporters. He resigned following coach Willie Donachie's move to Maine Road.

SPEIGHT, Michael

Midfielder/defender: 223+18 apps. 17 goals

Born: Upton, near South Elmsall, Yorkshire, 1 November 1951

Career: BLADES (apprentice, December 1967, professional May 1969), Blackburn Rovers (£40,000, July 1980), Grimsby Town (£25,000, August 1982), Bury (on loan, March 1983), Chester City (as player-coach, August 1984, later player-manager to June 1985).

An England 'B' international, Mike Speight was a tough tackling, gritty midfielder. He was also capable of playing in any back four berth and alway gave 100 per-cent effort out on the pitch. He made a further 129 League appearances after leaving Bramall Lane.

SPENCER, John Raymond

Forward: 30 apps. 12 goals

Born: Bradfield, 20 November 1934

Career: BLADES (amateur, June 1951, professional June 1954, retired through injury 1960).

An England Youth international, John Spencer made his debut for United against Barnsley in a County Cup game in October 1954. Unfortunately his career came to an abrupt halt following injury problems, suffered in 1957.

SPICER, Walter

Inside-forward: 4 apps.

Born: Sheffield, 7 May 1909. Died: 1981

Career: Norton Woodseats (1925), BLADES (April 1929), Rotherham United (August 1931-34).

Besides being a decent footballer, Walter Spicer was also a very useful cricketer. He failed to make headway at Bramall Lane but did well at Millmoor, scoring 15 goals in 66 League games for Rotherham over a period of three seasons.

SPOONER, Peter Goodwill
Outside-left: 18 apps. 2 goals
Born: Hepscott near Ashington, County Durham, 30 August 1910. Died: 1987.
Career: Newbiggin United, Ashington (1928), Newcastle United (on trial, 1929), Bradford Park Avenue (July 1930), York City (May 1931), BLADES (£500, May 1933), York City (June 1935), Gateshead (May 1939). Did not play after WW2. One of the heroes of York City's excellent 1937-38 FA Cup run, Peter Spooner was a talented left-winger who impressed with his skill, movement and temperament. He never really settled in at 'the Lane'; but during his two spells at Bootham Crescent he scored 48 goals in 207 competitive games

ST MIRREN
Blades' playing record against the Scottish club:
Others

Venue	P	W	D	L	F	A
Home	1	0	1	0	0	0
Away	1	0	0	1	0	4
Totals	2	0	1	1	0	4

St Mirren, formed in 1877, played the Blades in the semi-final of the 1979-80 Anglo-Scottish Cup competition and after a goalless draw at Bramall Lane, the Paisley club run the Blades ragged at Love Street to win 4-0 on aggregate.

STACEY, Alexander
Right-half: 71 apps. 3 goals
Born: London, 3 June 1904. Died: 1993
Career: Grove House Lads' Club, New Mills FC, Northwich Victoria, Leeds United (October 1927), BLADES (£2,000, November 1933), Kidderminster Harriers (season 1937-38).
Strong, resourceful wing-half Alec Stacey made 51 first-class appearances during his six years at Elland Road. He joined the Blades when injuries struck down Ernie Jackson and Tommy Sampy and did well during his first six months at 'the Lane' before Jackson returned to the side. He again held his position in the senior side for twelve months from January 1935 but was injured himself, subsequently replaced by Jackson, and as a result he missed the 1936 FA Cup Final.

STAINROD, Simon Allan
Striker: 68+12 apps. 15 goals
Born: Sheffield, 1 February 1959
Career: Sheffield & South Yorkshire Boys, BLADES (apprentice, June 1974, professional, July 1976), Oldham Athletic (£60,000, March 1979), Queen's Park Rangers (£275,000, November 1980), Sheffield Wednesday (£250,000, February 1985), Aston Villa ((£250,000, September 1985), Stoke City (£90,000, December 1987-May 1988), Racing Club Strasbourg (1988-89), FC Rouen, France (1989-90), Falkirk (player, June 1990, later player/caretaker-manager), Dundee (player/caretaker-manager), Ayr United (manager).
Capped by England at Youth team level, Simod Stainrod was an aggressive striker, easily losing his temper, but he had a knack of being in the right place at the right time to snap up the half-chances that came his way. He did well in European soccer before returning to the UK to round off his career in Scotland prior to taking up management. He helped QPR win the Second Division title in 1983 and during his career (in England) he netted 107 goals in 387 League games.

STANCLIFFE, Paul Ian
Defender: 341 apps. 20 goals
Born: Sheffield, 5 May 1958
Career: Rotherham United (apprentice, June 1974, professional March 1976), BLADES (August 1983), Rotherham United (on loan, September 1990), Wolverhampton Wanderers (free transfer, November 1990), York City (free, July 1991, later assistant-manager at Bootham Crescent, 1995-96, then City's Youth team manager).
Having helped Rotherham win the Third Division title in 1981, Paul Stancliffe was a promotion winner with the Blades on three occasions: 1984 & 1989 from Division Three & 1990 from Division Two, missing only a handful of games each season. He later skippered York to promotion from Division Three (1993). A tremendously effective defender, strong, determined and well conditioned, his career spanned 20 years during which time he accumulated an exceptionally fine record of 556 competitive appearances and 32 goals.

STANIFORTH, David Albry
Forward: 29+4 apps. 5 goals
Born: Chesterfield, 6 October 1950
Career: BLADES (apprentice, April 1967, professional May 1968), Bristol Rovers (March 1974), Bradford City (June 1979), Halifax Town (July 1982-May 1984).
A very good, positive goalscorer, especially in the lower Divisions, David Staniforth certainly made his mark after leaving Bramall Lane where he had been unable to hold down a regular position in the first XI. He netted 32 in 151 outings for Bristol Rovers and followed up by scoring 26 times in 128 games for Bradford City and then added another 25 in more than 70 starts for the 'Shaymen.'

STARBUCK, Philip Michael
Forward/midfielder: 27+13 apps. 2 goals
Born: Nottingham, 24 November 1968
Career: Nottingham Forest (apprentice, April 1985, professional August 1986), Birmingham City (on loan, March 1988), Hereford United (on loan, February 1990), Blackburn Rovers (on loan, September 1990), Huddersfield Town (£100,000, August 1991), BLADES (£158,000, October 1994), Bristol City (on loan, September 1995), Oldham Athletic (August 1997), Plymouth Argyle (March 1998), Cambridge City (June 1998).
There's no doubting that Phil Starbuck played his best football with Huddersfield Town, for whom he scored 47 goals in 177 League and Cup games in a three-year stay with the Yorkshire club. During his career he found the net 54 times in 306 competitive games. He was unable to hold down a regular place in the first XI with Forest or the Blades. He made his debut for United against Millwall soon after joining the club and had his best spell in the side at during the middle third of that season.

235

STAVELEY

United's playing record against Staveley

Midland Counties League

Venue	P	W	D	L	F	A
Home	1	1	0	0	5	0
Away	1	0	0	1	0	2
Totals	2	1	0	1	5	2

The Blades shared the spoils with Staveley in the MCL in season of 1890-91. Arthur Watson scored twice in thee 5-0 home win.

STEEL CITY CHALLENGE TROPHY

United met their arch rivals Sheffield Wednesday four times in the SCCT, their full record being:

Venue	P	W	D	L	F	A
Home	2	1	0	1	5	4
Away	2	1	0	1	3	5
Totals	4	2	0	2	8	9

Match details:

Season	Score	Venue	Att.
1990-91	Wednesday 3 United 0	Hillsborough	15,040
1994-95	Wednesday 2 United 3	Hillsborough	13,724
1995-96	United 1 Wednesday 3	Bramall Lane	13,254
1996-97	United 4 Wednesday 1	Bramall Lane	7,271

* Nathan Blake scored twice in the 3-2 win in 1994-95.

STOCKPORT COUNTY

United's playing record against the Hatters:

Football League

Venue	P	W	D	L	F	A
Home	7	6	1	0	17	2
Away	7	2	2	3	6	6
Totals	14	8	3	3	23	8

FA Cup

Venue	P	W	D	L	F	A
Home	2	2	0	0	5	2
Away	1	0	1	0	0	0
Totals	3	2	1	0	5	2

League Cup

Venue	P	W	D	L	F	A
Home	2	1	0	1	7	6
Away	2	1	0	1	2	2
Totals	4	2	0	2	9	8

WW2

Venue	P	W	D	L	F	A
Away	1	0	0	1	1	5

Stockport County began life as Heaton Norris Rovers in 1883, adopting its present title in 1890. They were elected to the Football League in 1900 and although failing to win re-election in 1904, they returned after just one season and have remained ever since. Nicknamed the 'Hatters, they moved to their current home at Edgley Park in 1902 having previously played at Nursery inn on Green Lane, Stockport.

The first meeting between the clubs was in the 3rd round of the FA Cup in 1926, united winning 2-0 with Billy Gillespie and Tommy Boyle the scorers.

The first League match followed eleven years later (on 25 October 1937) when again United came out best, winning 2-0 with Jock Dodds and Charlie Leyfield netting this time round. The return fixture at Stockport finished level at 1-1, Dodds again on target.

The Blades' first League win at Edgeley Park was claimed in December 2000, Paul Devlin and Wayne Quinn (penalty) securing a 2-0 scoreline.

United had two high-scoring League Cup contests against the Hatters in 1994-95 and again in 1996-97. They came through the first winning 6-1mon aggregate (5-1 at home, 1-0 away) but lost the second one 7-3 (going down 2-1 at Edgeley Park and 5-2 at Bramall Lane).

Danny Bergara, after leaving Bramall Lane, managed County for six years: 1989-95.

Andy Beattie managed County and later acted as assistant-boss at Bramall Lane.

Len Allchurch, Brett Angell, Steve Cammack, Gordon Cowans; David Davies, Joe Davies, Laurent D'Jaffo, Matt Dickins and Chris Downes (United reserves), Peter Duffield, Jeff Eckhardt, Keith Edwards, Tom Egan, George Farrow, Steve Faulkner, David Frain, Jim Gannon (United reserve), Barry Hartle, Fred Jenkinson, Alan Kelly, Phil Kite, Chris Marsden, Shane Nicholson, John Nibloe, Bernie Oxley, Bert Pearson, John Ryan, Lee Sandford, Paul Smith, Arthur Wharton and Paul A Williams are among the many players who have assisted both the Blades and County.

STOCKTON

Blades' playing record against Stockton:

Northern League

Venue	P	W	D	L	F	A
Home	2	1	0	1	7	3
Away	2	0	1	1	1	6
Totals	2	1	1	2	8	9

The Blades played Stockton in the Northern League in seasons 1891-92 & 1892-93.

After winning 6-0 at home in the first season, they surprisingly lost 5-0 away on 2 January 1893 - when the players were presumably still recovering from their New Year celebrations!

STOKE CITY

United's playing record against the Potters:

Football League

Venue	P	W	D	L	F	A
Home	45	23	13	9	73	48
Away	45	14	11	20	58	84
Totals	90	37	24	29	131	132

FA Cup

Home	2	1	1	0	3	2
Away	3	1	0	2	3	5
Totals	5	2	1	2	6	7

WW2

Home	1	1	0	0	4	0
Away	1	1	0	0	3	0
Totals	2	2	0	0	7	0

Other

Away	1	1	0	0	2	1

Formed in 1868 as Stoke Ramblers, becoming Stoke in 1870 and Stoke City in 1925, the Potters were founder members of the Football League in 1888, lasting only two seasons before returning on re-election only to lose their status again (through financial difficulties) in 1908 and not returning until 1919 when the competition was increased from 40 to 44 clubs.

United and the Potters first met in 1893-94 (Division 1). At The Victoria Ground (Stoke's home until 1997 when they moved to The Britannia Stadium) the Potters romped to an emphatic 5-0 win and then, despite struggling in the table, they forced a 3-3 draw at 'the Lane.'

United, who lost five of their first six League games at Stoke, were whipped 4-0 by the Potters at Bramall Lane in 1900-01.

The Blades registered their best home win over Stoke (5-2) in 1904-05 (Arthur Brown scoring a hat-trick0 while their best in the Potteries came in 1996, their final visit there ending in a 4-0 victory with Dutchman Michel Vonk netting twice.

Jack Pickering played game for United against Stoke City in June 1947 and scored one of the goals in Blades' 2-1 victory. If the Potters had won that match, they would have taken the First Division championship. A month earlier to this match Stoke boss Bob McGrory had accepted an offer of £11,500 from Blackpool for wing-wizard Stanley Matthews.

The clubs have, in fact, never met each other outside the top two Divisions. Since WW2 Stoke have been one of United's most frequent opponents, their 2002-03 meetings making it 29 out of 57 possible seasonal confrontations.

The teams met in the 4th round of the FA Cup in season 1945-46 when the Blades were beaten 4-3 on aggregate...despite Colin Collindridge's smartly taken hat-trick.

The following season United won a 5th round tie at The Victoria Ground, Harold Brook's smartly-taken goal deciding the issue.

United led the Potters at half-time in their 3rd round replay in January 1983 before losing 3-2 at Stoke.

Ex-Blades star Chris Kamara played for and managed the Potters; Howard Kendall played for Stoke and managed the Blades while Adrian Heath was also associated with both clubs along with Peter Beagrie, George Brown, Vic Busby, Tom Cowan, John Evans (United reserve), Steve Foley, George Gallimore, Fred Groves (United reserve), Adrian Heath (also Blades manager), Billy Hendry, Bobby Howitt, Roy John, Chris Kamara (also Stoke manager), Carl Muggleton, John Nibloe, Jack Peart, Paul Peschisolido, Paul Richardson, John Roxburgh, Geoff Salmons, Lee Sandford, Hans Segers, Simon Stainrod, Albert Sturgess, Mike Trusson (Stoke reserve), John Tudor and Billy Whitehurst.

Howard Kendall played for the Potters and managed the Blades; Walter Gould played for United and became coach/assistant-manager at Stoke.

STONE, Jack
Inside-right/centre-forward: 6 apps. 6 goals
Born: Yorkshire circa 1918.
Career: Norton Woodseats, BLADES (April 1939-February 1946), Boston United
A WW2 player with the Blades, Jack Stone netted five of his six goals in one game against Mansfield Town (h) in the Football League North in December 1942.

STRINGER, Edward
Right-back: 27 apps.
Born: Yorkshire, circa 1865
Career: Ecclesfield, BLADES (August 1889-May 1892).
Ned Stringer spent three seasons at Bramall Lane and was recognised as the Blades' first genuine right-back.

STUART, Graham Charles
Midfield/forward: 66+3 apps. 12 goals
Born: Tooting, 24 October 1970
Career: Chelsea (apprentice, April 1987, professional June 1989), Everton (£850,000, August 1993), BLADES (£850,000, in a deal that also involved Carl Tiler and Mitch Ward, November 1997), Charlton Athletic (£1.1 million, March 1999).
An England Youth international, Graham Stuart later added five Under-21 caps to his collection as well as winning the FA Cup with Everton in 1995. He moved to Bramall Lane in a three-player transaction and showed his versatility by appearing in several positions for the Blades. A broken hand meant that he missed the crucial Play-offs in 1998. After his big-money move to Charlton he helped the London club win the First Division championship (and reach the Premiership) in 2000 but was then sidelined during the 2002-03 campaign having reached the milestone of 450 career appearances.

237

STURGESS, Albert

Defender: 512 apps. 5 goals
Born: Etruria, Stoke-on-Trent, 21 October 1882. Died: 1957.
Career: Tunstall Crosswells FC, Stoke (1903), BLADES (with
George Gallimore, August 1908), Norwich City (July 1923,
retiring, May 1925)

Rangy and versatile but somewhat lightweight, Albert Sturgess
could and would play in any defensive position. A hard and
industrious competitor, he made his League debut for the Blades
(with his former Stoke team-mate Gallimore) against Bury (a) less
than a month after joining the club. He never looked back, going
on to amass more than 500 first-team appearances over a period
of 15 years before transferring to Norwich City. Capped twice by
England (v. Ireland in February 1911 and Scotland in April 1914)
he was an FA Cup winner with the Blades in 1915.
* Sturgess scored a stunning 40-yard goal for the Blades v.
Woolwich Arsenal in September 1911 (won 2-1).

SUBSTITUTES

* United's first substitute to be used was Tony Wagstaffe against Fulham at Craven Cottage on 8 September 1965. He replaced the injured Alan Birchenall in the second-half of a 0-0 draw.
* Alan Woodward, on for Tony Wagstaff, was United's first 'sub' in a League Cup-tie v. Sunderland (away) in September 1966.
* David Munks replaced Bernard Shaw to become United's first 'No 12' in the FA Cup v. Fulham (away) in February 1967.
* Ken Mallender had the pleasure of being the first 'sub' to score for United - doing so against Arsenal at Bramall Lane in April 1966 (Division 1).
* Steve Neville had the misfortune of being the first 'sub' to bet sent-off - dismissed in the League game at Scunthorpe in February 1982.
* Peter Duffield was the first 'sub' to be substituted, leaving the pitch at Fulham in April 1989 (replaced by Dane Whitehouse).
* Keith Edwards is the only 'sub' so far to have scored a hat-trick for United, obliging in the League Cup-tie v. Grimsby Town in October 1982.
* With 57 to his credit, Petr Katchouro holds the club record for most 'sub' appearances (competitive football). He is followed by Nick Montgomery 43, Andy Scott 38, Glyn Hodges 37, Gareth Taylor 35, Peter Duffield 34, John Francis 33, Alan Cork 32, Dane Whitehouse 32 and Gary Brazil 30.
* Katchouro was called off the bench 45 times in Football League matches (another club record) while Nick Montgomery 38, Andy Scott 36, Glyn Hodges 31, Cork 29, Francis 28, Taylor 28, Whitehouse 27, Carl Bradshaw 25 and Adrian Littlejohn 25 follow him in the League stakes.
* In the first season of the 'sub' (1965-66) United brought on their number '12' six times in League matches.
* Chris Downes made his debut as a 'sub' for United v. Portsmouth in an FA Cup-tie at Fratton Park on 1 February 1988. A week later Wally Downes played his first senior game for the Blades, also as a 'sub' v. Stoke City in a League match.
* Future United coach Geoff Vowden was the first 'sub' to score a Football League hat-trick - doing so for Birmingham City v. Huddersfield in 1968.
* Blades' manager Ian Porterfield came on as a substitute in the second-half of the friendly against Dallas Americans on 31 May 1985 (won 2-0).
* Technically George Aizlewood was the first 'sub' utilised by United. When Billy Mosforth failed to show up on time prior to United's home friendly game with Bolton Wanderers in November 1889, Aizlewood deputised for the first few minutes before Mosforth arrived.

SUFFO, Kengne Herve Patrick

Forward: 16+22 apps. 6 goals
Born: Ebolowa, Cameroon, 17 January 1978
Career: Tonerre Yaonde, CF Barcelona, Nantes/France, BLADES (£150,000, November 2000), Numancia/Spain (on loan April 2002, signed permanently, June 2003).

A Cameroonian international (29 caps won) Patick Suffo is a strong footballer with powerful shot, who unfortunately blotted his copy-book when he was sent-off (having been only on the pitch for just a couple of minutes) during the second-half of the Blades; home League game with promotion-chasing West Bromwich Albion in March 2003. The next month he was loaned out to the Spanish club Numancia and never returned to 'the Lane'. He helped his country win the African Nations Cup in 2002 (scoring in a penalty shoot-out in the Final to secure himself a winners' medal).

SUMMERS, Gerald Thomas Francis

Left-half: 305 apps. 7 goals

Born: Small Heath, Birmingham, 4 October 1933.
Career: Coventry Road & hay Mills Schools, Erdington
Albion (1948), West Bromwich Albion (amateur April
1950, professional August 1951), BLADES (£3,500,
May 1957), Hull City (£14,000, April 1964), Walsall
(October 1965; later appointed coach at Fellows Park,
February 1967), Wolverhampton Wanderers (coach,
August 1967), Oxford United (manager, July 1969-
October 1975), Gillingham (manager (October 1975-
May 1981), Southampton (scout, June 1981), West
Bromwich Albion (coach/assistant-manager, October
1981-May 1982), Leicester City (coach, October
1982-December 1986), Derby County (Chief Scout &
Youth team manager, December 1986, later
Community Officer).

A bargain buy from West Brom, wing-half Gerry
Summers replaced Jim Iley in United's middle-line. A
Second Division promotion winner with the Blades in
1961 (when he was an ever-present) he formed a
brilliant middle-line with Brian Richardson and Joe
Shaw, always pushing on, tackling with aggression, and
regularly delivering a defence-splitting pass for his
forwards to race on to. Tireless, unruffled and precise,
he was left 'out in the cold' at The Hawthorns (owing
to the presence of England international Ray Barlow)
but he certainly made up for lost time at 'the Lane' and
after touring the Far East & USA with the FA in 1962
he went on to give Hull City good service, appearing in
59 League games for the Tigers, followed by another 40
for Walsall. Summers was sacked as manager of Oxford
(bottom of the Second Division) and he was also
shown the door at Gillingham. He did well thereafter
as a coach.

239

SUNDAY FOOTBALL

The first League game played by United on a Sunday was against Bradford City at Valley Parade on 8 May 1983. The attendance was
only 4,811 and the Bantams won the Third Division contest 2-0.

SUNDERLAND

United's playing record against the Wearsiders:

Football League

Venue	P	W	D	L	F	A
Home	61	35	10	16	117	73
Away	61	9	14	38	65	133
Totals	122	44	24	54	182	206

Play-offs

Home	1	1	0	0	2	1
Away	1	0	0	1	0	2
Totals	2	1	0	1	2	3

FA Cup

Home	3	0	1	2	3	5
Away	4	1	0	3	4	7
Totals	7	1	1	5	7	12

League Cup

Home	2	2	0	0	3	0
Away	2	0	1	1	2	3
Totals	4	2	1	1	5	3

WW2

Home	2	1	0	1	4	1
Away	2	1	0	1	3	8
Totals	4	2	0	2	7	9

Other

Home	1	1	0	0	2	1

Sunderland, formed as the Sunderland & District Teachers' Association FC at a meeting held at the Adults School, Norfolk Street in 1879 (with help of Scottish-born schoolmaster James Allan who was working at Hendon Board School) were surprisingly not one of the original 12 members of the Football League. In fact, they were the '13th' when gaining election two seasons later when Stoke dropped out.

Described as a 'team of all talents' Sunderland (the other names were dropped in 1880) won three championships in the 1890s with a team almost entirely comprising 'Scottish professors.'

United's first meeting with the 'Black Cats' of Wearside was in the 2nd round of the FA Cup in 1893, a healthy crowd of 15,000 seeing the visitors win 3-1 at Bramall Lane.

The first League meeting took place in October 1893, and this time United won 1-0 thanks to a Fred Davies goal.

Both United and Sunderland were involved in a controversial 'club v. county' incident in 1987-98 with the pair locked in combat for the League championship. The key fixture fell on the same day as the annual England v. Scotland international match in Glasgow. United's Ernest Needham was released to play for England, but Sunderland chose to withhold their goalkeeper Ned Doig and key wing-half Hughie Wilson, much to United's (and Scotland's) annoyance. In the event United won by a goal from 'old' Harry Johnson, but the brilliance of Doig almost saved the day for the Wearsiders. United's win paved the way to the title before 23,000 fans at Bramall Lane.

The Blades' 1,000th match in the Football League was against Sunderland (home) in December 1924. They won 2-1, Harry Johnson scored both goals and the crowd topped 46,000.

United's 4th round FA Cup-tie at home to Sunderland in 1926 attracted a crowd of 62,041, an attendance bettered on only one other occasions at 'the Lane.' Unfortunately the Blades (Cup holders at the time) lost 2-1.

Dave Halliday scored all Sunderland's goals in their 4-4 League draw with the Blades at Roker Park in December 1928.

Sunderland held their top-flight status until 1958 (a remarkable achievement of 57 seasons) and in that time United met them 74 times in the League, a club record shared with the same number of fixtures against Aston Villa, Blackburn Rovers and Newcastle United. Yet since WW2, in 57 seasons, the clubs have met only on 24 occasions, all in the top two Divisions.

United's best win was 5 1 (h) in 1957-58 (when Harry Johnson and Fred Tunstall both scored twice) while their heaviest defeat was a 4-0 beating also at 'the Lane' in 1998-99. They also lost 5-2 at home in 1948-49.

The Blades have won only nine times at Sunderland in the League, only twice since WW2, and failing to win in 23 matches dating from 1928 to 1986. Their best victory on the road was an amazing 5-3 success in 1922-23 when Johnson rattled in a brilliant hat-trick. In the FA Cup. The clubs have met six times overall, United winning just once...a 2-1 triumph at Roker Park in 1901 when Fred Priest grabbed the winner.

At the end of the 1997-98 season the clubs battled against each other in the First Division Play-offs. Sunderland came out on top with a 3-2 aggregate win after gaining a 2-0 lead at The Stadium of Light following their 2-1 reverse at Bramall Lane.

Ian Porterfield scored the winning goal for Sunderland v. Leeds United in the 1973 FA Cup final and later managed the Blades.

Brett Angell, Kevin Arnott, Peter Beagrie, Joe Bolton, Peter Boyle, Arthur Brown, Alf Common, Jodie Craddock, Terry Curran, Andy Dibble (United reserve), Jock Gibson, Colin Grainger, Mick Henderson, Don Hutchinson, David Kelly, Sammy Kemp, Albert 'Tal' Lewis, Dennis Longhorn, John MacPhail,. Cliff Mason; George Philip & John Poole Blades WW1); Wilf Rostron, Keith Waugh, Billy Whitehurst, Cliff Whitelum and Bill Wood are among the many players who have served both clubs over the years. Jim McGuigan played for Sunderland and was later Blades' coach and Adrian Heath player for and managed United and was coach/scout at Sunderland.

SUNDERLAND ALBION

Blades' playing record against Albion:
Northern League

Venue	P	W	D	L	F	A
Home	1	1	0	0	2	1
Away	1	1	0	0	4	2
Totals	2	2	0	0	6	3

The Blades played 'Albion' in the NL in season 1891-92. Arthur Watson scored twice in the 4-2 away win.

SUPPORTERS' CLUBS

Sheffield United fans first formed a supporters' club in December 1929. Mr E Foster was appointed Chairman, with Councillor Fred Unwin its first President.

Over the next few years a handful of branches of the SUSC spouted up and by the mid-1930s membership had increased to around the 1,800-2,000 mark.

The Supporters Club was reformed in 1939 and 1969, and a District Supporters Club was also introduced.

SUSPENSIONS

United's Glyn Hodges received a six-match ban for an incident as the players left the pitch at the end of Blades' 1-0 First Division victory at Sunderland on 9 March 1991. During the same game Jim Gannon (United) and Kevin Ball (Sunderland) were both been sent-off.

Virtually every player who has been sent-off playing for the United duly served a suspension.

SUTCLIFFE, Charles Spencer

Goalkeeper: 53 apps.
Born: Bradford, 7 October 1890. Died: 1964
Career: Leeds City (August 1918), Rotherham County (November 1919), BLADES (Oct 1924-May 1927).

Sheffield United's 'keeper in the 1925 FA Cup Final win over Cardiff City, Charlie Sutcliffe admitted that he was 'lucky to gain a medal'...although he did save a vital penalty in the semi-final victory over Southampton. At the start of that season he was reserve to Ernie Blackwell and Albert Robinson but got into the side after eight League games and held his position. Reasonably sound - although at times he did give his defenders a few nervous moments - he eventually handed over his gloves to Jack Alderson before quitting top-class football in 1927, Sutcliffe played briefly for Leeds City directly after WW1 and made over 100 senior appearances for Rotherham before moving to the Blades in 1924.

SWANSEA CITY (Town)
United's playing record against the Swans:

Football League

Venue	P	W	D	L	F	A
Home	15	8	6	1	44	16
Away	15	7	2	6	24	24
Totals	30	15	8	7	68	40

FA Cup

Home	1	0	1	0	1	1
Away	2	1	0	1	3	6
Totals	3	1	1	1	4	7

Formed as late as June 1912 following a public meeting, Swansea Town gained entry to the Second Division of the Southern League immediately, were granted a place in the First Division in 1919 (without winning promotion) and then took Football League status a year later. The club changed its name from Town to City in 1970.

The first time the Blades met the 'Swans' was in the 3rd round of the FA Cup in 1932-33, United winning 3-2 at The Vetch Field with Jimmy Dunne scoring twice.

The first League encounter followed in 1934 (Division 2) and it finished in a 0-0 draw at Swansea, while the return game also ended level at 1-1.

United have an excellent home record against the Welsh club, losing only one of 15 League games played there (a 2-1 reverse in 1936-37). Of their eight wins United's best is 7-1, achieved in their 1952-53 promotion campaign); they also won 6-1 in 1950-51 and 5-1 in both 1951-52 and 1988-89. They also recorded a 5-3 victory at Swansea in 1937-38 when Jock Dodd scored a hat-trick.

Jimmy Hagan made his League debut for United against the Swans in November 1938 (Division 2). He scored twice late on to earn a 2-1 victory as the Welsh side missed a last minute penalty.

The Swans knocked the Blades out of the FA Cup in 1964, beating them 4-0 at the Vetch Field on their way to the semi-final.

Len Allchurch, Charlie Hartfield, 'Roy' John, Ray McHale, Jack Pears, Terry Phelan, Gil Reece, Paul Richardson, Bernard Ross, Billy Sampy, Dean Saunders and Jamie Thomas all played for both clubs while Colin Addison and Alan Cork played for the Blades and both later managed the Swans. John Burridge, John Harris and Ken McNaught were also associated with the Welsh club.

SWINDON TOWN
United's playing record against the Robins:

Premier League

Venue	P	W	D	L	F	A
Home	1	1	0	0	3	1
Away	1	0	1	0	0	0
Totals	2	1	1	0	3	1

Football League

Home	11	8	2	1	21	10
Away	11	2	3	6	16	23
Totals	22	10	5	7	37	33

FA Cup

Home	1	0	0	1	2	3
Away	2	0	1	1	0	1
Totals	3	0	1	2	2	4

Swindon Town, formed it is thought in 1881 with guidance from the Rev. William Pitt, and founder members of the Southern League in 1894, finally achieved Football League status in 1920, nine years after playing Manchester United in the annual FA Charity Shield game.

United first met the 'Robins' in 1sr round of the FA Cup in January 1908. The Wiltshire side held on for a 0-0 draw at home (The County ground) before humbling the Blades 3-2 at Bramall Lane. They again knocked the Blades out of the competition in 1920-21, winning 1-0 at home, again in the opening round.

The first League clashes took place in 1969-70 (Division 2), the Robins winning them both with 2-1 scorelines.

United's two wins at Swindon have been 2-0 in 1989-90 and 3-1 in 1994-95.

Four of the last five League meetings have ended in draws (the last three all 2-2).

Wayne Allison, Bill Batty, Frank Becton, Darren Bullock, Herbert Chapman, Glenn Cockerill, Mark Dempsey, Peter Dornan, Jan-Aage Fjortoft, Steve Foley, Jack Fountain, Chris Guthrie, Bernie Harris, Fred Hawley, Paul Heald (United reserve), Chris Kamara, Neil Logan, Tom McAlister, Ray McHale, Brian Marwood, David Munks, 'Iffy' Onuora, Tom Phillipson, Brian Richardson, Paul Richardson, Frank Talia and Carl Tiler all played for both clubs.

John Harris played for Swindon and managed the Blades; Lou Macari managed Swindon and was a scout for United.

241

TALIA, Francesco

Goalkeeper: 6 apps.

Born: Melbourne, Australia, 20 July 1972

Career: Sunshine George Cross/Australia (1990), West Bromwich Albion (on trial, season 1991), Blackburn Rovers (August 1992), Hartlepool United (on loan, December 1992), Swindon Town (£150,000, September 1995), Wolverhampton Wanderers (free transfer, August 2000), BLADES (free, September 2000, released July 2001), Wycombe Wanderers (2002).

Efficient goalkeeper Frank Talia, who won schoolboy honours back in Australia, never made the first XI at Blackburn, played 15 games for Hartlepool, 118 for Swindon, none for Wolves and just six for the Blades before his release. He was a Second Division championship winner at the County Ground in 1996.

TAYLOR, Charles Stanley

Inside-right/centre-forward: one app. one goal

Born: Sheffield, 1897.

Career: Atlas & Norfolk FC, Norfolk Arms FC, Sheffield Wednesday (August 1919), Norton Woodseats (1922), BLADES (1924), Denaby United (1925), Worksop Town (1926).

Stan Taylor, ex-Norton Woodseats, scored his only goal for the Blades in a League game against Notts County (h) in April 1924 (won 3-1). He made seven League appearances for the 'Owls.'

TAYLOR, Gareth Keith

Striker: 70+35 apps. 27 goals

Born: Weston-super-Mare, 23 February 1973

Career: Southampton (trainee), Bristol Rovers (professional, July 1991), Crystal Palace (£750,000, September 1995), BLADES (£400,000, player-exchange deal involving Carl Veart & Steve Tuttle, March 1996), Manchester City (£400,000, November 1998), Port Vale (on loan, November 2000), Queen's Park Rangers (on loan, March 2000), Burnley (free transfer, February 2002).

On transfer deadline day, 1996 Blades' boss Howard Kendall signed 6ft 2in striker Gareth Taylor from Crystal Palace (with Tuttle & Veart going in the opposition direction with a cash adjustment). He had not really established himself as a goalscorer at Selhurst Park (having netted 16 times in 58 games for Bristol Rovers) but he certainly gave a good account of himself at 'the Lane', striking up an immediate understanding with Scotsman Andy Walker. He later had to work hard for a place in the side when Brian Deane and Jan-Aage Fjortoft were playing but overall he gave the club excellent service before joining Manchester City in 1998. Taylor has been capped by Wales seven times at Under-21 level and on nine occasions by the seniors.

TEBILY, Olivier

Defender/Midfielder: 7+1 apps.

Born: Abidjan, Ivory Coast, 19 December 1975

Career: Chateauroux FC/France (1997), BLADES (£175,000, March 1999), Glasgow Celtic (£1.25 million, July 1999), Birmingham City (£700,000, March 20002).

Olivier Tebily, with strength and pace in abundance, surprisingly never really settled in at Bramall Lane nor at Parkhead, although he did help Celtic win the League Cup in 1999

He has also represented the Ivory Coast on four full internationals, having earlier played in three Under-23 games for France. He was the first Blues player to be sent-off in the Premiership, dismissed against. West Bromwich Albion at The Hawthorns in October 2002.

TEN HEUVEL, Laurens

Striker: 0+9 apps.

Born: Amsterdam, Netherlands, 6 June 1976

Career: Telstar FC/Holland (1998) BLADES (July 2002), Bradford City (on loan, March-May 2003).

Signed from in readiness for the 2002-3 season, Dutchman Laurens Ten Heuvel made his debut for the Blades as a substitute against Walsall in the second game of the season, replacing striker Wayne Allison during the second-half of the 1-1 draw. He was loan out to Bradford on 'deadline' day 2003.

TEXACO CUP

United played in this competition three times but never really threatened.

Their full record was:

P	W	D	L	F	A
7	1	2	4	6	12

In 1972-73, United were knocked out in the opening round by WBA (losing 2-1 on aggregate).

The following year it was Dundee United who went through in the first round, winning 2-0 over two legs (it was 0-0 at Sheffield) and over a period of one week in August 1974, following a 4-0 defeat at Oldham Athletic and a 4-1 home win over Manchester City, the Blades lost their sharpness and crashed to a 2-1 defeat at Bramall Lane at the hands of Blackpool, and as a result failed to qualify from their group.

United's biggest crowd for a Texaco Cup game was 13,381 for the home clash with West Brom (1-1).

In 1975, the Texaco Cup became known as the Anglo-Scottish Cup.

THICKETT, Henry

Full-back: 310 apps. one goal

Born: Hexthorpe near Doncaster, 28 March 1873. Died: Trowbridge, 15 November 1920.

Career: Hexthorpe FC, BLADES (April 1890), Rotherham Town (1892), BLADES (December 1893), Bristol City (player-manager, May 1904, retired as a player, May 1905, but staying on as manager until May 1910).

Well-built right-back Harry Thickett had two spells with the Blades, failing to get into the side first time round. He developed into a brave, quick, strong-kicking defender whose only blemish, at times, was his indifferent tackling (he was responsible for giving away far too many free-kicks in dangerous positions). However, he formed a wonderful partnership in the United defence with his fellow full-backs Bob Cain and Peter Boyle. A League championship winner with the Blades in 1898, he appeared in three FA Cup Finals, gaining winners' medals in 1899 and 1902 and collecting a loser's prize in 1901. He also won two England caps - against Wales and Scotland respectively in March and April 1899. He left his beloved Yorkshire to become player-manager of Bristol City, remaining at Ashton Gate until 1910. After retirement he became a licensee in Trowbridge, staying in that line of work until his death in 1920.

Sheffield United team group: (back row, l-r) Trainer Waller, Mick Whitham, Bill Foulke, John Docherty, Bob Cain (middle row, l-r) Jimmy Yates, Harry Hammond, Ernest Needham, Walter Hill, Arthur Watson (front row, l-r) **Harry Thickett**, Rab Howell

THOMAS, James Alan

Forward: 3+8 apps. one goal

Born: Swansea, 16 January 1979

Career: Blackburn Rovers (apprentice, April 1995, professional July 1996), West Bromwich Albion (on loan, August 1997), Blackpool (on loan, March 2000), BLADES (on loan, November-December 2000), Bristol Rovers (on loan, March 2002), Swansea City (signed, August 2002).

Capped 21 times by Wales at Under-21 level, Jamie Thomas, a willing worker with an eye for goal, found few opportunities at Ewood Park and after loan spells with four different clubs, including the Blades, he joined Swansea with whom he fought a successful relegation battle in his first season at The Vetch Field, scoring a hat-trick in the Welsh club's last match victory at home to Hull City which ensured their Third Division status.

THOMPSON, Charles Maskery

Centre-forward/centre-half: 104 apps. 70 goals

Born: Chesterfield, 19 July 1920. Died: 1997.

Career: Bolsover Colliery FC, BLADES (July 1937), Hereford United (August1947).

A fast, aggressive and energetic centre-forward, as brave as they come, Charlie Thompson was confident enough to chance his arm or rather foot, at shooting from angles ultra-prudent forwards wouldn't attempt. He was also a fine header of the ball and scored twice in the last four minutes to earn the Blades a 3-1 League Cup North win over Leeds United in March 1944. A month later he broke his leg playing against Aston Villa in the semi-Final of that Cup competition and was out of action for almost 12 month. He finally made his League debut for United v. Chelsea in September 1946.

A miner from Chesterfield, he actually played his first game for the club in April 1940 (three years after joining). After leaving Bramall Lane at the end of the 1946-47 season, he became the idol of the Edgar Street fans.

THOMPSON, Dennis

Forward: 118 apps. 24 goals

Born: Sheffield, 2 June 1925. Died: 1986.

Career: BLADES (amateur September 1941, professional August 1942), Southend United (July 1951).

An England Schoolboy international winger with fine ball control and good strike record Dennis Thompson played his first League game for the Blades against Stoke City in October 1946...his last was against Manchester City in April 1951. He netted 11 times in 51 League games for the 'Shrimpers.'

THOMPSON, Desmond

Goalkeeper: 30 apps.

Born: Southampton, 4 December 1928

Career: Gainsborough Trinity, York City (January 1951), Burnley (November 1952), BLADES (£4,250, May 1955, retired May 1964).

Goalkeeper Des Thompson had already appeared in 80 League games for York and 62 for Burnley when he moved into Bramall Lane following an injury to Ted Burgin. Highly professional, confident on his line, he remained decidedly loyal to the Blades for nine years during which time he made only 30 senior appearances as stand-in for Alan Hodgkinson.

THOMPSON, George Alexander

Winger: 42 apps. 4 goals

Born: South Shields, 23 March 1884.

Career: North Shields, BLADES (October 1906), Derby County (September 1908), Newcastle United (season 1911-12)

A busy, darting winger with neat ball control, George Thompson was at his best when chasing long balls deep into the corner of the field. He scored six goals in 55 games for Derby.

THOMPSON, John L

Winger: 25 apps. 3 goals

Born: Redcar, 22 July 1892.

Career: South Bank, Scunthorpe & Lindsey United (1912), BLADES (July 1914), Bristol City (November 1920-April 1922).

WW1 interrupted winger 'Jack' Thompson's career at Bramall Lane. On his day he looked good and may well have developed into a class player. He went on to score once in 29 League games for Bristol City.

THOMPSON, Philip Bernard

Defender: 44+1 apps.

Born: Kensington, Liverpool, 21 January 1954

Career: Kirkby Schools (Liverpool), Liverpool (apprentice, April 1970, professional February 1971), BLADES (on loan, December 1984, signed permanently March 1985-May 1986); returned to Liverpool as coach, July 1986, later appointed assistant-manager, while also acting as caretaker-manager).

Phil Thompson - who always looked a gangling figure on the pitch - possessed a hard tackle and was an authoritative player who skippered Liverpool for a while during his 16 years at the club. He used to stand on the kop as a boy and was overjoyed when offered a professional contract by manager Bill Shankly in 1970. He appeared in 336 games for the Merseysiders (7 goals scored), helping them win the European Cup twice (1978 & 1981), the UEFA Cup (1976), the Super Cup (1977), five First Division titles (1976, 1977, 1979, 1980 & 1982), the FA Cup (1974), the League Cup twice (1981 & 1982) and the Charity Shield on six occasions (1974, 1976, 1977 shared, 1979, 1980 & 1982), as well as four runners-up prizes for a tally of 22 medals in all. He also collected 42 full England caps (as well as earning Youth, 'B' & Under-21 honours) and it was the rise of Alan Hansen and Mark Lawrenson that finally brought his 16-year Anfield career to and end. He continued to performed disappointingly for the Blades, making 34 first-class appearances in his last season before returning to Liverpool where he has since been a very effective aide to manages Dalglish, Souness, Evans and Houllier.

THOMPSON, Steven Paul

Central defender: 23 apps. one goal

Born: Sheffield, 28 July 1955

Career: Frecheville FC, Worksop Town, Boston United (July 1975), Lincoln City (£15,000, April 1980), Charlton Athletic (£15,000, August 1985), Leicester City (£15,000, July 1988), BLADES (£20,000, November 1988), Lincoln City (August 1989, manager November 1990-May 1993), assisted with managerial duties at Doncaster Rovers (from January 1994).

A commanding central defender, Steve Thompson learnt his trade with Trevor Peake at Lincoln in the early 1980s. He made 154 League appearances for the 'Imps' (first time round), and 95 for Charlton, failed to get a single outing at Filbert Street, but played in 20 games when United won promotion from Division Three in 1989. He succeeded Allan Clarke as manager at Sincil Bank in 1990. A fine all-round sportsman in his schooldays, he represented Yorkshire at football, cricket and basketball.

244

THORPE, Percy
Right-back: 114 apps.
Born: Nottingham, 18 July 1899.
Career: Nottingham Boys, Sutton Town, Blackpool (July 1924), Connah's Quay & Shotton (July 1928), Reading (October 1928), BLADES (June 1930), West Ham United (August 1933), Accrington Stanley (1934), Port Vale (November 1934-May 1935).
A powerfully built defender with tree-trunk legs, Percy Thorpe could kick like a mule and was no mean tackler either! He made his League debut for Blackpool at centre-half and also played at right-half and inside-left for the Seasiders before settling down at right-back the following season. He had three excellent seasons at 'the Lane' when he partnered Jack Gibson, Harry Hooper and sometimes George Green. He made 115 appearances for Blackpool, over 70 for Reading but failed to make much of an impact with his last three clubs.

THORPE, Sam
Wing-half: 4 apps.
Born: Sheffield, 2 December 1920. Died: Sheffield, August 2002.
Career: Norton Woodseats, RAF, (WW2 guest for Liverpool, Tranmere Rovers, Southport), BLADES (December 1944, professional, April 1945-June 1949), Frickley Colliery, Gainsborough Trinity, Wisbech Town, Buxton (player-manager).
A fair-haired reserve wing-half, Sam Thorpe made his Football League debut for the Blades against Derby County (away) in March 1948 - having previously played in two WW2 games v. Mansfield Town and Manchester United in December 1944.

TIBBOTT, Leslie
Full-back: 100+3 apps. 3 goals
Born: Oswestry, 25 August 1955
Career: Ipswich Town (apprentice, August 19871, professional March 1973), BLADES (£100,000, March 1979, forced to retire through injury, summer 1983).
Welsh Under-21 international (two caps gained) full-back Les Tibbott's career was ended prematurely through injury - after he had made 175 League & Cup appearances (72 for Ipswich). He was a good, covering defender, possessed a strong tackle and was positive with his clearances.

TILER, Carl
Defender: 31 apps. 2 goals
Born: Sheffield, 11 February 1970.
Career: Barnsley (YTS June 1986, professional February 1988), Nottingham Forest (£1.4 million, May 1991), Swindon Town (on loan, November 1994), Aston Villa (£750,000, October 1995), BLADES (£650,000, March 1997), Everton (£500,000, November 1997), Charlton Athletic (£700,000, September 1998), Birmingham City (on loan, February 2001), Portsmouth (£250,000, March 2001).
A strong, tall, dominant defender, Carl Tiler had already gained 13 England Under-21 caps and made over 185 senior appearances as well as spending three years in the shadows at Nottingham Forest before joining the Blades for a big fee in 1997. He spent just six months at thee Lane and after leaving went on to appear in another 150 plus games, helping both Charlton (2000) and Pompey (2003) reach the Premiership.

TODD, Mark Kenneth
Midfielder: 87+11 apps. 6 goals
Born: Belfast, 4 December 1967
Career: Manchester United (YTS April 1984, professional August 1985), BLADES (free transfer, June 1987), Wolverhampton Wanderers (on loan, March 1991), Rotherham United (£35,000, September 1991), Scarborough (August 1995), Mansfield Town (non-contract, February-May 1996).
Mark Todd played in 39 games when the Blades won promotion from Division Three in 1989 and in 16 matches the following season when top-flight status was regained. A Northern Ireland Under-23 international one cap gained) he failed to get a game at Old Trafford but quickly made an impact at 'the Lane', his courage and commitment being admired by all. He made over 70 appearances for Rotherham.

TOMLINSON, Paul
Goalkeeper: 46 apps.
Born: Rotherham Town, 4 February 1965
Career: Middlewood Rangers, BLADES (professional, June 1983), Birmingham City (on loan, March 1987), Bradford City (June 1987-May 1995),
Paul 'Tommo' Tomlinson, 6ft 2ins tall, played in 30 games when United won promotion from Division Three in 1984. A fine shot-stopper, courageous and comfortable with high crosses, he was arguably the best 'keeper outside the Premiers League (1992-95). He set two new club records in his last season with Bradford City - a total of 71 clean-sheets and most League appearances by a Bantams' goalkeeper, 284 (beating Jock Ewart's tally which had stood since 1929).

TONER, William
Defender/centre-forward: 61 apps. 3 goals
Born: Glasgow, 18 December 1929.
Career: Queen's Park, Celtic (professional, February 1948), BLADES (free transfer, May 1951), Kilmarnock (£2,000, August 1954), Hibernian (April 1963), Ayr United (September 1963-May 1964), Dumbarton (manager, October 1964-September 1967).
The versatile Bill Toner (who preferred the centre-half berth but loved to play up front) was a calm, stylish footballer who, when in defence, produced some excellent displays alongside many fine wing-halves. Having appeared in only two League games for the Bhoys prior to his move to Bramall Lane, he then helped the Blades win the Second Division championship in 1953 before returning to Scotland. Toner was capped twice by Scotland (v. Wales and Northern Ireland in 1959) and represented the Scottish League on five occasions. He was also a Scottish Cup finalist with Kilmarnock in 1957 and 1960 and a League Cup runner-up in 1961.

245

TONGE, Michael William
Midfielder: 84+8 apps.* 11 goals*
Born: Manchester, 7 April 1983
Career: BLADES (apprentice, June 1999, professional March 2001).
Michael Tonge - never overawed despite his tender years - broke into the Blades' first team in September 2001 and during the next two seasons produced some splendid performances in midfield while also scoring some important goals. Occupying a key position in centre-field, with Michael Brown alongside, he received huge praise from the media in 2002-03 as United surged on to two Cup semi-finals and qualified for the First Division Play-off Final (v. Wolves). Tonge, unusually tall for a midfielder at 6ft, was voted the Supporters' club 'Young Player of the Year' in 2002.

TOOTILL, George Albert
Centre-half: 40 apps.
Born: Walkden, 20 October 1913. Died: 1984
Career: Chorley (1933), Plymouth Argyle (March 1937), BLADES (January 1938), Hartlepool United (September 1947).
'Alf' Tootill was a strong defender who helped the Blades win the Second Division title in 1939 (playing in 12 matches). Earlier he had performed adequately as a wing-half and centre-forward for the Pilgrims.

TORQUAY UNITED
United's playing record against the Gulls:
Football League

Venue	P	W	D	L	F	A
Home	1	1	0	0	4	1
Away	1	0	1	0	1	1
Totals	2	1	1	0	5	2

A football club was established in the Devon seaside resort in 1899 when a group of former pupils from Torquay and Torbay Colleges were sat in the Princess Gardens listening to a band. A proper meeting followed (at The Tor Abbey Hotel) when officers were appointed and entry was gained to the East Devon League. As an amateur club, it played on Teignmouth Road, at the Torquay Recreation Ground and Cricket Field Road before settling at the Torquay Cricket Club ground where rugby is now the featured sport. After switching to Plainmoor (1910) the club was officially registered as Torquay United in 1921 on the amalgamation with Babbacombe FC.
Immediately turning professional, the 'Gulls' were elected to the Football League six years later but as yet have never played above the Third Division.
United's only meeting with the 'Gulls' was in 1981-82. After a 1-1 draw at Plainmoor, Keith Edwards scoring in front of 5,126 spectators, the Blades carved out a comfortable 4-1 home victory in April, on their run in to the Fourth Division title. All of the Blades' goals came in a six-minute spell in the first-half.
Neil Warnock has managed both clubs (also a consultant at Torquay); 'Roy' John and Bruce Rioch both played for the Blades and later became managers at Torquay.
Of the handful of players who have served with both clubs were have Dickie Bird, John Brewster (Blades reserve), John Connaughton, Keith Curle, Tony Currie, Harold Gough, Paul Hall; Mark Hawthorne & Stewart Evans (both Blades reserves), John Matthews, David Mercer and Colin Rawson. Ex-Blades star Jack Alderson became trainer at Plainmoor.

TOTTENHAM HOTSPUR
United's playing record against Spurs:
Premier League

Venue	P	W	D	L	F	A
Home	2	1	1	0	8	2
Away	2	0	1	1	2	4
Totals	4	1	2	1	10	6

Football League

Home	38	19	13	6	85	53
Away	38	5	9	24	40	89
Totals	76	24	22	30	125	142

FA Cup

Home	1	1	0	0	3	1
Away	1	1	0	0	3	0
Neutral	2	0	1	1	3	5
Totals	4	2	1	1	9	6

League Cup

Home	1	0	0	1	0	2
Away	1	0	0	1	1	2
Totals	2	0	0	2	1	4

Like United, Tottenham Hotspur FC was formed by a group of cricketers...the Hotspur CC forming a football section in 1882, with the 'Tottenham' prefix being added in 1884.

After early games on Tottenham Marshes, Spurs switched to Northumberland Park in 1888, a ground later to become White Hart Lane. Spurs entered the Southern League in 1896, winning the title in 1900 and then capturing the FA Cup a year later, beating the Blades in the Final (after a replay).

The biggest crowd ever to watch United in action - a massive 114,815 (with record receipts amounting to almost £4,000 - attended that 1901 Final at Crystal Palace. The game ended all-square at 2-2. 'Sandy' Brown scored twice for then Southern League side (on 23 & 51 minutes) while Fred Priest (10) and Billy Bennett (52) netted for the Blades.

The replay at Bolton attracted a mere 20,470 fans (recs. £1,621) and this time Spurs came out on top, winning 3-1. Priest gave the Blades the lead in the 40th minute, but John Cameron equalised on 52, and then Tom Smith scored a second for Spurs on 76 before Brown finished things off with a late third.

The first League meeting followed in November 1909 - Spurs having gained election to the Second Division the season before and winning promotion straightaway. United lost 2-1 in London and were held to a 1-1 draw at 'the Lane'. Joe Kitchen scored in each match.

There have been some cracking games between the two clubs over the years, so it remains a disappointment, to a certain extent, that the clubs have met in only 40 seasons out of a possible 83 in the League.

Spurs were thrashed 6-2 at Bramall Lane in 1923-24 (Bert Menlove netting a hat-trick).

Three seasons later Spurs pulled back a three-goal deficit at Bramall Lane (March 1927) to earn a 3-3 draw, and then United recorded their 11th successive home win (8 League and three Cup) when they beat Spurs 3-1 on the last day of March 1928.

George Hunt grabbed all Spurs' goals when they beat United 4-1 in London in December 1933 and United's Jimmy Hagan was the star-performer weighed in with a treble as the Blades gleefully carved out a 6-1 home win in their promotion -season of 1938-39 (United's Harold Hampson had started the ball rolling with a 10-second opener).

In 1949-50 Spurs walloped United 7-0 at White Hart Lane (on their way to the Second Division title) and Johnny Gavin netted four times when Spurs won 5-0 in a First Division clash in London in March 1955.

Earlier that season United had beaten Spurs 4-1 at Bramall Lane, Colin Grainger having a hand in all his side's goals, setting up two for Alf Ringstead.

A 3-1 defeat at White Hart Lane in April 1956 condemned the Blades to relegation from Division One. Bobby Smith scored a hat-trick for Spurs.

Spurs recorded their first League win in 15 attempts at Bramall Lane when they defeated the Blades 3-1 on 28 December 1965 (their previous victory had come in 1926).

Twenty years later, in 1975-76, Spurs won 5-0 on home soil.

Blades' biggest win over Spurs came in the Premiership in 1992-93 when they ran up a splendid 6-0 scoreline at Bramall Lane (Ian Bryson scoring twice).

Since the 1901 Final, the clubs have met twice more in the FA Cup. In 1936 United won 3-1 at home to reach the semi-final stage and then goals from 'Doc' Pace, Billy Russell and Derek Hawksworth silenced the 51,000 White Hart Lane crowd when United won 3-0 there in the 4th round in 1958. Billy Hodgson dominated the midfield that afternoon, normally the sole preserve of the legendary Danny Blanchflower.

John Blair, Lycurus Burrows (United reserve), Bob Cain, Herbert Chapman, Jack Chisholm, John Cutbush (Spurs reserve), Pat Gilhooley, George Hunt (United trialist), George Hutchinson, Jim Iley, Andy Keeley, Phil Kite, John L Jones, Ken McKay, Roger Nilsen, Martin Peters (also Blades' manager), Hans Segers, David Tuttle, Joe Walton and Simon Webster are some of the players who have served with both clubs, while Stewart Houston, a United player, was Spurs assistant-manager. Jimmy McCormick and George Smith both played for Spurs and were later coaches at United.

TOWNER, Anthony James

Forward: 9+1 apps. one goal
Born: Brighton, 2 May 1955
Career: Brighton & Hove Albion (apprentice June 1971, professional January 1973), Millwall (£65,000, October 1978), Rotherham United (£100,000 plus John Seasman, August 1980), BLADES (on loan, March-May 1983), Wolverhampton Wanderers (£100,000, August 1983), Charlton Athletic (£15,000, September 1984), Rochdale (November 1985), Cambridge United (non-contract, March-May 1986), Gravesend (September 1986), Fisher Athletic (August 1987), Crawley Town (July 1989), Worthing (July 1990-May 1991).
Scorer of 53 goals in more than 400 League games accumulated over a period of 15 years, winger Tony Towner, on his day, was a very useful player (he could be brilliant), capable of turning any defender with one quick burst of speed, a clever pass or inviting cross. He made his debut in the First Division for Wolves v. Liverpool and later had his contract with Charlton cancelled by mutual consent.

TRACEY, Simon Peter

Goalkeeper: 379+3 apps.
Born: Woolwich, London, 9 December 1967
Career: Wimbledon (apprentice April 1984, professional February 1986), BLADES (£7,500, October 1988), Manchester City (on loan, October 1994), Norwich City (on loan, December 1994-January 1995), Wimbledon (on loan, November 1995).
Simon Tracey played in all 46 games when the Blades gained promotion to the First Division in 1990. Twelve years later he reached the milestone of 300 League appearances for the club and also set an 'unwanted' club record with his fifth sending-off!
Sure on crosses and smart off his line, he held off the challenge of Wilko de Vogt but then lost his place to new-signing Paddy Kenny at the start of the 2002-03 season.
Only Jack Smith (498) has made more first team appearances for the Blades than Tracey, while Tracey has now played in more League matches than any other United custodian (332).

247

Sheffield United's Simon Tracey takes a cross
under pressure from Blackburn Rovers'
Ashley Ward.

TRANMERE ROVERS

United's playing record against the Rovers:

Football League

Venue	P	W	D	L	F	A
Home	9	6	2	1	15	6
Away	9	3	4	2	16	13
Totals	18	9	6	3	31	19

The Wirral club came into being as 'Belmont FC' in 1884, changing its name to their present title a year later. In 1921 Rovers became original members of the newly-formed Third Division (North), after a single season in Division Two in 1938-39, they returned to the lower reaches until a remarkable surge took them from Division Four back to Division Two between 1989 & 1991, where they met United seven successive seasons, having met only twice previously.

The first League encounters took place in 1938-39, United winning both fixtures 2-0, Jock Dodds netting twice at Prenton Park.

In their only campaign in Division Four (1981-82) United were relieved to leave Tranmere with a 2-2 draw thanks to a stoppage time penalty save by Keith Waugh. The Blades won their home game 2-0 and have since claimed four more victories at 'the Lane' to Rovers' one (2-0 in 1995-96).

Wayne Allison, Nick Henry, David Kelly, Vince Matthews, Martin Pike, Shane Nicholson, Georges Santos, Paddy Sloan, Sam Thorpe and Steve Yates are some of the players who have assisted both the Blades and Rovers. Archie Clark played for Rovers and managed United while Dugald Livingstone was a Rovers player and later trainer at Bramall Lane.

TRANSFERS

This how the United's 'in and out' transfer records have been broken down the years:

Players 'In'

Fee	Player	From	Date
£1.2m	Don Hutchinson	West Ham Utd	Jan 1996
£250,000	Jamie Hoyland	Bury	June 1990
£375,000	Paul Beesley	Leyton Orient	July 1990
£650,000	Vinnie Jones	Leeds United	Sept 1990
£75,000	Tony Field	Blackburn Rovers	March 1974
£60,000	Colin Franks	Watford	July 1973
£60,000	Jim Brown	Chesterfield	March 1971
£65,000	John Tudor	Coventry City	Nov 1968
£15,000	Jack Chisholm	Brentford	April 1949
£12,000	Andrew McLaren	Burnley	April 1949
£8,000	Robert Reid	Brentford	Feb 1939
£5,000	Sid Gibson	Nottingham Forest	Aug 1928
£4,250	David Mercer	Hull City	Dec 1921
£1,000	Stan Fazackerley	Hull City	Mar 1913
£750	Ted Connor	Manchester United	June 1911
£700	Arthur Brown	Gainsboro' Trinity	Oct 1902

Players 'Out'

Fee	Player	To	Date
£1.75m	Nathan Blake	Bolton Wds	Nov 1995
£2.7m	Brian Deane	Leeds Utd	July 1993
£575,000	Vinnie Jones	Chelsea	Sept 1991
£400,000	Alex Sabella	Leeds Utd	July 1980
£180,000	Geoff Salmons	Stoke City	July 1974
£100,000	Alan Birchenall	Chelsea	Nov 1967
£100,000	Mick Jones	Leeds United	Sept 1967
£10,000	Jock Dodds	Blackpool	Mar 1939
£4,000	Stan Fazackerley	Everton	Nov 1920
£1,600*	Arthur Brown	Sunderland	June 1908
£520	Alf Common	Sunderland	June 1904

* A world record fee at the time.

Transfers Between United & Sheffield Wednesday

Players who have moved directly from the Blades to the Owls & vice-versa include the following...

To United: Joe Cockroft 1948, George Cole 1937, Terry Curran 1982, Jeff King 1981 & Wilf Rostron 1989.

To Wednesday: Billy Mellor 1892, Bernard Oxley 1933 & George Underwood 1951.

(See also under SHEFFIELD WEDNESDAY)

Two Spells At Bramall Lane

Among the players who had two separate spells with the Blades (including periods on loan) are: Bobby Davison, Brian Deane, Keith Edwards, Jonathan Hunt, Chris Kamara, Joe Kitchen, Adrian Littlejohn, Jim McCormick, Clive Mendonca, Trevor Ross, Geoff Salmons, Harry Thickett, Des Thompson, Arthur Watson & Chris Wilder.

Transfer Talk

* At the outset only two players were allowed to be signed on loan by any one club per season.

* Ex-United centre-forward Alf Common became the game's first £1,000 player when he was transferred from Sunderland to Middlesbrough in February 1905.

TRAVELLING MEN
Several of football's journeymen have served with United during their much-travelled careers, and among them we have the following (listed in A-Z order): Ian Benjamin (12 clubs), goalkeeper John Burridge (23 major clubs: 18 English, five Scottish), Terry Curran, Peter Duffield, Republic of Ireland striker David Kelly, Phil Kite (14 clubs), Jack Peart, Tom Simons (13 clubs: 1903-22), Billy Whitehurst (20 clubs in all, nine in the Football League) and Peter Withe, a 1982 European Cup winner with Aston Villa.

TRUEMAN, Albert Henry
Left-half: 58 apps.
Born: Leicester, April qtr 1882.
Career: Holy Trinity School (Leicester), Leicestershire County Schools, Leicester Fosse (amateur, August 1899), Grasmere Swifts, Hinckley Town, Coalville Town, Leicester Fosse (August 1905), Southampton (May 1908), BLADES (March 1911), Darlington (season 1913-14), Leicester Fosse (guest, September 1916). Did not play after WW1.
An England international trialist in 1911 (as a Blades' player) and honoured four times by the Southern League when with Southampton, Albert 'Nigger' Trueman was a regarded as a 'brilliant' juvenile footballer. Quick, resourceful and decisive in action, he was only 5ft 6ins tall but didn't let that worry him as he battled on gamely against more bigger and stronger opponents. He appeared in 92 first-class matches for the saints and almost 50 for Leicester.

TRUSSON, Michael Sydney
Forward/midfielder: 155+1 apps. 32 goals
Born: Northolt, 26 May 1959
Career: Plymouth Argyle (apprentice, June 1975, professional January 1977), BLADES (£60,000, July 1980), Rotherham United (December 1983), Brighton & Hove Albion (July 1987), Gillingham (September 1989-May 1992).
Well-built London-born utility player Mike Trusson missed only two games when United won the Fourth Division title in 1982 and played in 11 matches when promotion was gained from Division Three in 1984. A very consistent performer with every club he served, he scored 74 goals in a total of 434 League games (including 31 in 126 for the Blades and 19 in 124 for Rotherham).

TUDOR, John Arthur
Striker: 78+7 apps. 37 goals
Born: Ilkeston, Derbyshire, 24 June 1946
Career: Ilkeston Schoolboy football, Ilkeston Town, BLADES (on trial), Derby County (briefly), Notts County (junior), Chesterfield (junior), Nottingham Forest (on trial), Middlesbrough (played in reserves from August 1965), Coventry City (January 1966), BLADES (£58,500, November 1968), Newcastle United (exchange deal involving John Hope & David Ford, January 1971), Stoke City (September 1976), AA Ghent/Belgium (August 1977; retired through injury, May 1978; South Shields (manager, October 1979), Gateshead (coach, December 1980), Bedlington Terriers (coach, November 1982), Derbyshire Coaching School, Minnesota/USA Coaching School (June 1994).
After signing from Coventry City, blond haired striker John Tudor played in 21 games when the Blades gained promotion to the First Division in 1971. He was always an honest performer, unspectacular but capable of scoring and creating important goals. A knee injury ended his playing career and after that he became a highly respected coach, having been a licensee in Bedlington in 1982. A late developer in the game, he worked as a welder, truck driver and tile-maker before turning professional with Jimmy Hill's Coventry, having been rejected by several clubs prior to that (including the Blades).
Tudor was a Second Division championship winner with Coventry City in 1967, a runner-up Newcastle in the same Division in 1971 and an FA Cup finalist in 1974. He scored well over 100 goals (99 in the League) in more than 350 competitive games, netting 58 times in 187 when at St James' Park.

TUMMON, Oliver
Outside-right & left: 101 apps. 25 goals
Born: Sheffield, 3 March 1884. Died: October 1955
Career: South Street New Connexion FC (Sheffield), Gainsborough Trinity (briefly 1901), Sheffield Wednesday (March 1902), Gainsborough Trinity (June 1910), Oldham Athletic (£300, July 1912), BLADES (August 1919), Barnsley (June 1920).
Ollie Tummon was pen-pictured as a 'powerhouse winger with an explosive finish' whose direct approach proved to be the perfect foil to Stan Fazackerley and Joe Kitchen. He didn't have all that good a time with his major first club (Gainsborough), had limited opportunities with Wednesday but did much better in his second spell with Trinity, not missing a match for two years. He starred in Oldham's 1913 FA Cup run and then was a key member of the Latics' attack when they finished runners-up inn the First Division in 1915. During his career Tummon appeared in more than 250 competitive games and scored over 50 goals.

TUNSTALL, Frederick Edward
Outside-left: 491 apps. 135 goals
Born: Low Valley near Wombwell, Yorkshire, 29 March 1901.
Died: 1971.
Career: Darfield St George's, Scunthorpe and Lindsey United (April 1920), BLADES (£1,000, December 1920), Halifax Town (January 1933), Boston United (June 1936, remaining with the club after retiring, acting as a part-time player as well as being at various times, trainer, coach and, indeed, manager).
Fred Tunstall made an immediate impact at Bramall Lane. A dangerous, live-wire left-winger, direct in style, possessing loads of skill and a shot of 'abnormal velocity' he could centre splendidly on the run and gave the Blades excellent service for a shade over twelve years, scoring the winning goal in the 1925 FA Cup Final v. Cardiff City. He was an England international, capped seven times at senior level between 1923-27.

TURLEY, John William
Centre-forward: 5 apps. 3 goals
Born: Bebington, Birkenhead, 26 January 1939
Career: Ellesmere Port, BLADES (professional, May 1956), Peterborough United (July 1961), Rochdale (May 1964-April 1965).
A reserve centre-forward, who averaged one appearance per season with the Blades, John Turley scored on his Football League debut against West Ham in September 1957 (United won 2-1). He netted 14 times in 32 League outings for 'Posh' and five in 22 for Rochdale.

TURNBULL, Thomas
Goalkeeper: 2 apps.
Born: Stirlingshire, circa 1878
Career: East Stirling, Celtic, BLADES (October 1900), Stenhousemuir Partick Thistle.
Sadly Turnbull broke a leg playing for United against Aston Villa in a benefit match for Howard Spencer on 27 December 1900. He never played for then Blades again but later returned to action with Stenhousemuir Partick, albeit only briefly. He made 11 appearances for Celtic.

TUTTLE, David Philip
Defender: 68 apps. one goal
Born: Reading, 6 February 1972
Career: Tottenham Hotspur (apprentice, April 1988, professional February 1990), Peterborough United (on loan, January 1993), BLADES (£350,000, August 1993), Crystal Palace (March 1996), Barnsley (£150,000, August 1999), Millwall (£200,000, March 2000), Wycombe Wanderers (on loan, February-March 2002); retired through injury, January 2003.
An England Youth international and FA Youth Cup winner (1990), Dave Tuttle played 13 games in the top flight with Spurs before joining the Blades in 1993. Over the next ten years he went on to take hiss overall tally of senior appearances to 234 before announcing his retirement with problem groin/leg injuries. A commanding centre-half, strong in every department of defensive play, Tuttle replaced Brian Gayle in the Blades' back division before suffering serious a cruciate ligament injury that kept him out of the first XI for eleven months (although during that time he did have one outing as a substitute).

TWEDDLE, Frederick
Outside-right: 10 apps.
Born: County Durham, circa 1887
Career: Hartlepool United, BLADES (seasons 1909-11).
Fred Tweddle was a reserve right-winger who deputised, in the main, for Joe Walton.

TWISS, Michael John
Midfielder: 4+13 apps. one goal
Born: Salford, 18 December 1977
Career: Manchester United (apprentice, April 1994, professional July 1996), BLADES (on loan, August 1998), Port Vale (free transfer, July 2000), Leith RMI (July 2001), Chester City (May 2002).
Left-sided midfielder, nurtured at Old Trafford alongside David Beckham,
Paul Scholes, Ryan Giggs and others, Michael Twiss made just two first team appearances for the Reds and 17 on loan at Bramall Lane before going on to help the Valiants win the Auto-Windscreen Shield in 2001.

250

Right: Sheffield United v.s Wolverhampton Wanderers 28 October 1967
Left: Sheffield United v.s Nottingham Forest 22nd December 1961

UHLENBEEK, Gustav

Defender: 55+4 apps.

Born: Paramaribo, Surinam, 20 August 1970

Career: Ajax Amsterdam (July 1988), SC Cambuur/Holland (August 1992), Tops SV/Holland (July 1994), Ipswich Town (August 1995), Fulham (free transfer, July 1998), BLADES (free, August, 2000), Walsall (on loan, March-April 2002), Bradford City (season 2002-03).

An all-action defender, strong and mobile, Gus Uhlenbeek was 25 years of age when he moved into the Football League with Ipswich in 1995, having made over 60 appearances in Holland prior to his transfer. He helped Fulham win the Second Division championship in 1999 before having one good and one moderate season at 'the Lane.'

ULLATHORNE, Robert

Left-back: 29+1 apps.

Born: Wakefield, 11 October 1971

Career: Norwich City (apprentice, April 1988, professional July 1990), Osasuna/Spain (June 1996), Leicester City (£600,000, February 1997), Huddersfield Town (on trial), Real Zaragoza/Spain (on trial), Tenerife (on trial), Newcastle United (on trial), BLADES (December 2000, then on a non-contract basis, signed permanently March 2003).

An England Youth international full-back who took over from Shane Nicholson in the Blades' line-up, Rob Ullathorne gave some impressive displays when assisting Michael Brown to the full down the left hand side of the park. It was the injury, suffered during the infamous League game v. West Brom in March 2003 that caused the match to be abandoned.

UNCHANGED

For the first 21 League matches of the 1958-59 season the whole of the Sheffield United defence remained unchanged, so did the centre-forward position. The line-up was Alan Hodgkinson in goal; full-backs Cecil Coldwell and Graham Shaw; a middle-line of Brian Richardson, Joe Shaw and Gerry Summers, with Derek Pace leading the attack.

UNDERWOOD, George Ronald

Defender: 21 apps.

Born: Sheffield, 6 September 1925

Career: BLADES (professional September 1946), Sheffield Wednesday (October 1951), Scunthorpe United (June 1953), Rochdale (June 1954-April 1955).

A versatile reserve defender at 'the Lane', George Underwood had to wait until March 1950 before making his Football League debut, taking over at centre-half from Harry Latham for the game with Bury. He failed to make the first team at Hillsborough, made eight League appearances for Scunthorpe and 19 for Rochdale.

UNITED

When Sheffield United Cricket Club (q.v) was formed in 1854, it became the first sporting organisation to use the suffix 'united.' When the football club came into being in 1889, it used the same title, thus becoming the first senior football club to use the 'United' suffix.

Since then 'United' has become the most used football club 'name' in Britain. The Football League has had 18 clubs with the name United in their title with 'City' a close second (16). The Scottish League has also had several 'Uniteds', the first being Ayr United in 1910.

Blades' fans, however, can with some justification, sing: "There's only one United!"

UNITED COUNTIES LEAGUE

United played in this competition two seasons running: 1893-94 and 1894-95. Their full record was:

Venue	P	W	D	L	F	A	Pts
Home	7	2	2	3	11	15	6
Away	6	1	3	2	4	7	5
Totals	13	3	5	5	15	22	11

Their fixtures in the first campaign saw them beat Wednesday 2-0 at home, lose 2-0 at Derby County and 3-1 at Nottingham Forest and draw 0-0 at Notts County, 1-1 at Wednesday and 0-0 at home to Forest. The home clash with Notts County was not played. The 1894-95 competition was abandoned, but not after the Blades had been hammered 6-2 at home by Forest and lost 5-4 at Derby. They defeated Forest 1-0 away and Leicester fosse 3-2 at home and drew both games with Wednesday, 0-0 at home, 1-1 away.

UTLEY, George

Left-half/inside-forward: 240 apps. 24 goals
Born: Elsecar, Yorkshire, 16 May 1887.
Died: 1966
Career: Elsecar FC, Wentworth, Sheffield
Wednesday amamteur(1906), Elsecar FC (1907),
Barnsley (1908), BLADES (£2,000, November
1913), Manchester City (September 1922, retiring
within twelve months), Bristol City (trainer),
Sheffield Wednesday (trainer/coach in May 1924),
Fulham (as trainer, July 1925-27).
George Utley was a born leader who took over the
captaincy of the Blades. His forceful, commanding
presence and overall displays were a tremendous boost
to the side. A long-throw expert and a brilliant dribbler,
he scored a goal after a 60-yard mazy run against Bolton
Wanderers in the 1915 FA Cup semi-final at Ewood Park
and then gleefully lifted the trophy after the Blades had
beaten Chelsea 3-0 in the Final. An England international
(capped against Ireland in February 1913 after three
successful trials) he failed to make a single League
appearance for the Owls but after moving to Oakwell he
subsequently gained an FA Cup winners' medal with the
Tykes (1912) for whom he made 170 League appearances.
A fine club cricketer himself, for many years Utley was
employed as cricket coach at Rossall School.

VARADI, Imre

Striker: 8+4 apps. 4 goals

Born: Paddington, London, 8 July 1959

Career: Letchworth Juniors, Letchworth Garden City, BLADES (apprentice July 1975, professional, April 1978), Everton (£80,000, March 1979), Newcastle United (£125,000, August 1981), Sheffield Wednesday (£150,000, August 1983), West Bromwich Albion (£285,000, July 1985), Manchester City (player exchange deal, involving Robert Hopkins, October 1986), Sheffield Wednesday (player exchange deal, September 1988), Leeds United (February 1990), Luton Town (on loan, March 1992), Oxford United (on loan, January 1993), Rotherham United (March 1992), Mansfield Town (non-contract, August 1995), Boston United, Scunthorpe United (non-contract, September 1995), Matlock Town (player-manager, October 1995), Guiseley (player-coach), Denaby United (player-coach), Stalybridge Celtic (assistant-manager/coach),.

One of the great nomadic strikers in League football, Imre Varadi served with 13 different clubs (including Boston) after leaving Letchworth for Bramall Lane in 1979.

Certainly one who 'got away' from the Blades, he ended his senior career in 1995 with a haul of 178 goals in 5-2 senior matches, helping Leeds win the Second Division title in 1990. He netted 46 times in 121 outings for the Owls.

* Varadi's brother Fernando was a registered player with Fulham.

VEART, Thomas Carl

Midfielder/defender: 53+21 apps.18 goals

Born: Whyalla, Australia, 21 May 1957

Career: Adelaide FC/Australian, BLADES (£250,000, July 1994), Crystal Palace (£225,000, March 1996), Millwall (£50,000,December 1997-January 1998).

Two-footed Australian international (over 20 caps gained) Carl Veart was a member of Terry Venables' World Cup squad in 1997-98. A hard-working midfielder who could also be used as defender and at times (in an emergency) as an-out-and-out attacker, he was able to link up with his front men although at times he lacked conviction. Nevertheless he did well at 'the Lane' and followed up by scoring 11 times in 68 games for Palace after becoming the London club's second Aussie (behind Kevin Muscat).

VONK, Michel Christian

Central defender: 43 apps. 4 goals

Born: Alkmaar, Netherlands, 28 October 1968

Career: SVV Dordrecht/Holland, Manchester City (March 1992), Oldham Athletic (on loan, November-December 1995), BLADES (£350,000, December 1995), Maastricht/Holland (July 1998).

Solid Dutch defender Michel Vonk (6ft 3in tall & 13st 3lbs in weight) was United manager Howard Kendall's first signing from at £350,000 in 1995. A sound performer, who at his best was excellent in the air and a superb man-marker, he was out of action through injury for some 13 months (November 1996 to December 1997) and never really regained full fitness, being transferred to Maastricht in the summer of 1998.

WAGSTAFFE, Barry

Midfielder: 126+12 apps. 5 goals
Born: Wombwell, 28 November 1945
Career: BLADES (apprentice, April 1962, professional April 1963),
Reading (£17,500 with brother Tony, July 1969
1975-May 1976); later coach at Barnsley's Centre of Excellent.
A sound, constructive wing-half, Barry Wagstaffe spent eight years at
Bramall Lane, playing alongside his brother Tony (q.v) for five seasons
in the First Division (1964-69) before both players were transferred to
Reading for an overall fee of £17,500. He appeared in 235 competitive
games for Reading (adding class and guile to the Royals' midfield) and
almost 50 for Rotherham. He often left the pitch (after playing in the
muddiest of conditions) still wearing a clean pair of shorts! He had a
total of 419 League games all told.

WAGSTAFFE, Tony

Born: Wombwell, 19 February 1944
Midfielder: 164+3 apps. 23 goals
Career: BLADES (apprentice June 1960, professional March 1961),
Reading (with brother Barry, £17,500 joint deal, July 1969),
Cheltenham Town (May 1974).
Tony Wagstaffe and his younger brother Barry (q.v) played together in
almost 60 League and Cup games for the Blades during the 1960s before
both players moved to Reading. Tony was the more attack-minded and
scored his fair quota of goals while also creating chances aplenty for his
colleagues with his measured and precise passes. He went on to appear in
more than 175 first-class games for Reading before moving in to non-
League football with Cheltenham.
* Tony was the first to make his League debut (v. Middlesbrough in
April 1961); Barry followed three-and-a-half years later (v. Liverpool in
October 1964).

WAINWRIGHT, Harold
Outside-right/inside-forward: 2 apps.
Born: Sheffield, 1899.
Career: Highfields FC, Port Vale (amateur, December 1919, professional, January 1920), Highfields FC (May 1920), Doncaster Rovers (August 1920), Brodsworth Main (1922), Frickley Colliery (1923), BLADES (October 1924), Boston Town (July 1926), Scunthorpe & Lindsey United (July 1927), Newark Town.
Harry Wainwright, a reserve team player, made his League debut for United in April 1925, taking over from Albert Partridge for the away game with Bolton Wanderers, following his transfer from Frickley Colliery. He made only six League appearances throughout his career, four with Port Vale.

WALDOCK, Ronald
Inside-forward: 60 apps. 10 goals
Born: Heanor, Derbyshire, 6 December 1932
Career: Loscoe Youth Club, Coventry City (February 1950), BLADES (£6,000, May 1954), Scunthorpe United (February 1957), Plymouth Argyle (September 1959), Middlesbrough (January 1960), Gillingham (October 1961-May 1964).
Ronnie Waldock served with six clubs in ten years and in that time he scored 90 goals in 294 League games (45 in 97 for Scunthorpe being his best overall return), being the 'Iron's leading marksmen in 1957-58 when they won the Third Division (North) championship. His scoring record cannot lightly be dismissed, for he was a workhorse who enjoy a challenge and did very well during a very interesting career which saw him travel all over the country!

WALKER, Andrew Francis
Striker: 35+22 apps. 22 goals
Born: Glasgow, 6 April 1965
Career: Partick Thistle (juniors), Toronto Blizzard/NASL (summer 1983), Ballieston Juniors (September 1983), Motherwell (July 1984), Celtic (£350,000, July 1987), Newcastle United (on loan, September 1991), Bolton Wanderers (£160,000, February 1992), Celtic (£550,000, June 1994), BLADES (£500,000, February 1996), Ayr United (October 1997).
Scottish international Andy Walker was a natural goalscorer, fast, smart and pacy. He partnered Gareth Taylor in the Blades' attack and had a fine 1996-97 season, when he netted 14 senior goals. Capped three times at senior level, Walker also represented his country at Under-21 level. He won the Scottish League Division One title with Motherwell in 1965 and Celtic in 1988, was a Scottish Cup winner, also in 1988 (a finalists in 1990) and was a member of Celtic's beaten 1995 League Cup Final team, while also helping Bolton gain promotion to the Premiership in 1993 when he scored 33 goals. His record with Celtic was excellent: 69 goals in 195 matches.

WALLACE, Alexander
Inside-right/outside-left: 33 apps. 11 goals
Born: Scotland, circa 1868
Career: Abercorn FC, BLADES (November 1891), Middlesbrough Ironopolis (May 1893).
Alex Wallace was a resourceful player who, when in possession of the ball, was fast over the ground and difficult to tackle. He gave the Blades excellent service for eighteen months, scoring in the club's first-ever League game v. Lincoln City in September 1892 when he partnered Fred Davies on the left-wing.

WALLER, George
Left-half/outside-left: 11 apps. 2 goals
Born: Sheffield, 3 December 1863. Died: 1937
Career: Sheffield junior/intermediate football, Wednesday (1890), Middlesbrough (1890), BLADES (player/reserve-team coach, May 1892, first team trainer 1896, holding office until 1931).
Signed initially as reserve team coach, George Waller was enticed back to first team duty by the Blades when injuries and illness depleted the squad. During his 39-year association with the club, Waller saw the Blades win the League title (1898) and lift the FA Cup on four occasions (1899, 1902, 1915 and 1925).

WALLS, George
Centre-forward: 17 apps. 4 goals
Born: Scotland, circa 1872
Career: Heart of Midlothian (1891), BLADES (May 1896-June 1897)
Signed to partner Harry Hammond in the Blades' attack, George Walls was a strong, mobile attacker who did well initially (scoring on his debut in a friendly v. Lincoln City and later adding a hat-trick in a 7-0 home League win over Blackburn Rovers) before fading.

WALSALL (originally Walsall Town Swifts)
United's playing record against the Saddlers:

Football League

Venue	P	W	D	L	F	A
Home	7	3	2	2	10	5
Away	7	3	3	1	11	9
Totals	14	6	5	3	21	14

FA Cup

	P	W	D	L	F	A
Home	1	1	0	0	2	0

League Cup

	P	W	D	L	F	A
Home	1	1	0	0	2	1
Away	1	0	0	1	1	2
Totals	2	1	0	1	3	3

Birmingham Cup

	P	W	D	L	F	A
Away	1	1	0	0	5	2

Others

	P	W	D	L	F	A
Away	1	0	0	1	0	1

256

Walsall Swifts (established in 1877) and Walsall Town (1879) joined forces in 1888 to become Walsall Town Swifts, changing to Walsall in 1895.

Original members, with United, of the Second Division in 1892 (having played earlier in the Midland Association and Football Alliance) the Saddlers first opposed the Blades on 7 January 1893 at Bramall Lane. They lost 3-0, Harry Hammond (2) and Billy Hendry netting for the home side in front of just 1,000 spectators.

The league was not until November 1980 and with both teams based in the Third Division, they played out a thrilling 4-4 draw at Fellows Park. With the 90 minutes up, the scoreline stood at 3-3. Bu then Bob Hatton netted his second goal to give the Blades the lead but straight from the kick-off Walsall equalised.

The return fixture, on the last day of the League programme (played in front of a 16,000 crowd on 2 May 1981) saw both teams on the fringe of relegation. United needed a point to stay up, Walsall had to win to retain their status. With five minutes to go, the scoresheet blank, Don Penn tucked away a penalty to give the visitors to the lead. Stunned but not down, the Blades hit back and in the dying minutes they were also awarded a spot-kick. In tense, nervous stadium, Don Givens missed from the spot...Walsall stayed up, United went down to the Fourth Division for the first time in their history.

The last six League meetings have resulted in two wins for each side and two draws.

Ex-Blades player John Barnwell was Walsall's manager in 1989-90. Stewart Houston, ex-Blades, became assistant-manager of Walsall. And among the players who have served both clubs we have Brett Angell, Paul Hall, Mark Hawthorne (United & Saddlers reserve), Nick Henry, David Holdsworth, Roy John, David Kelly, Jeff King, Albert 'Tal' Lewis, Adrian Littlejohn, Marcelo, Derek Pace, Tom Phillipson, Paul Simpson, Gerry Summers, Gus Uhlenbeek, Walter Webster, Gary West and Chris Wilder.

WALSHAW, Lee
Midfielder: 9+1 apps. one goal
Born: Sheffield, 20 January 1967
Career: BLADES (apprentice, April 1983, professional January 1985), Worksop Town (June 1987).
Given his League baptism towards the end of the 1984-85 season, attacking midfielder Lee Walshaw was taken on tour to USA soon afterwards (to gain experience). He battled on in the reserves after that, coming back to score the winning goal in a 3-2 win at home to Leeds in April 1986.

WALTON, Joseph
Left-winger: 62 apps. 6 goals
Born: Lunes, Lancashire, 8 January 1881.
Career: Preston North End (1898), Tottenham Hotspur (May 1903), BLADES (April 1909), Stalybridge Celtic (July 1911-13). A tricky, mobile right-winger, Joe Walton was near to winning international honours, playing in three trial matches for England before joining the Blades ...after turning down the maximum wage offer made to him by Spurs. He joined Stalybridge for their first season as a professional club in the Lancashire Combination. He scored 51 goals in 218 first team matches for Spurs after netting just four times in 25 League outings during his five years at Deepdale.

257

WARBOYS, Alan
Forward: 7 apps.
Born: Goldthorpe, near Rotherham, Yorkshire, 18 April 1949
Career: Doncaster Rovers (apprentice, April 1965, professional April 1967), Sheffield Wednesday (£12,000, June 1968), Cardiff City (£42,000, December 1970), BLADES (£20,000 plus players, September 1972), Bristol Rovers (£35,000, March 1973), Fulham (£25,000, February 1977), Hull City (£20,000, September 1977), Doncaster Rovers (July 1979, retired through injury, May 1982).
Alan Warboys never settled at Bramall Lane, but either side his brief association with the Blades he performed exceedingly well as a swash-buckling, burly, all-action centre-forward, having the skill to beat his opponent and his fierce competitiveness made his a huge favourite with the supporters, certainly at Eastville and later when he returned to Belle Vue for a second spell. He formed a highly successful strike-partnership at Bristol Rovers with Bruce Bannister (the pair being dubbed 'Smash 'n' Grab' as the Pirates won promotion to the Second Division in 1974. He experienced life in all four Divisions and during his 17 years in League football he netted 137 goals in 479 appearances, including a fourtimer for Rovers in a televised and a hat-trick in the first nine minutes for Cardiff v. Carlisle United in March 1971...having stepped into John Toshack's boots at Ninian Park.

WARD, Mark Steven
Striker: 0+2 apps.
Born: Sheffield, 27 January 1982
Career: Sheffield Colleges, BLADES (July 2000), Stocksbridge Park Steels FC (August 2002).
Honoured by England as a schoolboy, Mark Ward was always on the fringe of first team football during his second and ultimately last season at Bramall Lane.

WARD, Mitchum David
Right-back/midfielder: 157+25 apps. 16 goals
Born: Sheffield, 19 June 1971
Career: BLADES (YTS, June 1987, professional July 1989), Crewe Alexandra (on loan, November 1990), Everton (£850,000, November 1997), Barnsley (£20,000, July 2000), Lincoln City (March 2003).
Right-sided versatile midfield ball-winner 'Mitch' Ward was one of the first names on the manager's team-sheet at Bramall Lane. A totally committed player, he grafted hard and long and never shirked a tackle, taking responsibility wherever possible. A great competitor, Ward was seriously injured towards the end of the 1994-95 season when he suffered a punctured lung and a broken rib playing for the Blades against Notts County. He also struggled with ankle injuries during his spell at Goodison Park (making only 29 first team appearances during his time on Merseyside).

WARHURST, Roy

Inside-left/left-half: 29 apps. 5 goals
Born: Handsworth, Sheffield, 18 September 1926.
Career: Atlas & Norfolk FC, Huddersfield Town (amateur 1943), BLADES (amateur, May 1944, professional, September 1944), Birmingham City (£8,000, March 1950), Manchester City (£10,000, June 1957), Crewe Alexandra (March 1959), Oldham Athletic (August 1960), Banbury Spencer (August 1961). Retired in May 1964.
Roy Warhurst was a stocky wing-half with a bone-crunching tackle and it is hard to believe that such a fine 'destroying' player could have begun his career as a winger. His hard-grafting style proved the ideal complement to the more artistic skills of Len Boyd at Birmingham, with whom he helped win the Second Division title in 1955 and reach the FA Cup Final a year later. Unpopular with opposition fans, he was appointed captain on his arrival at Oldham having amassed in excess of 300 League appearances prior to that, including 216 for Blues, 40 for Manchester City and 51 for Crewe. Possibly one who got away as far as the Blades were concerned, Warhurst later became a scrap-metal dealer.

WARREN, Henry

Centre/left-half: 2 apps.
Born: Newhall, spring 1902. Died: 1968
Career: Gresley Rovers, Blackpool (September 1924), Exeter City (July 1927), Merthyr Town (April 1928), BLADES (August 1929), Notts County (December 1929), Folkestone (1930-31).
Harry Warren made his first team debut for the Blades at centre-half in September 1929 but was given a testing time by the Leicester City centre-forward Arthur Chandler who scored a hat-trick for the Foxes in a 3-3 draw. He struggled after that and left 'the Lane' for Meadow Lane in 1930.

WARTIME FOOTBALL

This is United's playing record (first team level) during the two World War periods (friendlies & the FA Cup-ties from 1946 not included, but the three 1939 void League games are).
Key:
MS = Midland Section of the Principal Tournament; MG = Midland Group of Subsidiary Tournament.
FL2 = League Division 2 (void matches); REM = Regional East Midlands Division; LWC = League War Cup; NRL = North Regional League; LN1 = League North 1st competition; LN2 = League North 2nd competition; FLN = Football League North.

Seasons	P	W	D	L	F	A	Pts	Post.
1915-16 (MS)	26	12	7	7	51	36	31	2nd
1915-16 (MG)	10	4	3	3	17	11	11	2nd
1916-17 (MS)	30	11	7	12	43	47	29	10th
1916-17 (MG)	6	4	0	2	12	7	8	1st
1917-18 (MS)	28	20	1	7	66	27	41	2nd
1917-18 (MG)	6	2	1	3	9	12	5	3rd
1918-19 (MS)	30	12	6	12	56	47	30	8th
1918-19 (MG)	6	5	1	0	14	3	11	1st
Totals	142	70	26	46	268	190	166	-
1939-40 (FL2)	3	2	1	0	3	1	5	2nd
1939-40 (REM)	20	12	1	7	46	34	25	3rd
1939-40 (LWC)	4	2	1	1	4	3	-	Rd 2
1940-41 (NRL)	26	6	6	13	44	60	-	28th
1940-41 (LWC)	8	4	1	3	14	11	-	Rd 4
1941-42 (LN1)	18	7	4	7	39	38	18	18th
1941-42 (LN2)	17	8	4	5	39	33	20	-
1942-43 (LN1)	18	7	6	5	45	35	20	20th
1942-43 (LN2)	19	8	4	7	43	20	20	23rd
1943-44 (LN1)	18	8	5	5	30	26	21	14th
1943-44 (LN2)	21	11	2	8	53	35	24	18th
1944-45 (LN1)	18	6	3	9	27	25	15	36th
1944-45 (LN2)	24	9	3	12	56	48	21	30th
1945-6 (FLN)	42	27	6	9	112	62	60	1st
Totals	255	117	47	91	555	453	249	-
Combined Totals	397	187	73	137	843	643	415	-

War Cry
WW1
* The Blades finished runners-up to Nottingham Forest in the Principal Tournament (Midland Section) in 1915-16, gaining 31 points from their 26 matches.
* The following season they won the Subsidiary Competition (Midland Section), beating off the challenge of three other clubs.
* Runners-up of the Principal Tournament again in 1917-18 (behind Leeds City) the Blades won 20 of their 28 matches.
* A home game v. Chesterfield on Boxing Day 1916 could not be played on the soccer pitch at Bramall Lane and was therefore transferred across to the cricket field. United won 4-1 before 9,000 fans.
* David Mercer scored all of Hull City's goals in a 6-1 scoreline against the Blades in a WW1 game in January 1919, which had to be abandoned after an hour's play due to fading light. For this game the Blades had to borrow kit from the Tigers.
* David Mercer, later to play for the Blades, netted a double hat-trick (six goals) against United (whose players were all wearing borrowed boots) in January 1919 before the game was abandoned with the scoreline standing at 6-1.
* United scored four goals in the last 29 minutes to beat Leicester Fosse 6-2 in a WW1 game in February 1918.

* The Blades ended their WW1 activities by becoming champions of the Subsidiary Competition in 1918-19, winning five and drawing one of their six matches.
* United had to call on the services of a spectator to make up their team away at Leeds City in December 1916.
* Due to the late arrival of the team (owing to train delays) only 60 minutes play was deemed possible when the Blades visited Grimsby Town in December 1916 (they lost the game 2-0).
* Harold Pantling became the first United player to get sent-off twice in the same season (1917-18).
* United beat Barnsley 8-0 (home) in January 1919 ...their best result in WW1.
* Their heaviest defeat was a 7-3 drubbing at Lincoln in September 1915.

WW2
* United's three Division One games played at the start of the ill-fated 1939-40 season resulted a 2-1 win at home to Liverpool, a 1-0 win at Leeds and a 0-0 draw at Preston. All three were declared void but for the record purposes they are listed in the A-Z.
* In their first season of WW2 football, United finished third in the Football League (East Midlands Division), Chesterfield were declared champions.
* After that the Blades struggled to a degree throughout the hostilities - although they did reach the semi-final of the League North Cup (beaten by Aston Villa). They did, however, end on a high by becoming champions of the Football League (North) in season 1945-46. They won 27, drew six and lost nine of their 42 matches, had a goal-average of 112-62 and totalled 60 points, five more than second-placed Everton.
* In December 1940 Bramall Lane was severely damaged in a bombing blitz and from immediate effect all Blades' home fixtures were abandoned and transferred to Hillsborough with one being played at Millmoor. Football returned to Bramall Lane in September 1941.
* United's best wins in Wartime football were both against Lincoln City - 9-0 (h) in December 1941 and 10-2 (h) in January 1945. Their heaviest defeat came at Sheffield Wednesday in February 1943 when they lost 8-2.
* The biggest attendance for a United Wartime game was that of 50,859 for the FA Cup 4th round 2nd leg clash at home to Stoke City in January 1946 (won 3-2 - but out 4-3 on aggregate)

NB: During the two wartime periods United used several guest players (see GUEST PLAYERS) while a handful of professionals sadly were killed whilst serving their country.

FACT FILE
United's leading appearance-makers & goalscorers in wartime football:

WW1
Appearances: Albert Sturgess 129, George Utley 118, Bill Brelsford 117, Harold Pantling 112.
Goalscorers: Joe Kitchen 57, Harry Johnson 25, Oliver Tummon 23.

WW2
Appearances: Harry Latham 208, Walter Rickett 200, Jack Pickering 182, Albert Nightingale 151, Ernest Jackson 140, Bill Archer 134, Fred White 127, Fred Furniss 108, Jack Smith 107.
Goalscorers: Jack Pickering 74, Albert Nightingale 71, Charlie Thompson 67, Walter Rickett 56, Colin Collindridge 37, Harold Barton 26.

WATFORD

United's playing record against the Hornets:

Football League

Venue	P	W	D	L	F	A
Home	9	4	2	3	16	8
Away	9	3	3	3	11	11
Totals	18	7	5	6	27	19

FA Cup

	P	W	D	L	F	A
Home	2	1	1	0	4	3
Away	4	3	0	1	4	6
Totals	6	4	1	1	8	9

League Cup

	P	W	D	L	F	A
Home	1	1	0	0	4	0
Away	1	0	1	0	1	1
Totals	2	1	1	0	5	1

Watford FC emerged in 1898 (after amalgamating with Watford St Mary's). Playing at Cassio Road, the Hornets were elected to the Football League in 1920 and after steady progress eventually reached the top flight, playing in the 1984 FA Cup Final and appearing in Europe (with Graham Taylor as manager and Elton John as Chairman).
United did not meet Watford until 1960 when they despatched then 3-2 in a 5th round FA Cup-tie at Bramall Lane, Derek Pace netting a hat-trick.
The first League games followed in season 1969-70 (Division 2) when United won 2-1 at Vicarage Road (Tony Currie snatching a second-half winner) before drawing 1-1 at 'the Lane.'
The following season United clinched promotion to the First Division with a 3-0 win at Bramall Lane. However, things might have been different if Watford's Stewart Scullion had scored early on with a header that struck the bar. So impressed was the Blades' manager John Harris that within a week he had signed Scullion; he later added two other Hornets to his nest, Keith Eddy and Colin Franks, the latter signing for the unusual fee of £55,555. Earlier Harris had recruited Currie from Watford and in 1973 former Watford boss Ken Furphy took over from Harris at 'the Lane.' Since then Dave Bassett has also had spells as manager at both clubs.
The Hornets doubled up over the Blades in 2002-03, winning 2-1 at Bramall Lane and 2-0 at Vicarage Road...the only team to take six points off Neil Warnock's side that season.
Luther Blissett scored four goals in Watford's 5-0 drubbing of United in a 3rd round FA Cup-tie at Vicarage Road in January 1985.

259

United dumped the Hornets out of the League Cup in 1997-98 with a 5-1 aggregate victory.

Dave Bassett (a Watford junior player) and Ken Furphy managed both clubs while Ray Lewington was a United player and later Hornets' manager. Of the many players who have been associated with the clubs we have: Tony Agana, Wayne Allison, Billy Biggar, Joe Brooks, Tony Currie, Keith Eddy, Jack English, Willie Falconer, Colin Franks, Paul Furlong, Terry Garbett, Roland Gray (Blades reserve), Barry Hartle, Mick Henderson, Billy Hendry, Peter Hetherston, Glyn Hodges, David Holdsworth, Ted Hufton, Andy Kennedy, Peter Kyle, Martin Kuhl, John L Jones, Tommy Mooney, Mark Morris, Robert Page, Harold Pantling, Cliff Powell, Mel Rees, Wilf Rostron, Harry Savage, Stewart Scullion, Oliver Tummon and Keith Waugh (two complete teams!)

WATNEY CUP

United's record in the Watney Cup:

Venue	P	W	D	L	F	A
Away	5	3	1	1	13	1

United participated in this pre-season tournament on two separate occasions.

In 1970-71, after thrashing Aldershot 6-0 away in front of more than 9,500 fans, the Blades lost 1-0 away to Derby County in the semi-final when the attendance topped 25,000.

In 1972-73, after away wins at Notts County 3-0 and Peterborough United 4-0 (despite Tony Currie being sent-off) the Blades met Bristol Rovers in the Final at the Eastville Stadium. A crowd of 19,768 packed into the ground to witness the 0-0 draw, Rovers going on to win an exciting penalty shoot-out 7-6 to take the trophy. Unfortunately for the Blades, Ted Hemsley had his spot-kick saved.

WATSON, Arthur

Inside-forward/winger: 127 apps. 43 goals
Born: Ecclesfield, Sheffield, February 1868. Died: 1931
Career: St George's County School (Sheffield), Ecclesfield FC, Rotherham Swifts, BLADES (March 1890), West Bromwich Albion (1896-98).

Arthur Watson enjoyed 'fast dribbling' whether down the wing of through the centre; he possessed a long raking stride, powerful right-foot shot and whipped over dangerous centres, high or low. He was also able to fire in a 'screw shot' using the toe-end of his boot. He made his debut for the Blades towards the end of the 1889-90 season (in a friendly against Doncaster Rovers). He appeared on 15 League games in United's first League season of 1892-93, helping the team gain promotion to the top flight.

WATT-SMITH, Donald S

Forward: 17 'other' apps. 7 goals
Born: Yorkshire, July 1920
Career: Yorkshire Amateurs, BLADES (March 1940-April 1944), Yorkshire Amateurs.

An amateur player, Don Watt-Smith played for the Blades in five of the seven WW2 seasons, having his best campaign in 1942-43 when he scored three times in 12 League North & Cup encounters, all of them against Grimsby Town (2 games).

WAUGH, James

Centre-half: 143 apps. 3 goals
Born: Chopwell, 12 August 1898
Career: Chopwell Institute, BLADES (April 1921), Darlington (January 1927-May 1933).

Jimmy Waugh was a tireless competitor, a strong tackler, who grew in confidence after he was introduced to the first team following the withdrawal of Jim McCourt due to illness. Utterly reliable - until his lack of pace was exposed when the offside law changed - he unfortunately missed the 1925 FA Cup Final. He made 236 League appearances for Darlington (10 goals scored) in his six-and-a-half years at the Feethams.

WAUGH, Keith

Goalkeeper: 121 apps.
Born: Sunderland, 27 October 1956
Career: Sunderland (apprentice, April 1973, professional July 1974), Peterborough United (free transfer, July 1976), BLADES (£90,000, August 1981), Cambridge United (on loan, November 1984), Bristol City (on loan, December 1984, signed permanently, on a free transfer, July 1985), Coventry City (free, August 1989), Watford (free, January 1991-May 1992).

Goalkeeper Keith Waugh missed only one game when United won the Fourth Division title in 1982 and played in 16 when promotion was gained to the Second Division two years later. A fine shot-stopper, he appeared in well over 225 games for Peterborough before his transfer and after leaving Bramall Lane he went on to play in 224 senior games for Bristol City

WEATHER

* The hottest day ever recorded in England when Football League games were being staged was on 1 September 1906. The temperature in the shade was given as 75 degrees while at pitch level. It was in the low 90s. That afternoon United beat Derby County 2-0 at home.
* In June 1975 when on tour in New Zealand, the temperatures topped 100 degrees F.
* On 31 May 1985 when the Blades were playing Dallas Tornadoes in the USA, the temperature out in the centre of the pitch topped 93 degrees F.
* In mid-November 1894, Aston Villa's ground was completely water-logged but the referee ordered the League game against United to go on. Players on both sides were cold and soaked and at one point United were down to seven men while other players went off to change their shirts as well as taking hot drinks. Even a bottle of brandy was passed around (on the pitch!). Three members of the Villa team - Jack Devey, Charlie Athersmith and goalkeeper Tom Wilkes, both borrowed a mackintosh and umbrellas respectively from the fans. Villa eventually won 5-0.
* Two severe winters - 1947 and 1963 - caused the abandoned and/or postponement of so many matches involving Sheffield United (and of course other clubs).
* The temperature dropped to five degrees below freezing at Highbury when United lost 1-0 to Arsenal in a League game there on 31 January 1976. The fans knew something as only 14,477 turned out.
* On 19 January 1963, a pitiful Molineux crowd of less than 10,500 saw the Blades draw 0-0 with Wolves on a pitch covered in ice and snow with freezing winds gusting across the ground. The temperature was minus six and this was one of only five League games played that winter's day.
* United finished their First Division game at Blackburn on 29 October 1932 with only eight players - three having gone off (complaining of cold) due to the weather (torrential rain and driving wind). Rovers won 3-0.

WEBER, Nicolas

Left-back/midfielder: 5+1 apps.

Born: Metz, France 28 October 1970

Career: INF Vichy, Sochaux, Chateauroux, Le Havre (all in France), BLADES (on loan, August-November 2000), FC Grenoble/ France (June 2001).

A regular in the French First Division side, Le Havre, left-sided player Nicolas Weber joined the Blades on a three-month loan period following relegation at the end of the 1999-2000 campaign. He initially took over from Wayne Quinn, but was injured and duly returned to Le Havre.

WEBSTER, Simon Paul

Defender: 43+13 apps. 3 goals

Born: Hinckley, 20 January 1964

Career: Tottenham Hotspur (apprentice, April 1980, professional December 1981), Exeter City (on loan, November 1983), Huddersfield Town (£15,000, February 1985), BLADES (March 1988), Charlton Athletic (£50,000, August 1990), West Ham United (£525,000, June 1993), Oldham Athletic (on loan, March 1995).

Simon Webster fractured his leg playing against Mansfield in a 1st round FA Cup-tie at Field Mill on 19 November 1988 and was out of action for twelve months. Sadly he was later out for almost two years after suffering another broken leg in 1992. Despite his set-backs, Webster was still a durable defender, always totally committed who twice helped the Blades gain promotion, first from Division Three in 1989 (12 games played) and secondly from Division Two a year later (20 outings). He made over 375 senior appearances during his career.

WEBSTER, Walter George

Right-back: 36 apps.

Born: West Bromwich, 22 May 1895. Died: Sheffield, 15 September 1960.

Career: Kingsbury Colliery (near Tamworth), Walsall (1921), Lincoln City (June 1925), BLADES (£1,650, October 1925), Scunthorpe United (August 1930), Torquay United (August 1931), Rochdale (July 1933), Stalybridge Celtic (August 1934-35).

A well-built right-back, Walter Webster won junior international honours for the Birmingham FA against Scotland in April 1922 and after joining Lincoln and being made captain he was reported as being 'one of the finest backs in the Northern Section,' and a 'very classy type of full-back.' When he joined the Blades the transfer fee involved was a record for the 'Imps'. He returned to Sheffield on his retirement in 1935 and lived and worked there until his death.

WEIGHT

It is believed that goalkeeper Bill 'Fatty' Foulke was 25st 2lbs when he played for Bradford City in 1906-07. He may well have tipped the scales at 20st during his time with the Blades.

WELSH CONNECTION

United first ventured into Wales to play football in April 1900 when they defeated a South Wales XI 2-0 in a friendly in Cardiff.

The first time United played a League game in Wales was when they visited Ninian Park to take on Cardiff City in April 1922. A crowd of 15,000 saw the 1-1 draw.

The first time the Blades entertained a Welsh club at Bramall Lane was on 20 October 1894 when Chirk were defeated 5-1 in a friendly.

WEMBLEY STADIUM

United's playing record at the Empire Stadium:

Competition	P	W	D	L	F	A
FA Cup Finals	2	1	0	1	1	1
FA Cup SF	1	0	0	1	1	2
Play-off	1	0	0	1	0	1
Totals	4	1	0	3	2	4

Wembley Fact File

The Blades played three FA Cup matches at Wembley - beating Cardiff City 1-0 in the 1925 Final, losing by the same score to Arsenal in the 1936 Final and then going down to arch-rivals Sheffield Wednesday 2-1 in the 1993 semi-final (after extra-time).

In 1997, Crystal Palace beat United 1-0 in the First Division Play-off Final.

WEST, Gary

Defender: 89 apps. one goal

Born: Scunthorpe, 25 August 1964

Career: BLADES (apprentice, July 1980, professional August 1982), Lincoln City (£35,000, August 1985), Gillingham (£50,000, June 1987), Port Vale (£70,000, February 1989), Gillingham (on loan, November 1990), Lincoln City (on loan, January 1991, signed for £25,000), Walsall (on loan, September-November 1992), Boston United (March-May 1993), King's Lynn (season 1993-94), Gainsborough Trinity (August 1994-May 1995).

Gary West, an England Youth international, played in 24 games when the Blades were promoted from the Third Division in 1984. A confident player with a good attitude, he held his place in the first team until his departure in 1985. He made a total of 258 League appearances before drifting out of the competition in 1993.

261

WEST BROMWICH ALBION

United's playing record against the Baggies:

Football League

Venue	P	W	D	L	F	A
Home	49	23	14	12	77	47
Away	49	15	9	25	55	85
Totals	98	38	23	37	132	132

FA Cup

Venue	P	W	D	L	F	A
Home	3	1	2	0	4	2
Away	3	0	0	3	3	13
Totals	6	1	2	3	7	15

League Cup

Venue	P	W	D	L	F	A
Away	1	0	0	1	1	2

Others

Venue	P	W	D	L	F	A
Home	1	0	1	0	1	1
Away	1	0	0	1	0	1
Totals	2	0	1	1	1	2

West Bromwich Albion, one of the founder members of the Football League, started out as West Bromwich Strollers in 1878 (formed by a group of employees of Salter's Spring Works in the town who enjoyed a game of cricket in the summer). They changed their name to Albion in 1880, were founder members of the Football League in 1888 (after winning the FA Cup), became known as the Throstles on moving to their present ground at The Hawthorns in 1900 and acquired the nickname the 'Baggies' in 1905.

Matches between Albion and the Blades have been remarkably even over a period of 109 years. United have won 38 of the 98 'League' fixtures (Albion 37) while both teams have scored 132 goals. The Baggies have the upper hand regarding Cup meetings.

United first met Albion in 1893-94 (Division 1). They lost 2-0 at home and then succumbed to a 3-1 defeat at the Midlanders' sloping Stoney Lane ground.

The following season the teams opposed each other for the first time in the FA Cup, and again Albion came out on top, winning a 2nd round replay 2-1 after a 1-1 draw at 'the Lane.'

When Albion won the League championship in 1919-20 (scoring 104 goals) united were the only team to complete the double over them, winning 2-0 at The Hawthorns in February (Alf Jeffrey scoring twice) and 1-0 in front of 40,000 fans at 'the Lane' a week later.

A record crowd of 57,197 saw United beat Albion 2-0 at 'the Lane' in the 4th round of the FA Cup in March 1925 - on the way to lifting the trophy.

Albion themselves reached the 1935 FA Cup Final and en-route they beat the Blades 7-1 in a 4th round tie at The Hawthorns with future United player Teddy Sandford scoring twice.

A crowd of 55,847 saw the 1-1 draw between the Blades and Albion in a 5th round FA Cup-tie at Bramall Lane...United's biggest for 22 years.

The replay, which the Baggies won 4-1 despite losing right-winger Frank Griffin with a broken leg, attracted 57,503 spectators.

United's best League victory over Albion was claimed as recently as 2000 when they stormed to a 6-0 victory at Bramall Lane (Marcus Bent netting a hat-trick as the Baggies struggled to avoid the drop). A century earlier (in 1898-99) the Blades had won 5-0 with George Hedley scoring twice.

United have suffered two 4-0 defeats on Albion territory - in 1922-23 and 1987-88. In fact, they lost six consecutive League matches at The Hawthorns between 1921 and 1927 while during the same period they won five on the trot at home.

In a remarkable match at Bramall Lane in March 2002, three United players were sent-off - goalkeeper Simon Tracey, early on for hand-ball outside his area, and then substitutes Patrick Suffo and Georges Santos. United then went down to six men after two more had gone off injured. At this juncture (83 minutes) and with Albion, pushing strongly for automatic promotion, holding a comfortable 3-0 lead, the referee. Eddie Wolstenholme abandoned the match. There were suggestions that a replay could take place but in the event, the Football League decided to allow the score to stand and duly awarded the three points to Albion who went on to reach the Premiership.

Players with both clubs include Brett Angell, Paul Beesley, Ian Benjamin, Meynell Burgin, Franz Carr, Eddie Colquhoun, Andy Dibble (United reserve), Martin Dickinson, Paul Hall, Ian Hamilton, Billy Hendry, Ken McNaught, Shaun Murphy, Shane Nicholson, Paul Peschisolido, Mel Rees, Teddy Sandford, Georges Santos, Gerry Summers, James Thomas, Imre Varadi, Arthur Watson and Paul A Williams. Jimmy Hagan played for the Blades and managed Albion (1964-67) and Arthur Rowley played for Albion and later managed the Blades, while ex-United midfielder Dennis Mortimer was Albion's assistant-manager/coach. Andy Goran, Adrian Littlejohn and Martin Pike all started their careers at The Hawthorns while Lee Hughes and Reg Ryan had trials at 'the Lane' before later assisting the Baggies. John Deehan (Albion player, United coach etc.) and Stewart Evans have also been associated with both clubs.

WEST HAM UNITED

United's playing record against the Hammers:

Premier League

Venue	P	W	D	L	F	A
Home	1	1	0	0	3	2
Away	1	0	1	0	0	0
Totals	2	1	1	0	3	2

Football League

Venue	P	W	D	L	F	A
Home	35	20	7	8	76	46
Away	35	10	8	17	44	72
Totals	70	30	15	25	120	118

FA Cup

Venue	P	W	D	L	F	A
Home	1	1	0	0	4	2
Away	3	1	1	1	2	5
Totals	4	2	1	1	6	7

League Cup

Venue	P	W	D	L	F	A
Home	1	0	0	1	0	2
Away	1	0	0	1	0	5
Totals	2	0	0	2	0	7

Formed in 1895 as Thames Ironworks, the club adopted its present title (West Ham United) in 1900 and played in the Southern League before joining the Second Division straight after WW1. A strong Southern League side, the Hammers did not enter the Football League until 1919...four years later they contested the first Wembley Cup Final, losing 2-0 to Bolton Wanderers.

United first opposed the Hammers at League level in season 1923-24, the Londoners winning 2-0 at Bramall Lane on New Year's Day. The return match at The Boleyn Ground (Upton Park) in April resulted in a 2-2 draw, Harry Johnson and Billy Gillespie scoring first-half goals for the Blades.

The following season the Blades were thrashed 6-2 at Upton Park, this result vying with the 5-0 reverse at the same venue in 1989-90 as their worst ever against the Hammers.

At 'the Lane' United can reflect on three 'sixes'...wins of 6-0 in 1931-32 (Bobby Barclay scoring a hat-trick), 6-1 in 1951-52 (Derek Hawksworth grabbed a treble this time) and 6-2 in 1927-28 when Harry Johnson equalled Harry Hammond's club record by netting five times in a League game).

United's best win at West Ham came in September 1950 when they returned registered a 5-3 victory. There were three penalties and two own-goals scored in this Second Division fixture. The Blades who were behind three times, had full-back Fred Furniss to thank for their efforts. He belted in two spot-kicks. The Blades also struck the woodwork three times while the Hammers' right-back Devlin conceded two own-goals. Jimmy Hagan netted United's other goal.

A crowd of 32,403 saw United beat West Ham 3-1 at home in April 1953 to clinch promotion to the First Division.

Joe Shaw played his last game for the Blades in a 4-0 League defeat at West Ham in February 1966.

After a 0-0 stalemate at Upton Park, there was a five-goal thriller in the Premiership season at 'the Lane' where the Blades came back from two-down to win 3-2, thus picking up three priceless points in a vain attempt to stave off relegation.

On 14 October 1989, the Hammers plundered an extraordinary 2-0 win at Bramall Lane. United's supremacy was so comprehensive they forced 28 corners to West Ham's one...surely a record of sorts!

In the FA Cup, all ties have been post WW2. In 1952 the Blades won a 4th round replay 4-2 at 'the Lane' (Hawksworth scored twice) after a 0-0 draw; in 1968 they won a 5th round encounter at Upton Park by 2-1 and in 1987 the Hammers cruised into the 5th round with a 4-0 win in London.

The Blades were well and truly blunted by the Hammers in a League Cup-tie at Upton Park in 1971-72 - losing 5-0...their heaviest defeat in the competition to date.

Walter 'Cocky' Bennett, John Ball, Billy Barnes, Billy Biggar, Franz Carr, Joe Cockroft, Mervyn Day, Jim Holmes, Ted Hufton, Don Hutchinson, Alex Kay, David Kelly, Peter Kyle, Alf Leafe, Ken McKay, Fred Milnes, Martin Peters (also Blades manager), Jimmy Simmons, Percy Thorpe and Simon Webster are among then players who have been associated with both clubs. Lou Macari managed the Hammers and was later a scout for the Blades.

WHARNCLIFFE CHARITY CUP
United played for this local Cup on five occasions with there first team: 1889-94 inclusive.
Offering a reserve team for affairs in many later years.
Their full record in the competition was:

Venue	P	W	D	L	F	A
Home	1	1	0	0	1	0
Away	5	2	1	2	5	4
Totals	6	3	1	2	6	4

United were defeated 2-1 in the semi-final at Staveley in 1890; lost at the same stage to Wednesday, also away, by 2-1 in 1891; beat Attercliffe 2-0 to win the trophy in 1892; drew 0-0 at Wednesday to share the prize in 1893 and defeated Wednesday 1-0 (away) to take the Cup again in 1894.

WHARTON, Arthur
Goalkeeper: 2 apps.
Born in Accra, Ghana, 1865. Died: 1930
Career: Darlington, Preston North End (briefly), Rotherham Town (season 1893-94 season) BLADES (August 1894), Rotherham Town (July 1895), Ashton North End, Stockport County, retiring 1902)
Arthur Wharton was the first black professional footballer to appear in the Football League, doing so for Rotherham in 1893. He made his debut for the Blades against Sunderland (away) on 23 February 1895 when he replaced Bill Foulke in a 2-0 defeat. Basically a reserve at Bramall Lane for a season-and-a-half, he was also an AAA 100 yards sprint champion. He made a total of 34 League appearances for Rotherham.

WHARTON, Clarence Norman
Goalkeeper: 77 apps.
Born: Askam-in-Furness, Cumbria, 28 July 1903. Died: Askam-in-Furness, 13 July: 1961
Career: Askam FC (1919), Barrow (April 1920), Preston North End (May 1925), Barrow (August 1927), BLADES (£750, May 1928), Norwich City (July 1931), Doncaster Rovers (August 1935), York City (August 1936), Leeds United (August 1939-40). He did not player after WW2.
Norman Wharton, an agile and goalkeeper, spent 20 years in football playing in all four Divisions (1, 2, 3S & 3N) while amassing 380 League appearances, 226 after leaving Bramall Lane for Norwich City in Wharton's great joy was to meet a forward who did not know him and who tried to 'rush' through the goal. It was said that the player never tried twice!
* Wharton had seven brothers who all preferred to play Rugby League.

WHELAN, Michael
Outside/inside-right: 14 apps. one goal
Born: London, circa 1873
Career: Chesham, Millwall Athletic (August 1895), BLADES (July 1898), Bedminster (June 1899).
Signed as cover for the two right-wing positions in the front-line, Micky Whelan made his debut for the Blades on the opening day of the 1898-99 League campaign v. Everton and scored his only goal for the club in a 2-1 home win over Derby County in the November. He helped Millwall win the Southern League title in 1896 (netting 12 goals in 18 outings) and the following season scored five times in 14 games when the London club took the United League championship. He claimed a total of 30 goals in only 89 games for the Lions.

WHITE, David
Forward: 65+12 apps. 14 goals
Born: Manchester, 30 October 1967
Career: Manchester City (apprentice, April 1984, professional, November 1985), Leeds United (£2 million, December 1993), BLADES (November 1995, retired July 1998.).
An England international, capped once at senior level as a Manchester City player v. Spain in 1993, David White also represented his country's Youth, 'B' and Under-21 teams, playing in six games in the latter category. At 6ft 1in tall, he was a strong running forward who preferred the right side of the field. One of the most exciting players to watch when in full flight, his career was unfortunately dogged by injury and as a result he was forced to retire at the early age of 30. He scored 120 goals in 480 senior appearances for his three clubs (96 in 342 outings for Manchester City).

WHITE, Frederick
Goalkeeper: 179 apps.
Born: Wolverhampton, 5 December 1916.
Career: Wolverhampton junior football, Wolverhampton Wanderers (on trial, 1932), Everton (professional, May 1935), BLADES (May 1937), Lincoln City (£200, June 1950), Gainsborough Trinity (May 1951, retired through injury in May 1952), BLADES (reserve team manager, coach, scout, to 1972). He then became a salesman for a building company and at the same time held a scouting position with Leeds United. After that he did more scouting work for Colchester United, Blackburn Rovers, Birmingham City and Oxford United, before quitting football altogether in 1985.
Fred White, who stood well over six feet tall, was a brave and goalkeeper who made his League debut for the Blades against Aston Villa (away) in October 1947, after waiting ten years! He was signed in 1937 but with Jack Smith in such commanding form between the posts, he had to play second fiddle for quite some time, although he did perform regularly during WW2. He returned to Bramall Lane in 1952 and spent the next 20 years on United's staff. He employed as a scout by Jim 'Bald Eagle' Smith at Colchester, Ewood Park, St Andrew's and Oxford.

WHITEHOUSE, Dane
Midfielder: 244+33 apps. 50 goals
Born: Sheffield, 14 October 1970
Career: BLADES (apprentice, April 1987, professional July 1989, retired through injury, April 1999).
Diminutive central midfielder or wide-man Dane Whitehouse, who was always full of running, often providing the vital link between the defence and thee front-line, broke his leg v. Bristol City in a League Cup-tie in October 1992 and was out of action until March 1993.
A further injury problem suffered against Port Vale in November 1997 resulted in him giving up the game at the age of 28. Whitehouse helped the Blades gain promotion to the First Division in 1990 (playing in 12 games).

264

WHITEHURST, William
Striker: 13+10 apps. 2 goals
Born: Thurnscoe, Yorkshire, 10 June 1959.
Career: Retford Town, Bridlington Trinity, Mexborough, Hull City (on trial, signed as a professional for £2,800, October 1980), Newcastle United (£232,500, December 1985), Oxford United (£187,500, October 1986), Reading (£120,000, February 1988), Sunderland (£100,000, September 1988), Hull City (£150,000, December 1988), BLADES (£35,000, February 1990), Stoke City (on loan, November 1990), Doncaster Rovers (free, March 1991), Crewe Alexandra (on loan, season 1991-92), Hatfield Main FC, Kettering Town, Goole Town, Stafford Rangers (1992), Mossley, South China/Hong Kong, Glenntoran (January 1993), Frickley Colliery (later 1993), manager November 1994-May 1995).
As a 19 year-old brick-layer playing for Mexborough, Billy Whitehurst was selected to represent a Midland League XI against Nottingham Forest reserves. He impressed a scout from Hull City who attended the game and as a result was offered a trial at Boothferry Park (in a second team game against Notts County). Two days later (20 October 1980) he signed professional forms for the Tigers, made his Football League debut v. Gillingham five days after that and went on to play competitively until 1992, scoring 77 goals in 388 League matches while serving with nine different clubs. A strong, robust, wholehearted competitor, he helped the Blades win promotion to the top flight in 1990, having earlier twice been a promotion winner with Hull City (from Division 4 in 1983 and Division 3 two years later).

WHITELUM, Clifford

Centre-forward: 43 apps. 14 goals

Born: Farnworth near Bolton, 2 December 1919

Career: Doncaster Co-operative Sports Club (Bentley), Bentley Colliery, Sunderland (professional December 1938), BLADES (£7,000, October, 1947), King's Lynn (August 1949).

Signed to partner Albert Nightingale in the Blades' attack, former grocery assisant Cliff Whitelum was a lithe, elusive, quick-moving and aggressive centre-forward with a powerful shot in both feet. He scored 10 League goals in his first season at 'the Lane' after making his debut for the club in a 0-0 draw at Everton a few days after joining from Sunderland for whom he netted 18 times in 43 First Division outings as well as claiming 136 in 164 WW2 encounters when he was regarded as one of the best strikers in the country. He helped the Wearsiders reach the Final of the Wartime League Cup in 1942 (beaten by Wolves).

WHITHAM, Michael

Full-back/wing-half/centre-half: 160 apps. one goal

Born: Ecclesfield, Sheffield,baptised March 1868. Died: London, 6 May 1924.

Career: Ecclesfield FC, Rotherham Swifts, BLADES (February 1890), Rotherham Town (trainer), Gainsborough Trinity (trainer), Huddersfield Town (trainer), Brentford (trainer until his death at the age of 54).

Mick Whitham was a very capable, strong-tackling, robust defender, a zealot who certainly played a vigorous game. Teak-tough with a splendid shoulder charge, he could perform in midfield (as a wing-half), at the heart of the defence or as an exceedingly competent at full-back (where he began his career). United with Harry Lilley, he was capped at left-half against Ireland in Belfast in March 1892, setting up one of the goals for Notts County's winger Harry Daft in a 2-0 win. He played for the Blades in the last nine friendly games of the 1889-90 season before making his Midland Counties League debut against Burton Wanderers in September 1890. He later lined up in United's first-ever Football League game v. Lincoln City (September 1892). He remained at Bramall Lane until the end of the 1899-99 season when he took over as trainer at Gainsborough..

WIDDOWSON, John Robert

Goalkeeper: 11 apps

Born: Loughborough, 12 September 1941

Career: BLADES (junior, September 1956, professional, July 1959), York City (June 1968), Portsmouth (on loan, November-December 1969). Left Bootham Crescent, May 1970.

A dedicated and loyal reserve goalkeeper, Bob Widdowson spent almost 12 years at Bramall Lane during which time he appeared in just 12 senior games, having to wait until April 1962 before making his First Division debut (at 5-2 defeat Blackpool). He had 30 League outings with York.

WIGAN ATHLETIC

United's playing record against the Latics:

Football League

Venue	P	W	D	L	F	A
Home	4	3	1	0	7	3
Away	4	2	0	2	5	7
Totals	8	5	1	2	12	10

League Cup

Home	1	1	0	0	1	0
Away	1	0	1	0	2	2
Totals	2	1	1	0	3	2

265

Admitted to the Football League in 1978 (in place of Southport) Wigan Athletic are a different club to Wigan Borough who preceded them. Borough, in fact, were forced to resign part way through the 1931-32 campaign, having participated in the Third Division (N) for 10 seasons. Following a public meeting later that year (1932) Wigan Athletic was formed, playing its matches at Borough's old ground, Springfield Park, applying instantly, but unsuccessfully, to join the Football League. It was to take another 46 years before their dream was answered. These days Athletic play at the splendid appointed JJB Stadium, which they share with the town's highly-respected Rugby League club.

The first of the ten meetings between the Blades and the 'Latics' took place in 1981-82 (Division 4). United won 1-0 at Springfield Park (Tony Kenworthy scoring) and repeated the scoreline at Bramall Lane, thanks to Keith Edwards' goal

Ten years later the Blades squeezed past the Latics 3-2 on aggregate in a two-legged League Cup-tie.

Players Peter Beagrie, Paul Beesley, Ian Benjamin, Carl Bradshaw, Bobby Campbell and Paul Rogers have all been associated with both clubs. Steve Bruce was manager at both clubs while Malcolm Barrass and Bruce Rioch played for the Blades and also managed Wigan.

WIGGAN, Trenton Ashton

Winger: 33+5 apps. 5 goals

Born: Jamaica, 29 September 1962

Career: BLADES (apprentice, April 1978, professional, August 1980), Gainsborough Trinity (July 1982).

An England Schoolboy international, Trenton Wiggan made his senior debut for the Blades as a 16 year-old substitute against Doncaster Rovers in a 1st round League Cup game at Belle Vue in August 1979. His League baptism followed in May 1980 in a 4-0 defeat at Grimsby. A positive player, he played in 18 games during the relegation season of 1981-82 but was released by the club following promotion to the Third Division.

WIGLEY, Steven

Winger: 24+8 apps. one goal

Born: Ashton-under-Lyne, 15 October 1961.

Career: Curzon Ashton, Nottingham Forest (March 1981), BLADES (£90,000, October 1985), Birmingham City (player-exchange deal involving Martin Kuhl, March 1987), Portsmouth (£350,000, March 1989), Exeter City (August 1993), Bognor Regis Town (1994), Aldershot Town (March 1995).

A speedy winger, good on the ball, Steve Wigley made over 100 appearances under Brian Clough before transferring to Bramall Lane. He never really settled down at Bramall Lane and later teamed up at Fratton Park with former Blues player, Kevin Dillon. A good crosser of the ball, he did well at Fratton Park where he had the likes of Guy Whittingham and Colin Clarke as his strikers.

WILDER, Christopher John
Right-back/midfielder: 122+10 apps. one goal
Born: Stocksbridge, 23 September 1967
Career: Southampton (apprentice, September 1983, professional September 1985), BLADES (free transfer, August 1986), Walsall (on loan, November 1989), Charlton Athletic (on loan, October 1990 & November), Leyton Orient (on loan, February 1992), Rotherham United (£50,000, July 1992), Notts County £150,000, January 1996), Bradford City (£150,000, March 1997), BLADES (£150,000, March 1998), Northampton Town (on loan, November 1998), Lincoln City (on loan, March 1999), Brighton & Hove Albion (free, July 1999), Halifax Town (free, October 1999), Alfreton Town (free, May 2001), Halifax Town (manager, June 2002).
Reliable defender Chris Wilder was a model of consistency throughout his career despite switching from club to club. He helped the Blades gain promotion to the Second Division in 1989, playing in 29 games and when he came back to 'the Lane' for a second spell he was just as committed as had been first time round. He went on to skipper Rotherham for three years and when he quit Halifax (in 1999) his career in senior football was most impressive: 490 first-class appearances and 15 goals.

WILKES, Harry Theodore
Goalkeeper: 16 apps.
Born: Sedgley near Wolverhampton, 24 June 1907. Died: Derby, 5 April 1984
Career: Sedgley Congregationalists, Wellington Town, Derby County (February 1927), BLADES (March 1934), Rhyl Athletic (July 1935), Heanor Town (August 1936). Did not play after WW2.
Spotted initially by the former Aston Villa and England centre-forward Harry Hampton when he was playing for Wellington, it was thought that goalkeeper Harry Wilkes was too small for his position, but he proved everyone wrong and developed into a first-class custodian, one reporter to writing: 'He gets about his goal like a cat but that is not to confuse him with the dancing dervish type of player. His movements come of purpose backed by anticipation. There is no fuss.' Agile with expert anticipation, he appeared in 220 games for the Rams helping them finish runners-up in the First Division (1930) before winding down his League career at 'the Lane.' Tommy Davison, a former playing colleague at Derby, signed him for Rhyl and he later joined Heanor for £1-a-week.

WILKINSON, Bernard
Centre-half: 397 apps. 14 goals
Born: Thorpe Hesley, Yorkshire, 12 September 1879. Died: Sheffield, 28 May 1949.
Career: Thorpe Hesley RC, Shiregreen FC, BLADES (July 1899), Rotherham Town (June 1913-May 1915). He did not play after WW1 and later became a successful businessman in Sheffield
Relatively small for a defender, Bernard Wilkinson starred for the Blades in their 1902 FA Cup Final victory over Southampton. A part-time player throughout his career, he was a magnificent player, capable of outwitting the trickiest opponent. His tackling was hard but fair, his distribution first-class and his attitude towards the game A1. He was capped by England against Scotland at Hampden Park in April 1904 (performing splendidly in a 1-0 win) and many people thought that he should have received more honours. He spent 14 seasons at Bramall Lane.
* A fine cricketer himself, Bernard turned down a contract with Yorkshire for business reasons but his brother Bill Wilkinson did represent the county at senior level.

WILKINSON, Charles Edward
Left-back: 133 apps.
Born: Medomsley, County Durham, 7 May 1907. Died: Medomsley, winter 1975.
Career: Consett, Leeds United (September 1928), BLADES (£2,000, October 1933), Southampton (July 1938), Bournemouth (player-coach, August 1939-40). Did not play after WW2.
A totally reliable defender, strong in the tackle with a sure kick, Charlie Wilkinson, who was a member of the Blades' 1936 FA Cup Final side (v. Arsenal) was allowed to swap his red and white stripes for another set in 1938 after Albert Cox and Harry Hooper and had bedded themselves in as United's full-back partners. He suffered a serious knee injury in on his second appearance for Saints and had to have a cartilage removed. He never regained full fitness.

WILKINSON, John
Centre-forward: 30 apps. 17 goals
Born: Middlewich, Cheshire, 17 September 1931. Died: Winsford, 10 April 1996.
Career: Middlewich Athletic Rangers, Witton Albion, Arsenal (October 1953), BLADES (£5,000, March 1956), Port Vale (June 1957), Poole Town (briefly), Exeter City (£2,500, October 1959), Wellington Town (1961), Witton Albion (1963), Winsford United (player-coach, 1965).
Jack Wilkinson failed to make in-roads at Highbury but he certainly did well at Bramall Lane, averaging more than a goal every two games for the Blades. He later helped Port Vale win the Fourth Division championship in 1959. In his League career Wilkinson scored 81 goals in 158 appearances including 39 in 80 for the Valiants.

WILLIAMS, Bertram
Inside-forward/outside-right: 125 apps. 18 goals
Born: Merthyr Tydfil, 4 March 1907. Died: Sheffield, 1968.
Career: Georgetown County School (Merthyr), Cyfartha Stars, Merthyr Town, Bristol City (June 1927), BLADES (January 1932-May 1937). Later took employment with a tool company.
A 'brainy' winger, 5ft 6ins tall, 10st 6lbs in weight, 'Bertie' Williams, despite his trickiness, lacked pace and determination who at times could have perform with a little more gusto. When he moved to Bristol he was just a 'slip of a lad' and one director commented: '...that clever little beggar we got from Merthyr. You never saw such a box of tricks, the way he beat his man sometimes would have made a cat laugh.' He made his League debut (for Bristol) in February 1930, won an international cap for Wales in a 7-0 win over Northern Ireland that same year and was top-scorer at Ashton Gate (with 30 goals in 114 games) before moving to Bramall Lane. Unfortunately he was in and out of the Blades' first team for long periods (spending quite some time playing Central League football) but he did get a call-up for the 1936 FA Cup Final showdown with Arsenal, controversially preferred to Don Bird. He left the club after a dispute over terms.

WILLIAMS, Gordon
Centre-forward: 5 apps.
Born: Newcastle, 22 February 1929
Career: Army Service, BLADES (professional, September 1949), Darlington (June 1950-April 1951).
Reserve centre-forward Gordon Williams made his Football League debut for the Blades against QPR (h) in October 1949 when he deputised for Fred Smith in the 1-1 draw. His other four outings followed in quick succession before he returned to the reserves.

266

WILLIAMS, Paul Andrew

Striker: 9+5 apps.

Born: Sheffield, 8 September 1963

Career: Nuneaton Borough, Preston North End (professional, December 1986), Carlisle United (free transfer, July 1987), Newport County (free, August 1987), BLADES (£17,000, March 1988), Hartlepool United (free, October 1989), Stockport County (free, August 1990), West Bromwich Albion (£250,000, March 1991), Coventry City (on loan, October 1992), Stockport County (£25,000, January 1993), Rochdale (November 1993-June 1996), Doncaster Rovers (on loan, March-May 1996).

Tall, lanky striker, 6ft 3ins tall, 14st 6lbs in weight, Paul Williams never really settled down with any of his clubs and spent barely a month with Carlisle. Nevertheless, he was always a willing worker and gained one full cap for Northern Ireland (v. the Faroe Islands) as a West Brom player. He scored 38 goals in 203 competitive games for his 10 League clubs.

* It is thought that Williams was signed by West Brom boss Bobby Gould by mistake... the player who should have joined the Baggies' was Stockport's left-back Paul Richard Williams!

WILLIAMS, Victor

Right-half: 3 apps.

Born: Birmingham, 27 October 1901.

Career: Redditch Excelsior, Redditch Town, BLADES (with Harry Green, April 1925), Redditch Town (August 1927).

Reserve right-half Vic Williams made his League debut against Burnley just four weeks or so before his 25th birthday. He played in two more games against Cardiff City and Manchester United (the latter ending in a 5-0 defeat) and before the end of the season he had returned to Redditch while Harry Green moved to Nottingham Forest.

WILSON, Alfred

Right-back: 43 'other' apps. one goal

Born: Sheffield, 1895.

Career: Sheffield Wednesday (1912), Rotherham Town (April 1919), BLADES (WW1 guest: September 1915-March 1919), Rotherham Town (seasons 1920-21).

After failing to make the first team at Wednesday, Alf Wilson moved to Blues as cover for the regular full-back pairing, but alas he was restricted to only two outings on successive days over Christmas 1919. He did well whilst guesting with the Blades.

WIMBLEDON

United's playing record against the Dons:

Premier League

Venue	P	W	D	L	F	A
Home	3	1	2	0	5	4
Away	3	0	0	3	0	5
Totals	6	1	2	3	5	9

Football League

Home	8	3	1	4	11	7
Away	8	0	4	4	4	19
Total	16	3	5	8	15	26

Formed as Old Centrals FC in 1889 by ex-pupils of Central School, it is still difficult to believe that Wimbledon did not join the Football League until 1977, when Workington were voted out. Yet in their brief 26-season League history, they have spent 14 of them consecutively in the top-flight, including eight in then Premiership...and they won the FA Cup in 1988, beating mighty Liverpool 1-0 in the Final.

Blades' first meetings with the 'Dons' took place in 1979-80 (Division 3). With the London club facing relegation, United won 2-1 at Bramall Lane (John Flood and Pedro Verde the scorers) having earlier played out a 1-1 draw at Plough Lane, which was Wimbledon's home until 1991 when they moved in with Crystal Palace at Selhurst Park.

United's away record against the 'Dons' is abysmal. They have yet to win any of ten games, have been beaten on six occasions and scored only four goals, suffering two 5-0 hammerings (1984-85 & 1985-86). Their best home win is 4-0 on 24 August 1985 when Colin Morris scored twice.

Following Wimbledon's unlikely 3-2 win at Everton on the last day of the 1993-94 season, the Blades dropped out of the Premiership. When the Blades were defeated 1-0 by the Dons in April 2003, the attendance at Selhurst Park was 1,329 - the lowest League crowd the Blades had played in front of (home or away) for 102 years (since April 1901 at West Brom).

Over the last 20 years or so a 'complete team' of players (plus subs) has served with both clubs: Paul Heald (Blades reserve), Hans Segers, Simon Tracey (goalkeepers); Keith Curle, Kevin Gage, Brian Gayle, Jon Harley, Scott Fitzgerald, Mark Morris & Terry Phelan (defenders); Wally Downes, Vinnie Jones, John Gannon, Glyn Hodges, Ray Lewington & Jonathan Hunt (midfielders), Alan Cork, Stewart Evans (United reserve) & Francis Joseph (forwards). And there is Dave Bassett (who has been in charge of both clubs) and Peter Withe (United player & Dons' boss) as the management team.

WINS

* United's biggest win so far at competitive level in League or Cup (in terms of goals scored) is 11-2 v. Cardiff City (home) Division One, Friday, 1 January 1926.

Other Big Wins
Premiership
6-0	v. Tottenham Hotspur (home)	02.03.1993

Football League:
10-0	v. Burslem Port Vale (away)	10.12.1892
10-0	v. Burnley (home)	19.01.1929
8-0	v. Bury (home)	06.04.1896
8-3	v. Bootle (home)	26.11.1892
8-3	v. Manchester City (home)	26.10.1925
7-0	v. Blackburn Rovers (home)	09.01.1897
7-0	v. Hull City (home)	21.12.1935
7-0	v. Ipswich Town (home)	27.11.1971

FA Cup
6-1	v. Scarborough (away)	05.09.1889
6-1	v. Loughborough (home)	08.12.1891
5-0	v. Corinthians (home)	10.01.1925
5-0	v. Barrow (home)	01.01.1956
5-0	v. Newcastle United (away)	10.01.1914

League Cup
6-1	v. Lincoln City (home)	22.08.2000
5-1	v. Stockport County (away)	20.09.1994

Other Cup Competitions
9-2	v. Barnsley (home)	09.05.1931
7-0	v. Salamis (away)	06.06.1974

Wartime
10-2	v. Lincoln City (home)	27.01.1945
9-0	v. Lincoln City (home)	06.12.1941
8-0	v. Barnsley (home)	25.01.1919
7-0	v. Lincoln City (home)	18.03.1916

Friendlies/Tours/Testimonials etc.
12-1	v. Hagfors (away)	03.08.1988
11-1	v. Skegness Town (away)	05.08.1986
10-0	v. Ljusne BIK (away)	29.07.1992
9-0	v. Sheffield FC (home)	01.09.1890
8-0	v. Vassunda (away)	07.08.1988
9-0	v. Bracke (away)	02.08.1992
9-1	v. Select XI (home)	04.03.1990
9-1	v. Truro City (away)	22.03.1981
9-1	v. Guernsey XI (away)	12.05.1986
9-5	v. Sheff Utd All Stars (home)	07.05.2001
8-0	v. Gainsborough Trinity (away)	13.09.1905
8-1	v. Mount St Mary's (away)	15.12.1891
8-1	v. Arjang (away)	25.07.1997
8-1	v. Burnley (home)	28.03.1892
8-2	v. Aarhus (away)	28.05.1936
8-4	v. Aalborg (away)	31.05.1936
8-4	v. Select XI (home)	17.11.1980
8-5	v. West Yorks XI (away)	06.09.1903
7-0	v. The Casuals (home)	30.12.1890
7-0	v. Esjberg (home)	30.11.1954
7-0	v. Lucerne (away)	12.05.1960
7-0	v. Skegness Town (away)	28.07.1987
7-0	v. Kylbro IF (away)	06.08.1988
7-0	v. HBK Kronby (away)	01.08.1988

Victory Salute
* United have twice secured eight successive League wins, this (a) between February-April 1893 and (b) from the start of the 1903-04 season.
* They also won eight competitive games on the bounce between November 1890 and January 1891.
* United won 16 out of 22 League games in 1892-93; 17 out of 30 in 1897-98, 19 out of 34 in 1904-95, 26 out of 42 in 1960-61, and 27 out of 46 in 1981-82.
* Sixteen home League games were won out of 21 in 1958-59; there were 15 at home and 12 away in that total of 27 wins in 1981-82 and 16 at   home and nine away were claimed in 1988-89 (46 matches).
* The Blades won just six of their 42 League games in seasons 1920-21 and 1975-76 (Division One)...and they managed only eight victories in 46 matches in the Premiership in 1993-94 (six at home, two away).

WINDASS, Dean
Forward: 20 apps* 6 goals*
Born: Hull, 1 April 1969
Career: North Ferriby FC, Hull City (professional, October 1991), Aberdeen (£700,000, December 1995), Oxford United (£475,000, August 1998), Bradford City (£950,000, March 1999), Middlesbrough (£600,000, March 2001), Sheffield Wednesday (on loan, December 2001), BLADES (on loan November-December 2002, signed permanently, January 2003)
When he joined the Blades in 2002 Dean Windass was already vastly experienced having scored almost 140 goals in well over 475 senior appearances. His presence added a bit more firepower to the United front-line. He netted on his debut for United in a 5-0 win against his former club Bradford City in November 2002 and after that put in his fair share of effort as the Blades surged on towards the First Division Play-offs and a subsequent Final appearance at Cardiff's Millennium Stadium against Wolves, although he did not play in the latter, manager Neil Warnock preferring to use Messrs Asaba and Kabba to start with and naming Allison and Peschisolido as substitutes.

WINTERHALDER, Herbert T
Outside-right: 11 apps. 2 goals
Born: Kettering, 1880. Died: 1946
Career: Kettering Town (1900), BLADES (August1902), Plymouth Argyle (May 1903), Wellingborough (August 1904), West Ham United (September 1905-May 1906).
Signed as extra cover for 'Cocky' Bennett, Bert Winterhalder impressed in his first six outings for the Blades, scoring in successive wins over Wolves and Liverpool. He then returned to the reserves and made five more appearances during the second half of the season before moving to Plymouth.

WIRMOLA, Jonas
Central defender: 9 apps.
Born: Sweden, 17 July 1969
Career: Sparvagens/Sweden, BLADES (August 1993), FF Malmo/Sweden (February 1994).
With Brian Gayle sidelined through injury, Blades' manager Dave Bassett recruited Swedish defender Jonas Wirmola to strengthen his squad. After playing in Derek Dooley's testimonial game (as a sub) he made his Football League debut against Wimbledon three weeks later but was allowed to return to his home country once Gayle had reported for duty early in the New Year.

WITHE, Peter
Striker: 85+5 apps. 20 goals
Born: Liverpool, 30 August 1951.
Career: All Hallows School (Speke), Smith Coggins FC (1966), Skelmersdale, Southport (August 1971), Barrow (December 1971), Port Elizabeth City/South Africa (1972) Arcadia Shepherds/South Africa (1973), Wolverhampton Wanderers (£13,500, November 1973), Portland Timbers/NASL (1975), Birmingham City (£50,000, August 1975), Nottingham Forest (£42,000, September 1976), Newcastle United (£200,000, August 1978), Aston Villa (for a record fee of £500,000, May 1980), BLADES (July 1985), Birmingham City (on loan, September-November 1987), Huddersfield Town (July 1988, initially as assistant-manager/player-coach), Aston Villa (assistant manager/senior coach to Josef Venglos, January 1991, then reserve-team coach under Ron Atkinson, July 1991), Wimbledon (manager, October 1991 to January 1992), Evesham United (player, February 1992), Community Liaison Officer for the West Midlands and for Birmingham City(1993), Aston Villa (Youth Development Officer, August 1994), Thailand (national coach/manager & football advisor, from September 2000).
One of soccer's goalscoring nomads, Peter Withe (after leaving school) served with 16 different football clubs (at various levels) during his 20 years as a striker. In that time he chalked up a fine record - 232 goals in 640 games (all competitions). Big, strong and fearless, he never really established himself at St Andrew's where his power in the air seemed to be counter-balanced by his clumsiness on the ground. But under the guidance of Brian Clough at Forest he developed into a splendid target man, being a fine exponent of the chest pass. He played a major role in both Forest's and later Aston Villa's glory years, netting the winning goal for the latter in the 1982 European Cup Final.
With Forest he was a League championship and League Cup winner in 1978; adding a second League prize to his collection with Villa in 1981 while also helping them lift the Super Cup in 1982 and share the FA Charity Shield (when he scored twice in the 2-2 draw with Spurs at Wembley in 1981). He was also capped 11 times by England. He scored twice for Blues in a 2-0 win at Bramall Lane in October 1987 when he was on loan from the Blades!
* His brother, Chris, played for several League clubs, while his son, Jason, started off with West Brom and later served Burnley.

WOLVERHAMPTON WANDERERS
United's playing record against the Wolves:
Football League

Venue	P	W	D	L	F	A
Home	44	22	15	7	90	61
Away	44	10	14	20	54	85
Totals	88	32	29	27	144	146

Play-off

	P	W	D	L	F	A
Neutral	1	0	0	1	0	3

FA Cup

	P	W	D	L	F	A
Home	4	2	0	2	9	7
Away	7	1	3	3	7	11
Totals	11	3	3	5	16	18

Birmingham Cup

	P	W	D	L	F	A
Home	1	1	0	0	2	0

Others

	P	W	D	L	F	A
Home	1	1	0	0	1	0
Neutral	1	0	0	1	1	4

Wolverhampton Wanderers came into being in 1877 when a group of pupils and teachers from St Luke's School, Blakenhall chose to form a football team. Amalgamating with The Wanderers Cricket club, they were one of the founder members of the Football League in 1888 and in 1923 became the first of those early members to drop into the Third Division (North), yet the club bounced back under first Major Frank Buckley and then Stan Cullis to take over as one of the finest club sides in the country, winning three League titles in the 1950s and taking on and beating many of the top sides in Europe.

The Blades first encountered Wolves in a 2nd round FA Cup-tie in January 1892. Then a non-League club, having battled through the qualifying stages as well as defeating Blackpool, they found Wolves far too stronger opposition and went down 3-1 at Molineux.

The first League meetings followed in 1893-94, United winning 4-3 at Molineux (Robert Hill scoring twice) and 3-2 at the 'Lane;' to register a splendid 'double.'

These were the first of thirteen consecutive seasons of League fixtures prior to Wolves' relegation in 1906, United having notably won 7-2 in 1903-04, which remains as their best-ever victory over the Black Country club.

Between 1906 and 1946, there were only four League games, Wolves winning 5-1 at Molineux in 1932-33.

In 1948-49, one of Wolves' greatest-ever sides trounced United 6-0 at Molineux and in 1953-54, after returning to the top flight, the Blades were hammered 6-1 on the same ground as the Wanderers surged on towards their first League title.

By drawing 2-2 at Molineux on 9 May 1989, the Blades clinched promotion from Division Three (as runners-up to Wolves).

On 26 May 2003, the Blades travelled to Cardiff to play Wolves in the First Division play-off Final. The prize...a place in the Premiership. A crowd of 69,473 (half of them supporting United) packed into the Millennium Stadium to see the contest. Sadly, Neil Warnock's men were below par and lost 3-0, all the goals coming in the first-half.

Since WW2 there have been three six-goal thrillers at 'the Lane', all of which ended level at 3-3...in 1953-54, 1955-56 and 1994-95. United have lost only seven times at home in 43 meetings, their worst defeat coming in 1975-76 (beaten 4-1), On the other hand, they can boast only nine wins at Molineux in that time, the best 3-0 as long ago as 1894-95.

The 3-3 draw with Wolves at Bramall Lane in April 2003 was United's 2,000th home game in the Football League and their 4,000th in the competition overall.

In 1902, United knocked Wolves out of the FA Cup with a 4-0 scoreline in round three

An as holders of the trophy, Wolves were held to a goalless draw at Molineux in a 4th round tie in January 1950, but on a snow-covered, icy pitch at Bramall Lane, and despite a hat-trick from Harold Brook, the Blades slipped out of the competition, beaten 4-3 in a thrilling replay. Johnny Hancocks netted with two penalty kicks for the Wolves.

David Barnes, Pat Buckley, John Burridge, Gordon Cowans, Keith Curle, Mel Eves, George Farrow, Stan Fazackerley, Roger Hansbury, Bob Hatton, George Hedley, Charlie Henderson, George Henson, Martin Johnson, David Kelly, John McAlle, Chris Marsden, Archie Needham, Tom Phillipson, Dicky Rhodes (Blades reserve), Hans Segers, Bernard Shaw, Paul Simpson, Paul Stancliffe, Mark Todd, Tony Towner, Fred White (Wolves trialist) and Peter Withe are among the players who have served with both the Blades and Wolves. Ex-Blades player John Barnwell was manager at Molineux, John Harris and Arthur Rowley were both WW2 Wolves players and later managers of the Blades, Andy Beattie was assistant-manager at 'the Lane' and boss at Molineux and Gerry Summers, ex-Blades, became assistant-manager/coach at Wolves.

WOOD, Alexander
Left-back: 7 apps.
Born: Scotland, circa 1876
Career: Hibernian, BLADES (September 1900), St Bernard's FC (May 1902).
A reserve full-back at 'the Lane' to Peter Boyle, Alex Wood - a Football League debutant v. Stoke - spent two seasons in Sheffield before returning to Edinburgh to sign for St Bernard's.

WOOD, Paul Anthony
Outside-right/midfielder: 22+8 apps. 3 goals
Born: Saltburn, 1 November 1964
Career: Portsmouth (apprentice, April 1981, professional November 1982), Brighton & Hove Albion (£40,000, August 1987), BLADES (£90,000, February 1990), Bournemouth (on loan, February 1991, signed for £40,000, October 1991), Portsmouth (February 1994-May 1996), Happy Valley (Hong Kong), Havant & Waterlooville (September 1998), Hallam (season 2000-03).
Paul Wood played in 17 games to help United win back their First Division status in 1990. A workmanlike performer, very effective when driving forward, he made well over 350 senior appearances up to 1996 when he left Fratton Park having struggling with an ankle injury.

WOOD, William
Full-back: 5 apps.
Born: Barnsley, 28 December 1927
Career: Spen Juniors, Sunderland (professional, October 1948), Hull City (July 1951), BLADES (June 1952-May 1953), Wisbech Town (seasons 1953-55).
Having made just one League appearance for Sunderland and none for Hull, Bill Wood was recruited by the Blades as defensive cover for Graham Shaw and played in the opening five League games of the 1952-53 season before Shaw returned to duty.

WOODHOUSE, Curtis
Midfielder: 107+15 apps. 7 goals
Born: Beverley, Yorkshire, 17 April 1980.
Career: BLADES (trainee, June 1996, professional December 1997), Birmingham City (£1 million, February 2001), Bradford City (August 2002), Rotherham United (on loan, March-May 2003).
A First Division promotion winner with Birmingham in 2002 and capped four times by England at Under-21 level, having presented his country as a Youth team player, Curtis Woodhouse is a very combative midfielder with an excellent work-rate. He had to battle hard and long to gain a place in the Blades' first XI owing to the impressive form of so many other players of similar style.

270

WOODWARD, Alan

Outside-right: 639+4 apps. 193 goals
Born: Chapeltown, 7 September 1946.
Career: BLADES (apprentice, April 1962, professional, September 1963-May 1979), Tulsa Roughnecks (summer, 1979).

A powerful right-winger with pace and strong shot, Alan Woodward added to his armoury the ability to fire over accurate corner-kicks at speed and precisely the right height that defenders feared. He was an ever-present when United won promotion to the First Division in 1971, having also played in every game the two previous seasons. A tremendously hard-working footballer, totally committed he made his first team debut in the County Cup semi-final win over Rotherham United in April 1964 and the next month starred in the victory over Barnsley in the Final at Oakwell. He eventually took over the No. 7 short from John Docherty and established himself in the first XI the following season, making his League bow against Liverpool at Anfield in early October and scoring the first of his 158 League goals for the club in a defeat at Leeds later that month. He gave the Blades' 17 years loyal and dedicated service before rounding off his career in the NASL with Tulsa.

WORCESTER CITY

Formed in 1908, Worcester City were one of the strongest professional outfits playing non-League football when they were accepted into the Southern League in 1938.

They have had many great Cup runs over the years and a record crowd of 17,000 packed into their St George's Ground to see them face the Blades in a tightly contested 4th round FA Cup-tie in January 1959.

Having already dismissed Chelmsford City, Millwall and Liverpool (2-1) from the competition that season, Worcester were well-prepared to pull off another shock. Bit the Blades buckled down and soaked up early pressure before taking charge and going on to win 2-0 with goals by Kevin Lewis and Ron Simpson.

Worcester now play in Dr Martins Southern League (Premier Division).

WORKINGTON

Formed in 1884 by local steelworkers and elected to the Football League in 1951 when New Brighton resigned, Workington were managed by the legendary Bill Shankly for a while in the mid-1950s.

The Cumbrian side spent 26 seasons in the bottom two Divisions, up to 1977, and during that time they never met the Blades in League competition

The only time the clubs have done battle was in 1972-73 when United won a 2nd round League Cup-tie 1-0 at Borough Park in September 1972 in front of 7,188, Billy Dearden the goalscorer.

Workington share their ground with the Rugby League club Workington Town, and therefore it is not surprising that the soccer team is occasionally referred to, erroneously, as 'Workington Town.'

Ken Furphy was player-manager of Workington and later boss at Bramall Lane, and among the players who have served with both clubs are Bill Boyd, nomadic goalkeeper John Burridge, John Flynn, Gerald Hewitt (Workington reserve) and David Irving.
* Mick Heaton, ex-United, later managed Workington Town FC.

WRAGG, Peter

Inside/centre-forward/wing-half: 65 apps. 21 goals
Born: Rotherham, 1931
Career: Rotherham United (amateur, 1946, professional; April 1948), BLADES (£1,500, January 1953), York City (£4,000, July 1956), Bradford City (July 1963-May 1965), Haxby FC (manager), later Halifax Town (manager, season 1992-93).

Peter Wragg scored in seven successive League games for United - 17 September to 29 October 1955. An England Schoolboy international at the age of 15, he scored four goals in 31 League games for the Millermen before moving to Bramall Lane, signed to strengthen the attack options. He appeared in two senior matches in February 1953 against Birmingham City in the FA Cup and Lincoln City in the Second Division but it wasn't until the following season that he established himself in the first XI, scoring seven times in 24 outings. With Jack Cross and Jimmy Hagan, plus a handful of others, all doing well, he left 'the Lane' for York City in the summer of 1956, signed by ex-Charlton goalkeeper Sam Bartram who thus re-united him with his former Blades' colleague Arthur Bottom. He gave the Minstermen seven years outstanding service, during which time he netted 87 goals in 297 competitive appearances. He claimed three hat-tricks and one fourtimer (v. Carlisle United in 1961) and was the club's leading marksmen in two seasons (1958-59 & 1960-61), captaining the promotion-winning side in that first campaign. A fully qualified FA coach, he spent two years at Valley Parade (5 goals in 73 League games) and on his retirement he returned to York to take charge of Haxby FC in the local District League, later bossing Halifax Town.

271

WREXHAM

United's playing record against the Welsh club

Football League

Venue	P	W	D	L	F	A
Home	2	1	1	0	3	1
Away	2	0	0	2	1	8
Totals	4	1	1	2	4	9

FA Cup

	P	W	D	L	F	A
Away	1	1	0	0	5	1

League Cup

	P	W	D	L	F	A
Home	1	1	0	0	3	1
Away	1	0	1	0	1	1
Totals	2	1	1	0	4	2

Others

	P	W	D	L	F	A
Away	2	0	1	1	2	3

Wrexham, founded as long ago as 1872 by members of the town's cricket club, took almost half a century before gaining Football League status, becoming one of the founder members of the newly-formed Third Division (North) in 1921. The Welsh club briefly achieved Second Division status between 1978-82 but have otherwise played entirely in the bottom two sectors.

The Blades have played just four League games against Wrexham - losing two of them heavily, 4-0 (in February 1979) and 4-1 (in February 1983) both at The Racecourse Ground. United's lone win was achieved in October 1982 (2-0).

The Blades did, however, enjoy an excellent 5-1 FA Cup win at Wrexham in 1984 when Keith Edwards scored four times.

United also knocked Wrexham out of the League Cup in 1997-98, winning a 1st round tie 4-2 on aggregate.

Keith Bannister (United reserve), Steve Charles, Andy Dibble (United reserve), RE 'Bob' Evans, Colin Grainger, Michael Lake, David Powell and Ian Rush played for both clubs while Reg Matthewson (an ex-Blade) became a coach at Wrexham.

WYCOMBE WANDERERS

United's playing record against the Wanderers:

League Cup

Venue	P	W	D	L	F	A
Home	1	1	0	0	4	1

Formed in 1887, and a Football League club since 1993, the 'Chairboys' for many years were one f the south's most famous and enterprising amateur clubs, winning the FA Amateur Cup in 1931. It was not until 1974 that they became a professional body and since then they have improved greatly, gaining automatic promotion to the Conference in 1987 after winning the Isthmian League title. It was Martin O'Neill who guided them into the Football League as Conference champions six years later.

Th club's greatest day came on 8 April 2001 when they met Liverpool in the FA Cup semi-final at Villa Park, having already knocked Wolves, Middlesbrough, Wimbledon and Leicester City out of the competition under manager Lawrie Sanchez.

The only time the Blades have meet Wycombe so far was in the 2nd round of the League Cup in 2002-03 when Michael Brown's scored twice in a 4-1 win in front of just 4,398 loyal supporters at Bramall Lane. Michael Brown's strike in the 87th minute of this tie was the Blades' 200th goal in the competition.

Gary Ablett, Viv Busby, Mark Foran, Grant Smith, Frank Talia and David Tuttle are among the players who have served with both clubs.

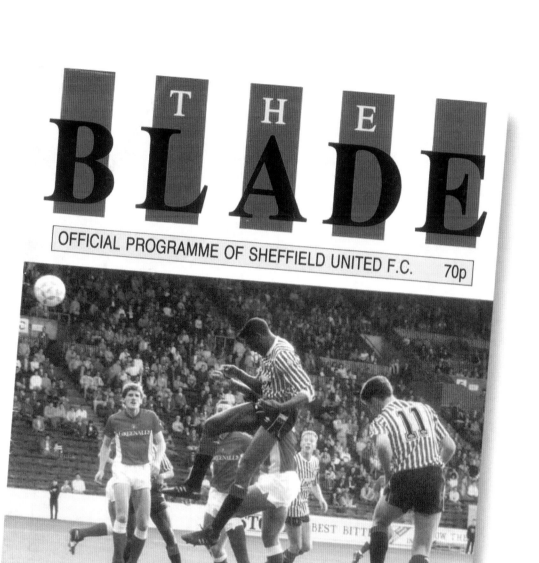

THE BLADE

OFFICIAL PROGRAMME OF SHEFFIELD UNITED F.C.   70p

LITTLEWOODS CUP, 2nd ROUND, 1st LEG

NEWCASTLE UNITED

Tuesday, 27th September, 1988
Kick-off 7.30 p.m.

SHEFFIELD UNITED F.C.
CENTENARY SEASON 1988-89
1889

Tonight's Match Sponsored
by
ANGLO-SCANDIA LTD.

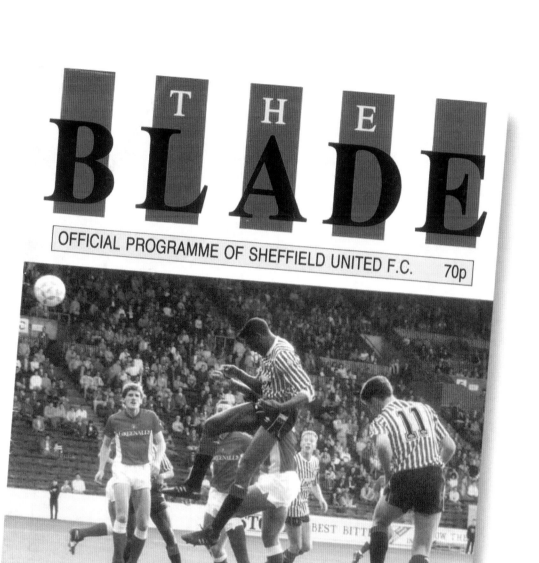

273

Littlewoods cup, 2nd round, 1st leg v.s Newcastle United 27th September, 1988

YATES, James
Forward: 104 apps. 9 goals
Born: Tunstall, 1869. Died: Southampton, 5 September 1922.
Career: Burnley (July 1891), Ardwick/Manchester City (November 1892), BLADES (December 1893), Southampton St Mary's (June 1897), Gravesend (July 1898), Southampton (March 1899), Hastings & St Leonard's United (June 1901), Copenhagen FC (Coach, 1903), Southampton (April 1905), Gravesend (August 1905), Hastings & St Leonard's United (January 1906), coached in Brazil & USA (1906-08), Salisbury City (season 1908-09).
A dapper, clever right-winger, Jimmy Yates was a regular in United's first team for three-and-a-half years before transferring to Southampton with whom he later won two Southern League championship medals (1899 & 1901), having returned to The Dell via Gravesend. He had a third spell with Saints and is the only player to this day to have been signed by that club on three separate occasions, scoring 22 goals in 77 outings. He developed into a very respected coach but on his return to England he took a job as a stevedore at Southampton Docks while also assisting Salisbury City. His health started to deteriorate in 1921 and a year later (following a period of unemployment) he committed suicide.

Sheffield United team group: (back row, l-r) Trainer Waller, Mick Whitham, Bill Foulke, John Docherty, Bob Cain (middle row, l-r) **Jimmy Yates**, Harry Hammond, Ernest Needham, Walter Hill, Arthur Watson (front row, l-r) Harry Thickett, Rab Howell

YATES, Stephen
Defender: 12+1 apps*
Born: Bristol, 29 January 1970.
Career: Bristol Rovers (apprentice, April 1986, professional July 1988), Queen's Park Rangers (£650,000, August 1993), Tranmere Rovers (free transfer, August 1999), BLADES (with Wayne Allison, July 2002).
A vastly experienced campaigner, with almost 525 games under his belt and a Third Division championship medal (gained with Bristol Rovers in 1990) Steve Yates arrived at 'the Lane' in a package deal involving striker Wayne Allison. Alas, he failed to establish himself in the side, although battling against injury, he remained an excellent squad member throughout the campaign, helping the Blades reach the First Division Play-offs by making 12 League appearances.

YORK CITY

United's playing record against the Minstermen:

Football League

Venue	P	W	D	L	F	A
Home	1	1	0	0	4	0
Away	1	1	0	0	4	3
Totals	2	2	0	0	8	3

FA Cup

Home	1	0	1	0	1	1
Away	1	1	0	0	2	0
Totals	2	1	1	0	3	1

League Cup

Home	3	3	0	0	5	2
Away	1	0	1	0	1	1
Totals	4	3	1	0	6	3

The present day York City club was formed in 1922 by a soccer enthusiast from Darlington and was elected to the Football League seven years later when Ashington was voted out.

United first met the 'Minstermen' in a 3rd round FA Cup-tie at Bramall Lane in January 1931. The visitors forced a 1-1 draw, Syd Gibson saving the Blades' blushes. The replay, at City's Fulfordgate ground, attracted a crowd of 12,721. This time United just scraped home, winning 2-0 with second-half goals from Gibson (again) and Jimmy Dunne.

The only League fixtures between the clubs took place in 1981-82 (Division 4). Title winners United won both - 4-3 at Bootham Crescent where Mike Trusson scored twice, and 4-0 at 'the Lane', Trusson again on target along with Keith Edwards (2) and Bob Hatton.

The Blades have knocked York out of the League Cup on three occasions - in 1971-72, when they won 3-2 at home, ten years later, in 1981-82, when they defeated them 2-1 on aggregate and in 2002-03 when they pipped them 1-0 in the opening round.

Players who have served with both clubs include: Colin Addison, Reg Baines, Jeff Birch (Blades reserve), Arthur Bottom, Ted Burgin (York reserve), Viv Busby, Cliff Calvert, Jim Coop, Tom Cowan, Graeme Crawford, Peter Duffield, Steve Faulkner, Jack Fountain, Wally Gould, Billy Hodgson, Ian Holmes, Howard Johnson, Andy Leaning, John MacPhail, Sam McNab, Alan Ogden, Ernie Robertson, Jack Smith, Peter Spooner, Paul Stancliffe, Des Thompson, Norman Wharton, Bob Widdowson and Peter Wragg. Neil Warnock played for City and later managed the Blades.

YORKSHIRE & HUMBERSIDE CUP

In seasons 1988-89 and 1989-90 the Blades entered the Yorkshire & Humberside Cup.

First up they beat Bradford City 1-0 (away), drew 0-0 at Doncaster, defeated Halifax Town 1-0 in the semi-final (staged behind closed doors at Huddersfield owing to The Shay being unplayable) before battling hard and long to overcome Scarborough 2-1 in the Final. The following season it was harder still. Scarborough were again overcome in the first match, United winning 3-1 away. Rotherham were held to a 1-1 draw at Bramall Lane before Halifax won a third match 1-0 in front of 1,500 fans at The Shay to dump the Blades out of the competition.

Full record:

P	W	D	L	F	A
7	4	2	1	8	4

YOUNG, Alexander Forbes

Forward: 29+3 apps. 13 goals
Born: Kirkcaldy, Fife, 26 October 1955
Career: Kirkcaldy YMCA, Oldham Athletic (professional, July 1974), Leicester City (£250,000, May 1979), BLADES (August 1982), Brighton & Hove Albion (£140,000, August 1983), Notts County (£55,000, September 1984), Rochdale (August 1986), Shepshed Charterhouse (player-coach, March 1988-90). Later ran an indoor cricket school and soccer centre at Thurmaston.

After scoring a hat-trick for the Latics against Leicester in 1979, Scottish schoolboy international striker 'Alan' Young became one of the first players to be transferred under the new freedom-of-contract regulations and have his fee set by an independent tribunal. The £250,000 tag placed on his head upset Oldham while at the same time he became Leicester's record signing. And he paid a fair amount of that money back to the Foxes by scoffing 29 goals in 119 games before switching to Bramall Lane in 1982. Unfortunately he wasn't quite as sharp with the Blades and although he did have some success at Hove, Meadow Lane and Spotland. He finally retired from competitive football in 1988 with well over 100 goals in his locker in almost 400 senior matches.

YOUNG, Charles Stuart Robertson

Goalkeeper: 4 apps.
Born: Falkirk, 23 August 1929
Career: Stalybridge Celtic, BLADES (May 1951-April 1952).
Signed as extra cover for goalkeeper to Ted Burgin, Stuart Young made his senior debut for the Blades against Southend in an FA Cup-tie February 1952 and played his last game two months later in a 4-1 defeat at Brentford as the Blades stuttered in mid-table in Division Two. He later returned to Scotland.

YOUNG, Richard Harker
Full-back/centre-half: 142 apps. 5 goals
Born: Gateshead, 17 April 1918. Died: Carlisle, 31 January 1989
Career: Wardley Colliery, Reyrolle's FC (Hebburn), Hebburn St Cuthbert's, Wardley Colliery (again), Bolden Colliery, BLADES (November 1935); (served in the RAF during WW2); Lincoln City (£2,000, March 1949, appointed player-coach at Sincil Bank during the 1951-52 season and club trainer on retiring in May 1954), Carlisle United (trainer, July 1956 to November 1975, then manager at Brunton Park for a year; assistant-manager (briefly); manager again: 1980 until his retirement in May 1982).
A six-footer, strong in defence with good heading ability, Dick Young - you filled eight different positions during his 14 years at 'the Lane' including one outing at centre-forward v. Blackpool in the FA Cup - helped the Blades gain promotion from Division Two in 1938-39 (playing in 11 matches) but unfortunately lost much of his playing career to the war. He served under Fred Emery when he first joined Carlisle and succeeded Alan Ashman as manager at the age of 57. On his own words he said: 'I loved Carlisle United Football Club and it was a sad day when I had to leave.'

276

YOUTH FOOTBALL

United have technically run a youth team since the 1940s when the local Oaks Field Youth Club acted as a nursery team for the Blades. United's teenagers joined the Northern Intermediate League in 1954 and held membership for 40 years until 1998, winning the championship three times, in 1963, 1964 & 1986. They also won the League Cup in 1962 & 1964.
The FA Youth Cup, introduced in 1952, the Blades' best effort so far came in 1973 when they lost in the semi-finals to Bristol City. In October 1968 the Blades' youngsters achieved their best-ever win - 16-0 over Doncaster Rovers.

United players who have represented their country at youth team include:
England: L Badger, Ian Benjamin, Steve Cammack, Phil Jagielka, Glyn Jones, Tony Kenworthy, Kevin Lewis, Lee Morris, David Munks, B Shaw, J Spencer, G West, C Woodhouse.
* Steve Cammack played for England Youth v. Spain at Bramall Lane on 15 March 1972.

ZAMBIA AIRWAYS TROPHY

In May 1972, United played in the sponsored Zambia Airways Trophy. They competed in three games against a Zambia XI, two of which were won - 3-1 in Lusaka when both Eddie Colquhoun and Len Badger were sent-off and 4-1 in Kitwe. The other, played in N'Dola, ended in a 1-1 draw, United's 'keeper Tom McAlister earning his corn by saving two penalties. United duly won the star prize.

ZENITH DATA SYSTEMS CUP

United's playing record in the ZDSC is:

Venue	P	W	D	L	F	A
Home	4	2	1*	1	11	5
Away	1	0	0	1	2	3
Totals	5	2	1	2	13	8

* Beaten on penalties.

277

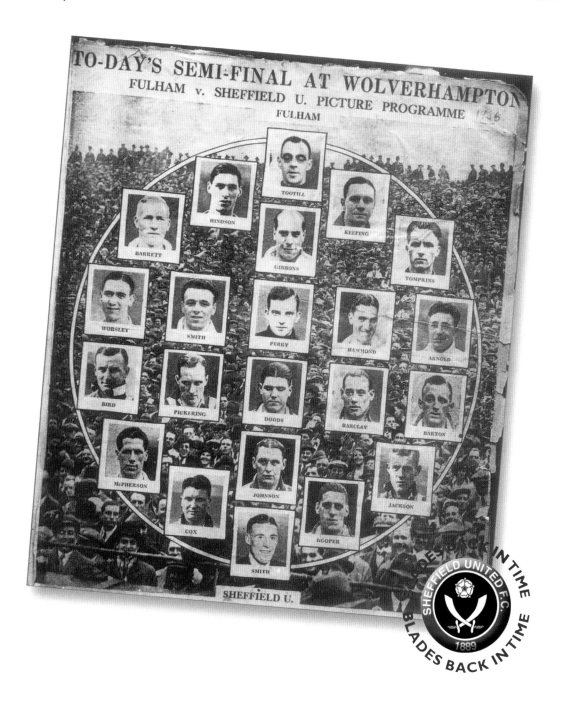

Fulham v.s Sheffield United Semi Final

278

Brian Deane of Sheffield United (left) and Martin Scott of Sunderland (right)

Sheffield United goalkeeper Alan Hodgkinson dives to make a save v Chelsea in 1955

britesp^ot
PUBLISHING SOLUTIONS

The Football Collection

Below is the range of publications available now from Britespot Publishing - one of the fastest growing sports publishers in the UK.

My Memories of Man Utd by Norman Whiteside
This fully illustrated hardback publication relives Norman Whiteside's outstanding career with Manchester United FC.
ISBN 1 904103 21 9   RRP £14.99 HB   130+ pages

My Memories of Everton by Kevin Ratcliffe
This fully illustrated book relives Kevin Ratcliffe's outstanding career with Everton FC from his early days to the famous Cup victories and his international career with Wales.
ISBN.1 904103 25 1   RRP £14.99 HB   114 pages

Today's the day Newcastle United FC by Andrew Henry and Paul Joannou
This officially endorsed publication is more than a diary, covering the club's complete history in 365 days of the year with facts, statistics, match of the day, birthdays, memorable matches and so much more.
ISBN. 1 904103 24 3   RRP £17.99 HB   320 pages

Wembley "the FA Cup finals" 1923-2000 by Glen Isherwood
This fully illustrated hardback publication covers the complete history of the Wembley Stadium FA Cup Finals 1923 - 2000, with rare unseen photo's and memorabilia.
ISBN 1 904103 17 0   RRP £19.99 HB   256+ pages

Old Gold Glory, Wolves League Champions 1953-54 by Steve Gordos
Available Now, this publication profiles all the players who brought the championship to Molineux. Surviving players talk candidly about their team-mates and a manager whose unique style and tactical views earned him a place in football's hall of fame. As well as the unfolding drama of a memorable season, Old Gold Glory contains reports and line-ups for every Wolves game in 1953-4, a host of pictures, plus results and scorers of every league match that season.
ISBN: 1 904103 27 8   RRP: £15.99   200+ pages

UpOver and DownUnder by Stan Rickaby
This autobiography is the life of Stan Rickaby - former England International and West Bromwich Albion Footballer, looking back over his childhood, wartime experiences, footballing career and his new life downunder.
ISBN 1 904103 18 9   RRP £10.99 PB   460 pages

Other publications include:-
100 Years of Test Match Cricket at Edgbaston by Brian Halford, My Memories of Wolves by Steve Bull, The Blues Who's Who, The Complete Encyclopaedia of Manchester Utd Football Club, Irish Reds by Iain McCartney, Duncan Edwards The Full Report by Iain McCartney, Tartan Reds by Iain McCartney, The World Cup Who's Who-50 years of England World Cup Football 1950-2002, 10 Tens by Glenn B Fleming, The Official Encyclopaedia of West Bromwich Albion 1878-2002, Smokin' Joe-Cyrille Regis, 25 years in Football, The Baggies Strip, The Official West Bromwich Albion Picture Gallery 1960's-1990's, The Official Encyclopaedia of Aston Villa Football Club by Tony Matthews, The Road to Rotterdam Aston Villa FC Champions of Europe 1982 by Rob Bishop, Today's The Day Birmingham City FC, The Forest Who's Who, The Official Spurs Comic Strip by Bob Bond, The Official Encyclopaedia of Tottenham Hotspur Football Club, My Memories of Spurs by Bobby Smith.

For ordering details or for further information on all the above titles contact:
Britespot Publishing Solutions Limited, Chester Road, Cradley Heath, West Midlands B64 6AB.
Tel: +44 (0) 1384 414170   Fax: +44 (0) 1384 414141   Email: info@britespot.co.uk   www.britespot.co.uk
Or visit your local bookshop.